Jewish Marriage and Divorce in Imperial Russia

Jewish Marriage and Divorce in Imperial Russia

ChaeRan Y. Freeze

BRANDEIS UNIVERSITY PRESS

Published by University Press of New England / Hanover and London

Brandeis University Press

Published by University Press of New England, Hanover, NH 03755

© 2002 by Brandeis University Press

Printed in the United States of America

5 4 3 2 1

The publication of this book was made possible in part by a generous grant from the Koret Foundation Jewish Studies Publications Program.

LIBRARY OF CONGRESS CATALOGING-IN-PUBLICATION DATA

Freeze, ChaeRan Y.
  Jewish marriage and divorce in imperial Russia / ChaeRan Y. Freeze.
    p. cm.— (Tauber Institute for the Study of European Jewry series)
  Includes bibliographical references and index.
    ISBN 1-58465-147-4 (cloth : alk. paper)—ISBN 1-58465-160-1 (pbk. : alk. paper)
    1. Marriage customs and rites, Jewish—Russia—History— 19th century.
  2. Marriage (Jewish law)—History— 19th century. 3. Divorce—Russia—
  History— 19th century. 4. Divorce (Jewish law)—History— 19th century.
  5. Jewish families—Russia—Social conditions— 19th century. 6. Jews—
  Russia—Politics and government— 19th century. 7. Russia—Ethnic relations.
  I. Title. II. Tauber Institute for the Study of European Jewry series (Unnumbered)
    BM713 .F719 2002
    306.81'089'924047—dc21   2001004217

The Tauber Institute for the Study of European Jewry Series

Jehuda Reinharz, General Editor
Sylvia Fuks Fried, Associate Editor

The Tauber Institute for the Study of European Jewry, established by a gift to Brandeis University from Dr. Laszlo N. Tauber, is dedicated to the memory of the victims of Nazi persecutions between 1933 and 1945. The Institute seeks to study the history and culture of European Jewry in the modern period. The Institute has a special interest in studying the causes, nature, and consequences of the European Jewish catastrophe within the contexts of modern European diplomatic, intellectual, political, and social history.

Gerhard L. Weinberg, 1981
World in the Balance: Behind the Scenes of World War II

Richard Cobb, 1983
*French and Germans, Germans and French:
A Personal Interpretation of France under Two Occupations, 1914–1918 /1940–1944*

Eberhard Jäckel, 1984
Hitler in History

Frances Malino and Bernard Wasserstein, editors, 1985
The Jews in Modern France

Jehuda Reinharz and Walter Schatzberg, editors, 1985
*The Jewish Response to German Culture:
From the Enlightenment to the Second World War*

Jacob Katz, 1986
The Darker Side of Genius: Richard Wagner's Anti-Semitism

Jehuda Reinharz, editor, 1987
Living with Antisemitism: Modern Jewish Responses

Michael R. Marrus, 1987
The Holocaust in History

Paul Mendes-Flohr, editor, 1987
The Philosophy of Franz Rosenzweig

Joan G. Roland, 1989
Jews in British India: Identity in a Colonial Era

Yisrael Gutman, Ezra Mendelsohn, Jehuda Reinharz, and Chone Shmeruk, editors, 1989
The Jews of Poland Between Two World Wars

Brandeis Series on Jewish Women

Shulamit Reinharz, General Editor

Joyce Antler, Associate Editor

Sylvia Barack Fishman, Associate Editor

Susan Kahn, Associate Editor

The Hadassah International Research Institute on Jewish Women, established at Brandeis University in 1997 by Hadassah, the Women's Zionist Organization of America, Inc., supports interdisciplinary basic and applied research as well as cultural projects on Jewish women around the world. Under the auspices of the Institute, the Brandeis Series on Jewish Women publishes a wide range of books by and about Jewish women in diverse contexts and time periods.

Marjorie Agosín, *Uncertain Travelers:*
Conversations with Jewish Women Immigrants to America, 1999

Rahel R. Wasserfall, *Women and Water: Menstruation in Jewish Life and Law,* 1999

Susan Starr Sered, *What Makes Women Sick:*
Militarism, Maternity, and Modesty in Israeli Society, 2000

Ludmila Shtern, *Leaving Leningrad: The True Adventures of a Soviet Émigré,* 2001

Pamela S. Nadell and Jonathan D. Sarna, editors, *Women and American Judaism:*
Historical Perspectives, 2001

ChaeRan Y. Freeze, *Jewish Marriage and Divorce in Imperial Russia,* 2002

For my husband, Gregory, and our son, Sebastian Aaron

Contents

Acknowledgments

During the past seven years that I have spent researching and writing this book, I have been very fortunate to have the intellectual support and encouragement of many colleagues and friends. I am particularly indebted to the members of my dissertation committee—Jehuda Reinharz, Antony Polonsky, and Gershon Hundert—for their careful reading and comments on my work and encouragement to revise the dissertation into a publishable manuscript. I owe a particular debt of gratitude to Marvin Fox of blessed memory, whose unstinting support and erudition were a constant source of help. When I found the meticulous signatures of his grandfather and uncles in a dusty archival file about the election of the Korostyshev state rabbi (Aron Ratner), I could not help but feel connected to my research in a more personal way. I am also grateful to Jonathan Sarna, who has been a true mentor in so many ways.

This book benefited tremendously from the constructive suggestions of Paula Hyman, who encouraged me to think more critically about the framework of gender. Special thanks to Shaul Stampfer, who not only shared his knowledge of Eastern European Jewish history with me but always had a word of moral support. I was also fortunate to meet Jay Harris as a Harry Starr Fellow at the Center for Jewish Studies at Harvard University. He has generously allowed me to use his personal translations of Moshe Leib Lilienblum, Yehuda Leib Gordon, and Pauline Wengeroff, for which I am most grateful. I am also indebted to Bernard Septimus for taking time to comment on the sections that deal with Jewish law. Of course, all the mistakes and broad generalizations made by a nonspecialist are mine. I also appreciate immensely the e-mail correspondence I had with Avraham Greenbaum, whose intellectual exchanges have added much to this book. I would like also to thank Todd Endelman for suggestions on the sections that deal with conversion and Kimmy Caplan for the comparative information about Eastern European rabbis in America. In addition, I am grateful to Shmuel Feiner, Benjamin Ravid, Aryeh Edrei, Ruth Wisse, Joshua Levison, Lawrence Fuchs, Reuven Kimelman, Bruria Nevo Hacohen, Verena Dohrn, Patricia Herlihy, Efim Melamed, Nerijus Udrenus, Benjamin Nathans, Lisa Epstein, Gerry Kadish, Alan Arkush, Lance Sussman, Shmuel Morell, and the wonderful members of the Binghamton University history department for sharing their knowledge of the *haskalah*, halakhah, family history, the Hebrew language, gender studies, and other topics with me.

A book based primarily on archival materials naturally owes much to a number of institutions and professional archivists in the former Soviet Union. In particular, I wish to thank Leonid Vaintraub (Moscow); Galina Ippolitova, Agnessa Muktan, and Serafima Varekhova (St. Petersburg); Ol'ga Belaia (Kyiv); Ruta (Vilnius); Marek Web, and Krysia Fisher (YIVO), as well as a host of others who cheerfully and expeditiously located and delivered huge quantities of unpublished materials. I am most grateful for the help of the Judaica Library staff at Brandeis University, especially Charles Cutter, Jim Rosenbloom, and Nancy Zibman, who spent hours with me looking up obscure citations.

This book could not have been completed without the generous support of the Memorial Foundation for Jewish Culture, which awarded me two special Mark Uveeler dissertation grants and several postdoctoral grants to travel and conduct archival research in the former Soviet Union (Russia, Ukraine, and Lithuania). I cannot express my deep and heartfelt gratitude for this support, especially during the years that I was ineligible for national grants with citizenship requirements. I am also grateful for the Harry Starr postdoctoral fellowship at Harvard University, which gave me the opportunity to use the rich resources at Widener Library. My research also received numerous grants from the Tauber Institute for the Study of European Jewry, the Near Eastern and Judaic Studies Department, and the Mazer grant at Brandeis University to conduct research at YIVO and St. Petersburg, Russia. The production of this book was made possible by a generous subsidy from the Koret Foundation, which helped to underwrite the production costs. I only hope that this final product merits the generous support that I have received from all my sponsors.

I would like to thank Boris and Irina Mironov for putting me up for two winter months in St. Petersburg. Irina's monster sandwiches gave me the energy to work long hours in the cold archive. Alla and Galina Ippolitova helped me find family photographs for this book, and their friendship made my visits to St. Petersburg extremely memorable. Galina Rokhlina, the Akselrod family, and Dr. Bernard Rattner were especially kind to let me use their family photographs as illustrations for this book.

I am sincerely grateful to my editor, Phyllis D. Deutsch, at the University Press of New England for her enthusiasm about this project, constructive suggestions, and patience. Working with her has been one of the greatest pleasures of completing this book. I am also deeply indebted to Sylvia Fuks Fried, executive director of the Tauber Institute, for our many discussions over the years about Jewish marriages and divorces. I cannot count the times that I have run to her for advice about everything from the title of the book to infant care. *A sheynem dank!* A sincere thank you to Shulamit Reinharz, director of the Hadassah International Research Institute on Jewish Women, for her constant encouragement and support throughout the years.

Some close friends deserve special mention for their moral support and kindness and as a reminder that there is much more to life than this book: Thank you to Jerry Schneiderman for giving me all of his Judaica books (rare and out-of-print editions) and for his optimistic outlook on life. Long late-night conversations with Svetlana Schneiderman and her lessons on Abkhazian cuisine added much spice and color to our busy schedules. Zhenia and Arina Finkelstein and Boris and Natasha Rumer were a constant source of support. Words cannot express my deep affection and gratitude to my Jewish family in Binghamton: Samuel, Shirley, and Marc Goldin. Homemade latkes, stories of Niesvisz, and Yiddish proverbs—all made my commute to and from Boston so much easier and gave me the courage to finish this book. Much appreciation also goes to Ruth Abusch-Magdar for her friendship and discussions about Jewish history, childrearing, and cookbooks.

I would have been lost without the encouragement and love of my family. I thank Paul and Mildred Freeze for the much needed breaks away from my work, especially for the memorable times in Mason. Katie and Christopher Freeze gave me the gift of music; one of their CDs was always at hand to enjoy while I worked at the computer. I am eternally grateful to my parents, Dr. Min Chul and Suk ZaYoo, who have supported my interest in Judaic studies all these years. Despite their anxieties about my foreign travels to faraway towns and cities in the former Soviet Union, they were always interested in my work and trusted my judgment. I owe a special thanks to my brother Jun (Ted), who has been a true and steadfast friend. He generously lent me his books on theory and baby-sat without complaint when I needed an extra hour to work.

Last but not least, I would like to thank my husband, friend, and colleague, Gregory Lee Freeze, who has been a source of good humor, emotional support, and intellectual stimulation. His thorough editing and critical suggestions are evident on every page. Without his good-natured laughter, his willingness to sacrifice his own work to let me finish my book, and his endless hours of child care, I would never have gotten this far. Our "little bear," Sebastian Aaron, arrived in the middle of my first draft and brought us immense pleasure with his little squeals, giggles, and smiles. I thank him for his patience as Mommy sat at her computer for hours, trying to finish her book. I dedicate my seven years of labor to you both.

Abbreviations

EE	*Evreiskaia entsiklopedia*
E.H.	*Even Haezer*
EJ	*Encyclopeadia Judaica*
ES	*Evreiskaia starina*
MVD	Ministry of Internal Affairs
PAAJR	*Proceedings of the American Academy for Jewish Research*
DAKhO	State Archive of Khar'kiv Oblast
DAKO	State Archive of Kyiv Oblast
DAOO	State Archive of Odessa Oblast
DAZhO	State Archive of Zhytomyr Oblast
DAmK	State Archives of the City of Kyiv
LVIA	Lithuanian State Historical Archive, Vilnius
RGIA	Russian State Historical Archive, St. Petersburg
TsDIAK-Ukraïny	Central State Historical Archive in Kyiv, Ukraine
TsDIAL-Ukraïny	Central State Historical Archive in L'viv, Ukraine
TsGIA-St. Petersburg	Central State Historical Archive, St. Petersburg
TsIAgM	Central Historical Archive of Moscow
REM	Russian Ethnographic Museum, St. Petersburg
YIVO	YIVO Institute for Jewish Research

Archival Notations

f.	fond (collection)
op.	opis' (register)
g.	god (year)
d.	delo (file)
l., ll.	list, listy (folio, folios)
ob.	oborot (verso)

A Note on Transliteration

I have followed the Library of Congress system in transliterating Hebrew, Russian, and Ukrainian with the omission of diacritical marks. All Jewish names in Russian archive documents have been transliterated according to this system, except for a few names like Iankel and Iakov, which appear as Yankel and Yakov for the sake of familiarity. In transliterating Yiddish, I have used the rules devised by the YIVO Institute for Jewish Research. All geographic names appear in their original historical context; hence L'viv is rendered as L'vov and Khar'kiv as Khar'kov. The most current names of the Russian and Ukrainian archives, which have gone through several changes in the past decade, have been used.

Jewish Marriage and Divorce in Imperial Russia

Introduction

In the summer of 1907, Ita Radin filed her first petition with the Rabbinic Commission[1] in St. Petersburg, protesting the inequities of her pending divorce suit: "In 1893, I married Isaak Meer Radin (who owns an apothecary in St. Petersburg) of my own volition and lived in harmony with him for fourteen years." "But last year," she complained, "he ran off with an unmarried woman to Odessa, and ever since he has refused to live with me, leaving me without any means of support." She claimed that her husband, after invoking every imaginable scheme to dissolve the marriage against her will, finally resorted to illegal methods. For that purpose he sought a change of venue, moving his machinations from St. Petersburg (his legal residence) to Nikolaev (Kherson province), "where he found a rabbi, who agreed to divorce us in spite of all the laws." The wife attested that "this rabbi now summons me [to appear in] Nikolaev" and, in the event that she failed to appear, he threatened to pass judgment in absentia and impose a monetary fine. With no other alternative, she beseeched the Rabbinic Commission to "deliver me from the constant fear of being divorced against my knowledge and will."[2]

Her husband, however, sharply contested that account and declared that their marriage had been anything but "harmonious." In a petition to the state rabbi in Nikolaev, he gave this account: "When I got married, I dreamed of finding purpose and meaning to my existence in family life, and devoted my life to cultivating a family and raising children, which I considered a sacred duty." During the course of their marriage, Isaak explained, his wife had two miscarriages, and "my house was as empty as the first day we got married."[3] Her childlessness, he argued, had effectively rendered their marriage null and void.

Local rabbis, however, informed him that obtaining a divorce would be difficult. According to Jewish law, if she did not agree to dissolve their marriage, he had to wait ten years from the time of his wife's second miscarriage to initiate a divorce hearing.[4] Apart from the legal obstacles, the couple could not agree on the financial terms of the divorce settlement. Hence, it was no coincidence that Isaak Radin journeyed from St. Petersburg to Nikolaev to seek the assistance of Rabbi Lev Kagan. The Nikolaevan state rabbi had a notorious reputation among local clients for his casual disposition to dissolve marriages illegally. Indeed, he even had the audacity to advertise himself in posters, pamphlets, and newspapers like *Odesskie novosti* and *Novoe obozrenie:* "The Chancellery of the Varvarov and Novo-Odessa rabbi L. A. Kagan will be open from 9:00 AM–2:00 PM and 5:00–7:00 in the evenings. Calling hours are available daily except for Saturdays."[5] The advertisements soon prompted an investigation by the governor of Odessa, who reported to superiors in St. Petersburg that "the rabbi increasingly expands his illegal activities, inculcating in the Jewish masses a belief that the law can be circumvented through illegal actions."[6]

"Family altercations between couples almost always create extremely unpleasant scenes," protested Rabbi Kagan in response to the inquiry by the Rabbinic Commission. "Thus the *Shulhan Arukh* [a codex of Jewish law] recommends that [couples] turn to a *beit-din* [rabbinic court] which is located neither in the husband's nor wife's legal place of residence."[7] Based on Isaak Radin's deposition, signed affidavits of other witnesses, and only a vague familiarity with Jewish law, which he misinterpreted to serve his own ends, the "rabbi" had already given Radin permission to remarry without an official hearing. He did obligate the petitioner to deliver the *get* (bill of divorcement) to his wife in compliance with Jewish law, and to return her dowry and *ketubah* (worth over 5,000 rubles). Convinced that the matter was settled, Isaak remarried and began life anew.

But as the correspondence of other rabbinic authorities indicates, the Radin case involved a host of thorny issues, not simply a divorce settlement between estranged spouses. "Concerning myself, I cannot take part in this case," wrote St. Petersburg rabbi Itskhok Dantsiger to the Odessa rabbi, Isaak Abel'son, a participant in Rabbi Kagan's *beit-din,* "all the more because they [the Radins] have a large family here [in the capital]." His own attempts to settle the case in a rabbinic court had failed because the wife had refused to accept the *get.* "Thus I completely recuse myself from this case," he declared. Family and communal pressures had prevented the St. Petersburg rabbi from taking further measures to dissolve the marriage, although he clearly sympathized with the husband: "From all appearances, he is right and she is an evil, shrewish woman and should be divorced as stated in *Even Haezer (Shulhan Arukh).*"[8]

The rabbi's scorn notwithstanding, Ita Radin had the law on her side, and she prevailed. Three years later the Rabbinic Commission ruled that

Rabbi Kagan had exceeded his jurisdiction and violated both Jewish and state laws; he was remanded to the state courts for criminal prosecution.[9] Since Ita Radin claimed that she never received the *get,* which her husband had entrusted to a calligrapher in Odessa for delivery, Isaak Radin's remarriage was declared a crime of bigamy. The commission ruled that if Ita still refused to dissolve their marriage, Isaak must divorce his second wife and that the child from the union was illegitimate. It also made the husband provide material support to *both* wives until the conclusion of the divorce.

Ita Radin's case, like many others, raised intense anxiety about the very survival of the traditional Jewish family. First and foremost, such public marital conflicts raised great alarm among contemporaries about what they perceived to be the disintegration of family values. "How chaotically these modern ideas whirled around through the minds of young Russian Jews!" wrote Pauline Wengeroff. "Traditional family ideals disappeared, but new ones did not arise in their stead."[10] A writer for the Jewish weekly newspaper *Nedel'naia khronika Voskhod* (1893) bemoaned "the demoralization of the family and purity for which the Jews have been distinguished for a long time."[11] Likewise, the Yiddish newspaper *Der shadkhon* (1906) declared that one need only to look at the divorce statistics among Jews or the growing number of deserted wives and unfaithful spouses to understand that "this is a frightening plague, an epidemic."[12] Prominent rabbinical authorities also expressed grave concerns about the fate of the Jewish family. As Rabbi Moshe Nahum Yersualimsky of Tomashpol' (Podolia province) observed, "For our many sins, there are some who have breached the bounds of decency. . . . They turn away from the path trodden by their fathers and forefathers throughout history."[13] With good reason, the controversial Radin case captured the attention of the Jewish press and public, for it graphically illustrated the complexities of family breakdown and the larger social ills that afflicted Jewish society.[14]

But the Radin case also exposed a broader issue—the bitter conflict between the state and national minorities, each deeply embroiled in the conflict between integration and autonomy. Since its founding, the Russian state gave each religious confession the authority to deal independently with questions of marriage and divorce. In the words of the main law code: "Each tribe and nation, including the heathens, is permitted to enter into marriage by the regulations of their laws and accepted customs, without the participation of a civil authority or Christian spiritual leader."[15] It further stated that "marriages of all religions tolerated in the Russian Empire (including the Muslims, Jews, and heathens) are legally recognized, if these have been conducted in accordance with the regulations and rituals of their faith."[16] Hence, rabbis and the traditional *batei-din* (rabbinical courts) retained complete and final authority to supervise circumcisions, betrothals, marriages, and divorces. Increasingly, however, the state had begun to question and, in practice, violate that autonomy. At the same time, a growing number of Jews (especially women) began to reject traditional means of redressing marital injustice; in contravention of community norms, they voluntarily turned to the Russian state to voice their grievances and to demand justice, as in the Radin case. Government intervention in private marital disputes not only violated the prerogatives of Jewish religious authorities but also abetted state intrusion into the domain of the family—a process with serious ramifications for Jewish law and society.

As the Ita Radin case suggests, the problem of marriage and divorce was exceedingly complex and raises a host of important and interesting questions. One is the formation of the family itself: what were the rules and customs of "making" the family—for example, marital age, social status, and gender expectations? Nineteenth-century Russia was an era of profound, accelerating change—from broader processes like industrialization and urbanization to assimilation and the regeneration of Jewish culture. How did these changes, both in the larger framework and inside the Jewish community itself, affect the ideals, methods, and expectations in the selection of spouses?

One must also examine the other side of the coin—the high rate of divorce among Jews. Contrary to the typical tendency for rates to skyrocket in Europe and Russia, modernization brought a curious decline in Jewish divorces by the late nineteenth century. To explain this unique pattern, it is essential to go beyond abstractions and normative laws to study concrete cases of marital dissolution, especially the records on divorce and separation and also to consider whether the statistics reflect a new stability in the Jewish family or conceal the real level of marital breakdown. For example, what obstacles—legal, social, financial—may have made it impossible or disadvantageous to obtain a legal divorce? Hence, it is important to examine the consequences of divorce, especially in matters such as child custody, division of property, and alimony. No less important is the impact of the "marriage and divorce question" on the Jews' relationship with the state. Whereas the state traditionally recognized the right of each confession to regulate family affairs, in the mid-nineteenth century it began increasingly to intervene, gradually imposing some regulation and opening its courts to litigation on a broad range of family disputes.

Historiography of the Jewish Family

This is not, of course, the first attempt to examine the "family question" in Eastern Europe. Starting in the 1940s, one of the pioneers of Jewish social history, Jacob Katz, initiated the study of the family and communal structures in Europe. In his classic work, *Tradition and Crisis*, he examined the autonomous institutions that helped sustain the "traditional" Ashkenazic family and the forces that challenged medieval customs, ideals, and practices.[17] Another influential work in shaping contemporary images of the Eastern European Jewish family has been Mark Zborowski and Elizabeth Herzog's anthropological study, *Life Is with People* (1952). Highly sentimental in content, the book seeks to capture the essence of a homogeneous, timeless "shtetl culture," which was destroyed by the Bolshevik revolution and Nazi occupation. Despite their underlying premise that most Jewish marriages "were made in heaven," they observe that divorce was an "extremely simple process" that allegedly occurred more frequently among the *prosteh* (common folk) than among *sheyneh* (upper-class) families.[18] The Eastern European Jewish family also has been the subject of American immigrant historians, who have been interested in the transition from the "Old World" to the "New World." Based primarily on oral histories and memoirs, works by Sydney Stahl Weinberg and Susan Glenn offer a less romantic picture of immigrant women's lives in Eastern Europe, focusing instead on their second-class religious status, economic burden of breadwinning, and complex family relations.[19]

More recently, influenced by new trends in cultural and gender studies, a small but growing number of studies have provided a more nuanced picture of Jewish society in Eastern Europe, challenging the idea of a single, homogeneous "Jewish family"—identical, immutable across space and time. Most obvious were the differences across space: Jewish family patterns in the Russian Empire varied profoundly, reflecting the immense differences in the society, economy, and religious life of individual Jewish communities. Immanuel Etkes's work on the *lomdim* (scholarly elites) in Lithuania, for example, examines the tensions between their obligations to study Torah and their marital responsibilities.[20] Jacob Katz suggests that similar tensions existed in Hasidic families because of the intimate bond between the Hasid and the *tsaddik*, although more research on this subject is needed.[21] Nor was there a timeless "traditional family," somehow juxtaposed to a "modern family.[22] In fact, the strands of continuity often merged so intimately with new ideologies that it was sometimes impossible to discern where one began and the other ended. As David Biale has so aptly put it, "The modern period always seems to exist in dialectical relationship to its predecessors and modern Jews define themselves in constant tension with their tradition, even if their knowledge of that tradition remains fragmentary."[23] Indeed, several important studies by Biale, Alan Mintz, Mordechai Zalkin, and others focus on maskilic critiques of these imagined traditions and their evolution.[24]

This exploration of Jewish marriages and divorces in Imperial Russia also has been greatly influenced by Paula Hyman's challenge to go beyond "filling in the gaps" of women's experiences (compensatory history) and examine the role of gender in Jewish historical development.[25] By *gender,* I refer to the "social organization based on sexual difference," which is specific to a certain historical context.[26] Groundbreaking work by Hyman, Shmuel Feiner, Iris Parush, Naomi Seidman, Shaul Stampfer, and Israel Bartal on the gendered system of education, literary bilingualism, and sexuality have all provided a new way of looking at the Eastern European past through the lens of women's experiences and gender.[27]

Scope of Present Study

This study seeks to combine the social historian's quest to understand "everyday life" with the postmodernist's close attention to language in examining the transformation of the Jewish family in Imperial Russia. In particular, it is interested in the impact of modernity on the different experiences of Jewish men and women in the context of marriage and family. How were gender expectations, roles and power relations in the Jewish family constructed, legitimized, and negotiated? Moreover, how did those relationships and power dynamics change as Jews (especially women) began to ask the state to intervene in private family affairs?

It is especially important to analyze the construction of divorce and separation narratives, to listen to the different stories told by spouses and witnesses, and to consider how each party constructed arguments in an effort to prevail. Individual cases, taken together, make a collective portrait of marital conflict and gendered responses to unfulfilled or violated expectations. The depositions and testimony graphically show how spouses negotiated gender roles, redefined family obligations, and dealt with domestic evils like spousal abuse and infidelity. As the foregoing suggests, this study attributes an important role to the agency of subjects. As Anna Clark (*Struggle for the Breeches*) put it, "Relations of power were always shifting but they shifted because real political actors, including women, negotiated and contested them."[28] Throughout, the overarching object of this study is to go beyond the mere juridical and theological and to explore the quotidian—how Jews perceived and constructed marital life.

Structurally, this book will combine a grass-roots case study of the Ukrainian and Lithuanian provinces, with attention to larger patterns in the Russian Empire as a whole. The Ukrainian provinces were dominated largely by Hasidism, whereas the Lithuanian provinces were influenced by a mitnagdic way of life, ethos, and culture. An in-depth examination of the Jewish family in these areas can provide a useful comparative perspective for other parts of the empire. The Jews in the Kingdom of Poland are not be included directly in this study (although some references will be made to their situation), since they were governed by a different legal and political system in the prerevolutionary period.[29]

I was able to make use of extraordinarily rich and diverse materials because of the fortuitous timing of my research. This project began as my dissertation in the summer of 1993, following the breakup of the Soviet Union two years earlier. Independence had brought profound changes, including the declassification of hitherto secret collections. That process encompassed not only classified repositories, such as the Ukrainian Communist Party archive, but also materials pertaining to national minorities, such as the Jews, which were gradually transferred from special storage *(spetskhran)* to the main collections. For the first time, researchers had access to materials that had been virtually inaccessible, allegedly to avert use by nationalists and to avoid "ethnic conflicts." I had the opportunity to work in various central and *oblast'* (district) archives in Russia (St. Petersburg and Moscow), Ukraine (Kyiv, Khar'kiv, L'viv, Zhytomyr, and Odessa), and Lithuania (Vilnius). The materials that are now accessible to historians provide a unique glimpse into the inner world of Russian Jewry in a way that is radically different from memoirs, diaries, and newspaper articles. For the first time, the individual "voices" of ordinary provincial Jews, particularly women, who have languished as the "masses," can be clearly heard. This study also draws upon YIVO archive's rich collection of documents and photographs pertaining to the history and culture of Jews in Eastern Europe.

The first set of sources are the central state records, located in the Russian State Historical Archive (RGIA) of St. Petersburg. The files of the Ministry of Interior (f. 1284), the Emperor's Chancellery for the Receipt of Petitions (f. 1412), and the State Senate (f. 1405), contain petitions from Jews for marital separation (separate passports), adoption of illegitimate children, residence rights, and other family issues. Still more important and interesting are the files of the Rabbinical Commission in the collection of the Department of Spiritual Affairs of Foreign Faiths (f. 821). These documents reveal how Jewish religious leaders reacted to controversial questions involving divorce, intermarriage, desertion, and the plight of the *agunah*. This collection also includes numerous petitions from Jews (mainly women) who, in contravention of community norms, turned to the state in their quest to overturn rabbinic divorce rulings that they considered unjust. The records of the Jewish Committee (f. 1269) include numerous reports and correspondence regarding Jewish metrical books (registers of vital statistics), the election of rabbis, and various other questions pertaining to Jewish communities in Russia. Finally, materials in the archive of the Chief Procurator of the Holy Synod (f. 797) contain valuable information on intermarriage and divorce between Jews and Christians.

A second set of sources are the local state records, including the Chancellery of the Kiev General Governorship (f. 442) and the Chancellery of the Vil'na General Governorship (f. 387), which address disputes over the validity of marriages and specific applications to overturn decisions of local rabbis. Civil and criminal court records from Zhitomir and Vil'na also contain invaluable information about the execution of wills, divorce settlements, infanticide, child abandonment, seduction, rape, and a host of other issues. Other important collections are the local Russian Orthodox consistories in Odessa, Zhitomir, and Vil'na, which shed light on conversions and "mixed" marriages, and the offices of the provincial boards and medical boards.

These materials do not carry any claim to being "representative." By their very nature, they are unique and personal; even the petitioners' willingness to appeal to the state was an act of rebellion against tradition and community. Nevertheless, their argumentation—and the response of defendants and testimony of witnesses—refer to accepted norms as their point of reference. The litigants, in short, inevitably spoke in the idiom of their subculture and thereby revealed the intricate construct of their world. Even extraordinary and sensational cases can be highly instructive, for they struck at the most divisive, sensitive and unresolved issues of Jewish society.

To be sure, legal suits and court records must be treated with caution: plaintiffs and lawyers wrote depositions and offered testimony, not for the sake of "sheer truth" but to "win the case." Indeed, it is often difficult to determine the "facts" of the case, and piecing together a divorce case can be an arduous task when both sides appear equally convincing. As Natalie Zemon Davis has shown, it is often the "fictional" elements of such documents that can be most revealing—that is, the way in which people shaped events into a story.[30] This does not necessarily mean forgery or fraud, but the choice of "language, detail, and order." At the same time, one cannot completely dismiss "experience" in favor of the postmodernist emphasis on language alone. Incidental details, such as a domestic servant's description of her daily routine, for example, can speak volumes about aspects of Jewish life that have yet to be explored.

A third complex of archival materials is the *lichnye fondy*, or private collections, of various Jewish personalities (e.g., Emmanuel Levin, Isaac Luria, Rabbi Jacob Maze of Moscow, Rabbi Isaac Roikhel and Sofia Roikhel of St. Petersburg, the lawyer G. B. Sliozberg). Apart from personal documents (e.g., private papers), these collections sometimes include correspondence (in Hebrew, Yiddish, and Russian), as well as newspaper clippings and other materials to which the owner attached particular importance. In particular, YIVO's large collection of family letters can provide a rare glimpse into private family matters, such as matchmaking, education, and emigration. For all their limitations, such papers provide a valuable counterpoint to the formalized documentation that pervades many official archival collections.

Valuable and dominant as the archival base may be, it is also imperative to tap the vast store of printed materials—law codes and proclamations, newspapers and journals, diaries and memoirs. The laws, Jewish and state, were important; even when violated, they defined the norms and, no doubt, exercised a constraining role, even in remote villages seemingly far removed from the tsar's undermanned government. The press is of particular importance. Although the family question was not the sole or even main interest of the mainstream Russian Jewish press, newspapers such as *Rassvet, Voskhod, Russkii evrei, Hamelits, Der yidishe folksblat,* and others nevertheless engaged in public debates about new family laws, intermarriage, women's rights, and the rabbinate. Finally, much valuable information also can be gleaned from diaries and memoirs about family life.

Although this first exploration can make no pretense at being definitive, it does allow a fresh new perspective on marriage and divorce, the family and the state, in Imperial Russia. This book is divided into five chapters. The first chapter examines characteristics of "traditional" Jewish marriage—its demographics (marriage rates and patterns), the linchpins of the traditional structures, and finally, the emerging critiques and transformation of the family. The second chapter explores the establishment of the Rabbinic Commission and provincial state rabbinate that were designed to "bring order to the Jewish family." The third chapter offers a systematic analysis of marital breakdown and divorce in order to highlight underlying conflicts in the nineteenth-century Jewish family. Chapter 4 addresses the aftermath of divorce (e.g., alimony, child custody and support) and the social problems stemming from unresolved marital issues (e.g., bigamy and the problem of the *agunah*). The final chapter deals with the struggle for domination by three major players: an embittered but optimistic Orthodox rabbinate, a discredited state rabbinate, and finally, the Russian state. Throughout, the overarching objective is to explore the quotidian—how the family "worked" or "broke down" on a day-to-day basis.

This study argues that while contemporary critics were wont to see the Jewish family as the victim of a sudden, radical crisis, in fact the processes of change were far more complex, long-term, and multifaceted. The changes were driven by both internal and external forces. Rebellion against traditional customs (e.g., arranged marriages, early nuptials) and the promotion of new ideologies had, again, gradually begun to challenge Jewish marital practices and expectations by the mid-nineteenth century. Tensions indeed ran high—from mundane conflicts over finances to new tensions over gender roles, female education, and religious observance—resulting in a high divorce rate. This social turmoil accompanied a steady decline in rabbinical authority (once a powerful influence in family life), and the emergence of the secular Russian state, which increasingly acted to undermine Jewish autonomy over marriage and divorce. That state intrusion, significantly, evoked support from a growing number of Jews (especially women), who voluntarily resorted to the government to resolve internal family disputes. Those exogenous factors—decline of rabbinical power and intrusion of state institutions—fundamentally changed the dynamics of marital conflicts and divorce. Indeed, what made the crisis of the Jewish family unique and intense was the combination of internal change and the realignment of external authority.

If formal marital dissolution once provided an easy solution to marital breakdown, that was no longer true in the late nineteenth century. New rules about residency, court intervention in divorce settlements (e.g., alimony and child custody), political instability (e.g., pogroms), and a social aversion to divorce all made formal marital dissolution increasingly less appealing, less feasible. Instead, more Jews opted for reconciliation, marital separation, desertion, even bigamy; these "marriages in limbo" were symptomatic of a family crisis that would prompt the Jewish intelligentsia, the Orthodox rabbis, and the state to seek a fundamental reform of this basic institution.

Chapter One

Marriage: Creating the Jewish Family

Both my grandfathers, on my mother's side and on my father's side, died before I was born, and I was named for both of them, and therefore their memories were dear and holy to me, almost like the memory of the great forefathers of generations past, Abraham, Isaac, and Jacob, for they were links in my chain of ancestry, and these—the last.

—Isaac Dov Berkowitz, *Beerev yom hakippurim*

Ven di vayb trogt di hoyzn, vasht der man di spodnitseh. (When the wife wears the pants, the husband washes the skirt).

— Yiddish folk saying

For Eastern European Jews, the family has been a basic institution, the critical unit for social bonding and cultural transmission. As Devorah Baron's short story "Mishpahah" (Family) emphasizes, the Jewish family is a "chain of generations . . . link after link in a chain that is never broken."[1] This self-conscious continuity encouraged both the custom of naming a child after a deceased relative and the abiding interest in family roots.[2] The family was also an important agency for the socialization of children and transmission of religion and cultural heritage. Pauline Wengeroff, raised in the Belorussian town of Bobruisk, fondly recalled the daily rhythm of her childhood: "In my parent's house, the day was divided and named according to the three daily prayers. . . . Jewish life in the first half of the 1800s was . . . very peaceful, comfortable, stern, and intellectual. There was no chaotic jumbling of customs, practices, and systems, as is now found in Jewish homes."[3]

Although the Eastern European Jewish family resisted the challenges of modernity, it was hardly immune to change and inevitably reflected the broader transformations in nineteenth-century society. Marriage, the central arena for redefining gender and authority, increasingly came under public scrutiny as critics (not simply from elites but also ordinary folk) questioned traditional values and customs. While everyday practices were slower to change, Jews emulated a distinct transition toward the "companionate marriage" based on mutual respect, emotional and intellectual compatibility, and affection. The new emphasis on self-fulfillment and individual feelings reshaped attitudes toward every aspect of marriage, from matchmaking to the gender division of labor in the household. Demographically, the most salient change was the sharp rise in age at first marriage: Jews married at a young age in the early nineteenth century, but by the end of the century, they married later than did the general population—a shift with major implications for fertility rates and marital relationships.

This chapter on family formation addresses five central questions. One was matchmaking: how were such unions arranged? What were the roles and rights of key actors—the parents, the matchmaker, and the partners themselves? A second focus is the criteria of a good match: what were the ideal qualities of a potential spouse, and how did these change over time? A third issue is demographics and the patterns of marriage—that is, the pattern of age, social and marital status, and seasonality. The fourth question pertains to the wedding itself: was there a common custom that Jews in different parts of the Russian Empire observed? Or was this rite of passage unique to each locality? Finally, what impact did all these changes—the methods and criteria of matchmaking—have on expectations about the respective roles of the husband and wife?

Shiddukhin: The Delicate Art of Matchmaking

Arranging marriage was one of the most critical decisions that a Jewish family faced: the outcome affected not only the couple but also their families, especially parents. In Jewish communities, an intermediary (e.g., a professional matchmaker, a relative, or a family acquaintance) usually met with the prospective parties to discuss the advisability of the match and to negotiate the terms of betrothal. But matchmaking was not a coldly calculated business deal; it had to navigate unpredictable human factors and complex religious laws about degrees of kinship and unlawful relationships.[4] Commenting on the difficulties of arranging such unions, one rabbi volunteered that "in heaven it is thought [to be] as difficult as the dividing of the Red Sea."[5] The task was especially challenging in Russia, which raised two additional hurdles: government restrictions on mobility and residency and deep religious divisions among the Jews (i.e., Hasidim and mitnagdim).

To arrange an advantageous match within a confined world, Jewish families could employ four main strategies: (1) hire a professional *shadkhan* (marriage broker); (2) attend annual fairs in large cities like Lublin and Khar'kov, where Jewish merchants gathered to trade but also negotiated potential marriages; (3) contract marriages with close relatives; and (4) resort to endogamous marriage within a small group of local families. This process unfolded under the watchful eye of parents or guardians, who had a large stake in the outcome.

Parental Authority

As elsewhere in Eastern Europe, Jewish matchmaking traditionally remained under strict parental control. To be sure, the *Shulhan Arukh* (a codex of Jewish law) required volition of the bride, forbidding betrothal until she was old enough to discern her own wishes.[6] Such admonitions notwithstanding, a woman was not expected to express prenuptial preferences. As one rabbinic authority wrote in the twelfth century, "It is the habit of all Jewish maidens, even if they be as much as twenty years old, to leave the arrangement of their marriage in the hands of their fathers; nor are they indelicate or impudent enough to express their own fancies and say, 'I would like to wed such-and-such a person.'"[7]

This parental control prevailed in the Polish-Lithuanian Commonwealth—areas that would eventually be annexed by the Russian empire in the late eighteenth century. In 1623 the Lithuanian Council issued a decree annulling any marriage contracted "without the knowledge of his father or close relative (in the absence of a father)."[8] Those who violated this law risked forfeiting the conditions in their *tenaim* (betrothal contract), a punishment fraught with grave economic and social consequences. In short, Polish law upheld parental right to organize children's marriages.

These basic principles remained in effect after the Russian Empire annexed these territories in the three partitions of Poland (1772–1795). Indeed, parental consent was also a fundamental tenet of Russian law; although the tsarist state forbade coercive marriage, it recognized the right of parental consent for those under age twenty-two: "If both parents are alive, the father's approval [to marry] is required; if he has died or disappeared, the mother's consent is required." Orphans in their minority required the permission of their legal guardians to marry.[9] Parents could even oppose the marriage of a grown child, although in that case they had to explain their reasons to a responsible institution (e.g., rabbinic authorities in the case of Jews).[10] This definition of parental authority and filial subordination reflected the patriarchal values of autocratic Russia.[11]

Submission to parental will was generally the norm in Jewish society. It was closely associated with the low marital age, which left children both psychologically and economically dependent. As Pauline Wengeroff has observed, "The thoughts and feelings of children in those times were so innocent as their parents made marriage plans for them."[12] Indeed, news about his impending marriage came as a total surprise to the *maskil* Moshe Leib Lilienblum (who became engaged at the exceptionally young age of fourteen): "On Sunday, 17 Ellul 5627 [1857], I awoke, but with the laziness of an only child I rested on my bed, until my father told me, 'Get up, groom! Why rest? Go say your prayers; your future mother-in-law is coming.' I did not understand him at all, nor did I try to for I thought he was joking." At the signing of the *tenaim* (betrothal contract), he noticed "a small girl, by appearance [only] three years old; I understood that she was the bride."[13]

Similarly, Puah Rakowski of Bialystok (b. 1865)[14] first learned that her parents had arranged her match when they announced that her groom's grandmother was to come for a visit. Although she reluctantly agreed to a disappointing match with a man ten years older, the young bride burst into bitter tears as they broke a plate sealing her betrothal. "Jewish daughters were not bold enough to wrench free from the restraint of unbending customs that in reality enslaved them," she remarked, reflecting back on her experience. "A girl did not even have the audacity to oppose the match that her father made for her."[15] Sometimes, the couple did not even meet before the wedding, a device used to avert remonstration and resistance. Miriam Shomer Zunzer recalled that her great-grandmother first caught a glimpse of her future husband "when he dropped the veil over her face before she was led under the *huppah* (wedding canopy)."[16]

Although the Russian state recognized the parental right to give or withhold consent, it gradually reduced this authority. Thus, while reaffirming the parental right of consent, the government forbade parents, regardless of class and status, to coerce their children to marry.[17] That policy derived from a Senate decree of 1722, which prohibited coercive marriage of people against their will.[18] Hence, involuntary marriage was invalid; for Russian Orthodox believers, it was prima facie grounds for annulment. To be sure, tsarist fiat did not automatically eliminate coercion among either Christian or Jewish families. Neither, understandably, could be expected to renounce their vested interest and observe a paper decree from remote St. Petersburg. Families had too much at stake; state officials had too little power to enforce. Local authorities also were well aware of the quotidian realities, where duress, if not physical coercion, was a fact of life. In 1893 the state tacitly conceded as much when the Ministry of Internal Affairs, without a tone of censure or disapproval, asked the Rabbinic Commission to explain Jewish laws and customs regarding the power of

FIG. 1. A venerable pair—Rabbi Moshe Yudel Reb Osher, the scribe, with his wife in Bershad (Podolia province), where he was also the cantor of the old town synagogue. *Courtesy of the YIVO Institute for Jewish Research.*

parents to marry off children without their consent.[19] The commission candidly replied that Jewish law forbade a father to marry a son against the latter's will but allowed him to betroth his underage daughter to whoever he pleased. Harsh penalties notwithstanding, the commission confirmed that the decree against involuntary matrimony did little to diminish parental authority.[20]

The memoir literature also shows that, despite the gendered nature of Jewish law on coerced unions, both sexes were vulnerable. When a son protested an arranged match with an older cousin, the father threatened to send him off as a recruit. Despite the youth's desperate effort to thwart the union (an anonymous letter to the bride's parents warning that "nothing good would come of the marriage"), the marriage took place.[21] Rabbi Shlome Yitshak Drozhd (1830–1904), orphaned at the age of twelve, had a similar experience when an uncle betrothed him to his daughter. His sister remembered how the young boy wept bitterly, complaining that "the bride did not please him because she was dark." His threats to flee to a yeshiva were to no avail; the unhappy groom had to marry the girl.[22]

While coercion sparked resistance in earlier times, defiance became much more pronounced and intense in the nineteenth century, partly because of the rise in marital age and partly because of new sentimental ideals.[23] It is also possible that the availability of more sources generates this impression. "Rebellion" assumed several forms, such as marrying despite parental opposition, running away from home, and even converting to Christianity to thwart an arranged marriage. Those who married without parental consent could be prosecuted by their parents in state courts for "disobedience and disrespectful behavior."[24] Some parents exercised this right. In 1859, Yosel and Yudes Eliashberg filed a suit against their twenty-six-year-old son Mordkhelia in a Vil'na state court for his "insubordination and insult to their parental authority." The infuriated parents not only had their son arrested by the Vil'na city police but requested that the court "terminate his association with his harmful acquaintances in Vil'na" by relocating him to a small town until he reformed.[25]

A counterpetition by the son's wife and father-in-law accused the Eliashbergs of being motivated by "their hatred toward us . . . because of [his] marriage to the petitioner Basia." Echoing new social attitudes, Ovsei Fridberg declared that the wedding had been performed "according to Jewish custom based on mutual agreement, good-will, and yes, even love. . . . The marriage, albeit without parental consent, cannot be considered a crime."[26] If love alone did not justify the union, Fridberg noted that his son-in-law, "Markus,"[27] had registered independently with his wife and two children from a previous marriage in the last poll tax census; hence, he should not be treated as a minor. In his own defense, Mordkhelia Eliashberg confirmed his parents' opposition to the union but stressed the importance of affective bonding: "It was well known to everyone in town, and even more so to my parents, that I have been in love with my present wife for a long time."[28] Although Eliashberg accepted exile to the town of Kovel (Zhitomir province), he insisted—contrary to his father's demand that he relocate alone—that he move together with his wife and children. Despite his age and legal status, the court upheld the Eliashbergs' right "to punish their son . . . for disobedience to parental authority" and sentenced him to three to six months in jail and voluntary exile with his family.[29]

Running away from home was another way to rebel against an undesirable match. For young bridegrooms, the yeshivot in Lithuania or the state rabbinical schools (in Vil'na and Zhitomir) occasionally served as safe havens from unwanted matches.[30] But flight was also becoming more popular among women. It coincided with the rise of radical political movements like nihilism, populism, and socialism; these close-knit conspiratorial circles functioned as ersatz families and helped single women contract the fictitious marriages that conferred internal passports and the right to reside outside the parental home. Gesia Gelfman of Mozyr (Minsk province) took that path: on the eve of her wedding she fled to the home of a Russian friend before the older women could "perform the repulsive rituals dictated by ancient Jewish customs."[31] Gelfman later joined the terrorist "People's Will" *(Narodnaia volia)* and participated in the assassination of Tsar Alexander II in 1881. Others replicated her actions by joining socialist movements like the Jewish Bund "to hide from parents who were trying to arrange speedy marriages."[32]

Jewish women from affluent families sometimes matriculated in the special schools, both to escape a match and to obtain professional training. Shmuel Leib Tsitron (1860–1930) recalled that it was not uncommon in the 1870s for residents of Minsk to hear the following: "The daughter of so-and-so fled her parents' home on the eve of her marriage, taking all her trousseau and jewels with her and vanished without a trace. . . . 'Twas not for love that the runaways had fled. No! The fugitive virgins were sitting and studying in schools for midwives in Mogilev or attending schools of dentistry in Kharkov."[33] Similar reports made their way into the Jewish press, such as *Russkii evrei:* "Ten young Jewish women from the most prosperous and religious families in the city of Mogilev, left for St. Petersburg to enroll in higher courses for women without the agreement of their parents."[34]

The most desperate recourse to avoid a match was conversion to Christianity. Apart from seeking to foil family plans, the converts were often women who preferred a Christian suitor to their parents' choice.[35] Conversion was also likely to elicit sympathetic treatment and protection from Russian authorities. Women like Sara Goldshtein of Grodno deliberately cultivated official support: she testified that she was "already spoken for by some young, rich Jew" but desired to be baptized because of her "disgust for Judaism" after reading the Gospels. Her mother denigrated the sincerity of Sara's conversion, claiming that her daughter simply wanted to marry a Russian soldier, who stole money and other valuables from the family when the two secretly left the house.[36] Whatever the truth, the case suggests that a higher level of female social interaction with non-Jews (mainly soldiers and peasants) sometimes led to clandestine romances and unions. The lack of Jewish education perhaps contributed to women's vulnerability to conversion, but even those with a strong Jewish upbringing sometimes chose a Christian spouse at the expense of their faith.[37]

Apart from a new culture valorizing affective ties, other factors in the mid-nineteenth century began to erode parents' power to arrange marriages. One was a decline in legal support—a response to the change of opinion among enlightened bureaucrats and educated society.[38] It was a matter of institutional change: in 1861, as part of the judicial reform, the government abolished the "conscience court" (sovestnyi sud) that had hitherto dealt with "contentious cases between parents and children over property and all types of litigation," such as the Eliashberg case cited above.[39] Although some parents appealed to district courts and justices of the peace, they rarely found a sympathetic ear. No less important, the government drastically curtailed parental and community power by outlawing the traditional Jewish methods of disciplining—the flogging and ostracism (excommunication) that had ensured conformity and obedience.

Another challenge to parental authority came from the Jewish enlightenment movement (haskalah), which aimed to modernize Jewish society by fundamentally changing the inherited values, institutions, and power structures.[40] Whether they actually functioned as initiators of change or as rationalizers for a transformation already underway, the maskilim (enlightened Jews) played a critical role in articulating and disseminating the attack on traditional Jewish culture.[41] The maskilim attached particular importance to reforming the Jewish family, which they regarded as a major impediment to modernization. As early as the 1790s, enlightened thinkers like Jakub Kalmanson of Warsaw enjoined parents to cease arranging marriages for their children, since "this step requires complete freedom of choice and very serious thought."[42]

Later maskilic writings also elevated individual feelings over parental authority. In Peretz Smolenskin's Reward of the Righteous (1905), for instance, Miriam and Bathsheba bitterly bemoan the fate of Jewish women, who are "led to the marriage canopy like sheep to the slaughter": "In giving their daughters in marriage, they [the parents] forget that these daughters are living beings with heart and desire. . . . No, they march them off like captives at sword point to a home contrived by a matchmaker."[43] While Smolenskin likened parental tyranny of arranged marriages to the brutal treatment of captives, his contemporary, Judah Leib Gordon, described it as a violation of a woman's honor. His famous epic poem, "The Tip of the Yud" "Kotso shel yud," portrays the fate of Bat-Shua, whose parents callously marry her off without regard for her emotions: "What does delightful love give, what does it add? Our mothers knew not this kind of love. Shall we make our sister into a prostitute?" the writer protests. The allusion, of course, is to the response of Jacob's sons, who slaughtered their sister Dinah's rapist rather than allowing him to marry her in accordance with the custom in ancient Israel.[44] This "invocation and inversion of sacred Biblical images," Michael Stanislawski aptly notes, made his critique all the more scathing.[45] While not all arranged marriages precluded love and affection,[46] the *maskilim* emphasized its less appealing side and the gap between individual rights and parental will. In effect, they portrayed the problem as a generational conflict and clash of irreconcilable values.

Demographics also subtly undermined parental authority: as the average age of first marriage increased, the children were no longer legal minors but young adults, with their own will and capacity to support themselves. Whatever the dynamics of deferred marriage (longer education, economic necessity, or a willful decision to defer and exercise one's own will), the main point is that those taking the marital vow were often independent adults, not dependent children. They were, predictably, less inclined to submit to parental will, especially in such vital matters as marriage. They were also emboldened by a growing sympathy in government and religious authorities; some grooms even succeeded in dissolving undesirable matches by turning to sympathetic rabbis.[47]

As a result, while parents often dominated the matchmaking process, at the very least, they were increasingly obliged to solicit their children's cooperation and consent.[48] As Rabbi Eliyahu ben Yehudah Feldman, a professional matchmaker from Gel'miazkov (Poltava province), observed in 1913, "In these days, one must discuss the match more with the children than with the parents."[49]

The *Shadkhan*: The Marriage Broker

Jews used marriage brokers to find an eligible partner from a different geographic region. It was not only the affluent who could afford to organize long-distance marriages; as Jacob Goldberg has demonstrated, even "simple and less prosperous Jews" used matchmakers to broaden the sparse selection of partners in their own village.[50] In the seventeenth and eighteenth centuries most marriage brokers plied their trade at the great fairs in Krakow, Lublin, and other commercial centers. These fairs provided a convenient venue to arrange matches and, above all, to tap a richer pool of potential candidates.

Traveling from village to town with a well-worn *pinkas* (ledger) in hand, the Eastern European matchmakers were descendants of the illustrious intermediaries of medieval Europe who served as agents of "reunification"—to link the scattered Jewish communities through marriage. By the sixteenth century, however, this profession had lost its erstwhile prestige and moral authority, and some communities even began to adopt laws to regulate the fees and activities of marriage brokers, a group that included not only rabbis and lawyers but also "traveling merchants who hawked hearts as well as trinkets."[51] The distrust of unscrupulous matchmakers became a stock theme in Jewish culture. In his satirical *Tractate of Poverty (Masekhet aniyut)*, Aizik Meyer Dik (1814–1893) warned: "All of Israel are qualified to be matchmakers, cantors and teachers, even someone who has never in his life read the Torah or even attended school. Rav Batlan says: even someone who stammers and emits bad odors."[52]

Given regional differences, the *Shulhan Arukh* let local custom dictate the fees of marriage brokers.[53] For example, if the *shadkhan* insisted on immediate payment but the groom wanted to wait until the marriage, local custom was to resolve the dispute. If the local community had no rule, the will of the prospective husband, not the matchmaker, prevailed.[54] The price for *shadkhanut* varied by region, but in Eastern Europe it reflected mainly the geographic distance between the parties.[55] For example, the Lithuanian Council ruled that, for arranging a betrothal within a forty-mile radius, the *shadkhan* was to receive "forty-eight Polish groszy for every hundred and hundred [*sic*] [groszy of the dowry]." To prevent misunderstandings, the marriage broker was to accept only the amount stipulated by both parties at the commencement of the deal. Since the *shadkhan* could not subsequently raise his fee, he had to anticipate all possible expenses (e.g., travel) and justify their inclusion in the original agreement.

Matchmaking often involved multiple marriage brokers. A Lithuanian Council ordinance of 1623 even provides for their financial settlement: "The one who begins [the deal] and the one who concludes [it] shall divide [the fee] between them." In the event of a dispute between the two matchmakers, a *beit-din* or "reliable people" *(neemanim)* was to decide "who started and concluded the match or if they worked on it together."[56] No other intermediaries were to be compensated, both to protect the rights of the *shadkhan* and to avoid encumbering the negotiations with too many players. As Sholom Aleichem's fictitious matchmaker, Menachem Mendel, once complained, the failure of his business was due to "strangers mixing in."[57]

Not surprisingly, the devious *shadkhan* became a prime target of the *haskalah* movement, which denounced him as an "unproductive parasite" who turned marriage into a business transaction—a practice "unsuited to the modern world."[58] According to the *maskil* Abraham Baer Gottlober (1811–1899), matchmakers rapaciously saw young Torah students like himself as prize merchandise, reserving them in their ledgers for the daughters of the finest and wealthiest families. To earn the coveted commission, he noted, these unscrupulous brokers, who possessed Promethean powers of exaggeration, routinely deceived the prospective parties. Thus, a *shadkhan* might receive a letter from a fellow matchmaker describing "the daughter of so-and-so, an illustrious officer of a town such-and-such for ten years." He would then be carried away by his own excitement and declare that the bride was a stunning beauty, skilled in prayer, adept at reading and writing, and even versed in accounting. He would add that the father pledged to give a huge dowry and provide ten years of *mezonot* (material support) in order to obtain a Torah scholar for his daughter. Only when parties met to negotiate the specific terms did they discover that "the words of the *shadkhan* were a lie and a falsehood."[59]

Not only acculturated *maskilim* but also ordinary Jews distrusted the matchmaker. As a wary Sheine Elke Yaffe of Pskov wrote to Rabbi Shlome Drozhd of Shebiz in 1903, regarding a proposed match for her daughter with a young man from the latter's hometown, "I know that I can rely upon you to advise as a good friend . . . because one cannot really believe the *shadkhan*."[60] Yiddish folksongs also reflected a popular animus toward the matchmaker's nefarious dishonesty and indifference to affection and personal feelings. In one poignant song, a young bride bitterly cursed her marriage broker:

Shadkhan, shadkhan,	Matchmaker, matchmaker
a klog tsu dir	woe to you!!
Vos hostu gehat tsu mir!	Oh, what did you want with me?
Tsugenumen di shadkhones	You took my dowry,
Opegekoylet on rakhmones	And slaughtered me without pity,
A klog tsu dir, a klog tsu dir!	A curse on you, a curse on you![61]

Women were not only victims but also perpetrators: female *shadkhaniyot* (female marriage brokers) also plied the trade of matchmaking. Simon Dubnow makes a passing reference to *svati* and *svakhi* (the Russian terms for male and female matchmakers, respectively) and observes that they helped to organize "secret meetings between couples without the knowledge of the bride's parents."[62] In the family itself, women—especially if they were the primary breadwinners—often played a central role in selecting spouses for their children. That is, in fact, a major theme in the abundant memoir literature. The popular Yiddish writer Nahum Meyer Sheikewitz (better known as Shomer, 1846–1905), like many of his generation, credited his mother and grandmother—both diligent businesswomen, fluent in Polish and Russian—for organizing his marriage. His father, the "impractical" rabbinic scholar whose ignorance of secular matters allowed him to be swindled out of his inheritance, played no role in the process.[63]

If a family did not hire a professional marriage broker, it might resort to less expensive options. In the case of Chaim Aronson, for example, a relative (employed full-time as a weaver) negotiated the terms of his marriage with the bride's family.[64] Jewish merchants acted as their own marriage brokers, using their trips to the large fairs in Lublin or Khar'kov to marry off a son or daughter. Abram Sagal, for instance, personally negotiated the terms of his own marriage with a local merchant family. Tsarist residency laws also figured in his marital calculations: Segal wanted not only to find a wife but to acquire the right to reside in Khar'kov and to set up a business there.[65]

Inroads of Modernity: New Rituals and Patterns

Although parents tenaciously defended their prerogative, they could not halt the steady erosion of custom and tradition. Some sought to influence, if not to control, the shock by permitting some courtship. Letter writing, a medium fostered by the rapid expansion of postal services, became increasingly popular, especially among the privileged. Some did not immediately welcome this literary romanticism. No sooner had S. Y. Abramovich (Mendele Moykher Sforim) written his fiancée that he had no interest in a romantic correspondence, than he received his first love letter from her. "Believe me, my dear Pauline," he later confessed, "what ecstasy I experienced when I read your letter, what an impression it made on me."[66]

Nahum M. Sheikewitz (Shomer) posted love letters during his engagement and later published a sample collection in Yiddish for those in need of guidance. "The letter plays one of the most important roles in a person's life," he informed his readers. "The words of a letter make a much greater impression when they are wise, good, and sensibly written, than all the words that come forth from [one's] mouth." In the letter "From a Bride to a Groom Who Is in America," he advised the woman to express her utter dependence on her partner: "You know, Hershele [or the name of the groom], that my life depends on you alone, that you are my 'all' in this world." After the groom departed for America, the bride compared herself to a millionaire who had lost all his possessions in a fire.[67]

Letter writing was not always rewarding; it could be a painful experience. It only compounded the misery of those with an intolerable arranged marriage. As Puah Rakowski wrote, "Then there began for me another plague—the correspondence with the groom *(khosn)*. What could be a greater pain than to write love letters to a person who is a stranger to you?"[68] This new ritual also could bruise egos. When Isaak Simkhovich Lur'e was still a student in Paris, he corresponded with a female cousin from Vitebsk, who was auditing medical courses in St. Petersburg.[69] At first, she firmly rejected his fervent declarations of love and proposals of marriage: "You say that you do not want any pity from me but, at the same time, you demand my consent, knowing that except for pity, I have absolutely no feelings for you. . . . I have decided once and for all, *never, under no circumstances* [will I love you]. I would rather remain unmarried, then at least I would be true to myself. I know that this is a brutal way of saying it, but I do not have any other alternative. Don't you understand at last that I am strong and imperious by nature and I will fall in love only when I am attracted to someone."[70] She finally had to threaten to terminate their correspondence if he did not drop his unwelcome intentions.

Not only the post but more informal sociability (at least in some quarters) lowered the social boundaries between the sexes. Rakowski recalled that in her youth it was improper for young men to pay visits to the daughters of pious families, let alone to carry on a full-fledged romance.[71] Yiddish etiquette books warned: "A woman should not be with a strange man without a chaperone."[72] But these rules fell increasingly into disuse, even in strict Orthodox homes. Rabbi Chaim Tchernowitz (b. 1870), for instance, recalled how the young people of his town used to meet at his house to discuss their romances with his mother, an avid reader of Yiddish literature and newspapers. As a young boy, he participated in their schemes to divert his father to the *beit-hamidrash* so that they could openly confide in her.[73] Much to the dismay of parents, daughters fell in love with their young tutors, family friends, and sometimes even non-Jews—a phenomenon captured so vividly in Sholom Aleichem's *Tevye the Dairyman*. As education and schooling increased, such interaction naturally rose, breaking down gender walls and removing boys and girls from family control. One can also assume that the parallel changes in non-Jewish society, where new values (even in sexual mores) were increasingly evident, also had an impact, especially on the more acculturated and secular segments of Jewish society. And the belle-lettres of nineteenth-century Europe and Russia only fueled such expectations and desires.

Politics played an important role, too: movements like the Bund provided a common forum in which single men and women could meet. Drawn together by a shared ideology and social activism, the men and women in such movements often developed intense loyalties and romantic bonds.[74] The account of Daniel Charny (b. 1888) emphasizes the importance of affective ties in these underground movements. When he went to Minsk to bail his older brother out of prison and witnessed the comradely intimacy at a banquet held on the latter's behalf, he was utterly amazed: his brother warmly embraced both male and female comrades as if they were lifelong friends. "Some of the girls kissed me as well," Charney admitted sheepishly, "although I did not know why."[75] Although the "sexual revolution" and family question were central to the radical movements, some parties felt obliged to regulate relationships. The unprecedented intermingling of the sexes impelled the Bund, for instance, not only to reject the idea of sexual license espoused by some radicals but also to uphold a strict code of morality that essentially mirrored the norms of traditional Jewish society.

The secular press, which exploded in sheer volume in the postreform era, also had a major impact on matchmaking. By the turn of the century, the Yiddish newspaper *Der shadkhon* (published in Vil'na) featured a "personal ads" section, which often included information about the dowry, education, and profession of the prospective bride or groom, and sometimes a physical description as well. Singles from every station of life sent in personals that reflected new marital and gender expectations. Men often advertised their higher education (with the promise not only of wealth but also residency outside the Pale of Settlement) in exchange for financial security. Kh. Kom of Moscow offered this immodest self-description: "A student from Moscow University who is studying medicine, a handsome and good man, but not from a wealthy family, wishes to marry an educated woman from a rich family." He was, if not modest, at least candid. He might have been tempted by a woman from Melitopol (Tavride province), who admitted being "not extremely pretty, but not ugly" and promised a dowry of twenty-five thousand to thirty thousand rubles for a merchant or a young man who had graduated from school.[76] Other personals stressed more traditional qualities, such as an Orthodox background, strict observance, respectable lineage, and even rabbinical ordination.[77] Female divorcées and widows posted personals more frequently than did males, who found it easier to remarry and had less need of advertisements. One recently divorced woman from Vil'na admitted that the divorce settlement had ruined her financially but assured her prospective suitor (preferably a merchant) that her commercial and linguistic talents (Hebrew, Polish, German, and French) would more than compensate for her small dowry (300 rubles).[78] Although the newspaper fulminated against "marriages for money rather than love," the personals show that even the most romantic suitors were attentive to the financial dimension.

Although self-made matches gradually became more accepted, some families insisted on observing traditional formalities to lend respectability to the betrothal. Golda Meir's grandparents summoned a *shadkhan* to negotiate the technical arrangements after their daughter had already met and become engaged to a young army recruit on her own.[79] The contradiction between "modern" love and the matchmaker's role invited ridicule from Yiddish writers like A. Bukhbinder, who wrote chapbook romances. In *A Bride on Installments* (1889), friends mock "Boris" (a newly "acculturated" Hasid from Galicia) when he reveals his plan to send a *shadkhan* to the girl he loves, instead of proposing to her himself. "What a nonsensical idea that is," they exclaim with contempt. "What young man or woman obtains a bride [or groom] through a matchmaker these days? This only happens among the simple yids."[80] The parody of Boris suggests that, despite all the maskilic propaganda, old customs persisted and provided a good foil for a Yiddish satirist.

As the foregoing suggests, the traditional method of matchmaking, with a predominant role for parents and often with the assistance of professional matchmakers, did not disappear but did experience growing challenge and change. Above all, the future bride and groom increasingly assumed an important role, tempering if not abrogating the parentally arranged marriage. As with other groups in Russian society,[81] parental authority—emblematic of patriarchy more generally—suffered a steady attrition as youth became more assertive and independent. Although the generational crisis was less intense among Jews, the era of untrammeled parental tyranny and involuntary marriage was less prevalent in law or everyday social reality.

An Evolving Marriage Market

The criteria for choosing a spouse also underwent a significant transformation. Earlier, Jewish families had weighed four major factors: (1) family lineage (*yikhus* in Yiddish); (2) family wealth; (3) the male's learning; and (4) the female's commercial talents, ability to run a household, and personal morality. Physical attractiveness, an auxiliary consideration, sometimes played a role in discussions but was not a principal determinant. From the mid-nineteenth century, however, other factors gradually began to have an impact, a reflection of the growing influence of the bride and groom but also of medical science, secular education (especially for women), new cultural trends, and changing social and economic realities. The cultural and religious divisions in Jewish society itself also played an important role. Quite apart from seeking a spouse from a similar background (whether Hasidic or mitnagdic background), families also considered an individual's religiosity and devotion to Jewish tradition, especially after the emergence of the *haskalah* movement.[82]

Yikhus (Family Lineage)

"As is well known, Jews are excessively picayune about good lineage," wrote a commentator in *Evreiskoe obozrenie,* and thus "*yikhus* plays an extremely important role in marital matters."[83] One need only peruse the genealogical histories of famous Hasidic dynasties or rabbinical families to ascertain the importance of lineage in marital unions.[84] Despite the adage that "a shoemaker's son does not marry a rabbi's daughter," it was possible, if rare, for someone of modest descent to marry into a distinguished family. For example, Mikhel Bertsinsky (Shomer's father-in-law), who was wealthy but lacked genuine *yikhus,* managed to marry his eldest son to the daughter of an illustrious rabbinic family from Brisk. Only when the groom stepped under the *huppah* did he understand why his venerable in-laws had deigned to allow the match; the bride was not only much older but also "ugly and pockmarked, and Moshe remained unhappy his entire life."[85] Such matches inspired A. M. Dik to satirize parents who allowed their hubris and avarice to overlook "flaws and deformities" in their lust to associate with elite families. As his widely read *Boruske der shomer* (Boruske the watchman) warned, "It is best that each person should be matched only with his equal."[86] Sometimes a child prodigy *(iluy)* won access to a respectable family on the basis of his potential as a distinguished Torah scholar. Thus, a rich family from Plotsk, with a venerable lineage, elected to overlook the lowly background of R. Yehoshuale to obtain this "extraordinary *iluy*" for their daughter.[87]

The emerging class of Jewish entrepreneurs, intent on gaining elite respectability, placed a high premium on family status in choosing partners. According to Aleksandr Poliakov, his grandfather's cousins—the illustrious bankers and railroad financiers Iakov, Samuel, and Lazar Poliakov—married off their daughters to "different dynasties of European bankers, as well as French and German aristocrats." Bound by commercial as well as cultural ties, upper-class Jews often met in salons or over intimate Sabbath dinners, where their children were introduced to one another. Aleksandr Poliakov's own father met his wife, Flora Shabbat, the daughter of a prominent first-guild merchant, over a Sabbath meal in Moscow.[88]

No matter how distinguished the family lineage, it had to be "pure"— that is, there was to be no suspicion that "he or she was the offspring of an illicit union" or a convert from Judaism.[89] One way to avoid a "tainted" individual was to limit marriages to relatives or a close circle of known families. Judaism even encouraged cousin marriages, particularly during the Middle Ages, when relatives were given priority over strangers.[90] These marriages were deemed advantageous not only because they strengthened common bonds but also because they provided an opportunity to combine assets and expand markets.[91]

Although data on consanguineous marriages in Russia are lacking, contemporaries claimed that they were "very common," largely because of the narrow circle of eligible partners for any given class of Jews. This geographic endogamy impelled one Jewish observer to write that "the expression '*Kol Yisrael ahim*' or 'all Jews are brothers' is true in this sense, that Jews [who] belong to one strata of society and reside in one area, always find out that they are related when discussing their family backgrounds."[92] The strategy of marrying relatives was particularly pronounced in small towns. It was due to concerns about family lineage, as well as to restrictions on geographic mobility (i.e., legal restrictions on residency, poor communications and transportation, and the high costs for travel).

That observation indeed finds confirmation in the metrical records. These archival materials are unusually complete for Korostyshev, a small town in Kiev province with 2,657 Jewish residents in 1847.[93] Unlike many Ukrainian towns where the metrical records were destroyed during World War II, Korostyshev preserved metrical books from the mid-nineteenth century to 1915, thus representing some of the most complete runs of Jewish metrical books in the entire Ukraine. Significantly, they reveal that most residents married locally—that is, to people from Korostyshev or, at most, from nearby villages and towns (Zhitomir, Berdichev, and Radomysl').[94] Still more striking were the marital bonds between small family networks—for example, the countless marriages among the Fuksmans, Gershengorens, Trakhtenbergs, and Ratners (all of whom lived in Korostyshev or nearby Zhitomir).[95] Another network included the Vinikurs, Tsiponiuks, and Abrumovichs; this cluster overlapped with a group that included the Kagans, Umerskiis, and Peigers. And so on until, several decades later, many Korostyshev residents were distant or even close relatives.[96] Devorah Baron's description of small shtetl families was indeed perspicacious: "In our little town, families joined together by marriage ties often resembled well-fitted but separate sections of a garment; all that was needed was the skillful hand that would join the seams."[97]

In the late nineteenth century, Jewish reformers castigated this consanguinity as detrimental to family health. The developments in contemporary medicine (especially eugenics and clinical psychiatry) had a profound impact on public discourse; as physicians joined in, the debate on Jewish marriage became increasingly medicalized. "Owing to heredity," warned the *Evreiskii meditsinskii golos* (The Jewish medical voice), "all physical defects appear in the offspring with particular force, since the deficiencies of both parents are aggregated."[98] Invoking Western science, Jewish physicians ascribed the increased rate of "nervous disorders," such as hysteria, epileptic seizures, imbecility, and insanity, among the Jews in Russia to their pernicious inbreeding.

Samuel Gruzenberg (1854–1909), who held a degree from the Medical-Surgical Academy in St. Petersburg, publicized a series of essays in an influential Jewish journal. Representing the views of the medical establishment, he warned parents that "nervous illnesses" and hereditary diseases, such as blindness, deafness, and muteness, posed a threat not only to the immediate offspring but also to subsequent generations. Endogamous unions, he declared, also produced a large population with unhealthy "national physical features"—namely, "a short [body], weak muscles, and especially . . . a high level of nervousness."[99] Citing a study on army conscripts, he noted that nearly half of the Jewish recruits failed to meet the physical requirements and exhibited "extreme forms of the Jewish physical type."[100]

It was no accident that Gruzenberg cited the Jewish recruit to demonstrate the evil of consanguineous marriages: the physiognomy of male offspring greatly concerned reformers. In contrast to the modern ideal of man, who displayed "virility, proportion, and self control," the asthenic Jewish conscript embodied all the traits of the effeminate Jew so despised in European society.[101] Whereas Jewish society had long associated a pale, slender Jewish body with Torah scholarship and *edelkayt* (nobility), reformers now scorned this model as passive, cowardly, and feminine, a clear indication that the reformers had embraced the new European construction of masculinity.[102] The inbreeding affected not only the body but the mind: "Moral sickness and physical sickness were thought to be identical—the latter leaving an imprint on body and face."[103] As George Mosse has pointed out, the Jewish stereotype included a purported predisposition to nervousness, even hysteria, conditions traditionally associated with the weak female constitution. When exhibited in men, as French physicians argued in the 1880s, this "irritable weakness" led to profound exhaustion during the sexual act and ultimately led to "sterility and extinction."[104]

For Gruzenberg, nervousness constituted the "fundamental trait of the Jewish physical type" and greatly endangered the prospects for survival. A hypersensitive nervous system, he argued, made Jews more vulnerable to mental illnesses and numerous physical disabilities. For want of statistical data on Russia, he cited European statistics showing that the rate of deaf and dumb among German Jews was three times that of the general population. Gruzenberg also cited an 1861 German study, claiming that 1 in every 673 Jews suffered from this disability (compared to 1 for every 2,215 Christians).[105]

These data, he wrote, show the urgent need for a radical transformation of Jewish marital practices and even intermarriage *(smeshannye braki)* if the transmission of nervous disorders to future generations was to be averted. He argued that Darwin's studies of the mestizo (half breeds) produced important findings and directly applied to the Jews. But Gruzenberg refused to sacrifice Jewish religion and culture on the altar of genetics: "To be sure, on the one hand, the health of Jews would gain a lot from mixed marriages with adherents of different confessions *(inovertsy)*; on the other hand, however, it goes without saying that a lot would be lost as well." Gruzenberg concluded that, until more studies had been conducted on "all the physical peculiarities of the Jews—both beneficial and harmful," it was premature to leap to a radical solution like intermarriage.[106] In the interim, however, it *was* critical to avoid the intense inbreeding so common in the shtetls and small towns.

Although this public debate did not reduce the frequency of consanguineous marriages, it did popularize new medical ideas about infant mortality, mental illness, and other diseases. And this did percolate down to the general population. Rabbi Tchernowitz's grandmother on his maternal side gave birth to thirteen children, nearly all of whom died in her lifetime. Rather than invoking conventional interpretations of tragedy (i.e., the angel of death), he recalled that family members secretly whispered that the misfortune was due to "the close blood relations of the couple."[107]

Publicity about the rising threat of "nervous disorders" may also have struck a chord with the general Jewish population. It could cite some hard and worrisome official data. Thus, the census of 1897 showed that .098 percent of Jews suffered from mental illness, a rate higher than the national average of .094 percent.[108] In response, Jewish families began to dispatch mentally ill relatives to Jewish colonies in Lithuania and Belorussia; they apparently believed that the fresh air would have "a salutary effect on nervous, disturbed people," that the "calm, almost phlegmatic colonists" would not harm the patients.[109] The petitions from Jews to the medical office of the Vil'na Provincial Board, seeking to institutionalize mentally ill spouses and children whom they called "dangerous," also reflected the growing concern about nervous disorders.[110] These concerns were real and deeply personal. The tragedy of mental illness pervades the petition of Zusel Mendik in 1900, asking the Vil'na governor to commit his wife to the Jewish hospital:

My wife Sora Ginda Mendik has been periodically losing consciousness for a certain period of time; now, however, she has begun to fight and throw whatever comes into her hands—pots and jugs; she has [also] started to run out into the street and it is with difficulty that [we] bring her back to the apartment. She breaks the dishes at home and creates scandals with the neighbors. For this reason, I am afraid that she will kill someone at night, or perhaps murder me or one of the children. I am very poor and lack the means to care for her, for I must earn the daily bread to feed my poor children.[111]

Despite the "scientific" debate, *yikhus* remained an important consideration but underwent a change: it was commercialized and medicalized. For social climbers, wealth and sometimes Torah learning could be exchanged to attain a venerable lineage. That process was hardly unique to Jews; new professionals and entrepreneurs in Russian society also sought suitable connections with an economically distressed nobility. Among Jews, however, the medicalization played a particularly salient and interesting role, intensified by the high degree of endogamous marriages. The new sciences, especially eugenics and psychiatry, cited "objective" evidence on the need to sunder old family networks, even consider the possibilities of intermarriage.

Family Wealth

A second key attribute was family wealth, as reflected in the dowry, engagement gifts, and room and board from parents (*kest* in Yiddish, *mezonot* in Hebrew). Under Jewish law, the dowry *(nedunyah)* consisted of assets that the wife brought to the marriage and entrusted to her husband.[112] Some rabbis viewed it as her share of the paternal estate, circumventing the rule that Jewish women could not legally receive an inheritance.[113] The dowry, of course, reflected family wealth; the Talmud specified that each daughter was to receive one-tenth of her father's assets, thereby assuring her at least a share of the family wealth.[114] In late-nineteenth-century Russia a typical dowry ranged between one hundred and several thousand rubles. According to Ezekiel Kotik (1847–1941), wealthy tavern keepers and property owners in Kamenets (Grodno province) generally provided dowries of one thousand rubles for each daughter.[115] That was a huge sum; domestic servants in Vil'na province, who earned thirty to fifty rubles a year (during the 1870s and 1880s), worked to save one hundred rubles as a dowry.[116]

If the marriage was dissolved through divorce or the husband's death, the entire dowry reverted to the wife as her lawful property. In fact, the Mishnah required the husband to pay not only the principal but any profits from the dowry.[117] As a result, the dowry was a substantial deterrent to a hasty divorce. The deterrent was still greater if the dowry had been used to finance a business, as was the common practice in tsarist Russia.[118]

Predictably, dowries were a continuous source of conflict: pressure to inflate dowries to attract the best suitor encouraged misrepresentation and outright deception. According to Moshe Leib Lilienblum, his future mother-in-law, without her husband's knowledge, promised a three-hundred-ruble dowry and six years of *kest;* when her husband learned of the prenuptial agreement, he demanded that the dowry be reduced to two hundred silver rubles and the *kest* to five years.[119] Violation of prenuptial agreements inevitably provoked conflict between the in-laws and grooms, particularly when the young couple sought to establish their own household and independence.[120] Perhaps reflecting such tensions, *Shulhan Arukh* warned men not to marry for money alone.[121]

To assist poor families, a special communal association (called *hakh-*

nasat kallah in Hebrew and *hakhnoses kalleh* in Yiddish) provided dowries to enable the marriage of "poor brides." Jewish society regarded such assistance as a commendable deed for someone who "enjoys the fruits in this world, while the stock remains for him in the world to come."[122] Families could also apply to private Jewish philanthropies, which provided poor girls with dowries. The scale of such activity in Russia is difficult to ascertain, for the archival record is minimal. Just across the border, however, the records of these private philanthropics in L'vov (Galicia) provide rich insight.[123] Applicants had to present the following documents: "a birth certificate, attestation of morality *(Moralitätszeugnis),* declaration of poverty, kinship certificate [affirming that no impediments to the marriage existed], and, finally, the betrothal agreement."[124] The applicant provided information about her age, social status, geographic origin, family background, sexual status (including confirmation of virginity), and some data about the groom. For example, thirty-year-old Gittel Deiner described herself as "maternal, moral, and desirous of getting married," and to demonstrate her poverty she included a copy of her father's death certificate.[125] Once a foundation elected to assist an applicant, it required her to present a certificate of banns *(Verkundigungschein)* before the wedding.[126] Naturally, the amount of the dowry varied considerably, but in most cases the sums were modest.[127]

The other main financial consideration was *kest,* the obligation of the bride's or groom's parents to provide room and board for the new couple for a specified period.[128] *Kest* enabled couples to accumulate the means to establish an independent household or allow the husband to immerse himself in traditional Torah studies[129] The institution of *kest,* which had deep roots in the Polish Commonwealth, remained an important institution for Jewish families in tsarist Russia.[130] Data on family structure in Kiev for 1843 reveal that the majority of Jews lived in complex or multigenerational households (46 percent) and nuclear families (43 percent); only a small proportion formed extended families (11 percent), composed of the married couple, their children and unmarried relatives.[131] Immanuel Etkes has observed that, for the scholarly elites *(lomdim), kest* represented a rare opportunity for them to study without financial concerns.[132] The support generally lasted for two to five years, although sometimes longer.[133]

The *haskalah* movement was especially critical of *kest,* denouncing it as an unproductive custom that only encouraged the husband to shun work and shamelessly sponge off his in-laws and wife.[134] Devastating caricatures of the parasitic groom appeared in novels such as Peretz Smolenskin's *Wanderer in the Paths of Life (Hatoeh bedarkhei hahayyim):* "Is my mother-in-law paralyzed that I should have to earn a living? Until the day the worms take up residence in her corpse, she will go on working and supply our needs."[135] Calls for "productivization"pervaded Aizik Meyer Dik's popular etiquette book, *Seyfer hilkhoys derekh erets* (The customs of conduct). This guide to interpersonal relationships, based largely on traditional Jewish sources, praised the "clever man" who first took up a trade, purchased a home, and then considered marriage—the exact obverse of the *kest* system.[136]

Kest, whether from maskilic satire or vicissitudes of the Jewish economy,[137] apparently became less widespread. Nevertheless, as the personals featured in *Der shadkhon* suggest, young Jewish couples still desired some measure of financial security. While they embraced the ideals of independence and self-assertion, like their gentile peers, they were less willing pay a financial price for them.

Male Religious Learning

Jewish families in tsarist Russia esteemed a candidate for his learning in the Torah and Jewish law.[138] The prestige of rabbinic scholarship, which reflected the religious identity of Jewish society, profoundly affected familial expectations in the search for a suitable groom and future in-laws. From birth, a young girl would hear her mother sing: "Sorele's groom will be a wise scholar, a wise scholar with fine virtues; Sorele's groom will know how to solve problems."[139] Even early Yiddish romance novels, such as the popular *Mordechai and Ester: A Beautiful and Wonderful Story of a Bride and Groom* (1829), valorized the sharp-witted Talmud scholar as a heaven-sent bridegroom. The archetypical plot forces the hero, Borukh Fridman, to endure various trials; but upon arriving at the yeshiva, he exhibits his erudition by secretly solving the Talmudic problems that the rabbi, seeking the best scholar for his daughter, leaves daily on a slip of paper. Naturally, once Fridman's identity is revealed, the match made in heaven is consummated on earth.[140]

Erudition in Jewish law could even outweigh worldly considerations of wealth and family lineage. Hence, knowledge of the Torah not only served to sustain family piety but also functioned as an instrument for upward social mobility. Artisan families in the northern provinces may have deliberately enrolled their sons in the renowned yeshivot of Lithuania in hopes of obtaining a "good match" *(shiddukh tov)* and a generous dowry.[141] As one observer pointed out, "the dowry of a girl is proportional to the scholarship of the prospective bridegrooms."[142] Even if the motive for religious studies was this-worldly, students had to take their studies seriously; it was essential to dazzle prospective in-laws with their knowledge of Torah. Clever families often made the test challenging, dispatching a rabbi or sharp-witted *melamed* to examine the future groom. Although some men allegedly passed the test by bribing the examiners, students could hardly count on such venality and had to display a modicum of learning to impress future in-laws.[143]

By the late nineteenth century, however, Jewish brides took little interest in the effete, studious grooms who bore no resemblance to the cosmopolitan males lionized in popular romance novels. As Isaac Bashevis Singer recalled, the world of his pious father revolved around the sacred texts, but that was "out of fashion" in the marriage market. What could an unsophisticated Talmud scholar offer to the "daughters of rabbinical families, who read modern books, dressed modishly, visited spas, walked about unchaperoned, spoke 'German' and even occasionally wore modern hats?"[144] As Paula Hyman and Iris Parush have shown, the cultural gap between husbands and wives stemmed largely from the gendered system of education and socialization in Eastern Europe.[145] Regardless of social class, Jewish sons attended the *heder* (elementary school) from the tender age of four or five, where they learned from Torah and the sacred texts of the Talmud. Some later traveled to distant yeshivot (rabbinical academies) to pursue their studies.

By contrast, daughters were more likely to study secular subjects, such as mathematics and foreign languages, partly because of rabbinical indifference, partly because they often played the role of primary breadwinner so that their husbands could devote themselves to study.[146] In the late nineteenth century, as marital age rose, increasing numbers of women pursued a formal education in secondary schools (gymnasia).[147] Apart from formal schooling, girls were freer to indulge in secular literature, unlike their brothers, who read "like thieves in the night . . . books whose contents they understood but imperfectly."[148] Even women with no formal education devoured romantic chapbooks by Yiddish writers such as Aizik Meyer Dik and Shomer, who deliberately addressed their books to a female audience.[149] Whereas the earlier romance tales had hailed the Torah scholar as the coveted husband, the new maskilic novels now shunned him as an *unmentsh,* a nonperson, despised by his cultured bride.[150] In his stead stood the enlightened Jew, who could navigate his way through the modern world with ease.

By the early twentieth century, rabbinical authorities in Lithuania, struggling to defend *haredi* (Orthodox) society from the processes of acculturation, turned their attention to the declining role of Jewish learning in matchmaking.[151] "Life and its demands are knocking on the gates of our houses of learning," warned Rabbi Isaac Jacob Reines (1839–1915), who was better known for his leadership in the Mizrachi movement. "If we do not open them, they will force their way in. The whole house is in danger."[152] At stake were the traditional marital alliances between Talmud

FIG. 2. Outdoor portrait of students and teachers at a *heder metukan* (a progressive Jewish elementary school for boys and girls, where they studied secular subjects), Lithuania, 1900. *Courtesy of the YIVO Institute for Jewish Research.*

scholars and the wealthy elites, which had reinforced rabbinic cultural hegemony and communal power.[153] In the second half of his *Two Lights (Shnei hameorot)*, Rabbi Isaac Reines conceded that there was little hope that the "cultivated and enlightened" daughters of wealthy merchants and *balebatim* (householders) would be attracted to the present yeshiva student. His solution, however, was not to recast female education but to establish a modern yeshiva in Lida (Grodno province) that would offer not only traditional knowledge but also general subjects, including vocational training, and thereby acquaint male scholars with "the ways of the world."[154] In his view, only through the modernization of the yeshiva student could *haredi* society ensure his attractiveness in the new marriage market, which Reines viewed as vital to the preservation of Judaism in the home. "In the event that the daughter [of the wealthy elites] marries one of the free-thinkers," Rabbi Reines cautioned, "her husband will also endeavor to influence his father-in-law's house and, in a short time, change the leadership of the house so that all become free-thinkers; from this one sees the great value in the marriages of daughters to the Torah scholar *(talmid-hakham)*."[155]

But the Lida yeshiva did less to halt the acculturation than to recognize its inroads. Ironically, women, often viewed as vehicles of religious preservation and renewal, were the instruments of secularization in Jewish society.[156] In this case, rabbis like Isaac Reines sought to refashion the yeshiva student according to the spirit of the times to preserve those traditional marital alliances that had sustained the cultural esteem for Talmudic scholarship and religious observance.

Female Economic Talents and Domestic Skills

Another valued attribute was a woman's capacity to support the family. That consideration was hardly peculiar to Jews; other groups, especially the underclass, gave women a key role in the family economy, whether through agriculture or cottage industries.[157] In the Jewish family, however, women were not simply additional labor inputs but sometimes the primary breadwinners. As A. B. Gottlober observed, "women of valor" in his time earned the livelihood while their husbands studied in the prayer house *(beit-hamidrash)*.[158] Given this structure of gender roles, it was imperative that female candidates demonstrate their ability to support the family, traditionally in trade or business. Hence, a matchmaker's claim that a woman spoke fluent Polish ("Zi redt Poylish vi a vaser!") carried great weight at the bargaining table: Polish was the main language of business in the western provinces and hence a major asset. Although the female economic role did not necessarily translate into social prestige, it was a significant factor in the calculus of matchmaking.

But traditional gender expectations were still in evidence: just as a groom was tested in his Talmudic erudition, a bride could anticipate that her in-laws would visit and assess her intelligence, beauty, and other virtues. They would judge her ability to perform housework, produce clothing, cook and preserve food, and perform other domestic chores. Little wonder that Ezekiel Kotik's pious mother, a rabbi's daughter, who spent her day reading literature like *Khoyves halevoves* (Duties of the heart),[159] fell short of the expectations of her energetic mother-in-law. In her son's words, "Mama was not an efficient housewife, nor could she cook or bake like the traditional wives. . . . She could not even sew what a small girl was able to do. Mother just could not do anything."[160] In contrast, his aunt Yocheved (the favored daughter-in-law) was admired for her sumptuous salted goose dishes, cracklings *(gribenes)*, schmaltz, and turkey meatpies.[161]

Nevertheless, while families still prized a woman's business and domestic skills, the processes of acculturation and education were producing a different kind of woman. Ezekiel Kotik's mother was hardly unique; women from the emerging Jewish *Bildungsbürgertum*[162] or *obshchestvennost'* (educated society) began to reflect *embourgeoisiement*—adoption of "bourgeois" values characteristic of an emerging class of educated professionals.

Personal Morality

A quality of rising concern and a target of verification was personal reputation, primarily of female candidates. As in many European communities and peasant society in Russia itself, Jews attached great importance
to a bride's virginity.[163] That demand was more easily sustained in societies that had a lower age of nuptiality and that restricted the interaction
of adolescents. In Jewish society, unmarried girls who accidentally lost
their virginity were to report the incident to the *beit-din* so as to avoid
any questions about their virtue later. One communal *pinkas* alone contained thirty-two cases of *mukat ets,* or "the accidental deflowering of a
virgin."[164] To cite one such record: "Let it be recorded this day of the mis-
hap that occurred to so-and-so, the daughter of so-and-so. By an act of
heaven she fell from the stove and impaled herself on a sharp-edged bedpost standing nearby. There was blood on that spot and blood on the
bedpost. Therefore, lest it be questioned, God forbid, in the future should
there not be a sign of virginity, we, the undersigned have inscribed this
event in this pinkas as evidence of accidental loss of virginity."[165] Without
evidence of *mukat ets,* a nonvirginal bride ran the risk of humiliation,
even abrogation of the marriage.

As elsewhere in Imperial Russia, by the late nineteenth century those
norms had begun to lose their force, with premarital sex (especially after
a promise of marriage) becoming more common, though not widespread.[166] This was particularly true when nuptials had to be postponed
for economic and legal reasons.[167] Illicit relationships sometimes came to
light when vigilant neighbors monitored women whom they suspected of
moral laxity, hoping to detect signs of pregnancy.[168] Rumors of secret
births or deliveries less than nine months after a wedding triggered gossip
and even denunciations to the state police—a striking violation of the
rule against informing on coreligionists to gentile authorities.[169] What is
important here is not some great increase in frequency, which was not the
case, but the perception and preoccupation with what appeared to be a
qualitatively new phenomenon.

One poignant case arose in 1861 when Aizik Svidler accused eighteen-
year-old Khana Kenigsberg (a resident of a small village in Vil'na province) of murdering a newborn child, allegedly conceived prior to her marriage. "In order to conceal [evidence of] her loose morals *(bludnaia
zhizn'),*" he asserted, "she claimed that the infant was born prematurely
and died a few hours after his birth."[170] Svidler's close familiarity with
the details her life suggests that he held a grievance against the bride, perhaps as a jilted suitor. Whatever his motive, the denunciation led to a
court investigation and her admission of premarital sexual relations with

her present husband, Mendel (a fact she had concealed from her parents). She adamantly denied the charges of infanticide, however, attributing the infant's death to an accidental fall two days before giving birth. A Jewish midwife confirmed her testimony, stating that "after a long labor, she [Khana] gave birth to a live baby, but was weak with blood-shot eyes."[171] Since her child was not born out of wedlock, the state dropped the case but not before forcing the woman to admit premarital sexual relations.

Accusations often proved completely groundless yet initially seemed credible enough to warrant an investigation. In 1881, on the basis of rumors spread by a female neighbor, Gavriel Dlugin accused Feiga Gordon, from a town in Vil'na province, of giving birth to an illegitimate child.[172] The court required her to undergo a medical examination but found no evidence of a birth (i.e., her sexual organs were normal and her breasts showed no signs of milk). Nevertheless, the state medical examiner revealed that "Feiga Gordon lost her hymen a long time ago and has repeatedly and frequently had sexual relations with men."[173] He offered no clinical proof for the alleged promiscuity, evidently reflecting a general bias against women who were no longer chaste.

The investigation of infanticide, often triggered by the discovery of an infant's corpse, led to few convictions but to some admissions of sexual indiscretion. When several workers found a dead infant in the Azvolinskii's outhouse in 1885, a servant working for the family accused the neighbor's domestic servant of perpetrating the crime, given a marked change in her physical appearance: "When I visited the Ratners [earlier], Shendlia [their servant] was obese, but after the baby was discovered, she became thin. I was sure she had been pregnant."[174] The woman, in fact, admitted to the pregnancy and described her desperate attempts, whether from shame or fear of losing her job, to conceal her awkward condition: "I hid my pregnancy from everyone; not even my employers knew that I was pregnant. I live alone in the kitchen, [so] the birth of my baby was concealed from everyone. Upon throwing my baby in the outhouse, I went about my work; I prepared the samovar and cleaned the floors. . . . I hid the baby in the outhouse because I was afraid and did not know what to do with the dead baby."[175] Seeking to retain a semblance of normalcy, she apparently resumed her domestic chores as though nothing had happened. Concealing the death, however, greatly increased suspicions that the child was not stillborn but the victim of a deliberate homicide.

Shendlia, however, denied committing infanticide and insisted that the baby died because the birth was three months premature. She emphasized that "I did not hear the baby cry after she was born and I was certain that she was dead." She appealed to a medical truism of the day: prematurity (namely, the absence of hair and nails) was generally accepted as evidence of a stillbirth and grounds for acquittal. In this case, however, an autopsy found that the infant had been born "fully formed" and alive but died from "exposure and inhalation of harmful gases" in the outhouse. Despite the damning medical evidence, Shendlia did not offer details of the relationship (or the identity of the father) to prove that the birth was indeed premature. Rather, she stressed her moral character, arguing that her actions were "unintentional" and motivated by "fear and shame" (strakh i styd). Her credibility vitiated, the court found her guilty and meted the standard sentence—four to eight months in prison.

Although such cases were not common and convictions rare, they reveal the intense pressure for a woman to conceal her loss of virginity. Allegations that women murdered their babies "out of shame and fear" (a phrase routinely used in court) reflected a deep bias against women who lost their chastity prior to marriage, even as mores and sexual behavior were beginning to change.[176] Predictably, the social stigma and legal responsibility lay with the female, not the male, even in cases where the relationship was plainly consensual.[177] Although men occasionally suffered ridicule for premarital affairs, the censure was negligible compared with the ostracism experienced by women. Chaim Tchernowitz described one man in his hometown who was nicknamed "the evil inclination" (yetser hara) because his wife gave birth too soon after their wedding.[178] Worse still, women faced not only village gossip but serious legal consequences, compounded by public interrogation in court and involuntary gynecological examinations by the state medical board. In Russia, as in the West, women's bodies became "sexualized, pathologized, and medicalized," making them all the more vulnerable to public intervention and social control.[179]

Women who engaged in premarital sex did so at great risk, but neither the community nor the law was likely to punish the man who reneged on a promise of marriage. In a few exceptional cases, Jewish women sued their lovers for seduction (obol'shchenie) or rape (iznasilovanie) when they reneged on their word. But few did so, which is hardly surprising, given the onerous process and dismal prospects of success. Russian law defined seduction as "luring a single, honorable woman into a mutual [sexual] relationship with a solemn promise to marry her."[180] In effect, the plaintiff had to prove that her lover expressed "a serious intention" of marriage, a formidable task given the clandestine nature of such relationships. Thus, although the court punished the seducer with a prison sentence (namely, 1.5 to 2 years), it neither required him to fulfill his promise of matrimony nor to provide any monetary compensation (the only exception being child support if, indeed, paternity was clearly established).

One typical case unfolded in Vil'na in 1873, when Traipel Kul'kin sued his employee Itsko Leib Kit for impregnating his daughter and reneging on his promise to marry her. The deposition of the sixteen-year-old Leah Kul'kin stressed that the defendant had always made "affectionate advances" toward her and repeatedly voiced his desire to marry her.[181] One September night, when she was upstairs with two sleeping children, Kit (who lived in their house) entered her room half-dressed, locked the door behind him, and embraced her. For an entire hour he vowed to marry her if she would only submit. When she resisted, he simply raped her. When she became pregnant, Kit supposedly gave her "a liquid to destroy the fetus"—a proposal that she rejected in favor of giving up the child to a Jewish family to raise. Such, at least, was her account.[182]

Kit, like most male defendants, sought to impugn the accuser's reputation. Although numerous witnesses claimed that Itsko Kit had confessed to causing Leah's pregnancy and had also expressed his desire to marry her (a union supposedly thwarted by his mother), in court he vehemently denied all the charges. He claimed that Leah's father treated his daughter so harshly that she often fled the house and took refuge with a lover (a Jew from Kovno named Israel), not returning home until late at night. When her father found out, he allegedly beat her and cut her hair. Although Kul'kin denied this story (claiming that the doctor ordered it to cure a rash on his daughter's head), he was unable to disprove the spirited denials by his former employee and to convince the court that Kit offered a "solemn promise of marriage."[183]

Some men filed a preemptive lawsuit to discourage hostile litigation. In 1909, Yakov Khaskes charged his former companion, Basia Gutman of Vil'na, in criminal court of pouring sulfuric acid on his face that left him permanently disfigured. His deposition laid great emphasis on her flirtatious behavior: "Two months ago, I met the girl Basia Gutman at a Pushkin conference; the latter, passing by me, smiled and I, a single man, went over to her to get acquainted. Gutman told me that she was a teacher of German language, who lives in the house no. 20 on Tatar street (third district); that recently, she was without work and in light of [her] critical position, she was forced to streetwalk, that is, to be a prostitute."[184]

Khaskes claimed that he gave her money on several occasions out of pity. When he sought to break off his liaison, however, she allegedly complained to his father that he had infected her with syphilis and "spread rumors that he promised to marry her." By accusing the unemployed teacher of prostitution (the "archetypal female sexual transgression"), Khaskes sought to impugn her morality and thereby demolish her credibility. By the late nineteenth century, prostitution had increased markedly and was a growing source of official and public concern.[185] Tapping into this pool of public anxiety, Khaskes sought to portray

Gutman's alleged sexual advances as "professional" and thus to cast himself as the innocent victim.

Basia Gutman (who went by the more acculturated name, Berta) admitted throwing acid in her lover's face during a heated moment of anger and humiliation. She testified that "Yasha" (Yakov's russified name) had a three-month sexual relationship with her based on a promise to wed her. Hence, in her view, their sexual liaison was a prelude to marriage, not wanton behavior as the plaintiff claimed. Letters to her lover (which Khaskes had delivered to the court as proof of her aggression) reveal Gutman's anguish at his sudden decision to break off their relationship:

To my incomparable Yasha,
    . . . I cannot express to you in words my emotional state; my soul is overflowing with bitterness. I am totally alone. I thought that I had met a kind and good person, who is responsive to the bitterness of my entire soul. But you did not understand me. I beg you dear to answer my letter—what do you think of me and what the reason was for our separation? Your sympathy toward me touches me to the depths of my soul and I cannot be reconciled to the thought that we will not meet anymore. I beg you to answer me quickly. Berta[186]

The court investigator reported that Khaskes offered her fifty rubles to "settle all their accounts," which, because of her financial plight, she reluctantly accepted. Arriving at his lawyer's office to sign the agreement, however, she flung the acid on him—a premeditated act, by her own admission. Surprisingly, the twelve-man jury (including one Jew) acquitted her, despite her own admission of guilt; the plaintiff's failure to make a court appearance may have played a role in the verdict, as well as the twenty-six-year-old defendant's ability to demonstrate that she was the victim of seduction by the son of a wealthy merchant.

Even when a woman did win a seduction suit (a rare event in itself), a former partner sometimes pressured her into renouncing the court settlement. Hence, when the Vil'na district court awarded Ita Zarkh five rubles a month to pay for her illegitimate child until he reached his maturity, her former lover, Itsko Kantor, filed an appeal. He presented a surprising letter signed in Yiddish stating that "I, Ita Khana Zarkh, have the honor to add that I have received complete satisfaction from Itsko Kantor and never will consider it right to demand support from him, either for myself or my child."[187] The letter is all the more surprising because the court record clearly attests to her financial difficulties. The court record is silent on her motive—whether because she received a lump-sum payment, or because she wanted to curb his relentless attack on her moral reputation (as evidenced in his letters to the court).[188]

In effect, personal morality was still important for women: evidence or mere rumors of improprieties could ruin the marital prospects for a woman but had little impact on a man. In most instances, the paramours not only came away unscathed but even married a few years later. Although premarital sex became more common and ceased to be a target of state prosecution, women were still subject to the traditional gender norms and found little protection either within the Jewish community or in the secular state courts.

The Religious Factor: Hasidim versus Mitnagdim

A final factor in matchmaking was the cultural background of a prospective spouse. Traditional Eastern European Jewish society consisted of two major groups—the Hasidim, primarily concentrated in the southwestern provinces (i.e., Ukraine, Poland, and certain regions of Belorussia), and the *mitnagdim* (*misnagdim* in Yiddish) in the northwest (Lithuania and Belorussia).[189] Both adhered to the basic tenets of Judaism but represented two distinct cultural movements with different modes of worship, teachings, and customs. The Hasidim elevated prayer (even over Torah studies) as the primary means to achieve *devekut* (cleaving to God) and expressed their piety through emotional fervor and ecstasy.[190] They imbued mundane, daily activities with spiritual meaning so that "the profane sphere of any Hasid could become sanctified into one single sphere of the holy, leaving no room for the concept of a 'profane action.'"[191] Through the mediation of the *tsaddik* (a righteous man), the center of Hasidic life, even simple folk could achieve communion with God.[192] Pilgrimages to the *tsaddik* or rebbe, special Sabbath rituals and clothing, singing, dancing, and storytelling—all constituted a unique Hasidic subculture.[193]

The *mitnagdim* (the opponents) rejected the Hasidic emphasis on prayer and reaffirmed Torah studies as the highest ideal. The Gaon of Vil'na, the cultural icon of this movement, apparently knew no sleep, devoting himself to twenty-two hours of study a day. His was a society anchored in learning. Chaim Tchernowitz asserted that if one could characterize the major difference between the Hasidim and *mitnagdim*, the former were "fearers of heaven" and the latter were "fearers of the book."[194] He recalled that, in his neighborhood, Torah scholars were always studying in the synagogue. Prominent members of the community also belonged to study groups or associations: Hevrah Shas (by far the largest and most prestigious), Hevrah Mishnayot, Hevrah Ein Yaakov, Hevrah Tenakh, and Hevrah Tehillim.[195]

During the early conflict between these two movements, in the late eighteenth and early nineteenth centuries, mitnagdic leaders strictly prohibited marriage with the "sectarians" (Hasidim) and even prescribed harsh punishment for social interaction with them.[196] Although the two maintained

FIG. 3. The ascetic. Portrait study of a Hasidic Jew sitting with his book in the mid-nineteenth century, Podolia province. *Courtesy of the YIVO Institute for Jewish Research.*

separate communal institutions, such as synagogues and ritual slaughters, their mutual animosity abated in the face of a new challenge—the *haskalah* movement that posed a threat to Orthodox Judaism. As a result, marriage between Hasidic and mitnagdic families became more acceptable in Lithuania but still capable of igniting family conflicts. As Pauline Wengeroff (who married into a Hasidic family) has observed, the differences between the Lithuanian Hasidim and mitnagdim were limited despite their distinct rituals and customs, for both venerated learning and the Talmud. The former, in her view, were "more sober" and practical than their Polish brethren, "whose life floated between heaven and earth."

Still, spouses had to adapt themselves to the religious rituals of the new household. As Wengeroff recalled, "I, the mitnagid daughter, saw and heard much that was new here and had to adapt myself gradually to much that was strange."[197] Due to the kindness of her in-laws, she not only developed strong bonds with her family and community but even grew fond of the Hasidic rhythms of life. Such was not always the case. Ezekiel Kotik, for instance, recalled that his mother, who had unwittingly married a Hasid, never really adjusted to her new circumstances: "Mother, who was raised in a pious home of *gaonim* and *tsaddikim*, unfortunate soul, had entered a house where not a word of Torah was heard." Empathy for his mother's plight probably stemmed from his own painful marriage. Even before the wedding had taken place, his father and grandfather became embroiled in a dispute because the latter opposed, to no avail, his grandson's marriage to a Hasidic woman. Kotik, who had already taken his grandfather's side, resisted efforts by his father and new wife to turn him to Hasidism. On one occasion, when he rashly pronounced a curse on the rebbe's father to spite a young Hasid, he deeply offended his wife, who tearfully told him: "I love you Hatzkel. . . . Only now I wish I were dead and not your wife. Don't think I want a divorce, God forbid! But if you could find it in your heart to curse the father of Yankel's rebbe, I am afraid to live under the same roof."[198] Blaming his father for turning his wife against him, Kotik decided to leave home and resume his studies at the Volozhin yeshiva, a haven for many unhappy grooms.

Although the cultural divide between Hasidim and *mitnagdim* remained, it paled by contrast with the antipathy toward the *haskalah*. Although slightly more tolerant to the other sect of Orthodox Judaism, parents took great precautions against a union with reputed "Berliners" or "heretics" (*apikorsim*)—derogatory terms for the maskilim. As Lilienblum's future mother-in-law asked his father, "The majority of gifted youth (*iluyim*) are being led astray from the path by their sharp minds that mislead them and they become heretics. What guarantees do I have that my son-in-law will not be changed, God forbid, into a heretic?"[199] Her fears were not completely unfounded; the yeshiva, the institution that trained future rabbis and scholars, often served as a breeding ground for the *haskalah*.

In any event, religious subculture remained an important factor even if the particular line of division had shifted. Faced with the threat of *haskalah*, acculturation, and secularization, Orthodox families attached great significance to religiosity, showing more tolerance toward each other as they sought to ward off the menace of the irreligious.

The Rites of Passage

The wedding ceremony remained largely unchanged, even amid the transformations in matchmaking and criteria for selective mates. Jewish folkways in the Russian Empire were highly heterogeneous, reflecting local traditions, but they did share some basic features. Although Jews had no centralized, institutionalized instruments to regularize rites and make them uniform (in contrast to the various Christian confessions), they did follow common rituals rooted in centuries of tradition and reinforced by interregional marriages.

Once the family had weighed these factors and settled upon a match, the next step was to formalize the betrothal through a verbal agreement or written document (the *tenaim*) that stipulated the precise terms of the marriage. After this formality, "the two fathers, holding the opposite corners of a handkerchief, exchanged symbolic tokens," a ritual followed by a feast and celebration.[200] It was also customary for a wealthy bride's parents in Ukraine to send the groom "small gifts," such as "a silver or gold watch, a silver box for tobacco powder, a headpiece covered with gold, a small *Humash* (the Pentateuch) bound in silver."[201] Right before the wedding, he received more "substantial" gifts, such as a prayer shawl and *shtreimel* (a hat with fur trim). For her part, the bride could expect to receive jewelry and head coverings from her future in-laws. Other kinsmen were likely to give the bride silverware and special candles for the Sabbath.[202] For their part, the groom's parents sent the bride a small chain for a watch. According to the ethnographer I. M. Pulner, only the poor gave each other clothes as presents.[203]

One major consideration was the wedding date. Just as the peasants planned their weddings around the agricultural and ecclesiastical calendars, Jews timed their ceremonies around religious holidays and festivals.[204] The Jewish wedding calendar, however, was quite different. Whereas Orthodox peasants held their weddings in late fall (October–November) and winter (January–February), with some coming in late spring after Lent, most Jewish weddings, according to the Kiev archival records from

1866 to 1870, occurred in late spring after Passover (25.4 percent) and summer (34.2 percent). The month with most weddings was August (17.8 percent).[205] That clustering resulted from the traditional ban on weddings between Passover and Shavuot (with some exceptions) and for three weeks in the summer between 17 Tammuz and the Ninth of Av. Following the Ninth of Av, there was a rush of weddings prior to the High Holidays in the fall, when a ban on marriage was again in effect.[206] Apart from the religious calendar, parents also sought to ensure that the wedding would not coincide with their daughter's menstrual period, which would make her an "unkosher bride" in the sense that she could not sleep with her husband until she was ritually "clean."[207] It was also advisable to avoid important state and Christian holidays, as Moishe Tsyvin learned when a drunken peasant mob disrupted his daughter's wedding, held on the anniversary of Tsar Nicholas II's coronation.[208]

According to ethnographic reports, Jewish weddings in the southwestern provinces usually took place on a Friday.[209] Although there was no Talmudic requirement for this custom, it caused less disruption to economic activities and accommodated patterns of household meals. Lewittes speculates that this practice afforded some economies, since it enabled families to "combine the Friday night Sabbath meal with the wedding feast."[210] He notes that the indigent Jews in Ukrainian towns and villages had a poor diet during the week (consisting of bread, herring, onion, and fish with pepper) but "indulged on the Sabbath," making that a particularly propitious time for a wedding feast.[211] A Friday wedding did, however, raise the problem of rupturing the hymen on the Sabbath (by causing a flow of blood), which was categorically forbidden by some Talmudic authorities.[212] Jews in Belorussia had a somewhat more flexible pattern, with weddings on a Tuesday or Friday (occasionally Sunday); like their coreligionists in the south, however, they avoided Mondays, which they considered an "unlucky day."[213]

Whatever the date, the prenuptial week had its own rituals. Thus, on the Sabbath before the wedding *(Shabes oyfrufenish)* the groom's friends escorted him to the most coveted seat by the eastern wall; there he awaited his turn to be called to make a blessing over the Torah, an event that his parents savored with pride. "Even a poor man, who does not have a seat in the synagogue," was deemed worthy of this honor.[214] To ensure that the groom's mother witnessed this important event, the women escorted her to the synagogue, showering her with candy and nuts along the way. After the blessing, the women in the balcony (or the female section of the synagogue) would cast nuts down onto the congregation, and in most Ukrainian towns the poor children would run in to gather them up.[215] Afterward, while the friends of the groom purchased wine and appetizers and entertained him until the evening, parents and relatives "drank wine, spirits, and beer, eating and passing the time in happy conversation and drunkenness."[216]

The future bride also observed various rituals to prepare her for the *huppah* (the wedding canopy). One joyous celebration was the *forshpil*, or *zmires* (the "merry entertainment") on the Sabbath night preceding the wedding, a celebration by the bride's friends and relatives, with food and dance. P. Chubinskii reported that because Jews were not permitted to play instruments on the Sabbath, some families invited Christian musicians to entertain the guests.[217] In the first half of the nineteenth century, the musicians' fee varied according to the dance: five kopecks for a polka or waltz, ten for a mazurka, and twenty for a quadrille. According to ethnographic reports, Jewish families in Minsk often organized a meal for the poor on the morning after the *forshpil*. In Ukraine, the indigent enjoyed a meal of "fish, meat, and other dishes with beer" on the Sunday or Monday before the actual wedding; wealthy families even provided wine and honey to the impecunious guests.[218]

At the close of the week, the bride's closest friends led her to the bath house for the *mikveh* (ritual bath), where the attendant cut her nails and recited the prayers.[219] The bride-to-be took this opportunity to mourn the passing of her childhood and the onset of a new life. Devorah Baron offers the apt metaphor of the bride who wept before her wedding day "as Jephthah's daughter had done—the passing of her youth": "'Alas, I'll see no more of the world!' she wailed, as her childhood friends, like their Biblical counterparts, wept with her."[220] Following the *mikveh* the bride invited her friends for another meal *(di meydn mol)*, where the klezmer bands entertained the guests with song and dance. In Grodno, in the second half of the nineteenth century, the bride was also expected to invite the female relatives on the groom's side.[221]

The wedding day usually began with the *badkhn*'s serenade of the groom and then the bride at their respective homes. During the ceremony of "seating the bride" *(di kaleh bazetsn)* friends dressed the bride in a special outfit (usually white); then they seated her in a chair, surrounded by a myriad of candles, so that they could unbraid and cut her hair (ignoring Nicholas I's ban on this ritual).[222] Shortly thereafter, the bride's family and friends visited the groom to present him with the wedding gifts (often a *kittel* and yarmulke). In Minsk it was customary to bring a saffron cake with raisins. When all the guests were finally seated, the groom delivered a short sermon *(drosheh)*, although this was not a part of every family's rituals. The bride's family then returned home for the veiling ceremony *(di kaleh badekn)*.[223]

The wedding itself consisted of two discrete rituals: the formal betrothal and the rites of marriage.[224] The betrothal ritual was rich in religious symbol and meaning. To prepare properly for this rite, both bride and groom were expected to fast as a symbol of repentance (as on the Day of

FIG. 4. The fourth day after the wedding, Berdichev, 1883. *Courtesy of the YIVO Institute for Jewish Research.*

Atonement).[225] The fasting also served to keep them "sober" for the approaching ceremony.[226] At the wedding itself the new couple were led under the wedding canopy *(huppah),* where the groom then recited the following words: "Behold thou art consecrated unto me by this ring in accordance with the laws of Moses and Israel," and then he placed the ring on the forefinger of the bride's right hand. Once a man presented a woman with a ring or "any article worth a *perutah*"[227] and repeated the words of consecration in the presence of two witnesses, the betrothal *(kiddushin)* became permanently binding and could be dissolved only through a formal divorce. Because of the religious meaning of the ritual, it was binding even if performed in jest and could be reversed only by a formal divorce.[228]

Following the betrothal benedictions, the marriage contract *(ketubah)* was read aloud, signed by two witnesses, and handed to the bride for safekeeping. This important document contained a statement on the mutual obligations of the spouses and stipulated the monetary compensation due to the wife in the event of a divorce or her husband's death. In most cases, the husband was also to pay the value of her trousseau and an additional sum called the *tosefet ketubah,* depending on the nature of the marriage contract. This financial arrangement was intended to prevent rash divorces and to protect "the divorcée against financial disaster."[229] In 1893 the Rabbinic Commission reported that the amount of the *ketubah* varied according to geographical regions in Russia. For those marrying for the first time, the customary sum was seventy-six rubles in the northern provinces and forty-eight rubles in the southern provinces; the amount for those entering marriage for the second time was half of those sums.[230]

After a brief interlude came the formal rites of marriage, performed by a rabbi or any individual upon whom this honor had been bestowed. The ceremony itself consisted of the "seven blessings," including the benediction over the wine.[231] Once the solemn benedictions were concluded, the groom took a glass and broke it under his feet, symbolizing "the fragility of marriage" and the destruction of the Temple in Jerusalem. Only then did "the whole crowd explode" with shouts of "mazel tov" and laughter.[232] Afterward, guests joined the wedding parties at a festive feast to celebrate the new marriage.

Apart from the presence of hired musicians and professional jesters the wedding party included traditional dances and songs replete with allusions to the tensions between the new in-laws. During the "quarreling dance," for example, "the new mothers-in-law . . . stamp, grimace, and lunge at one another, dramatizing a mock quarrel," although at the end they embrace.[233] One Yiddish folksong of the bride's anxious mother warned: "If you prove to be a nasty mother-in-law, then my daughter too can be a shrew!"[234] As these celebrations proceeded, the bride and groom retired to a private room to share a meal, symbolically consummating their marriage (also known as *yikhud*).[235] In Minsk and Starokonstantinov (Volhynia province), celebrants usually shared a bowl of chicken soup, known as the "golden bouillon." In Grodno and Propoisk (Belorussia), the couple usually had some pastry with coffee or tea.[236] Soon, if not immediately afterward, the rabbi registered the event in the metrical books—the first and only nexus between the marriage and the secular state.

Wedding celebrations of prominent Hasidic families were particularly elaborate, lasting for several days.[237] In a secret memorandum (12 November 1865) the Kiev governor described the wedding of Borukh Meier of Makarov, which was attended by his grandfather, Rabbi Aron Twersky of Chernobyl and Itsko Twersky of Skvir:

A crowd met them [the latter two *tsaddikim*], some on foot, others in carriages and on horseback. . . .and together they headed for Makarov with shouts, noise, and [a great] tumult, while the tsaddikim's carriage was escorted by an orchestra of Jewish musicians. . . . The wedding banquet lasted four days, attended by local inhabitants and [guests] from out of town—over one thousand Jews; counting those from out of town [who came only to express their] congratulations and make donations, the total was probably more than three thousand people.[238]

The wedding feast was lavish, especially by Ukrainian standards: three *pud* (108 pounds) of fish, three times that amount in beef, and alcoholic beverages for all the local residents, regardless of their religious confession.[239] As a result, the governor declared in disgust, "The peasants and Jews got completely drunk together." Despite the ban on their participation, the peasants presented the bride and groom with bread and salt (a Russian custom), explaining that "the rabbi is our benefactor; he helps us [when we are] in need with money." To add to the festivity, "acrobats and masked Jews" provided entertainment for the guests.[240]

What did all this ritual—from the prenuptial ceremonies to the post-nuptial feast—mean? Nineteenth-century ethnographers, seeking to record "folk culture" for posterity, provided lavish descriptions of such rituals (emphasizing their heterogeneity and complexity) but were far less inclined to explain what all this signified to participants. In fact, this complex "rite of passage," with all its myriad diversity, proceeded at several different levels. Above all, it firmly grounded the marriage in religious symbol; the fasting, benedictions, and religious allusions served not only to consecrate the union but also make participants cognizant of its deep spiritual significance. Although lacking the theological sacramentalism and attendant "indelibility" doctrine of the Catholic and Orthodox churches, the betrothal and wedding draped the new union in religious meaning.

The ritual also was permeated with rich social meaning. Above all, it was an ostentatiously public, communal event and an antithesis to the "clandestine" marriage. Thus, from the prenuptial customs to the post-nuptial celebrations, the community was an active participant and witness. Communal involvement also served to attest to the terms of the union—hence, the public reading of the *ketubah,* which was not buried in a government or other institutional repository but given over to the bride herself. Save for the postnuptial registration in the metrical book, at no point did the wedding invoke the presence or recognition of the secular state.[241]

Naturally, the marriage ceremony held particular meaning for the new couple and their families. The religious symbolism and public involvement served to emphasize the gravity of the event and to make due recognition of this "rite of passage." In effect, the wedding ritual (including such rites as shaving the woman's hair) symbolized the momentous transition from childhood to adulthood, with new responsibilities and expectations. Even if buffered by a short period of *kest,* the groom and bride now had very different status and obligations.[242] The wedding also formalized and publicized the bonds—and mutual obligations—of the two families. In some measure the ritual also served to reduce tensions between them, mostly through the carnivalistic elements in the postnuptial celebrations: by verbalizing and satirizing in-law tensions, the celebrations served to recognize, relativize, and thereby defuse the inevitable stress and strain between the various in-laws.

Demographics

When the state rabbi inscribed the wedding into the metrical book, he generated the basic source needed for modern demographic analysis. The compilation of vital statistics was a belated phenomenon in the Russian Empire; although mandated from 1702 by Peter the Great, metrical books (records of births, deaths, and marriages) did not become routine until decades later, and even then were replete with errors of omission and deception.[243] For Jews, such records did not become obligatory until 1826, when the government imposed the responsibility of record keeping on the state rabbis. The standard form of Jewish marital records included information about the ages and names of the bride and groom, their marital status (single, divorced, widowed), the name of the rabbi who performed the ceremony, the date of marriage, obligations of the marital contract (usually the amount of the *ketubah),* and the signatures of the two witnesses.

For all its importance, demographers can offer only approximate data on the marital age of Jews in the Russian Empire. Not until the second quarter of the nineteenth century did metrical books and poll tax censuses *(revizskie skazki)* significantly improve; until then, oral declarations served as the primary verification of age. But knowledge of one's age was at best an approximation; as one townsman confessed, "I have lived many years, [but] how many years, I do not know." All this makes precise demographic calculations, even for such rudimentary phenomena as age at marriage, highly problematic. To compensate for these deficiencies, demographers use the device of pentennial units; such aggregates serve to offset errors, since the information (especially for younger people) had to remain within certain parameters based on the individual's physical appearance.[244] This method is particularly useful for determining marital age; although it does *not* provide a precise arithmetic mean, it does compensate for any potential tendency to exaggerate marital age and thus comply with the minimum age requirement for Jews first set by the Lithuanian Council in 1793 and later raised by Nicholas I in 1835.[245]

These data, notwithstanding their limitations (especially for the earlier years), do allow one to go beyond the memoirs and belles-lettres to address several important issues. One is marital age. Were child marriages common? Did marital age rise, as in other segments of society, and if so, why and with what consequences? But marital age is also of great social significance. Most obviously, it bore enormous demographic implications, functioning as a close correlate with fertility: early marriage naturally meant earlier (and higher) fertility rates; later marriage served as a form of birth control and family planning (as, for example, among elites in early modern Europe). No less important, marital age also had significant implications for family structures and relations. In particular, early marriage tended to produce young couples who were more dependent and pliable, thereby buttressing parental control and dominance. And deferred marriage, contrariwise, tended to have the opposite effect.

Child or Young Marriages?

Marital age has long been a subject of much speculation and mythmaking, especially in the history of Eastern European Jews, where the image of "child marriages"—between youths as young as eleven—has long held sway. This stereotype derives largely from the autobiographies of the maskilic elite, many of whom were married off at an exceptionally early age.[246] Avraham Baer Gottlober even claims that boys who were still single by their eleventh birthday were ashamed in the presence of their married peers.[247] His contemporary, Moshe Leib Lilienblum, was but a child of fourteen who still delighted in climbing on the beams of the synagogue when his father engaged him to a wealthy family from Marislav. In his classic *History of the Jews in Russia and Poland*,

Simon Dubnow also portrayed child marriages as the dominant pattern: "Just as firmly established was the old-fashioned scheme of family life, with its early marriages, between the years of thirteen and sixteen, with the prolonged maintenance of such married children in the parental home, with its excessive fertility in the midst of habitual poverty, with its reduction of physical wants to the point of exhaustion and degeneration."[248]

As recent demographic research has shown, child marriages—that is, boys under age sixteen and girls under thirteen—were exceedingly rare and limited to a special subgroup, the scholarly elites.[249] The poll tax records and Jewish metrical books confirm that conclusion.[250] Marital records from Vil'na and Korostyshev (Ukraine) show that, from the first half of the nineteenth century, the earliest age of marriage was sixteen for women and eighteen for men, thus corresponding to the minimum legal age. In 1837–1838, for instance, twenty-five of ninety-nine single brides (25.2 percent) in Vil'na were sixteen, and twenty-six of seventy-nine single grooms (32.9 percent) were eighteen years old; the remainder were all older.[251] Although some dissimulation is possible, the recent improvement in state records made falsification risky, since it was easily exposed by comparison with the birth date previously entered in the metrical records and in the most recent poll tax revision.

Significantly, these records show that the mean age for first marriage in both towns was much higher than previously thought.[252] In 1851, for example, the mean in Vil'na was 19.5 for women and 23.4 for men, although the latter figure is slightly skewed because of the large number of older, retired Jewish soldiers marrying for the first time (10.8 percent of first-time grooms being over 30 years old).[253] In 1854, Korostyshev Jews reported slightly lower averages (18.6 for females and 20.1 for males), a pattern more typical of a small Ukrainian town.[254] Although these rates are comparable to those of females and higher for males in the Russian Empire (largely because of Jewish soldiers), they are considerably lower than was the case in contemporary Europe.[255]

There were several reasons for this relatively youthful marital age. One was religious: a young man was to fulfill the mitzvah of procreation ("to be fertile and multiply").[256] Second, early marriage enabled parents to direct sexuality into legitimate channels and thus avoid indiscretions deemed intolerable in communities that placed a high premium on chastity. As the rabbis said, "He who marries off his sons and daughters close to their coming of age (samukh lefirkan) is one of whom it is said: 'And you shall know that your tent is at peace.'"[257] As nineteenth-century Europe discovered, late marriage meant skyrocketing illegitimacy; early marriages, by contrast, served as an effective means to control sexuality.[258] Third, the system of kest made early marriage feasible: newlyweds

TABLE 1.1

Mean Age at First Marriage in Vil'na and Korostyshev, 1837–1895

	Vil'na			Korostyshev	
Year	Female	Male	Year	Female	Male
1837	18.0	19.8	—	—	—
1844	19.7	21.5	—	—	—
1851	19.5	23.4	1854	19.7	20.1
1860	20.1	24.2	1861	19.2	20.5
1864	20.6	23.7	1865	19.3	20.2
1870	21.3	23.1	1876	19.1	20.0
1880	21.6	25.9	1881	19.1	20.3
1885	22.8	25.6	—	—	—
1890	22.9	26.9	1890	19.4	21.7
1895	23.2	26.3	1895	21.1	23.1

Source: LVIA, f. 728, op. 2, dd. 2, 27, 270; f. 728, op. 3, dd. 6, 12, 13, 77, 1087, 1088, 1100, 1101, 1440, 1441, 1474; TsDIAK-Ukraïny, f. 663, op. 1, dd. 63, 69, 73, 81, 83, 87, 92.

remained in the parental household and need not postpone marriage until they could establish an independent household, as was the case in Western Europe. Finally, early marriage served to offset the low life expectancy caused by a poor diet, bad hygiene, and lack of medical case in pre-reform Russia. Indeed, mortality was particularly high for infants and women (in the latter case, because of the frequent and hazardous nature of childbirth). As Jacob Goldberg suggests, these realities forced Jews to practice early marriage in order to offset the high mortality rate.[259] Significantly, the higher rate of female mortality persisted in the second half of the century. The 1897 census shows a substantially higher mortality rate for Jewish women in the cohort aged twenty-one to fifty, compared not only with Jewish males but also with the general population.[260] Early marriage, together with the high fertility rate, probably accounts for the higher toll on Jewish women.

Similarly, the high rate of infant mortality also encouraged early marriage: given the extremely low chances of survival in infancy, it was essential to bear as many children as possible. Although some believed that Jewish children had a lower mortality rate because "parents sacrificed themselves to nourish [them]," Russian demographers claimed that, in fact, the contrary was true.[261] Based on census data from Kiev, I. Pantiukhov reported that mortality of children under age ten represented 50.2 percent of all Jewish deaths in 1873 and 68.9 percent the following year, whereas child mortality in the Russian Orthodox population decreased from 54.1 to 50.1 percent in the same period.[262] Such data must be treated critically, however. Quite apart from the problem of Pantiukhov's polemical motivations, the years 1873–1874 were hardly representative: a recent cholera epidemic in Kiev left a deep imprint on public health.[263] That said, infant and child mortality for Jews as for most segments of the population in Imperial Russia *was* high. The natural response was to start having children at an early age, in hopes that some might survive the deadly diseases and epidemics that periodically claimed so many lives.

By the first national census in 1897, infant mortality rates among Jews had declined significantly and was lower than those of the rest of the general population. By modern standards, of course, it was still significant— Jewish male infants constituting 26.9 percent of all male deaths, and infant girls making up 22.1 percent of female deaths. Similarly, M. Ptukha's study of death in European Russia showed that the probability of Jewish newborn males living to age ten was 80.8 (the maximum probability being 100.0 for Estonians); for Russians, the survival rate was much lower at 59.1.[264] If high infant mortality had previously encouraged a lower marital age to ensure higher fertility, the decline in the rate in the late nineteenth century made it possible to defer marriage and reproduction to a later age.

PANIC MARRIAGES

Although child marriages were rare, there was one exception: the "panic marriages" *(nisuei behalah)* triggered by rumors of state plans to raise the minimum age of marriage.[265] According to Israel Aksenfeld's novel *The First Jewish Recruit,* the first *behalah* in tsarist Russia coincided with the conscription edict of 1827.[266] Alarmed by rumors about an impending ban on juvenile marriages, parents hastened to marry off not only sons who were liable to the draft but also small children, including young girls (for fear that they would be conscripted to work in factories).[267] The peak in panic marriages came several years later, just prior to the promulgation of the new Statutes on the Jews *(Polozheniia o evreiakh)* in April 1835, which did indeed raise the legal minimum age of marriage.[268] Aksenfeld's dramatic account drew upon this later, more widespread *behalah*—a response not only to the usual rumors but to false reports that Jews married before the decree would be exempt from the draft.[269]

The best-known satirical account of this later event was Aizik Meyer Dik's *Habehalah,* which takes place in the town of Niesvizh (Grodno province). On the morning of Tisha b'Av (commemorating the destruction of the Temple), a prominent Jew comes to the synagogue to warn about plans to raise the minimum age of marriage. By nightfall the town had divided into two camps—matchmakers and prospective in-laws. The poorer families, mostly Hasidim, were the first to organize makeshift weddings, dispensing with the customary musicians and jesters *(badkho-nim)*; after all, it was a day of lamentation (Tisha b'Av), and the tsar's edict was still a secret. They also jettisoned the traditional rituals of the seating of the woman on the bridal chair *(bazetsns)* and the veiling prior to the ceremony *(badekns)*. Some families even dispensed with the min-yan (a quorum of ten men) because of the profusion of weddings in a sin-gle night. As the panic spread, wealthy families—initially scornful of the rumors (who could trust a matchmaker and his "18,000 lies"?)—realized that a critical shortage of bridegrooms was imminent and frantically began to organize their own weddings. The town quickly turned into a "wedding depot" that eradicated the boundaries of age, lineage, and class. A ten-year-old boy became the surprised groom of an eighteen-year-old maiden; a ten-year-old girl became the bride of a young widower; the rich were intermarried with the indigent; commoners became kinsmen of families with *yikhus*.[270]

While not all participated in this marital orgy, the pandemonium created a matchmaker's paradise, where "each minute was gold."[271] One matchmaker shamelessly exploited the situation by terrifying residents with the claim that the state would forbid Jewish women to marry be-fore twenty-five and men before thirty. Another beneficiary was the town cantor; the *behalah* represented a "golden moment" in his career: when not writing marriage contracts or singing at a wedding, he was busy with his duties as the town's ritual slaughterer. In Dik's apt phrase, "He slaughtered the children *(kinder)* with the cattle *(rinder)*, with the poultry *(hiner)* all together." When the real edict was finally announced, the flabbergasted residents of Niesvizh learned that the government merely reaffirmed the minimum age for girls (sixteen) and boys (eigh-teen). In a word, they had become exemplars of utter foolishness, now confronted with a mass of *agunot* (grass widows), mismatched couples, and divorce suits.

THE RISE IN MARITAL AGE

The latter decades of the nineteenth century witnessed a substantial de-cline in the traditional pattern of youthful marriage. This tendency to defer marriage, while also true for the general population, was especially salient in the case of Jews.[272] In the 1860s the average marital age for Jews was still low; in 1867, for example, 43.0 percent of Jewish grooms and 60.8 percent of Jewish brides were under the age of twenty-one, as table 1.2 shows.[273]

Although the decline was especially marked for males (from 43.0 per-cent to 5.8 percent), it was also true of women (60.8 percent to 25.0 percent). At a lower, disaggregated level, the metrical books for Vil'na and Korostyshev similarly show that, by 1895, the mean age of first marriage among Jews had risen to 23.2 for females and 26.3 for males in Vil'na.[274] The small district town of Korostyshev reported slightly lower averages but also showed a significant increase from the first half of the century: 21.2 for brides and 23.1 for grooms.[275]

In 1910, Sara Rabinowitsch observed that "in our time, not one religious confession in Russia has experienced such a sharp [increase in marital age] and the almost exceptional predominance of older people entering into marriage.... Between 1888 and 1892, the average age of Jewish brides was lower than any other religious confession, except Muslims; at present, however, it is higher than all other confessions."[276] Even by the time of the 1897 census, the age of marriage of Jews, particularly among women, was the highest in the Russian Empire.[277] This revolution in marital age bore momentous consequences for family structure, relations, and fertility.

How is this dramatic rise in the marital age to be explained? Part of the answer is cultural: the *maskilim,* bitter about their lost youth and unhappy marriages, waged an unrelenting campaign against adolescent marriages. Thus, the influential autobiography by Mordechai Aaron Guenzburg (1795–1846) castigated early marriages for forcing "nature to flower prematurely," which in his case meant sexual dysfunction.[278] Even before the wedding night, he recalled the mutual embarrassment (like an "iron wall") between the bride and himself, a mere child who had not even experienced sexual desire. His humiliation only deepened when his wife and mother-in-law forced him to imbibe a potion to cure his impotence (aptly described as "a perverse version of the *sotah* ritual").[279] Like the adulterous wife whose body contorts from guilt (i.e., yellow face, bulging eyes, swollen veins), the groom failed the "ordeal of bitter waters" and fell ill, unable to gain his virility. On the basis of his traumatic experiences, Guenzburg sought a middle ground between premature marriage in East-

TABLE 1.2

Percentage of Married Jews under Age 21

Year	Male	Female
1867	43.0	60.8
1877	25.4	54.7
1887	10.9	42.2
1897	5.8	25.0

Source: Sara Rabinovich, "K voprosu o nachal'nom remeslennom obrazovanii evreiskikh zhenshchin," *Novyi voskhod* 5 (4 February 1910): 9.

ern Europe and late nuptials in Germany (which he blamed for encouraging men to frequent prostitutes). The ideal age for the first marriage, in his view, was twenty for men and fifteen for women—a point, he believed, when both sexes attained physical and sexual maturity.[280]

Ironically, the Orthodox establishment also came to favor later marriage, independently of the *haskalah* movement.[281] According to Rabbi Naphtali Zvi Berlin (1817–1893), the head of the Volozhin yeshiva, early marriages were harmful for both sexes: "Girls who begin giving birth when they are young become weak and sickly. And the same is true of males who use their sexual organs for procreation in the days of their youth; their health also fails."[282] Medical arguments for a higher marital age among Jews were hardly new, but they had greater appeal when justified in terms of Torah studies.[283] Indeed, in the course of the nineteenth century, the marital age of students at the Volozhin yeshiva (i.e., the scholarly elite) rose from thirteen to twenty.[284]

Higher education also caused the marital age to rise. The Moscow metrical books from 1870 to 1887, for example, reveal that Jewish men seeking to obtain their professional degrees (i.e., in medicine, law, and economics) often postponed marriage until their late twenties and early thirties.[285] Likewise, pharmacists *(provizory),* who were required to complete university courses in their profession, generally did not marry until their mid-or late twenties.[286] By contrast, their assistants *(aptekarskii pomoshchniki),* who needed only four years of gymnasium and apprentice training, married several years earlier.[287] Similarly, Jewish women who pursued secondary and higher education in pedagogy and midwifery deferred marriage until the ages of twenty-two to twenty-five.[288] The majority, moreover, married fellow students or graduates of the professional faculties.[289] As the number of Jewish female auditors steadily increased, they formed the largest minority group in the universities of Moscow, St. Petersburg, and Kiev. Their desire to learn for its own sake (rather than to become better wives and mothers, as the *maskilim* envisioned) and to achieve economic independence inevitably created new tensions in the family over gender roles.

At the other end of the social scale, declining economic opportunities and growing impoverishment in the Pale tended to cause later marriages. This was especially true for the increasing number of Jews who migrated from rural areas to the cities, where they huddled in large concentrations.[290] By the time of the 1897 census, nearly 48.7 percent resided in the prescribed set of urban centers,[291] where they dominated crafts like tailoring, weaving, shoemaking, carpentry, and the production of food and beverages.[292] Most of these Jews found their lot in the city a hard one. The dense concentration of Jews in the consumer goods sector increased competition and ethnic tensions in a market already being reshaped by a belated industrialization.[293] Domestic demand grew slowly; given their limited purchasing power, consumers restricted expenditures to the bare "necessities."[294] The result was a superabundance of Jewish artisans; as one contemporary observed, "there were enough Jewish tailors to supply clothing for half the urban population of the Russian empire."[295] The weak demand made master artisans increasingly vulnerable to the caprice of the marketplace; they in turn responded by exploiting their journeymen and apprentices even more ruthlessly.[296] Long working hours (16 to 18 hours a day in the northwest cities), meager wages, and seasonal employment left many workers in dire poverty.[297]

These conditions bore significant negative implications for the Jewish underclass and traditional family order. The meager income forced young men and women to defer marriage; neither they nor their parents could afford a wedding, much less support a family with children.[298] Three rubles per week (the wages of a Lodz weaver or Bialystok carpenter in the 1860s) barely covered the basic necessities, making it increasingly difficult to consider marriage, even with the assistance of communal charity.[299] By the late nineteenth century, men who had married were unable to support their families on their wages alone and had to rely on what their wives and children earned in the nonmechanized shops and factories. The cramped housing conditions, exacerbated by the rapid growth of urban areas, drove many families to share "the semi-darkness of cellars or similar hovels that had wet walls and floors."[300] Such limited living space not only produced inter- and intra-family conflict but also rendered the traditional system of *kest* all but impossible.

In sum, cultural and religious opposition to adolescent marriages, the priority accorded to education over marriage (both in the yeshivot and secular institutions), and growing immiseration of the Jewish underclass all contributed to the significant rise in the age of marriage.

FERTILITY

In the nineteenth century the Jewish population experienced an extraordinary rate of growth, increasing from slightly more than over 1 million in 1795 (the fifth revision census) to 5.1 million in 1897.[301] High rates of nuptiality and early marriage in the first half of the century produced very high fertility rates. A Russian Geographical Society survey (published in 1858) estimated approximately 4.5 Jewish births per marriage during a five-year period (1848–1852), a figure slightly higher than all the other religious confessions, with the exception of the Orthodox population (4.7 births per marriage).[302] The average number of Jewish births

FIG. 5. Modern natal care in Melitopol (Tavrida province). Consultation for nursing babies at the "Drop of Milk," a subsidiary of the JOINT, established by the Society for the Preservation of the Health of the Jewish Population in the early twentieth century. *Courtesy of the YIVO Institute for Jewish Research.*

may have been even higher, given their disinclination to register. The paucity of female entries in the metrical books suggests that parents neglected to register their daughters, presumably to avoid the costs (usually 1 to 5 rubles) and the inconvenience. As Rebecca Himber Berg (b. 1878) remarked, "With a boy, it was different. The Jewish community and the Russian government collaborated in observing his birthdays [i.e., to determine his bar mitzvah date and conscription]. . . . But a girl! It was enough if one reckoned that she was born some time before the 'big fire.'"[303]

Stereotypes of Jewish fecundity were widespread in the Russian medical establishment, which attributed high rates of fertility to Jewish women's propensity for quick labor and deliveries. According to a comparative study of births at Russian and Jewish hospitals in Kiev from 1854 to 1864, the average time of labor for all patients was twenty-six hours for first-time births and eleven to twelve hours for subsequent children.[304] Among Jewish women, 35 percent gave birth in five hours, 34 percent in five to ten hours, 18 percent in ten to twenty hours, and only 13 percent required more than twenty hours.[305] Jewish physicians explained the low rate of stillbirths and miscarriages by a long tradition of skilled midwifery, dating back to biblical and Talmudic times.[306] These reports that Jews were exceedingly fruitful were not so farfetched. The Demographic research has shown that the Jewish population in tsarist Russia (including Congress Poland) increased at a higher rate than the general population between 1825 and 1850: 1.55 percent per annum compared to 0.85 percent among the non-Jewish population in European Russia.[307]

In the second half of the century, however, Jews underwent a major demographic transition. Thus, the 1897 census showed that the fertility rate among Jews—once the highest—was now almost the lowest (surpassed only by the Protestants). There was a parallel decrease in mortality rates, making the Jewish rate the lowest in the empire. Thus, in spite of the lower fertility, Jews nonetheless showed a natural increase of 14.7 percent between 1896 and 1904. Infant mortality and illegitimacy rates were also noticeably lower than for other groups (table 1.3).

Aggregate data compiled by the Russian government suggest that Jews began to limit their families around the mid-1860s, when the number of births decreased sharply. The Jews in Vil'na province, for instance, reported 51.3 births per 1,000 of the Jewish population in 1858; by 1869 that figure had plummeted to 23.7. Likewise, their coreligionists in Kiev province had 41 births per 1,000 of the population in 1858 but only 36.6 in 1869. By 1896–1897, the birth rate for the Jewish population in European Russia was 30.6, and the death rate was 16.0, allowing a 14.6 rate of natural increase (See table 1.4). Despite the decline, the rates were still high compared to Jews in Western Europe; the rate for the Jews in Prussia, for example, was 33 births per 1,000 of Jewish inhabitants in 1866, and then declined to 23.75 by 1890.[308]

TABLE 1.3

Demographic Reproduction in European Russia, 1896–1904, by Religious Confession (per Thousand Members of Each Confession)

Confession	Mean age of marriage Male	Female	Nuptiality	Fertility	Childhood mortality	Mortality	Illegitimacy
Orthodox	24.2	21.3	8.7	51.1	34.8	263	2.4
Catholic	29.1	23.3	6.9	36.5	22.3	151	3.4
Protestant	28.5	24.6	6.8	29.2	21.0	161	3.7
Jewish	27.5	24.1	7.3	30.7	16.0	116	0.4
Muslim	27.6	22.2	10.9	43.9	27.7	158	0.2
Empire	25.1	21.8	8.5	50.1	30.9	224	2.3

Source: A. Novosel'skii, *Obzor glavneishikh dannykh po demografii i sanitarnoi statistike Rossii* (St. Petersburg, 1916), 26–53.[309]

TABLE 1.4

Births, Deaths, and Natural Increase in the Jewish Population, 1858–1869

Year	Province	Jewish population	Births	Births per 1,000	Deaths	Deaths per 1,000	Rate of natural increase
1858	Kiev	222,074	9112	41.0	6072	27.3	13.7
	Vil'na	75,802	3873	51.1	3315	43.7	7.4
1862	Kiev	247,842	8816	35.6	6259	25.3	10.3
	Vil'na	81,832*	3081*	37.7	2396*	29.3	8.4
1865	Kiev	258,525	8692	33.6	6934	26.8	6.8
	Vil'na	103,958*	3000*	28.9	2991*	28.8	0.1
1869	Kiev	267,867	9792	36.6	6427	24.0	12.6
	Vil'na	108,191*	2554*	23.6	2756*	25.5	1.9

Source: RGIA, f. 821, op. 8, d. 480, ll. 25, 37; d. 484, ll. 13–15, 28; d. 487, ll. 7–8, 22; d. 490, ll. 20–23, 27–28.

*For some years the data included Karaites; the data have been adjusted to cover Jews only.

The sharp decline in the birthrate, especially in Vil'na province, was at least partly due to the rising age at first marriage among women (see table 1.1). Indeed, deferred marriage had long been a form of family planning in premodern Europe. But it may also have been partly due to the use of birth control; court records sometimes refer to various methods to prevent or terminate pregnancies. In one seduction case, for example, the paramour purportedly offered his pregnant partner "a potion" (supplied by his mother) "to destroy the fetus." In another suit, a domestic servant from Dubno denied taking "substances to destroy the fetus" after learning that she was pregnant from a liaison with a Jewish soldier.[310] Reference in both cases may have been to the mercury, sulfur, and various herbs then used to abort a pregnancy.[311] Rabbinic literature in Eastern Europe also refers to oral sterilizing potions, which are originally discussed in the Talmud (Yevamot 65b); in 1875, for example, Rabbi Shneor Zalman of Lublin (d. 1902) described a "cup of roots" *(kos shel ikkarin)* that allegedly "despoiled the uterus."[312] Earlier responsa by Rabbi Sirkes in Poland cited the case of a woman who tried to abort an illegitimate child by taking a liquid concoction.[313] Jewish wives, like their gentile peers, may also have prolonged lactation to reduce fertility, as scattered allusions in the court records suggest.[314]

A traditional method like coitus interruptus, the method most common among German Jews, may have been current in Russia, given the close ties and diffusion of Western culture in Russia.[315] More modern methods, notably the condom, also made some inroads, especially among the educated classes in the late nineteenth century, and they were advertised in major newspapers.[316] Given the Jewish religious injunction against "spilling the seed" *(hashhatat zera),* this method appealed less to religious Jews than the more acculturated residing outside the Pale.

A few desperate women resorted to the illegal device of abortion.[317] In indicting the barber Leizer Lindenblit and his wife, Basia (a midwife), for performing illegal abortions in the Vil'na area, the prosecution used depositions from several Jewish female domestics. Mikhlia Leibova Biryshnikova, who had been raped by her employer and then fired without pay, turned to the couple to help rid herself of the shame and unwanted child. She claimed that the "treatment" lasted eight to ten days as Basia Lindenblit tried to "dig out" the fetus with a "white, bent metal rod with the thickness of a pencil, and then with a white bone rod, which was slightly curved." Although the domestic claimed that the treatment was not "too painful" and that there was "just a little blood," her mother testified that her daughter had changed completely.[318] Whatever the case, such illegal abortions were doubtless becoming widespread, reinforcing demands, especially from the medical community, to decriminalize the procedure and thus save young, desperate women from the harrowing ordeal of amateur surgery.

WIDOWHOOD AND DEATH

Death and widowhood also had significant implications for Jewish marital patterns. A low life expectancy meant that nineteenth-century Jews not only married but frequently remarried.[319] Remarriage was an economic necessity in a society where the family was also a production unit and childrearing a principal domestic task. Indeed, the marital statistics show an astonishingly high proportion of widows and widowers. In 1861, for example, the metrical records for Korostyshev reveal that nearly half of the marriages (11 of 24) represented a second marriage for at least one of the spouses.[320] During one four-year period in Kiev (1866–1869), 41.7 percent of Jewish marriages involved a widow or widower, compared to 26.0 percent for the Russian Orthodox population.[321]

Second marriages, whether due to widowhood or divorce, profoundly affected family dynamics if children from a previous marriage were involved. Remarriages after widowhood, particularly among men with young children, were so frequent that a special prayer for the stepmother was included in women's Yiddish prayer books.[322] The stepparent or stepchild was a stock figure in memoirs and belles-lettres. The writer Judah Loeb Katsenelson explained that, when he was but one year old, his father died and his mother (his father's second wife) remarried a man from Gomel; from that day on, Katsenelson lived with his grandfather in Chernigov.[323] S. Y. Abramovich (Mendele Moykher Sforim) also recalled the feeling of abandonment after his father died. His widowed mother remarried and moved away with the younger children to another town, leaving him behind. "I remained alone and forlorn in Kopyl," he wrote. "I was very miserable then and life was unbearable for its pain and despondence, for I was still a boy, young in years and old in troubles."[324]

Remarriage also produced substantial age gaps between the new spouses. In Korostyshev, for example, the age discrepancy of remarried couples was consistently large; in 1861, for example, it ranged between nineteen and thirty-one years.[325] This differential was markedly greater than for couples entering into their first marriage; that same year in Korostyshev, for example, age difference among first-time spouses was zero to five years.[326] In some cases, the bride was even a year or two older than her groom. Such marriages in which the male was significantly older and the primary holder of assets tended to buttress traditional patriarchy.

Summary

Thus, the Jews in the Russian Empire experienced a far-reaching change in marital age, fertility, and mortality. Child marriages were as rare as they were sensational; the principal exception was the infamous episode of "panic marriages." Nevertheless, from a European perspective, Jews did marry at a relatively early age in the first half of the nineteenth century. That, however, changed dramatically in the latter part of the century, as the mean marital age rose substantially. It accompanied and in large measure caused a concomitant decline in fertility. Although the birthrate fell, so too did mortality; hence, the natural increase remained high. Even so, the Jewish population had a large number of widows and widowers; the result was a high rate of remarriage, exacerbating the problem of stepchildren and tangled family relations.

Gender Roles and Power Relations in the Household

Each confession, including Judaism, had its own normative ideals of spousal relations and appropriate gender roles. Interestingly, the normative roles, whether traditional or "bourgeois," were remarkably similar: the male was the provider and patriarch, the wife, the homemaker and dependent. Jewish law unambiguously ascribed specific duties for the husband and wife. His basic responsibility was to provide food and raiment for his wife and to perform his conjugal duties with the frequency prescribed by the Talmud.[327] Her obligation was to perform household duties: "She grinds, bakes and washes; she cooks and nurses his child; she makes his bed and spins wool."[328]

In reality, however, these ideals bore little relevance to the quotidian realities of Jewish life in the Russian Empire, where the gender division of labor was far more complex. Here the nexus of work, power, and cultural prestige was deeply embedded in the socioreligious structures of Jewish society, which differed—and evolved differently—for each segment of Jewish society. The *mitnagdim,* in particular, turned the Talmudic model on its head. They prescribed an arrangement that allowed the husband to study Torah and gave the wife the task of earning the livelihood. Chaim Tchernowitz recalled that his grandfather devoted his entire life to study and "remained dependent on the wages of his wife, my grandmother, who was the housewife, merchant, and trader all her life."[329] In the southwestern provinces, Hasidic wives were likewise expected to support their families, while their husbands passed their time in prayer houses or made pilgrimages to the rebbe that lasted up to two months or longer.[330] To be sure, this allocation of roles was more ideal than real; the vast majority of men were not Torah scholars and in fact toiled as artisans, tradesmen, and merchants. Nevertheless, these cultural ideals served to legitimize women's work outside the household.[331]

This "inverted" structure of work gave Jewish women distinct spheres and corresponding authority.[332] One site of female activity was the marketplace, where women interacted on a daily basis with the non-Jewish world, as they ran small shops, traded in bazaars or markets, and peddled dairy products and foodstuffs. Ezekiel Kotik recalled that in the small shops of Kamenets, "the only people who engaged in business are the women, old and young, maidens and girls. And here all the wives sat, one against the other, excited and agitated" as they vied for customers.[333] These business activities brought them periodically into the courtroom. In 1894, for example, Mariam Beizer of Uman sued the local rabbi for seeking to ruin her business; she claimed that he had proclaimed a *herem* on anyone who bought milk from Russian peasants—her suppliers.[334] The court docket in Vil'na was jammed with charges filed by police and customers that Jewish shopkeepers and petty traders (most of whom were female) used false scales to defraud buyers. A typical charge was filed against twenty-four-year-old Khasia Solomonova Levin of Sirot Street, who ran her own grocery and purportedly had used her scales to cheat; although she adamantly denied the accusation, the court ruled otherwise. It sentenced her to the usual punishment—a five-ruble fine or, if she could not pay the fine, two days in detention.[335]

Jewish women were also active in the tobacco and alcohol trade, a business that frequently brought them into conflict with state inspectors and tax collectors. These feisty businesswomen stood their ground; many court cases involved accusations that Jewish women had insulted the honor of the officials.[336] At any rate, the court records confirm a common theme in the memoirs: it was the wife, not the husband, who usually handled everyday relations with state authorities. That was due not only to their role in the business but also to their ability to converse in the Russian language.

Then, too Jewish women enjoyed special advantages: while most women were wise enough to invoke public transcripts of deference and subordination, the hotheads who ended up in the courtrooms, read from the "wrong transcript."[337] Gender ("defenseless woman") and ethnicity (religious minority) gave women protection that their spouses could hardly invoke, a fact that served to reinforce further their public role. Even when the husband operated the business, he often chose to have his wife serve as the intermediary with the state. That strategy was apparent in a typical incident that took place in a Jewish tavern in Vil'na province. When an official came to collect an excise tax, the owner abruptly left the room and his wife appeared to deal with the odious official. The owner's wife, Sore Leia, asserted that "she had already paid the tax several times, and then proceeded to call him a 'robber bandit' *(razboinikii grabitel')*, an insult that caused her to be hauled into court."[338] Other women on trial for "insulting the honor" of state officials had showered them with such acolades as "scoundrel" *(svoloch')*, "drunkard" *(p'ianitsa)*, "tramp" *(brodiaga)* "thief" *(vor)*, "swindler" *(moshennik)*, and "son-of-a-bitch" *(sukyn syn)*.[339] Seventy-seven-year-old Khaia Gurvich offended a tobacco inspector by using the informal "you" *(ty)* and allegedly scorned his threats of litigation in "your shitty court" *(govennyi vash sud)*.[340] That outburst cost her a fifty-ruble fine and a month in detention. Such cases impelled state officials to denounce Jewish women as grotesquely "masculine" in their vulgar language, aggressive behavior, and dominant role as "mistress of the home" *(khoziaika)*—a critique echoed in maskilic discourse as well.

Jewish women also had to deal with the non-Jewish customers who patronized their stores, inns, and taverns. The role was not without its risks. In a suit before the Vladimir-Volhynia district criminal court, a Jewish woman complained that an inebriated peasant customer became violent and kicked her in the stomach, causing a miscarriage; witnesses confirmed that the blow caused a premature birth, with the infant dying almost immediately.[341] In another case, a patron claimed that Khana Pitukovaia, who operated a tavern with her husband in Troki district (Vil'na province), had given him a counterfeit ruble. In her defense, the twenty-year-old woman testified that so many people passed through her tavern that she had no idea where the false bill came from. Pitukovaia added that since she was illiterate, she could hardly distinguish between a real and fake ruble, an argument so cogent that the court dismissed the charges.[342]

The court records also show that Jewish women, not just men, frequently engaged in money lending and had to file numerous suits against clients who had failed to repay their loans (usually in the form of promissory notes). For instance, Rivka Ryndziunskaia sued Shlema and Nekhama Ryndziunskii for defaulting on a loan (2,350 rubles at a 12 percent annual interest rate). According to the written agreement, they promised to pay her 282 rubles a year (or 23.50 rubles a month) until the debt was retired. But the couple was already embroiled in legal difficulties and could not afford to repay the borrowed money. The case involved, interestingly, not only a bad debt but also bad blood; the plaintiff was the defendant's own daughter-in-law.[343] In any event, such cases demonstrate that women acted as moneylenders, often alone, and had the full status of a litigant before state courts.

However, Jewish women's roles in the public sphere—as traders, merchants, and moneylenders—was not a unique feature of Jewish life, as the historiography sometimes implies.[344] This division of labor was common in imperial society, especially among townspeople. One study of Kiev in 1875 claimed that women comprised over three-quarters of those engaged in trade. Although perhaps an exaggeration, the report confirms that in general women were highly active in the region's commercial life. In the postreform era that role tended to increase as women also assumed a growing presence in the artisan class, especially in the needle trades.[345] Their business and artisan activity, interestingly, created tensions with male counterparts, who sought to stem the unwelcome competition. When Khaia Laiman opened her seamstress shop in Zhitomir in 1901 and neglected to secure permission from the local artisan board, her competitor, Hirsh Mermil'shtein seized on the oversight to file a formal denunciation with state authorities.[346]

Within this largely female domain of small trade and business, some husbands were "mere lackeys in the shops."[347] As Puah Rakowski put it, her grandmother's third husband was, throughout her life, her helpmate (*ezer kenegdo*), a term usually reserved for women.[348] Chaim Tchernowitz's father, who used his wife's dowry to open a store, "sat in the store most of the time, with the *Gemara* open before him, studying to a melody, and all the customers who passed through the store thought that it was a Talmud Torah." Although his father rarely involved himself in the daily business affairs, he insisted that his wife strictly follow rabbinical laws (e.g., the prohibition on excessive competition with neighbors), much to the detriment of her business. "And so one can imagine how great a profit the store made!" Tchernowitz remarked. "In the end, after a year or two, the trade was done and the store was closed and . . . he returned to the table of my grandfather as before."[349]

Due to the perils of travel, however, it was primarily the men who transported merchandise, procured liquor, and traveled to distant towns to peddle their wares.[350] Despite his inexperience, Tchernowitz's father insisted on journeying to Dvinsk to purchase goods since "it was customary for the head of the household to travel to buy the merchandise." According to A. M. Dik, when the men departed to peddle goods or to conduct business in another town, "the hamlet looks dead during the entire week; it resembles a gynecocracy, that is, a kingdom inhabited only by women. In the hamlet itself remain only women, children, communal officials, students and a few . . . unemployed men."[351] Amid the industrialization of the late nineteenth century, men also left for seasonal employment in the factories (as *otkhotniki,* migrant laborers), leaving their families behind.

While both spouses often shared the role of breadwinner, the traditional chores of housekeeping and child care remained in the woman's domain. The wife had to shop for food and supplies at the market, prepare the meals, clean the house, and trudge to the nearest stream to wash the laundry. The onus of such daily toil was a common refrain in memoirs, belles-lettres, and folksongs.[352] More prosperous families had domestic servants, cooks, gardeners, and stewards to perform household chores, take care of the children, maintain the garden, clean the outhouse, and attend to myriad other tasks. Although Russian law forbade Jews to employ Christians as servants, incidental references suggest that the practice was in fact not uncommon.[353] In Bella Chagall's home, for example, a Russian domestic servant and a Jewish cook worked side by side in the kitchen, the former as conscientious as the latter about maintaining a Jewish home.[354]

The ban on using Christian domestics ("Jews are not to take Christian slaves or servants of either sex into their homes") was initiated in the Ministry of Education and Spiritual Affairs by Prince A. N. Golitsyn in January 1820. Golitsyn contended that "women of the Christian faith, living in Jewish homes as servants, not only forget and leave [their religion] without fulfilling their responsibility to the Christian faith, but take on the customs and rites of the Jews." He claimed that the problem was a menace in Kherson and other provinces and had inspired a dangerous sectarian group called the Judaizers (who emulated many Jewish ritual practices, such as observance of the Sabbath). Golitsyn claimed that he not only sought to prevent the "conversion" of Christian domestic servants to Judaism but also to provide more opportunities for poor Jews to become domestics for their own coreligionists.[355] Despite the categorical terms, the law was not strictly observed; when the Jewish Committee reconsidered the question in 1881, it discovered that a significant number of Christians served in Jewish homes, although it did not provide specific figures. In defense of Jewish families, the learned Jew of Ekaterinoslav argued that Christian wet nurses and nannies performed a valuable acculturating role: "In our time, there are many Jewish families in which Yiddish has been forced away by the Russian language. . . . Thus, if the Commission will enforce the prohibition . . . regarding Christian servants . . . , then Jewish children will again be taught to speak in Yiddish."[356] Despite the clever appeal to the state's assimilationist ambition, the law stood—at least on the books. The fact that the Senate reiterated the ban on Jews' hiring of Christian domestics on 27 March 1910 suggests that the law was still being observed more often in the breach.

The woman's role in the household economy naturally had an impact on domestic relations between husbands and wives. That is abundantly apparent in the massive memoir literature, which is replete with images of strong, sharp-tongued wives and obsequious, browbeaten husbands. Chaim Tchernowitz, for instance, recalled that his paternal grandmother, Chaya Deich, made all the important decisions in the household, while her husband followed her obediently from town to town. At the end of his life, when his grandfather finally established himself as the head of a yeshiva or Talmud Torah in Kherson (thanks to his wife's family connections), he was "anxious to show her that he was also a man, that she had risen to greatness because he had allowed her [to do so]." Despite his desire to reverse the power relations in the household, "his dream was never realized and he remained under the power of his wife all his life."[357]

In multigenerational families, the matriarchal mother-in-law ruled the home, at least from the perspective of young bridegrooms. "My father-in-law did not wear the pants in his house," Lilienblum scornfully observed, "but was subordinate to his wife." He then proceeded to explain that "this accursed woman extended her dominion to a fifteen-year-old boy . . . with her curses, fiery tongue, and contentious screaming."[358] This negative portrayal of the mother-in-law was partly due to the system of *kest*, which squarely placed the young groom under the authority of his bride's parents. Immanuel Etkes has shown the deep tensions between the new husband and the wife's family that formed precisely during this period.[359]

The power that women exercised over the household, however, did not necessarily translate into cultural prestige or authority.[360] As Daniel

FIG. 6. Russian wet nurse (*left*) and nanny (*right*) for the Dymshits family in St. Petersburg at the turn of the century. *Courtesy of Galina Markovna Rokhlina of St. Petersburg.*

Boyarin and Naomi Seidman point out, in a society where Torah study represented "a system for the domination of women," only men enjoyed real social value.[361] In fact, one could even argue that "female power was not fully legitimate," given the male hegemony over the religious institutions and laws that governed family life.[362] As we shall see, women's vulnerability in matters of marriage and divorce increasingly impelled them to turn outside this authority structure and appeal to the state for a defense of their rights and interests.

In the second half of the nineteenth century, the *haskalah* movement launched a massive assault on Jewish women's roles in the family economy and castigated this gender division of labor as "abnormal" and "exploitative." They combined their call for men to take up productive occupations with sharp criticism of women's presence in the marketplace. One writer for the *Vestnik russkikh evreev* repudiated the justification that it was a mitzvah and privilege for women to support their scholar-husbands, mourning the physical toll that it took: "The woman resembles some kind of a dressed-up skeleton with sunken eyes and an almost green, thin face rather than a healthy person."[363] In fact, the Russian Jewish press routinely printed articles urging an end to "female participation in the so-called male sphere of activities—namely trade."[364] That trade should be defined as an exclusively male occupation implied not only the desire to eliminate women but to remove their very culture from this arena, which the *maskilim* (like state officials) viewed as "masculine" and vulgar.[365]

This most famous critique appeared in S. Y. Abramovich's satirical novel, *The Brief Travels of Benjamin the Third* (1878), which exaggerated the traditional gender division of labor to reveal the "subverted sexuality" of Jews in the fictional town of Tuneyadevka ("town of parasites"). The emasculated male is represented by Senderl the Dame *(Senderl di yidene)*, whose wife "wore the pants in the house." On holiday eves, "tying a kerchief around his beard, she ordered him to whitewash the house, peel potatoes, roll and cut noodle dough, stuff fish, and kindle the oven."[366] Senderl's passivity and "stolen masculinity" are imposed on his wife, the breadwinner, "disfiguring" her and making her violent (i.e, prone to husband beating), coarse, and dominant.[367]

In lieu of the traditional roles, the *haskalah* movement propagated the cult of "bourgeois domesticity" that would shelter Jewish wives from the corrupting influences of commerce and feminize the private sphere of the home.[368] Here they were to assume the role of educated mothers, wives, and efficient homemakers. David Biale suggests that behind this "revolt against a perceived matriarchal family" lay a desire on the part of the *maskilim* to usurp power from the very women who had dominated them in their adolescent marriages.[369] Whatever the motive, this new ideal ran contrary to the nascent feminist movement in Russia, which argued that women should have an independent source of income as a first step toward their emancipation. Even the few radical *maskilim* who espoused equality for women in the family and society ultimately desired to control their new roles and status. As Shmuel Feiner aptly points out, the *maskilim* perceived the "modern Jewish woman" as a threat to sexual morality and Jewish national identity and therefore sought to contain her within the model German bourgeois family.[370]

Conclusion

The inroads of modernity within the Jewish family generated new expectations about self-fulfillment and individuality that stood in stark contrast to the system of dependency and strict parental and communal control of the past. As the age of first marriage rose dramatically in the late nineteenth century, some "children" insisted on their right to choose their spouses, set up their independent livelihoods, and even determine where they were going to live. This growing self-reliance left many parents bewildered. As Pauline Wengeroff put it, "We must now obey our children and submit completely to their will, just as once obedience to our parents was inviolable. . . . When our parents talked, we listened respectfully." Although she expressed indignation at the brazenness of the new generation, Wengeroff could not conceal a little admiration for the open manner in which the children "talk about themselves and their ideals."

While the ideology of the "companionate marriage" gained ascendancy in the mid-nineteenth century, actual marital practices and customs were slower to change. Most Jews remained attentive to "traditional" qualities, such as family lineage, wealth, male learning, commercial talents, and morality. At the same time, they were not immune to the influence of medical science, secular education, and new socioeconomic realities, all of which challenged gender hierarchies and relations. In particular, these "modern" forces of change began to undermine the system of cultural prestige and male domination associated with Torah studies. Although Jews still esteemed close endogamous unions with families of great rabbinic lineage and learning, they became increasingly cognizant of hereditary genetic disorders, especially the rise of mental illnesses. If Torah studies had once served as a means of upward social mobility, a university degree, which promised the right to reside outside the Pale of Settlement, now played a similar role among some strata of Jewish society. Little wonder that, by the early twentieth century, Jewish men began to advertise their diplomas in medicine and law to attract wealthy partners.

Women's secular education and socialization also challenged the traditional marriage market. The rabbinical establishment especially feared the loss of the marital alliances between Torah scholars and the acculturated daughters of the economic elites, unions that had traditionally buttressed its authority and cultural hegemony. Although as yet relatively few women had the opportunity to acquire elite education and pursue professional careers, their numbers were increasing. It is indeed arguable that the transition to such professions was particularly easy for Jewish women, whose mothers had routinely plied a trade or business, providing a model and ethos that were easily transferred to the new professions. Their new *mentalité* and assertiveness would generate severe tensions in the household, forcing spouses to renegotiate gender roles. Even the *maskilim,* who had advocated women's education, neither anticipated nor approved of these new attitudes. In fact, their desire "to revolutionize politics of marriage and family along lines of romantic love and bourgeois marital relations," tended to reinforce traditional gender relations.[371]

Amid this reconstitution of marriage and family—and indeed a key factor in the process of transformation—was yet another agent of change: the Russian state. As we shall see in the next chapter, it increasingly endeavored to wrest control over the Jewish community and family, establishing its own institutions and seeking to arbitrate and regulate Jewish life.

Chapter Two

⚜

Bringing Order to the Jewish Family

In a six-point memorandum to the Ministry of the Interior in 1854, the Jewish Committee sought to explain why the state had repeatedly been unable to transform Jews into "productive agricultural producers." Part of the problem, it argued, was Judaism itself; its various religious holidays and customs (such as the Sabbath, Passover, and the seven-day mourning period for the dead) "distracted" the Jews from farming and hindered the success of state reforms.[1] But no less detrimental was the unordered Jewish family, especially the utter lack of regulation and control over Jewish marital practices—above all, underage marriages and hasty divorces.[2] Although there were no hard data, local reports and, indeed, the very lack of strict governmental control predisposed the state to believe that both phenomena—so reprehensible to Russian Orthodox—were rampant among Jews.

The Jewish Committee[3] was particularly concerned about underage marriages. It contended that the custom prevented Jews from establishing and maintaining an efficient household economy. Instead, it claimed, young couples quickly became burdened with the need to support large families and hence, from the outset, had to devote all their energies to eking out a bare existence. Their children either died from deprivation or grew up "in a feeble condition, with little capacity for hard labor demanded by agriculture."[4] The committee proposed to emulate the practice of European states, which had discerned a similar nexus between early marriage, reproduction, and poverty (and antisocial behavior) and therefore sought to prevent early marriage and hence the growth of the "dangerous classes," or *Pöbel*.[5]

The committee also voiced deep concern about the high divorce rate among Jews.[6] It warned that "divorces among the Jews occur without proper grounds [and] so frequently that out of one hundred Jews, perhaps twenty divorce their wives." The committee claimed that it was even common for a Jew to divorce his second wife and remarry the first. Apart from the jarring dissonance (divorce was all but impossible for the Russian Orthodox) and the conservative view that a stable family was the bedrock of the existing political and social order, such divorces were also fraught with significant economic consequences: they had a "harmful influence on household economies, which remain without female heads for entire months at a time and suffer complete ruin."[7]

This rampant disorder in the family, declared the Jewish Committee, was due to the lack of uniform supervision over Jewish marriage and divorce. It therefore recommended that the government tighten control over the formation and dissolution of the Jewish family. That control, in its view, was the surest means for raising economic productivity and improving moral standards among Jewish colonists. While the memorandum dealt primarily with the Jews in agricultural colonies, similar criticisms of the Jewish family had circulated in the government ever since the late eighteenth century.[8] That the state viewed the Jewish family as the breeding ground for religious "fanaticism" and "unhealthy" practices (e.g., strict observation of Jewish rituals and an "oppressive" upbringing) inevitably had a profound impact on government strategies for Jewish reform. To be sure, the government did not adopt a systematic set of laws to regulate the Jewish family; as in the case of other subjects, government allowed the religious authorities of each confession to control marriage.[9] However, imbued with the spirit of the Petrine *Polizeistaat,* the state did seek to establish administrative uniformity over marriage and divorce (e.g., in such matters as officiation of ceremonies and record keeping) and even tried to eliminate practices that it deemed "pernicious."

This chapter focuses on state attempts to impose "order" on the Jewish family, first through a series of ad hoc laws and ultimately through the creation of two "Jewish" institutions—the Rabbinic Commission and the state rabbinate (both under the jurisdiction of the Ministry of Internal Affairs). These attempts proved abortive, partly because the state failed to understand the Jewish family and the underlying social and economic forces and partly because it was ambivalent about creating a separate "Jewish officialdom" within the state bureaucracy. Ironically, the government inadvertently created a contradictory "dual rabbinate" ("spiritual" and government rabbis) that served to increase, not decrease, tension and "disorder" in the Jewish family. More important, as the government deprived rabbinical law of the very mechanisms that allowed it to function (i.e., the power of enforcement), Jewish family law became increasingly dysfunctional, especially in spheres where Jews were less inclined to heed rabbinical injunctions.

The Russian Orthodox Paradigm

The notion of "bringing order to the family"—especially by establishing institutional control over marriage and divorce—was neither new nor peculiar to Russia. Ever since the sixteenth century, largely in response to the Reformation and the need to separate the faithful from the errant, both Protestant and Catholic countries had gradually constructed elaborate systems to record and regulate marriage. The subsequent growth of the secular state, especially in its "absolutist" forms, laid an ever greater emphasis on its right and duty to supervise the family and marriage. That impulse intensified in the eighteenth century, when states were seized by "demomania"—a frantic desire to increase the number of subjects (hence taxpayers and conscripts) at any cost. The zeal to regulate persisted into the nineteenth century, as in Napoleonic France, where the state required that all citizens (regardless of religious persuasion) submit to a formal "civil marriage" to ensure proper registration and order. In part, intrusion into the private sphere of the family was only a natural extension of its boundless faith in the power of law; the states, especially in Central and Eastern Europe, believed that only the government could create anew, extirpate "dark custom," and modernize. Regulating and ordering the family was but a natural extension of this boundless hubris about the creativity and beneficence of the "well-ordered police state." Finally, the attitudes of European elites toward the family also reflected Enlightenment thought, especially the secular notion that marriage was not a sacrament but a contract, a microcosm of the larger "social contract."[10]

Similar ambitions to regulate the family came to shape official policy in the Russian Empire, first in the case of the official confession, Russian Orthodoxy. Although the Orthodox Church—in modern times—held the exclusive authority to make and unmake marriages, until the mid-eighteenth century it lacked the records (metrical books), administration, or even coherent law to realize this prerogative. As a result, marital unions were made and dissolved with scant regard for superior authorities or even canon law; priests married young peasants and divorced old ones, with their bishops rarely interceding to assert control or enforce canons. All that began to change in the mid-eighteenth century, as Church authorities expanded and improved their administrative control over marriage and divorce. By the 1770s the Church required regular record keeping, subjected all divorces to episcopal and central review, and began to systematize the complex of canon and central laws. As a result, by the end of the century the Church had come increasingly to control marriage and divorce, not just de jure but de facto. Significantly, here too the secular state became increasingly assertive and intrusive. Although the Church's monopoly over marriage remained intact, the state displayed a waxing interest in this nuclear institution, much as its peers in Western Europe did. Hence, the government sometimes intervened directly (e.g., when it set the minimum marital age of thirteen for females and fifteen for males in 1774) but more often indirectly, by insisting that the Church tighten its control over the family.[11]

An obsession with administrative uniformity, however, was only one impulse to state policy: the French Revolution profoundly politicized the family question and especially the question of liberal divorce. The French divorce law of 1792 had been socially and psychologically revolutionary, transforming the marital sacrament into an easily dissoluble contract and unleashing a veritable avalanche of divorces until its abrogation in 1803. The breakdown of the family, of which the divorces seemed emblematic, reinforced conservative fears of a fundamental breakdown in the social order. As Europe emerged from the trauma of revolution and the Napoleonic wars, the need to reestablish the sanctity of the family became a principal leitmotif in social and political discourse. Determined to preserve stability and order, restorationist Europe castigated the French divorce law for promoting the "immorality, social and national degeneration" that had all helped to fuel political upheaval. Divorce, wrote an avid apologist of the Restoration, "weakened the authority of the father in the family, and also decreased fertility—thus stunting the vital forces and growth of the French population."[12] For the regimes of restorationist Europe, strict control over the family and divorce became synonymous with morality and stability.

Similar sentiments also pervaded contemporary Russia. In the last quarter of the eighteenth century the Church had gradually tightened its control over marriage; politics now impelled it to adopt a far more conservative policy, one that saw marriage as an "indelible sacrament" and that regarded divorce as utterly abhorrent.[13] The political subtext, reflecting conservative views in contemporary Europe, was transparent. Prominent state officials, such as the influential A. N. Golitsyn[14] and the ranking prelate in the Russian Orthodox Church, Metropolitan Filaret (Drozdov), defended marriage and family as "the best defense against moral degradation" and "the bedrock of political stability." The result was not only tighter control but a conscious campaign to prevent illegal marriages, to punish priests and parishioners who perpetrated them, and to thwart divorce and separation—regardless of the circumstances. New rules and their restrictive application made annulment and divorce all but impossible in pre-reform Russia. Thus, between 1836 and 1860 the church permitted an average of only fifty-eight divorces per year; the rate in most contemporary Protestant lands was markedly higher, as much as six hundred times higher in Saxony.[15] Even Catholic lands, despite the ban on divorce, offered ample opportunities for terminating a marriage through annulment or separation. Thus, Catholic France, which did not again legalize divorce until 1884, permitted separations (forbidden in Russia) at twenty-five times the divorce rate in Russia [16]

Authorities likewise tightened controls over marriage, not just its dissolution. Armed with fuller documentation, the Church could easily verify whether the betrothed satisfied the various canonical and legal requirements on kinship, age, and the like.[17] The mania to control extended to those on the fringe of the Church, such as the schismatic Old Believers, whose common-law marriages *(svodnye braki)* were a source of rising concern for ecclesiastical and state authorities. By the 1840s, bishops and bureaucrats, who previously had no control over marriage and divorce among the schismatics, became increasingly preoccupied with asserting their authority over this important minority.[18]

In short, in the first half of the nineteenth century, Russian authorities manifested a growing determination to establish stricter institutional control over marriage and divorce. In the case of the majority of the tsar's subjects, the large mass of Russian Orthodox, the state achieved an unprecedented level of control. Significantly, it did so by operating through the traditional ecclesiastical institution, the Russian Orthodox Church, which was all too ready to apply the stringent new rules and regulations to defend the sacrament and family.[19]

"Governing" the Jews, Regulating the Family

In principle, the ancien régime in Russia—down to its final overthrow in 1917—made marriage the responsibility of each religious confession. In contrast to most European countries, which gradually put marriage under the control of the secular state, the Russian government left this sphere under the control of each individual confession. State intrusion, however tempting, elicited adamant opposition from the Orthodox Church, jealously seeking to protect its remaining prerogatives and privileges. Then too, the state had to deal not only with the Russian Orthodox but with the myriad of other confessions and cultures; the task of producing a standard marital code for a multinational, multiconfessional empire was as mind-boggling in its complexity as it was provocative in its political implications. As a result, the state's new legal code—the *Svod zakonov Rossiskoi Imperii* (Digest of laws of the Russian empire), first promulgated in 1833—remained remarkably laconic and circumspect with respect to marital questions. It formally recognized the right of each religious confession (including Jews) "to marry according to its own laws and customs." At this point, at least, Russian legislation broached Jewish family law only in rare instances and, when it did, only as part of a more general family and marital policy—for example, in the minimum age established for all subjects in 1830. Although some ambitious bureaucrats did want to secularize marriage and divorce and although the state did include some matters under criminal law (e.g., bigamy), the government generally left marital questions for the religious authorities to sort out and resolve.

The problem in the case of Jews, however, was that they did not have an institutional or clerical hierarchy to standardize policy, supervise practice, and enforce either halakhic rulings or state laws. Indeed, the breakdown of Jewish communal institutions made it exceedingly difficult for the community, much less the state, to regulate marriage and divorce among Jews.

Traditional Communal and Judicial Institutions

Institutional control had not always been lacking; at the height of Jewish communal autonomy in Poland-Lithuania, an elaborate administrative system had governed the communities.[20] Bernard Weinryb has shown that communal responsibility mandated strict control over each individual; the effect was "to make him dependent upon the whole community or upon its representatives."[21] Offenders faced severe sentences, including "fines, imprisonment, corporal punishment, being placed in pillory and confiscation of property."[22] As a rule, Jewish religious authorities opposed "outside" interference in their private communal matters; in some instances, however, they did appeal to state courts or local magnates to enforce their decisions.[23]

Domestic matters of a "religious-legal-ceremonial character," including family issues, belonged to the competence of an official rabbi elected by the community.[24] He served as the head of the local courts *(av beit-din)*, adjudicated civil cases, prepared divorce documents, and supervised various ceremonies such as marriages and circumcisions. According to the decree of 1551, the "official" rabbi had the unequivocal authority "to hurl bans and impose punishments according to the customs and law of Moses in all matters related to religion."[25] He drew his salary directly from the *kahal,* usually from special collections rather than from the community treasury.[26] In addition to this official income, the rabbi collected fees for overseeing various ceremonies. The fee was a progressive levy: in Opatów, for example, to grant a divorce the local rabbi assessed eighteen zlotys from rich couples, twelve zlotys from middle-income people, and six zlotys from the poor.[27]

Although policies regulating family life (e.g., quotas on marriage) varied from town to town, Polish rabbis often convened to consider and resolve difficult halakhic questions. According to Edward Fram, rabbis sometimes assigned "problems that evaded easy solutions" to one of the attendees for a fair resolution. For example, Rabbi Joel Sirkes described a 1632 meeting in Lublin at which everyone agreed to accept his final decision on a problematic bill of divorce, which he was to investigate thoroughly at home.[28] In general, rabbis relied upon lay leaders, whose authority stemmed not only from tradition but from the Polish government, to enforce their rulings.[29] Nevertheless, the flouting of rabbinical decrees was common. Rabbi Solomon Luria even went so far as to claim that "the hand of the masses has grown more powerful than the voice of the rabbis even in halakhic matters."[30] In some cases, violation of the law was unintentional; for example, women who heard that their husbands had been killed sometimes remarried without rabbinic consent, a practice that was apparently widespread in early modern Poland.[31]

These problems became still more acute after the annexation of Jewish areas into the Russian Empire, where the intense zeal to regulate inspired attempts to rebuild and control the infrastructure from above. The pre-reform state, especially under Nicholas I, had a strong penchant to regiment and regulate. It sought incessantly to control all spheres of social and cultural life; it constructed a plethora of new institutions and rebuilt old ones.[32] The regime had similar ambitions with respect to the Jews; the fact that it encountered enormous difficulties (especially in controlling family practices) only impelled it to intensify its intervention. That intrusion, however, did less to impose state control than to erode Jewish communal institutions and to fan new religious divisions.

Disintegration of Jewish Communal Institutions

Even before the Polish partitions and the incorporation of a substantial Jewish population into the Russian Empire, the Jewish communal and religious structure had begun to lose its effectiveness. One factor was an apparent decline in the moral authority of the rabbinate. From the mid-eighteenth century the common people became increasingly disillusioned over a perceived moral decline in their communal leaders, especially the official rabbinate; that negative attitude undermined the rabbi's legitimacy and authority in the community. The main cause of this degeneration, in popular perception, was a corrupt election process whereby those "with ties to the overlords and princes" used bribes and other machinations to gain control of vacant positions. In some towns, people described the rabbinate as "a profit-making job, virtually synonymous with farming the customs tolls." In Dinur's apt phrase, "it was not that rabbis became wealthy, but rather that the wealthy and powerful became rabbis." Such perceptions fueled numerous complaints that rich magnates "influence the verdict in [civil suits] and give biased judgment, favoring their friends and taking revenge on their opponents."[33] Solomon Luria even complained that the rabbinic elites and their scribes profited unfairly from their flock by requiring a bill of divorce from couples who were not even married; they had exchanged gifts but later broke off the engagement.[34] As a result, people became increasingly resentful and distrustful of these rabbis in positions of power; some preachers even fulminated against "ignorant and wicked people who hate the rabbis more than gentiles hate the Jews."[35] Given the rabbi's pivotal judicial power, this image of "degeneration" undermined rabbinical authority and bore significant implications for daily life.

A second factor undermining the supra-*kehilla* system was the steady decentralization that followed the dissolution of the Council of the Four Lands (1764) and the partitions of Poland (1772–1795). The breakdown of central authority enabled each *kahal* to assume full responsibility over its own community; administrative coordination between communities, however, virtually ceased, a pattern that would persist throughout the nineteenth century. During the first decades of Russian rule (until 1844), the state promoted this process as it recognized and legitimized the authority of the *kahal* over the tsar's Jewish subjects. The *kahal* thus functioned as a tool of the state (e.g., bearing responsibility for collecting taxes and delivering military recruits). That role, understandably, made it the focus of deep resentment in Jewish society.[36]

The *beit-din* (rabbinical court, translated as *sud ravvinov* in Russian sources) operated alongside the *kahal,* just as it had done in Poland, albeit with more narrowly circumscribed jurisdiction.[37] In theory, only those cases that involved "Jewish religious laws, rites and liturgy" were to come before the rabbinic courts; all other civil and criminal matters belonged to the purview of state magistrates and municipal councils.[38] In practice, however, the *beit-din* exercised much broader power in resolving disputes within the Jewish community. As one hostile observer (a Jewish convert) complained, "This court examines all Jewish cases; and in spite of the fact that it is not invested with any state authority, it judges Jews in a dictatorial manner—decisively, without an appeals [court] and so severely that there is probably nothing like it."[39]

Although the *beit-din* operated quite independently of state control (even after the abolition of the *kahal*), it came under the scrutiny of central authorities, who increasingly questioned its "usefulness." Local government authorities, however, tended to defend the *beit-din* and its utility. Thus, in response to an inquiry from the Ministry of Internal Affairs in 1854, the governors of Kherson, Ekaterinoslav, and Bessarabia all described these Jewish courts in a positive manner and emphasized that the *beit-din* "freed the state from having to deal with petty suits."[40] For example, one official pointed out that the rabbinic court in Odessa resolved issues like ritual slaughter, kashrut, reconciliation of marital disputes, regulation of property relations, and officiating the rite of *halitsah*.[41] Not until the judicial reform of 1864, which established a new Westernized legal system, did the *beit-din* encounter a serious challenge to its authority and jurisdiction.

Another decentralizing force was the rise and spread of Hasidism in Ukraine and in some areas of Belorussia and Lithuania.[42] The emergence of new rituals, customs, and alternative leadership posed a threat not only to traditional Judaism but to the integrity of communal Jewish life. Although the teachings of the new movement "emphasized its adherence to tradition," Hasidism inevitably represented a direct challenge to the existing establishment and authority structure.[43] In a poignant case brought before Russian authorities in 1800, Rabbi Avigdor of Pinsk complained bitterly that "the sect" (Hasidism) had usurped his position as *av beit-din* before his term had come to an end and "chose one of their own persuasion" in his place.[44]

David Assaf suggests that the influential institution of the authoritative *tsaddik* became "an alternative to the old communal institutions," even the *beit-din,* which had lost prestige and trust. The fragmentation of Hasidic leadership, whereby "every *tsaddik* and group had a great deal of independence," significantly intensified the process of decentralization. To accommodate Hasidim who could not visit their leader because of long geographic distances or legal obstacles to travel, the position of a secondary *tsaddik* was established.[45]

As Jewish society fragmented into local communities, with differing patterns of social and economic development, it became increasingly difficult to impose uniform control over communal life, particularly in private practices like marriage and divorce.[46] In short, not only did Russian Jewry lack a centralized institutional authority (which the state might co-opt for its own purposes), but even the existing institutions at the infrastructure gradually lost the power that they had once wielded in the Polish-Lithuanian Commonwealth.

A related obstacle to state control over the Jewish family was the lack of either a juridical "clergy" *(dukhovenstvo)* or a modern "professional clergy" comparable to that of the Christian faiths. Unlike the other religious orders, Judaism did not have a professional service group with institutional, educational, and sometimes hereditary claims to monopolize the right to interpret Jewish law and to officiate at ceremonies.[47] In fact, traditional practice permitted "anyone versed in Jewish law," not just rabbis, to perform marriages and divorces.[48] Indeed, Jewish law required only two witnesses for a valid marriage, not a special ceremony performed by a professional cleric. Hence, in some remote villages and hamlets, men with no claims of expertise in halakhah performed these ceremonies.

Such anarchy had not, of course, been the case before the breakdown of Jewish communal structures, at least in the major Jewish centers. Hence, the communal records of Poznan from the late eighteenth century indicate that the official rabbi presided over all domestic matters and that strict rules regulated marital practice (not least because of the housing and economic constraints). That is why males from other towns required the approval of the community administration to marry Poznan citizens. Such rules enabled communal leaders to scrutinize not only the petitioner's "moral standing" but also his social-economic background. In the same vein, Jewish communal authorities in Poznan would approve a marital petition from a woman only if she had a dowry of at least four hundred Polish zloty. Later, the community established a quota for "marriages among people of limited means" (i.e., six marriages per year for women with dowries of less than 400 zloty); domestic servants and other employees (the so-called *meshartim*) could marry only with "the consent of at least two-thirds of the communal administration."[49] The purpose of such rules, of course, was to ensure that couples not become a financial or moral problem for the community.

In Imperial Russia, by contrast, Jews were free to marry at will, without any semblance of communal or state control, even without a verification of prior marital status (an open invitation to bigamy).[50] Such practices found expression in Mendele Moykher Sforim's satires of traditional Jewish life. In *Dos kleyne mentshele* (The little man), the main character, Itskhok Abram, deserts his pregnant wife, Golda, to seek his fortunes in the neighboring town of Berdichev. Not long after his arrival, the local marriage broker (who erroneously assumes that Abram is a widower) proposes a match with the daughter of the local communal official. The father of the potential bride, however, stipulates that there be no children from the first marriage. Only after Itskhok Abram shakes hands on the bargain does he "begin to think in earnest about ridding himself of Golda in so quiet a fashion that never a soul should know and never a cock should crow."[51] Such deceit was easy in tsarist Russia: no single institution was responsible for registering births, deaths, marriages, and divorces and hence detecting potential bigamists like Abram. The government's lack of reliable, basic information on Jews contrasted sharply with the elaborate records it routinely compiled about its other subjects.

That lack of centralized, authoritative institutions led, in the midnineteenth century, to the formation of the Rabbinic Commission in St. Petersburg.

Creating a Jewish Supreme Court:
The Rabbinic Commission

In 1840 the government formed the Jewish Committee *(Evreiskii komitet)* from ranking Russian bureaucrats in St. Petersburg to consider how to achieve "a complete transformation of Jewish life."[52] After examining information compiled by previous commissions, the committee concluded that "the religion of the Jews is the principal, and possibly the sole, force shaping the social and family position of this people." So pervasive was Judaism in every aspect of Jewish life, the committee noted, that Western European governments deemed it the most effective "instrument by which to transform the Jewish people."[53] Given this premise, some states established religious consistories in the capitals and provinces as an administrative tool for governing the Jewish population. According to the committee's chairman, Count P. D. Kiselev, this approach not only succeeded in consolidating authority into one central institution but also helped to eliminate "previous biases that alienated the Jews from the rest of civil society."[54] The fundamental question was how to attain similar results in Russia.

After five years of deliberations, in 1845 the committee concluded that "the Jews, given the tenets of their religion, cannot respect civil authority in religious matters." The committee therefore proposed to establish a "special central institution, which would have a moral influence on the Jews," and that could "give force to the decrees promulgated by the government to reform this people."[55] That rationale underlay the formation of a consistory-like administrative system based on French institutional models, headed by the Rabbinic Commission and augmented by a provincial rabbinate operating under the supervision of the Ministry of Interior.[56] The new institution was to "direct the Jewish masses to merge with civilian society *(grazhdanskoe obshchestvo)* and to engage in useful labor."[57]

Surprisingly, the Rabbinic Commission, which the Jewish Committee had deemed critical to reforming internal Jewish life, has attracted little interest from historians. Simon Dubnow and Iulii Gessen, for instance, all but ignored it.[58] Isaac Levitats devotes a single paragraph to the Rabbinic Commission and concludes that "most of [the sessions] were consultative, dealt with cases of divorce . . . and generally bore no practical results." Eli Lederhendler also refers briefly to the Rabbinic Commission and, citing Max Lilienthal and other Jewish reformers, observes that "the Rabbinic Commission never became a legitimizing force for political activity." That assessment stems in part from maskilic writings; the *maskilim* had hoped that the Rabbinic Commission "would not deal with petty specifics, such as marriage and divorce" but would "become the basis for a central permanent Jewish consistory."[59] The historiography on Russian Jewry, which has focused narrowly on political matters, has discounted an institution that failed to raise the issue of Jewish rights or to alleviate their legal disabilities.

But such was not the purpose or charge of the Rabbinic Commission. As Lederhendler correctly points out, its agenda was restricted to "matters such as divorce law, schools, the synagogue, and the status of the rabbinate."[60] Yet that charge *was* important, especially in the everyday lives of Jews. The commission archives, moreover, also afford a fresh new perspective on Jewish society, which was often shielded from the outside (especially from the government) by its cultural distance and alienation from tsarist state and society. In particular, the commission files shed valuable light on critical religious and family issues, suggest why Jews invoked secular authority against rabbis, and offer a new perspective on the interaction of Jews and state authority.

Establishment of the Commission

In February 1847 the Jewish Committee submitted a comprehensive proposal to establish a rabbinic commission in the town of Zhitomir.[61] The memorandum organ was distinguished more by its proscriptive style (declaring what the Rabbinic Commission should *not* do) than by a positive definition of its legitimate functions and responsibilities. Thus, while instructed to occupy itself exclusively with "religious" issues, the commission was forbidden to deal with the censorship of books, monetary collections, and payments for grave diggers. Rather more peculiar was the admonition, given the commission's explicit charge to deal with religious issues, not to broach "the rules of various Jewish sects in light of the fact that the state is not obliged to support the independence of the Jewish religion." The memorandum further instructed the Rabbinic Commission not to treat private divorce suits, "because these cases have hitherto been decided definitively by local rabbis, who have been selected by the agreement of both spouses."[62] It did, however, allow the commission to examine cases involving ambiguities in Jewish law or complaints by one party against a local rabbi for an unjust decision in a divorce suit. Interestingly, the Jewish Committee thus evinced a striking reluctance to question the authority of local rabbis in family matters. To be sure, that cautious approach hardly stemmed from a veneration of Jewish customs and law; it indicated, rather, a realistic awareness of the limits of state intrusion and a tacit recognition that autocracy, with its soft underbelly of weak provincial institutions, was in no position to replace rabbinic authority. Assuming responsibility over the immense number of Jewish divorce suits was simply unthinkable, for it inevitably entailed a monumental administrative burden on the Ministry of the Interior. It would have required the ministry not only to investigate all divorce cases before turning them over to the Rabbinic Commission but also to review the final resolutions to ensure due justice, a task for which it had neither the administrative capacity, time, nor incentive.[63]

The Jewish Committee unanimously agreed that "the Jews will not have confidence in people who are appointed [by the state]." It therefore concluded that, if the members of the Rabbinic Commission were to have legitimacy and authority, it was essential that they be elected by Jewish communities.[64] That in itself was a remarkable conclusion, especially for Nikolaevan Russia, traditionally celebrated as the "apogee of autocracy."[65] The recommendation reflected, significantly, an acute awareness of the peculiar status of Jews, the limitations of state power, and the need to induce local communities to cooperate voluntarily. Concretely, the Jewish Committee proposed that each provincial governor be responsible for organizing elections—to be sure, with the charge of finding three "loyal candidates." The franchise, moreover, was carefully restricted to three categories of Jews: rabbis, honorary citizens *(pochetnye grazhdane)*,[66] and merchants *(kuptsy)*.[67] In other words, this electoral system disenfranchised the mass of Jews—that is, the petty townspeople *(meshchanstvo)*. Interestingly, this provision also replicated the French model, which restricted consistory elections to the top stratum of taxpayers and the most respected citizens of the Jewish community.[68] The list of candidates from each province would be sent to the Ministry of Internal Affairs, which in turn selected the members of the Rabbinic Commission.

This proposal underwent substantial modification before the final text of the law was issued on 1 July 1848. In this final version the government sharpened its definition of the new organ's relationship to the central bureaucracy. Namely, it situated the Rabbinic Commission in the ever growing Ministry of Internal Affairs (MVD)—specifically, as the "fourth section" in the Department of Spiritual Affairs for Foreign Confessions (Departament Dukhovnykh Del Inostrannykh Ispovedanii).[69] That decision was entirely consistent with the treatment accorded other non-Orthodox confessions. Although one historian of this ministry has asserted that "Jewish society received a separate organization from the rest of the population," the establishment of the Rabbinic Commission in fact conformed to the general state policy of centralizing the "religious" administration of foreign confessions in a single department.[70] Such "consistories" already existed for Catholics and Lutherans, with similar institutions for non-Christians like Muslims and Karaites. Thus, as in other matters, Jewish policy here was an extension of a more general approach to dealing with other minorities. The 1848 law required that the chairman and four members take an oath of loyalty before a *beit-din* and a councillor of the governor's provincial board *(sovetnik gubernskogo pravleniia)* in the local synagogue. This curious amalgamation of religious and state representatives was presumably intended not only to ensure their compliance with state law but also to enhance their legitimacy with the Jewish community.

As foreseen in the original memorandum, the Rabbinic Commission bore responsibility "for matters of the Jewish faith." It had three principal functions. First, it was to serve as an advisory organ and overseer for local rabbis; in the words of the decree, the commission was "to examine and render opinions on questions pertaining to the laws and customs of the Jewish faith and the activities of rabbis." Second, the commission was to function as a higher "court of appeals" in Jewish divorce cases, with the duty "to investigate cases pertaining to the dissolution of marriages when a rabbi encounters ambiguities in the law or when a complaint is lodged against him due to an erroneous decision." Finally, it was obliged "to fulfill other missions that the MVD considers necessary to place on it." In resolving cases under its jurisdiction the commission was "to be guided by the laws of the Jewish faith."[71]

The decree also stipulated how the commission was to operate. It was to conduct sessions in Russian and to operate in a "manner of collegiality." A clerk was to record each of its meetings and its daily activities. The decree laid particular emphasis on the obligation to provide a formal, legal explanation of *how* the commission arrived at its conclusions, a procedure long since de rigueur for the rest of the Russian bureaucracy. Namely, the clerk was to compile an extract of the case, cite the relevant Jewish religious and state laws, and present the commission's final resolution. At the close of the deliberations, the commission was to file a copy of its journal with the Ministry of Internal Affairs for confirmation, a step intended to provide oversight and to ensure that justice had been served. If the ministry challenged the decision, it could remit the case to the same commission or to a newly elected one. This rule thus deprived the commission of final authority; it served to prevent the Rabbinic Commission from developing into a "quasi-government" like the Jewish consistories in France and thereby pose a challenge to the Russian bureaucracy.

Given its new status as a subordinate of the Ministry of Internal Affairs, the commission was to be situated in St. Petersburg, not Zhitomir as the Jewish Committee had originally intended. While this venue increased its proximity to central authority, it also made convening the commission more cumbersome and costly. As a result, the commission did not become a permanent institution, operating on a continual basis, but convened on special orders from the ministry. Altogether, the commission met only six times between 1848 and 1910, each time addressing a plethora of difficult cases that had accumulated since its last session.[72]

The First Meeting (1852)

The first session of the Rabbinic Commission in 1852 proceeded under a veil of secrecy so characteristic of the Nikolaevan state. "No information has been preserved about the opening or activities of the first commission, either in the files of the MVD or the former Jewish committee," complained an official in the Ministry of Internal Affairs who had the unenviable charge of drafting a general history of Rabbinic Commission in 1909.[73] A writer for the Jewish press echoed similar sentiments when he claimed that the activities of the Rabbinic Commission were so "shrouded in mystery" that it did not have any influence on Jewish life.[74] Why indeed did four years pass between the decree of 1848 and the first meeting? The surviving documents indicate that the delay was due to the "indifference and inattentiveness of the Jewish societies to the election of the candidates for the commission."[75] Given the tenor of state and Jewish relations in Nikolaevan Russia, the distrust and resistance were hardly surprising. When the communities finally acquiesced to demands for an "election," the government complained that the Jews "chose people who did not meet the expectations of the state."[76] Shortly thereafter, the Jews of Dinaburg sent a complaint to the MVD denouncing the candidates for incompetence—particularly "the one from Berlin, who does not know Jewish dogmas or believe in God or observe the customs, and who with malicious talk and slander directs the people to hate Adjutant-General Ignat'ev."[77] Another source claims that none of the members had adequate knowledge of Jewish law; Bernshtein, the only Russian-speaking member of the commission, had not studied Talmud in over twenty years. Matters did not stand much better with Dr. Cherol'zon, who had to ask scholars in Vil'na for citations from the Talmud ("which he had not studied in a long time").[78] As one state official conceded, "Not only were the members of the committee obscure to the Jews in Russia for their authority [in religious and social matters], but they were completely unprepared to work out the questions presented to them."[79]

The ministry's agenda was complex and comprehensive. It included queries about the censorship of Jewish books (e.g., midrashim, Haggadot, prayer books and commentaries), "secret rabbis" *(tsaddikim)* and Hasidic sects, the Jewish oath, registration in metrical books, and marriages of Jewish military servicemen.[80] Although the archival records provide little detail about the deliberations, the agenda shows that the state was mainly seeking to obtain more information about the internal life of Russian Jewry—from the kinds of books being printed to the marital practices of Jewish soldiers. Any attempt to reform Jewish society obviously required basic information about religious leadership, customs, and the patterns of birth, marriage, and divorce; precisely these concerns underlay the preoccupation with the role of the *tsaddikim* and the maintenance of metrical books *(metrichiskie knigi)*. The latter also reflected a broader ambition to improve the registration of social groups and thereby assist the state in keeping a fuller account of each individual, family, and community.

The marital rights and family privileges of Jewish soldiers was a recurring issue for state authorities. A decree of 1834 permitted Jewish servicemen to marry, so long as their wives and children did not don "Jewish clothing" but wore contemporary "German" dress. Jewish soldiers who married also had to enlist their sons as cantonists *(kantonisty)* in the army. In conformity with the general state principle that "superiors" must approve marriages of those in service (including Russian officers for ordinary soldiers), the state required that the commanding officer authorize all marriages of Jewish soldiers.[81] The very fact that the ministry raised the issue in 1852 suggests a recognition of the need for some revision in the existing law.[82]

Notwithstanding later assertions about the "secret operations" of the Rabbinic Commission, such was not the case. According to one disapproving report from the Ministry of Internal Affairs, the meetings "not only stirred up the general interest of the Jews (generally in the western provinces), but [also] attracted many of them to come to St. Petersburg, under the pretext of [bringing] private matters [to the Rabbinic Commission]." The sudden innundation of the capital by provincial Jews greatly distressed state officials and prompted them to caution the government that "this should not be duplicated under the new assembly."[83] Whether from a visceral aversion to any uncontrolled movement or from fear that the commission might provide a pretext for illegal Jewish travel and migration to St. Petersburg, the state had further cause not to convene the Rabbinic Commission on a frequent basis.

By all accounts, the first commission achieved far less than the state expected. Instead of returning to their respective communities and propagating the new decisions of the Rabbinic Commission, the members simply disappeared into oblivion. To quote one official in the ministry: "The activities of the first Rabbinic Commission were fruitless and unsatisfactory."[84] Disappointment with the results, concern about the unwelcome influx of Jews to the capital, the outbreak of the Crimean War—all these factors combined to dissuade the government from convening a new session the following year (in contravention of the decree of 1848). Another five years passed before the next commission was assembled.

The Second Meeting (1857)

When P. D. Kiselev wrote to the Minister of Internal Affairs in 1855 for permission to convene the second Rabbinic Commission in St. Petersburg, he reiterated that the "lofty" purpose of this institution was to function as a vehicle of social and family reform.[85] His immediate concern, based on prior experience, was the election of candidates—a process that had exasperated provincial governors because of the Jews' refusal to cooperate. Although the governors had no choice but to organize the elections, some expressed reservations. In particular, the governor-general of Kiev, Podolia, and Volhynia complained that his task was the most difficult because, in contrast to Lithuania, "the Jewish masses here have the lowest level of general education." He conceded that "those who devote the entire or vast part of their lives to studying Jewish spiritual books, religious laws and Talmudic interpretations are venerated among the Jews, defining all the conditions of family, social and civil life." By contrast, however, people with a general education were rare; those who did boast broad secular knowledge did not enjoy the respect of fellow Jews, who "scornfully" dismissed them as "Frenchmen or Germans."[86]

Of the eighteen candidates, the ministry chose five who were deemed influential in their respective communities and thereby best suited to assist the government in reform and to persuade their coreligionists.[87] The new assembly included Dr. Abraham Neumann, a Bavarian-born Jew who had served as a state rabbi and director of a Jewish school in Riga;[88] the merchant Yekutiel-Zisl Rapoport of Minsk, a prominent Jewish politician;[89] a merchant from Odessa by the name of Gurovich; a merchant from Kremenchug, Chlenov; and finally, Rabbi Iakov Barit of Vil'na (who replaced a first-guild merchant from Kovno, Shlima Feinberg, who could not attend because of illness).[90] When the governor of Kiev discovered that not one member was chosen from his provinces, he urged his superiors in St. Petersburg to reconsider: "In light of the immense Jewish population, who are educated in a more fanatical [manner] than the Jews in Lithuania," he urged that they have a representative on the commission, preferably one of the merchants he had recommended.[91] His appeal fell on deaf ears; St. Petersburg refused to change the composition of the commission.

Significantly, the ministry instructed the commission to consider how to establish state schools for Jewish women in the major towns, using Vitebsk and Mogilev as models. This agenda reflected a widespread definition of the "women's question" in the 1850s: how to educate Jewish women so that they would make better mothers who, in turn, could favorably influence the rearing of the next generation.[92] As in the case of the lower gentile classes, the task was not so much to design a suitable curriculum as to persuade the Jews to accept the idea of schooling and, especially, to bear its costs. Hence, the ministry considered it "useful" to charge the commission with the task of "propagating a healthier understanding of this subject among the Jews [and] transmitting it through educated rabbis."[93]

The ministry did not underestimate the difficulties that the rabbis would face. It reported that the Rabbinic Commission was well aware that "the Jewish masses still maintain eastern prejudices (which stem from the Talmud) against the education of women and their social situation in general."[94] As a preliminary step, the commission resolved to assemble all the halakhic references to Jewish women's education that appeared to support popular misconceptions and prejudices. Despite the wide range of opinion in rabbinic literature, Rabbi Eliezer in the Mishnah was identified as the main source of biased attitudes. "To teach your daughter the Law (Torah)," the rabbi stated, "would be to direct her path toward worldly vanities." This statement, the commission contended, could be interpreted as a prohibition against women's education in general. It added that since "the activities of women were limited to the sphere of the family, such scholarly study of the law would appear to be completely useless, and in many respects, harmful."[95]

To counter these assumptions, the commission proposed a strategy that sought not only to dispel biases against women's education but to demonstrate its practical utility. To overcome traditional prejudices, it proposed to disseminate excerpts of its own proceedings to rabbis, preachers, and teachers of Jewish law in state schools, with the expectation that these would then transmit its enlightened ideas to the rest of the Jewish community. The goal, declared the commission, was "to inspire, in the hearts of the young and in their parents, an aspiration to educate their children, regardless of sex." The commission also proposed to require that preachers and rabbis give advance notice of sermons that would deal with the education of the young, both male and female. To elicit the interest of the girls themselves, the commission directed that "daughters, between the ages of eleven and twelve years, attend Sabbath and religious holidays, and also be present at ceremonies to hear these edifying sermons."[96]

The commission's criticism of the lower classes, especially for failing to educate their daughters, elicited a sharp rejoinder from M. Morgulis. He castigated the commission for its naive analysis and judgment, which sought to find the roots of every Jewish "deficiency" in the Talmud and, moreover, demonstrated complete ignorance of the social and economic realities in the Pale of Settlement. He noted that, in fact, Jewish women often played a key role in the Jewish household economy, especially in family businesses and trade. Because of their extreme poverty, "they were obliged to take positions as servants and nurses in order to support their families." The furthest thing from their immediate concern, declared Morgulis, was general education. The commission's proposal that Jewish women attend religious services to hear preachers expatiate on the importance of education, he added, "met with smiles that completely characterized the [commission's] failure to grasp the conditions that enveloped their lives."[97]

While Morgulis may have been right about the commission's naïveté, the effort to propagandize new values may well have had some impact, if only to introduce the topic into public discourse. It also bears noting that, in stressing the "practical utility" of schooling, the commission did reveal an awareness of the basic economic impediments, not just religious barriers, that discouraged the lower strata from sending their daughters to school. The commission also showed some prescience, for secular female education would indeed have a significant impact on Jewish marriage and family life in the coming decades.

The Third Session (1861–1862): From Sanhedrin to Beit-din—
the Gelefonova Divorce Case

The third session of the Rabbinic Commission (lasting from 15 November 1861 to 13 March 1862) marked the beginning of a significant transformation. In essence, the commission began to evolve from a "French Sanhedrin" body that merely responded to government queries into a "supreme court of appeals" to review rabbinic decisions—above all, for cases involving Jewish divorce. As a result, subsequent sessions gave their main consideration to questions of marital dissolution and family issues. In strictly quantitative terms, the number of family-related suits before the commission increased from one in 1861 to thirty-three in 1910. Interestingly, that practical role as a supreme appellate court impelled religious leaders—from both the Orthodox and the "enlightened" camps—to request that the commission meet at least once every two years.[98]

Of all its cases, none attracted more public attention than the first divorce suit, which, after crawling through a bureaucratic maze, finally came before the Rabbinic Commission. It began on 5 April 1857, when Feiga Dina Gelefonova filed a complaint with the governor of Ekaterinoslav against the local rabbi, Shaperinskii, for unjustly dissolving her marriage. According to her testimony, in 1853 she had married a townsman from Vil'na, Leib Meerovich Passov, who disappeared shortly after the wedding. After receiving written confirmation of his death from relatives, the plaintiff moved to Ekaterinoslav and married Kel'man Itskhovich Gelefonov. In compliance with state law, she reported the marriage to the Novomoskovskii rabbi, who promised to record the deed in the metrical book.

Her woes began when the Ekaterinoslav state rabbi (Shaperinskii), "wishing to torment her" (in her own words), informed the local police that "she had left her first husband in Vil'na and had remarried illegally." To refute these accusations, Gelefonova traveled to Vil'na to obtain the death certificate of her first husband. By the time she returned with the requisite documents, she discovered that her second husband had already remarried—without a formal divorce but with the permission of the very same Rabbi Shaperinskii. With no other venue in which to appeal the rabbi's decision, Gelefonova turned to the Russian state and asked that a Jewish rabbinical court review the case. Alluding to her past conflicts, she also requested that the rabbinical court not include Shaperinskii or "any other rabbis from the province, who are dependent on him." She obviously feared the collusion of local rabbinic authorities and suspected, no doubt rightly, that their testimonies would carry more weight than that of an ordinary Jewish woman.

In response to Feiga's deposition, Rabbi Shaperinskii put up a spirited defense of his actions. He claimed to have received word in October 1856 that a certain Meer Kopeliovich had officiated at the marriage of Feiga Passova and K. Gelefonov in the village of Popova (Novomoskovskii district). He complained that the marriage not only violated state law (which permitted only state rabbis and their assistants to perform marriages) but also Jewish law (which forbade an *agunah* to remarry). Even if she could prove her husband's death, the rabbi pointed out, she still needed a certificate confirming that the ceremony of *halitsah* had been performed on her behalf, since she was childless at the time of her husband's disappearance. A few days after the rabbi reported the "crime of bigamy" to the local police, Khaikel Likhtenshtein (a Jewish soldier) arrived in town with a document in Hebrew confirming that the rite of *halitsah* had indeed been performed in the presence of a *beit-din*. To confirm the authenticity of the death certificate and the affidavit of the *beit-din,* Rabbi Shaperinskii advised the state to question the rabbi of Vil'na.[99]

Rabbi Amsterdam of Vil'na confirmed that he had issued the death certificate on the basis of the document from the *beit-din* (submitted by Gelefonova) and the testimony of "one person who was later sentenced to Siberia."After consulting with the rabbi of Ekaterinoslav, he now declared that the *beit-din* document had been forged and "that the handwriting belonged to the Jewess Feiga." He also asserted that the four signatures on the document were forgeries: "The signatures had striking mistakes (which violate Hebrew orthography), demonstrating that it was done by people not versed in Hebrew grammar." In addition, Rabbi Amsterdam pointed out that the residents of Vil'na could not recognize the names of two signatories on the certificate (rabbis Movshi Omerovich and Gershon Yakovlevich)—further proof, in his view, of a fabrication.

The court investigator interviewed local Vil'na residents and discovered that Gelefonova had a daughter, Dveira, by the first marriage, who lived with her husband in the province of Saratov. The plaintiff confirmed this fact and explained that the only reason she requested the ceremony of *halitsah* was to avoid any complications in the event that her daughter suddenly died; hence, she did not even require the *beit-din* certificate to remarry.[100]

Due to the complexities of the case, the governor of Ekaterinoslav first sent it to the city magistrate for review. The latter was sympathetic to the wife's cause and sent the case to the local criminal court for final disposition. On 11 November 1860, however, that court ruled in favor of the state rabbi (contrary to the magistrate's recommendations) and concluded that Meer Kopeliovich, who had performed the "illegal" marriage, should be judged separately since "he could not be found to give a deposition."[101] The court permitted Feiga Gelefonova to collect her belongings from her husband's house but ignored her protestations about the undelivered *get* that the Pavlograd rabbi had prepared (at the request of Rabbi Shaperinskii) but had not presented to Feiga, as required by Jewish law.

In defiance of both state and rabbinical courts, Feiga Gelefonova appealed to the Senate, which in turn sent her appeal to the Rabbinic Commission. The case was significant, not only because it was the first divorce suit to come before the commission but also because it had been initiated by a provincial Jewish woman. Rather than simply rendering an opinion on abstract questions about the status of Jewish women, the commission had to confront the real-life situation of a Jewish divorcée.

To "guide" the commission, the Senate sent a list of questions that transparently reflected the primary interests of the state in Jewish marital matters. First, "did the Jew Kapeliovich have the right to officiate at the marriage of Feiga and Kel'man Gelefonov?" That was a circuitous way of asking whether this marriage, even if contrary to state law, was valid under Jewish law. Second, the Senate wanted to know whether Rabbi Shaperinskii had the right to dissolve the marriage and permit the husband to remarry another woman. Finally, it asked for the commission's opinion on whether a rabbinical court should try Rabbi Shaperinskii.[102]

Interestingly, the commission ignored these queries and reformulated the basic issue: did Gelefonova have the right to remarry? Armed with the *Shulhan Arukh* (a codex of Jewish law) in one hand and the "evidence" collected by state investigators in the other, the commission endeavored to resolve this highly tangled case. Apart from the particulars of the case, it established the basic procedures that became the model for the adjudication of future suits.

Basing its decision on Jewish law, the Rabbinic Commission ruled that mere "rumors about a husband's death do not give the wife the right to remarry." This ruling was fully consonant with Jewish and secular state law. Hence, a *beit-din* must first have written confirmation of the death; only after it verified the authenticity of the signatures could it authorize remarriage.[103] In this case, because no documents had confirmed the death of Gelefonova's husband, the commission accepted the testimony of the Vil'na rabbi and rejected the plaintiff's claim to have written confirmation from her relatives.[104] The commission also invalidated the testimony of her so-called witness on the grounds that he had been sentenced to hard labor and exile in Siberia (for some unspecified crime). To be sure, the commission noted, "Jewish law does not require a thorough scrutiny of a witness's testimony about the death of a husband, when there is no reason to suspect deception." However, when there are grounds to suspect dishonesty, as in this case, a thorough investigation is mandatory.[105]

The fact that Gelefonova did not request the certificate of her first husband's death until *after* remarriage was a further cause of suspicion. The commission also invoked the principles of the *Shulhan Arukh*, which forbade relations with a woman (let alone betrothal) if there were any doubts about a previous marriage or divorce. All this gave the commission grounds to challenge her testimony: "If a woman says in the presence of her [first] husband, "you divorced me, she is believed," because it is presumed that she would not dare lie in front of him. . . . But if she married another in the absence of her [first] husband (even though she says in the presence of her husband, "you divorced me"), she is not believed. Since she was already married, she is treated like a prostitute."[106] In other words, the commission emphasized that Gelefonova had *already* remarried when she first began to seek evidence of her first husband's death. Under these circumstances, it concluded, she had a motive to lie about her divorce. It therefore concluded that Gelefonova's second marriage violated both Jewish and state law. The commission also indicted Kopeliovich for officiating at the ceremony (even though he was not a state or assistant rabbi) and recommended that he be punished according to state law. Thus, it exonerated Rabbi Shaperinskii of wrongdoing, save for the *herem* he had pronounced on the wife.

This ruling outraged some contemporary observers, such as M. Morgulis, who denounced the decision as "retrograde." Despite this disappointment, Morgulis himself recognized the potential capacity of the commission to reform Jewish life. "From the viewpoint of the government," he argued, "the Rabbinic Commission could have far more influence on the civil and family life of Russian Jewry, thereby indirectly on their enlightenment, if its activities are directed at bringing Jewish family laws into alignment with Russian laws." Moreover, he argued, issues such as marriage, grounds for divorce, conversion of one spouse to Christianity, *halitsah,* and the *agunah* had an important meaning in domestic and religious life; by using this institution to "bring order" to the Jewish family, the state could "free a whole class of people from personal caprice."[107] But the transformation of Jewish society at the grass-roots level required not only a central institution in St. Petersburg but an effective administrative structure at the grass roots: only then could the government hope to regulate the daily life of the Jewish family. That was to be the central mission of the "state rabbi."

An Official Clergy for Jews: The State Rabbinate

Apart from establishing the Rabbinic Commission, the Russian government established a new hierarchy of officially recognized "state rabbis." The purpose was to create a new institutional nexus between the state and Jewish society. Rather than rely on the traditional imperial method (i.e., co-opt local elites, recognizing their prerogative in exchange for executing government policies), in this case the Nikolaevan state chose to construct an entirely new institution of state rabbis. The ambition was not unique; Kiselev had been no less vigorous, for example, in rebuilding the administrative infrastructure for state peasants. But the task here was far more daunting; this official had spiritual, not merely bureaucratic, duties and, indeed, required acceptance and salaries from the local community.

Establishment of the State Rabbinate

What became known as the state rabbinate or crown rabbinate *(harabanut mitaam)* was not the product of systematic reform but of ad hoc laws seeking to define the functions and responsibilities of Jewish rabbis.[108] As early as 1804, the Statute on the Administration of Jews decreed that "by 1812, anyone who is not literate in one of the aforementioned languages [Russian, Polish, and German] cannot be appointed to a communal post or to the rabbinate."[109] A decree of 1826 made rabbis responsible for maintaining registers of births, deaths, marriages, and divorces—a duty analogous to that of clergy from the other confessions.[110] These Jewish metrical records differed in two significant respects: they were to be in Hebrew as well as Russian, and they were also to record divorces.[111] However, none of these laws provided a systematic description of the rabbi's obligations either to his community or to the state. Not until the statute of 1835 did the government define the rabbi's precise role and describe rabbis both as "the supervisors and interpreters of Jewish law" and as state servants.[112]

FIG. 7. State rabbi of Korostyshev (Kiev province) Aron Ratner and his wife, late nineteenth century. *Courtesy of Dr. Bernard Rattner.*

According to the new regulations, coreligionists elected the rabbi for a three-year term (subject to confirmation by the provincial governor) to perform a host of religious, administrative, and police duties. As a religious leader, he was to supervise religious services and ceremonies, explain Jewish law to his flock, and "teach them the true meaning of the law." Under no circumstances, however, was he to resort to coercion; he must, rather, rely on "persuasion and exhortation."[113] In that respect this statute reflected laws in Western Europe, where, in the spirit of absolutism, monarchs acted "to curb the judicial and coercive powers of the rabbinate."[114]

The rabbi's duties of principal interest to the state pertained to marriage and record keeping. Thus, effective in 1835, only the official rabbi and his assistant had the right to perform marriages, divorces, circumcisions, and burials. In 1853 the state dotted the i's and crossed the t's by adding the fateful clause that "marriages and divorces not performed by the rabbi and his assistant will be considered illegal."[115] To prevent "bigamy" among Jews, the government ordered the state rabbi to require that all newcomers bring written permission from their local rabbis before they dare to officiate at any marriages. As a further guarantee of legality, marriages between Jews from two different towns also required the approval of the local police chief—a rule that was mainly observed in the breach. Those seeking to remarry had to prove that they had no obligations from a previous marriage and to present a registration of divorce from their state rabbi.[116] Such rules, an extrapolation of procedures required of other confessions, nonetheless represented a significant intrusion and change for Jewish society.

The Russian state also attempted to establish order in the thorny question of Jewish divorce. Thus, divorces, "whether or not they involved repayment of the *ketubah*," required the supervision of an official rabbi or a "learned Jew" whom the couple had selected by mutual agreement.[117] In contrast to the prolix instructions on other marital issues, however, the passages on divorce were remarkably laconic and vague. That circumspection persisted until the last quarter of the nineteenth century; it reflected the state's general policy of recognizing the authority of each confession, as well as its reluctance to become mired in questions of family dissension. It was only in the wake of a reformed court system in 1864 that the state began to broach these matters and to seek radical changes in the Jewish rules on divorce.

The state rabbi had the important task of maintaining the metrical books of births, deaths, marriages, and divorces. The assignment was hardly accidental; it coincided with a systematic attempt by the Russian state to standardize and enforce registration to improve the reliability of record keeping.[118] Specifically, the clergy of each confession now received published, bound volumes with individual entry numbers. This new standardized format made it all but impossible to "doctor" the records by ripping out or inserting pages *ex post facto*. Such fabrication was further impeded by the requirement that each year the rabbi deposit a copy of the metrical books with the provincial board, which made it impossible for him to alter retroactively information about births, marriages, and divorces.

The final set of obligations concerned the rabbi's "police" duties. Although elected by the Jewish community, he was nonetheless an official of the state and obliged to perform its charges and assignments. As a public servant, the rabbi was explicitly responsible for ensuring that "the Jews observe their moral obligations and obey general state laws and appointed authorities."[119] In particular, many took offense at the requirement that the rabbi pledge his allegiance to the government.[120] In other words, the government sought to utilize rabbis as agents of the state as indeed it attempted to do with other religious authorities. That approach reflected not only the Nikolaevan distrust of society but its ambition to rule (and also to reform) from above. For that, it needed reliable "insider" information like that gathered by a rabbi. This secretive approach gave Jews good reason to fear that the state intended to transform their religious leaders into "tools of the tsarist police."[121]

Personnel

The first generation of state rabbis consisted of Jews who knew enough Russian to maintain the metrical books but were not viewed as actual rabbis by their communities. According to Yitshak Baer Levinson, "Some of the small towns have elected, quite cleverly, people who can just about write and sign their names in Russian and are ostensibly called 'rabbis,' while the real rabbi, an expert solely of the Torah, remains in his place; the two of them [being] grafted together like the lame and the blind." Some, like Rabbi Meir Berlin, actually learned how to sign their names in Russian to obtain the post.[122]

In the future, however, both the government and the *maskilim* envisioned a "rabbi" who more closely approximated the model of an educated German rabbi. To this end, the government agreed (if reluctantly) to establish state rabbinical seminaries, which were opened in Vil'na and Zhitomir in 1847. However impressive the seven-year program might have been on paper,[123] in fact the standard of religious education was low, partly because the faculty lacked proper training (many faculty members were autodidacts) and partly because of the poor preparation and quality of the students. Orthodox Jews suspected a government scheme to convert the students and therefore refused to send their children. The resulting shortage of students forced the schools to matriculate youths who were not qualified to study difficult religious subjects. I. Levanda, who began teaching at the Vil'na Rabbinical Seminary in 1849, pilloried most students as "riffraff—the most loathsome of Jewish youths in all the districts of this land."[124] Mendele Moykher Sforim ridiculed the schools as "shelters for the sons of the poor, for young men who live a life of suffering in the yeshivot, for grooms who sneak out and run away from the house of their fathers-in-law, for married men who become tired of their wives and leave them and their children."[125]

While recent scholarship has modified such one-sided portraits by emphasizing the number of distinguished and influential alumni of these schools, the seminaries did fail to achieve their principal task: to train young men to staff a modern rabbinate in Russia.[126] To be sure, the seminaries did produce a new generation of *maskilim* eager to transform Jewish life. But these graduates lacked the erudition, skill, and legitimacy needed to establish their authority and their moral right to resolve such matters as divorce, *halitsah*, the *agunah*, and other religious questions.

No doubt to their dismay, most graduates discovered that this seminary education did not necessarily guarantee them the position of state rabbi in their hometowns. The state itself was partly responsible, since it failed to require that the state rabbi have professional training at a rabbinical school, even after the creation of the state seminaries. Instead, according to a decree of 13 May 1857, candidacy for the post of state rabbi was open not only to graduates of "rabbinic seminaries [and] secondary Jewish state schools" but also to those who had completed a degree in "secular institutions of higher, secondary, and primary education."[127] That rule probably reflected a desire to encourage the selection of thoroughly secular, even assimilated Jews—that is, those alien to Jewish "fanaticism." Interestingly, this rule often was an extension of a broader policy, not a measure fabricated specifically and solely for Jews. In this instance, the tsarist government was applying a basic principle of the Great Reforms, namely, the desire to reduce (though not dismantle) institutional and even social-estate *(soslovie)* barriers and to use education to encourage greater mobility.[128] However, the decree allowed the choice of utterly unqualified candidates; even if armed with a higher education, they were unqualified to perform the spiritual duties of a rabbi.

Although this decree did not specify a preference for any particular educational qualification, some state officials *did* recognize the need for religious training and regarded pupils from the Vil'na and Zhitomir rabbinic schools as the best qualified. A particularly enthusiastic supporter of the schools was Vladimir I. Nazimov, the governor-general of Vil'na, who predicated the success of the Jewish reforms on the establishment of a modern religious leadership. In a lengthy memorandum to the Ministry of Internal Affairs in 1861, he emphasized that reform could be achieved only by "uprooting the influence of backward and fanatical rabbis" and by replacing them with enlightened minds versed in both secular *and* religious subjects.[129] Nazimov also noted that, apart from serving the interest of reform, the law obliged all rabbinical students, who received state stipends to support their training, to serve in any community that elected them.

Nevertheless, as Nazimov was painfully aware, most communities did not *want* such rabbinical candidates, for the simple reason that the two state rabbinical schools enjoyed scant respect among Jews. As long as that was true, of course, there was little prospect that Jewish communities would select students from the two seminaries as state rabbis. Compounding the bias against the seminary students was a sheer dearth of candidates. That had indeed been Nazimov's own experience during the recent elections (in 1859–1860) in the provinces of Vil'na, Grodno, and Kovno: "Taking into consideration that the election of 236 rabbis has been entrusted to me, [be advised] that there are only fifteen graduates from the rabbinical school for this post; practically no other aspiring candidates have emerged."[130] In response, Nazimov proposed to select candidates not only from the religious division of the rabbinical schools but also from their pedagogical section. Although the latter were intended for teaching careers, Nazimov believed that the need for qualified candidates in the state rabbinate was so acute that the students could more effectively be used to fill the vacant rabbinical posts. To facilitate their candidacy, he even proposed to exempt them from the regular examinations. The Ministry of Internal Affairs replied tersely that "the law of 1857 does not differentiate between pupils of the religious and pedagogical divisions" (hence, implicitly authorizing the appointment of candidates from the pedagogical division), but it did reject his proposal for a special exemption from examinations. In short, as the Nazimov case made clear, the schools had failed to supply the kind of professional rabbis, with sufficient training or even in sufficient numbers, to fill the large number of vacancies. Yet the government did not modify its original definition of the state rabbi's role; it still expected him to "oversee religious rituals and to arbitrate all disputes pertaining to Judaism." That mandate hardly squared with the fact that neither state law nor educational institutions required formal rabbinic training as a requirement for eligibility to serve as state rabbi.[131]

Above all, it bears emphasizing that Jewish communities did not want these professional rabbis. And the choice was theirs: the Jewish communities held the power of selection and the purse. No amount of persuasion or coercion could induce them to choose graduates from the rabbinical state schools, whom they castigated as "ignorant in Jewish law" or, still worse, as "renegades."[132] The well-known bibliographer, Isaac ben Yaakov, in a letter to a fellow *maskil,* Yitshak Baer Levinson, bitterly censured the students' appalling behavior: "Their mouths were filled with derision and mockery of the Jews and of all that was at the root of Judaism. And among them were those who dined at the gentile's table on the Ninth of Av, ate crabs and *trefot* [unkosher food], and those who laughed at their [own] Law."[133] The low repute of the rabbinical school graduates was dramatically evident in the Vil'na elections of 1859–1860: a dismayed Nazimov had to report that "all of the pupils of the rabbinic schools received many more votes against than for [them]." Of the fifteen pupils, not one was deemed acceptable by Jewish communities.

Government officials found the election results all the more puzzling, "since some local Jews are absolutely fair and treat them [the students] with respect." Apart from the students' low reputation, communities were probably fearful of selecting an outsider—someone more likely to represent the state than local interests. The very fact that state authorities promoted their candidacy only reinforced such fears and suspicions. Moreover, many Jews complained that the students were exceedingly presumptuous and arrogant, not least because the students condescendingly described their task of reforming coreligionists as a "mission." The following letter from Vil'na students to the government was as supercilious as it was typical: "Joyously, we take our posts because we have been presented with the opportunity (in consort with the will of the state) to further the education and to raise the morals of our coreligionists."[134] Statements like that, even if sincere, were bound to be exceedingly offensive to most Jews. Even the *maskil* I. L. Kantor complained that, once a student arrived at the seminary to learn to become a *maskil*, "a different spirit entered him. . . . In shame and disgust his soul looked upon the people from whom he descended."[135] Like the Russian intelligentsia, the very self-consciousness and self-importance of rabbinical students tended to build thick walls of distrust and enmity around the very people they were intended to serve.

The battle over rabbinical appointments eventually came to the attention of authorities in St. Petersburg. To counter strong pressure from the influential Nazimov, the Jews of Vil'na sent a petition to the Minister of Internal Affairs, Sergei S. Lanskoi, explaining why they had rejected the state rabbinical students. They claimed that, "in contrast to other Jewish communities," Vil'na had always had the most renowned rabbis of each century, duly famous for their "erudite scholarship, high merit, and other qualities."[136] Rather than accept inexperienced students, they proposed to select Yankel Barit, "an erudite scholar educated in Europe" and a prominent member of the Rabbinic Commission in St. Petersburg.[137] Nazimov in turn ridiculed their claims to have "famous rabbis with profound erudition," noting that in the last election they chose "a destitute trader, a person with no education or significance." He emphasized that Barit had not passed the required examinations and therefore was not qualified to hold the position of state rabbi. Given Nazimov's own proposal to exempt the pedagogical students from the examinations, the complaint about Barit was rather disingenuous.

Not only Nazimov but also the seminary graduates were dismayed by the outcome of the elections. With the support of the faculty at the Zhitomir Rabbinical School, the students urged the state to annul the elections and simply appoint them as state rabbis.[138] "Given the aversion of the majority of Jews toward European education and toward those with a European education," they argued that "it is impossible to wait for the new rabbi to be elected voluntarily by the community." They also placed some blame on the decree of 13 May 1857, which "inadvertently opened a wide field of abuses" by failing to differentiate between the graduates of rabbinical seminaries and those of other institutions: "Why should the state expend [resources] in vain to support rabbinical seminaries, when graduates from the elementary and secondary schools suffice as rabbis?" The students felt that they had been unfairly treated, that their seven years' study in a seminary was ignored, and that preference was given to those who had spent a mere two to three years in a secular secondary school.

The student proposal elicited little enthusiasm in the Jewish Committee, the interministerial body charged with engineering reform among the Jews. Reflecting past experience with Jews and the new spirit of the Great Reforms, the committee warned that depriving Jewish communities of the right to free elections would "fail like other coercive measures applied to the Jews." While reaffirming the need for elections, the committee nevertheless did enjoin local government officials to exert a proper "influence" and do what they could to arrange for the selection of rabbinical school graduates.[139]

Rabbinical students, moreover, had to compete not only with graduates from secular schools, but also with Western European rabbis trained in the elite universities of Germany and Prussia. Although only a small handful of European rabbis had ever come to Russia, rabbinical school students became deeply concerned when two former classmates suffered a crushing defeat in the elections held in Odessa in the fall of 1859. As the governor of Odessa reported to St. Petersburg, the two candidates from the Zhitomir Rabbinical School (Barats and Bliumenfel'd) had excellent academic records but failed to receive a single vote from the Odessa Jewish community. Evidently, both had been entered as candidates only because of state pressure; the fact that both failed to receive a single vote could hardly have been a more humiliating rejection. The governor, however, placed part of the blame on the students themselves: "Perhaps this was to be expected, given the youthfulness of Barats and Bliumenfel'd, who failed to present themselves as models of how one should act in the office of rabbi."[140]

With both state candidates repudiated, the Jews had to call new elections, and this time chose S. L. Schwabacher, a rabbi from Lemberg

(L'vov) with a doctorate in theology.[141] His election was a veritable land-slide: Schwabacher received 96 of 99 votes. That stunning victory im-pelled the governor of Odessa to conclude that graduates of Russian rab-binical schools might have some chance "in one of the small and undeveloped communities of the empire" but certainly not in Odessa, where Jews were educated on a "far higher level, with many people, even entire families, possessing a thorough European education."[142] In other words, when a Jewish community *did* want a learned state rabbi, they preferred one with a European university degree, not the suspect and ill-educated products of the rabbinical schools in Vil'na and Zhitomir.

During the last quarter of the nineteenth century the secularization of the state rabbinate proceeded even further. The rabbinic schools pro-duced relatively few candidates, but even this tiny contingent vanished when the state decided in 1873 to close both schools. A further factor was antisemitic educational policy—above all, the quotas on Jewish ma-triculation in secondary schools and universities in the 1880s. That re-striction led to a further reduction in the number of "qualified" candi-dates for the post of state rabbi. Moreover, some Jews who had a higher education but were denied access to state service chose the state rabbi-nate as a livelihood. Enticed by the alluring incentives of this semiofficial post (e.g., the status of a first-guild merchant, medals, and exemption from the poll tax), the new generation of state rabbis often made no at-tempt to camouflage their mundane motive for seeking the position.[143] The Nikolaevan state rabbi, Yehuda Leib Vilenskii, delivered a devastat-ing but informed assessment of the new generation as "ignoramuses who could not succeed in another profession—jurists, pharmacists, doctors, and engineers who turned to the rabbinate as a means of living or as a part-time supplement to their occupations."[144] Hence, though still charged with performing religious functions, the state rabbinate had be-come essentially an army of secular bureaucrats.

This bureaucratization of the state rabbinate proceeded in an ad hoc, incremental fashion. Whenever local authorities rejected the application of "dubious" candidates (e.g., pharmacists, veterinarians, and dentists), the latter appealed to the Senate and won reversals that provided a prece-dent for the whole empire. Thus, when the Provincial Board of Kiev re-jected an application by the pharmaceutical assistant Rudol'f Rakobshchik to compete in the elections for the rabbinic post in Lysia (Zvenigorod dis-trict), he appealed the decision on the basis of an earlier Senate ruling. Cit-ing the Oksman case of 1892, Rakobshchik claimed that the Senate had allowed a pharmaceutical student (who had completed only four classes in a gymnasium) to occupy the post of state rabbi. If a mere student was eligible, argued Rakobshchik, then he, as a pharmaceutical assistant, also had the right to this post.[145] The Senate agreed, ruling that the Kiev authorities had no legal grounds to reject Rakobshchik's petition and ordered that his application be reconsidered.[146]

By the mid-1880s the Russian state had abandoned its clumsy attempts to promote candidates with both religious and secular education. By this time, the ethos and policies of the Great Reforms had long since dissipated; in their place was a reassertion of *étatisme* and state authority, with an unabashed emphasis on the need for powerful, willful bureaucrats.[147] In the case of the Jews, this meant a state rabbinate composed of dutiful *chinovniki* (officials), not necessarily of those with more religious education. The government further abetted this process in 1886, when it forbade the selection of foreign (i.e., German) rabbis, thereby eliminating those candidates who promised to possess some religious education. Although the decision reflected other tendencies (such as fear of Western influence and growing tensions with Germany),[148] it also indicated that the earlier commitment to creating a modern rabbinate had largely expired.[149]

By most accounts, the earlier generation of rabbinical school graduates were Talmudic savants compared with the new state rabbis, many of whom could not even read Hebrew, let alone navigate the intricacies of marital and divorce laws.[150] Their deficiencies were grist for the mill of the traditional religious establishment, which exploited the ill repute of state rabbis to bolster the moral authority of the spiritual rabbis. The ideal candidate for the state rabbinate, according to some spiritual rabbis, was someone who "ate pork in public." They not only sought a government rabbi whose notorious behavior precluded any respect from the community, but more important, one who "would not be bold enough to occupy himself with matters of *gerushin* [divorce], *Gittin* [a Talmudic tractate on divorce], and in other religious matters."[151] The journalist Shmaryahu Levin recalled how the Vil'na community resorted to every conceivable device to prevent the state rabbi from meddling in its social or religious life. When the governor's aide complained that, in the 1880 rabbinate elections in Vil'na, "the Jews had elected a rabbi who stuttered," communal leaders retorted that "this way the rabbi would not interfere in general public matters."[152] Rumors that state rabbis sometimes transferred Jewish divorce suits to secular courts redoubled the determination to restrict them to the bureaucratic tasks of record keeping.

The criticism of state rabbis turned into merciless vilification, maligning not only their educational but even their moral qualifications for the lofty title of rabbi. A typical article in the Jewish press dismissed as a "fallacy" the notion that "a veterinarian, pharmaceutical chemist, or student in the sixth class of a Realgymnasium [technical secondary school], who holds the modest position of a clerk, has the right to bear the official title rabbi—i.e., teacher and spiritual leader of the society." A true rabbi, declared the author, was "a specialist in Jewish law, trained in the strict spirit of religiosity and morality—preparations that begin in childhood."[153] By the mid-1880s, correspondents of *Voskhod* (a liberal Jewish weekly) sent candid reports that state rabbis enjoyed absolutely no public support or sympathy; if there were one or two exceptions, "they were the fortunate ones."[154] The community's view of state rabbis as state bureaucrats found reflection in the aphorism that "the way to insult a state rabbi is to call him 'the administrator of the four books'—the metrical books of births, deaths, marriages and divorce."[155]

By the 1870s, even the *maskilim,* who had previously supported the ideal of a learned, professional state rabbinate, ceased to defend the institution or its personnel. In part, this shift in opinion stemmed from an internal transformation within the Jewish intelligentsia. Confronted with profound upheavals and social crises in Jewish society (the product not only of state repression but of other forces, such as the economic depression of the 1870s, recurring famine and hardship, and a burgeoning emigration), the *maskilim,* who sought to ameliorate the conditions of their coreligionists, began to "mature." While still faithful to the basic principles of enlightenment, they now became more empathetic and protective of traditional Jewry, tempering their youthful arrogance and condescension.[156] Still more important, they grew more critical and wary of the Russian state; the shift from Great Reforms to counterreforms brought particular hardship on Jews, with a new wave of infamous discriminatory laws and policies.

But perhaps the principal reason for the *maskilim*'s disillusionment with the state rabbinate was the institution itself. It was hard to defend an office that, according to contemporary newspaper accounts, had been "purchased," a vice so reminiscent of practices under the Polish *szlachta.* Daniel Khvol'son, a convert, sarcastically denied any risk of selecting candidates familiar with the literature of Israel, "for the incompetent men working in the apothecaries, who so wish, can buy the rabbinate by advertising that they will sell their medicine more cheaply if they are appointed rabbis."[157] Others complained that state rabbis were often guilty of moonlighting; their second jobs (such as insurance and banking agents) caused them to neglect their main responsibilities. "They do not even consider public opinion of themselves," charged one critic, "for state rabbis are confident that, if dismissed from one place, they will be elected somewhere else."[158] In all fairness, however, it must be said that most state rabbis had little choice; given the meager salaries of state rabbis, they needed a second income to make ends meet. The economic duress no doubt exacerbated the situation: With the renewal of bureaucratization, the enhanced power of bureaucrats, and the vital importance of paperwork gave the state rabbi more leverage, a change that only redoubled disgruntlement and enmity in the Jewish community.

In effect, the state rabbi assumed a greater presence precisely because of his bureaucratic duties, since official paperwork—for example, a certificate on birth or divorce—loomed ever larger in the lives of ordinary people. At the same time, however, the state rabbinate forfeited whatever spiritual claims it might have had in the Great Reform generation; if anything, respect for the rabbinate declined so sharply that it provoked disparagement even among the *maskilim*.

Conflict in the Dual Rabbinate

Despite low public esteem and diminished religious training, the state rabbinate did not renounce its claim to the prerogatives of spiritual rabbis. To be sure, this corps of former doctors, dentists, and pharmacists did not dare to storm the lofty chambers of Talmudic polemics and discourse; by all accounts, they knew little and cared still less about such matters. But in matters of "secular" import—above all, family law and practice—they *did* claim competence in a sphere traditionally assigned to the spiritual rabbi.

The state rabbis had strong incentives to assert their power and to challenge the role of the spiritual rabbis in the familial sphere. In some cases the goal was to combat hidebound tradition; imbued with the maskilic ethos, they aspired to vanquish injustice, superstition, and all that was antithetical to their enlightened European values. Material incentive also played a role; whether from a desire to monopolize the rites of passage (and the attendant fees) or to extort illicit "gifts" for a favorable decision, the state rabbi had strong incentives to seize control over marriage and divorce. It was also a matter of status and power: as long as the spiritual rabbi continued to officiate at ceremonies, perform circumcisions, and resolve family disputes, ordinary Jews considered him, not the state rabbi, to be the legitimate authority. If the state rabbinate was to establish its authority, it was essential to control the rites and rituals of the family sphere.

It was not only naked self-interest that drove state rabbis to challenge spiritual rabbis. They were legally bound to denounce violators of law, including those who flouted the statutes on marriage and divorce. The duty was no mere formality; local officials expected state rabbis to exercise a monopoly over religious and marital matters and to enforce state law in these matters. In 1892, for example, the governor of Odessa gave the city rabbi a blistering reprimand for permitting spiritual rabbis, "who are distinguished by their extreme fanaticism . . . to perform marriages, dispense divorces, and circumcise Jewish children." What particularly enraged the governor was the fact that entries in the metrical books, based on the notes of spiritual rabbis, were replete with errors, even in the spelling of Jewish names and surnames. In those days, such errata, whether they involved Jews or Gentiles, were the source of great confusion, endless petitioning, and boundless irritation on the part of state officialdom. The dour governor warned the state rabbi that he must report any violations of the law by spiritual rabbis and that, if "he did not take serious measures," the governor would press charges against him for insubordination and dereliction of duty.[159]

The intrusion into the complex sphere of family law, with state sponsorship and imprimatur, posed a direct threat to the existing communal order. Fundamental questions—"Who is a rabbi?" and "Which rabbi, state or spiritual, has authority over religious ceremonies?"—aroused deep consternation and confusion. The disarray was most apparent in matters involving marriage and divorce. As already noted, the decree of 1853 declared that "no other person, except confirmed state rabbis and their assistants, can perform religious rites (e.g., circumcisions, marriages, and divorces)." Hence, under state law, rites conducted by anyone other than state rabbis were illegal and invalid.[160] Although Jews might informally give precedence to the spiritual rabbi, in the event of a dispute one party could appeal to the only legally recognized authority—the state rabbi and his superiors in the Russian state administration.

In some regions the state and spiritual rabbis collaborated to preserve peace and harmony on day-to-day matters. This was generally the case in the Lithuanian provinces; disputes were evidently rare there, to judge from the archival records.[161] Such was not the case in Ukraine, where disputes were more common, but even there state rabbis—perhaps in the teeth of communal pressure—tended to shield the spiritual rabbi. Thus, when the police chief of Ovruch (Zhitomir district) filed charges against Iosel I. Shneierson for officiating at the wedding ceremony of his daughter, the state rabbi (Isaak L. Tsveifel) promptly came to the defense of the fifty-two-year-old Hasidic leader, testifying that he, not the spiritual rabbi, had performed the marriage: "I was not only present at the marriage, but also performed the wedding ceremony." He assured the court investigator that he, not the Hasidic rabbi, had read the prayers and handed the ring to the groom to put on the bride's finger in accordance with Jewish law. Another witness testified that Tsveifel had indeed performed the entire ceremony, as relatives stood nearby, and that after the wedding Shneierson had merely brought out the wine, toasted the newlyweds, and pronounced a blessing on them.[162] The state rabbi asserted that so many guests came to the wedding that it was almost impossible for most of them to see the ceremony (actually performed in a courtyard) and that vision was obscured for those standing by the gateway, the vantage point of the police chief. Tsveifel stressed too that he had recorded the marriage in the metrical book, as required by state law. On the basis of such evidence, the Ovruch district civil court terminated the case. The court record makes it impossible to determine the facts of the case (the testimony against the police chief may have been orchestrated); in any case, whatever the motive, the state rabbi spurned an opportunity to expose the spiritual rabbi to prosecution.

Some state rabbis formally, in oral or written form, authorized spiritual rabbis to perform marriages, perhaps to mollify relations with the community or perhaps to avert the intercession of government officials. Such actions, which were patently illegal under the decree of 1853 periodically elicited demands from the government that the law be strictly observed. In 1874, for example, the Kievan provincial board received an anonymous denunciation against the state rabbi in Smela (Cherkassy district) for permitting a merchant's son to conduct numerous marriages in the village. The state rabbi strenuously denied the accusation, claiming to have performed all the marriage ceremonies save two weddings where illness had left him incapacitated. In the latter cases, he recorded the marriages beforehand and gave written permission to Srul' Lieberskii, a "teacher in religious matters," to officiate at the ceremonies.[163] The latter confirmed this testimony, volunteering that the services had taken place in his courtyard, not the synagogue, since both couples were marrying for the second time.[164]

Unable to determine the rabbi's guilt, the provincial board solicited the opinion of the state rabbi of Cherkassy (Korenblit). The latter did not reply in the spirit of an obsequious servant; he wrote that although the law required the state rabbi to perform such rites, this rule was contrary to Jewish law and tradition. In his words, "In the absence of a Jewish 'clergy' in the strict sense of the word, anyone versed in Jewish law is permitted to perform religious ceremonies." Indeed, Jewish custom regarded the invitation to perform this religious ceremony "an honor," not the sanctifying act of an official cleric. While admitting that problems of registration were grounds for concern, the state rabbi denied that "self-officiated marriages, composed of prayers and blessings" constitute a crime, especially if the state rabbi had been informed beforehand.[165]

That argumentation carried no weight with government authorities in Kiev. The governor refused to pardon the hapless rabbi and remitted the case to the procurator of the Kiev criminal and civil court for formal prosecution. This time, the outcome was not so fortunate as in the Shneierson case: cooperation brought calamity for both the state and spiritual rabbis of Smela, who were sentenced to prison. The harsh verdict was doubtless intended to as a warning that the state expected total compliance with state law.

Although the state and spiritual rabbis sometimes collaborated, elsewhere their relations were often far more acrimonious. In such confrontations, the state rabbis could invoke government power; they had little difficulty crushing rivals in state courts, where all the cards were stacked in their favor.

Such battles were both ubiquitous and vicious. A typical case in 1876 involved a spiritual rabbi (Berlo Khamer) who had purportedly officiated at the marriage of Meer Kosmacher and Khana Leia Shekhet.[166] The issue was neither tradition nor law but rubles: the state rabbi had demanded such an excessive fee that the family decided to summon the spiritual rabbi. According to the groom's testimony, the state rabbi lived in a nearby village but had demanded ten rubles (and travel costs) to perform the ceremony. A poor man, Kosmacher had beseeched the state rabbi to accept one ruble but in the face of the latter's refusal asked Rabbi Khamer to conduct services.

The sixty-year-old spiritual rabbi admitted performing the ceremony but claimed that the state rabbi had personally commissioned him to perform weddings and circumcisions in his absence. When the case came to trial in May 1877, the state rabbi denied that claim: "I never gave you written or oral permission to perform rites of the Jewish faith and I do not know you at all and have never seen you before." Although the spiritual rabbi backtracked on his original claim ("I have never seen you before, rabbi, and you never commissioned me to perform the marriage"), he still insisted that the state rabbi had given permission "to officiate the marriage ceremony in the groom's home village." Confronted with the contradictions in his testimony, Rabbi Khamer sought refuge in the claim that "I do not understand the Russian language very well."[167] The court found the accused guilty of violating the state rabbi's jurisdiction and, in accordance with the criminal code, sentenced him to forty days in prison.[168]

To sum up, the postreform state rabbinate bore less resemblance to agents of Jewish transformation than the newly assertive state bureaucracy. Like the state and autocracy, which reaffirmed its right and duty to dominate, the state rabbinate vigorously asserted its authority over the unofficial spiritual rabbis. The motives were variable and multifarious— zeal, greed, status anxiety, and state pressure. The result was an ambiguous and highly conflictive dyadic structure of religious authority that invited manipulation from below.

Dual Power and the Jewish Family

The Power of Paper: The Metrical Books

The power of the state rabbi rested, first and foremost, on his monopoly over the metrical books—the official documentation for recording the crucial facts of birth, marriage, divorce, and death. The state rabbi's authority in these matters was firmly grounded in state law: the 1857 statute specifically warned that "the head of the family for whom a rite has been performed will be subject [to a fine] of twenty rubles; marriages and divorces that are not performed by state rabbis or their assistants will be considered illegal."[169] Hence, only those rites that had been duly entered into the metrical books were due legal recognition. If, however, a state rabbi failed to make such an entry, for whatever reason, the consequences were serious. These omissions sometimes involved divorces but usually concerned marriages, births, and deaths.

In some cases, the omissions stemmed from a feud between the state rabbi and the spiritual rabbi, as was apparent in a case from the town of Zaslav. When Borukh Rebel'skii and Reizel Kharif turned to the state rabbi to officiate at their wedding, he summarily refused but gave no explanation for his conduct. He later testified before the provincial board of Volhynia that a local spiritual rabbi (the bride's father) had married the couple in his absence, but he noted that the marriage had not been recorded in the metrical books. Now that the couple sought "to legalize" their marriage, he decided to take his vengeance. He refused to register the marriage, thereby denying the couple the benefits of lawful matrimony. That would make the children illegitimate and deprive them of their parents' social status, the right of inheritance, and all associated privileges.[170] Not surprisingly, the state rabbi prevailed, with the court upholding his decision not to record an "illegal" marriage.

The rabbis in the town of Vasil'kov (Kiev province) became ensnarled in a typical court case. The suit was commenced when a Jewish couple petitioned the governor to take action against their local state rabbi (Dobrov), who refused to enter their marriage in the metrical books. They claimed that Rabbi Dobrov had attempted to extort one hundred rubles for performing the ceremony—far in excess of the fee stipulated in his written agreement with the community (two rubles). But Dobrov remained adamant; the couple finally agreed to make a down payment of twenty-five rubles and promised to pay the balance after the ceremony. The state rabbi then declared that "in all his twenty years of service, he personally had never performed a marriage." He gave them a note in Hebrew, authorizing the cantor at the synagogue to officiate at the wedding.

When they returned to the rabbi for the metrical certificate, he refused to issue the document until they paid the other seventy-five rubles. The couple first brought their complaint to the governor's provincial board, but the latter upheld the state rabbi and declared their marriage void. The desperate couple then appealed directly to the governor himself. "After this, our desperate position became clear," they wrote, "all the more since we had a baby from our marriage . . . and the child who is without guilt will be considered illegitimate."[171] They implored the governor to intercede on their behalf.

State rabbi Dobrov offered a radically different version of events. He claimed that, in the winter of 1891, the couple had repeatedly asked him to officiate at their marriage. However, because they were newcomers to the town, he demanded that they show him their passports and written permission from their hometown rabbi (as required by the law).[172] But the couple's papers were not in order: the woman did not possess a passport (needed to verify her identity), and neither had a letter from their state rabbi (certifying that there were no legal impediments to the union). As a result, the state rabbi claimed, he had been forced to deny their request. On the evening of 30 December 1891, the prospective groom announced that his parents and friends would arrive that night on the 11:00 P.M. train from Kiev and bring all the necessary documents. He requested that the rabbi immediately make arrangements to hold the ceremony the next morning, to allow the family time to make wedding preparations. Reassured by this statement, the state rabbi handed him a note for the cantor that read: "Prepare the necessary arrangements for the marriage of groom Lipa Leib Itskov Isserlis and bride Mariam, daughter of Raikhmil Tseitlin, on 31 December."[173] The rabbi repeatedly warned Isserlis, however, that the note would be void if he did not produce the requisite documents. Rabbi Dobrov waited for the documents until midnight, and when the groom failed to deliver them, he assumed that the wedding had been postponed.

Once again the government upheld the state rabbi. The governor denied the couple's appeal and even initiated criminal charges against the cantor, Mordko Krupnik, for violating the state rabbi's jurisdiction. That decision left the marriage of Isserlis and Tseitlin void and their child illegitimate. Although the evidence is murky, especially the claims of extortion by the rabbi, the government found the rabbi's testimony compelling and, most important, consistent with his formal duties and obligations, especially with regard to proper documentation. While many Jews viewed the request for documentation from outsiders as cumbersome bureaucratic red tape (and an opportunity to extort bribes), the law, which applied to *all* confessions, served to prevent invalid marriages and especially bigamy (since the passport included information about current

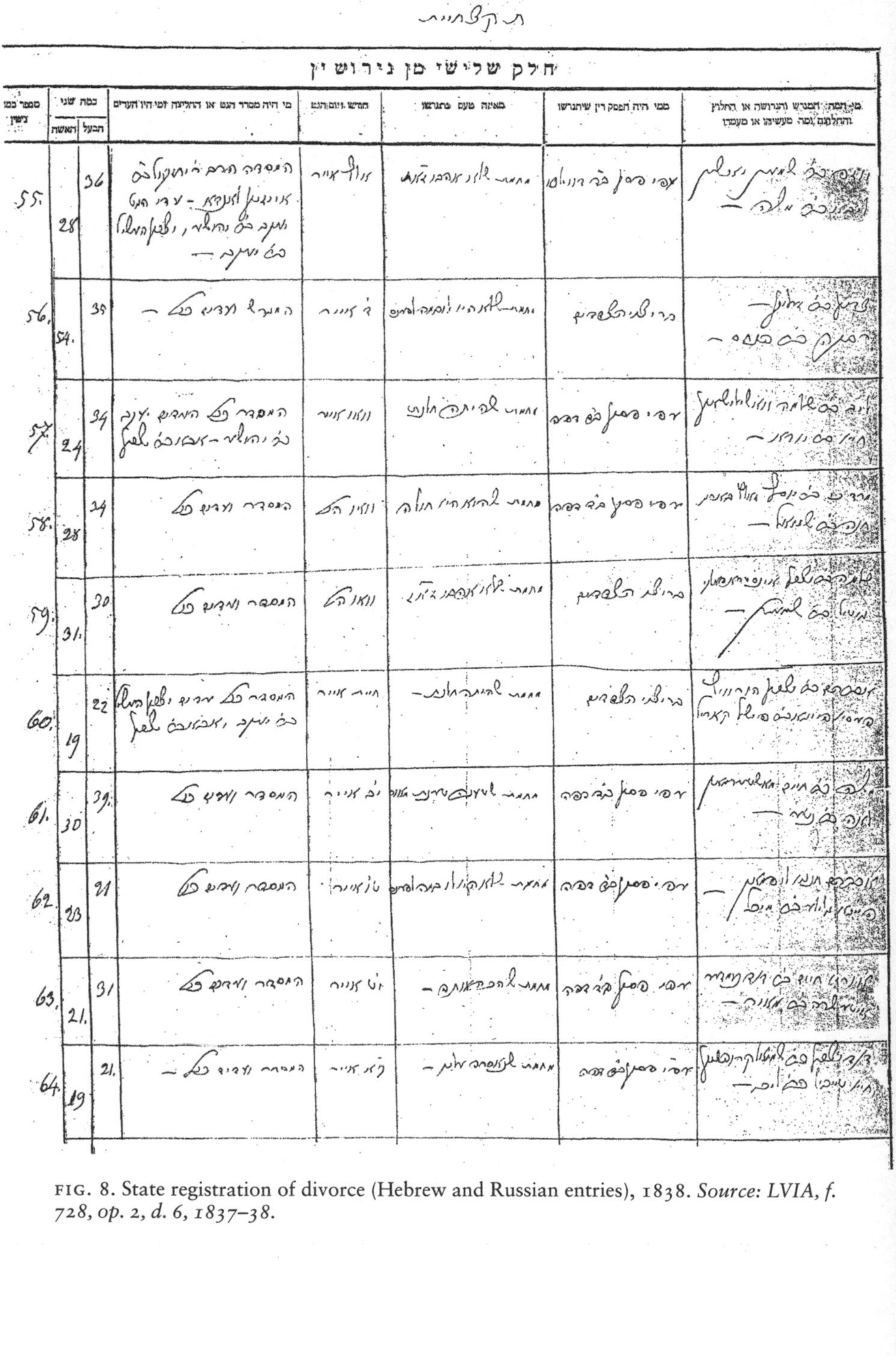

חלק שלישי מן גירושין

מספר כמו נישן	כמה שני		מי היה מפרד רעם או הרמיזה ומי היו העדים	חדש ויום ושנה	באיזה מעם נתגרשו	מתי היה חפסק רין שיתגרשו	מתימת: דמערש ותגרושה או הרלגין
	הבעל	האשה					והתלחמה נמר מעשישו או מעמדן
55.	36 / 28	*(handwritten)*	*(handwritten)*	*(handwritten)*	*(handwritten)*	*(handwritten)*	*(handwritten)*
56.	39 / 54.	*(handwritten)*	*(handwritten)*	*(handwritten)*	*(handwritten)*	*(handwritten)*	*(handwritten)*
57.	34 / 24	*(handwritten)*	*(handwritten)*	*(handwritten)*	*(handwritten)*	*(handwritten)*	*(handwritten)*
58.	34 / 28	*(handwritten)*	*(handwritten)*	*(handwritten)*	*(handwritten)*	*(handwritten)*	*(handwritten)*
59.	30 / 31.	*(handwritten)*	*(handwritten)*	*(handwritten)*	*(handwritten)*	*(handwritten)*	*(handwritten)*
60.	22 / 19	*(handwritten)*	*(handwritten)*	*(handwritten)*	*(handwritten)*	*(handwritten)*	*(handwritten)*
61.	39 / 30	*(handwritten)*	*(handwritten)*	*(handwritten)*	*(handwritten)*	*(handwritten)*	*(handwritten)*
62.	21 / 23	*(handwritten)*	*(handwritten)*	*(handwritten)*	*(handwritten)*	*(handwritten)*	*(handwritten)*
63.	31 / 21.	*(handwritten)*	*(handwritten)*	*(handwritten)*	*(handwritten)*	*(handwritten)*	*(handwritten)*
64.	21 / 19	*(handwritten)*	*(handwritten)*	*(handwritten)*	*(handwritten)*	*(handwritten)*	*(handwritten)*

FIG. 8. State registration of divorce (Hebrew and Russian entries), 1838. *Source: LVIA, f. 728, op. 2, d. 6, 1837–38.*

ЧАСТЬ III. О РАЗВЕДШИХСЯ

№	Число и Мѣсяцъ	Кто именно съ кѣмъ разведенъ разводнымъ или чрезъ Халицу	По чьему рѣшенію	По какимъ причинамъ	Кѣмъ совершается обрядъ разводный или халицы и кто были свидѣтелями при совершеніи онаго	Лѣта Муж.	Лѣта Жен.
			по рѣшенію Виленскаго Раввинскаго Духовнаго Суда			36	28
			по Согласію обоюстороннему			35	54
			по рѣшенію Духовнаго Раввинскаго Суда			34	24
			по рѣшенію Духовнаго Суда			34	28
			по Согласію обоюстороннему			30	31
			по Согласію обоюстороннему			22	19
			по рѣшенію Духовнаго Суда			39	30
			по рѣшенію Духовнаго Суда			21	23
			по рѣшенію Духовнаго Суда			31	21
			по рѣшенію Духовнаго Суда			21	19

marital status). The very fact that the couple failed to produce a letter from their local state rabbi only increased suspicions that there were indeed impediments to the marriage.

However irksome (and costly) such documentation might be, Jews increasingly came to realize the importance of timely and proper registration in the metrical books. The importance of such entries became painfully clear to the widow Lipa Froima Gol'dberg when she later sought to prove the legality of her marriage to Leib Gol'dberg. As so often happened in these cases, trouble began when a spiritual rabbi officiated at their wedding but neglected to report the marriage to the state rabbi (perhaps to avoid questions or fees). Whatever the reason, the wedding was never recorded in the metrical books.[174] That oversight was to cost Lipa Gol'dberg dearly. After her husband's death she applied to receive his military pension and asked the state rabbi for a copy of her marriage certificate. When the metrical book showed no record of the marriage, however, the state summarily rejected her petition on the simple grounds that she had no proof of their marriage.

Such cases proliferated in the postreform era and became a major issue in the Russian-Jewish press. By the early twentieth century, journalists noted that a couple had two legal ways to legalize a marriage *ex post facto*.[175] One approach, possible after 1903, was a direct appeal to the Senate; if this highest court of appeals rendered a favorable decision, the couple could then apply to their district court and have their marriage formalized. But this procedure entailed much time and expense and did not guarantee a successful outcome. The second method, far more attractive to ordinary Jews (who had little experience with the state), was to request a hearing before a Jewish *beit-din* for a ruling on the legitimacy of their marriage. In 1910 the Rabbinic Commission ruled that, if a *beit-din* confirmed the union, the state rabbi was to issue the marriage certificate.[176]

Both procedures represented a significant loophole in the system of registration that defined an individual's hereditary status and served as the regime's main instrument of social control. These exceptions were a remarkable concession; they reflected the growing angst about family stability and the urgent need to make some accommodations.[177] The awareness of the need for such concessions was neither new nor limited to Jews; ever since the 1870s the government had periodically showed a growing inclination to adapt the civil registry to facilitate the integration of subjects into imperial society. Such was the case, for example, with respect to religious dissenters like the Old Believers; although the church denied the validity of their marriages, in 1874 the government began to register Old Believer marriages, in effect establishing a kind of "civil marriage" (*grazhdanskii brak*).

But the "four books"—the metrical records on births, marriages, divorces, and deaths—continued to play a major role in the everyday lives of Jews. Omissions and errors, whether accidental or with malice aforethought, were fraught with catastrophic consequences for the parties involved. In general, state law strictly prohibited "any corrections in Jewish metrical books, with the exception of errors made by a clerk."[178] But the burden of proof to document that exception lay with the victim; amendment to the metrical books depended on the caprice of local officials. While the original law may have intended to ensure proper registration and to penalize those who flouted the authority of the state rabbi, it did not easily accommodate human error or foresee the popular aversion to the bureaucrats serving as state rabbis. As a result, every year the government found itself inundated with a flood of petitions requesting the retroactive insertion of entries or, no less frequently, the correction of names, birth dates, and the like.[179]

Although the metrical records bolstered the power of the state rabbi, they did not enhance his prestige and status among fellow Jews. Although most state rabbis refused to alter the record books, due to legal barriers rather than out of malice, their image as the malefic masters of the four books invariably alienated them not only from the impoverished underclass, but also from the affluent and educated in Jewish society. The verses of the popular writer Y. Raikher captured the disdainful attitude toward the "keepers of the four books" as execrable traitors to their faith and people.[180] Such enmity was ubiquitous and intense. For many, the state rabbi was the very incarnation of the state; an agent of the oppressive, alien state, he was a natural lightning rod for discontent. Even his very title—*kazennyi ravvin*—was a revealing oxymoron. The lofty, spiritual image of *ravvin* was preceded by the adjective *kazennyi*, which invoked images of money, being derived from the root word for "treasury" *(kazna),* and bureaucracy (in modern parlance, bearing the connotation of the state).

LIMITS OF POWER

In contrast to the state's own vision of a powerful, reformist state rabbinate that was to transform Jewish life, state rabbis found that they had neither the time nor the authority to play such a dynamic role. Critics, to be sure, were wont to ascribe the failings of the state rabbis to the officeholders themselves, emphasizing the lack of proper education, professional training, and rudimentary knowledge of Jewish law and traditions. While there is much truth to such criticism, it bears emphasizing that even the most zealous and learned rabbi was hardly in a position to reshape Jewish religious life and practices. There were two

reasons for this: (1) excessive responsibilities, that is, a surfeit of onerous responsibilities ascribed to the state rabbi; and (2) limited powers
of enforcement.

EXCESSIVE RESPONSIBILITIES

Much of the problem rested in the overambitious job description: the state
rabbi had too many responsibilities and served too large a community to
perform all his many duties—at least, in a consistent and efficacious manner. This difficulty was apparent, for example, in a case from 1889, where
a district police chief reported the complaint from state rabbi "M" that he
could not possibly perform all the Jewish ceremonies in his town without
assistance. That statement triggered a formal investigation, which revealed that the rabbi often commissioned a *shokhet* (ritual slaughterer) to
perform circumcisions and marriages. Appalled by this violation of his
statutory duties, the provincial board initiated criminal proceedings
against the hapless rabbi. The presiding procurator, however, concurred
with the state rabbi that he could not possibly circumcise every male child
on the eighth day after birth and terminated the prosecution.[181]

As the case of "Rabbi M" indicates, state rabbis found it physically impossible to perform the traditional ritual tasks, let alone enlighten and
transform coreligionists. As one sympathetic observer noted, state rabbis
were to maintain the register books, write numerous reports, oversee military conscription, explain the laws to the Jews, perform the sundry rituals,
and attend to myriad other duties.[182] Some also assisted their coreligionists in many other matter–for example, on behalf of an *agunah*, sending a
description of a missing husband to Jewish newspapers such as *Hamelits*.
As the official link between state and community, the government summoned the state rabbi to deal with a host of utterly unrelated matters:
"They were called from time to time by court investigators, the police, and
different administrative institutions; they wrote letters to the various institutions of the government, translated documents from Hebrew to Russian
[i.e., if they knew Hebrew]."[183] They were also burdened with the impossible task of prohibiting Jewish women from shaving their hair after they
married.[184] A state rabbi in Volhynia province, in a letter to the local governor, similarly stressed that the vast spectrum of his official duties was
simply unrealizable: "You can be certain, kind sir, that to explain the law,
to teach, persuade and exhort Jews, to direct them morally, to guide them
to obedience to the authorities, to speak and read instructions [to them] at
all times, in places of worship for prayers—that all this is not only the law
but the direct responsibility of the rabbi . . . but to put up with hundreds
and thousands of Jews alone is physically impossible."[185]

A writer for *Rassvet* criticized the government for being too harsh on state rabbis for neglecting their duties. Nonfeasance, he added, was hardly unique to the state rabbi: "Undoubtedly, rabbis sometimes breach the confidence but then again, most of these acts have been committed by other *chinovniki* [government officials] around the world."[186]

To ease the burden on the state rabbi, the Russian government permitted the Jewish community to elect one assistant rabbi for every thousand residents.[187] Apart from the ambivalence of state rabbis toward the appointment of an assistant, the Jewish community generally had little desire to appoint a second rabbi. One reason was financial: many Jews did not wish to assume the costs of maintaining yet another rabbi. Moreover, there was even a clear advantage to having an overworked state rabbi, as long as he handled the paperwork properly: it limited his capacity to play a broader role. Given the animus that many Jews felt toward the state rabbi, they obviously preferred to restrict his activities to record keeping. While it was essential to have a state rabbi in close proximity, there was no incentive to ease the lot of an overburdened rabbi so that he could engage in more than bureaucratic record keeping.

LIMITED POWERS OF ENFORCEMENT

In addition to the plethora of responsibilities, the state rabbi lacked the authority to impose his decisions. Ironically, the very regime that used coercion to maintain order strictly denied state rabbis the coercive means to influence coreligionists. Indeed, state law prescribed severe penalties for any Jew who imposed "fines, the *herem*, or expulsion from the community": fifty rubles for the first violation, one hundred rubles for the second, and dismissal from their post for the third. Moreover, anyone who resorted to the *herem* at least three times could be taken as a military recruit without a physical examination.[188] Instead, the only means of enforcement at the disposal of state rabbis was "persuasion and exhortation"—hardly of much effect given the state rabbis' lack of influence and respect in their communities.[189]

The severe limitation on the state rabbi's effective power was dramatically evident in the Poliakov lawsuit from the late 1880s. The case commenced when Ester Poliakov complained to the state rabbi that her husband "was living a depraved life and engaging in marital infidelity."[190] In 1887 he had signed a pledge to initiate divorce, but later reneged, presumably because of the financial burdens that the divorce inevitably entailed. Whatever the motive, he simply deserted his wife and young children, without any provision for their support, and vanished abroad. When he returned to Russia in 1891, the state rabbi confronted him about the broken pledge and the failure to support his wife and family. Such remonstrations were to no avail; the rabbi had no power to compel the miscreant to fulfill his sworn promise. Given the state rabbi's low esteem in the community, it was well-nigh impossible for him to invoke community censure, let alone impose his will by force.

The erosion of rabbinical power was exacerbated by the increasing geographic mobility in the second half of the nineteenth century. Although the processes of migration (and emigration) affected virtually every segment of imperial society, they had a particularly strong impact on Jews, a group closely linked to commercial and industrial development. The partial relaxation of residence restrictions on certain categories of Jews (e.g., first-guild merchants, university students, artisans, and soldiers) facilitated the rapid exodus of these select Jews from the Pale to the empire's capitals and eastern cities.[191] Such movement made it all the more difficult for the state rabbi to exert his authority. In a case from Khar'kov province, one merchant simply ignored the verdict of the *beit-din* to provide material support for his family and moved to another province, confident that he could avoid such payments altogether.[192] As Jews left their hometowns, communal leaders—not to mention the ostracized state rabbi—found it difficult to put moral pressure on the obdurate, let alone the absent.

A Controversial Spiritual Role

Despite the lack of time and power, some state rabbis did seek to become more than mere "religious bureaucrats" mechanically entering information in the metrical books. Not many, to be sure, became transformers seeking (in accordance with the state's maximalist vision) to eradicate "superstition" and bring "enlightenment" to the empire's Jewish population. But all had clear responsibilities in the spiritual domain; according to state law, they alone had authority over the basic rites for betrothals, marriages, divorces, and the like. Predictably, the lack of proper training created serious problems in performing this role: ignorance of halakhah (Jewish law) easily led to egregious errors and transgressions against the most rudimentary codes and customs.

The zealous reformers encountered particular difficulties, as a case from Georgia in 1895 illustrated. The chief protagonist was the assistant state rabbi, Shalashvili, who had handled the divorce of a couple called Adzhiashvili. Following the wedding in her parents' home in Kulash (Kutaiskii District), Rivka Adzhiashvili moved to her husband's village of Bandza.[193] Not long afterward, against the wishes of her husband, she moved back to her hometown. Although she did not want a divorce, she declared that she was homesick and simply could no longer tolerate the conditions in her husband's village. The husband countered that, to support his family and ply his trade, the family had to live in Bandza. Dismayed by her departure and determined to stay in his home village, he asked the local rabbi to dissolve their marriage.[194] The rabbi made a public announcement in the local synagogues and prayer houses that the wife was "unfaithful" to her husband[195] and ordered Adzhiashvili to return to her husband before the end of the year. When she refused to comply, he granted the divorce without further consultation or her consent.

In defiance of the assistant rabbi's edict, she appealed to the provincial governor. In this case the chief state rabbi in the province, Reuden, upheld her appeal, declaring that the divorce was illegal under Jewish law on several counts. First, a wife betrothed and married in her parents' home was not obligated to move to her husband's place of residence.[196] Second, if the request for divorce was not based on mutual consent, the rabbi was obliged to announce her "rebellion" publicly for four consecutive weeks. She then had one year to return to her husband and resume their marital relationship. At the end of this period, the spouses could divorce by mutual agreement; if the wife rejected the divorce and returned, the husband could neither dissolve the marriage against her will (even if he returned her entire dowry) nor remarry.[197] Finally and most important, the rabbi ruled, the husband's relatives had served as witnesses for the delivery of the *get*; the use of such partial witnesses rendered the divorce null and void.[198] "It is evident that Shalashvili does not have an adequate understanding of Jewish law," declared Rabbi Reuden, "and I am persuaded that in the event that he is summoned to Kutaisi, [I will] invite him personally and explain Jewish law to him."[199]

Even learned rabbis could run afoul of the law, especially if disposed to support a liberal reinterpretation of Jewish law and tradition. In 1910 the Rabbinic Commission reviewed one such case involving a liberal state rabbi, Perel'man, who had attempted to prevent Borukh Pekker from divorcing his wife on the grounds of her childlessness. After twelve years of childless marriage, the husband asked Rabbi Perel'man to issue a divorce. Although infertility was traditionally a valid ground for divorce, the rabbi cited the "more progressive responsa" (which extended protection to women in such circumstances) and denied his request. The exasperated husband thereupon appealed to the Rabbinic Commission to overturn what he deemed an unjust decision. By rejecting his petition, argued Pekker, the rabbi prevented him from fulfilling the mitzvah (commandment) to "be fruitful and multiply."[200] Rabbi Perel'man defended his position by citing the responsa literature of Rabbi Chaim Hezekiah Medini (*Sedei hemed*) on the subject.[201] He argued that while the ancient authorities granted divorce on the grounds of infertility, "the majority of authors in contemporary times" rejected this view. The Rabbinic Commission, however, overturned Rabbi Perel'man's well-meaning attempt to defend the childless woman. It explained that the wife's infertility *did* constitute legal grounds for divorce after ten years of uninterrupted cohabitation. Moreover, it reprimanded the rabbi for exercising such discretion in the matter: it declared that in any case that raised issues about the interpretation of Jewish law, the rabbi was duty-bound to bring the matter before a *beit-din* composed of one hundred rabbis from three different districts.[202]

No less damaging to the reputation of the official rabbinate were instances involving the flagrant abuse of power. The disproportionate number of complaints about illegal activities of state rabbis from southern Ukrainian cities like Odessa, Kherson, and Ekaterinoslav reflected several distinctions between these "new areas of settlement" and traditional centers of Jewish residence. "Judaism was not scholarly here as in Lithuania," observes Shochat, nor had Hasidism ever taken root, as it had in Volhynia, Podolia, and Belorussia.[203] These cosmopolitan cities had no religious or cultural tradition to restrain the inroads of modernity, and hence (in the words of one writer), there were many here who "threw off the yoke of Torah and *mitzvot*."[204]

Probably the most infamous state rabbi of all was Lev Kagan (rabbi for the city of Nikolaev in Kherson province), who performed unlawful ceremonies behind the deceptive veneer of his charming and authoritative personality.[205] He openly provided two illegal services that aroused great concern among state officials as well as the Jewish community. The first was to register in his metrical books acts like birth and marriage that previously had gone unrecorded. For example, O. M. Gurvich, realizing that he had neglected to register his daughter's birth (five years after the event), appealed to his local rabbi to amend about the oversight. Although this state rabbi was too cautious to comply, he advised him to "visit Rabbi Kagan," and Gurvich was pleasantly surprised to find that the rabbi recorded the birth in his metrical book without the slightest hesitation.[206] So brazen a violation of state law promptly provoked an investigation by the governor of Odessa, who recommended that the rabbi be exiled "as a person harmful to the peace of society."[207]

That was not Rabbi Kagan's only foible: he also displayed a tendency to perform patently illegal Jewish ceremonies, especially for people outside his legal jurisdiction. For example, when local rabbis refused to grant Abram Malamud a divorce, he took his case to the obliging Rabbi Kagan of Nikolaev.[208] As in the Radin case,[209] Rabbi Kagan summoned Malka Malamud (a resident of Odessa) to appear before a rabbinic court for a divorce hearing in the town (Gorev) where her husband resided. If she failed to appear, he warned, judgment would be passed in absentia. Frustrated in her attempts to settle the matter with the stubborn rabbi,

FIG. 9. Studio portrait of a family in Nikolaev: a couple and five children (1900). Mother holds a book; father, a hat. The youngest boy, wearing a school uniform, sits on a footstool with a cap at his feet. *Courtesy of YIVO Institute for Jewish Research.*

she appealed to higher-ranking state authorities (the provincial board of Kherson province) to ban the hearing in Gorev and to force her husband to pay child support. Eventually, after a direct appeal, the governor of Kherson categorically rejected the legality of this so-called rabbinic court. The astonished governor wrote that "Rabbi Kagan does not appear to be an imposter, but he has illegally usurped authority to establish a rabbinical court [outside his jurisdiction]."[210] Rabbi Kagan, if the most notorious, was hardly the only state rabbi to violate Jewish law.

Nor were women the sole victims of rabbinical arbitrariness, as the case of Il'ia Shumbroit illustrates. The husband's tale of woes began when he received a warning from the state rabbi of Kherson that, if he failed to attend the divorce hearing initiated by his wife, a decision would be rendered in absentia.[211] The husband protested that this summons violated Jewish law in multiple ways. First, the rabbi had initiated the divorce case solely at his wife's behest and without—as Jewish law requires—prior consultation with the husband. Second, the rabbi threatened to dissolve their marriage without his consent—yet another transparent violation of Jewish law, which gave the husband the sole right to accept or reject a proposal for a divorce. Finally, the rabbi overstepped his geographical jurisdiction by judging a case that involved residents of Odessa—that is, people who were manifestly outside the Jewish community in Kherson. The Rabbinic Commission concurred with the husband's remonstrations. It reiterated the rule (common to imperial law more generally) that a divorce suit involving defendants from another district must be transmitted to the hometown rabbi for resolution.[212]

Not all violations of Jewish law were innocent errors or misguided philanthropy: some state rabbis used their position for personal gain. Apart from blatant corruption (bribes and extortion), state rabbis were known to demand exorbitant fees for performing and registering various religious ceremonies. For example, several Jews from the village of Lugan (Ovruch district) denounced their state rabbi, Pinkhas Vainerman, for assessing inordinate fees for various rituals.[213] State rabbis occasionally admitted such practices. One state rabbi, Manus Shur, cheerfully confessed to levying high fees on the residents of Kolkov (a village in Volhynia province) but explained that he did so only when the community refused to conclude a contract to regulate his fees.[214] And a few state rabbis allegedly committed criminal offenses—for example, pilfering funds from the kosher meat taxes *(korobochnyi sbor).*[215] Still more notorious was Rabbi Yankel Twersky, who purportedly was embroiled in contraband, false credit, and various illicit financial machinations.[216]

To be sure, corruption was more the norm than the exception in prerevolutionary Russia, where a marginal economy and underfinanced administration routinely sustained the traditional ethos of *kormlenie* (feeding) upon the subordinate population. Such obtained as well in the case of state rabbis, where the responsibilities were great but the salaries meager.

Although the regime periodically prosecuted officials, including state rabbis, for malfeasance, government officials often extended their protection to the state rabbi. In one famous case, the police chief of Ovruch district consented to the illegal marriage of an underage couple, ignoring the fact that the poll tax census clearly showed the groom to be just fourteen years old. When another local official learned about plans for the illegal marriage, he urged the police chief to intercede. The latter, however, pretended to have no knowledge of the matter and took no further action. In the meantime the couple were married in the village of Slavech, with the personal approval of the same police chief.[217]

Such cases, broadly publicized in the contemporary press, raised serious concern in Jewish society. At one level the malfeasance of state rabbis was subversive: it threatened to undermine the traditional pillars of law and order in Jewish society, for the rabbi Kagans were sending a dangerous message: if marital problems could not be resolved through the customary procedures of Jewish law, then Jews could resort to extralegal methods to settle their case.[218] No doubt, many such cases never came to the attention of authorities; only if one spouse raised a legal challenge would the misdeeds of the state rabbi come to light. But the misapplication of Jewish law, whether from ignorance or corrupt motives, was a flagrant challenge to traditional norms and values.

Still more disturbing for many Jews was the impact on community solidarity: the misdeeds of state rabbis impelled an increasing number of Jews, especially women, to seek justice from secular authorities. It became a source of deep concern for spiritual leaders that Jews (particularly women like Malka Malamud and Ita Radin) appealed to the Russian government to combat unjust rulings by state rabbis. In many respects, such appeals offered their only effective recourse for dealing with rogue rabbis like Kagan, since their very source of legitimacy stemmed from the state itself. Thus, despite an abiding distrust of the Russian government, discontented Jewish litigants petitioned provincial and central administrators (even the emperor himself) for justice, expressing hope, however qualified, that the state's protective and mediative powers would prevail. Women's petitions, in particular, addressed the state as a guardian or father figure; they routinely invoked such phraseology as "Thus I come under your protection, Your Excellency" or "I implore you to take mercy on me, an unfortunate and unhappy woman."[219] While women often employed the idiom of official patriarchy to press their cases, the very fact that they appealed to the state, despite the financial and personal costs, reveals a growing confidence in the efficacy of such litigation.[220] In such cases the state assumed its professed identity and role as a "supra-class, supra-ethnic entity," to reconcile and arbitrate disparate interests in marital conflicts.[221]

The intercession of non-Jewish authorities in matters of marriage and divorce significantly vitiated the authority of spiritual leaders. As it became more convenient and productive to appeal to state officials, the role of spiritual rabbis in mediating disputes gradually declined. Indeed, some observers even blamed the spiritual rabbis for the misconduct of state rabbis, claiming that the spiritual leaders failed to defend the honor of Judaism and had thereby opened the Pandora's box of appeals to non-Jewish state authorities. Such criticism impelled the spiritual rabbis of Odessa to publish the following complaint in a local newspaper: "In the local Jewish community, accusations circulate against us—and are also echoed in the local press—that we silently tolerate the numerous violations of ritual ceremonies (i.e., the validity and legality of marriages and divorces) by Odessa state rabbis." According to Jewish law, they argued, "anyone who is not well-versed in the law does not have the right to conduct marriages and divorces. [Those] violating these enactments are 'worse than the generation in the days of the Flood.'"[222] Interestingly, the writers bemoaned the fact that such violations occurred only in Odessa, whereas in the rest of the empire they claimed that "spiritual rabbis maintained strict control over religious customs and ceremonies." Frustrated by the lack of response on the part of communal leaders to the "antireligious disorders," the Odessa spiritual leaders complained, "Unfortunately our voice remains unheard, like a 'voice crying out in the wilderness.'"[223]

Manipulating the Rabbinate: "Illegal Marriages"

It was, however, not only incompetent and corrupt rabbis who sowed turmoil in the Jewish family; individual Jews exploited the weaknesses of the state rabbinate for personal gain. Just as the spiritual rabbinate feared, Jews who sought to circumvent Jewish law—above all, to obtain a quick divorce or to remarry without a formal divorce—took advantage of corrupt rabbis and ambiguous laws. In no case was this more dramatic or devastating than in the phenomenon of illegal marriages. That phrase, which had gained broad currency by the late nineteenth century, pertained to marriages that observed the requirements of Jewish rites but in some respect violated state law (e.g., not performed by a state rabbi or not inscribed in the metrical books). In the aftermath the husband could void the union in civil law, thereby eliminating any financial or other obligations to his former spouse. However, because Jewish law still deemed the marriage valid, the woman could remarry only if the man agreed to provide the obligatory *get*.

One typical case involved Abram Sagal, the son of a merchant from Kremenchug. When the Litovchins penned the marriage contract between their daughter and Sagal at the annual Khar'kov fair, they thought the match was made in heaven.[224] Just three months after the wedding, however, the husband suddenly took all his valuables (some 800 rubles in silver) and abandoned his pregnant wife, leaving her without any means of support. The woman's father confronted Sagal at the Elizavetgrad fair and demanded that he either return to his wife or at least provide monetary support. When Sagal refused, Litovchin appealed to the provincial governor, who commissioned the state rabbi Tseitlin to settle the dispute. Sagal at first denied even having such a wife but after witnesses testified that they attended the wedding, he acknowledged that Sura Litovchin was indeed his legal wife and agreed to appear before a *beit-din* to resolve the dispute.

The *beit-din* concluded that, notwithstanding "Sagal's malicious desertion" and "indecent insult to his wife's honor," Sura Litovchin had agreed to live with him if he would return to Khar'kov and escort her to his new place of residence. When Sagal refused (saying "So be it, let her come here herself"), the *beit-din* concluded "that he had no intention to resume his marital life with her." It therefore ruled that Sagal should compensate his in-laws for the two years they supported her, in addition to the gifts he gave her at the wedding (worth 60 rubles). As long as he lived separately from his wife, the court ordered him to pay twelve silver rubles a month in alimony and an equal amount for child support.[225] Confronted with that ruling, on 7 August 1866, Abram Sagal signed an agreement whereby he promised to escort his wife to Kremenchug in ten days and "to lead her through life with love."[226] In a second statement, signed in September 1866, he pledged that "at this time, having spoken with my wife Sura about our future family life, I have been reconciled with her and will provide for her, and I am obliged to love and honor her."[227] To ensure that Sagal complied with this verdict, the governor of Poltava sent a copy of his statements to the police in Kremenchurg.

Rather than travel to Khar'kov as promised, Sagal instead sent a countercomplaint to the governor of Poltava, requesting an annulment of the verdict by the *beit-din* on the grounds that his marriage was illegal by state law. Before the governor had time to reply, the police in Kremenchug had already arrested Sagal for violating the governor's orders and demanded that he pay the 144 rubles he owed his wife.[228] His father pressed the appeal on his behalf and sent a petition directly to the Ministry of Interior, claiming that "my son's wedding was not officiated by an established state rabbi, but by some nameless Jew and not recorded in the metrical book." Thus, he argued, "the marriage of my son with the daughter of Litovchin should be considered illegal."[229]

In response to an inquiry by the ministry, the governor of Poltava angrily reiterated the facts of the case and added that "because Sagal was married for over two years to Litovchin's daughter and has not said anything about illegality or deceitfulness until the present time, I recommend that Sagal's petition to invalidate the decision of the *beit-din* be rejected."[230] The case eventually reached the Senate, which remanded the matter back to the rabbinical court but first defined the parameters of a final resolution. Namely, if the *beit-din* judged the marriage valid, Sagal must pay twelve rubles in alimony and twelve rubles in child support payments; if, however, it found the marriage invalid, the court was to arrange some means of support for the mother and any "illegitimate" children from the union.[231] In other words, if Sagal could demonstrate that the marriage failed to satisfy the requirements of *state* law, it would void the union and leave him immune to any major obligations.

Numerous cases like the Sagal suit sparked a vigorous debate in the Jewish press about the so-called illegal marriages. B. Bogrov, a correspondent for the Jewish weekly *Voskhod,* defended the state laws that regulated Jewish marital practices. In his opinion, the institution of marriage in the modern age, "quite apart from its religious and social meaning," was central to the definition of "civil, personal, and property rights." By restricting the officiation of Jewish ceremonies to state rabbis, he argued, the government sought to prevent bigamy and protect the interests of women. His study of illegal marriages (i.e., marriages performed by people other than the state rabbi) in the city of Nikolaev revealed that the "abuse was so great that this question is even more serious than is generally believed." And such illegal unions all too frequently provided a facile pretext for annulment, freeing the male from the usual financial obligations. His investigation showed that illegal marriage provided grounds for 5 of 24 divorces in 1890, 4 of 31 divorces in 1891, and 6 of 27 divorces in 1892—that is, 15 of 82 divorces during a three-year period.[232]

Bogrov concluded that those who entered into an illegal marriage were more likely to treat it casually and to divorce at a whim. Apart from undermining the institution of marriage, such illegal unions left the deserted wives in an "abnormal position," since often their only proof of marriage was "an illiterate *ketubah*" (marriage contract). The female victim had no legal recourse if her husband deserted to remarry: the state did not recognize such marriages, and the spiritual rabbinate lacked the moral authority to compel spouses to grant a proper divorce under Jewish law. "It is impossible to listen without shuddering to the complaints of unhappy deserted women," lamented the writer, "and to see their tears and protests." Such woes, he wrote, only aggravated the desperate impoverishment of Jews that intensified the suffering of Jewish women: "Life becomes so hard that it is difficult to support a large family, and they [parents] begin preparing to sell their daughter [to prostitution]." That duress, he suggested, underlay the willingness of families to enter into such illegal—and ruinous—unions as the illegal marriages.[233]

Bogrov recommended several measures to combat the phenomenon of illegal marriages. First, the rabbi should enter such unions into passports in order to prevent remarriage without, at least, first obtaining a formal

Jewish divorce. Second, Bogrov proposed to clarify the ambiguous language in state law, which had allowed those who officiate illegal unions to elude due punishment. Thus, instead of punishing "those who performed Jewish ceremonies," the law would specifically punish "those who read the prayers," a phrase that did not presuppose a legal union and dealt properly with the real perpetrators. Finally, he urged the Rabbinic Commission to take steps to protect the civil, personal, and property rights of deserted wives and children of illegal marriages.

Illegal marriages also created serious legal problems for Jewish women, especially with respect to their right of residence in restricted areas. That was apparent, for example, in an 1888 case involving Malka Zel'vin of Moscow. Although the case initially concerned an entirely different matter (accusations that she and her family operated a pawnshop, not a tailoring service, as their residence permits indicated), the court learned that Zel'vin's marriage to her husband Isser Khodykel was illegal and had not been recorded in the metrical books. Although the judge found her innocent of the crimes for which she had been indicted, the state expelled her from Moscow because she was no longer the legal wife of a retired soldier (who did have the right to reside in the capital). The problem was that her husband refused either to move to Vitebsk (her hometown) or to grant her a divorce under Jewish law. According to religious authorities, Zel'vin could not remarry until she received the obligatory *get* from her husband. "On the one hand, the court verdict states that I was not married to him," Zel'vin complained, "and, on the other hand, Jewish law does not allow me to remarry without a divorce from my husband Khodykel." She could neither use his social status nor require him to grant her a divorce: "I am twenty-two years old and in a hopeless position. Can I remarry without a divorce?"

The Rabbinic Commission concluded that Malka Zel'vin's marriage to the townsman Khodykel complied with all the requirements of Jewish ritual but not civil law. It thus concluded that while the marriage was void under civil law, it was nevertheless binding under Jewish law: "Marriages which are considered illegal [by civil law] are considered valid by Talmudic law and the only way to dissolve the marriage is through a formal divorce." Although Zel'vin no longer lived with her husband, Jewish law did not free her from her marital union with Khodykel. Her only hope was that the local state rabbi might persuade her husband to grant her a divorce. Although the commission felt obliged to rule against the woman, it was plainly alarmed by the abuse of state law by ordinary Jews. "In light of the information which has come before the Ministry about the considerable number of such illegal marriages among Jews," the commission concluded, "it would be desirable for the Rabbinic Commission to find positive measures to diminish, or completely eliminate, these kinds of marriages, which have pernicious consequences for the family."[234]

Another writer in *Voskhod* sharply censured any intervention of state law into Jewish autonomy, arguing that this was a blatant violation of the regime's own principle that "each tribe and nation is permitted to marry according to their own laws or customs without the participation of a civil authority." By restricting the officiation of Jewish ceremonies exclusively to state rabbis and their assistants, he contended, the government had in fact appointed a "civil authority" over private rituals. The result, he warned, was that the state attempt to impose its own standards in marital matters not only violated centuries of traditions and customs but also was doomed to fail. From the very beginning, Jewish society distrusted the ability of the new rabbis to perform religious rites. "No threat of the law," he argued, "will compel them to turn to the state rabbi to perform marriages, divorces and other rites."[235] In effect, the state itself had fabricated these illegal marriages by seeking to regulate the Jewish family and had unwittingly punished the very victims it sought to protect. The only solution, he concluded, was to give the Jews complete autonomy to handle marital issues.

Conclusion

As the Russian state maneuvered to govern its Jewish population, one of the last and most distinctive groups to join the empire, it found that it could not easily resort to the traditional "imperial method"—that is, to co-opt existing elites and institutions as instrument for control and rule. At both the regional and community level, Jewish society showed a pronounced tendency toward disaggregation, a pattern already apparent before the partitions but accelerated by the policies of the Russian state.

In response, the regime attempted to build a new authority structure and to establish an official clerical hierarchy. The Rabbinical Commission was the apogee of that new system; based on a foreign (French) model but adapted to Russian needs, it was to serve as the supreme court for Jewish affairs. Although initially charged with a broad spectrum of responsibilities, by the 1860s it began to focus on what would become its single primary sphere of concern—regulating a plethora of marital and divorce questions. At the lower echelon the government undertook to establish a new clerical hierarchy to perform the administrative functions required of the clergy of other faiths, such as registration and officiation of ceremonies. Like other schemes to "transform" the Jews, it met with strong oppsition. In the late 1870s, Judah Leib Gordon penned his scathing critiques of the state rabbinate and castigated a graduate of the rabbinic school for the callous and avaricious manner in which he abused his training in Jewish law. In his poem "Shomeret yabam" (A widow waiting the levirate rite), Gordon described the plight of a poor, childless couple who turned to the state rabbi for a divorce when they discovered that the husband's death was imminent; without a legal *get,* the widow could not remarry until a brother-in-law (or closest kin) performed the ceremony of *halitsah.* "But Satan came to them from another place, in the image of a maskilic rabbi," and demanded two hundred zuzim (silver coins worth one-fourth of a shekel) for arranging the *get.*[236] As the official state rabbi, this young man had the power to grant the divorce so that the widow would not become an *agunah,* but out of greed and heartlessness he refused. This poem, reminiscent of Gordon's famous mock-epic poem, "Kotso shel yud" (The tip of the yud),[237] underscored the writer's view, shared by many disillusioned *maskilim,* that the new state rabbis were no better than the "obscurantist" traditional rabbis whom they were to replace.

The shortcomings of the state rabbinate in postreform Russia were indeed significant. Above all, the new state rabbis failed to achieve the "professionalization" that was to emulate Western models and make them more effective servitors; indeed, after the two rabbinic schools were dismantled in 1873, state rabbis became little more than religious *chinovniki* (bureaucrats), armed with a secular education and charged mainly with compiling the obligatory metrical books. As many coreligionists complained, they had neither the time nor the training to engage in spiritual matters; indeed, the former or part-time dentists, doctors, and apothecaries often had only a dim grasp of Jewish law and teachings. Even if well-meaning and honest, they were utterly unfit to carry forth the "mission" of reforming Jewry as originally envisioned by the state and *maskilim.*

At the same time, their failings—from incompetence to malfeasance and corruption—were fraught with serious consequences. Their inadvertent blunders and deliberate machinations, after all, inflicted great harm; mistakes in the metrical books and fallacious decisions in divorce had a devastating impact on the individuals involved. Moreover, the state rabbis had a powerful corrosive impact on Jewish community and religious life, not only undermining the credibility of basic institutions but even bringing the spiritual rabbis into disrepute. The misdeeds and low repute of state rabbis encouraged a growing number of Jews (especially women) to seek justice and protection from the secular state, at once undermining the authority of both state and spiritual rabbis.

The spontaneous breakdown of traditional authority, compounded by the abortive attempt to construct a new religious hierarchy, had the dual consequence of empowering Jewish women and at the same time making them more vulnerable to the caprice of husbands and rabbis. In this conflictive, confused order, where authority was uncertain and the rules ambiguous, individual Jews could and had to articulate and defend their own vision of marriage and family life as we shall see in the next chapter.

Chapter Three

❧

Marital Breakdown and Divorce

Inasmuch as you can change one's nature by force, divorce is considered in itself a strange thing, and every person who walks righteously will distance himself from it.
—Yehudah Edel Shereshevskii, *Kur lezahav* (1858)

"Well, so whyn't you get a divorce?" says Alter, interrupting Fishke in his own person this time. "I mean that's what Jewish folks get divorces for, ain't it!"
—S. Y. Abramovich, *Fishke the Lame* (1869)

In our home, which served as the communal office, there was no joy on the day of a divorce. The *sefer kritut* is called the 'bill of excision,' my father explained, because one soul is torn asunder from another."[1] Devorah Baron, whose father served as the rabbi and head of the *beit-din* in the town of Ozdah (Minsk district), was no stranger to divorce. Throughout her childhood she watched local residents present their marital grievances to the rabbi, as a crowd of people shamelessly pressed into her father's court to hear the latest case. Baron's short stories, first published in the Hebrew newspaper *Hamelits*, captured not only the vivid detail of these events but also the emotional pain of the female litigants. Her graphic account recorded the anguish of the wife who shivered silently as the scribe drafted the bill of divorcement, the humiliated woman whose husband publicly demanded a divorce because she failed to bear a son, or the childless divorcée who watched enviously as her ex-husband's new wife caressed a newborn infant in the synagogue.[2] Such accounts stand in stark contrast to modern idealization of Jewish family life in pre-revolutionary Russia.[3] On the contrary, contemporary writers like Abraham Mapu warned that "only one in a thousand will derive joy from family life and even that will be a facade."[4] Another *maskil*, Mordechai

Aaron Guenzburg, even claimed that divorces were so common among Jews that one out of every two Jewish women was married at least twice.[5]

Such negative representations of Jewish marital life raise several important questions. First, were unhappy marriages, marital breakdown, and rampant divorce indeed the norm in Jewish life? Or were such claims merely the distorted perception or antitraditionalist propaganda of an intellectual elite determined to secularize and modernize? Second, however high (or low) the divorce rate, what were the principal causes of marital breakdown? After all, divorces do not correspond with marital breakdown; the two phenomena, while closely related, must be treated distinctly.[6] Finally, it is essential to analyze divorce and marital breakdown diachronically—that is, to see how these processes evolved over time and why.

To put the Jewish case into comparative perspective, this chapter first examines the laws on divorce—for the non-Jews and then for the Jews. This confessional framework affected not only Jewish perceptions of changes in their institutions but also state attitudes and policies as it attempted to deal with the non-Orthodox and, especially, non-Christian segments of the population. The next task is to chart the dynamics of divorce—that is, reconstitute statistical data on incidence, age, social status and occupation, and duration of marriage at the time of divorce. But the principal issue is *why*—how indeed does one explain marital breakdown among Jews in the Russian Empire. Here it is important not only to draw inferences from the statistics but to analyze closely individual divorce files in the archives. While divorce is predictably a complex phenomenon, it is argued here that spousal conflict and marital breakdown grew particularly intense as gender roles and expectations underwent change and that this conflict prompted spouses to reassert control over their traditional spheres.[7]

Divorce in a Multiconfessional Empire

No country in Europe had such complex, differing attitudes toward marital dissolution as did the multinational and multiconfessional Russian Empire. Whereas most European states had secularized and standardized laws on marriage and divorce, the tsarist empire still permitted each religious confession to regulate its own marriages and divorces.[8] Predictably, as in Western Europe, divorce rates reflected the law: the more liberal the grounds for divorce, the higher the rates of divorce.[9] In the Russian case the regime set certain parameters, but in the end it allowed each confession, from the official Orthodox Church to the non-Christian faiths, to determine the grounds and procedures for marital dissolution.

For its part, the regime (but not every religious group) recognized four grounds for marital dissolution.

1. *Death of a spouse.* Although this was, of course, a universally recognized ground for marital dissolution and remarriage, each confession had its own nuances and restrictions.[10] The Russian Orthodox Church recognized the first marriage as transcendent but acceded to the "weakness of human foibles" by tolerating a second or third remarriage for widows and widowers. But there it drew the line; it categorically prohibited a fourth marriage and, in the case of widowed priests, categorically prohibited a second marriage.

2. *Legal divorce.* A second form of marital dissolution was a legal divorce, or a *divorce a vinculo matrimonii* (divorce from the marriage bond). In that sense divorce meant the termination of a validly contracted marriage based on a legal process before a competent religious authority.[11] Its principal import was not only to terminate current relations but to permit remarriage. Partners could always desert one another, but they could remarry, legally and free of prosecution, only if they first obtained a legal divorce. In the case of the majority of subjects in the Russian Empire, members of the Russian Orthodox Church, legal divorce was extremely difficult to obtain, and even when possible, it was fraught with qualifications until a reform in 1904 permitted the "guilty" party to remarry.

3. *Annulment.* Annulment "presupposed that the marriage concerned did not exist"; that is, the marriage itself was invalid because religious or state law (e.g., concerning consanguinity, affinity, minimum age, or other impediments) had been violated.[12] Historians have tended to treat annulment as a "quasi-divorce"; in the case of the Roman Catholic Church, annulment has functioned as an operational ersatz for legal divorce. In the Russian Empire, annulment often came at the instigation of state authorities, not the married couple; and therefore served to enforce religious or state law, particularly in matters of consanguinity and minimum age.

4. *Separation.* A de facto form of marital dissolution was "separation from bed and board" *(a mensa et thoro)*. Although separation did not formally dissolve the marriage, it permitted the respective spouses to have separate domiciles and freed them from their conjugal duties; however, neither party had the right to remarry or legally cohabit with a third party.[13] Although widespread in European states, separation was all but impossible in the Russian Empire, which used the passport and residence registration in its never-ending campaign to control population movement and hence formally banned separation. Only toward the end of the nineteenth century did the government (through personal edicts of the emperor in each individual case) make this solution to marital discord

somewhat more broadly available. Not until March 1914 did the government formally establish separation as a regular, legal option.

Divorce: The Christian Confessions

Of the main confessions in Imperial Russia, the Catholic Church had by far the most restrictive policy on marital dissolution.[14] Above all, it essentially denied the possibility of dissolving a properly consecrated marriage, on the basis of Christ's teaching that "what therefore God hath joined together, let not man put asunder" (Matthew 19:6). The Catholic Church elevated this teaching to the status of obligatory canon law in 1563, a decision fraught with significant implications for Church policy on the family and marriage.[15] The Church also based its notion of the "indelibility" of marriage on the fact that marriage was one of the seven holy sacraments conferring grace to the couple. That dogma led the Catholic Church to deny completely any divorce, even in the case of adultery, which meant that "even the innocent one . . . cannot contract another marriage during the lifetime of the other."[16]

The Catholic Church did, however, recognize annulment and separation. In the Russian Empire, Catholics could seek annulment on six grounds: (1) bigamy, (2) consanguinity or affinity, (3) conversion to a different faith, (4) spiritual vows of priesthood that one party had taken earlier, (5) offense to public decency *(honestas publicá)*, and (6) crimes of adultery and murder committed against a former spouse to enable the new union. The Catholic Church also recognized several grounds for granting separation; these included adultery, cruel treatment of one spouse by the other, and punishment for criminal activities (prison or exile).[17] Although the Church apparently applied this dogma to its believers in Poland and Russia, modern scholarship is yet to provide a detailed picture.

The Russian Orthodox Church, which held power over nearly three quarters of the Tsar's subjects, retained its monopoly over marriage and divorce of its faithful. Perhaps more important, the Orthodox Church gradually constructed a more elaborate administration (a prerequisite for ongoing institutional control) even as it adopted an increasingly restrictive teaching on marriage and divorce.[18] At least until the mid-eighteenth century it was fairly easy to arrange divorce, which required only a "divorce letter" from the local priest, on such grounds as adultery, sexual incapacity, desertion, bigamy, prolonged illness, attempts on the life of a spouse, and monastic vows taken by one spouse. The latter four gradually faded in importance, although the Orthodox Church added two new grounds that doubtless reflected contemporary concerns: Siberian exile and the conversion of one spouse from Orthodoxy to the proscribed sectarian and Old Believer faiths.[19] Doctrinally, however, the Orthodox Church became more restrictive, especially in the wake of the French Revolution, as it embraced the doctrine of the "indelibility or permanence" of the marital sacrament.[20] Although in theory the Orthodox Church, in contrast to the Catholic Church, allowed divorce on a fairly broad set of legal grounds, in practice it made divorce all but impossible.

It did so by resorting to an array of devices: procrastination, caviling objections, and new legal impedimenta. To avert fraudulent testimony, the Orthodox Church not only applied the principle of marital fault (forbidding remarriage of the guilty party until 1904) but also required two eyewitnesses in adultery cases—a deliberate attempt to humiliate and thereby discourage divorce. To obtain a divorce on grounds of "sexual incapacity" it was necessary to obtain not only verification from a qualified physician but proof that the physical condition existed *prior* to the marriage. Desertion involved lengthy investigation and high costs; such suits, moreover, could be initiated only after five years and applied only to spouses whose whereabouts were unknown. As a result, the Church granted very few divorces—a mere seventy-one in 1860, for example.[21] Not for want of demand: each year the church—first at the diocesan level, then with a still more vigilant review by the Holy Synod—rejected the overwhelming majority of divorce applications on a variety of technical and doctrinal grounds. And in contrast to Catholic countries, where annulments provided a de facto substitute for divorce, the Russian Church granted very few annulments, an annual average of just 32.8 from 1836 to 1860. In an effort to maintain a tight grip on divorce, in the late nineteenth century the Orthodox Church showed some flexibility but still failed to satisfy elite and popular expectations of a significant liberalization in divorce law and practice.[22]

The Protestant churches generally took a far more liberal view of marital dissolution and divorce. They did so primarily because they rejected the doctrine of the sacramentality and hence "indelibility" of marital vows.[23] In practice, however, the Protestants were ambivalent about the indissolubility of the marital bond, but they did accept divorce "as a response to matrimonial offense," although not to marital breakdown.[24] In the eighteenth century, however, the waxing power of the state and Enlightenment teachings encouraged many Protestant theologians and states to adumbrate a "contract theory" of marriage, whereby marriage was essentially seen as mutual contract that, by implication, could also be sundered without reference to any "indelible" sacraments.

While practice varied kaleidoscopically in Western Europe according to denomination and country, Protestant churches in the Russian Empire recognized several grounds for divorce: adultery (on condition that the plaintiff be innocent), malicious desertion, disappearance of a spouse for five years or more, sexual incapacity, incurable and contagious diseases, a debauched lifestyle, insanity, criminal behavior leading to the death penalty or a severe prison sentence, and cruel treatment and behavior that threatens a spouse's life. In the last case, a wife could not sue her husband for divorce if the abuse had been "due to her evil conduct, which gave him a reason to treat her cruelly."[25] The husband had the right to "chastise" his wife but only in moderation. Because the Protestants did not define cruel treatment and behavior, its governing agency (the consistory) had discretion in determining what was acceptable as "chastisement." Although the Protestants (following the German model) clearly had more liberal grounds for divorce, they still placed primary emphasis on a reconciliation of the spouses and permitted divorce only in cases of irretrievable breakdown. Information on divorce among Protestants in Russia is wanting, but in all probability the rate was high, especially among the Evangelical Lutherans, who emulated the Prussian model.

Muslims and Karaites

Two important non-Christian confessions—Muslims and Karaites—took a far more liberal position on divorce than did the Christian churches. Interestingly, both embraced a "modern" conception of consensual divorce—that is, dissolution through mutual consent without attributing fault to either party ("no-fault divorce" in contemporary parlance).[26] Hence, it sufficed for the couple to proclaim irreconcilable differences and irretrievable breakdown to terminate a marriage. Both groups recognized a broad set of grounds for divorce, such as adultery, childlessness, abuse, sexual incapacity, and insanity.

Significantly, however, this "liberality of divorce" was principally orchestrated in favor of the male. Although a Muslim or Karaite woman could theoretically initiate a divorce on certain grounds, disposition of the case ultimately depended on the husband. Whatever her grievances, he alone had the power to grant or deny her request. Hence, the marital laws of Muslims and Karaites were extremely patriarchal, according extraordinary power and privilege to males and effectively authorizing the husband to dissolve a marriage unilaterally.[27]

Multiconfessionality and Divorce

As the foregoing survey indicates, the Russian Empire, which delegated authority over marriage and divorce to each individual confession, tolerated an enormous variety in terms of dogma, procedure, and rates of marital dissolution, whether through divorce, annulment, or separation. To some degree, Russia was a microcosm of European practices, with state policy itself deeply informed by contemporary policies and ideologies in Western Europe. Above all, despite the liberality of certain confessions (Protestants, Muslims, and Karaites), the dominant tendency, especially in the western provinces, with large populations of Catholics and Eastern Orthodox believers, was definitely toward tighter institutional control and measures to thwart marital dissolution (in whatever form). That "pro-family" policy accorded fully with the conservative ethos of the Russian state, eager to avert the kind of social flux and moral decline that was held responsible for the French Revolution and its nineteenth-century epigones.

The foregoing has omitted one other ethnic group, important in the western provinces and, increasingly, in the cities of central Russia itself: the Jews.

Marital Dissolution in Jewish Law

In Judaism, marriage was "neither elevated . . . to the position of a sacrament" nor reduced to "a mere contract in civil law."[28] Rather, it constituted a voluntary union entailing mutual responsibilities and benefits.[29] Unencumbered by Catholic or Orthodox canon law, which sanctified marriage as a spiritual bond consecrated by God, Jewish law allowed dissolution if either or both of the spouses failed to fulfill the obligations and violated the marital contract. Nevertheless, divorce was no trivial matter, particularly if it involved a first marriage. The Jewish sages warned that "anyone who divorces his first wife, even the altar sheds tears over him, as it is said, 'you cover the altar with tears, weeping, and moaning.' But you ask, because of what? The Lord is a witness between you and the wife of your youth with whom you have broken faith."[30] Interestingly, the law was strikingly less stringent for dissolution of subsequent marriages: while a man could dissolve the first marriage only for good and sufficient reason, the law was far less exacting for successive marriages.[31]

The Husband's Prerogative

Jewish law affirmed the husband's prerogative to divorce his wife, even, under special circumstances, against her will.[32] It was not until the eleventh century, however, that a ruling attributed to Rabbi Gershom of Mayence formally abolished the husband's absolute right to divorce his wife at will. Although this practice was evidently rare during the Talmudic period, "Gershom's" teaching marked a signal innovation in Jewish law. Nevertheless, the new teaching was subject to significant qualifications in the responsa of Rabbi Meir of Rothenberg: "If he [the husband] divorced his wife against her will and she remarried, he is innocent of all blame. If he divorced his wife with her consent, and the act was declared void [e.g., because of an error in the *get*], he may give her a second divorce even against her will." In Rhineland communities a man could divorce his wife only after he had obtained "the sanction of the three communities," on pain of expulsion were he to divorce without such approval. Thus, divorce was a public matter, ensuring that "no man might be a law unto himself and proceed without official authority."[33]

Notwithstanding such Talmudic teachings, the practice in Imperial Russia was less restrictive. As the Rabbinic Commission pointed out, divorce remained essentially a private matter, a circumstance that enabled Jewish husbands to jettison their wives at will, despite "the ban of Rabbi Gershom."[34] Men also had the exclusive right to grant or deny a wife's suit for divorce. Indeed, the refusal of a capricious husband to grant a divorce, despite the irretrievable breakdown of the marriage and even separation, was one source of the tragic fate of the *agunah,* a wife who remained "anchored" and forbidden to remarry.[35]

According to two official reports by the Rabbinic Commission, Jewish law permitted the male to divorce on several grounds. One was the charge of "antenuptial sexual activity" of a wife who had claimed to be a virgin before the marriage.[36] In such cases, Jews who belonged to the priestly class of the *cohanim* were not only permitted, but sometimes *obligated* to divorce the woman in order to shield themselves from sexual impurity; others could remain married if they so chose.[37] A second ground for divorce was the husband's suspicion that his wife had committed adultery.[38] Unlike the Russian Orthodox Church, which required eyewitnesses to prove the accusations,[39] Jewish law recognized that adultery was normally secretive, and hence "there is no witness against her." As a result, strong suspicions, not eyewitnesses or proven guilt, sufficed as grounds for divorce.[40] Whereas in ancient times the unfaithful wife was subjected to the ordeal of drinking bitter water (to test her innocence) or even capital punishment, the penalty was now a humiliating divorce and a strict prohibition on her marriage to the adulterous partner.[41]

The third and most controversial ground for Jewish divorce in tsarist Russia was the husband's accusation that his wife was a *moredet,* or a rebellious wife. Much of the problem lay in the term "rebellious wife," for the language of the original law was ambiguous and vague. The text read as follows: "If a wife rebels against her husband, the [lump sum] alimony provided in her marriage contract is to be reduced seven *dinarim* a wcck."[42] The critical issue was the meaning of the word *rebel*. Some rabbinic authorities interpreted the term to include the wife's refusal to perform "the seven types household duties" specified in Jewish law.[43] Another interpretation in the *Shulhan Arukh*, the most commonly used codex of law in Eastern European Jewish society, stated that "a woman who denies her husband sexual relations is the one who is called a rebellious wife."[44] This passage recognized two motivations for the woman's rebellion. In one case, the wife issued the following statement: "I am repulsed by him and I cannot willingly have sexual relations with him."[45] Normally, the aim here was to obtain divorce and alimony, both based on cogent proof of her husband's physical shortcomings or disease. In the second case, the rebellious wife did not seek to secure divorce but to "gain certain concessions" from her husband by "causing him pain." If wives did "rebel" against their husbands in either of the foregoing ways, this rule gave the husband a broad license for divorce. Thus, the husband could easily cite a wife's brief absence from the home (e.g., to visit to her parents) to secure a divorce based on rebellion.[46] The husband also had strong material incentives for seeking to convince the rabbinic court of a purported "rebellion"; in that event, his wife forfeited rights to alimony and other financial support.

A fourth ground for divorce was childlessness—more precisely, the wife's failure to bear children after ten years of marriage. The argument was particularly cogent if the husband had no children from a previous marriage.[47] If she had had a miscarriage, the ten-year term was reckoned from the day of the miscarriage.[48] If the wife contested the husband's claim of a miscarriage, rabbinic authorities gave her word more weight: "If she had really miscarried, she herself would not have sought to acquire the reputation of a barren woman."[49]

Finally, Jewish law provided the husband with various miscellaneous grounds on which to sue for divorce. Some pertained to religious issues: in the event a wife converted to another faith or proved lax in religious observance, thereby causing him to commit transgressions against the faith, these provided due grounds for terminating the marriage. The husband could also sue for divorce if the wife proved to have concealed premarital physical defects or sexual abnormalities or if, after the marriage, she contracted an incurable disease that made intercourse impossible or dangerous.[50]

Although Jewish law provided a liberal definition of male rights for divorce, it did establish three limitations. First, some rabbinic authorities denied insanity as grounds of divorce. In essence, they argued that the husband could not deliver the bill of divorcement to an individual who was not mentally competent and therefore capable of consciously "receiving" the *get*.[51] But other authorities disagreed. Maimonides, for example, permitted divorce in such cases, arguing that the "principle that the ancient legal right of the husband [to divorce his wife] could not be abrogated."[52] As the archives in Imperial Russia indicate, Jews sometimes did dissolve marriages on grounds of insanity by securing the signatures of one hundred rabbis *(heter meah rabbanim)*.[53] The second restriction pertained to an underage wife: like the insane woman, she was deemed "too young to understand the meaning of the *get*."[54] Since child marriages were rare, however, this rule was actually of little significance in Russia. The third restriction pertained to women taken captive in war. In such instances, the husband was obliged to ransom her and could not elude his duty by divorcing her. This rule admitted no qualifications, but it was of little relevance in modern Russia. The land no longer suffered incursions from steppe peoples, and although the pogroms caused much devastation and death, prisoners were not taken. In short, the limitations on male-initiated divorce were of little significance.

The Wife's Right to Sue for Divorce

In theory, Jewish law recognized several circumstances where the woman had the right to initiate a divorce. As already pointed out, however, these "rights" were contingent on the consent of the husband, since rabbinic courts could not use coercion but, in the case of males, had to act through "persuasion and exhortation." That rule stemmed not from Jewish law but from the Russian government, which, on pain of harsh penalties, strictly forbade coercion (even expulsion from the community, let alone physical punishment). As a result, women found it increasingly difficult to secure a divorce, especially in cases of wife beating, because rabbinical courts had no legal means to enforce their will. With this reservation, however, women did have several specific grounds for seeking divorce.

One involved husbands who became repugnant because of a physical ailment or an occupation. According to the *Shulhan Arukh,* men must divorce their wives if they emitted "intolerable odors" from their mouths or noses of if they suffered leprosy (sometimes translated as boils) or a polypus. Nor need these deficiencies be postnuptial; most rabbis agreed that a wife could sue for divorce even if she knew about the conditions prior to the marriage because "knowing about [them] from a distance was not like living with them every day." In one case, the rabbis did make it mandatory for the male to divorce his wife: contraction of leprosy.[55]

A second ground for woman-initiated divorce was a husband's failure to fulfill basic marital obligations. Above all, that included his duty to provide food, raiment, and shelter. Rabbis like Solomon ben Adereth even contended that a man who had a single day's ration must give up everything necessary to support his wife.[56] In fact, failure to provide support did figure as grounds for divorce in Russia; the metrical books from Khar'kov and Vil'na, for example, listed "inadequate support" as the reason for the dissolution of a marriage.[57] To judge from the *get* that one husband sent his wife from Lugansk (a small town in western Ukraine), the couple had separated prior to the divorce for lack of material support.[58] In the event that the husband declared outright that "I will neither maintain nor support [my wife]," a woman was entitled to divorce because her domestic situation would be like "dwelling in the same basket with a serpent."[59]

A third ground on which women could demand divorce was the husband's refusal to cohabit for more than six months.[60] That rule derived from another—that conjugal duties were "the obligation of a husband toward a wife, not vice versa."[61] To be sure, rabbis sought to grant some latitude for men who spurned sexual pleasure in order to study the Torah; nevertheless, most authorities found it difficult to deny the wife's right to sexual satisfaction.[62]

Physical abuse, according to Jewish law, was a violation of the husband's obligation to honor his spouse. According to Rabbi Moses Isserles, "A man who beats his wife commits a sin, as though he had beaten his neighbor, and if he persists in his conduct, the court may castigate him and excommunicate him and place him under oath to discontinue this conduct." If an abusive husband refused to obey the court's injunction, it could require him to divorce his wife in order to demonstrate that Jewish society would not tolerate such behavior. As Rabbi Isserles noted, "It is not customary or proper for Jews to beat their wives; it is a custom of the heathen." However, like the Protestant legal code, Jewish law recognized the husband's right to "chastise" a wife moderately for subjecting him or his parents to invective and verbal abuse.[63] If neither spouse could adduce conclusive evidence in a dispute, the court was to accept the wife's version on the grounds that "all women are presumed to be law-abiding."[64] As will be seen, however, in practice that was not always the case.

A fourth ground for female divorce was male impotence; after ten years of childless marriage the wife could charge her husband with sexual impotence and demand a divorce. Although a man could also sue for divorce in such cases, the woman adduced a different argumentation. Whereas the husband could claim that the childless marriage prevented him from fulfilling the commandment of procreation (a duty ascribed only to men), the wife contended that she needed children to support her when she grew old. That claim "was elevated to . . . a quasi-right."[65]

As in the case of males, Jewish law also provided for sundry other grounds to demand a divorce. While one ground, conversion to another faith, was similar to that of the male rights to divorce, the Jewish woman could also sue for divorce if her husband committed crimes that culminated in exile to Siberia or if he led a dissolute and licentious life.[66] Interestingly, the latter grounds also applied to the Russian Orthodox majority and therefore found support in formal state law. Still, even in these cases where state law was implicitly invoked, the woman's right to sue for divorce was contingent: she first had to obtain her husband's assent before the rabbi could proceed with the formalities of dissolving their marriage.

In the real world, women's status appeared much better in law than in practice, at least in some rabbinical courts of Imperial Russia. Their disadvantage was particularly striking in the case of contested divorce, where, as will be seen, male testimony carried greater weight than did that of a woman. No less important was the impact of patriarchal bias and male networking; it was very difficult for a woman to prevail against an influential husband who enjoyed the friendship and trust of rabbinic authorities. This discrimination in formal law, compounded by the discrepancy between nominal right and everyday reality, drove increasing numbers of Jewish women to seek protection from the Russian state by petitioning to have their cases reviewed by rabbis from different geographical regions or even that the government itself intervene to correct an injustice.[67]

Seder haget: The Procedure of Divorcement

The first step for a Jewish couple seeking to divorce was to appear before a *beit-din* (rabbinical court) for a legal hearing.[68] The rabbinic authorities had the duty to review the petition and determine whether a divorce was warranted. According to the *Shulhan Arukh,* only those who were "learned in the law of marriage and divorce" could supervise a divorce proceeding; if the presiding official was not deemed competent, warned Rabbi Joseph Caro, "I am of the opinion that his acts should be declared null and void."[69] Such indeed happened. In 1873, for example, the Rabbinic Commission invalidated the divorce of Getsel Borshch from Minsk because competent religious authorities had not presided.[70] According to Jewish law, the divorce proceedings must include the presence of a scribe and two witnesses, none of whom can be related to one other or to the divorcing couple. The presiding rabbi was responsible for ensuring that the witnesses understood the proceeding, particularly in the event that they were illiterate.[71] Any Jew (save "a deaf-mute, an idiot, a slave, an idolater, an apostate, or one who openly desecrates the Sabbath") might serve as the scribe.[72] Neither the husband nor the couple's relatives were to prepare the bill of divorcement; only if there was no alternative might an exception be allowed.[73]

Compared with other religious confessions in the Russian Empire, the procedure for divorce in Judaism was unique in one major aspect: the

באחד בשבת בששה ועשריב ועשרים יום לירח אדר שנת חמשת אלפים ושש מאות ושמנים וחמש

לבריאת עולם למנין שאנו מנין כאן בראסטאוו מתא דיתבא על נהר דאן ועל נהר

טעמערניק ועל מי מעיינות אנא צבי המכונה הירש בן עזיאור זכמן דמתקרי זכ — בי

העומד היום בראסטאוו מתא דיתבא על נהר דאן ועל נהר טעמערניק ועל מי מעיינות

צביתי ברעות נפשי בדלא אניסנא ושבקית ופטרית ותרוכית ליד — זיכי ליכי אנתי

אנתתי מרים דמתקריא מערי בת אריה ליב הכהן דמתקרי ליבא ד — יהוית

אנתתי מן קדמת דנא וכדן פטרית ושבקית ותרוכי — תי ידתיכי ליכי

דיתיהווייין רשאה ושלטאה. בנפשיכי למ — הך כל ה תנסבא

לכל גבר דיתיצביייין ואנש כל א ימחא בידיכי מן יומא דנן

וכ — ל — ב ויד — די אדת מותרית לכל אדם

ודן די יהוי ליכי מנאי ספר תרוכין ואג — רית שבוקין וגט פטורין

בד — ת בדיד — ה. וישר — אכ

אליהו אהרן בן שמואל עד

אליעזר בן שניאור זל מן עד

special rule regarding the *get* (bill of divorcement). Whereas other religious groups treated the judgment of religious authorities as definitive and final, Judaism held that the divorce became valid only when the husband physically delivered the *get* (either personally or through an appointed agent) to his wife (or her agent), an act that had to be attested to by at least two eyewitnesses.[74] The *get* itself could be composed at the divorce proceeding or in the woman's absence if the witnesses could identify her. When the court concluded that reconciliation was impossible, the presiding rabbi asked the husband if he was delivering the *get* of his own free will or because of coercion. To demonstrate that he desired the divorce, the husband handed the scribe parchment, pen, and ink and in the presence of the two witnesses asked him to "write for me a bill of divorcement for my wife, so-and-so, the daughter of so-and-so."[75]

This initiated the complex procedure for preparing the text of the *get*, which had to satisfy a whole series of detailed requirements. The parchment was first cut so that its length exceeded the width; only then could preparation of the text begin. The document itself had to consist of twelve lines; the last line consisted of two smaller ones, where the witnesses were to affix their signatures.[76] The scribe had to prepare the text carefully so as to ensure that the handwriting was clear, "not crooked or confused." Each letter was to be separate, not adjoined to other letters. Erasures were absolutely forbidden, even in the case of accidental ink spots. It was also critically important that all the names be spelled correctly, even those transliterated into Hebrew. It was also customary to identify a town by the closest river so as to preclude any misunderstandings or ambiguities. Only if the written text satisfied all these requirements was it deemed valid; in the contrary case, it was null and void.

Once the ink had dried on the parchment, the witnesses were to sign the document in legible handwriting. The rabbi and witnesses were then to examine the document closely and affirm its validity; once that was done, it was given to the husband. If his wife was present, the rabbi ordered her to remove any rings and to extend her hand to receive the *get*. Then, in the presence of ten male witnesses, the husband placed the document in her hands and recited the following words: "Behold, this is your *get*; thou art divorced by it from me and thou art [hereby] permitted to marry any man." The rabbi took the bill of divorcement and tore it "lengthwise and crosswise" to indicate that the divorce had been finalized. He then warned the woman not to marry another man during the next ninety days, a waiting period intended to avert any disputes about the paternity of a newborn child. To comply with Russian state law, the divorced couple was to pay the rabbi for recording the divorce in the metrical book.

Not surprisingly, this corpus of detailed, obligatory rules afforded bountiful opportunities for one party to contest the legality of a divorce, whether because the procedure had been violated or because the *get* contained an error. The responsa literature, for example, is replete with questions about misspelled names, inkblots, improper transfer of the *get,* and so forth. When rabbinical authorities could not agree on the validity of the *get,* it sometimes fell on the Russian state to mediate the disputes. One such case, involving a couple in Kiev, occurred in 1865. Although the wife, Sara Shnaper, had duly received a bill of divorcement through her husband's agent, she claimed that it violated Jewish law on several counts.[77] First, the *get* itself contained an error: it incorrectly transcribed her father's name (as "Khaim" instead of "Khaim Khaikel"). Second, she claimed that her husband's emissary delivered the document but declined to read it to her or to recite the requisite words, purportedly because it had not been written in accordance with the law. Finally, she complained that her husband made no arrangements to provide material support for her and their six-year old daughter. In response to the wife's complaint, Rabbi Tsukerman (the state rabbi of Kiev) immediately consulted with several religious authorities from neighboring towns. They noted that although the name "Khaikel" was a nickname, the wife's father had always signed his name "Khaim Khaikel" and was even called up to the Torah reading in the synagogue by the two names. If people used only "Khaim," it was not clear to whom they were referring. Hence, they concluded, the *get,* which failed to include both of her father's names, was invalid. Thereupon Rabbi Tsukerman duly apprised the husband that his divorce was void. To his surprise, however, the husband spurned the admonition and proceeded to remarry a woman from Berdichev.

For his part, Iankel Shnaper explained that his wife had agreed to a divorce because of his "hostile attitudes" toward her. Because the state rabbi Tsukerman could not supervise the proceedings (due to his wife's funeral), he had commissioned the spiritual rabbi Khaskel to preside. According to the husband, his wife did not want to wait for the scribe to finish preparing the final document; hence, he remained behind to ensure that everything be done properly. He denied that the *get* contained errors; if the scribe had written only "Khaim" rather than "Khaim Khaikel," it was because they were identical, "Khaikel" serving only as an affectionate nickname. In addition, Shnaper declared that he had in fact provided for his wife by establishing a tavern for her in Kiev. Naturally, the husband had no written evidence to substantiate his claims. Shnaper's agent supported his testimony but did not deny that only "Khaim" had appeared on the *get.*

Because Jewish rabbis could not agree on the validity of the *get,* the governor of Kiev sent the case to the Rabbinic Commission in St. Petersburg for final disposition. Here the husband's side prevailed. Speaking on behalf of the Rabbinical Commission, Dr. Neiman (Neumann) overruled the Kiev state rabbi and declared that a bill of divorcement was defective only if the name was completely changed. "Taking into consideration that Khaikel is not a special name but identical with Khaim, the name of the plaintiff's father," the commission concluded that "the absence of this name . . . cannot be considered a violation."

The Shnaper case was only one of countless disputes over the validity of the divorce procedure and bill of divorcement. A defective *get* and botched divorce could have devastating consequences for women; it could "anchor" them in eternal solitude (the plight of the *agunah*), denying legitimacy to any children from a second marriage, and could lead to a conviction and prison sentence for committing bigamy (i.e., remarriage without a legal divorce). With good reason, *Shulhan Arukh* warned that only those well versed in Jewish law should supervise a divorce proceeding: "It is easy for a man to err therein, and it would result in invalidating the proceeding and in bastardizing children, and may the Rock of Israel save us from all error."[78]

David Amram once suggested that the complex procedure of divorce "acted as a check on the theoretically unrestricted right of the husband to divorce his wife at his pleasure."[79] But to what extent did it prevent hasty divorces in Russia? How did the relatively liberal grounds for divorce, especially for men and for couples who mutually agreed to dissolve their marriage, affect the frequency of divorce in Russia? Although many factors determine divorce rates, a liberal divorce law could certainly play a major role, especially when compared to the huge impediments placed by most other confessions. That is all the more true when, as argued in the previous chapter, the creation of a new state rabbinate created rich new opportunities for abuse.

The Demographics of Divorce

In his encyclopedic history of divorce, Roderick Phillips observes that "divorce on any significant scale must be treated as a recent phenomenon, a characteristic of little more than the past century."[80] While that generalization may be true for twentieth-century Europe and the United States, it does not apply to the Jews of Imperial Russia: in the nineteenth century, they already reported astonishingly high, "modern" rates of divorce. Still more interesting, the Jews followed a pattern that was diametrically opposed to the dominant tendency in Europe—a steady, inexorable increase in the rate of marital dissolution. Instead, the Jews showed the *contrary* tendency with modernization: from astronomically high divorce rates in the early nineteenth century, they demonstrated a striking tendency to *reduce,* not increase, the divorce rate in the late nineteenth and early twentieth centuries.

It should be emphasized, however, that quantification of Jewish divorce rates is fraught with enormous difficulties and perils; state records on Jews were neither accurate nor complete. First, the Russian government compiled its statistics from the divorce registers of the state rabbis. Such records, however, were replete with inaccuracies and marked by a pronounced tendency toward underestimation, reflecting the Jews' general aversion to such state records, which, inevitably, were used for conscription, tax, and other purposes. Likewise, Jews had strong disincentives for recording marital age accurately in the case of underage marriages, performed in contravention of state law on minimum marital age (eighteen for males, sixteen for females). Although such illegalities were evidently decreasing, they impelled Jews to falsify the ages or even not report the marriage at all. Second, the government compiled data only on selected provinces; it often neglected sizable Jewish populations (e.g., in Kovno, Volhynia, Kherson, Ekaterinoslav, and Tavrida). Hence, global statistics for *all* Jews are nonexistent until the first all-Russian census of 1897, which in fact did assemble data on marriage and divorce for Jews all across the Empire. Moreover, the state did not even begin to assemble general data until 1857. Marital patterns, including divorce, going back before the mid-nineteenth century are hard to establish given the paucity of records (save for exceptions such as Vil'na). Nor is it feasible to reconstruct aggregate data from the extant metrical books; even in the best local repositories, only scattered and broken runs have survived. While these are useful and contain important information, they do not suffice for purposes of family reconstitution.

Nevertheless, important sets of data have been preserved and, in some cases, aggregated. Thus, the state did assemble comprehensive data on Jewish divorce for some provinces in selected years (1856–1858, 1860–1867, 1869, 1897, and 1901). While far from comprehensive, they cover a broad spectrum, temporally and spatially, to give an instructive statistical picture of Jewish marriage and divorce. To complement these general statistics, this study draws on records from the metrical books of Vil'na, Korostyshev (Kiev province), and Khar'kov. Although it cannot be claimed that these are typical of Jews throughout the empire, the records provide a valuable grass-roots picture of Jewish life in an important mitnagdic center, a small Ukrainian town, and the sixth largest city in the empire. Taken together, this corpus of aggregate data and local metrical records make it possible to analyze the demographic patterns of Jewish divorce—that is, to map the absolute numbers and rates of divorce, the age and social status of those who divorced, the duration of their marriages, and geographic distribution. Moreover, they reveal differences between mitnagdic and Hasidic patterns of marital dissolution, at least as presented in the data.

The Divorce Rate

In the nineteenth century, Jews had the highest rate of divorce among all the religious confessions in the Russian Empire, but that gap began to close by the early twentieth century, partly because the divorce rate of non-Jews (especially Orthodox) increased sharply but also because divorce among Jews declined.[81] This section will examine the huge initial difference in the first half of the nineteenth century and the remarkable turnaround in the late nineteenth and early twentieth centuries.

DATA FOR 1837–1853 (VIL'NA)

The earliest data in this study come from the Vil'na metrical books of divorce, which are extraordinarily detailed. A survey of Jewish divorce between 1837 and 1853 shows fluctuations from year to year but an overall rate that was high even by modern standards (see table 3.1). To take the first full set of data (for October 1837 to December 1838), Jews reported 133 divorces against 158 marriages—an astonishing rate of 841.8 divorces per 1,000 marriages.[82] Even that extraordinary rate was exceeded in 1845, when the state rabbi recorded 107 divorces against 98 marriages (a rate of 1,091.8 divorces per 1,000 marriages).[83] Although the divorce rate dropped to 549.5 divorces per 1,000 marriages in 1853, even that rate was positively astronomic compared to that of the Russian Orthodox population, where, for example, in 1848 the divorce rate was 0.05 divorces per 1,000 marriages, 31 divorces against 595,426 marriages.[84]

TABLE 3.1

Jewish Divorces and Marriages in Vil'na, 1837–1853

Year	Number of divorces	Number of marriages	Divorces per 1000 marriages
1837–38	133	158	841.8
1844	88	157	560.5
1845	107	98	1091.8
1846	62	120	516.7
1851	48	124	387.1
1852	32	92	347.8
1853	50	91	549.5

Source: LVIA, f. 728, op. 2, dd. 6, 27, 28; op. 3. dd. 6, 8.

The first question is whether these data represent a statistical anomaly—that is, a "spike" due to some transient, accidental factors. It is unlikely that these figures were inflated or forged by the state rabbi, who meticulously recorded each divorce (including the names of the couple, their ages, grounds for divorce, the authority who issued the *get*, and the eyewitnesses). Although the records may have included some "out-of-town" Jews who came to Vil'na for a divorce hearing, these must have been quite rare, given the costs of travel and state laws mandating registration in the hometown. Although in exceptional cases (often those with dubious legality) some Jews did seek to arrange a divorce away from home, that whole procedure was not only expensive but also invited litigation and invalidation. No less important is the fact that the divorce rate remained consistently high throughout this period (1837–1853). Despite some annual fluctuations, divorce was ubiquitous and a common feature of Jewish life.

Not only numbers but narratives sustain this picture of a high rate of divorce. Thus, Mordechai Aaron Guenzburg, who began his autobiography, *Aviezer*, in 1828, flatly declares that every Jewish woman was married at least twice because of frequent divorces.[85] A *maskil*, Yehudah Shereshevskii, similarly confirms these divorce patterns in Vil'na in his commentary *Kur lozahav* (1858). In reference to an aggadic statement about the difficulty of obtaining divorces (Baba Batra 22a, Babylonian Talmud), he writes: "This statement shall remove from us the embarrassment that many have thought about us—that divorce is a small and light matter for us Jews." Shereshevskii goes on to explain that although the Torah permitted divorce, the Sages made it difficult and even discouraged it. "Inasmuch as you can change one's nature by force," he added, "divorce is considered in itself a strange thing, and every person who walks righteously will distance himself from it."[86]

The available evidence, significantly, suggests that these high divorce rates reflected a long-standing, even centuries-old pattern of marital dissolution, not some peculiar aberration induced by the Jewish experience under tsarist rule. Apart from the fact that the tsarist regime had but limited control or even influence in the Jewish community, marital breakdown antedated the Polish partitions and the Jews' absorption into the Russian Empire. At least, such has been the principal finding in the historical scholarship. Israel Yuval has shown, for example, that divorce and remarriage were common and evidently provided a lucrative business for local rabbis in fifteenth-century Germany.[87] Indeed, that very frequency inspired the jeremiads by Rabbi Seligmann Bing (c. 1395–1491) against the proliferation of divorce, indicating that the "traditional" institution of marriage was not anchored in granite and indeed was far more vulnerable and fragile than previously imagined.

At the same time, principally as a foil to familial problems in their own society, some non-Jewish writers constructed highly positive, idealized images of the "Jewish family." Indeed, for some in eighteenth-century Poland, the Jewish family represented the very ideal model of marriage.[88] As the prominent member of the Polish enlightenment, Stanislaw Staszic (1755–1826) wrote in his *Ród ludzki* (The human race): "[E]ven now, among these few remaining, wandering Jews, . . . we find certain relationships closely linked to serenity, family happiness, the real aspirations of marriage and the value of national customs."[89] Although Staszic himself earned notoriety for a vehement anti-Jewish position at the Four Years Sejm (1789), just three years earlier, he now expressed his admiration for the "virtues of Jewish marriage." Such declarations, however, represented less an informed description of Jewish life than a widespread literary trope—to castigate coreligionists (in this case, Polish Catholics) for a growing problem of marital breakdown by contrasting them to the marital stability prevailing "even" among the Jews.[90]

That is why, such idyllic descriptions notwithstanding, sources on pre-partition Poland indicate a rise in illicit sexual relations (i.e., premarital sex and adultery), abandoned wives, and other domestic problems.[91] Goldberg attributes these changing mores to socioeconomic changes in Polish-Jewish life, especially the frequent travel undertaken by men for study or trade. Given the lack of statistics on divorce for this period, however, it is difficult to quantify the problem of marital dissolution.

Whatever the underlying dynamics and degree of severity, the problem of marital dissolution clearly persisted after the partitions and the inclusion of a large Jewish population in the Russian Empire. Perhaps the most striking, even sensational, evidence of family conflict comes from the "conscience court" *(sovestnyi sud),* that new institution established by Catherine the Great and charged with handling such as issues as family strife and sexual behavior. Apart from some sensational matters like infanticide,[92] the conscience court was busy mediating family conflicts, often in matters involving finances and personal honor. Apart from acute conflict over inheritance and various other family conflicts, the conscience court sometimes dealt with the problem of marital breakdown. In one case, for example, Mordukh Bershtel sued his widowed mother, Pesia, in 1853 for failing to pay a promissory note that she had allegedly given to him as a wedding present. But as the merchant Girsh Kliachko (who drew up the contract) testified, the parents had given their son the monetary gift on the condition that he stay married to his wife, Sora Gershonova, who hailed from a respectable family. However, a few weeks later he nevertheless divorced her (without their consent or knowledge) and remarried; he soon divorced the second wife and remarried yet again. The mother admitted that "I spoiled him" against his father's wishes.

Although her son had studied an honorable trade, she asserted, he was lazy and preferred to "hang out on the street."[93]

These files from the conscience court suggest that high rates of marital dissolution in Vil'na were only part of a broader "crisis of the family." At the same time, it should be noted that some grounds for marital dissolution in 1837–1838, such as childlessness (10.5 percent of divorces), wife beating (11.3 percent), and a husband's illness (7.5 percent) were obviously not new to Jewish life (see table 3.2) and had deep roots in Jewish law and earlier experience.[94]

TABLE 3.2

Grounds for Jewish Divorces in Vil'na, 1837–1838

Grounds (as recorded in Russian)	Number
Childlessness	14
Husband's illness	7
Husband's illness and inability to have children	2
Husband's illness and inability to live together	1
Wife's illness	10
Wife's illness prior to marriage	2
Mutual desire to divorce	2
They do not love each other	26
He did not like her	1
She did not like him	1
Inability to live together	3
He cursed her parents	1
She cursed his parents	4
She cursed him	2
He behaved indecently	1
He cannot support her	32
Promiscuity of the wife	2
Halitsah	2
Husband was recruited into the military	3
He beat her	15
She could not live with her stepchildren	1
A religious prohibition prevents him from having sexual relations	1
Total	133

Source: LVIA, f. 728, op. 2, d. 6, 1837–38.

While the continuities between pre- and post-partition times clearly dominate, there may be some reason to suppose that the rate of marital breakdown nonetheless did rise. That inference is suggested by the reasons adduced for divorce, as indicated in tables 3.2 and 3.3. Thus, a substantial number of divorces reflected harsh economic realities, such as the husband's inability to support his wife (24.1 percent in 1837–38 and 30.8 percent in 1844), as well as changing marital expectations, such as "the lack of love between them" (19.5 percent and 23.4 percent respectively). While Jews may have divorced for these reasons earlier, such factors appear to have gained in significance with changes in economic conditions and cultural values. Thus, the economic displacement of Jews from traditional occupations (e.g., the liquor industry, leasing, and petty trade) in the first half of the nineteenth century, due to government restrictions and changing markets, intensified pauperization among the lower strata of Jewish society. As Michael Stanislawski has argued, the economic life of Jews in 1825 "was unhealthy but viable," but by 1855 "the disease had metastasized to the point where only radical new cures could prevent utter disaster."[95] Little wonder that divorces for insufficient livelihoods constituted such a large proportion of Jewish divorces in Vil'na.

TABLE 3.3

Grounds for Jewish Divorces in Vil'na, 1845

Grounds (as recorded in Russian)	Number
Childlessness	9
Husband's illness	3
Wife's illness	5
They do not like each other	25
No means of livelihood	33
Halitsah	4
Husband was recruited into the military	1
He beat her	4
She could not live with her stepchildren	15
He does not want to live with her children from the first marriage	1
The wife does not want to move with the husband or wait for him to return home	3
He intends to convert to Christianity	2
He violated Jewish laws	1
She has become crippled	1
Total	107

Source: LVIA, f. 728, op. 2, d. 27 (1845).

In short, the divorce rate among Jews was exceedingly high, reflecting long-term continuities but also, no doubt, the impact of economic stress and the intrusion of new sensibilities and values, however slight. Significantly, the frequency remained high despite some countervailing forces, above all, the declining capacity of rabbinical authorities to enforce their decisions, especially in suits initiated by women, thereby making such appeals less effective and less appealing.[96] Notwithstanding that factor, the Jewish metrica reveal an extraordinarily high rate of marital dissolution, especially when compared with people belonging to the other confessions in Imperial Russia.

DATA FROM 1857–1869

As in so many other spheres, from midcentury the data gradually become more complete and verifiable. A large set of data in 1857 omitted some important Jewish communities in the Pale of Settlement, but it does encompass sixteen Russian provinces and confirms that the rate of marital dissolution was still high (if less astronomic than the Vil'na data from the 1830s and 1840s).[97] In absolute numbers, Jewish records show 1,734 divorces (against 11,773 marriages); that represents 147.3 divorces per 1,000 marriages among 1,046,136 Jewish residents (see Appendix, table A.9). Significantly, the 1857 data are remarkably similar to those reported in 1860, namely, 145.2 (with 1,708 divorces against 11,762 marriages).[98] The 1860 data, moreover, are far more comprehensive, providing information on Jewish communities in twenty Russian provinces and thus representing the most complete picture of Jewish divorces in tsarist Russia before the onset of the Great Reforms.[99]

Though lower than the previous decades, the figures for 1857 and 1860 were nonetheless high, especially when compared with those of the Russian Orthodox or indeed other populations in contemporary Europe. That is a divorce rate 1,472 times higher than in the case of the Russian Orthodox Church which reported only 54 divorces against 563,599 marriages in 1858, a divorce rate of 0.1 per 1,000 marriages.[100] In Sweden, Belgium, England, and Wales, the absolute number of divorces did not increase to such levels until well after 1910. The only Western country that had a higher absolute number of divorces than did the Jews of Russia in 1860 was the United States, which had 7,380 divorces—a rate of 1.2 divorces per 1,000 existing marriages.[101]

The highest incidence of marital dissolution was in the southwestern provinces of Bessarabia and Kiev, particularly in the large Jewish social and economic centers, and in these areas steep divorce rates persisted throughout the nineteenth century. For example, S. Y. Abramovich's "Glupsk" (a Russian word connoting stupidity), better known as Berdichev, with a total Jewish population of 42,141, reported 151 divorces to

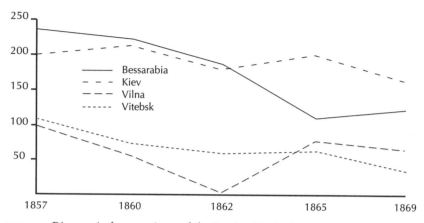

FIG. 3.1. Divorces in four provinces of the Russian Empire (per 1000 marriages, 1857–1869. *Source:* RGIA f, 821, op. 8, dd. 479, 484, 487, 490, 492.

376 marriages—a divorce rate of 401.6 divorces per 1,000 marriages, or nearly three times the Jewish average in the empire as a whole. The divorce rate for Jews in Kishenev was still higher— 412 (with 103 divorces against 250 marriages). By contrast, Jews in northwestern cities had a significantly lower rate of marital dissolution. Vil'na, for example, reported only 36 divorces to 246 marriages, a divorce rate of 146.3, although this rate also began to rise in the mid-1860s, presumably under the impact of the Great Reforms.[102] A survey of the divorce rates for a thirteen-year period between 1857 and 1869 in the southwestern provinces of Bessarabia and Kiev and the northwestern provinces of Vil'na and Vitebsk, as shown in Figure 3.1, indicates the striking geographic differences.[103]

These statistics indicate not only a high frequency of divorce but also substantial regional differentials. Although the issue is a complex one, some tentative explanations can be suggested. One obvious factor was religious and cultural differences, above all, the famous difference between Hasidim in the south and *mitnagdim* in the north. Although the latter also experienced family strains (since devotion to Torah study could lead to a neglect of family responsibilities), some contemporaries have argued that the Hasidim were even more prone to family conflict. Immanuel Etkes, for example, contends that marital breakdown in the south was due to the "intense and intimate bond between the Hasid and the *tsaddik* [that] weakened the Hasid's responsibility to his family."[104]

Attitudes toward divorce in official "rabbinic" circles was a further factor. State rabbis in the southwest, particularly in the "new areas of settlement," proved considerably less averse to granting a divorce, especially when initiated by men. Indeed, as we have seen in the preceding chapter, officials like Rabbi Kagan of Kherson actually encouraged divorces in order to earn extra income. By contrast, state rabbis in the north were better versed in Jewish law and less inclined to grant divorce on demand, especially in contravention of rabbinic law. Also, the rabbinical disinclination to grant divorce coincided with social realities: the financial question made divorce far more difficult in the north, where the *ketubah* was 58 percent higher than in the south (76 silver rubles in the north compared to 48 silver rubles in the south). While that may have reflected some differences in the cost of living, it nonetheless posed a substantial deterrent, especially for the poor of the Jewish underclass.[105]

Interestingly, urbanization, often associated with high divorce rates, was *not* a factor at midcentury. That certainly runs contrary to the general pattern, not only in Western Europe but also in the Russian Empire, whereby divorce rates correlate closely with levels of urbanization, with the highest rates in urban areas and the lowest in the countryside. In the case of non-Jews, the higher divorce rate for urban inhabitants reflected such factors as higher mobility, anomie (weakening community control and norms), easier access to legal advice and courts, independent employment opportunities for women, and the impact of secular values and attitudes. In the case of Jews in the Russian Empire, however, the relationship between urbanization and divorce rates was actually inverse: frequency was higher among Jews in the southwest (where only 38 percent resided in cities) than in the northwest (where 58 percent were city-dwellers).[106] Finally, registration may have been more lax in Vil'na province, where official attitudes toward record keeping were not as vigilant as in the Ukrainian provinces.

Although the question of regional patterns is complex and may even reflect discrepancies in recording divorces,[107] the difference between the northern and southwestern provinces formed a striking contrast in Jewish culture and family life.

DATA FOR 1870–1914

The Ministry of the Interior ceased to assemble data on Jewish divorces in 1869; hence, for the subsequent period (1870–1914) it is necessary to rely upon samples from metrical books—above all, the relatively well preserved metrica from Korostyshev, Khar'kov, and Vil'na. These three cases represent very different kinds of Jewish communities. Korostyshev, a small Hasidic town in the province of Kiev, was a typical southwestern Jewish shtetl. It had two artisans' prayer houses for shoemakers and tailors, the local *beit-hamidrash* (the house of study), the Ruzhin *kloyz* (house of worship), the Twerskii *beit-hamidrash,* and two synagogues.[108] As noted earlier, marriages in Korostyshev were highly endogamous and linked many of the residents into broad kinship networks. By contrast, the city of Khar'kov lay outside the Pale of Settlement and had a distinctive population of Jewish merchants, students, and soldiers. It was the location of the spectacular commercial fairs, thriving markets, army garrisons, and the famous Imperial Kharkov University. Vil'na, better known as the "Jerusalem of Lithuania," was the cultural and spiritual center of the *mitnagdim*. It also became the locus of the radical working-class movement in the late nineteenth century, in which impoverished artisans, small traders, and factory workers dominated the population. In a word, these three cities represented three different microcosms of Jewish society, economy, and culture.

Until the late 1890s the divorce rate in Korostyshev and Khar'kov remained relatively high. Korostyshev usually reported between eight and fourteen divorces and twenty-one to thirty-three marriages per year.[109] In 1872, for example, there were twenty-nine marriages and twelve divorces, a rate of 413.8 divorces per 1,000 marriages. The rate among Jews in Khar'kov was slightly lower—approximately thirteen to sixteen divorces against some thirty-five to fifty-four marriages per year.[110] To be sure, some years were anomalous; 1881, the same year that Alexander II was assassinated, both communities registered an unusually low number of divorces (only nine divorces and fifty-four marriages in Khar'kov and five divorces and twenty-two marriages in Korostyshev). Although the divorce rate steadily declined in the 1880s and 1890s, a far more radical shift took place after the turn of the century. For example, the Jews of Korostyshev registered only 1 divorce and 48 marriages in 1900; the Khar'kov community reported 12 divorces and 108 marriages the following year. Although these later showed some upward fluctuation (in 1910 there were 2 divorces against 15 marriages in Korostyshev and 22 divorces against 182 marriages in Khar'kov),[111] the rate nonetheless remained exceedingly low, especially when compared with the mid-nineteenth century. Moreover, the per capita divorce rate (divorces per 1,000 inhabitants) showed an even more striking decline, given the general population increase.

In Vil'na, the divorce rate, which had already leveled off at midcentury, remained relatively low in the following decades. Thus, in 1870, Vil'na reported only 39 divorces to 247 marriages in 1870 (a rate of 157.9 divorces per 1,000 marriages),[112] and in 1881 it recorded a drop in the absolute number of divorces *and* marriages (27 divorces against 175 marriages), but the divorce rate remained essentially constant (154.3 per 1,000).[113] The next year showed a sharp increase (to 285.1 per 1,000), perhaps because the political tumult of 1881 caused temporary delays or perhaps because of the economic dilemmas caused by the May Laws of 1882 (which restricted Jewish commerce on Sundays and

Christian holidays, the right to lease real estate in rural areas, and the registration of property and mortgages).[114] The divorce rate remained slightly elevated in the 1890s (e.g., 184.1 divorces per 1,000 marriages in 1896), but this level was nonetheless considerably lower than in the first half of the nineteenth century, especially if measured in per capita terms. By the turn of the century, rates in Vil'na began falling again: by 1901 the metrica show 96 divorces to 620 marriages (a rate of 154.8) for a total population of 80,266, or 1.2 divorces per 1,000 of the Jewish inhabitants.[115]

It is, of course, essential to make the usual caveats about three case studies: as concrete as they may be, they *may* not be representative. That typicality could be established only on the basis of broad statistical runs or full sets of reliable metrical books from other communities. Unfortunately, the state did not assemble long-time series; although it did begin to assemble vital statistics for Jewish communities in Lifland, Enesei, and Vil'na, it did not compile information on divorce. The most comprehensive imperial data on vital statistics are in the 1897 census; although this does show a high proportion of divorced Jews, it is a snapshot at a particular point in time, with no indication of temporal dynamics. Still, for the long series in two very different Jewish communities (Korostyshev and Khar'kov), the data clearly demonstrate a gradual decline in divorces in the 1880s and 1890s, followed by steep decrease after the turn of the century.[116] In Vil'na there was a slight rise in the 1880s and 1890s, followed by a decline, as in the Ukrainian towns.

That pattern is all the more striking when compared with the non-Jewish population in the Russian Empire. Despite opposition from the Orthodox church, which resisted attempts by the state to secularize marriage and to liberalize divorce, even ecclesiastical authorities gradually acceded to the growing demand for less restrictive policies. Thus, the number of divorces among Russian Orthodox jumped from 58 in the 1850s to 1,171 in 1900 (a divorce rate of 1.41) and more than tripled over the next fourteen years, rising to 3,714 divorces in 1914 (a divorce rate of 4.20).[117] At work were a host of factors: urbanization, secularization, new job opportunities for men and women (often away from home), better legal advice, and the growing reluctance of nervous clergy to antagonize their parishioners. The sharp increase in divorce among the Russian Orthodox population may have also reflected the de facto recognition of separations, with the easing of restrictions by the church. As in Western Europe, divorce rates soared, along with growing fears about the very survival of the traditional family.

The anomalous decrease in Jewish divorce rates probably reflected a variety of factors. In part, it may have resulted from the sharp rise in the age of first marriage for both sexes. As we shall see, it was mainly the youthful who divorced, often within the first five years of marriage. It also may have reflected growing ethnic identity, as evidenced by the growing Zionist movement[118] and a desire to buttress traditional bonds of family and community. That was all the more urgent in the face of threats from without (both popular and official antisemitism) and from within (secularization and acculturation). The falling divorce rate also resulted from a decline in rabbinical authority, making it more difficult for women to obtain a divorce from recalcitrant husbands for abuse and other reasons. Moreover, as the metrical books of Vil'na indicate, divorces on traditional grounds, such as childlessness, began to decrease, perhaps an indication that "love" or marital compatibility took precedence over the religious duty of the procreation. "Compassionate" divorces—granted by sick husbands without children or military conscripts who did not want to leave their wives as *agunot* in the event of their death or disappearance—also declined. The difficulty of paying the financial settlement no doubt also served as a deterrent against hasty divorces. As women increasingly turned to the state courts to settle their claims (i.e., to enforce payments), husbands may have become more reluctant to embark on marital dissolution. Finally, the processes of "modernization" may have contributed to the cultural and religious aversion to marital dissolution. As early as the 1850s, individuals like Yehudah Edel Shereshevskii denounced high divorce rates as a source of "embarrassment" for the Jews. By the late nineteenth century, Orthodox rabbis also began to advocate the preservation of the family as a bulwark against the inroads of assimilation and political "unreliability." As we shall discuss in the final chapter, they sought to convince the Russian state to grant them authority to instill traditional family values in the youth, thereby weaning them away from the "harmful" revolutionary movements.

To some degree, the official data showing a decline in divorce may be slightly misleading: they record the behavior only of those who remained in the Jewish community, not those who emigrated nor those who converted to another confession. Both paths, emigration and conversion, short-circuited the traditional need for a divorce procedure; they permitted spouses (especially men) simply to restart their lives and families, never bothering with the costs, aggravation, and risks of a legal divorce. In turn, such large-scale desertion led to a serious *agunah* problem, as husbands simply abandoned their wives without a divorce and emigrated to the United States or other foreign countries. In other words, Jews most affected by the modernizing processes—cultural change, mobility, and the like—were more likely to leave the traditional Jewish community, simply ceasing to figure in metrical books, their change in family status going unrecorded.

That qualification notwithstanding, in the second half of the nineteenth century the Jewish divorce rate did decline from the high levels in the pre-reform era, in striking contrast to the rest of the Russian Empire and Western Europe.

Age at Divorce and Remarriage

Among the Jews it was primarily the youthful who divorced. According to the metrical books of Korostyshev for 1854–1912, a majority (54.2 percent) of the men and women who divorced were under age 30. More precisely, 31.7 percent were between the ages of twenty-one and twenty-five, and another 22.5 percent were between twenty-six and thirty.[119] Although the data do not indicate how long the divorcing couple had been married, the statistics on the age at first marriage (see Appendix, table A.8) indicated that the divorcing couple had been married, at most, five to ten years, if not less. This early divorce age suggests the impact of Jewish law and rabbinical practice, which made possible a relatively prompt divorce—in contrast to the incredible procrastination of the Russian Orthodox church, which required years, even decades, before it finally approved and finalized marital dissolution.

The data from Khar'kov are similar, if somewhat less dramatic. For the period 1870–1915, the metrical books show that 25.9 percent of Jewish women and 12.8 percent of men divorced between the ages of twenty-one and twenty-five; another 23.3 percent of the women and 24.9 percent of the men divorced between the ages of twenty-six and thirty.[120] In other words, 49.1 percent of Jewish women were divorced between the ages of twenty-one and thirty, indicating that marital breakdown and formal dissolution occurred within the first ten years of marriage. As in the case of Korostyshev, the divorce records do not indicate length of marriage, but the data on marital age again indicate that divorce for most came after just a few years of marriage. Somewhat anomalous is the low proportion of men aged twenty-one to twenty-five in the divorce records, but this probably reflects the tendency for men to marry at an older age. Similarly, males tended to dominate among those who divorced after age forty (see Appendix, table A.20), presumably reflecting both their older age at marriage and, especially, the higher probability for remarriage and multiple divorces. The oldest to divorce in these records was Leizer Mordko Binovich of Korostyshev, who, at the ripe old age of eighty-six, terminated his marriage with a thirty-five-year-old wife in 1895.[121]

Similar patterns of divorce can be found for Vil'na, where 65 percent of women and 45 percent of men divorced by the time they were twenty-five years or younger in 1837–1838 (see Appendix, table A.25). In fact, the majority of these spouses were in their teens or early twenties. This meant that their marriages usually lasted between one and five years, given that the average age of first marriage during the same period was 18 for women and 19.8 for men.[122] By 1860 the largest proportion of women who divorced were under twenty-five years old (47.5 percent); for men it was between thirty-one and forty years (39.0 percent). The latter reflected the higher mean age at first marriage among men (24.2) compared with that for women (20.6). As in the Ukrainian towns, more men than women divorced when they were over forty years old, mainly on the grounds that they could not support their younger wives.

Although the state records do not show how quickly or how often Jews remarried, they do indicate strong gender differences. Significantly fewer women than men remarried; in 1867, for example, only 3.7 percent of women entered into a second marriage, compared with 10.8 percent for men. This difference persisted in later years. Thus, remarriage rates for women remained lower in 1885 (2.9 percent for women and 8.9 percent for men) and in 1910 (2.4 percent for women and 8.2 percent for men).[123] The discrepancy also was apparent in the 1897 census, which reported a far larger number of divorcées (12,589) than divorced men (3,975).[124] Similarly, the census showed that the number of widows (155,729) was several times that of men (44,969); while that may partly reflect different life expectancies, it also reflected a lower rate of remarriage among women. The differential can probably be ascribed to a variety of factors, including the disinclination of men to marry widows or divorcees with children (given the added financial burden of providing dowries and support), as well as preference for younger women, whether for physical appearance, greater fertility, or stronger economic partnership.

Causes of Marital Breakdown: Models and Sources

Historians have interpreted the relationship between marriage and divorce in two main ways. The traditional school sees "marriage breakdown and divorce as [simultaneously] rising over time so that divorce trends reflect trends in marriage breakdown." The second theory, dominant in recent historiography, holds that marital breakdown is fairly constant, but the divorce rate has risen so that it "more closely resembles the rate of marriage breakdown in society." In other words, it was not a sudden explosion in marital dissolution but greater accessibility and acceptability of divorce, because of changes in law, society, economy, and culture, that "permitted more broken marriages to be dissolved by divorce."[125]

The Russian-Jewish experience defies both models. Above all, the statistical curve of divorce directly contravenes the linear projection of a steady increase in the divorce rate.[126] Throughout the imperial period, Jews, especially men, could obtain a divorce with relative ease, with no need to dismantle the impediments that faced Christians. Rather, a more accurate model for Jewish divorces in tsarist Russia charts a growing *discrepancy,* not congruency, between marital breakdown and the divorce rate. In a word, a host of obstacles—legal, financial, social—made it increasingly difficult, even undesirable, to seek the formal dissolution of a marriage. This was particularly true for Jewish women and not simply because Jewish law recognized the husband's unilateral prerogative to dissolve the marriage. More important was the breakdown of rabbinical control over those broad rights that had previously served to protect women. As will be seen, Jews also chose marital separation over legal divorce to avoid confrontations with state authorities over residence rights and social status.

Archival Sources on Marital Breakdown

There are four principal archival sources that shed light on the causes of marital dissolution and help to explain why people embarked on the costly, painful, and sometimes humiliating path and how they presented their suits. One major source consists of the 104 cases reviewed by the Rabbinic Commission between 1852 and 1910. Of these, eighty-one cases pertained directly to problems of marriage and divorce. Twenty-one were brought forth by the state (in response to queries from provincial governors, state courts, and the like); another seven emanated from local state rabbis seeking elucidation on how to apply Jewish law to various divorce cases. The remaining fifty-three cases were filed by individual Jews throughout the Russian Empire; thirty-six were initiated by Jewish women, fifteen by men, and two by both spouses. Given the fact that only a small percentage of petitions survived the red tape of the Russian bureaucracy and reached their intended destination, the actual numbers of appeals filed at lower echelons remains unknown.[127]

The second source comprises petitions by Jewish women to His Imperial Majesty's Chancellery for the Receipt of Petitions (henceforth, the Imperial Chancellery). Established in May 1884,[128] this imperial office began to grant women separate passports in "exceptional cases of abuse and neglect," circumventing state laws that denied wives the right to reside apart from their husbands or gain employment without their permission. In the late nineteenth century the number of petitions seeking legal separation rose dramatically, more than doubling between 1881 and

1896 (from approximately 1,500 to 3,469 per year).[129] The majority of requests originated from the wives of peasants and unprivileged urban estates (80 percent), while the petitions from privileged groups, such as the wives of the nobility and servicemen, constituted only 12 percent; from honorary citizens and merchants, 4 percent; and from *raznochintsy* (people of various ranks), 4 percent. Although these figures are not proportionate to the general population (with the nobility strongly overrepresented and the peasantry underrepresented), the data do show a significant democratization; the great majority stem indeed from the underclass, not elites, even if not in exact proportion to their share of the population. The motive of women for seeking legal separation varied; some could not obtain a formal divorce, whereas others wanted to retain their social, residential, and legal rights (based on the husband's status)[130] but be free from reciprocal conjugal obligations.

The third major source consists of the court records from Vil'na and Zhitomir, as well as petitions to various administrative officials (i.e., the general governor and police). These fascinating files afford a rare glimpse into everyday Jewish domestic life as portrayed by spouses, relatives, neighbors, officials, and rabbinic authorities. Incidental but revealing information also appears even in files that seem to have no direct relation to marital questions.

Finally, metrical books of divorce contain data on the cause of divorce. Although the state rabbi often recorded a standard formula ("by mutual agreement" or "mutual hatred"), such was not always the case. Thus, until the 1850s the metrical books of Vil'na provided fairly detailed reasons for divorce, allowing for a limited quantitative assessment of marital breakdown. While the standardized phrases (e.g., "she could not live with her stepchildren" or "they did not have any children") do not provide the story behind each entry, nonetheless, when combined with other sources, they do indicate a broad palette of complaints voiced by husbands and wives.

To be sure, these sources must be used with due caution and skepticism. Although the files include first-person depositions, especially in provincial archives, documents in central repositories are often in the form of "extracts"—detailed summaries, with detailed paraphrases or even quotations of original testimony. Still, however proficient the extract, it nonetheless mediates the original, whether through excisions or summaries, which conflate and obfuscate the original narrative (as a whole document). Hence, the extract, while convenient, inevitably becomes an official filter, its weaknesses further compounded in the event of a language barrier (e.g., where petitioners and witnesses spoke Yiddish). Even in cases where state rabbis, learned Jews *(uchenye evrei)* or other Russian-speaking representatives acted as translators, the abstract invariably emasculates the language and distorts the perspective. Moreover, any court document was part of the public domain, a fact that encouraged silence on whatever might be personally humiliating. Also, litigation was adversarial; the plaintiff and defendant naturally sought to exaggerate or rearrange facts in order to win the case. Still, the main predisposition is to emphasize what was legally valid and what was more demonstrable or more publicly credible.

Nonetheless, the archival records contain invaluable information and much testimony about the causes of marital breakdown, providing an extraordinary window on Jewish life more than a century ago in tsarist Russia. To be sure, the "causes" of marital breakdown were manifold, some direct and consciously recognized, others less readily perceived but powerfully corrosive all the same. The following section attempts to identify, principally on the basis of the actors' own statements, what loomed as the main factors, whether direct or indirect.

The main source of marital stress was not the "isms" and "zations" of broad cultural or social change but quotidian tensions at home. Contrary to the ideal of *sholom bayis* (peace at home), some marriages were a dismal chronicle of conflict. Often, it was a matter of differing expectations or, at least, the perception that the other party had miserably failed to satisfy the basic desiderata of marriage or had committed an intolerable grievance. The notion of a companionate marriage underlay many divorce petitions, especially among Jewish women, who protested what they deemed a violation of their cherished ideals. Indeed, from the mid-nineteenth century, the idea of a companionate marriage, disseminated earlier in Western Europe, steadily gained in popularity in Russia. In essence, this conception went beyond the ecclesiastical dogma of marriage as a sacramental union and the Enlightenment idea of a legal contract and instead envisioned marriage as a partnership with mutual obligations and affection. It specifically attacked arranged marriages, as well as the patriarchal authority of men. In so doing, the companionate marriage required a reconsideration, a renegotiation of traditional roles and responsibilities for the spouses.

Causes of Marital Breakdown and Divorce

In general, the sources of marital breakdown, some of which were also legal grounds for divorce included several main categories: (1) failure to meet economic responsibilities and the dissipation of family finances; (2) the absence of "love"; (3) inability to tolerate in-laws, stepchildren, and other relatives; (4) childlessness; (5) physical and psychological abuse; (6) adultery and sexual misconduct; (7) insanity; (8) religious conversion; (9) aspirations for female education; and (10) different views about religious observance. In most cases, it was a multiplicity of factors that led to domestic strife and the eventual dissolution of the marriage.

Economic Responsibilities and Family Finances

Different expectations about economic responsibilities and the control of family finances was predictably, an important cause of marital breakdown. Thus, the most common reason for divorce in the Vil'na metrical books was "the husband's inability to support his wife "(25 percent of divorces in 1837–38 and 31 percent in 1845). The Hebrew translation (on the opposite page of the record in Russian) was more mutual in its wording, without the gendered connotation: "They did not have a livelihood [parnasah]."[131] One underlying cause of conflict was the perceived failure of spouses to meet their financial obligations or their squandering of mutual assets. A poignant case involved Sara Shternfel'd of Kovno in 1881, who complained of being ruined by her husband's financial irresponsibility. Citing his duty to contribute to the family economy, she declared that "from the time that Rafail Shternfel'd became my husband, he did not earn a single kopeck and was incapable of earning a living." Indeed, she complained, he not only failed to support his family but proved to be "a great spendthrift, used up all the money . . . and accumulated a lot of debts." Because the husband failed in his responsibility, the wife pronounced herself "an unfortunate woman" and explained, "I have been tormented with the burden of earning a living to support myself and to pay off the debts." Prominent local merchants confirmed her testimony, adding that after her father's death she had become impoverished because of her ne'er-do-well husband.[132] It is revealing that over half the Jewish women in Vilna who divorced due to insufficient support between 1837 and 1864 were in their early twenties. Unfortunately, expectations of a better future with a new spouse were not always realistic. As one writer for the Jewish newspaper Russkii evrei lamented: "Whoever is closely acquainted with the Russian-Jewish masses knows that every divorce deals a grave blow to the material welfare of both spouses."[133]

Changing ideas about the gender division of labor also were prominent in marital complaints. For instance, Grigorii Bagrov testified before a rabbinical court on 29 April 1870 that his wife, Rivka, had impinged upon his business interests by ruining his honorable reputation. More specifically, he accused her of "becoming closely acquainted with his enemies in Simferopol, disgracing his honor, ruining his credit, and creating

FIG. 11. The marketplace; with people posing in the street near shops. Women and children stand on a balcony: *Arrow* points to the house where the Yiddish writer Lamed Shapiro was born and raised. *Courtesy of YIVO Institute for Jewish Research.*

such a domestic scandal that . . . everyone ran away from him." In reply, Rivka concurred that for years there had been "no harmony between them," but she denied his accusations and instead put the blame for marital discord on her husband. The result was a complete marital breakdown, including an end to conjugal relations; according to the testimony of a local rabbi, "[Rivka] Bagrova had not been to her husband's room in ten years."[134] Whatever the truth of the husband's accusations, he drew upon new gender delineations of commerce as an exclusively male sphere, treating any involvement of his wife as intrusive, even harmful.

For women, who were accustomed to participating in the family business, the husband's refusal to consult was an outright affront to their self-esteem and sensibilities, especially when the capital came from their own dowry. As Pauline Wengeroff recalled, "My husband devoted himself more to business and, with my dowry, started his own business where he lost all our money. I was allowed no opinion in business affairs. He called my advice interference and wanted to hear nothing from me. He was of the opinion that no woman, especially his wife, had any ability in this sphere and regarded my attempt to help as insulting." Her husband's position was all the more incomprehensible because his own mother had been a successful businesswoman. But, she observed, his attitude was "widespread among Jews throughout most of Little Russia [Ukraine] especially among the concessionaires who in their arrogance saw themselves as autocrats, [and] tolerated no advisors."[135] As gender roles began to shift in the marketplace, women sought to reassert their traditional power in the commercial sphere. Husbands, however, viewed their attempts to intercede as a challenge to male authority and rejected their advice altogether, even if to the detriment of the family economy.

Quite apart from the issue of breadwinning, spouses also expected to share mutually in the management of household resources—an important facet of the companionate marriage. The majority of female petitioners for separate passports, who came from affluent families and brought large dowries to their marriages, held such expectations. Little wonder that Ester Saet was enraged when her husband accused her of squandering *his* money on clothes and refused to leave her an allowance during his business trip to St. Petersburg. She informed the court investigator that *her* family had provided a dowry worth over ten thousand rubles and that her husband had promptly lost it in his jewelry business. To the dowry, she had added another thirty thousand rubles during their fifteen-year marriage (through family gifts and other sources). In her view she was entitled to control their resources, especially when it affected their children's upbringing.[136]

The daily struggle over the purse strings was no less intense in impoverished households. In his memoir, *Horeve veltn* (Worlds that passed), Abraham Sachs recalled that "the worst day in the *heder* was Thursday

. . . the day when the rebbitsin would nag the rebbe to death with her eternal questions about the provisions for Sabbath." The rebbitsin believed she had a right to the few kopecks she had earned so that she could buy the flour for her challah—all the more since the other wives in the shtetl had already purchased their fish and meat for the Sabbath. The rebbe responded by accusing her of being a spendthrift: "*Marshas* [shrew]! A bad plague! From where should I get the money for you? Who do you think I am? Shakhne Tsalels? Rothschild?"[137]

The financial question was particularly acute when the couple came from different socioeconomic backgrounds. The case of *Meerson vs. Meerson* is a good illustration. In 1903, Anna Meerson (born Eliasberg) of Riga petitioned the Imperial Chancellery for separation from her husband Solomon because of his "evil and cruel treatment of me and my children." Among the many sources of marital discord, she cited deep financial conflicts. Revealingly, the couple (who married "for love" in Warsaw in 1892) exhibited strikingly different social backgrounds: whereas the bride came from an exceptionally wealthy family in Riga, the husband had worked his way up from humble origins to become an engineer-mechanic. Shortly after the wedding, they moved to the industrial town of Ivanovo-Voznesensk in Vladimir province, where her young husband assumed an excellent position as engineer in a local factory.

Although both spouses confirmed that they passed the first ten years in harmony, money matters were clearly a source of conflict, at least in the husband's view. "If we had minor squabbles," he said of those early years, "they were of a monetary nature." Tensions mounted after Solomon had a mental and physical breakdown in 1894 (from overexertion at the factory) and had to resign his post. Almost simultaneously, their oldest son fell seriously ill with cancer-like symptoms. When Russian doctors pronounced his case hopeless, the desperate couple left home in search of a miraculous cure; for a full six months the couple and their son lived in the Crimea and later on the French Riviera. Because Solomon remained unemployed during all this time, his in-laws disparagingly declared that they were "wasting their money to cure the child." In 1896 the family moved to St. Petersburg, where Meerson obtained a position in the technical division of a metallurgical society. But he claimed that his wife came under the influence of her brother and returned to her former way of thinking: "She became extremely niggardly and anxious about the future. . . .I came to realize that, to a considerable degree, she began to look upon me as a source of income; hence my prestige in her estimation rose or fell depending on my salary."

In the fall of 1901, Meerson fell ill and was again left jobless. Unable to support his wife and children, he sent them to live with her family in Riga. At this point, Anna Meerson—without her husband's knowledge—put all their capital (from her dowry and their savings) solely in her name. The wife's petition concedes that her husband continually sent money from St. Petersburg, but unlike most women who applied for marital separation, she was determined to support herself and did not seek child support or alimony payments: "I have lived independently all this time [one year]. . . . I do not use the material support from my husband either for me or the children; I refuse any help from him as long as he lets me use the house for the children and leaves me in peace." She finally asked her husband for a divorce because he insulted her verbally in May 1901—even struck her the next month in Karlsbad when she tried to shield her son from a spanking— and for earning "too little for someone of his specialization." The husband conceded that "it is true that I do not earn a lot," explaining that "until 1901, my earnings were quite respectable, but I began to earn less and less for the last half year due to the crisis in Russian manufacturing."[138]

As the Meerson file makes clear, the couple had an extraordinarily high standard of living until 1901. Not only did they go abroad several times and vacation at resorts in Russia for extended periods, but they also rented some of the most expensive apartments in St. Petersburg (between 86 to 110 rubles a month). Affluence did not secure affection; their different attitudes toward money and lifestyle contributed to the breakdown of the marriage that, ironically, was originally based "on love." As one close friend of her family candidly testified, "The wife comes from a family in which money is their God and their whole way of life." Still, in the end, Anna asked for neither monetary support nor a division of their assets. That decision perhaps reflected her determination to obtain a separation at any cost or at least was part of her strategy to win her case and custody of the children.

The Lack of Love

The "absence of love" between the couple—a broad category to describe incompatible personalities and lack of sexual attraction—was another common source of marital breakdown. Expectations of love were clearly present in the traditional Jewish family but became more prominent after the mid-nineteenth century with the popularization of romantic ideals. In 1837–1838 the Vil'na rabbi granted twenty-six divorces (19.5 percent) on the grounds that "they do not love each other"; the rate rose to 23.4 percent in 1845.[139] Some Jews even divorced because they found their spouses "repulsive" (מחמת שטענת מאוס).

From the outset, some couples expressed great disappointment with their arranged marriages. As Anna Mikhlinaia of Rostov informed the Imperial Chancellery in 1909: "I categorically told my mother that I will not live with my husband because I do not love him and that I could not possibly love him after our three-day acquaintance." Her mother had allegedly retorted, "Get used to him and you'll come to love him."[140] Rabbi Chaim Tchernowitz, who grew up in the town of Shebiz (Belorussia), described how his learned mother, who was an avid reader of secular Yiddish novels, was married off against her will to an otherworldly Talmud scholar: "My mother was another type altogether, completely the opposite of Father. It is difficult to understand how two people as remote as east and west could live together. . . . But she made peace with her destiny, for such is the way of the modest maidens of Israel, who bear their sorrow in their hearts."[141] Such resignation did not characterize Ida Velen, who complained that after ten years of marriage "we did not have anything in common." Although her husband promised to give her a divorce, he took no active steps to fulfill his word, and the wife eventually turned to the Imperial Chancellery for a separate passport. The state investigator noted that the couple still lived together and had no visible problems, perhaps except for "incompatible characters," and recommended that her application be denied.[142] Many marriages like this case terminated in divorce on the grounds of "mutual consent" or "mutual hatred" with little if any information about the nature of the incompatibility.

Meddling In-laws, Siblings, and Stepchildren

A third proverbial source of marital conflict was the unwelcome intercession of in-laws, stepchildren, and other kin. Still, even though the memoir literature highlights conflict between Jewish men and their in-laws because of the matrilocal arrangement of *kest,* divorce because "he cursed her parents" was rare—indeed, grounds for 1 of 133 cases in Vilna between 1837 and 1838. More divorces resulted when the wife insulted her in-laws (4 out of 133 divorces). But here the metrica probably understated conflict with in-laws and instead submerged these tensions under other language. Memoirs suggest that social norms dictated some "tolerance" toward a husband's mistreatment of his in-laws (more specifically, his mother-in-law), but it certainly did not go unanswered. When M. L. Lilienblum mocked his mother-in-law after her memorial candle blew out during the Yom Kippur prayers, she responded with a barrage of curses—to which he, of course, answered in kind.[143]

While society expected tensions between a groom and his mother-in-law, it was less tolerant of a wife's mistreatment of in-laws. The husband routinely criticized his wife for failing to uphold his parents' honor and argued that she was unfit to be a good mother. In the Bagrov case (1870) the husband claimed that throughout their tumultuous marriage his wife,

Rivka, had not only objected to giving assistance to his elderly parents but had even subjected them to such suffering (under his own roof!) that they were forced to move away.[144] Citing patriarchal norms to assist needy parents (indeed, a statutory duty in Russian law), Grigorii Bagrov contended that his wife had violated the basic rules of conduct.[145] In his own words, she "had not been obedient to him, acted against his rights and interests, and even hindered the education of the children." Similarly, Solomon Meerson complained that his young wife initially remonstrated when he sent money to his indigent parents in Warsaw and later changed her negative view about charity, not only toward his parents but also toward others in need.[146] He also recalled how deeply he had been offended when his wife visited Warsaw but refused to live with his impoverished parents, preferring instead to stay with her sister. Only when their son contracted scarlet fever, ironically at her wealthy sister's home, did she appear at their residence suddenly and without prior warning. Significantly, the narratives of both recast such details to expose their wives' "poor mothering" and hence their inability to fulfil basic marital duties.

In-laws, however, were not only the victims but also the alleged perpetrators. In the case of Yankel and Sheine Maizil'son the young groom claimed that his father-in-law had forced him to divorce his wife, an accusation that was not uncommon at the time. The reason was their arrangement of *kest*: according to Yankel, he married the twenty-year-old daughter of Meir Aizinshtat in 1855 after the family promised to provide five years of *kest*. After the wedding the young groom moved from his hometown (Minsk) to Cherikov, where he "did not have a single relative or protector." On the evening of 15 March 1856 (one year after the marriage), Yankel claimed, his father-in-law gave him a severe beating and demanded that he give his daughter a divorce. Nor did the torment end there; the next day, he wrote, "I was subjected to cruel torture [and] physical punishment that left me desperate and feebleminded." At this point his father-in-law allegedly summoned the local rabbi to execute the divorce. During the formal investigation of this case, witnesses from the wife's hometown challenged this version of events, testifying that the husband himself had summoned the rabbi and scribe in order to proceed with the divorce. They admitted, however, hearing rumors of "discord and disagreement between Aizinshtat [the father-in-law] and Maizil'son," and that such conflict is "usually the cause of divorce." The plaintiff continued to deny initiating the divorce since he would be totally ruined by the obligation to return immense funds (more than 2,000 rubles) to the bride's family. The Rabbinic Commission, however, overruled his appeal to annul the divorce, explaining that it had been legally recorded in the metrical books on grounds of "mutual hatred" and in the presence of two witnesses. The commission added that Yankel had not filed his complaint until a full year after the event, raising doubts about his claim. Given the unresolved contraction in the case, the commission doubtless found it difficult to determine the rightful party and relied on the criteria of "formal evidence."[147] Even if Maizil'son lied, the very fact that he constructed an argument against his father-in-law suggests cultural assumptions about the credibility of in-law tensions.[148]

In the case of the *maskil* Abraham Baer Gottlober, family and even communal pressure forced him to divorce his first wife. During his sojourn in the town of Tarnopol, where he had fled to avoid the military draft, Gottlober came under the influence of the Galician *maskil* Joseph Perl, who introduced him to the teachings of Moses Mendelssohn and the Jewish enlightenment. Aware that most of this literature was not in the "spirit of Hasidism," the newborn *maskil* decided to leave the books at his mother's house in Starokonstantinov (Volhynia province) before returning to his wife and son in Chernigov. Much to his dismay, his mother unwittingly sent him the books through Rabbi Aron Tshodniver as an act of kindness, unaware of their contents. During the journey, the curious Hasid examined the contents of the box and was horrified to find several books by enlightenment thinkers. Before long the entire town knew that the heretical books belonged to the son-in-law of Nachman Leib the Hasid. The *tsaddik* of Zhitomir forced Gottlober to divorce his wife, even though they had lived in harmony, and expelled him from the town. Gottlober bitterly recalled the divorce, particularly because his young wife had no say in the matter: "But who gives the daughter of Israel the privilege and right to choose what she pleases?"[149]

Older siblings who assumed a parental role also caused marital tensions between couples. Avraham Mapu meddled incessantly in his brother Matityahu's first marriage, divorce, and subsequent remarriage, as evidenced in his "letters of advice" on a variety of matters. Although Matityahu's mother-in-law held Mapu solely responsible for destroying her daughter's marriage, Benzion Dinur has argued that the older brother only facilitated the breakup of a damaged relationship. Apparently, difficulties began in the early years of their marriage because of gossip about the wife's behavior and doubts about her chastity. The estrangement only increased when the husband left his wife and child in Vil'na and went to work in Paris for the Gintsburg family.

Regardless of whether Mapu directly influenced his brother to divorce his wife, his correspondence shows that he discouraged reconciliation and poured oil on the flames of conflict. Despite the urging of Matityahu's mother-in-law that the couple live together (emphasizing her daughter's ill health and loneliness), Mapu opposed the idea and worked to prevent a reunion. He also urged his brother to take control over his family finances—more specifically, to prevent his wife's "extravagance" and careless dissipation of their assets. The letters suggest that the older Mapu's importunate interference played no small role in hastening the final destruction of Matityahu's marriage.[150]

Solomon Meerson also candidly complained of poor relations with his wife's siblings and cited class differences as the source of tension: "Almost all her brothers looked down on me when we first met, and they never deemed it necessary to visit my parents in Warsaw, even though that would have been appropriate." The husband further complained that, when they moved to St. Petersburg in 1896, his wife's brother took charge of everything, from purchasing furniture to designating a date for his son's birthday party. A bitter Meerson recalled that whenever her family came to visit, his wife suddenly became hostile and capricious; once they departed, however, her antagonism promptly subsided. In his view, the loss of authority over his own household—from the choice of decor to the planning of family events—contributed to his alienation from his wife.[151]

Quite apart from intrusive in-laws and siblings, stepchildren were a major source of tension, not surprisingly in view of the high rate of remarriage among Jews. Notably, the number of divorces due to wife's "inability to live with her stepchildren" (מחמת שהיא לא יכלה לגור ביחד עם בנים שיש לו מאשתו הראשונה) in Vil'na rose from 1 percent in 1837–1838 to 21.3 percent by 1851. In most cases, the age difference between the couple was enormous. In 1845, for example, more than half of the divorced couples in this category reported a twenty-year age gap, the greatest being thirty-six years. Hence, "children" were usually the same age as or even older than the new wife.

Legal suits filed in the Vil'na conscience court (sovestnyi sud) and orphan's court (sirotskii sud) reveal that conflicts between the new wife and stepchildren were primarily of a financial nature. In 1845, for instance, the stepchildren of Leah Grushka of Vil'na filed a lawsuit against her for misappropriating nine hundred rubles that their mother had allegedly left for them in her will. They also blamed her for wrecking a lucrative match proposed to the daughter Beilka for lack of a dowry, the funds for which were tied up in a promissory note held jointly by the stepmother and father. All this led the stepchildren to wail that "we the poor orphans . . . saw how our stepmother succeeded in turning our father against us, depriving us of all honor." One stepson invoked patriarchal values in his portrait of a domineering wife: "She herself carries out the business not allowing father to participate in household or commercial decisions."[152]

Interestingly, divorce on the grounds of the husband's refusal to live with his stepchildren was rare in the Vil'na metrical books, especially when compared to those initiated by women (see table 3.3). One such case was recorded in 1845, when Khaim Shalomovich Dines divorced Khasia Businskaia because he refused to accept her children from the first marriage. Whatever his motive for marriage in the first place, Dines presumably hoped—and failed—to convince his new wife to abandon the children.[153]

As these cases illustrate, the union of two families through marriage led to tensions over authority and especially over finances. The files also show the significant impact of cyclical patterns of marriage, divorce, and remarriage, which inevitably promoted tensions between couples and in-laws, between stepparents and stepchildren. Obviously, such conflicts were not omnipresent nor automatic; some families merged together so successfully into one cloth that, even in remarriages, stepsiblings displayed no differences in their backgrounds. What was new was the public airing and litigation in state courts, where the venue, overt and latent, mandated explicit articulation and rationalization. These narratives, interestingly, reveal that attitudes were changing toward patriarchal expectations of assistance to elderly parents and that such challenges impelled husbands (and even wives) to reassert traditional norms.

Domestic Violence

A fourth cause of marital breakdown was domestic violence, which was understood to mean physical, verbal, or emotional abuse. These cases are particularly interesting because petitioners (all women) rebelled against traditional authority and appealed to the secular Russian state. That directly contravened the traditional taboo in Jewish culture on allowing "evidence of dissension to get abroad"; to violate the "norms of silence" and community boundaries was deemed a disgrace.[154] More interesting still, the women who dared file such complaints articulated their own perception of spouse relations and explicitly challenged the power that the husband might legitimately exercise in asserting his hegemony in the family. In appealing to judicial authorities and describing their suffering and woes, the female litigants postulated new norms of conduct that implicitly rejected the pretensions of traditional patriarchy.[155]

It is particularly important to stress that wife abuse emerged as a major public issue in the 1870s and indeed became a primary concern of the Imperial Chancellery for the Receipt of Petitions. The latter functioned to circumvent the state passport law, which denied the right of separate residency, and on an ad hoc basis granted special imperial permission for battered women to reside apart from abusive spouses.[156] In theory, the male had the legal right to demand that authorities return his wife, even one who had fled physical and emotional abuse. Although few males evidently exercised this right,[157] the Imperial Chancellery acted to provide women with the documents needed to reside separately.

The 1911 case of Dora Shliomova Faivilevich (née Kofman) is typical. Already living separately from her husband for four years, she petitioned state authorities to recognize her status and to grant a separate passport to go abroad for treatment of diabetes. The file is not just a long tale of marital conflict and unhappiness but of incessant maltreatment by her husband. She explained that she married as "a very young girl" and hence was unprepared "to understand the character of my groom." Her parents, in fact, had arranged the marriage, basing "their choice on the fact that my groom was a man with means." To her dismay, however, he proved to be "a person with the highest measure of pettiness, maliciousness, rudeness, and a deficiency in his moral and spiritual development." Her first years of marriage revealed "all the horrible injustices of marriage," as her husband continually provoked fights and "ignored my human and feminine attributes." Her plight was only aggravated by the in-laws, especially the husband's sister and mother, who made no secret of their animosity. Isolated and friendless, "I was not able [to tell] anyone of these complaints and to shame my close ones, [so] I [alone] carried this heavy cross" (an unusual metaphor for a Jewish petition). Nevertheless, she endured all these travails for the sake of her son. When her mother attempted to intercede, that only provoked a "cruel" response from the husband, who moved to his mother's apartment and took all the silver and his wife's dowry of two thousand rubles.

The investigator from the Imperial Chancellery confirmed that the husband had "a crude and severe character" and that he denied his wife permission to go abroad for medical treatment (contrary to the doctor's recommendation). He also found that the husband had taken the wife's entire dowry, derived his living from this capital, and refused to support his wife and son. Not surprisingly, the investigator's final report spoke on behalf of the plaintiff. Endorsing his recommendation, the Imperial Chancellery ordered that Dora Faivilevich be given a separate passport to go to Karlsbad for medical treatment. Although the file does not explain why the husband beat his wife (except for references to his violent character), the fact that he did not have an independent livelihood and lived off his wife's dowry may have impelled him to translate failure in the economic sphere into a violent assertion of power at home.[158] Whatever the motive, the key point is that even the conservative state, by acting in defense of abused women, was acting to undermine traditional patriarchy.

Although Faivilevich prevailed, her case reveals several factors that deterred a woman from seeking a divorce or even separation, however severe the maltreatment. No doubt, children—and custody—were a critical factor; this petitioner explicitly cites her son's welfare to explain why she tolerated abuse for so long. That argument was probably sincere and, unquestionably, was effective.[159] Moreover, even on the eve of World War I, the stigma attached to divorce was still a factor, even if not a deterrent. Here the wife was ashamed to discuss her plight with close friends or to publicize her marital problems by a scandalous separation; only when the husband abandoned her and denied her permission to travel did she turn to the state to legalize the de facto separation.

In an earlier case, Sara Shternfel'd wrote a long letter to her local rabbi on 30 June 1881 that disclosed confidential information previously shared only with her father: "He [Raphael Shternfel'd] treated me in an extremely evil, crude and barbarous manner. One can say that my position was without end [because] as a mother who would sacrifice her life gladly for her children, I was compelled to stay with them." The anguished woman wrote that her husband "drove me to the point where I turned to others for help and I experienced such shame that I would have preferred to die." Like Dora Faivilevich, she tolerated the abuse for the sake of her children; if she had turned to her others for assistance, it was with great shame and humiliation. To make matters worse, Sara Shternfel'd claimed that her husband suffered from a physical disease (halitosis) that was severely harmful for her own health. She added, darkly, that there were other "horrible things that I deemed inappropriate to write [on paper]."[160]

Uncertain about how to settle the case, the local rabbi asked the prominent Rabbi Yitshak Elhanan Spektor of Kovno, author of *Beer Yitshak* and *Ain Yitshak,* for advice. Evidently for want of a reply (none is in the file), the local rabbi decided to resolve the case on his own. He ruled against the plaintiff: she had provided no "proof" of cruel treatment and a medical certificate (from a certain "Doctor Shenberg") confirmed that the husband's mouth and teeth were neither damaged nor malodorous. When she remonstrated that her husband had beaten her publicly on the streets of Kovno but failed to produce eyewitnesses, the rabbi reaffirmed his decision. The Rabbinic Commission upheld the rabbi. It ruled that witnesses failed to confirm her claims of abuse and that the doctor's certificate was sufficient evidence of her husband's good health.[161] As this case shows, it was not enough to make claims about spousal abuse; evidence, such as eyewitness testimony, was essential.

Naturally, it was not always easy to provide such evidence, especially if the cruel treatment occurred at home or, at most, in the presence of the wife's in-laws. In such cases a woman was particularly vulnerable, but perhaps especially so in the case of Jews: the woman who refused to cohabit could be deemed a "rebellious wife" *(moredet),* liable to forfeiting her *ketubah*. One such case concerned a woman named Khaia Giller in Warsaw. When the rabbi of Warsaw ordered her to leave her relatives' home and return to her husband, she protested that "she could no longer return to her husband because he would murder her at night, and she was afraid." However, because she could not prove the alleged abuse, the local rabbi ruled that she was a "rebellious wife" for refusing to cohabit with her husband and in the event of divorce she would lose her claims to the *ketubah*.[162]

As these two cases reveal, divorce on the grounds of wife beating was possible but by no means automatic. While Jewish law banned such behavior, some rabbinic authorities were particularly stringent about demonstrating the physical abuse. It was, understandably, difficult to prove what normally occurred behind closed doors or, indeed, to expose family scandal to the community, much less to state authorities. Hence, judicial protection fell far short of the bold statements of Rabbis Isserles that wife beating was a transgression that deserved severe punishment.[163]

For some women, especially the well educated, the threshold of tolerance was much lower. Anna Meerson of Riga, for example, cited two incidents of abuse that led her to declare that her husband represented a physical threat. In the first case, she claimed that he insulted her verbally, an accusation that the husband did not deny. During a short period of unemployment, she disparaged his abilities as an engineer and predicted that he would never succeed in life. He admitted that, at this point, he shot back that she was an *alte skrande* (an old hag). In the second incident, she claimed that in the summer of 1901 her husband "struck me with all his might when I protected my young two-year-old son from a spanking, so that my back ached for a whole month." If such a blow had landed on her son, she contended, it would have "maimed him for life." It was not merely the physical violence that offended the wife but the husband's denigration of her ideas on child rearing.[164]

A wife's refusal to tolerate physical abuse was especially pronounced for younger women. Revealingly, most women who initiated divorce for wife beating were relatively young: 53.3 percent in 1837–1838 were between the ages of seventeen and twenty-three; 57.1 percent in 1844 were between twenty and twenty-two. In fact, relatively few wives were over thirty-five years old.[165] On the basis of this limited data, it appears that if women did not initiate divorce within the first few years of marital abuse, they became reluctant to do so, whether out of consideration for their children or for other reasons.

Although there are no official figures on domestic violence, the archives do show a decline in divorces on the grounds of wife beating. In 1837–1838, for example, the metrical book of Vil'na cited wife beating (מחמת שהוא מכה אותה) for 11.3 percent of divorces in Vil'na (see table 3.2). This relatively high figure undoubtedly reflects the fact that women were more successful in their suits, for they could rely upon the effective sanctions of an autonomous *kahal* that still existed until 1844. Despite government restrictions on the use of coercive measures, Jewish communal authorities often employed a secret persecutor *(rodef haneelam)* "to bend the disobedient like a reed."[166] Not only did offenders undergo severe ostracism (i.e., no ritual rites were performed for them, such as circumcision and burial), but they also experienced public humiliation in the synagogue. Under these circumstances, women had strong inducement to seek communal protection and, if need be, could offer this evidence in support of a divorce claim.

Significantly, wife beating as a grounds for divorce in Vil'na dropped to 8.0 percent in 1844, 3.8 percent in 1845 (one year after the dissolution of the *kahal*), and 2.0 percent in 1851; it was negligible by the 1860s. The dynamics of this decline are unclear: it may represent an actual decrease in wife abuse or a diminished willingness to seek divorce on these grounds. It may be, as Nancy Tomes suggests in the English case, that there was a growing disapproval of marital violence as "unmanly" behavior.[167] Perhaps more pertinent, however, especially in view of the earlier timing of the decline, was diminishing capacity of Jewish women to obtain divorces from abusive husbands as the system of enforcement weakened. The other legal option for a separate domicile was to apply to the Imperial Chancellery for a separate passport—a route taken by a small minority of women, given the obstacles of cost and social pressure. Alternatively, some women may not have desired a formal divorce, just an end to the beatings, as was the case among battered wives around the turn of the century in England.[168] Finally, among the relatively wealthy, the declining ability to provide *kest* for extended periods of time certainly diminished the protective gaze of the extended family, which could serve as eyewitnesses and pressure a husband to divorce his wife.

"Drunkenness, Licentiousness, and Depravity"

A related cause of marital breakdown was dissipation. In general, it was mainly women who filed these complaints and stressed the detrimental impact of male drunkenness, which they claimed not only depleted family assets but led to violent, even criminal behavior. Accusations of alcoholism clearly resonated with religious and state authorities, who were no doubt sensitive to the public discourse and campaigns to combat this social malady.[169] In addition, female petitioners contended that the offending party had violated not only norms of tolerable behavior but their vows of marital fidelity and basic morality. Apart from the drunkenness, women routinely alleged that their husbands consorted with prostitutes and criminals as they squandered family resources.

The case of Dveira Elka Aizikovich shows that such appeals evoked considerable resonance in government circles. Her tale began on 3 June 1882, when she petitioned state authorities to compel her husband to divorce her because of his intolerably sordid behavior. She claimed that since their wedding eight years ago, "my husband [Eliazar] Aizikovich has led a depraved and drunken life, without any kind of occupation to support the family, only his drunkenness." One night, she recalled, her husband came home "with a drunken look" and, while she was still in bed, "threw away my last pair of boots, forcing me to go around barefooted." In no time the husband had squandered the family's resources on alcohol, forcing his wife and two children to live with his parents. That only made matters worse, since his parents compounded the tensions between the couple: "I tolerated everything as long as my strength would allow . . . until I could no longer endure the beatings; I then decided to leave their house and my own children, wandering here and there [both] day and night because no one would take me in without a passport." To add insult to injury, her husband began a scandalous affair with a prostitute. One month after filing the divorce petition, Dveira Aizikovich, despairing over the prospects for success, filed another petition, merely asking for a separate passport. Eliazer Aizikovich was in no haste to respond: not until two years later did he deign to reply, claiming that his wife had deserted him without cause and had left him with two underage children. Despite the husband's statement that he intended to divorce his wife and claim that she had even abandoned her children, the Imperial Chancellery conducted its own inquiry and found her claims warranted and granted her a separate passport to remain in St. Petersburg.[170]

But the charge of a "depraved way of life and marital infidelity" did not necessarily prevail within the Jewish community, as Ester Poliakov's divorce case demonstrated. Khaim Poliakov had signed a pledge in 1887 agreeing to divorce but then reneged, probably because of second thoughts about the material support he would have to provide. He thereupon simply abandoned his wife and young children, left them without any means of support, and vanished abroad. When he returned to Russia in 1891, the rabbi confronted him about his broken pledge and his responsibility to support his wife and family. Poliakov ignored the rabbi's demands and persuaded his wife to give *him* a large sum of money to "compensate" him for the divorce that he again promised to provide. After squandering his wife's entire dowry (an immense sum, exceeding 6,000 rubles), he once again reneged. In this case, the rabbis found clear and incontrovertible grounds for divorce but lacked the power to enforce their decision: only the husband could "grant" the divorce—a fact that was perfectly clear to Poliakov as he extorted huge sums from his wife.[171]

Still, the accusation of depravity did work, especially in state courts, to arm women with a powerful weapon. The homogeneity, thematic and linguistic, of texts is striking: women constructed their petitions around the familiar image of the archetypal drunken, dissolute male to elicit support for marital separation or dissolution. They argued that their husbands' conduct was not only intolerable to their personal sensibilities but was ruinous for family finances, specifically referring to the difficult responsibility of supporting their minor children. As in the wife-beating cases, these suits revealed the declining power of rabbinical authority; once it became illegal to enforce rabbinical decrees through coercion, women were forced to turn to the Russian state for an extraordinary redress of their grievances.

Adultery

Another cause of marital breakdown was adultery, "the breach of sexual exclusivity."[172] Jewish law drew a sharp gender distinction between the treatment of adultery on the part of men and women. As in many other societies, it upheld a double standard that punished married women far more severely than men.[173] The Rabbinic Commission even formalized the double standard; it defined adultery as the "illegal sexual relations between a married or single man with a married woman." It added that "an illicit affair between a married man and unmarried woman is simply considered fornication, . . . not adultery." In other words, whereas any extramarital affair for a woman was adulterous, such obtained for the male only if the female also was married.[174] The distinction was important, since the penalties for adultery were incomparably greater.

The double standard applied directly to divorce. Whereas a Jewish man could demand and obtain summary divorce if his wife committed adultery, matters were far more complicated when the husband was the guilty party, as the case of Khaia and Girsh Zak reveals. When Khaia Sima Zak discovered that her husband, Girsh, was having an affair with a young student from a dental school in Warsaw, she claimed that the shock made her consider returning to her parental home and that only concern for her daughter's welfare dissuaded her from taking so public a step.[175] The couple had met when she was sixteen years old, just as Girsh was completing his law degree at the Moscow Imperial University. "At that time, he was poor, with only a few acquaintances, and without any means," she recalled. As distant relatives of the young law graduate, her family took him into their home in Gomel and gave him generous financial and material assistance. Khaia's infatuation with the young lawyer led to marriage, despite her parents' disapproval. Soon after the wedding, however, Khaia began to feel exploited: while she looked after the family business, her husband "went outside the house in search of worthless entertainment." She tolerated this for about ten years, until her husband began an affair with a young woman and made no attempt to be discreet. Emphasizing that her husband had betrayed her family, which had supported him during his student years, and had dealt a severe blow to her "pride and self-esteem," she despaired of obtaining her husband's consent to divorce and applied to the state for a separate passport. Interestingly, she simultaneously enrolled in a women's dental school, clearly intending to start a new and independent life of her own. After a thorough investigation confirmed her claims, the state granted a temporary separate passport and instructed the couple to negotiate child visitation rights.[176]

State intercession, however, was more aggressive if the man had committed adultery with a Christian woman. In a sensational case at midcentury, Itska Kushelev was indicted for having an affair with a young peasant girl in 1854.[177] Eventually, his case came before the Governing Senate (the highest secular appellate court). It not only demanded that Kushelev be punished as a "criminal" but also be subjected to some form of "spiritual penance"—that is, be subjected to the kind of religious penalty applied to the Russian Orthodox population.[178] The decision reflected a deep ignorance of Judaism but was apparently an exception; in only one other case (involving a Jewish soldier who had an affair with the wife of a Finnish soldier) was the issue raised again.[179]

By the end of the century, amid a broad public debate about liberalizing divorce and separation, the Imperial Chancellery demonstrated a distinct leniency toward adultery.[180] That policy was strikingly evident in the case of Ioisif and Leia (Sonya) Broun, in which an adulterous wife appealed for separation from a vengeful Jewish husband who refused to exercise his right to divorce. According to the wife, the couple had lived in harmony until the husband suffered a stroke and became paralyzed on his left side. "As a result, my husband began to behave in an intolerable manner: he was capricious, cursed in indecent language, [and] displayed a strong hatred toward me. . . . Living with him became impossible." She claimed that her husband moved out and left her with two children, whom she supported through work as a seamstress and assistance from relatives. Ioisif Broun denied her allegations, claiming that the marriage had broken down because of his wife's affair with a local Russian doctor and that she attempted to commit him to a lunatic asylum when he refused to give her a divorce. The husband explained that he went to stay with relatives out of fear that she would carry out her threats, adding that she had convinced the police of her claims. To substantiate his accusations, he included a telegram (written in Russian) from his wife's father, admonishing her to end the affair. According to the secret police, Leia

Broun "maintains an intimate relationship with Doctor Dmitrii Mal'-shevim, and people in town openly say that she is having an affair with him, that she intends to convert to Orthodoxy and leave her husband, but it is impossible to confirm these facts."

The state, however, ruled in favor of the wife. Although the investigator confirmed that Ioisif Broun was "psychologically healthy, but physically ill" and showed some commiseration ("he cries all the time and curses his wife because of her affair with [the doctor]"), he described the husband as unintelligent and uncultivated, someone who became repulsive to his wife once she had gained some familiarity with educated circles. One could hardly expect her to resume conjugal relations with him: "Making her live with her husband could lead her to commit suicide." Perhaps influenced by hints of a religious conversion, the Imperial Chancellery granted the wife a separate passport for a four-year term. Ioisif Broun vociferously protested this unseemly leniency, noting that Jewish "religious law permits divorce on grounds of mutual consent and hence there is no need to issue a separate passport to a wife (in contravention of a husband's legal rights)." He warned that his wife needed the divorce only "in order to remarry or to carry on her illegal cohabitation, given her constant striving for a luxurious and disgusting life." Nevertheless, responding to the investigator's recommendation, the greater sexual liberality of the early twentieth century, and the lure of religious conversion, the Imperial Chancellery ruled in his wife's favor and granted the separate passport.[181]

A husband's accusation of infidelity, even if bogus, nonetheless was a hardship for the woman. In 1908, Anna Kagan of Dubno testified that she was willing to tolerate her husband's cruel treatment until "he dared to question the legitimacy of my daughter."[182] The wife recounted bitterly how the father spread this vicious rumor around town and even sent a denunciation of his own daughter to the local police, "thus blackening my name and my daughter's reputation." Kagan enclosed copies of letters from her husband when their daughter was born, wishing her love and happiness. In another case, although David Saet had allegedly spread rumors of his wife's "indecent behavior" with Kronshtadt navy officers, the court investigator found no evidence of adultery. Ester Saet wrote that her marriage of twenty-two years had been "the most miserable union." She added that in recent years, "his attitude toward me has been hostile and contemptuous and for four years we have lived together, not like man and wife, but like complete strangers."[183]

As Lynn Abrams has shown in her study of family life in one German district, such accusations might have nothing to do with sexual infidelity but "could be a reference to women's increasing sphere of influence and autonomy."[184] Indications of such a subtext emerge in both the Kagan and Saet files. In the Kagan case, the wife had moved to her parents' home because she could no longer turn a blind eye to her husband's criminal business dealings. As she put it, his "ruthless methods of settling accounts with commercial contractors" and corrupt business practices (which eventually landed him in prison) represented such an affront to her moral sensibilities that she found it impossible to live with him. That moral stand no doubt appeared, in the husband's eyes, as a sign of rank insubordination. In the Saet case, the wife refused to stand at the cash register of the family store while her husband made business trips to St. Petersburg. Her demand to control her own leisure time was a direct challenge to her husband's authority and control.

Hence, accusations of adultery sometimes involved more than a breach of sexual norms, rather changing power relations in the household. It was not solely the growing autonomy of women that generated anxieties but also male independence from the wife's household. Hence, Khaia Zak expressed dismay when her husband, who had been penniless and friendless when he arrived in Gomel after their wedding, sought the company of new acquaintances. While her accusations of adultery should not be dismissed, the husband's declining dependence on her family and his newfound "entertainment" outside the home clearly generated suspicions about his commitment to the marriage and sense of personal indebtedness. A growing cultural gap between spouses and their involvement in different social circles also fostered mistrust and fears of infidelity. Regardless of Sonya Broun's guilt in the alleged affair, the husband defined the moment of marital breakdown from the time she became acquainted with members of the Russian intelligentsia, who were far removed from his world. Her success in obtaining a separate passport no doubt confirmed his fears that the state was colluding with his wife's lover to convert her to the Orthodox faith and to abandon him in his illness.

Childlessness

Another cause of marital breakdown and divorce was childlessness. According to the biblical commandment, one of the central purposes of Jewish marriages was procreation.[185] In tsarist Russia it was not uncommon for childless couples to turn to their spiritual leaders as mediators between earth and heaven for their coveted offspring. A packet of Yiddish letters, which the Vil'na censors accidentally confiscated, revealed that Jews sent requests for a blessing (kvitlekh) around the High Holidays. In 1839 a certain Nokham, son of Feiga, who had lost all his children through miscarriages and early death, wrote to his rabbi: "We ask you on Yom Kippur to pray to God that He would send me a live and healthy infant through my wife this year. Long have I lamented about this [and] no help could I find; so now, at this time of goodwill, I ask you to obtain God's love for me, so that I may be counted among the people of Israel, to be given a live baby."[186]

Jewish law, reinforced by the worldly need for assistance in old age, thus placed a high priority on procreation. It accordingly permitted a man to divorce if his wife failed to bear children in ten years. The male's prerogative was unequivocal, leaving a childless wife in an "emotionally vulnerable, but also legally precarious" situation.[187] In fact, the community expected such a couple to divorce, even if they had a stable marriage, so that the husband could fulfill his religious duty to "be fruitful and multiply." The situation was exacerbated by Russian laws that made legal adoption possible only with the personal permission of the emperor himself.[188] That was an onerous and expensive process, but some Jews did attempt to adopt children through the Imperial Chancellery. In 1909, Moishe and Zel'da Zel'manovich petitioned for permission to adopt the son of the wife's late cousin: "Because we have no children of our own (and apart from helping an unhappy orphan), we have decided to adopt one of [the cousin's] children and to raise him like our own child." They had already spent an enormous amount of time and money in the lower courts but to no avail; in desperation they appealed to Nicholas II, "our kind father—the emperor."[189] The absence of a final resolution suggests that their petition was denied. A Jewish couple from Tomsk also sought to adopt a deserted peasant baby, but the local court had rejected their petition on the grounds that Jewish parents could not raise a Christian child.[190] Given these virtually insurmountable barriers to adoption, Jewish men often insisted on their right to divorce and remarry.

Women's fate in these divorce suits served as a common theme in the works of Devorah Baron. In her short story, "Mishpahah" (Family), Baron describes the childless Dinah, who sat silently by her window as she awaited the dreaded divorce hearing.[191] While silence was the norm, some childless women, like Khaia Grinshtein, sought a more active role in their relatively powerless positions. When her husband, David, married her, he stipulated that, if his "crippled" wife did not bear children during the first ten years, she would agree to a divorce based on mutual consent. Berko Iudovich testified that he was a witness at the signing of this prenuptial agreement. When the couple failed to have children and the husband duly terminated their marriage, Khaia filed a suit against him in state court for divorcing her against her will (in order to remarry another woman) and for leaving her without material support. She provided a list of five people who had witnessed the "coercive delivery of the *get*." The first witness, Mordukh Leizer Rozenberg, stated that the husband "placed the bill of divorcement on his wife's neck because she was not capable of receiving it with her hand." He noted that the wife did not shout or make any noise but accepted the divorce. The remaining four men either concurred with Rozenberg's testimony or denied any knowledge of the matter. If any doubts still remained, the state rabbi of Pinsk clarified the matter by notifying the Commission that he had recorded the divorce in the metrical book in 1875 on the grounds of "sexual incapacity." The husband explained that his first wife was offended because he married her niece just six weeks after the divorce (however, "as Khaia had suggested"). If such testimony was true, Khaia apparently changed her mind after the divorce, perhaps because her husband reneged on a financial agreement (hence the reference to leaving her without "material support").[192]

Although Jewish law clearly stipulated childlessness as grounds for divorce, some rabbis were plainly sympathetic toward Jewish women and sought to deter husbands from divorce. This was not entirely a new position; according to Judith Baskin's reading of aggadic texts on procreation, the rabbis favored prayer over divorce in the case of childlessness.[193] Hence, in February 1910, Rabbi Perl'man refused to grant Borukh Pekker a divorce and cited the "more progressive responsa of Rabbi Chaim Hezekiah Medini of Karasubazar" *(Sedei hemed).*[194] Unlike most divorce cases, this archival file has no statement from the wife, Sara; like the childless wife Dinah in Devorah Baron's "Mishpahah," she waited silently for the cruel termination of her ten-year marriage. The Rabbinic Commission rejected the rabbi's attempt to protect the woman, ruling that he had no right to interfere with the male's desire to fulfill his religious duty to "be fruitful and multiply."

The statistical record provides some insight into the pattern of divorce on the grounds of childlessness. Significantly, the number of such divorces based on childlessness, to judge from the Vil'na files, was relatively small and even declined from 11 percent in 1837–1838 to 8 percent in 1845 and 2 percent by 1851. Nor did the couples necessarily wait the ten-year term; in 1837–1851 the majority of childless couples divorced in their early twenties, meaning that they obviously divorced before the ten-year minimum. Husbands may simply have been impatient and spouses agreeable to divorce; or perhaps the wives demanded a divorce on the grounds of male sexual impotence. In the latter case, however, the Vil'na state rabbi usually used the phrase, "because the husband is impotent" (מחמת שאין לבעל כח גברא) rather than the general entry, "because they did not have children" (מחמת שלא היו להם בנים).[195] According to the Babylonian Talmud, the court was to support a woman who questioned "his ability to shoot like an arrow" (Yevamot 65a). Whatever the cause, divorces prior to the ten-year waiting period were clearly authorized, whether reluctantly or tacitly, by the Vil'na *beit-din* that presided over each case. The haste to dissolve such childless marriages appears to have abated by the 1860s. In 1864, for example, the age of childless couples rose: the three women who divorced were 42, 38, and 32 and their husbands were also older—namely, 47, 50, and 28, respectively.

The memoir literature suggests tacit disapproval of childless divorces if the couple had been married a long time perhaps because procreation was less compelling for people of advanced years. Thus, when Gabriel Goldberg of Niesvizsh decided in his sixties to divorce his childless wife whom he loved and to whom he had been married for over fifty years, the rabbis refused to give him permission even though the couple satisfied the ten-year minimum. According to Sheikewitz's daughters, the story of R. Gabriel's divorce stirred up such an uproar that it was allegedly recorded in the town's *pinkas*. In the end, the Neisvizsher rabbi Nahum Meyer reluctantly approved the suit but solemnly warned the sixty-nine-year-old Reb Gabriel and his sixteen-year-old bride, Sorke, under the *huppah:* "If the marriage is against the will of God, may your wife, Gabriel, remain childless, fruitless like the sand of the desert; if however, I have done God's will, may your union be blessed with children and you, Gabriel, be worthy of marrying off even the youngest of them."[196]

Insanity

Mental illness, whether temporary or chronic, caused great stress and, with the development of psychiatry, increasingly came to be regarded by Russian society as a legitimate ground for divorce.[197] Rabbinic authorities in Russia recognized a "one-sided right" to divorce on grounds of insanity: only men, not women, could divorce on grounds of the spouse's insanity. That rule derived from the fact that only the male could initiate the divorce proceeding; as rabbinical authorities reasoned, a man who was mentally incompetent could not perform the divorce act.[198] In addition, Jewish law did not formally recognize the authority of institutions and professional psychiatrists. To overturn the "herem of Rabbi Gershom" that an insane woman could not be divorced (since she has no "will"), the law permitted a man to remarry without a divorce, granted that he obtain the signatures of one hundred rabbis. In essence, the so-called *heter meah rabbanim* allowed a man to abrogate the provisions of "Rabbi Gershom's" ruling so that he would not become an *agun* (a chained man). A woman, on the other hand, had no such possibilities since she was prohibited by biblical law from having two husbands.

By the early twentieth century, however, amid growing public debate, the unequal treatment of women came under criticism. At issue was the question of whether a mentally ill woman could consciously "receive" the

get. That was a central issue in a 1903 case, in which the father of a mentally ill woman protested a recent divorce, which, in conformity with Jewish law, had recently been approved by Rabbi Luria of Kiev. The case
eventually reached the Rabbinic Commission, which asked the Kiev provincial board to determine whether the husband (Yankel Lozban) had remarried, whether the wife was institutionalized in the psychiatric division
of the Kiev-Kirillovskii hospital, and if she was sufficiently mentally competent to receive the *get.* The first question was practical: were the husband remarried, it was much more complicated to reverse the decision,
dissolve the second marriage, and to reaffirm the validity of the first. The
latter two questions were more suggestive. The query about her institu-
tionalization, rather than demand of proof that the husband had secure
the signatures of one hundred rabbis, suggests that the Rabbinic Commission, like the Russian state, expected professional, not rabbinical, certification of insanity. More interesting still is the fact that the commission
even posed the question of her capacity to receive the *get.* For reasons that
remain unclear, the commission ultimately upheld the rabbi's decision and
pronounced the divorce valid. More significantly, the commission promulgated no formal changes in policy and left intact the one-sided principle
that only female, not male, insanity afforded a valid ground for divorce.

These insanity cases generated growing controversy about the inequity
of Jewish law toward women. In 1907, the physician Birshubskii presented a provocative paper on "Jewish law of divorce in the case of mentally ill" at the Pirogov Conference of Doctors in Moscow, a liberal national association of doctors in the Russian Empire.[199] Birshubskii,
sensitized to women's issues by medical colleagues active in the feminist
movement, vehemently denounced the treatment of mentally ill women
in Jewish religious law. He argued that psychiatric illnesses were no different from serious medical disorders and that both required proper
consultation and treatment from a qualified physician or psychiatrist.
"The principles of Jewish law," declared Birshubskii, "ignores the elementary demands of modern psychiatry." He warned that it failed to protect the interests of the divorced spouse or to determine "which partner
was responsible for the insanity." Moreover, he observed, "the very process of convening one hundred [rabbinic] signatures for the divorce in the
case of a mentally ill spouse is only available to wealthy and influential
individuals." He challenged the Rabbinic Commission to prevent further
abuse and to require all rabbis to demand an expert opinion of a psychiatrist before permitting such divorces.

In response, the Rabbinic Commission staunchly defended Jewish religious law and pointed out that the halakhah "strives to safeguard the
honor and position of women." It also explained that, contrary to Dr.
Birshubskii's claims, Jewish authorities in fact require medical certifica-

tion from an "expert" to demonstrate the mental illness of a wife. If the law additionally demanded the opinion of a rabbinic court, it was only to ensure that religious authorities be fully persuaded of the illness of the spouse. The commission explained that the final verdict of rabbinical courts sought to take into consideration the interests of *both* parties: (1) the interests of the husband, who might be tempted to pursue a "disorderly extra-marital life with all of its evil consequences," and (2) the interests of the wife, who should not be deprived of her material security in the event of divorce. In reality, the commission argued, it was extremely difficult for a Jewish husband to divorce on the grounds of insanity because of the many preconditions he had to fulfill. He was, for example, responsible for paying his wife's medical bills and for providing complete support until she was cured. In addition, he had to return her entire dowry and *ketubah,* as well as all of her personal belongings. And above all, he needed the signed approval of one hundred rabbinic authorities from three different districts.[200]

The onus of obtaining the signatures of one hundred rabbinic authorities could indeed deter or at least delay divorce on grounds of insanity, as in an earlier case involving Bentsel Shmuilovich Kissin of Kovno. In 1872 he sent a petition to the Rabbinic Commission challenging his local rabbi's decision to deny him a divorce because he failed to obtain permission from one hundred rabbis. The husband complained: "Upon my marriage to the daughter of the merchant M. Mysh, [my wife] resumed her fits of madness, which she had had before the marriage, but which they [the parents] concealed from me (exploiting my youthfulness and inexperience)." He had already spent large sums in a futile attempt to find a cure, but the endeavor had brought him only financial ruin. And because of her mental incapacitation, his wife failed to perform her maternal duties: their children suffered neglect and were growing up "without a mother's care and without a father's supervision and education." Declaring that he could no longer tolerate this situation, the husband asked not for a divorce but for annulment, on the grounds of his wife's premarital mental illness and the concealment by her parents.[201] The local rabbi, however, ruled that their marriage could be terminated only through a legal divorce, including the confirmation by one hundred rabbis. Although Kissin provided several medical certificates confirming his wife's mental illness, the Rabbinic Commission ruled against his petition and upheld the traditional ruling.[202] Kissin's apparent attempt to transfer Russian legal practice, including the rule of annulment for premarital insanity, to Jewish law thus fell on deaf ears in the commission.

The controversy over insanity as grounds for divorce formed part of a much broader debate in Western Europe and Russia. In part, it pertained to the general attempt to liberalize and especially to secularize divorce, that is, to see marriage as secular institution based on partnership and mutual relations, not as a sacrament. Interestingly, the insanity issue also drew strength from the eugenics movement, which argued that "divorce of the insane was a measure of defense for the sane and of preservation of society against procreation of the mentally abnormal."[203] For Russian Jews, this issue took a different form: it was the unequal application of insanity, compounded by the onerous requirement of approval by one hundred rabbis, that generated debate. At least on paper, the Jewish practice was more enlightened than formal rule might suggest, since authorities like the Rabbinic Commission did require medical certification and did attempt to protect the material interests of women who were mentally ill. Like their Christian counterparts, however, Jewish authorities found it much more difficult to revise core principles or, most important, to challenge the male's exclusive rights.

Religious Conversion

Religious conversion (apostasy) provided certain and speedy grounds for divorce, not only because of religious incompatibility with the spouse who remained loyal to Judaism but also because Russian authorities clearly favored dissolution of such mixed marriages. The converts themselves were often eager to take advantage of this policy, which allowed them to remarry without requiring a formal divorce, since the Russian Church did not recognize the validity of non-Orthodox marriages. If the convert was male, the remarriage required no Jewish divorce and thus left the wife in the unenviable position of an *agunah*. The Church was favorably inclined to a prompt, easy remarriage, perhaps to shield the new convert and any children from the pressure of coreligionists to reconvert, but perhaps also to coerce the spouse to convert as well. Apart from Church missionizing, conversion did inevitably disrupt not only family harmony but also unity, since converts often relocated, either to avoid persecution by their former coreligionists or to take advantage of their new right to leave the Pale.[204]

More problematic was the case of converted Jews who elected *not* to divorce. Here state law was unequivocal: according to a statute of 1835 (reiterated in 1851), in such mixed marriages "neither the husband nor wife are permitted to maintain permanent residency outside the Pale of Settlement."[205] In other words, although baptized Jews normally had the right to reside in St. Petersburg or Moscow, they forfeited that privilege if they chose to remain married to a Jewish spouse. This rule, understandably, created an enormous problem and dilemma for Jewish converts: either divorce or forfeit the new residency rights. For example, when Iosef

Rubenshtern (originally from Mitav) and Aleksandr Brozgal (from Vitebsk) converted to Orthodoxy, they obtained the right to register in communities in St. Petersburg and Orenburg, respectively.[206] However, once they informed local authorities that they had no intention of divorcing their Jewish wives, both immediately lost their new residence permits.

This law revealed deep ambivalence on the part of authorities. On the one hand, they did not require divorce if one spouse converted; unless one party insisted, the marriage remained intact. The state did mandate, to be sure, that converted spouses swear that they would proselytize to the "unbelieving spouse" and ensure that their children not be "led away to the Jewish faith." This qualified tolerance of interfaith marriages between Jews and converts gave lip service to the Pauline principle "that if any brother has a wife who is an unbeliever, and she is pleased to dwell with him, let him not send her away" (1 Cor. 7:12). On the other hand, the law clearly penalized those who chose to remain with a Jewish partner, perhaps from fear that communal pressure would cause the converts and their children to revert to Judaism. Such concerns were paramount for church authorities, who could find suitable scriptural justification, such as Paul's injunction not to be "bound together with unbelievers; for what partnership have righteousness and lawlessness" (see 2 Cor. 6:14–18). It was not until a flurry of similar cases reached the Holy Synod and Senate starting in the late 1890s that the state began to reconsider these contradictory positions in the law regarding interfaith marriages.

One such suit involved Dr. Mikhael Niurenberg, who had converted from Judaism to Christianity in 1899 with the expectation of enjoying the full rights and privileges of the tsar's Orthodox subjects. To his dismay, however, he discovered that the Moscow police would not give him a passport until he brought a certificate verifying that he had divorced his Jewish wife.[207] As Niurenberg explained in his appeal, prior to baptism he had enjoyed the privilege of residency in Moscow as a physician, as did his wife, who had obtained residency in the capital before their marriage. If the police's decision stands, he complained, this means that he had had more rights as a Jew than as a new Christian. In a second case, the first-guild merchant Isaak Gurkov complained that the police expelled him from St. Petersburg when they discovered that he had converted to Lutheranism but had not divorced his Jewish wife.[208]

Authorities were reluctant to revise the 1835 rule. Amid growing skepticism about the sincerity of such conversions (especially if only one member was baptized) and the growing antisemitism in popular and official circles, authorities took a hard line. Thus, in 1901, the chief procurator of the Synod (representing the Church) and the Senate initially rejected the Niurenberg's appeal on the grounds that tolerance of "mixed marriages" would have a "morally harmful" impact on the rest of the population.[209] Two years later, however, secular authorities again took up the issue for new consideration. To be sure, some senators reaffirmed the earlier ruling and defended the "religious-moral character" of the original law. They noted that the law applied only to those converts who chose "to maintain the marital union with an individual of the Jewish faith"; in other words, the converts forfeited their rights by making a morally "wrong" decision to remain married to the non-convert.[210] But this time a strong alternative view emerged, with adherents from the Senate and even from the Church. They noted that the 1835 law predated later legislation (from the 1850s and afterward) liberalizing the right of certain categories of Jews (e.g. retired soldiers, first-guild merchants, university graduates, and artisans) to reside outside the Pale of Settlement. The law of 1835, they argued, should be modified to take into account these new legal realities. Specifically, they rejected the decision to deprive the Niurenberg couple of their residency rights in Moscow. In 1904 the Senate formally ruled in favor of the Niurenbergs, recognizing their right to reside as an interfaith couple in Moscow.[211] Similarly, the Senate decided in the Rubinshtein and Brozgal cases to allow the wives, Tsira and Gita, to register in their husbands' town of residence but enjoined the local police to verify that the wives actually resided with their husbands.[212]

Modernity: Social and Cultural Framework

While the foregoing factors provided the immediate cause of individual marital breakdown, much broader forces were at work to reshape popular attitudes toward marriage and divorce in Russia.[213] The Great Reforms—in particular, the establishment of Western courts (1864), the liberalization of censorship, the expansion of schools and universities, and improvement in the legal status of Jews—had a profound impact on the Jewish family. Despite all the vagaries, contradictions, and partial retractions of later decades, the new order created immense new opportunities for mobility, education, litigation, and careers for men and women. All this inevitably had far-reaching repercussions on the institution of the family, marriage, and gender relations and expectations. The new order enhanced intellectual and economic independence, fostering not only a greater sense of individuality but also a more critical view of traditional Jewish values and customs. Contemporary intellectual movements in Russia shifted the emphasis from "economic and social considerations in marriage" to the importance of "individual emotions, feelings and self-fulfillment," a shift in values that inescapably affected spousal expectations and relationships.[214] Whereas couples had once tolerated certain forms of behavior and lower levels of affection, they now insisted that marriages embody the ideals of mutual love and respect being promoted by educated society.

Women's Education and Its Impact on Marital Breakdown

Nothing so typified the new milieu as the emergence of the "women's question" in the late 1850s and 1860s, not only in Russian society but also among Jews.[215] That new spirit informed *haskalah*'s indictment of traditional Jewish society, which it condemned for relegating women to an inferior position. The *maskilim* thus sought to heighten public consciousness of Jewish women's issues and the need for fundamental changes to improve the woman's role and status in the family, workplace, and religious sphere. One powerful spokesman for Jewish women was the writer Judah Leib Gordon, whose mock epic poem "Kosto shel yud" (The tip of the yud) bitterly castigated the position of women as equal only to enslavement.[216] As already pointed out, some *maskilim* proposed to improve women's lives by protecting them from the need to work outside the home, often as primary breadwinner, and to return them to the home and domestic sphere— an ideal deeply influenced by a Western "bourgeois" model.[217]

Others proposed the diametrical opposite, favoring greater rights of education to free women from their traditional bonds of subordination.[218] But, echoing a common theme in Russian feminism, such education was not intended to impart knowledge for its own sake but to create more compatible partners for educated husbands and better "qualified" mothers. As one writer for a Russian-Jewish weekly contended, "An uneducated mother can give her children neither an education nor a rational upbringing."[219] In 1851 the Rabbinical Commission further contended that parents who failed to educate their daughters only invited the husbands "to free themselves from this unhappiness." In the words of the report: "He [the husband] gives her a divorce according to the law and she returns to her own father, to the culprit of her unhappiness, who neglected her upbringing in her youth [by] not educating her, not permitting her [to have] any religious and noble sensibilities."[220] The commission concluded that female education would enable women to fulfill their triple role as wives, homemakers, and mothers.[221] Thus, from this rather conservative perspective, Jewish women's status would be raised in the eyes of society primarily through their contribution as mothers and wives. This limited vision for women's education would inevitably come into conflict with the broader aspirations of Jewish female students who strove to attain higher goals even at the expense of their marriages and families.

Institutions devoted to women's secondary education expanded dramatically in the second half of the nineteenth century. Indeed, that growth commenced from the very onset of the Great Reforms: between 1856 and 1868 the Ministry of Education opened 125 new schools, with an enrollment of over 10,000 students.[222] One type of school, the gymnasia, offered a six-year program (later increased to seven years) that included courses in "the Russian language, religion, arithmetic, penmanship, needlework, and [some] science." Those who completed an additional year received a supplementary degree that entitled them to become domestic teachers or tutors. The less ambitious progymnasia, a three-year program, offered a similar but more modest curriculum; its graduates were eligible to teach in elementary schools.[223] Both schools received a partial subsidy from the state but depended heavily on local funding. Wealthy Jewish families supported the new schools, and by the late nineteenth century established numerous private Jewish gymnasia for women.[224] For example, the Odessa educational district had several private female gymnasia, all founded by families such as the Goldins and Gold'denbergs.[225]

FIG. 12. Shul Marud, female artisan school in Chernigov. *Courtesy of the YIVO Institute for Jewish Research.*

According to one observer, Kishinev had more private women's schools because Jewish Orthodox families were more inclined to give their daughters a secular education than their sons, who were encouraged only to study the Torah and Jewish law.[226] Many upper-class Jewish women were keenly interested in taking full advantage of the opportunities to study, as is evident from sensational reports in the Jewish press. The Odessa branch of *Russkii Evrei,* for example, reported that "a Jewish girl ran away from her home to receive further education." The fourteen-year-old daughter of a merchant, it claimed, "took the necessary documents with her and six hundred rubles. She ran away on Yom Kippur."[227] A prominent feminist writer, Sara Rabinovich, argued that Jewish women had been excluded from participating in Jewish culture, and as a result, a large number now enrolled in secular Russian schools, sometimes even outnumbering Jewish male students.[228]

Jewish women, like their Russian peers, viewed their secondary degrees as a stepping stone to higher education. Although the government refused to grant women full admission rights, from the late 1850s it did permit progressive-minded professors to open their lectures to female auditors. Given the costs and legal obstacles, the number of Jewish auditors in the Lubianskie courses in Moscow's Third Gymnasium, which "boasted a curriculum equivalent to the physical-mathematical faculty of Moscow University," was astounding: between 1882 and 1885 the gymnasium enrolled eighty-one Jewish women (16.3 percent of the total auditors), by far the largest minority group in the school.[229] Similarly, Jewish auditors were highly visible in the women's higher courses in Kiev; between 1878 and 1882 they composed 15.8 percent of the students (112 of 708) in 1878–1882 and ranked second only to the Russian Orthodox students. Jewish auditors in the women's medical courses in St. Petersburg composed more than 20 percent of the admissions, compared with 4.8 percent for Roman Catholics and 2.1 percent for Lutherans.[230] This rigorous four-year program offered courses in general science and lectures in "gynecology, ophthalmology, dermatology, syphilis, and children's diseases," as well as practical training in midwifery.[231]

These educational aspirations often clashed with parents' plans for marriage and husbands' expectations for their role as mother and wife. One Jewish weekly reported that "ten young women from the most prosperous and religious families [in Mogilev] left for St. Petersburg to enroll in the women's higher courses, without the agreement of their parents."[232] In the case of the Jewish orphan, Varvara A. Kashevarova, the first woman to receive her medical degree in Russia, her marriage to a wealthy merchant in St. Petersburg collapsed when he reneged on his promise to "further her education" and opposed her plans for a career in medicine.[233]

In another case, Khaim Grinshtein complained to the Imperial Chancellery that his wife left him and her two children to study dentistry in Odessa, and he demanded that the government force her to return. The couple had initially renegotiated the division of gender roles to allow the wife to complete her studies while he managed the household and cared for the children. Now he complained that he himself suffered ("I get worked up every day over my trade [and] I have lost my head") and that his "small children suffer worse than orphans, being left without the tenderness and care of their natural mother." He complained that his wife's decision to practice dentistry was simply "unnecessary" and the "fruit of [her] capriciousness." In an effort to reassert traditional roles he invoked popular views about the innate nurturing abilities of women and insisted that his wife perform her natural duty. His wife, Rivka, however, categorically refused: "I was especially oppressed by the disagreement that became manifest between us regarding the moral world view with respect to the meaning of the family, the role of the mother, and concern about the upbringing of the children." She also denied that her career in dentistry was a caprice and openly voiced her desire for economic independence: "My striving for development and self-reliance met with desperate opposition from my husband, and I decided to study dentistry in order to [satisfy] my thirst for knowledge and to be able to support myself and my children in the event of a divorce." She included a copy of an agreement that her husband had signed, granting her a separate passport to receive

FIG. 13. A first-guild merchant family in St. Petersburg: Bella Dymshits and her children. *Courtesy of Galina Markovna Rokhlina of St. Petersburg.*

FIG. 14. First-guild merchant Isaac Dymshits with his wife, Bella Dymshits of St. Petersburg. *Courtesy of Galina Markovna Rokhlina.*

her dental training. Given his written consent, the Chancellery had no choice but to permit her to remain in Odessa.

This file graphically attests that educated Jewish women were becoming conscious of their own abilities, ambitions, and identity as separate from that of their husbands. That Rivka openly expressed her goal for obtaining an independent source of income, so as to support herself and her children in the event of a divorce, indicated a determination to control her own fate. Rivka Grinshtein, representative of a small but growing elite of educated women, had plainly reordered priorities, giving far more weight to personal self-realization than to her role as wife and mother. Her behavior, while exceptional, was particularly iconoclastic and subversive for traditional patriarchy.[234]

Decline in Religious Observance

Spousal relations also were greatly influenced by changing attitudes toward Jewish religious customs. When the *maskil* Yeshaya Heshl Perelstein (b. 1870) wrote his memoir in 1889, he observed that Jews had already become lax in their religious observance. In Bialystok, for instance, he saw "people who were undeniably Jewish, but who behaved like civilized Europeans and who abandoned customs that stood in their way." His own uncle's home was considered "modern" and was by no means exceptional for his community: "His home life was conducted in the European manner: people sat down to meals bareheaded, no one made a fuss over the preliminary ritual of hand-washing, and no care was taken to recite the blessing either before or after the meal. Likewise, they paid no heed to the stricter Sabbath restrictions; they carried handkerchiefs in their pockets, even money; and they combed their hair and polished their shoes on the Sabbath. For all that, my uncle was a good Jew."[235] Such transformation, however, inevitably ignited conflict in homes where one spouse defended traditional customs and resisted a more acculturated lifestyle.

One contention was observance of religious rituals at home. Pauline Wengeroff has emphasized how the decline of religious observance generated a "strange, mixed tension in the air on Sabbath." She claimed that

FIG. 15. Between tradition and modernity: the Akselrod family in the Pale of Settlement. The studio photographer pasted in the photo of a family member who was unavailable for the formal sitting. *Courtesy of the Akselrod family of St. Petersburg.*

women clung to Sabbath rituals (i.e., light the candles and recite the blessing) "because their very inner being still clung to the old," whereas the enlightened husband "lit his cigarette, turning her otherwise contented face
into a painful grimace."[236] Although her statements incorporated popular
assumptions about women's "natural" proclivity toward religiosity, they
also reflected her view of women's role as "guardians of tradition" against
a rising acculturation and assimilation. As Marion Kaplan has shown from
German Jews, women successfully maintained separate holidays, rituals,
and customs at home ("domestic Judaism"), not only because bourgeois
culture encouraged female spirituality but also because they "experienced
less of a contradiction between their daily lives and religious practice than
men."[237] For women who were more acculturated than their husbands (because of the gendered education), Wengeroff's experience was not representative. In such cases, it was the observant husband who maintained traditional
customs (like Isaac Bashevis Singer's father, who constantly endured jeers
from his wife's family for "excessive" piety). "Since he never looked at a
woman," wrote Singer in jest, "he could not recognize my mother and might
easily have mistaken Grandmother or a sister-in-law for his wife."[238]

Secularization also meant changes in physical appearance and dress.
Wengeroff's husband shaved off his beard, much to his parent's dismay,
and demanded that his wife stop wearing her wig. "At this point, my husband and I had our first truly severe conflict," she recalled. "All the other
women, even the older ones in our group had long ago freed themselves
of their wigs. I was uneasy. The concept of following the others was foreign to me, although I knew that my own hair could be more attractive.
. . . I did not comply and wore the wig for years."[239] Singer recounted the
story of Todros the watchmaker, who divorced his pious wife and married "a wigless modern girl."[240] Family photographs from the second half
of the nineteenth century also reveal generational changes in dress, with
couples outfitted in the latest fashion but the parents still donning traditional "Jewish clothing."

Another flashpoint of conflict was the upbringing of children. For
Wengeroff and other observant wives, it was essential that their children
learn the basics of Judaism—Hebrew, the Bible, and the sanctity of the
Sabbath and Holy Days. "But to all pleas and arguments,"she recalled,
the observant wives "always received the same answer from their husbands: the children do not need any religion!" Pious males had their
grievances too; Ioisif Broun complained bitterly that his wife, from
whom he was separated, was raising their son to become revolutionary
instead of a good, pious Jew.[241] Following the onset of pogroms in the
1870s and the increase of conversions among the Jewish youths, even
enlightened Jews like Wengeroff's husband had to reconsider the need
for a Jewish education. In fact, when the latter opened a new trade

school for impoverished boys in Minsk (with the help of a certain Rabbi Chaneles), it offered not only courses in useful trades but also in biblical and other Jewish subjects.

Industrialization and Urbanization

In addition to cultural change, broader forces like industrialization and urbanization also tended to erode traditional family bonds, especially among the lower social strata. A significant increase in migration from rural areas to factories and mills inevitably had a major impact on family structures and relationships, especially since employment was usually seasonal and affected only the individual, not the family. Migrant factory labor inexorably undermined the patriarchal and family control over individual members.[242] As noted earlier, the new industrial economy also wrought an important change in marital age, which rose markedly by the late nineteenth century as many Jews deferred marriage until they had achieved an independent livelihood.[243] The rise in the age of first marriage coincided with the emergence of a sizable artisan class composed of Jewish women.[244] Others worked as domestic servants, sometimes in distant towns far away from their families. The 1897 Russian census estimated that approximately 35 percent of gainfully employed women were registered as household or domestic servants. Although Arcadius Kahan suggests that this figure was exaggerated, in light of the fact that many so-called domestic servants were actually live-in apprentices, the archival records of Zhitomir indicate that prosperous Jewish families did in fact employ several servants (usually two or three), thereby distributing their workload in cooking, cleaning, mending, child care, and so forth.[245]

Later marriage and the growing economic independence of Jewish women had a profound impact on marital relationships and divorce. The pursuit of economic self-sufficiency sometimes came at a high price. In 1905, Dveira Zaets petitioned the Imperial Chancellery for a separate passport from her husband: "Six years ago, I married the townsman Shimshelia Zaets—a decrepit old man *(starik)*—because of difficult material circumstances and lack of a livelihood," she wrote. Shortly after the marriage, however, she found him so physically repulsive that she could not abide living with him. She left him, with his consent, but on the condition that each month she pay him a certain sum for the separate passport. "Until now, I have had steady work sewing neckties and could afford to give my husband the money in return for my passport," she wrote. Because of the recent economic recession, however, she declared that she no longer had the means to pay her seventy-three-year-old husband.[246]

Indeed, hardships that resulted from the economic recessions were a recurring theme; deals made earlier were hard to satisfy when the economy crashed. In turn, the husband complained that his wife had deceived him; despite her promise to cohabit, almost immediately she deserted. She spurned his suggestion of a divorce—in his opinion, because she would lose right to live in St. Petersburg, a privilege based on *his* status as a retired soldier. In response, she admitted to marrying Shimshelia Zaets because her chances of "earning a crust of bread" were better in the capital than in the Pale of Settlement. After a cursory investigation, the Chancellery rejected her petition, presumably because it looked askance at marriage that enabled a provincial Jewish woman like Dvira to live in the capital. The commission added that the wife earned fifty rubles a month, while "the decrepit old man who is blind in both eyes . . . lives on his pension of six rubles a month and on the assistance from his son; the price for the renewal of her passport according to their agreement is five rubles."[247] Although clearly a *mariage de convenance* (at least for her) that did not beget any children, it reveals that Jewish women with an independent means of income were less constrained by financial necessity to remain in their unhappy marriages. That was the very reason why early Russian-Jewish feminists like Sara Rabinovich advocated professional artisan schools for women. By assisting women to become economically self-reliant and educated, she argued, activists could induce a radical transformation in Jewish women's dependent position in marriage, as well as their exclusion from active "participation in Jewish culture."[248]

Conclusion

Abraham Mapu's indictment of Jewish marriages was surely hyperbole when he wrote: "Only one in a thousand will derive joy from family life and even that will be a facade."[249] But for those individuals who were caught up in a painful divorce, his words certainly rang true. The interaction of social and cultural change is complex. As David Biale once wrote, "We cannot know whether the high divorce rate was a consequence of haskalah or if, conversely, haskalah may have been one result of unhappy marriages."[250] The above discussion, at least, suggests that unhappy family life gave rise to *haskalah* and its general disenchantment with traditional Jewish life. The earlier divorce rate was astronomically high, even by modern standards; yet even these rates did not include many marriages that had broken down but (for reasons to be considered in the following chapter) had not been formally sundered. To be sure, not all divorces resulted from "unhappy marriages." Some stemmed from parental or communal pressures (e.g., coerced divorces like that of Abraham Baer

Gottlober or the dissolution of childless marriages); others were "conditional divorces" that a husband granted to his wife before he embarked on a long journey or entered the military so that she would not become an *agunah* in the event of his death. Some ailing husbands who were childless also granted their wives a conditional divorce to save them from the complications of a levirite divorce *(halitsah)*.

Still, the majority of divorces did ensue from deep tensions in the Jewish family, some immediately traceable to everyday domestic problems (the "precipitants" discussed above), as well as to less transparent but powerful forces of broader social, economic, and cultural transformations. The key was the decision to divorce—that is, to dissolve the marital union. That resolution reflected change in marital tolerance, expectations of marriage, and external constraints. The opportunity and facility to divorce was also important, especially the presumed willingness of the state to intercede on behalf of women.

The late-nineteenth-century decline in the divorce rate (contra the typical tendency for rates to skyrocket among the rest of the population) was due to several factors, including the rise in the age of first marriage (the majority of divorces were between young couples), the diminished power of rabbinical authorities to enforce female-initiated divorces, the specter of the financial settlement (especially as women learned to use the secular courts to secure their claims), and a growing cultural and religious aversion to divorce. The surge of antisemitism (pogroms; blood-libel cases) may have served as an additional deterrent toward family dissolution, compelling Jews to look "inward" for security and shelter. Despite the decline in the absolute number of recorded divorces, the sources (archival, memoir, and belles-lettres) suggest that the level of marital breakdown and tension did not decrease and perhaps even rose during the same period, suggesting a growing disparity between the number of divorces and marital breakdown.

Chapter Four

Kritut: Negotiating the Divorce Agreement and Unresolved Issues

For our many sins, there are some who have breached the bounds of decency and have cast off the obligation to support their families. . . . Among them are men who know no discipline, and who have taken themselves other wives in place of those they betrothed according to the law of Moses and Israel. . . . An outcry has reached us from many towns and cities from living widows, left without support from their husbands and without anyone to hear the wailing of their tender children asking for food, when there is none to give: a voice of weeping that pierces the heart!

— Rabbi Moshe Nahum Yerusalimsky to Western rabbis (undated letter)

Tsu a khasene geyt men, tsu a get loyft men [To the wedding one walks, to the divorce one runs]. —Yiddish folk saying

The previous chapter has suggested that spouses were often reluctant to embark on formal divorce proceedings, even long after the marriage had clearly and irrevocably broken down. Although Russian state officials and *maskilim* were wont to imagine an avalanche of hasty divorces, in fact, many spouses demurred for a long time before formalizing the marital breakdown. Rates *were* high, but so were the levels of resistance and procrastination. The case of the Jewish merchant Grigorii Bagrov was not unusual: reluctant to seek a formal divorce, he chose to live in a separate room for almost ten years before finally resolving to dissolve the marriage.[1] A similar reluctance was true for many women. Thus, although the marriage of Dveira Elka Aizikovich disintegrated shortly after the wedding (because of her husband's drunkenness and physical abuse), more than eight years would pass before she finally left him and petitioned the Imperial Chancellery for a separate passport.[2] While some marriages did end quickly and abruptly, the number of cases in which the spouses were estranged and separate but not formally divorced indicates the presence of serious impediments and disincentives. Couples increasingly found the consequences of divorce even more unpalatable than the continuation of a bad marriage.

This chapter explores the aftermath of divorce—both the consequences for the partners and the broader issues raised by formal divorce. It first examines the mundane but important issues of alimony, division of property, and child custody and support. However, in the Russian Empire, divorce entailed a host of additional problems for Jews—above all, residency and social status of the wife. If a woman had the privilege of residing outside the Pale prior to marriage but had married and resettled in the Pale, the question was whether she might regain that right in the event of divorce. Could she reclaim her original (paternal) legal status, or did she retain that of her husband? Questions like these poured into the offices of the Russian-Jewish press and government bureaus, as divorced Jews sought to clarify their new legal position vis-à-vis the state. The final section of this chapter focuses on the "unresolved" cases of marital breakdown, which ended in desertion, bigamy, and the tragic plight of the *agunah*. Such problems, no less than the high rate of divorce, defined public and official perceptions of a crisis of the family and ignited an outcry about the breakdown of family values and, by extension, social order.

Severing the Marital Bonds: Consequences and Quandaries

Marital dissolution involved much more than the divorce proceedings in rabbinic court or the delivery of the bill of divorcement to the wife. It also severed the ties that bound the couple together as an "economic partnership," with a sharing of assets, real estate, and personal belonging. Depending on the circumstances, divorce might entail alimony to provide support for the former wife. Divorce also required a determination of child custody and support. With laws vague and much done ad hoc, these issues were laden with enormous emotion and invited a torrent of acrimonious litigation.

Negotiating the Financial Settlement

A writer for the journal *Russkii evrei* lamented the high rate of marital dissolution among the Jews, estimating that approximately one-quarter of all marriages ended in divorce. He decried this "extremely deplorable phenomenon," particularly because it entailed tragic economic consequences for all concerned. "Whoever is closely acquainted with the Russian-Jewish masses," he declared, "knows that every divorce deals a grave blow to the material welfare of both spouses and . . . affects the upbringing of children in a detrimental [manner]."[3] Even when the legal requirements were unambiguous, they still left room for negotiation over specific terms, which often fueled bitter conflict and interminable legal wrangling by divorcing couples.

According to the Jewish marital contract, the husband was potentially liable for three types of payment in the event of a divorce: (1) restitution of the entire value of his wife's dowry *(nedunyah)*; (2) the *ketubah* payment, usually a lump sum, as a one-time divorce settlement; and (3) the *tosefet ketubah,* any additional monies on which the two parties agreed. The dowry consisted of all assets that the wife brought to the marriage and remained her exclusive property even if she voluntarily entrusted it to her husband's care and management.[4] In Imperial Russia the dowry included not only assets in the narrow sense (tangible material and monetary possessions given on the occasion of the wedding) but also any other gifts. If a marriage was dissolved through divorce or death, the husband or his heirs were bound to restore the full amount of the dowry to the wife, supplemented by an increment of "no less than one-half of the sum specified," the standard rate of appreciation in Russia. In 1893, for example, the Rabbinic Commission ruled that if a wife brought a dowry of 100 rubles to the marriage, the husband was obliged to repay to her, in the event of divorce, 150 rubles to comply with the rule of a 50 percent increment.[5]

While a Jewish woman forfeited her dowry only in the most exceptional cases, that was not true for the *ketubah;* she could lose a portion or the entire sum if the charges brought against her in divorce court involved a monetary penalty. As noted earlier, the minimum *ketubah* settlement for the northwestern provinces of Russia was 76 silver rubles for virgins and 38 rubles for previously married women; the equivalent minimum in the southwestern provinces was 48 and 24 rubles, respectively. To deter rash divorces, wealthier families stipulated significantly higher sums in the marital contract, but they did so in vain if the wife had to forfeit her right to full compensation. In essence, "the wife's right to claim the amount of the *ketubah* depended on her good conduct."[6] In the case of an adulteress—whether she was caught in the act, discovered in a "compromising" position, or simply suspected of having illicit relations—the penalty was swift and merciless: she was to be "driven off," with the total forfeiture of her *ketubah.*[7] A woman suffered similar consequences for various misdemeanors that violated Jewish customs, such as "appearing in public places with exposed shoulders or arms or [an] uncovered head, bathing in men's bathing [areas] . . . indulging in conversation with men or flirting with them, acting familiarly with her slaves or neighbors, being loud-mouthed on private matters, or cursing her husband's parents in his presence."[8] Moreover, a wife who made her husband "objection-able" to his neighbors by vowing that she would not "lend or borrow household utensils, not attend weddings or funerals," could also be de-prived of her monetary settlement in a divorce.[9] Predictably, men were often disposed to find grounds to annul the *ketubah*. For example, when M. L. Lilienblum's father divorced his first wife, he was able to abrogate the *ketubah* "because she stayed in the home of a gentile without a chaperon."[10] Another husband succeeded in divorcing his wife without her *ketubah* on the grounds that his wife did not observe the laws of *niddah* (ritual purity).[11]

The *ketubah* also could be reduced in the case of the *moredet,* the "re-bellious wife." The *Shulhan Arukh* warned that a woman who denied her husband sexual relations could be divorced without any alimony and was not permitted to take anything that belonged to her husband: "She must remove even the shoe on her foot and the kerchief on her head and she re-turns to him anything he had given her as a gift."[12] If, however, the wife convinced the court that her husband was repulsive for legitimate reasons (e.g., "he did not follow a proper path [of conduct] or he squandered money"), then she retained the right to her dowry and property.[13] But if she had rebelled out of anger or ulterior motives (e.g., to extract money from her husband), the court could "return to her husband even that which she had taken from her own property [dowry]."[14] It was also to a man's advantage if the wife had deliberately and deceitfully concealed physical defects before their marriage, including "a bad odor from the body or mouth, excessive perspiration, a wart on the face, a masculine voice, oversized or misplaced breasts, epilepsy, or irregularity in men-strual periods."[15] If he could prove this fraud, the wife lost her *ketubah*.

Although these rules voided the *ketubah* under specific circum-stances,[16] most husbands had to pay the full amount when they divorced. Not that they were eager to fulfill their obligation willingly; on the con-trary, negotiations over the divorce settlement elicited numerous claims and counterclaims that could be resolved in several ways. According to the Rabbinic Commission, the dispute could be settled by the couple pri-vately or through the mediation of parents and relatives; if that failed, they could appeal to a rabbinic arbitration court *(ravvinskii treiteiskii sud)*. Increasingly, however, couples did neither and instead appealed to state courts for adjudication, especially after the creation of the new court system in 1864. The Rabbinic Commission itself observed: "Since the establishment of the judicial statute of 1864, Jews have almost always resorted to the decision of a general [state] court in matters of this kind."[17] The commission complained that Jews were "more inclined to turn to these institutions with their civil suits, rather than to the rabbinic courts, because the decision of the latter lacks any executive power" to ensure implementation and enforcement.[18] As couples quickly discovered, the word of the rabbi was only as good as his ability to enforce the decision of the *beit-din*. Unable to impose his ruling and limited to "persuasion and exhortation," the rabbi could not compel a husband to return his wife's dowry or to pay the *ketubah*.

This growing reliance on state courts was thus due to two main factors. One was the decline of traditional Jewish authority, which in turn was due to the breakdown of communal discipline, the circumscribed authority of rabbinic courts, the greater social and geographic mobility of Jews, and a loss of religiosity among the more secularized strata of the Jewish population. The second factor was the judicial reform of 1864: the new court system was not only more efficient and equitable but also more accessible "not only in formal rights, but also in costs."[19] As for other groups in late Imperial Russia, the courts thus not only brought greater justice but also inspired a spirit of "litigiousness."[20] Indeed, local archives, such as the materials in the Zhitomir and Vil'na civil and criminal courts, show that Jews were actively taking advantage of the new courts. By the early 1870s literally thousands of Jews, both men and women, submitted their civil cases to the new courts to settle a host of disputes. Countless suits, for example, were filed by widows and legitimate heirs against avaricious relatives seeking to deprive them of their *ketubot* or inheritance.[21] Domestic servants charged their employers with failure to pay their salaries;[22] relatives litigated over every imaginable personal or financial conflict;[23] one man took his neighbor to court for constructing a window that faced his house and deprived him of privacy;[24] wives even sued their husbands for money.[25]

To finalize divorce settlements, Jewish couples often hired a lawyer to prepare a legal agreement delineating their respective rights and obligations.[26] If the couple had been married very briefly and had no children, such agreements were fairly simple. The use of lawyers was especially common in the capitals of Moscow and St. Petersburg; legalistic language routinely informed divorce petitions to the state rabbi Jacob Maze of Moscow. A typical request from Isaak Estrin and Feiga (born Malkin) of Moscow in 1914 read as follows: "Wishing by our mutual agreement to dissolve our marriage, which was concluded in Moscow on 23 November 1912, we humbly ask you, Sir, to issue the appropriate order for the dissolution of our marriage. Moreover, we have no present or future claims against each other."[27] The reliance on lawyers was apparently not only limited to the two capitals. According to a report by the Jewish Committee in Volhynia, Jewish lawyers had allegedly appeared in "every town and village," with promises to help provincial Jews draft petitions and other legal instruments.[28]

Couples embroiled in more complex financial disputes were especially inclined to use the secular court. In December 1864, Lipman and Gitla Aingorn asked the rabbi of Ekaterinoslav to convene a *beit-din* to mediate their conflicting interests regarding the division of property and alimony. Beforehand, each spouse agreed to binding arbitration, signing an acknowledgment that "the decision of the rabbinic court regarding their case shall [be considered] definitive."[29] Apparently, the *beit-din* had no intention of devoting its erudition and time to the case only have its decision challenged by a secular court. They eventually ruled that if the husband desired to divorce his wife, he must return all her belongings and 250 rubles (presumably the amount of her *ketubah*) and to re-deed to her their small store in the village of Nikopol (presumably, part of her dowry), worth a reported 160 rubles. He was also obliged to pay Gitla Aingorn fifteen silver rubles a month for maintenance—an unusual stipulation, since the husband in principle was to pay his wife a lump sum (to cover the dowry, *ketubah,* and any other monetary obligations), and therefore owed no alimony payments.[30] However, in Russia, husbands in fact often had to pay alimony because they were unable to repay the wife's dowry at the time of the divorce.[31]

This divorce settlement doubtless spelled economic hardship for Lipman Aingorn. At a time when two hundred to four hundred rubles was the total income of petty bureaucrats, priests, and others below the privileged and affluent, the husband's obligation to pay fifteen rubles per month (180 rubles per year) was clearly a large sum.[32] Aingorn's plight was all the worse since he lost his wife's capital and his primary source of income—the family store. Little wonder that he contested the binding arbitration and appealed the decision of the *beit-din* before state authorities. In petitions to the provincial governor, civil court, and later to the Senate, he argued that the rabbinic court had no authority to regulate the financial settlement since "a rabbi is only [permitted] to resolve misunderstandings in Jewish law," not to "meddle in civil affairs."[33]

In response to Aingorn's complaint, the Ministry of Internal Affairs made a formal investigation. It concluded that the *beit-din,* even if lacking official status, could function as an arbitration court *(treiteiskii sud)* in civil suits. The only stipulation was that the *beit-din* comply with the basic rules of arbitration promulgated in 1844.[34] Those rules provided that an arbitration court should be composed of mediators chosen by the litigants themselves (usually an odd number to avoid a deadlock) to resolve civil disputes concerning personal status rights, children or other dependent wards, real estate, and other issues. To prevent abuses and appeals, the law required that litigants sign a document called an arbitration declaration *(treteiskaia zapis')* stipulating the conditions of the hearing. Only on rare occasions could parties appeal the decision of the arbitration court; in such cases, the litigant could ask a state civil court to reexamine the suit.[35] Although the Aingorn archival file has no clear resolution, the state evidently upheld the decision of the rabbinic court, thereby setting a precedent for future litigation. The Rabbinic Commission therefore advised Jewish petitioners to choose an arbitration court to settle any monetary and property disputes.[36] It strongly recommended, however, that the rabbi who presided over the divorce proceedings not participate in any property suits, since that contradicted his primary duty to reconcile the couple.[37]

In principle, the financial arrangement was to provide the divorcée with capital for support and maintenance. In most cases, however, such capital was not sufficient and could not replace the husband's income. That was especially true if the marital union was also a business partnership in which both spouses cooperated to earn a living. This economic interdependence underlay a Yiddish folksong that warned the future bride of the hardships if she married an artisan or worker instead of a rabbinic scholar (the traditional ideal): "Cobblers' wives must make the thread. Tailors' wives must sit up late. Coachmen's wives must tar the axles . . ."[38] Since Jewish women often shared their husbands' occupation, divorce not only deprived them of their main source of income, but also their own job. Even when the wife acquired the family tavern, inn, butcher store, or shop (as in the Aingorn case), it was difficult for a single person to manage the business. As a result, some divorced women chose to seek new employment in the cities. All this explains why the 1897 census reported that nearly four times as many divorced women lived in cities as in the countryside.[39]

Despite the protection extended by Jewish law, divorcées faced economic ruin if the husband deserted (after squandering the dowry) or was unable or unwilling to fulfill his financial obligation. Khaim Arieh Poliakov, for example, dissipated his wife's dowry of six thousand rubles to support a "debauched" lifestyle and then abandoned his wife, leaving her in dire financial straits. He refused to initiate the divorce until he had extracted her last kopeck; by then he had presumably found a prospective wife to support him. Whatever the truth about his extortion, the files do demonstrate that he had exhausted his wife's resources.[40] In 1911, Dora Faivilevich faced even more trying circumstances: her estranged husband, from whom she had separated, withdrew two thousand rubles from their bank account (her dowry) and refused either to initiate divorce proceedings (since he would have to repay the sum) or to support her and their twelve-year-old son.[41]

Other husbands resorted to legal technicalities, claiming that the *ketubah* had not been signed by witnesses, thus rendering it null and void as a legal document in state law. In 1893, Rabbi Elin of Novogrudok (Minsk province) sent an alarming letter to the Rabbinic Commission, warning that an unsigned *ketubah* was no longer legally binding in state courts. The reason was a rule in Russian civil law whereby "testimonies of witnesses can be accepted only if no written documents are required." If the *ketubah* was unsigned, the wife could not use witnesses to confirm its validity. Rabbi Elin objected that state courts should be "guided by local social customs," an alternative principle cited in the same statute. The Rabbinic Commission ruled that a *ketubah,* whether signed or not, "should have juridical significance not only for the Jewish spiritual courts but also for the general [state] courts." It conceded, however, that "all too often, the judicial institutions do not recognize the binding power of the *ketubah* document, either due to the absence of signatures . . . or due to the inaccuracy of the witnesses' signatures." Powerless to change the rulings of the state courts, the commission recommended that, henceforth, the witnesses to the *ketubah* include their first names, patronymics, family names, and places of residence so that courts might more easily locate them to verify their testimonies. In addition, the Jewish groom was now to sign beneath the signature of the witnesses or on the back of the document, thereby confirming his accountability for fulfilling all the stipulations in the marriage contract. In the case of an illiterate groom, the person bearing power-of-attorney could sign the *ketubah* for him.[42]

It is important to underline the dynamics of intrusion by secular courts. As the above cases suggest, the state intervened not because of some abstract desire to assimilate or standardize but in response to judicial appeals by Jews themselves. That initiative from below is all the more striking in the Great Reform era, when the state abjured its belief in *étatisme* and sought to foster "self-development" from below. In short, it was not state ambitions but the attractiveness of postreform courts that stimulated petitions, suits, and legal appeals against Jewish courts and Jewish law. Little wonder that so many divorce agreements included a disavowal from both parties on pressing future claims.[43]

Faced with the harsh economic realities of divorce, Jews sometimes attempted to claim misapplication of Jewish religious law. Instructive is the 1870 case of Meita Liubich. In a petition to the Rabbinic Commission she claimed that "after twelve years of marital life, my husband evicted me from my home without cause [and] kept not only my dowry, but also my entire wardrobe, pearls, and various valuables worth one thousand rubles." She alleged that her husband feigned a quarrel with his mediator, Srul Friedberg, who then offered his services to Liubich. As she prepared to leave the "mediator's" apartment, however, Freidberg grabbed her while another man sat her down in a chair and shouted: "Your husband and the state rabbi have sent you a *razluka* [separation]."[44] Apparently, they then handed her the bill of divorcement. Meita declared that she refused to acknowledge such a humiliating divorce, given only to "women with loose morals." She claimed that, contrary to Jewish law, she held the *get* in her hand for less than five minutes, making the divorce invalid.

The local state rabbi, however, claimed that the wife, not the husband, had initiated the divorce. According to him, in February 1870, Meita Liubich had told several people that "she had long felt a strong hatred for her husband"and was confident that she had sufficient material wealth to choose another husband at her discretion. She allegedly told the rabbi about her plan to pressure Zel'man Liubich to grant a divorce by suing him for support in a Grodno state court on the grounds that he evicted her. However, the scheme backfired when the court denied her petition. In the end, the husband decided to acquiesce, "sacrificing a significant sum of money."

After a lengthy investigation, the Senate dismissed Meita Liubich's claims as totally groundless.[45] According to several witnesses, she initiated the divorce, eventually prevailing upon her husband to agree, and allegedly seized a substantial share of his personal assets (500 rubles). For all her claims of "destitution," officials noted that she had traveled all the way from Grodno to St. Petersburg to press her case and hence had sufficient resources to pay for transportation, passport, a temporary residence permit, and lodging in the capital. If the testimony of the rabbi and other witnesses was accurate, Meita had demanded a divorce on the assumption that she would receive a handsome settlement and then remarry someone of her own choice. Once the Grodno civil court rejected her petition for alimony, she evidently began to reconsider her demand for the divorce. Her designs for remarriage also went awry, casting doubt on her future economic security. It was difficult for a forty-eight-year-old Jewish woman with three children to remarry, given the patterns of remarriage among Jews. She evidently did not receive child support for the two older sons. Although the file does not include the details of the financial settlement, it clearly lowered her standard of living.[46]

Finally, some women obtained a monthly alimony as an "incentive" for agreeing to a voluntary divorce. Such concessions were more likely when the state rabbi (like Jacob Maze of Moscow) refused to grant a divorce against a wife's will. The case of the Bialo family is indicative. In May 1910, Boris Bialo, who had a law degree, explained to the rabbi that he had been living separately from his wife by mutual consent since January and now desired a formal divorce.[47] He announced his willingness to pay 150 rubles a month for the rest of her life, notwithstanding the fact that her personal assets (money and jewelry) were worth approximately 20,000 rubles. Next came the threat: if she declined his offer, he would reduce her support to 50 rubles a month. He also threatened to seek a unilateral divorce hearing on the grounds of childlessness (either at the rabbi's *beit-din* or before the Rabbinic Commission in St. Petersburg). He thus presented an ultimatum: either she accept the alimony or face a humiliating trial as a childless wife.[48]

In short, the complex rights and rules allowed, even encouraged, the two parties to negotiate and seek some kind of mutually acceptable trade-off. The litigation lever worked both ways, as the Bialo case shows: its threat could force a husband to volunteer a more generous alimony, but it also could subject the wife to public humiliation.

The Children: Custody, Visitation, and Support

Arrangements for child custody and support varied kaleidoscopically, depending on the parents' economic and social circumstances.[49] Such was

FIG. 16. Children of Anna Dymshits-Person in St. Petersburg, turn of the century. *Courtesy of Galina Markovna Rokhlina.*

FIG. 17. Studio portrait of a little girl with a ball. *Courtesy of the Akselrod family.*

true as well for Jews until 1893, when the Rabbinic Commission attempted to standardize practice in a report to Ministry of Internal Affairs. According to Jewish law, the commission declared, the mother had the sole right of custody of the son until he was six years old (when he became the father's ward) and of the daughter until she was married; the father was to provide support as long as the children were minors and lived with their mother.[50] If the divorced wife agreed to nurse her infant, the husband had to pay her for the service, whether in kind (e.g., food and clothing) or in money. The mother could, however, refuse to nurse her child, except when the infant refused to take another woman's milk. When a son turned six, the father had the right but not the obligation to claim custody in order to educate him in Jewish law or to teach him a trade; unless the couple decided otherwise, the daughter almost always remained with the mother.[51] Thus, the parents divided the children according to gender, a practice not uncommon in contemporary Western European countries (e.g., France).[52]

Such prescriptions notwithstanding, archival sources reveal that the majority of Jewish mothers in Moscow gained sole custody of their children, regardless of their ages, after divorce.[53] But there were exceptions. In contrast to the usual arrangement, Itsko and Roza Rozin of Moscow signed an agreement that the oldest daughter Khaia (age 5) would remain with the father while the son, Moise (4 years old) would live with his mother. The father promised to pay five rubles a month (starting in 1908) for his younger child's maintenance.[54]

Divorced couples often signed prolix agreements that detailed the responsibilities of the custodial and noncustodial parents, and reflected contemporary concerns about child rearing. One primary issue was assimilation. Clearly alarmed by the rising number of Jewish conversions to Christianity in Moscow,[55] Zelman El'birt obtained a pledge from his wife that she would not convert their son Avram to another faith after their divorce.[56] If she violated their agreement, the mother was required to return the son to the father's custody. This precaution was judicious, given the complications that arose when one parent converted to Christianity. In that event, Russian law generally mandated a gendered division of the children between the spouses. "Upon the baptism of Jews, they can baptize their children as long as they are under seven years old. If only the father or mother converts, in the former case, the sons can be baptized; in the latter case, the daughters can be baptized."[57]

In reality, however, the Church routinely dismissed these requirements and granted child custody of both sexes to the converted parent. Hence, the Lithuanian Orthodox Consistory approved Iosel Stengrod's petition to baptize his son *and* daughter. The monastery reported, however, that the father arrived "with his eight-year-old son and without his daughter Khana, who remained with her mother due to an illness." Apparently, the wife prevailed in her struggle to retain custody over her two daughters— the oldest who adamantly refused to convert, and the one-year-old girl who mysteriously fell ill just before the father entered the monastery.[58] The Tevners in Moscow came up with a compromise based on age. When Yankel Tevner, a dentist, converted to Russian Orthodoxy along with his three oldest sons (Viktor, Anatolii, and Iurii), he agreed to give his wife custody of their youngest son, Avram, who would be raised in the Jewish faith. According to their divorce agreement, the father promised to pay twenty rubles a month for his maintenance.[59]

Another concern was the child's daily upbringing and care. Although some spouses accorded an important role to the extended family, they insisted that the custodial parent provide the primary care. Hence, Tsiva El'birt promised to "bring up the child under my direct supervision and, under no circumstances, will I give him up to be raised by relatives, let alone by strangers." The issue was particularly sensitive in the event that the custodial parent remarried. In the El'birt case the husband reserved the right to contest his wife's sole custody, especially if she had children from the second marriage and thus might neglect his own child's interests.[60]

The issue of material support also generated much bitter conflict and litigation. Aware that only the state could coerce compliance, many Jewish couples ignored the rabbinical courts and resorted directly to state courts or binding arbitration.[61] At stake were questions about the amount and duration and also stipulations to ensure that the agreement was legally binding and enforceable.[62] Still, a court verdict did not guarantee automatic compliance; a determined father had various options for evading his financial responsibilities. Thus, a father like Nakhim Israel'son entertained ideas about emigrating and renouncing Russian citizenship to free himself from the obligation to support his ex-wife and children.[63] Others simply refused to pay until faced with serious retribution by state authorities. For example, David Mordukh Saet, received an order from the St. Petersburg court of appeals *(sudebnaia palata)* to pay nine hundred rubles per year to support his wife (from whom he was separated) and their son Herikh, effective on 9 August 1906. Nonetheless, he ignored the court and refused to support his family; he also continued what his wife called "a depraved lifestyle." Four years later, having received not a single payment from her husband, Ester Saet asked the Rabbinic Commission to intercede. It instructed the local rabbis in Vil'na to use moral persuasion and, if that failed, to enlist the assistance of state authorities.[64] Others appealed directly to local authorities to enforce child support payments and to threaten recalcitrant fathers with imprisonment for noncompliance.[65]

But child support also was negotiable; some wives renounced their claims to child support in order to gain sole custody. Hence, Khana Kopel'man of St. Petersburg signed an agreement that she would not seek any monetary assistance from her former husband, Zelik Iudelevich. In exchange he promised not to interfere in the child's maintenance, upbringing, and education.[66] Minna Luntz and her husband, a medical doctor, reached a similar arrangement when they divorced in St. Petersburg. The doctor complained, however, that his ex-wife constantly asked for money to support their son and not only created "scandals" in his apartment but also threatened to sue him. Rather than provide assistance, he proposed to take custody of the boy and promised to "give him a good upbringing." Unwilling to risk losing custody, Minna enrolled in a trade school to become a seamstress so that she could earn an independent living and support the boy and herself.[67]

In exceptional instances, fathers had minimal or no obligations of child support. When Jewish soldiers converted to Orthodoxy, the state promised to provide special assistance: "children of low-ranking soldiers of the Jewish faith are eligible for aid from the state treasury in the event that one of the spouses converts to Russian Orthodoxy and the couple gets divorced."[68] This offer was certainly attractive to the impoverished soldiers, although the state did not keep records on how many actually took advantage of this offer. Statistically more significant was unproven paternity: if men sired children out of wedlock but the fatherhood was ambiguous, they had no legal obligation to assist the mother. The plight of illegitimate children was indeed tragic. It drove at least three Jewish women who lived in the same building on Rybnaia Street in Zhitomir (evidently a Jewish birthing home for poor women) to ask a local Christian orphanage to take custody of their children.[69] "Not having any means [of support], I gave birth to a girl at the Zhitomir birthing home on 9 March 1892," wrote Sura Rivka Kavruka, who asked the administrators to baptize her newborn girl so that she would be eligible for the orphanage.[70] Although the files give no motive for leaving their children in a Christian institution, one can speculate that either they could not obtain assistance from a Jewish orphanage (for whatever reason, perhaps as nonresidents) or that the fathers were of the Russian Orthodox faith.

Other Jewish women without child support left their children with family members while they worked to support them. In 1879, Shendlia (no family name) came to Starokonstantinov (Volhynia province) to leave her six-year-old daughter Khaia Sura with her older brother, a Jew who had converted to Russian Orthodoxy as a cantonist. Desperate, the mother beseeched him to take her daughter while she went to Odessa to work as a cook; her employers refused to hire her if she brought along the child. A younger brother had cared for Khaia, but he could no longer afford to do so any longer. The brother's wife recalled that day vividly: "Two years ago, a Jewish woman came to me and claimed that she was the sister of my husband (who had converted from Judaism) and asked if I could take care of her daughter—a small, sickly girl—explaining that she did not have the means to support her." In the end, despite vigorous protests, they took the child but on the condition that Shendlia send five rubles a month.

In the ensuing months, Khaia Sura allegedly suffered physical and emotional abuse at the hands of her "Aunt Volkov," who renamed her Liuba and planned to baptize her into the Russian Orthodox church. Word of the cruelty eventually reached Khaia's grandmother, who had just left her position as a domestic servant to live with her youngest son.

When the grandmother arrived in Starokonstantinov to take custody of grandchild, Volkov refused to give her up, claiming that she had no proof of the grandmother's identity (the husband was in Kiev for medical treatment). The grandmother then petitioned the Starokonstantinov district court with this description of Khaia Sura: "She always looks dirty and Volkov beats her because she wants her to speak only in Russian. What a strange demand of a six-year-old [girl], who does not know how to speak Yiddish very well, let alone Russian. Now she has completely changed and cannot understand either Yiddish or Russian."[71] Numerous witnesses confirmed rumors that Maria Volkov abused the child, locked her up in a room all day, and starved her "without mercy." As a schoolteacher who boarded at the Volkov residence, testified, "We noticed her because sometimes she would run to us . . . and ask for bread and it was clear that the child was suffering from hunger." Another witness confirmed to the court: "This is to confirm that [Maria] Volkov is very cruel to the girl." Most revealing was the girl's own testimony:

My name is Liubuchka and before that it was Khaia. I do not know who my parents are, but they say that they are *zhidi* [a pejorative for Jews]. How old am I? I do not know. It has been almost a year and a half since I was taught to read. I do not know how to write. I do not know how long [it has been], but I think it was a long time ago that my mother brought me and left me with Aunt Maria who taught me how to read and write. . . . Sometimes she leaves me all alone and forbids me to eat all day, and sometimes the cook gives me a piece of bread. . . . I would like to live with [my uncle], but not with my aunt.

The court gave the grandmother custody of the child and sentenced Maria Volkov to permanent exile in Tobol'sk, with deprivation of all personal rights and social status. Apart from the extraordinary denouement, the child's experience was doubtless emblematic of poor children without support and in the care of strangers.[72]

But not all fathers left their illegitimate children without any material support, and some even attempted to adopt their illegitimate children. Adoption, however, was exceedingly difficult and expensive, since the Russian state strongly resisted adoption;[73] in fact, it required a personal order of the emperor. Nevertheless, some fathers attempted to adopt illegitimate offspring and change their status in order to shield them from legal and social discrimination. For example, Rafail Veisman sent a petition to the Imperial Chancellery in 1902 admitting that he had sired two children with a Russian Orthodox widow (Elizaveta Iakovlevna Mal'shevskaia); conceding that adoption was unthinkable, he implored the emperor at least to allow his children to use his patronymic and family name, if adoption was not an option.[74] In another case, Peisakh Moiseev Vul'fovich asked that his illegitimate daughter use his surname, and he promised to provide material support. He admitted that the mother was the wife of a certain Viktor Pavlovich de-Briuks, who had registered the girl under his name.[75] Since the file had no positive resolution, the petition was doubtless denied on the grounds that Jews could not adopt Russian Orthodox children. Even without this complication, the appeal, without connection in high places, had little chance of success.[76]

Since most women had custody of the children, the main bone of contention was the father's visitation rights. One of the more "permissive" agreements read as follows: "I am obliged not to prevent your visitations with our [child] at any time, at my place of residence. I shall not limit the time of the visitation without determining beforehand how and where you meet."[77] In this legal twilight zone, however, disputes were ubiquitous, for a tidy legal arrangement on paper gradually became an opportunity for some women to ignore prior agreements and deny visitation rights. The desperate, predictably, often ended up in secular courts, as with the separated Zaks couple. On 9 December 1899, Khaia Zak signed a document at the St. Petersburg gendarme office confirming that she was obliged "to give my daughter Agnessa to him [her husband] for visitation two times a year for two weeks." According to their separation agreement, the husband could take his daughter to his own apartment during those designated periods as long as he returned her promptly to his wife. However, just five months later, the husband sent a complaint to the Imperial Chancellery stating that "my wife categorically refuses to comply with this document [the agreement on visitation rights] without any reason."

Outraged by her husband's infidelity and concerned about her six-year-old daughter's "mental health," she fiercely refused to comply. In May 1899 she had a certain Dr. Butkevich send an official medical report to the Imperial Chancellery describing the results of medical examination of her daughter after the last visit with her father. The doctor claimed that "due to the influence of unusual circumstances and the forceful separation from her mother after . . . her mental illness," he had discerned "the appearance of nervous irritation, insomnia with general anaemia." The father confirmed that five years ago his daughter had some kind of brain illness and, as a baby, "did not begin to develop mentally." The doctor concluded that the child was suffering from *neurasthenia et anaemia* and advised the Chancellery to deny the father's visitation rights because of the deleterious impact on the child's "physical and psychological development." In August, Khaim Zak traveled from Moscow to St. Petersburg, where his wife then resided to study medicine, and attempted to see his daughter, but he was rebuffed again. He claimed that his wife tore up a photograph and smashed a toy that he had sent, in front of the child, with tears pouring down her face. Such behavior, he asserted, "instills the monstrous idea that 'papa will murder you,' instead of 'go to [your father].'"

FIG. 18. Studio portrait of a father and son. *Courtesy of the Akselrod family.*

State authorities were disinclined to untangle such conflicts. The state investigator reported that the marriage disintegrated because of Chaim Zak's love affair with a young student but observed that, while the husband has a "hot temper and is coarse," the wife has a "nervous and unrestrained character." The Imperial Chancellery concluded that, given the "mutual mistrust and extreme enmity" between the couple, "it is impossible to expect a resolution to their dispute over their daughter through a voluntary agreement." It therefore advised the couple to take their case before a civil court.[78] While such disputes were natural in the aftermath of a divorce, the temptation was especially acute in prerevolutionary Russia because of "dual power" and conflicting authorities of rabbinical and state courts.

Under these circumstances, custodial conflict was as vicious as it was ubiquitous. In one instance, a wife accused her estranged husband of "kidnapping" their oldest son and castigated her husband's "evil sentiments."[79]

Embittered, fathers had their own sympathy-seeking narratives. In a letter to his twelve-year-old son, one father expressed profound anguish that he could not see his children, blamed this on the hostility of his estranged wife, and accused the son of betrayal for associating with his wife's lover and friends:

Dear child, Vitiusha!
  You cannot know how tortured I have felt [because] I have not been able to see my dear children, but I endure [it] and will live. . . . You are not little anymore and should understand that Shaika, Dasheka, Malyshev, and the others [the latter was the wife's lover and the former were her friends] have destroyed your father and thus are your enemies; if you continue to meet with them, you are committing a crime against your ailing father.[80]

Even in this patriarchal society, the husband felt so disempowered that he had to exploit the dual loyalty of his child in a vain effort to assert his rights.

When divorced or widowed parents remarried, young children also confronted the dilemma of conflicting loyalties: some clung to the past, whereas others sought a place in the new family unit. Such a fusion was not easy. State law, which automatically ascribed the name of the biological father, institutionalized the differences in a mixed family with natural and stepchildren. This impelled one mother, Dyshel Khaimova Vurgraft, to seek permission to change her daughter's last name. She had three children: one from her former marriage (her daughter Broina) and two from the present one (Polina and Mark): "My husband is accustomed to considering my daughter Broina as his own daughter and she, in her own turn, lives in the family and does not know that the other two children are not really her own [siblings], only that they are from the same womb and have a different family name." The couple wanted permission for thirteen-year-old Broina Shapiro to adopt their family name, emphasizing that the child, who was extremely ill, desperately wanted to change her name. The knowledge "that she is not a Vurgraft, but a Shapiro," they added, "has a very marked impact on her health and brings discord to our peaceful family life."[81] The file has no final resolution, indicating that, as in most such cases, the state declined to make an exception.[82]

The Legal Maze: Residency, Citizenship, and Conscription

The legal consequences of divorce vis-à-vis the state primarily affected Jewish women, for Russian law traditionally made their status dependent on their spouses (for non-Jews as well). Nevertheless, the very complexity of *Digest of Laws (Svod zakonov)*, with its "numerous exceptions . . . for nationality, ethnicity, region, religion or social status," not only intimidated many Jewish women but also invited much confusion about the application of general laws to specifically "Jewish" cases. Indeed, the disparity between formal law and everyday realities baffled even the best-informed judges. One significant indicator of the incongruity was the sharp increase in the suits brought before the Civil Cassation Department of the Senate, which, as the supreme court of appeals for civil suits, had the power to clarify ambiguous laws and elucidate their application to "situations unforeseen by the legislators." Between 1881 and 1914 the annual number of cases submitted to the Civil Cassation Department rose from 5,792 to 16,188; the department more than kept pace as the number of cases resolved rose from 5,594 to 18,969.[83] To apprise readers of the latest developments in the Senate, Jewish journals and newspapers like *Rassvet, Evreiskii mir,* and *Budushchnost'* created their own juridical columns.

In terms of state law, divorce raised four main legal issues: (1) estate status and residency outside the Pale of Settlement, (2) questions of citizenship, (3) conscription of children from former marriages, and (4) the right to remarry.

Estate Status and Residency outside the Pale of Settlement

Juridical status was a critical issue confronting Jewish divorcées or widows, since their juridical status determined their social estate *(soslovie)* and residency rights (whether inside or outside the Pale of Settlement). Russian law, as noted above, ascribed a woman's legal status first according to her father and then her husband ("unless, in the latter instance, she belonged to a higher estate than her husband").[84] Heeding this principle, the Senate ruled that "a Jewish woman, who was divorced from her husband, retains [his] status *[sostoianie]* and rank *[zvanie]* until she remarries," whereupon she assumes the status and rank of the new spouse.[85]

Despite this clear ruling, Jewish women had to fight for their rightful status, largely because of numerous loopholes in state law. This problem bedeviled Anna Shor, the ex-wife of a pharmaceutical chemist who, because of her husband's rank, had the rare privilege of residing in Kiev, outside the Pale of Settlement.[86] The local police, however, seized upon the fact that her passport erroneously listed her as the *wife* (not *former* wife) of a pharmaceutical chemist. They insisted that she assume her paternal surname if she still wished to apply for a residence permit. With the assistance of a Jewish lawyer, Anna Shor appealed to the Senate that these demands had no legal grounds and that they contravened Russian law, which did not require a woman to change her family name, especially one that she had used for almost thirty years. "A divorced Jewish woman (like a widow)," Shor pointed out, "has the right to be registered according to her husband's rank and status," and as the former wife of a pharmaceutical chemist, she had the right to reside in Kiev or any other city outside the Pale of Settlement. Her lawyer, the assistant barrister Sliozberg, emphasized that "nowhere does the law differentiate between the rights of a divorced Jewish woman and those of other confessions." In short, the law contained no specific provisions about the applicability of these principles to Jewish women. Persuaded by this argument, on 10 June 1897 the Senate informed the Kiev provincial board that the laws regarding divorced women applied equally to Christian and non-Christian confessions, thus allowing Anna Shor to reside anywhere in the empire. It specifically forbade the police to expel her from Kiev or to force her to assume her paternal surname.[87] Thus, the Senate decision created a precedent that guided decisions on similar cases.

A related question was whether a Jewish woman who had the right to reside outside the Pale of Settlement *before* her marriage could reclaim that privilege after a divorce. This issue was critical for women who planned to return to their parents' home—a common recourse for young Jewish divorcées. In this case, the Senate was not so generous; in 1902 it ruled that women who married men without this privilege could not reclaim their earlier status.[88] The case involved Sore Ester Fridman, the daughter of a retired soldier from Kronshtadt, who married a Jew from Dokshits (Minsk province).[89] After her divorce she petitioned the St. Petersburg Revenue Department *(kazennaia palata)* to register in her hometown with her mother but was rejected on the grounds that she lost her former privileges when she married a Jew from the Pale of Settlement. When the Ministry of the Interior rejected her petition, she turned to the Senate; the latter offered a split decision. Four senators and the chief overseer *(ober-prokuror)* argued that women automatically forfeited their previous status upon marriage, with one special exception: if the wife had a higher social status than her husband.[90] The *ober-prokuror* argued, however, that this exception did not apply to Jews: their right to reside outside the Pale of Settlement was an entirely different question.[91]

At first blush, the ruling seemed categorical: "The right to live anywhere [in the empire] cannot be restored after the dissolution of the marriage, either [through] the death of the husband or [through] a divorce from him." Perhaps reflecting the more liberal spirit of some jurists in the Senate, the new ruling explicitly reminded such women of exceptions.[92] One category of women exempt from these laws consisted of those who had a "personal" right to live outside the Pale of Settlement on the basis of their "higher educational degrees, [or] occupational status as artisans, traders, and first-guild merchants." They not only retained the right of

FIG. 19. Seventeen- and eighteen-year-old seamstresses in Starokin. Among them is Soma Hofnitz, Slutz, 1910. *Courtesy of YIVO Institute for Jewish Research.*

unrestricted residence for the duration of their marriages (even if their husbands lacked this privilege) but after a divorce or the death of a spouse, could "live unhindered" anywhere in the empire.[93] When a woman lacked a personal claim to this right, the Senate cited the possibility of a personal petition to the emperor: "Sometimes by appealing to the mercy of the monarch, [one can] regain the right of one's childhood family."[94]

Marital dissolution raised serious dilemmas for Jewish women with respect to their children's residence. If a mother moved to areas that precluded or restricted Jewish residency, she had to obtain state approval to bring in children from a previous marriage. Caprice in such matters was boundless. When Cherna Shliomovna Duvinskaia sought to have her children accompany her, authorities refused. She had remarried (to a Jewish soldier from Kiev) in hopes of starting a new life but had no idea that stringent residency laws forbade her to bring two children from a previous marriage. Despite repeated appeals to the governor, emphasizing that the children had never lived apart from their mother, local authorities adamantly refused to make an exception. Her second husband also invoked his exemplary military record but to no avail.[95] Sometimes, however, authorities *did* permit the children to accompany the mother.

For example, Motel Pavalotskii petitioned the governor of Kiev to permit his wife's two children from her first marriage (seventeen-year-old Elia Borukh and eighteen-year-old Sara) to come to Kiev. After the Kiev police reported that the children had no means to live on their own and supported the petition, the governor approved the request. In short, ambiguities in state law and practice left Jewish families at the mercy of the local officials, a powerful stimulus for extortion.[96]

Jewish women depended on men not only for their status but also for their paperwork. In 1880 the procurator of Volhynia province, burdened with numerous petitions for new passports from divorced Jewish women, asked the Senate to register these women in their fathers' hometowns, using the paternal family name. The general-governor of Kiev concurred but added that the passport should indicate that the woman was "the divorced wife of so-and-so." The primary aim here was to prevent Jewish sons from evading the draft by registering with their divorced mothers (whose last name was now different) and qualifying for the only-son exemption from the military. While the Senate supported the idea of allowing a divorced wife to return to her parental home, it raised concerns that the husband might seek to neglect his financial responsibilities because his family lived in another town. It therefore ruled that a Jewish divorcée could designate either her father's or her ex-husband's hometown as her place of permanent residence, as well as the choice of family name, on her passport.[97]

Not only divorcées but women deserted by their husbands had difficulties in obtaining a new passport. The husband usually took his passports with him, leaving the wife without documentation as she tried to explain to police why she was living separately from her husband. The plight of Braina Tevelevna is instructive. In 1900 she married Zal'man Gengenstein, who, as a skilled artisan, had the right to move to St. Petersburg. "To my unhappiness," she wrote to the Imperial Chancellery, "my husband turned out to have weak moral principles." He deserted her with two young children (a five-year-old son and a ten-month-old daughter) "with the intention of settling down with another family." To make matters worse, the husband informed the police and passport office that he was leaving St. Petersburg, deliberately subjecting his wife and children to expulsion from the capital. The Imperial Chancellery, sympathetic to the woman's plight, granted her a separate passport for one year, the term normally granted in such cases. She must then reapply to extend her residency.[98]

Another case involved Maria Edelshtein, who complained to the Senate in 1892 that the Moscow police refused to extend her passport because her husband's whereabouts were unknown. Local state authorities reported that the wife operated her own fashion-design store and resided in the capital on the basis of her husband's status as a veterinarian. Unless she possessed the personal right to reside outside the Pale of Settlement (e.g., through higher education), the Senate ruled that she was subject to expulsion.[99] Given the residency issue, women like Rokha Novshovna (Berosa by her first husband) found it easier to purchase a false passport (for 1.5 rubles in the 1880s), than to obtain an official document.[100] Lack of an authentic passport, however, could be disastrous. Novshovna, for example, was arrested in Dinaburg and deprived of all her personal rights. In the another case. Khaia Bronshtein, caught without a passport and charged with vagrancy, was sentenced to three years in Siberia and thirty to forty lashes; the latter punishment was commuted on the grounds that corporal punishment could not be applied to women.[101]

Questions of Citizenship

Jewish women who married and divorced foreigners had to reestablish Russian citizenship.[102] In 1856 the Jewish Committee received a Senate inquiry regarding two Russian-Jewish women who had married foreign Jews, subsequently divorced, and then sought to regain their status as Russian subjects. Their former husbands (Faiman and Gol'denshtein) had been living in Kishinev on foreign passports but were expelled from Russia in 1845, leaving their wives, Kaufman and Berov (native residents of Kishinev), behind.[103] The Senate, which initially heard the case *before* the two women divorced, decided the case strictly on the basis the *Digest of Laws:* if a Russian woman married a foreigner who did not have a legal permit to work and reside in the empire, she was to be expelled from the country, since her status depended on that of her husband. It also ordered that their houses be sold within six months. The women appealed that ruling, arguing that they had since divorced their husbands and raised anew the question about their citizenship. The Jewish Committee reviewed the case, and a majority concluded that both women had permanently forfeited their status as Russian subjects by marrying foreign Jews.[104]

The women pressed their appeal in the Senate, where a minority of senators supported their case. They compared the status of these women to that of those who had married Asian soldiers; according to the *Digest of Laws*[105] these women retained Russian citizenship even if their husbands left the empire. This liberal minority also emphasized the humanitarian dimension: "These Jewish women have neither relatives nor acquaintances abroad and will [therefore] be subjected to pitiful conditions."[106] They stressed that the petitioners had never left Russia and owned property in Bessarabia. Significantly, this view won the support of the Ministry of Finance, which cited a similar 1843 precedent involving several foreign Jews who received permission to live in Odessa and married Russian subjects. After the husbands died or were expelled (for unspecified reasons), the government allowed the wives to remain with their children in Odessa because of the difficulties they would face in a foreign country "not knowing the language" or culture.[107] On that basis the government agreed to restore the women's citizenship.

This precedent governed subsequent cases. In 1900, Eidlia Aizenberg, a Jewish widow, complained to the Senate that the Bessarabian provincial board denied her status as a Russian subject because she had been married to a Moldavian.[108] She had lived with him in Kishinev throughout their entire marriage and left that city only once (in 1877) to "conduct business" in the Moldavian city of Iassy. Due to complications in her pregnancy, she remained there for three months, until her daughter was born. Citing the above precedents, the Senate summarized the operating principle: "If a Jewish woman marries a foreign Jew and does not leave her fatherland, she has the right to reclaim her status as a Russian subject." It interpreted the phrase "leave the fatherland" liberally; it meant physical departure from the country with the *intention* of changing residency. Thus, Aizenberg's trip to Iassy on business was temporary and should not be treated as "a departure from the fatherland." On that basis the Senate overturned the decision of the Bessarabian provincial board and reinstated Aizenberg's citizenship.[109]

Conscription

Remarriage raised questions about the status of sons and their liability to conscription. Until the adoption of universal military training in 1874, this issue weighted heavily, not only because the government was determined to obtain draftees but also because it subjected Jewish conscripts to coercive conversion.[110] And even after the 1874 conscription reform, the government made an exception for "only sons," ensuring that at least one son be left to support parents in their old age. Remarriage cast this only son status into a legal limbo, especially if the spouses had sons by a previous marriage: which son had the coveted draft exemption was critically important.

The issue naturally led to bitter disputes between spouses. In 1834, for example, Gershko Shor registered his wife's son from a previous marriage in the family poll tax register but not his own sixteen-year-old from a previous marriage. To all appearances, he had given her son sanctuary from conscription because her boy would appear as the only son. As Rukhli Shor told the governor of Kiev, her husband agreed to "pay the [poll] tax for my son until he came of age, and I, as a woman, placed my hopes on this, being naive [about] this kind of deceptiveness." In fact, her husband had registered four other male "souls" in the family census (presumably in exchange for bribes), thereby depriving her son of his only-son exemption. The *kahal* thereupon turned her son over to the military as part of its recruit quota. Because she had lost some key documents in a fire, Rukhli Shor had no basis for a legal suit and could only ask that the Emperor intercede: "Your Highness, as a defenseless widow and complete orphan, I beseech you to protect my son from illegal recruitment in place of another family."[111] The file contains no resolution, indicating that the appeal probably failed, perhaps because Rukhli lacked documentation or because the government had no desire to undo how the *kahal* met its recruitment quota.

The universal military training act of 1874 did not eliminate the problem of the only son. In 1890 the Kiev newspaper *Kievlianin* reported a sensational case involving David Vekker of Radomysl, who was married and had a single son. Having decided to divorce his wife, Vekker started an "intimate relationship" with another woman and produced an illegitimate son. When, however, the local rabbi recorded the birth in the Jewish metrical book as the lawful son of David Vekker and his paramour, that jeopardized the only-son status of Vekker's first male offspring and prompted his legal wife to file suit in state court. The husband had not initiated the false metrical record, which the court found to be bogus; it was presumably the result of his lover's attempt to shield her infant son from the stigma of bastardy.[112] Similar complications still overshadowed second marriages that resulted in new male progeny, since they bore important implications for previous children, above all, for the legal status of an only son.

Laws for Cohanim

Any Jew deemed to be a descendant of the priestly lines (i.e., certain people, though not all, bearing the family names Cohen, Levi, or Katz) faced special restrictions based solely on their family name. Specifically, Jewish law forbade the males, deemed to be members of the priesthood, to marry a divorcée. The rule was based on a passage in Leviticus 217:7: "They [the priests] shall not marry a woman that is a harlot or profaned, nor shall they marry one divorced from her husband, for they are holy to their God."[113] This prohibition, which reflected the "strict laws of purity by which the priests were bound" (because of their service in the Temple), was still binding on Jews in tsarist Russia, much to the bewilderment of state officials.[114] As a result, such divorced men could marry a single woman but none of the numerous divorcées in the Jewish community.

The rule was so strictly applied that it even precluded a man from remarrying his ex-wife. In March 1905, the governor of Tavrida received a complaint from Iudeliia Aronovna Katz [Kats], who accused state rabbi Perel'man of Simferopol of permitting his son Boris to remarry his ex-wife, Fruma. He argued that "Katz" fell under the "Cohen" laws and that the remarriage was a blatant violation of Jewish law.[115] As the state learned, the couple divorced on 25 August 1903, but a month later they reconciled and decided to reunite. Aware that a conscientious rabbi would deny remarriage, the couple traveled from Kiev to Simferopol, where they found a compliant state rabbi.[116] For his part, Perel'man testified that he had examined the couple's passports, as required by state law, and found no legal impediment, particularly since the groom had claimed to be neither a "Cohen" nor a "Levi." The Simferopol rabbi questioned the connection between the name "Katz" and the Aaronic line, especially since Jews had "no genealogical books or documents."[117]

The Rabbinic Commission flatly declared that the remarriage was void. It noted that Perel'man, as a state rabbi, needed a written statement from the rabbi who had performed the divorce; had he done so, he would have known that the couple could not remarry. Although the commission decided not to prosecute the rabbi for wrongdoing,[118] it dissolved the marriage as ordered in the *Shulhan Arukh*.[119] To avoid similar problems in the future, it advised rabbis to make a special note in the metrical book that read "a divorcée of Aaronite or Levitic descent."[120] In short, the laws on *cohanim* were strictly enforced, imposing constraint on purported descendants of the priestly class.[121] For a select few, these laws restricted the choice of a second spouse and created particular difficulties in small Jewish communities with a limited number of eligible and desirable partners.

All these impediments had several important implications. First, they induced many couples to remain nominally married, with or without separation, even if the marriage had irretrievably broken down. It is likely that these obstacles became more substantial in the postreform era, since state authority and secular courts could be invoked to enforce financial requirements and issues of legal residency. Thus, while the legal grounds for divorce remained liberal and unchanged, the stricter procedure and enforcement of terms (e.g., alimony, child support) served to dissuade couples from divorce. And when they did divorce, the stakes were now higher, generating bitter acrimony, legal battles, and growing public concerns about the issue of marital dissolution.

Bigamy

The travails of divorce, compounded by the state's limited institutional control over Jews, encouraged some to seek a shortcut solution to a failed marriage—bigamy. Hardly unique to Jews,[122] bigamy became an increasing source of concern and figured prominently in government reports and in the Russian-Jewish press. Significantly, it was not data showing a high rate of bigamy (such figures are virtually nonexistent),[123] but the question of polygamy that so exercised bureaucratic and journalistic circles. Nor was the polygamy issue merely a red herring raised by the antisemitic press; even a Russian Jewish journal, *Vestnik russkikh evreev,* carried headlines asking, "Does Judaism permit polygamy [*mnogozhenstvo*]? And do Jews desire polygamy?"[124] The Rabbinic Commission also held several discussions about "the question of polygamy among the Jews."[125] The sensational and well-publicized cases that came before state courts and the Rabbinic Commission helped to reinforce public perception that bigamy was indeed a widespread phenomenon among Jews.

Was Bigamy a Crime?

As the government and press raised the question of Jewish bigamy, state law itself was unclear: the only distinction made between bigamy *(dvoe-zhenstvo)* and polygamy *(mnogozhenstvo)* was numerical (two versus multiple wives).[126] Implicitly, however, there *was* a difference in connotation if not in formal law. Thus, the concept of bigamy stemmed from the teachings of the Russian Orthodox Church; it referred not to a harem but to remarriage without the formal termination of a prior union. By contrast, polygamy denoted the lawful cohabitation with multiple wives as practiced by Muslims and some other minorities.

This ambiguity in law stemmed from the fact that the state left the issue of polygamy, like all questions of marriage and divorce, to individual confessions. Hence, bigamy was a criminal offense only if the perpetrator's own faith condemned it or if the victimized spouse belonged to such a faith: "Individuals of the non-Christian faiths who remarry despite the existence of another marriage when this is contrary to the laws of their faith, or those of mixed marriages between Protestants and Muslims, are subject by state laws to incarceration in a house of detention *(smiritel'nyi dom)* for eight months to one year and four months, with the loss of some rights and property."[127] If, however, both spouses belonged to a confession that tolerated polygamy, if its rules for the making and dissolution of a marital union posed no problem, state law did not prescribe any secular punishment.

After the 1860s, as Jews filed complaints about bigamy in state courts, the government sought guidance on whether the Jewish faith prohibited polygamy or bigamy. The critical appeal came in 1879 from the procurator of an appeals court in Odessa, who asked the Rabbinic Commission to rule whether "polygamy [*mnogozhenstvo*] is permitted among the

Jews in the present time from a religious point of view? . . . Should individuals of the Jewish faith [who commit this crime] be prosecuted in criminal court?"[128] A ruling by the Rabbinic Commission would bear significant consequences for ordinary Jewish bigamists who had thus far gone unnoticed or at least unpunished by the state. The commission appointed one member, Dr. Neumann, a learned Western European rabbi, to prepare a memorandum about Jewish law on bigamy.

Rabbi Neumann emphasized the high ethical standards of the Jewish people, evidently seeking to rebut innuendos about Jewish marital practices. In his words: "The moral principle constitutes the fundamental [and] dominant foundation among the Jews from the religious point of view on marriage."[129] Although he did not deny that Judaism once tolerated polygamy, he attributed the practice to the fact that most Jews lived in the "east" (vostok) and had been influenced by the customs of the surrounding peoples. Still, even where polygamy was lawful, it had been subject to restrictions that reflected the moral concerns of rabbinic authorities. As an illustration he cited a passage from the Talmud: "A man may marry wives in addition to his first wife, provided only that he possesses the means to maintain them."[130] Hence, polygamy was not an unqualified right even in the Jewish communities that tolerated the practice.

However, as Rabbi Neumann stressed, some Jewish authorities explicitly prohibited plural marriages. Indeed, their teachings were essentially monogamous: before a man could take a second wife, he must formally divorce his first wife and pay her ketubah. Neumann cited no authority but may have been alluding to a passage from Rabbi Ammi: "I maintain that whosoever takes, in addition to his present wife another, must divorce the former and pay her the amount of her ketubah."[131] Neumann further cited Jewish authorities who permitted a second wife only with the knowledge of the first, the purpose being to prevent unintentional incest among the husband's offspring. While this Western European rabbi did not gainsay that Jews, like their Eastern neighbors, had earlier practiced polygamy, he emphasized that it had followed strict moral guidelines and that some authorities had either restricted or banned polygamy.

More important, Neumann argued that for hundreds of years European Jews had abandoned polygamy. While conceding that Christians observed monogamy, one should not assume that "this concept of monogamy as a moral safeguard was alien to the Jews."[132] Such concerns informed the official interdiction attributed to Rabbi Gershom of Mayence, who denounced polygamy "as contrary to [the standards] of moral purity." The result was an official ban on polygamy (circa 1025). Most important, monogamy was obligatory for Jews in Imperial Russia because of Joseph Caro's principle, which held that, in societies that permitted only monogamy, a second wife was not permissible.[133]

Punishing Bigamists

That conclusion empowered the Russian state to criminalize and punish Jewish bigamy. Henceforth, state rabbis were to require that Jews from other towns produce documents confirming their single status before performing marital ceremonies.[134] Jews convicted of bigamy in state courts were now subject to penalties, including imprisonment. Thus, when a court in Vitebsk found Efroim Myshind guilty of bigamy on 27 October 1883, it sentenced him to five months and ten days in prison and the forfeiture of his personal property.[135] The state made an exception for "mountain Jews" *(gorskie evrei)*, those who lived in the Caucasus and traditionally practiced a limited polygamy.[136] Their "backward" marital customs became the symbol of a polygamous society to the *maskilim* critical of their "eastern" coreligionists. "Forever locked up as in a harem, enslaved in the kitchen, shackled in chains [performing] a woman's *mitzvot*," one writer lamented, "the mountain Jewish woman never dares to raise her voice, to laugh aloud or to sing [a song]."[137] Save this special subgroup,[138] the Jews in the Pale were liable to prosecution for bigamy.

One case involved Sara Aizikova from Kremenchug (Pultava province). When her husband, Rafael Isaev, discovered that she was still married to a townsman, Khaim Iakhnovits, in Bialystok, he immediately demanded a divorce. Given a witness's testimony about the first marriage and the lack of a divorce entry in the metrical book, the first marriage—under state and Jewish law—was therefore still in force, and the second marriage was bigamous. After the rabbi dissolved the second union, Sara Aizikova requested a copy of this order to obtain a new passport and permission to remain in Kremenchug. To her dismay, she discovered that the rabbi had inserted a provision in the document forbidding her to remarry until she received a proper divorce from the first husband.

She decided to contest the rabbi's action, claiming that the insertion of such a stipulation was "unfair." Her appeal proved disastrous: the Rabbinic Commission not only endorsed Rabbi Bramberg's ruling but also ordered that she be punished for committing bigamy. Specifically, it ruled that she be deprived of her first husband's social status and rank and that, in the event of divorce, she be denied material support. Although the commission did not specify her new status, presumably she was to assume her original paternal status. Thus, apart from depriving her of the customary claim to a financial settlement, it may have jeopardized her right to reside in Kremenchug. Most important, the decision reveals the Rabbinic Commission's concern about the bigamy issue and its determination to apply draconian measures. Apart from depriving her of the customary claim to a financial settlement, it may have negatively affected her legal status and, in particular, her right to retain residency in Kremenchug.

The Rabbinical Commission also acted decisively against male bigamists. For example, Yankel Zonis, who had married and emigrated to America, later returned to Russia; evidently frustrated by problems and delays in obtaining a divorce, he simply remarried with full observance of the customary Jewish rites (e.g., by placing the ring on her finger and crushing the glass after the wedding ceremony). When the Rabbinic Commission reviewed the case, it affirmed that the state law against bigamy applied to Jews in the Russian Empire. Because of doubts about the testimony of witnesses (who could identify neither the individual who performed the marriage nor the purported bride), the commission made no ruling and instead directed that a *beit-din* determine his guilt. If Zonis did commit bigamy, however, the new marriage was to be dissolved, but he was to provide material support to the second wife until the divorce was granted; if the first wife agreed to a divorce, he could remain with his second wife.[139]

While similar, these two cases show revealing differences in gender policy. The Rabbinic Commission dealt differently with the two bigamous unions: it summarily divorced the female bigamist but recommended exhortation for the male. The penalties were also radically different: it deprived the woman of a financial settlement from the first husband but made the male liable neither for compensation to the first wife (other than the customary return of the dowry and *ketubah*) nor to the second wife, who lost all support once the divorce was finalized. While the Rabbinic Commission left the final disposition to the *beit-din,* it plainly gave favorable treatment to the male offender. That leniency may have been due partly to the evidentiary matter but more likely reflected gender bias and greater tolerance for male than for female bigamy.[140]

The Agunah Question

Apart from bigamists, Jewish society also debated a unique social problem—the tragic *agunah*. She was literally an "anchored" woman, that is, someone bound in marriage to a husband with whom she no longer lived but who, for a variety of reasons, had not formally "released" her from the marital union.[141] Whatever the cause, she was forbidden to remarry and doomed to languish without material support or even the prospect for a change in fortune and status.

A "New" Agunah Crisis?

The historiography has conventionally attributed the acute *agunah* problem to the mass emigration of Jews, chiefly to the United States, from the

1870s on. Arthur Hertzberg, for instance, writes that almost one hundred thousand Jewish husbands deserted their wives and departed to the "promised land" without granting them a divorce.[142] Another classic study of the Jewish immigrant community likewise observes that "the most severe sign of disturbance was the persistent desertion of families by immigrant husbands." Such desertion wrought havoc on the moral condition of the Jewish community. In an open letter to "rabbis in the west," Rabbi Moshe Nahum ben Binyamin Yerusalimsky (b. 1855) declared that "mass departure" had inflicted great hardships on the "families in Israel . . . a nation that has, from time immemorial, excelled in the purity and wholesomeness of its way of life."[143] Similarly, contemporaries complained that males even replicated the desertion in America. A writer for the Yiddish paper *The Forward* argued that desertion, unthinkable in the Old World, proliferated in America because the young men were "without spiritual roots" and hence abandoned wives and children with total impunity.

In fact, however, the problem of the *agunah* was hardly as novel as contemporaries thought. Although the issue in American discourse formed part of a larger debate about immigrant mores and assimilation, the *agunah* question was an age-old problem for European Jewry. It figures prominently in the responsa literature; Rabbi Yitshak Elhanan Spektor's nineteenth-century collection of responsa in *Beer Yitshak* alone has over eighteen specific references to the *agunah,* not to mention the numerous *sheelot uteshuvot* (questions and answers, or responsa) written during the Polish-Lithuanian period on the subject.[144] To be sure, the mass emigration to America intensified desertion but not to the degree once assumed.[145] In any event, mass emigration did not cause the *agunah* problem but simply exacerbated an older problem.

Origins of the *Agunah* Problem

The *agunah* problem was so complex precisely because it was actually an umbrella term for women who became "anchored" under different conditions: (1) refusal of husbands to grant a divorce, (2) malicious desertion, (3) unconfirmed disappearance and death, (4) conversion of the male spouse, (5) childless widows who awaited the ceremony of *halitsah,* and (6) Siberian exile.

RECALCITRANT HUSBANDS

Some *agunot* were the victims of husbands who refused to divorce, even though the marriage had disintegrated and the couple lived apart. Often, the man simply wanted to avoid the travails of divorce and especially its costs—the obligation to repay the dowry and provide the *ketubah*. By living separately and avoiding divorce, the man avoided the costs of a formal divorce, so long as he did not want to remarry. Sometimes, as in the Ester Poliakov case, the male exploited his right to initiate divorce and blackmailed the desperate woman into making major financial concessions. In another instance, Rabbi Yerusalimsky wrote to Rabbi Yehoshua Segal in New York regarding Miriam-Devorah of Kielce, whose husband not only refused to send her support from America but had the temerity to demand one thousand rubles for the divorce. "I have spoken to the woman's father, who is a poor man," the rabbi wrote. "Nevertheless, he told me that to secure her release from the bonds of *igun* [the status of an *agunah*], he would sell everything he has and would give the man 100 rubles. If that is not enough, he will try to obtain help from his relatives, perhaps another 200 rubles." He urged the New York rabbi to persuade the "renegade husband" that his reward from heaven would "double" the amount he obtained from this poor family if he released the woman. Finally, some husbands refused to divorce even unfaithful wives as an act of revenge.[146]

Whatever the motive, the husband's refusal to divorce precluded remarriage. Before 1879, when state law on Jewish bigamy was ambiguous, the problem was less acute, although conscientious rabbis would have refused to allow an *agunah* to remarry. The criminalization of bigamy, however, made it dangerous for women to remarry without the requisite divorce from the husband.

DESERTION AND EMIGRATION

Malicious desertion and emigration, where the man simply vanished without divorcing, was a major cause of the *agunah* problem. A typical victim was Vera Portugalova of Poltava province, who appealed to state authorities in 1894 for assistance in locating her husband. "Four months ago, my husband Avram Portugalov left me and my children," wrote the wife. Since then she had "not received any word of his location or money to support myself and my children."[147] Despite rumors that he was living illegally in Kiev, the chief of police reported that he was apparently not in Kiev and that he had even avoided registration in his hometown. As a result, it was virtually impossible to trace his whereabouts. A month later, Vera Portugalova informed local police that her husband was now reportedly in Ekaterinoslav, but authorities again failed to snare the light-footed spouse.

As a result, Vera Portugalova joined the hapless women "anchored" to absentee husbands. Although data on the rate of desertion among Russian Jews were not assembled, the frequent announcements about "missing husbands" in the Jewish press suggest that the problem was not uncommon. The Hebrew newspaper *Hamelits* published one or two descriptions daily:

The request of an *agunah*. It has been two years since my husband left me and my child in deprivation and great poverty because, six weeks after our marriage, he deceptively took [our] money, saying that he was going for a few days to the town of Bialystok to purchase instruments for his work; he settled down [evidently in another town], and from then on I do not know where he has gone. . . . My husband's name is Eliezer Zeidman, born in the town of Brisk. He is twenty-three years old, tall, with black hair, a short black beard . . . , a long nose, with one crooked and short leg.[148]

The prospects for finding such deserters were, to put it mildly, extremely remote, especially if the husband did not register in his new place of residence, as often happened.

Even when the deserting spouse attempted to divorce officially, the wife sometimes had serious difficulties in obtaining official recognition. Thus, the state rabbi pronounced invalid a *get* that one woman received from abroad, thereby making her an *agunah*. The case began in 1901, when Khaim Aronov Mezhibovskii emigrated to America, leaving behind his pregnant wife, Tema Iankelevna, with two young children. Two years later he sent her a *get* that she, in turn, presented to two rabbis to obtain the formal divorce. The state rabbi Kligman, however, refused to recognize and register the divorce, although spiritual rabbis confirmed the reception of the *get*, without written conformation from her husband in America. "Considering myself divorced," Tema Mezhibovskaia wrote to the Rabbinic Commission, "I live by my own labor and raise my two children; but it has been three years and I have not received a metrical certificate of [my] divorce." As a result, she complained, "I am now deprived of the possibility to remarry, and I live under the oppressiveness of being an illegally divorced woman."

The Rabbinic Commission did intercede. It noted that, although the state laws required the permission of the state rabbi or his assistant in the dissolution of Jewish marriages, "this kind of case is actually supervised by those who know Jewish divorce laws (the so-called spiritual rabbis), according to the regulations of the Jewish legal proceedings." In fact, this liberal ruling directly contradicted state law, which allowed no exceptions to the competence of state rabbis. The commission, however, ruled that the courier's delivery of a *get* in the presence of two witnesses fully complied with the *Shulhan Arukh* (Gittin 140–41) and that the state rabbi's demand for a written confirmation from the husband was unwarranted. It instructed Rabbi Kligman to reexamine the case and permit the petitioner to remarry.[149] This case, so reminiscent of Judah Leib Gordon's mock epic poem "Kotso shel yud" (The tip of the yud) about the tragedy of a defective *get* (save for the happy ending), exposed the vulnerability of women

FIG. 20. *Letter from America,* by Yehuda Pen, 1903. *Vitebsk Regional Museum.*

to the caprice of individual, especially state, rabbis. For Jewish women not so fortunate as Tema Mezhibovskaia, the dreaded words *haget posul* (the *get* is invalid) heralded lifelong marital solitude and economic hardship.

Desertion was hardly unique to Jews and, indeed, in Imperial Russia became more pronounced after the Great Reforms, when mobility became considerably easier.[150] The Orthodox Church had a minimal term:

five years had to pass before the Church granted divorce on the grounds of "absence of the spouse for unknown reasons." Jewish law had no time limits; no matter how long the husband had been missing, it forbade the wife to remarry and doomed her to the fate of an *agunah*.

Emigration, chiefly to America, Canada, Argentina, and South Africa, only exacerbated a problem already rooted in growing geographic mobility and family separation.[151] Distressed by the *agunah* problem, Rabbi Moshe Yerusalimsky blamed the dire economic and political circumstances in Russia for driving men "away from the path trodden by their fathers and forefathers." In an emotional appeal to Western rabbis, he wrote: "An outcry has reached us from many towns and cities from the living widows, left without support from their husbands and without anyone to hear the wailing of their tender children asking for food, when there is none to give: a voice of weeping that pierces the heart!" He urged the leaders in New York to establish a special organization to ascertain the whereabouts of such husbands and persuade them to divorce their wives: "Talk to them with reason and persuade them gently, with the help of rabbinical courts, to leave the path that tempts them and to return to the proper path, or else to grant a proper divorce."[152] Indeed, the creation of the National Desertion Bureau in 1911 by the National Council of Hebrew Charities reflected growing social concerns about the fate of deserted wives and their children, who were forced to rely on communal aid.[153] Financial aid for *agunot* constituted the second largest item in the United Hebrew Charity's budget (14.5 percent in 1905).[154] But even the National Desertion Bureau could do little to extract support from husbands, let alone help unfortunate wives obtain a divorce.

DISAPPEARANCE AND DEATH

The involuntary disappearance of a husband because of an unreported death, homicide, or status as "missing in action" in war was another source of the *agunah* problem. When Abram Borisov Freizerov left for the Caucasus to find a cure for his grave illness, his wife expected him to return within a few months. After some six years passed without a word, she published descriptions of her husband in three Hebrew newspapers *(Hamelits, Hamagid,* and *Levanon)* and asked for information about his fate. Still young and anxious to resume a normal life, she also appealed to the Rabbinic Commission: "I am compelled to acquaint you with my pitiful condition, the position of a twenty-five-year-old woman in good physical health, living as a burden in her parental home." Despite her "extreme poverty and youth," she had avoided an immoral live ("for the sake of public opinion and the reputation of my parents") and inquired whether the commission had the authority to permit her to remarry. The local authorities confirmed that she had lived with her impoverished parents since her husband's disappearance in 1877. The commission rejected her request, albeit with regrets, on the grounds that Jewish law categorically forbade an *agunah* to remarry.[155]

As announcements in Hebrew newspapers show, missing Jewish husbands usually traveled extensively within the Pale of Settlement. One wife reported in 1881 that her husband, a bookseller, had last been seen in Warsaw.[156] Another woman, who lived in a small village near Vil'na, reported that her bookseller husband was last seen in Poltava.[157] Numerous reports of robberies, assaults, and murders in the very same newspaper, as well as court records of unidentified Jewish male corpses found in the forest, suggest that many a Jew met a tragic end on the road.[158] Given the weakness of the Russian police and the difficulties in identifying victims (who were normally stripped of their papers as well as their money), many women never learned about the fate of their husbands.

In response, husbands gave their wives a "conditional divorce" before embarking on a trip or entering military service. In the event that they did not return, a designated agent was to deliver the bill of divorcement. According to the metrical books from Khar'kov, some husbands, mostly Jewish soldiers, divorced their wives before they left for military duty and remarried upon their return.[159] While "conditional divorces" prevented some tragedies, they caused much confusion.[160] Moreover, this preventive measure was not accessible to Jews who were *cohanim* because they were not permitted to marry divorcées and therefore could not remarry their ex-wives.

To establish death, Jewish law required the testimony of two competent witnesses,[161] but some authorities went to extraordinary lengths to help widows. Perhaps the most lenient was Rabbi D. Menkis of Sokol (Galicia), who ruled in favor of women even when firm evidence of their husbands' deaths was lacking. In one instance, he recalled that during the Polish rebellion against Russia, a Jew and his son were killed near the town of Sokol and buried in the forest.[162] Although government officials permitted a secret reburial of the bodies in a Jewish cemetery, the victims' wives and the Jewish community had been too terrified to go and identify the corpses. As the rabbi testified, "Only I, together with some younger people, attended the reburial, but I was not able to obtain proper testimony [as to the identity of the bodies]." Three years later, the widows sought to remarry but were told that the decision depended on Rabbi Menkis; as was his wont, he showed his customary mercy and granted their request, citing the unusual circumstances of their husbands' deaths.[163]

Also influential was the responsum of Rabbi Yitshak Elkanan Spektor of Kovno regarding an *agunah* whose *levir* (brother-in-law) had been killed in military combat before he could return home and perform the ceremony of *halitsah* (levirate divorce) for his sister-in-law.[164] Although one Jewish soldier and an army report confirmed his death, the issue was whether a non-Jewish report was valid in a Jewish court of law. Rabbi Spektor declared that "their [the official] testimony is more worthy than that of the first witness" because "they would not record that he was killed except after careful investigation of the matter."[165] He argued that the official report was all the more credible since military officers were unlikely to falsify records for fear of punishment and shame. His astute decision eased the requirements on witnesses and greatly facilitated the resolution of cases generated by war, pogroms, and the like. Not all rabbis, however, were so accommodating. An overly fastidious rabbi (whether from conscientiousness, circumspection, or corruption) could impose insurmountable demands for evidence.[166]

CONVERTED SPOUSES

The requirement of formal dissolution also applied to males who converted to Christianity but failed to divorce their Jewish wives. If the husbands refused to grant a Jewish divorce, rabbinic authorities deemed the marriage to be binding and forbade the women to remarry, even if the male had already married a Christian wife.[167] Neither the Russian state nor the Orthodox Church had compassion for such *agunot* and did nothing to induce converts to ease the lot of their Jewish spouses. Hence, the rabbinical authorities *could* not and the gentile authorities *would* not act to formalize the end to the Jewish marriage and set the *agunot* free.

This tragedy was poignantly apparent in the case of Fedor Ivanov, formerly Khaim Salomanskii. On 13 January 1886, the diocesan consistory in St. Petersburg gave permission for Ivanov to marry a Russian Orthodox woman without divorcing his Jewish wife. Church policy there partly reflected the view that only an Orthodox marriage was "real" (as a sacrament) and partly a desire to shield converts from interaction and abuse by "fanatical" coreligionists. When Ester Salomanskaia learned of her husband's conversion and remarriage, she complained to the state that she needed a formal Jewish divorce to remarry. The Ministry of Internal Affairs was not unsympathetic. It noted that "a Jewish marriage dissolved by a Russian Orthodox consistory is no longer considered legitimate." But by permitting the convert to remarry without the dissolution of the first marriage, the law in effect "induces one spouse to commit bigamy and unjustly condemns the other to celibacy." If the final resolution had rested with the Ministry of Internal Affairs, which had more experience with Jewish marriage and divorce than any other branch of the government, it might have forced converts to divorce their Jewish spouses. The jurisdiction, however, rested with the Church, which was concerned principally about the new believers, not an unconverted spouse. As the Church's top lay official replied: "I cannot help but notice, that although the petitioner was prompted to [send] her request on the grounds that it was impossible for her to remarry, . . . not only does she lack evidence for this [assertion] . . . but she does not appear to have attempted to obtain permission to remarry."[168] As that official response reveals, he had not the slightest grasp of the *agunah* problem and the fact that the role played by the Church could be overtly callous.

YEVAMOT: CHILDLESS WIDOWS

Other *agunot* were women whose husbands had died before they had borne children. Jewish law "chained" such women to the husband's brother; according to ancient Israelite custom, the husband's brother had to marry the childless widow and to name the firstborn after the deceased "so that his name is not obliterated from Israel."[169] The only exception was release through the ceremony of *halitsah* (the levirate divorce), sometimes called the "unshoeing" ceremony. In Eastern Europe, the option of marriage *(yibum)* was never available so the levirate divorce was the only alternative. The ceremony of *halitsah* required that the widow remove a shoe from her brother-in-law, spit on the ground, and declare: "Thus shall be done to the man who will not build up his brother's house!"[170] If, however, the surviving brother-in-law refused to perform this ritual, the widow automatically became an *agunah*.

While bigamy laws and conversion[171] were occasionally an impediment, some *levirs* refused to perform the ceremony of *halitsah* out of pure greed. When the widow Gitla Mogilevskaia asked her brother-in-law to grant her a levirate divorce, he demanded a large sum of money. "If I had this sum at my disposal," the widow wrote, "I would not think twice about satisfying Mogilevskii's avaricious plan."[172] But because she had to support her indigent parents, she rejected his demand: "If it were not for my parents, for whom I can endure a lot of grief, I would not insist on this divorce. I can live my young life in celibacy until the end of my days."[173] She therefore appealed to the state in an attempt to force her brother-in-law to acquiesce to her request.

The appeal eventually came before the Rabbinic Commission, which was sympathetic to her request. In a report to the Ministry of the Interior, it conceded that "this symbolic rite *(halitsah)* often plays into the hands of unscrupulous people as an instrument of extortion from widows, dooming them to live in celibacy."[174] Fearful that the state might ban this ritual, the commission promised to devise measures to ensure the cooperation of obdurate brothers-in-law.

Simultaneously, the commission also had to review the case of twenty-

one-year-old Roza Pergamenshchik Varshavskii, who faced a similar dilemma when her husband suffered a fatal illness. Once again the dispute
was purely monetary. When Roza married Eli Varshavskii on 25 February 1893, her husband had used her dowry of five hundred rubles to open
a soap factory jointly with his brother Aron Dovid in the town of Gadiach (Poltava province). But when the husband fell ill, her father summoned
a spiritual rabbi to the dying man's bedside, and together they tried to
persuade him to divorce his wife and save her from the fate of an *agunah*.
But the man unexpectedly died before the divorce proceedings began,
and his brother declined to return the three hundred rubles paid to hasten
the divorce. Indeed, the brother demanded an additional five hundred
hundred rubles to perform the ceremony of *halitsah*.

The local rabbi explained that he had urged the *levir* to perform his
duty but to no avail: "I immediately spoke with Aron Dovid Varshavskii
to let him know how unjust it was to turn against his sister-in-law Roza,
wounding the young woman . . . and depriving her of the possibility of
remarrying." No doubt he feared that a levirate divorce would mean not
only losing half the founding capital of his soap factory but also having
to pay the total sum of her *ketubah*. He therefore refused to renounce his
monetary claims. The widow's father then wrote to the governor of Poltava, begging him "to save my daughter from eternal solitude with all of
its terrible consequences . . . to persuade Aron Dovid to perform the [cer-
emony] of *halitsah*, without which her young life will be in danger of
moral degradation." Like Gitla Mogilevskaia, the father exhausted all
options within Jewish communal norms and turned to government officials to enforce the rabbinic decree.

In response, the Rabbinic Commission issued a new set of sanctions
against recalcitrant levirs. Specifically, it proposed that the government
adopt three rules: (1) if single, the *levir* could not marry until he freed his
brother's widow; (2) he forfeited any inheritance claims to his deceased
brother's estate; and (3) he had to support the widow from his brother's
death until he granted the levirate divorce. Since the commission had no executive powers and its proposals required state confirmation and enforcement, the main responsibility lay with the state. Although the latter did not
act on these recommendations, the commission demonstrated its sensitiv-
ity and made an earnest attempt to intercede on behalf of the *agunah*.[175]

SIBERIAN EXILE

The final source of *aginut* was uniquely Russian: the exile of a *levir* to Siberia. In 1861, Pesia Iur'evich appealed to the very state that exiled her
brother-in-law, Zalman Iur'evich, to Iakutsk in Eastern Siberia, having
exhausted all other options to change her anchored status. She explained

that after her brother-in-law had served his sentence, he voluntarily re-married and settled down in a village in the Verkhneudinskii region. Al-though it was her responsibility to go to the *levir* for the *halitsah* ritual, she cited several reasons that she could not do so. One was the need to obtain permission and documents to travel outside the Pale of Settlement. That was virtually impossible for a provincial Jewish woman in 1861. The ceremony itself required the presence of a Jewish *beit-din* with at least three members; since no Jews lived in the *levir*'s village, that too was an unrealizable condition. The Rabbinic Commission agreed with her ap-peal, ruling that Zalman Iurevich must travel to the town of Minsk in order to perform his duties. In this case too, especially since no male pre-rogative was threatened, the Rabbinic Commission showed considerable empathy for the plight of the *agunah*.[176]

A Male *Agun*?

If the *wife* disappeared, making it impossible for the man to deliver the bill of divorcement, could the husband remarry? Rabbi Berger had to consider that very question when Ios' Khaim Davidov Osel'ka came to see him on 20 December 1904.[177] The petitioner explained that his wife Malka deserted him thirteen years ago, and he now wanted to remarry. To his amazement the state rabbi refused on the grounds that his wife was not "missing" but lived in New York and hence had the option of returning to Russia to resume marital relations.[178] The rabbi also noted that, although the husband had attempted to send a *get* to his wife in America, through an agent, he had no evidence that she received it. Therefore, he declared the marriage still intact and binding. Frustrated by the rabbi's obstinacy, the deserted husband appealed to a different *beit-din*.

In this new venue, the plaintiff found a more sympathetic audience. All the members of the rabbinic court—rabbis Khaim Berlin of Elisavetgrad, Yekhil Mikhel Halevi Epstein of Novgorod, and Malkiel Tanenbaum of Lomzhi—unanimously concurred that Malka Osel'ka was a "rebellious" wife and authorized the husband to remarry, especially since he had sent a bill of divorcement. Unlike the state rabbi, they ignored the issue of the re-ception of the *get*. The *beit-din* ruled: "Here is the proof that Iosef Khaim, son of Duvid Osel'ka, is permitted to remarry according to our law, the Torah, without any danger. In this case, there are no oaths or prohibitions; on the contrary, he will be blessed one hundredfold when he marries for the second time."[179] The Rabbinic Commission upheld this decision, cit-ing the principle that if a wife refused to cohabit, the husband could dis-solve the marriage without her consent. Although Osel'ka did not collect the obligatory signatures of one hundred rabbis to make the decision of the *beit-din* binding, the commission allowed him to remarry on the condition that he send a new *get* to his wife, Malka Leibova Diner.[180]

The Rabbinic Commission was also sympathetic to a man whose wife was of ill repute. A state rabbi, uncertain whether to permit a deserted husband to remarry, had forwarded the case, along with the husband's petition. He testified that his wife had behaved "indecently" with other men from the very outset of their marriage and eventually left him to live with another man.[181] In May 1893 he went to Ialta, where his wife was rumored to be living, to deliver the *get*. Upon arrival he learned that his wife had lived there for only one year and had left for parts unknown with another man. Citing numerous corroborating depositions, the Rabbinic Commission ruled that "the unknown whereabouts of a wife gives the husband the legal grounds to remarry," with the qualification that this was valid as long as "he himself did not behave in such a manner as to drive his wife away."[182] Furthermore, it required the husband to prepare a bill of divorcement for his first wife in the event that she returned.[183]

Conclusion

This chapter has attempted to argue that the repercussions of marital dissolution were so onerous that many Jews postponed divorce either until they could no longer tolerate the nominal ties or until they wished to remarry. For men, the primary deterrent to an official divorce was financial—the restitution of the dowry, the *ketubah* payment, child support, and any other monies as stipulated in the marriage contract. Hence, although Efroim Myshkind of Minsk claimed that "it is not at all difficult for a Jew to divorce his wife, especially if she does not have a good reputation," he found it more convenient to remarry without divorcing his first wife in order to retain her assets.[184] The reluctance to initiate a divorce was compounded by the fact that Jewish women, not only in the capitals but also in the provinces, increasingly resorted to the state courts to settle their claims. This growing reliance on secular institutions to resolve private family issues attests to the steady decline in the authority of Jewish rabbis and the breakdown of internal communal discipline in tsarist Russia. It also reveals that some members of Jewish society no longer bothered to fulfill requirements of Jewish law if they found them disadvantageous. Hence, avaricious brothers-in-law refused to perform the ceremony of *halitsah* unless they were rewarded with a significant sum of money, and some fathers rejected their obligations to pay child support to maintain their own "lavish" lifestyles.

Divorce, for women, not only meant financial loss but social ostracism (the term *gerushah* meant "driven out") and single parenthood. According to the 1897 census, there were three times more divorced Jewish women than men, indicating that the former found it more difficult to remarry. Although many received child support until the children reached their majority (with the amount varying according to class), a few voluntarily forfeited that right to gain sole custody. Hence, it is not surprising that the majority of divorced women relocated to large urban centers in search of work in the factories or small artisan shops. Women also confronted a host of legal problems regarding their juridical status (e.g., social status and residence rights), which they ordinarily derived from their fathers or husbands. As we have seen, the problem was especially critical for women who sought to return to their parental home or to relocate their children from a previous marriage outside the Pale of Settlement. Legal issues also forced some Jewish women to remain married to abusive or undesirable husbands for fear of losing their residence rights outside the Pale. Indeed, the numerous cases in the Senate archive reveal that these problems only increased as the gap between formal law and new realities widened.

It is thus not surprising that a growing number of Jews chose to avoid the legal and financial consequences of divorce by resorting to informal or extralegal means of terminating the marriage, such as marital separation, desertion, or bigamy. Although these methods did not dissolve the legal marriage bond (i.e., neither spouse could remarry), it terminated the couple's sexual and sometimes financial obligations. Separation, however, was especially detrimental for Jewish women, who were dependent on their husbands for their legal status and paperwork, making them more vulnerable to unfair conditions (e.g, forfeiting material support for a separate passport). It was precisely these "marriages in limbo" that fueled contemporary perceptions that the Jewish family was in the throes of a profound crisis and prompted prominent Orthodox rabbis to call for unity to "repair the breach for the sake of Torah and the faith."[185]

Chapter Five

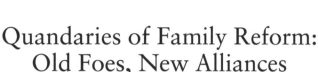

Quandaries of Family Reform:
Old Foes, New Alliances

This is the time for the faithful ones of Israel to join forces and strengthen ourselves for the sake of raising the cause of Torah and faith.

—Rabbi Moshe Nahum Yerusalimsky (1909)

In a clever pun on a familiar Talmudic aphorism, Rabbi Yaakov Halevi Lifschitz of Kovno once wrote: "Ten measures *[kabin]* of bureaucracy descended to the world; ten were taken by our new maskilim."[1] Instead of the nine *kabin* given to a particular subject and one measure to "the rest of the world," as expressed in the original saying, the *maskilim* received the entire allotment without a single portion left for the Orthodox rabbinic leadership.[2] From the mid-nineteenth century until the late 1890s, Lifschitz's mordant play on words offered a fair description of reality. The *maskilim*, or more precisely, non-Orthodox Jews, did indeed dominate positions of authority, monopolizing virtually all the official positions as state rabbis, learned Jews *(uchenye evrei)*, censors of Hebrew and Yiddish books, and members of the Rabbinic Commission.[3] It bears noting, however, that these were not all *maskilim* in the true sense of the word, despite the Orthodox tendency to tar and feather them as a single group; rather, the non-Orthodox leadership also included secular professionals (physicians, dentists, lawyers, journalists), wealthy merchants (e.g., the Gintzburgs and Poliakovs), philanthropists, and intellectuals, who did not necessarily ascribe to the ideology and "internal cultural codes" of the *haskalah*.[4] To make the distinction that the Orthodox camp did not make, we will use the term *maskilim* in its strictest meaning, and "Jewish intelligentsia" for the broader non-Orthodox leadership (who advocated sociopolitical change), of which the *maskilim* were only a subset.

By the turn of the century, Orthodox religious leaders began to reassert their claim to leadership in Jewish society and to demand that the state recognize them as the legitimate representatives of the Jewish people.[5] Their claim to authority came amid profound political and social crisis; virtually every group in the Russian Empire, even the most backward, began to organize, articulate their demands, and establish their own recognized leadership.[6] The breakdown of autocracy, which even spasms of repression could not reverse or even contain, provided the opportunity for Orthodox religious leaders to mobilize and press their claims to represent the Jews. To a weakened and frightened autocracy they offered a platform of conservatism and loyalty, with a promise to instill traditional religious and family values in the Jewish youth and thereby wean them from revolutionary movement. As one "public appeal" (kol koyre) issued by the rabbis in Vil'na (1903) proclaimed, "The aim of these agitators [Jewish socialists] is to lead the people astray from the proper path. But we, children of Abraham, Isaac, and Jacob, have been commanded to do only that which is good and right ([in the Yiddish text] and fully to observe the laws and statutes of the government under whose protection we dwell) and to accept willingly and wholeheartedly the rule of the government."[7]

That attempt to reclaim authority and to reassert traditional values collided head-on with the reform aspirations of "enlightened bureaucrats"—above all, the progressive jurists in the Russian Senate. Indeed, acutely sensitive to the dangerous volatility of a multiconfessional empire, leading officials (even the so-called modernizers) accepted the urgent need to integrate national and religious minorities into the empire. That integration meant, in the first instance, a common set of legal codes and administrative structures; it often included attempts at cultural Russification and conversion to Orthodoxy. In the case of Jews, the reformers sought to wean Jews away from their traditional spiritual leaders and bring them under the direct control of the state. This struggle for domination found its most poignant expression in the sphere of family law and practice, where the aspirations of the government, the Jewish intelligentsia, and the Orthodox religious leadership increasingly clashed, and helped to create a unified Jewish front against the intrusive state.

This conflict was central to Jewish politics and state policy in the last decades of the ancien régime. This chapter first examines the emergence of a conservative Orthodox movement that came to dominate the Rabbinic Commission in its final session. It next considers an important national congress of rabbis, convoked at the behest of the state and summoned to examine the whole spectrum of problems affecting Jewish religious life—above all, the problems of the dual rabbinate and the family (in particular, the problems of marriage and divorce). While the Jewish intelligentsia and Orthodox rabbis debated the prospects and desiderata of reform, the state itself became increasingly determined to assume responsibility and to promulgate a new order for all the tsar's subjects, including Jews. This chapter suggests why reform in the twilight of the ancien regime, whether from within or from without, failed to resolve the critical problems of Jewish family and religious life.

Religious Politics: The Rabbinic Commission

Between the 1870s and 1910, Russian Jewry experienced a profound shift in power and influence in the arena of family and religious politics: the ability to influence the state gradually shifted from the leadership of the Jewish intelligentsia to the Orthodox rabbinate. Most important, the religious conservatives gradually gained control of the Rabbinic Commission, the one institution with the authority to address a broad range of issues, especially those pertaining to the family.

1879: A Session Dominated by Enlightened Jews

When the government announced the new elections for the Rabbinic Commission (with a scheduled meeting in 1879), the Jewish intelligentsia seized upon this opportunity to rally the people to their cause of legal emancipation for Russian Jewry. The elections and meeting came in the midst of a profound "crisis of autocracy," triggered by a destructive terrorist campaign and deep discontent among many segments of society.[8] Although the government as yet gave no hint of plans for new reforms favorable to Jews, members of the Jewish intelligentsia nevertheless regarded the convocation of a new Rabbinic Commission, the first in seventeen years, as an indication of the government's willingness to consider giving full equality to the Jews.[9] To discourage participation by Orthodox leaders, the secular Jewish press launched a journalistic campaign against its ideological rivals. A typical fusillade came from Moshe Leib Lilienblum; writing for *Hakol,* he warned that the fate of the Jews could not be left to the hidebound rabbis, men utterly incapable of comprehending the contemporary status and needs of their coreligionists:

Anyone acquainted with the spirit of our rabbis knows how ill-equipped they are to comprehend what is in the Jews' best interest; they do not know the suffering of their own people. . . . I have no doubt whatsoever that the rabbis would be satisfied if the Jews did not win equal rights, just as long as every iota of the prayers inherited from our ancestors could be preserved. . . . The word "exile" *[galut]* is for them like a toy in the hands of a child: They do not want it to be taken away from them. For the real truth is that the Jews without their *galut* are like a body without a soul.[10]

That the *maskilim* felt it necessary to rebut the Orthodox stalwarts was already an indication of growing anxiety that, indeed, the latter's prestige and influence, partly because of the scandalous failure of state rabbis, had actually increased in recent years.

The Orthodox aggressively campaigned for influence in their own right. One leading figure was Rabbi Yaakov Lifschitz, a staunch supporter of the Orthodox camp, who repudiated the aspersions of the *maskilim* and reasserted the duty to defend Jewish tradition from the corrosive effect of the *haskalah* and acculturation among the Jews. In response to Lilienblum's accusations, Lifschitz emphasized that the Orthodox spiritual rabbis were the real leaders of the Jewish community: "To whom does an anguished and distressed man turn to first [as do] the poor and wounded in spirit, every widow and orphan, every oppressed and discouraged individual, and so on—but to the local rabbi?" In his view, the purpose of the Rabbinic Commission was not to secure equal rights for the Jews but rather to address religious questions involving marriage and divorce. Little wonder that the rabbi expressed his disgust at "the foolish wickedness of the Jewish intelligentsia, who elect their own—those who are distant from the Torah."[11] If the *maskilim* were to have any role in state service, wrote Lifschitz disparagingly, it was merely to register Jewish vital statistics in the metrical books. The resolution of religious questions—matters of *real* importance—should be left to spiritual rabbis, those "real" rabbis learned in the Torah and halakhah.

Testifying to the shift in popular mood, Jews showed a strong inclination to elect spiritual rabbis, not members of the Jewish intelligentsia. The Orthodox camp, in particular, enjoyed significant victories in several important Jewish centers, including Kovno (e.g., rabbis Eli Levinzohn of Kratinger and Eliezer Simhah of Suvalk) and Vil'na (Rabbi Eli Chaim Maizil). The elections were a plebiscite against the state rabbis and those who upheld the banner of acculturation and Russification. And the result was a resounding defeat for the non-Orthodox camp.

The final selection of members to the Rabbinic Commission, of course, depended not on popular votes but on bureaucratic calculation: the state chose members from the list of candidates selected by the various Jewish electoral districts. Despite the strong vote for the Orthodox camp, the Ministry of the Interior chose only non-Orthodox representatives; that decision doubtless reflected the predilections of bureaucrats with roots in the Great Reform era. The discrepancy between the composition of the Rabbinic Commission and the elections did not escape the attention of well-informed Russian observers. Even a liberal newspaper like *Golos* took exception, deriding the Rabbinic Commission as an "assembly of rabbis without rabbis."[12]

That mordant characterization was no exaggeration. Apart from state rabbi G. F. Bliumenfel'd of Odessa (appointed to chair the commission) and Dr. Avraham Harkavy (an erudite Orientalist from Vil'na), the other five members were all secular professionals: (1) Hirsh Shapiro, a pharmacist from Kovno; (2) Zel'man Liubich, a civil servant in the city administration of Minsk; (3) Meier Levin, a merchant from Pinsk; (4) Baron Goratsii Gintsburg, an entrepreneur from St. Petersburg; and (5) I. I. Kaufman, a representative from Odessa.[13] While the non-Orthodox camp duly celebrated these selections, the composition of the Rabbinic Commission was naturally a source of great distress for the Orthodox rabbis. As R. Yitshak Elhanan Spektor, the influential rabbi of Kovno, observed in a letter to Dr. Avraham Harkavy, once again the government had not selected "any of the great *gaonim*" to serve on the commission, he questioned the moral integrity and ability of its members to address issues involving Jewish law.[14] That acerbic remark, like the strong showing of spiritual rabbis in the preliminary elections, reflected a waxing interest of Orthodox leaders in what was unfolding in St. Petersburg.[15] This politicization of Orthodox Jews derived, in good measure, from the fact that enlightened Jews, despite their ignorance of Jewish law, were clearly determined to transform the Jewish way of life *(byt)*, especially the received norms and teachings on marriage and divorce. Nor could the spiritual rabbis overlook the increasing importance and intrusiveness of the state (especially the secular courts) in issues of family law. It therefore became essential, from their perspective, that the Orthodox, not reform-minded Jews, shape state policy pertaining to Jewish law and religion. By 1879 it was already clear that state rabbis and an "enlightened" commission had had a major impact on state policy and legal precedent; for example, state officials utilized their judgments as precedents to resolve Jewish suits in state courts that involved critical issues like bigamy.[16]

In any event, the fourth assembly of the Rabbinic Commission (1 February–12 April 1879) examined just seven cases; most of them concerned questions of divorce.[17] How the commission resolved such cases was bound to have a major impact on the Jewish family.[18] It was no accident that the Rabbinic Commission gave so much attention to these issues: they had become a primary focus of disputes at the local level and resonated strongly with the broader "family question" *(semeinyi vopros)* that loomed so large in public discourse.

Apart from a concern about family issues, Orthodox Jewish leaders began to regard the Rabbinic Commission as a potential instrument to exert a broader influence over the Jewish population. Here the Orthodox rabbis had an unrestricted opportunity; unlike the office of state rabbi (open only to candidates with a general Russian education), membership in the Rabbinic Commission presupposed no specific qualifications, at least according to the terms of the original decree of 1848. In striking contrast to the "enlightened" camp, the Orthodox rabbis recognized that the commission could fulfill an important national mission of preserving tradition, shaping a common future, and representing the Jewish nation. That vision impelled them to organize a grass-roots campaign, long before their opponents did, to promote their own candidates for the next meeting of the commission.

A Mixed Committee of 1893–1894

"Who is eligible to be elected [to the Rabbinic Commission]?" inquired one headline of the *Vilenskii vestnik*.[19] In a pamphlet devoted to the impending election, David Beithilel (Beit Hillel) noted that, while the pertinent statute imposed no specific requirements, in fact members *should* have certain qualifications if the Rabbinic Commission was to discharge its assigned duties properly. To be sure, the candidate must be familiar with Russian civil laws as well as general political juridical matters. However, he also insisted that all must have a thorough understanding of Jewish law; only then would they be qualified to "to examine and render opinions on questions pertaining to the laws and customs of the Jewish faith and the activities of rabbis." Although the intelligentsia might satisfy the first requirement, many manifestly lacked a fundamental knowledge of Jewish law and tradition.

Beithilel's main argument was that only the candidate who had *both* could carry out the principal mission of the Rabbinic Commission: to resolve the growing contradictions between Jewish and secular law on marriage and divorce. What he meant by "resolving," of course, was a staunch defense of Jewish law, which of late had been consistently undermined by civil courts. As an example, he noted how state courts were now routinely dissolving Jewish divorces in the district of Warsaw, in utter disregard of the mandates of Jewish law. But such verdicts were invalid until the basic requirements of Jewish law were satisfied—for example, the husband's obligatory delivery of the *get* to his wife. Beithilel complained that this requirement was now routinely flouted: "It is common that the court decides to divorce the couple, but the guilty [spouse] evades [the obligation] to fulfill the rite according to Jewish law and the decision of the court turns into a dead letter." Since such a "divorce" violated the basic requirements of Jewish law, rabbis forbade either spouse to remarry even if, in the eyes of the secular court, the couple had been legally divorced. Furthermore, the author challenged the legal monopoly of state rabbis over religious rites; it was wrong to prosecute Jews who performed private marriage ceremonies simply because they were neither state rabbis nor their assistants. In this instance too, state law violated the teachings and spirit of Judaism, which did not even require "rabbis" to officiate at weddings. Hence, Beithilel declared that the primary mission of the Rabbinic Commission must be to rectify these "abnormal" conditions, which had gradually accumulated over the past few decades. For that task, only the most qualified candidates—men who knew Jewish law—were suited.[20]

Being qualified and being chosen, however, were very different things. To win the coveted seats in the Rabbinic Commission, traditional rabbis understood that they must campaign more intensely than they had in the elections for the session of 1879. As Yaakov Lifschitz later recalled, this time the Orthodox faction worked diligently to mobilize voters on their behalf—distributing, for example, campaign materials throughout the Pale of Settlement and urging franchised Jews to vote for their candidates.[21]

In contrast to the Orthodox activists, the Jewish intelligentsia took considerably less interest. Although the election generated the usual polemics, the latter did little to mobilize and enlighten the electorate. In part, they had been disillusioned by the previous sessions, which had done little to realize their own agenda: legal emancipation of the Jews. The fact that the session of 1879 had concentrated on mundane questions of marriage and divorce made it clear that the commission would do nothing to address the question of equal rights. That was all the more true in the early 1890s after years of political repression and blatant anti-semitic policies. As a result, members of the Jewish intelligentsia, like their Russian counterparts, spurned any collaboration with the autocracy and looked elsewhere to advance their political aspirations. And the alternative opportunities were manifold: socialism, Marxism, and Zionism or some combination of these.[22]

Indeed, the very engagement of liberal Jewish intelligentsia in the "liberation movement"[23] enabled the Orthodox camp to appeal more powerfully to the Russian state and to hope for strong representation on the next Rabbinic Commission. In essence, the Orthodox activists could now argue that their very religious conservatism was a guarantee of social and political stability; not "enlightened Jews" but spiritual rabbis would instill political loyalty, protect the family order, and restrain Jews from joining the anti-state movements.

This new rhetoric of religious and political conservatism had already begun to emerge in the early 1880s. It figured prominently, for example, in a letter sent in 1882 from a group of Orthodox Jewish émigrés in London to K. P. Pobedonostsev, the leading public spokesman for autocratic statism and chief procurator of the Holy Synod. The main thesis in the letter was that the state, in its own political self-interest, should support the Orthodox, not the *maskilim*[24]—who, they warned, sought only to erode the foundations of faith and tradition. The consequences were dangerous for both state and society: "The lack of faith among the Jews not only encourages nihilism, but spreads atheism [which leads to] a corruption of morals among the general population." The letter admitted that "the Jewish people are convinced that the government is hostile to the Jewish faith" but attributed this attitude to the preferential treatment accorded to the *maskilim*: "Indeed, government authorities always patronize the educated, aristocratic Jewish party, while oppressing individuals of the Orthodox religious party, who exhort the people to be true to their faith." The last election of the Rabbinic Commission in 1879, they emphasized, was a clear case in point. Although the Jewish population had overwhelmingly chosen "spiritual rabbis," the machinations of the *maskilim* had induced the governors to select only "those without any religious learning." If the Russian state desired to eradicate the harmful influence of revolutionary nihilism and to overcome the general disaffection of the Jewish people, it must allow the spiritual rabbis to educate Jewish children from a young age and "to entrust them with independent authority over Jewish religious issues," such as marriage, divorce, *kashrut,* and the like.[25]

In this event, the government compromised by including both Orthodox and non-Orthodox representatives for the session of 1893–1894. Specifically, the Ministry of Interior chose four enlightened Jews, as well as three prominent Orthodox leaders from the northern provinces:

Rabbi Tsvi Hirsh Rabinovich[26]	the illustrious preacher at the main synagogue in Vil'na, designated chairman of the commission
Rabbi Samuil Mogilever[27]	a leading Orthodox leader from Belostok (Grodno province)
Rabbi Iuria Hillel Mileikovskiia	theologian from the province of Mogilev
Herman Barats	a jurist from Kiev
Iakov Gottesman	a merchant from Volhynia
Samuil Simkhovich	a merchant from Mink
Avraam Katlovker[28]	the state rabbi of Kishinev

The assembly met for two and one-half months (from 19 November 1893 to 28 January 1894) and examined a total of twenty-seven cases, most of which pertained to "marriage, religious rituals, and divorce—all of which had a personal character."[29] The learned Talmudic scholars immediately made their presence felt: journal entries now contained more detailed explanations of Jewish law, with detailed references and citations from various halakhic sources as well as the more commonly cited *Shulhan Arukh*.[30] The commission also prepared special memoranda on the ritual of *halitsah,* the meaning and form of the *ketubah,* and the grounds for divorce in Judaism.[31]

The presence of Orthodox rabbis in the commission evoked a strong resonance in the Jewish community, arousing far more interest and trust than had the preceding sessions. Indeed, the commission also stirred expectations that the spiritual rabbis would intercede with the government and promote Jewish religious interests. Such heightened expectations about the rabbis' influence, for example, informed a petition from a group of printers in Vil'na to Rabbi Tsvi Hirsh Rabinovich. Specifically, they urged him to "endeavor to remove the prohibitions on the printing of two sections of the *Shulhan Arukh,* namely, *Hoshen Mishpat* and *Even Haezer,* as well as select writings of the *poskim* (rabbinic authorities) that are banned in Russia."[32] According to Yaakov Lifschitz, the rabbi addressed the issue in the context of other religious questions and obtained permission to publish the requested books. Such actions reinforced the belief among many Jews that the commission could function as a mediating institution between the state and people and that it must be dominated by Orthodox rabbis if it were to have a salutory impact on family and religious life.

1910: An Orthodox Session

Although the next (and final) session of the Rabbinic Commission did not convene until 1910, in the interim the Orthodox faction actively worked to mobilize their resources and to promote their influence. That activism became particularly intense during and after the Revolution of 1905–1907, when Jews, like other groups, used the new Law of Associations to organize and to hold national conferences.[33] The Orthodox rabbis similarly began to plan a conference to discuss the future of Judaism and Jewish communal life in Russia, as well as their strategies for the next elections to the Rabbinic Commission. Finally, in September 1908, Rabbi Itsko Girshov Liubinskii sent a petition to the Ministry of the Interior, asking permission to convene a conference of twenty-five rabbis in Vil'na. Its purpose was to discuss important questions pertaining to Judaism and particularly to marital law. To persuade the ministry that the conference was politically well intentioned, Rabbi Liubinskii emphasized that the conference would also endeavor to "find the means to maintain faith and religion among the Jewish youth, who have almost all fallen under the influence of revolutionary agitation in the previous years." The list of participants included a colorful combination of Hasidic and mitnagdic rabbis, four of whom would later serve on the Rabbinic Commission of 1910.[34]

Before granting approval, however, the ministry directed each provincial governor to investigate the proposed participants and report on their background and political reliability. The responses were almost universally positive. Thus, the governor of Grodno informed central authorities that "the sixty-one-year-old Khaim Iosef Soloveichik has not participated in any political movements and has conducted himself in a proper and moral [manner] as a spiritual rabbi." The governor of Odessa sent a similar assessment: "This is to certify that Iosif Gal'perin [Halperin], who is sixty years old, has served as a spiritual rabbi in Odessa for thirty-one years and has had a tremendous influence on the Jewish masses. . . . He is moral, orthodox, and conservative." Virtually all the reports bore the same tone, emphasizing that the individual rabbis under their jurisdiction were "conservative," "have no record of political activity," or "have not participated in any revolutionary movements." Only one report contained an implicitly negative note: according to the governor of Poltava, Rabbi E. Rafailovich, "an honorary citizen *(pochetnyi grazhdanin)*[35] and the spiritual rabbi of Kremenchug, has participated in a Zionist organization."[36]

Given the loyal political record and the promise to help the government combat the revolutionary spirit among Jews, the Ministry of the Interior gave permission for the conference to convene. That decision was in itself telling, for it came amid the most repressive years of the Stolypin era, when the government reneged on the concessions of 1905, systematically violated its own law on associations, and banned most meetings of this kind. Elated at the good news, R. Moshe Yerusalimsky informed the Gerer Rebbe (R. Avraham-Mordecai of Gur) that the conference "comes at an opportune moment, for the Torah and piety have fallen on bad times; [we are plagued with] trouble upon trouble and [Jews have begun] imitating the ways of the gentiles." He admitted that he had been skeptical about the entire affair, until he learned that the subjects to be discussed "rest on the most sacred foundations." He added that the conference would provide the perfect opportunity to consider joining the Knesses Yisroel, a formal Orthodox association founded in 1907 in Vil'na with the blessing of the government.[37]

The conference finally met in early 1909 under the leadership of Rabbi Katsenelenbogen of St. Petersburg and included thirty-one other rabbis (hence, more than the number specified in the petition).[38] The agenda had several items that reflected the primary concerns of the Orthodox camp:

- questions concerning marriage and divorce,
- *kashrut,*
- observance of the Sabbath,
- the education and upbringing of Jewish youth,
- legalization of the status of spiritual rabbis, and
- a detailed program for the forthcoming elections to the Rabbinic Commission.

Similar issues had been discussed at a rabbinic conference held a few months earlier in Warsaw. According to a St. Petersburg newspaper, one participant in that conference had argued that the Orthodox faction could provide a counterweight to the "radical and left-wing elements" in Jewish society, not only in terms of "religious, but also political conservatism." He thus struck a familiar refrain: only by allowing a conservative religious leadership to regain control over the fundamental aspects of Jewish domestic and religious life could the Russian government hope to stem the participation of Jewish youth in radical, antigovernment movements.[39]

By the time the Ministry of Internal Affairs announced the elections for a new session of the Rabbinic Commission, the Orthodox coalition had mobilized for the struggle against their enlightened opponents. The Jewish press reported that several rabbis in tsarist Poland had already begun urging the Jewish masses "to elect only [Orthodox] rabbis to serve in the Rabbinic Commission." The motive for such a call, the writer ventured, stemmed from the fact that "they [the Orthodox rabbis] are powerless to do anything about the secular interests of the Jewish population, [but] they can do something in the sphere of religious life.[40] To the shock and dismay of the non-Orthodox camp, their rivals won a smashing victory in the elections. Save for one jurist from Kiev (Moishe Savel'ev Mazor), all the other members chosen to the Rabbinic Commission were prominent rabbis and *tsaddikim*: Rabbi Yehuda Leib M. Tsirel'son of Kishinev, Rabbi Khaim Soloveichik of Brest-Litovsk, Rabbi Khaim Oizer Grodzenskii of Vil'na, Rabbi Sholom Shneerson of Liubavich, Rabbi Shmuel Polinkovskii of Odessa, and Rabbi Mendel David Khein of Nezhin.[41]

The consternation of the opposing camp pervaded reporting in the Russian-Jewish press. A provocative article in *Rassvet,* written by Vladimir Temkin, put the blame for these results squarely on the shoulders of the "Jewish intelligentsia." He noted that, at the outset of the elections, they had been "completely indifferent to the Rabbinic Commission," believing that it would address only "a few narrow questions about marital laws"—matters of little interest to most of the intelligentsia. By the time the activists realized that they were "poorly informed" about the potential importance of the Rabbinic Commission, it was too late to change the direction of the elections. Temkin noted that the Orthodox, by seizing control over family and religious issues, had not only gained official control over important issues in the everyday lives of Jews but had attained unparalleled power to reconsider the general rabbinate question, an issue that was of equal importance to their opponents. The author expressed a begrudging admiration for the political skill of Orthodox representatives in campaigning for the elections. He noted that, long before the elections, Orthodox agents distributed pamphlets about the upcoming struggle, whereas "the St. Petersburg Jewish intelligentsia was occupied with its own internal affairs; they slumbered and did not consider it necessary to be informed about the remote Jewish Pale of Settlement." Temkin also emphasized the surprising show of "unity and single-spiritedness [between] two different sects of Orthodox Jewry, namely the Polish and Liubavich Hasidim, who were not long ago at odds with one another, and contemptuous of one another—an enmity that has endured for one hundred years."[42]

As is clear from that article, Vladimir Temkin, like others of the intelligentsia he criticized, was utterly unaware of the earlier political activities of the Orthodox rabbis that presaged their startling triumph in 1910. Hence, he found it "strange" that the Orthodox leadership, "who have always stood inert and passive about any social work, who have shown little interest in Jewish life, suddenly showed such energy" in the recent elections. He speculated about the potential motives of this "sudden" involvement. "Could it be that the Orthodox elite believe that they can investigate and decide all the public and social aspects of internal Jewish life by force without the participation of the cultural strata of Jewry?" Or, he wondered, "did they perhaps fear that the enlightened elements want to make changes in some parts of our customs, marital laws and so forth?"[43]

Another writer for the Russian-Jewish press, A. Davidson, also admitted that he had been totally unprepared for the emergence of what he called "the clerical movement." In fact, he confessed, his latest article[44] had argued that "Jewish Orthodoxy as a social-political party with a specific, distinct proclivity does not exist" in Russia. Only in retrospect did Davidson recall the series of rabbinic conferences held the previous year. He now recognized as well that the militant character of rabbinic publications, along with the organization and agitation in the elections for the Rabbinic Commission, should be seen as "signs of this movement." In his view, clerical movements began "only when the representatives of a religion wish to acquire some secular power (whether it be in the government, community or in a local institution)," their main objective being to find some way to buttress their religious authority. So too in the case of the Orthodox political movement: the primary motivation was to combat the growing religious apathy among the general Jewish population and the powerlessness of the rabbis and their declining influence. In a sense, he claimed, this political activity violated the rabbis' principal responsibility: "Until now, religious shepherds have remained within the framework of their calling; until now they have been concerned about fulfilling the spiritual needs of their flock."[45] Indeed, he argued, the spiritual domain was the only sphere in which the rabbi should seek to exercise an influence. That argument was not, of course, new to Jewish discourse.[46] Even if the Orthodox rabbi had the right to be involved in political matters, Davidson argued, "secular power can only merge with the *dukhovenstvo* (clergy) when the latter displays some strength [and] independent influence," which he believed the Russian rabbis lacked. Perhaps to conceal his own miscalculation, the writer concluded that all the distress on the part of the Jewish intelligentsia was unfounded: the Orthodox rabbis had no political influence and remained nothing more than "uncultured *batlanim* (poor men who sat in the synagogue all day and lived on alms). They remained just as they were a half century ago."[47]

The writings by Temkin, Davidson, and other members of the Russian-Jewish press reveal that the intelligentsia not only misjudged the influence of the Orthodox rabbis but also the attitudes of the Russian state.[48] In the wake of the Revolution of 1905–1907, the government was deeply concerned about the decline of piety; the "liberation movement," they believed, had deeply eroded the faith—and political loyalty—of the tsar's most pious and reliable subjects. Such sentiments were characteristic not only of the bureaucrats in St. Petersburg but also of civil servants in the provinces, including those in the Pale of Settlement. In a meeting with the spiritual rabbi Shmuel Polinkovskii in 1909, the governor of Odessa (I. N. Tolmachev) observed the "strong decline in belief among the Jews of Odessa" and expressed his confidence that the rabbi and "older religious Jews would strengthen the religious spirit among the Odessa-Jewish population." That view underlay the governor's advice to the Ministry of the Interior: representatives from the Jewish community in Odessa to the Rabbinic Commission should be selected "only from the Orthodox strata."[49]

That represented a 180-degree shift in attitude toward a group of Jews that Russian officialdom had, for decades, disparaged for its "fanaticism." It was a telling sign of the fear, uncertainty, and desperation of Russian autocracy that, at this late hour, it should favor the very people it had so long abjured and denigrated. Confronted with a powerful, surging revolutionary movement, the tsarist government found the political and social conservatism of Orthodox Jewry a welcome respite and potential pillar of support. By enhancing the power and authority of the Orthodox party, the government could at once combat revolution. That the Ministry of Internal Affairs selected a rabbinic majority to represent Russian Jewry in the Rabbinic Commission was indeed one indicator of this new position. To quote one embittered writer: "The Orthodox did not let any chance go by without remarking that the government would support the spiritual rabbis as a conservative and loyal element that can serve as a bulwark against any changes in Jewish life."[50]

The session of the Rabbinic Commission met from 2 March to 4 April 1910. It dealt with thirty-three total cases, of which twenty-three pertained directly to marriage and divorce. The other issues included questions about burials and cemeteries, the spelling of Jewish names, the censorship of books, and the Jewish oath in civil matters. Under the nearly total domination of the Orthodox faction, the discussions about marital laws were more complex and authoritative. The journal entries referred to various responsa and commentaries of numerous rabbinic scholars.[51] In short, the Rabbinic Commission lived up to its appellation, lending more credibility to the institution than it ever had in the past.

The Rabbinate and Reform

Behind those ferocious battles for power in the Rabbinic Commission was a long-festering but increasingly grave crisis in the system of the dual rabbinate. That problem, more than any other dimension of state policy, impinged powerfully—and destructively—on the daily lives of Jews all across the realm, regardless of status, region, politics, or conviction. A reporter for the Jewish periodical, *Khronika voskhoda* did not exaggerate when he wrote that "the rabbi question . . . occupies one of the most painful places in the life of Jewish society today."[52] Another writer described the problem as "abnormal" and a primary issue in Jewish life, one that required immediate and fundamental reform.[53]

As we have seen,[54] the state rabbinate was indeed the source of much acrimony, crisis, and confusion. Although created to regulate and transform Jewish family and religious life, the rabbinate not only maintained the metrical books, but intervened sporadically into complex questions of marriage and family. Based on their official jurisdiction in family matters, some state rabbis—educated not as Talmudic scholars but as pharmacists, dentists, doctors, and the like—boldly pronounced verdicts on divorce, permitted husbands to remarry without dissolving the first marriage, and remained impervious to harsh accusations that they were unqualified to serve as "guardians and interpreters" of Jewish law.[55] As one critic of the state rabbis fulminated, "There is nothing worse in the world, than to be in a false position, playing someone else's role." He went on to add that "if it were unpleasant to be unmasked at a masquerade party, how much more so it was to wear the mask constantly knowing that one was not concealing [anything]." Such, he cried, was the position of a state rabbi—someone who "knows very well that he serves the society only as a masked [rabbi], but that he is only a spiritual person in the eyes of the government, [a position that was] far from enviable."[56]

Quite apart from the disruption that the state rabbinate caused in the family, many Jews simply viewed this institution as entirely superfluous. As one observer put it, "the Jews [already] have their own clergy *(dukhovenstvo)* to fulfill religious demands and spiritual acts." Each community had at least one cantor to recite the liturgy and lead synagogue services, a *mohel* to perform circumcisions, and a *dayyan* (rabbi) to expound on religious questions and to decide divorce suits.[57] They did not need, he wrote, a bureaucrat in rabbi's clothing to usurp the traditional division of labor among the established leaders. In addition, this institution was an unnecessary financial burden: by diverting the income from the kosher meat tax to pay the salaries of the state rabbis, it left little for the "spiritual rabbis" who actually performed the majority of responsibilities for the community, leaving many of them impoverished and dependent on communal charity.

Although most Jews wanted to abolish the state rabbinate altogether, the intelligentsia still hoped to create a modern, professional rabbinate. "If the conditions of Jewish life only demanded . . . order in the metrical books and decisions about questions of *kashrut* and *trefot*," remarked Yakov Katsenel'son in his lengthy study of the rabbinate in Russia, "then it would not be such a great misfortune to have two special individuals to serve the Jewish community to fulfill these two obligations." One would be responsible to register civil acts and secular matters, while the other (the genuine rabbi) would occupy himself with the interpretation and application of religious-ritual laws to daily life. The author contended, however, that the dual rabbinate did not serve the needs of the people, a failing that he vaguely attributed to the complex and broader demands of Jewish society. Whatever the cause, Katsenel'son also recommended that the secular and spiritual functions be combined in a single rabbi, someone who was an "experienced and knowledgeable pilot, a leader and mentor who would be led by spiritual and secular interests."[58]

Proposals like these about how to solve the rabbinate question would become more clearly articulated in the empire-wide conferences that would be convened at the initiative of both Jews and the Russian state.

Early Encounters

The anomaly of "dual power" *(dvoevlastie)* and all the problems it spawned inevitably impelled some members of the intelligentsia and Orthodox rabbis to meet (albeit reluctantly) and discuss various solutions to the problem. Both believed it important to devise a solution before the Russian state did so.[59] Such encounters, however, invariably ended in frustration and distrust, revealing the deep divisions between the two sides and their radically different visions about the role and primary functions of the rabbinate. The cultural divide, underlying values, conflicting interests, and competing objectives were simply too great to allow even a modicum of organized cooperation. While these meetings failed to produce a "solution" to the crisis, they did reveal much about the crisis itself and how each party sought to resolve it.

The first assembly met in 1887 on the initiative of the wealthy entrepreneur Samuel Poliakov, who invited fourteen delegates to St. Petersburg to discuss various questions important to Russian Jewry. The participants included five members of the intelligentsia (including Poliakov himself) and ten Orthodox rabbis from the Pale of Settlement.[60] The central issue was how to narrow the gap between the state and spiritual rabbis. Their goal was to seek an institutional change (abolition of the state rabbinate, for example) and to establish new cultural and professional bonds between the two types of rabbis.

In essence, the intelligentsia proposed to "enlighten" the Orthodox with more secular learning. One delegate proposed to introduce several hours a week of Russian and mathematics into the general course of study in the yeshivot; thus, its curriculum was similar to that of the secular progymnasium, thereby making the rabbinic students eligible to hold the office of state rabbi. Despite his persuasive oratory skills, the very suggestion of incorporating secular studies in the yeshivot was anathema to the rabbis; they summarily rejected the proposal without further consideration. Shmuel Poliakov recommended that, if the proposal to combine secular and religious studies was unacceptable, the students could take the requisite secular courses in a special school outside the yeshiva or in a "single-class school" *(odnoklassnoe uchilishche)*.[61] That would avoid "tainting" or compromising the strictly religious spirit and image of the rabbinic schools. This proposal similarly failed to find favor with the rabbis. It was hardly surprising, however, that the Orthodox camp should have responded so negatively: the enlightened Jews sought not to change the state rabbinate but to transform the Orthodox rabbis into state rabbis.

The common thread in all these proposals was the attempt to induce their Orthodox coreligionists to undergo some measure of secular education. The intelligentsia would frequently recycle these proposals over the next few years. In 1887, for example, the Society for the Promotion of Enlightenment among the Jews,[62] organized a special conference in Odessa to discuss the problem of the dual rabbinate. The participants considered a array of ideas, including the creation of special rabbinic seminaries with both secular and religious subjects and the establishment of an institution of higher education for rabbinical training. The key element behind these proposals, whatever the particulars, was the notion that the ideal rabbi should have not only a religious but also a secular education.[63]

Although the Orthodox rabbis initially rejected such proposals at the Poliakov session, they gradually showed some willingness to compromise. In his memoir, Yaakov Lifschitz recalled that "the rabbis recognized the spirit of assimilation" from the beginning, but "[they] did not want to kindle the fury of the aristocrat [Poliakov] against them at a time when the Jews lived in danger." They therefore proceeded in a "diplomatic" manner and sought a compromise that would address their main concerns.[64] If Lifschitz's assessment is accurate, the Orthodox leadership recognized that they were politically powerless to thwart any government legislation that their enlightened opponents might seek to initiate. In the 1880s, at least, the government was not yet ready to discern the positive, stabilizing role that conservative Orthodox rabbis might play. Indeed, ministerial reports from the 1880s still described Orthodox rabbis as "fanatic" and decried their "harmful influence on the Jewish masses."[65]

In the end, the Orthodox representatives agreed to supplement the yeshiva education with secular study but only with several important qualifications. The students would take two classes at the special auxiliary school as long they did not have to study at the yeshiva "under the supervision and administration of a [secular] curator." In addition, the secular subjects were to be voluntary; no student would be forced to take them. Nor were the secular courses to affect the general "operation of the yeshiva or its spirit."[66]

None of these proposals were ever realized. Much of the responsibility here rests with the intelligentsia themselves, who remained adamant about the need for an obligatory secular component in rabbinical education. Still, acting under their influence, the state not only rejected proposals to establish such schools and the auxiliary secular curriculum, but even *raised* the minimum educational requirement for eligibility to serve as state rabbi. The original law had permitted *any* level of secondary education, including the four-year progymnasium program. Specifically, two Senate rulings increased the minimum educational requirement for eligibility in the state rabbinate elections, raising the minimum to six years of study (in 1895) and then to eight years (in 1902).[67] Although some were willing to settle for just a modicum of secular education among the Orthodox rabbis, which they would have deemed a considerable achievement, the government became more exacting and, at least before the great upheavals of 1905, showed little concern about religious training.

Convening: The Rabbinic Congress of 1910

The next significant encounter did not come until 1910, although this is not to say that there were no other attempts to rectify the problem of the rabbinate during the intermediate years.[68] As Azriel Shochat has pointed out, the efforts of the enlightened faction "continually encountered the opposition of the Orthodox," who refused to compromise the religious upbringing of their youth. In a sudden display of concern about the internal life of Russian Jewry, the Ministry of Internal Affairs summoned forty-two Jewish representatives to come to St. Petersburg for a "Rabbinic Congress" in 1910. Significantly, the rabbis met under the personal supervision of Count P. A. Stolypin (chairman of the Council of Ministers) and A. N. Kharuzin (the director of the Department of Spiritual Affairs of Foreign Faiths). The government's motive for organizing the assembly was transparently political. Stolypin himself explained that the Jews in the revolutionary movement and in the Bund possess "a terrible inclination," and he suggested that the question of religious leadership was as much about maintaining political loyalty among the people as it was about spiritual guidance. Significantly, the month-long conference (2 March–4 April) coincided with the session of the Rabbinic Commission, perhaps to increase the visibility of pro-regime Jewish conservatism. The participants included all seven members of the Rabbinic Commission, as well as an array of prominent Orthodox rabbis, merchants, honorary citizens, and state rabbis. Geographically, the composition was extraordinarily diverse: thirty-two representatives came from the Pale of Settlement, five from Tsarist Poland, and two each from Moscow and St. Petersburg.[69]

The agenda of the Rabbinic Congress was long, inclusive, and diverse. It included such important issues as the reorganization of the rabbinate, registration and metrical books, transformation of the Rabbinic Commission, marriage and divorce, and the kosher meat tax *(korobochnyi sbor)*.[70] It was to be the most wide-ranging national assembly ever convened; its resolutions would address the most important critical problems in Jewish religious life.

The "Rabbinical Question"

The controversial problem of the dual rabbinate dominated the meetings—indeed, so much so that Stolypin complained that the participants made little progress on the other issues. To mollify the prime minister and solicit his sympathy, Leizer Poliakov reminded him that the spiritual rabbis were often "dismissed as artisans and merchants," even though they were the true "pastors of the Jewish nation and preserve the Jewish religion." Stolypin softened his tone as he remembered one spiritual rabbi whom he held in high regard—Rabbi Yitshak Elhanan Spektor of Kovno, whom he evidently knew from his service in Kovno province and who had made a deep impression on such leaders as the governor of Kovno and the Metropolitan of St. Petersburg.[71] He asserted that "if the Jews were brought up in a religious spirit in the future . . . perhaps one could expect a constant improvement in their position."[72]

It was hardly surprising that the question of the dual rabbinate, given its complexity and significance, should have so engaged the participants. Particularly contentious was the issue of whether the state should "legalize" the status and role of spiritual rabbis. The most ardent advocates argued that spiritual rabbis should not only be granted official status but even be recognized as superior to those educated in secular schools ("in the Russian spirit"). They were referring, of course, to the state rabbis, who had a higher education but lacked formal knowledge in matters of the Jewish faith. Their opponents categorically rejected the proposal: legalizing spiritual rabbis would mean giving "people who are uneducated and fanatical" unlimited power over the Jewish population. "They [the spiritual rabbis], along with the capitalist Jews, purposely try to keep the Jewish masses in ignorance and superstition," they argued, "and also demoralize the established state rabbis."[73]

A related issue was educational requirements for the position of state rabbi. Although the majority of participants concurred that candidates for the post must be learned in Jewish law, they disagreed sharply over the specific requirements. Some contended that the nominees should pass a special test by an examining committee to determine their competence in halakhah. Others believed that an individual's degree from a rabbinic seminary or any "theological institution" should suffice as evidence of training in Jewish law. Predictably, the enlightened Jews insisted that candidates not only have this religious training but also hold a diploma from a secular school (either a gymnasium or institution of higher education).[74]

Once the discussion turned to the "language requirement" for rabbis, any semblance of civility and comity dissolved as the participants became embroiled in a fierce fight. The enlightened faction and some Hasidic rabbis viewed the knowledge of Russian language as an essential prerequisite for anyone seeking to serve as a state rabbi. Tsaddik Shneerson of Bobruisk, for example, delivered an emotional speech, claiming that ignorance of Russian had brought much misery on the Jewish people: "If the Jews [rabbis] know the state language, will they not be able to intercede on behalf of the people to the authorities?" The *tsaddik* of Bobruisk reminded listeners that knowledge of Russian did not go against the calling of the rabbi. Tsaddik Shneerson of Liubavich, however, vehemently rejected such arguments. "No qualification is needed for the spiritual rabbi!" he shouted passionately. Secular knowledge of any sort, in his view, was positively dangerous for the spiritual rabbinate; it could only serve to alienate them from the Torah and draw them closer to the intelligentsia. Amid this dispute among the Hasidic rabbis, the lawyer G. B. Sliozberg ventured a compromise: that all state rabbis must know Russian in order to fulfill their administrative tasks, but the assistant rabbis, being responsible solely for the regulation of religious and family life, would be exempt from the requirement.[75]

In an exclusive interview given afterward, a reporter asked the Liuba-vich *tsaddik* why he had so vehemently opposed the requirement that rabbis be competent in the Russian language. "I did not say that I was against the *knowledge* of Russian," Rabbi Shneerson maintained. "On the contrary, I believe that it would be often useful for rabbis to speak Russian, but I am opposed to [the notion] that rabbis must be *obliged* to know Russian."[76] He explained, furthermore, that the requirement to study Russian would distract rabbis from their present duties, certainly a more pressing and important obligation. In addition, he argued that the state language was hardly essential for rabbis to carry out their religious responsibilities: "When they tell me that rabbis should know how to preach in Russian in the synagogues, I reply that a *Jewish* rabbi should read his sermon in *Yiddish* and that every Jew should understand Yid-dish," he insisted. In essence, the *tsaddik* envisioned a very different role for the rabbi than what the enlightened faction had in mind. A rabbi, in his view, was someone who "occupies himself exclusively with religious matters" and does not become mired in secular activities. His authority must come from within; he must not resort to the secular authorities for assistance to enforce his word. In the *tsaddik*'s view, "If, for example, the Jews in my town opened their store on the Sabbath, I would never em-ploy the assistance of the police to close them down [for] I assure you, the government is not inclined at all to side with us." Rabbi Shneerson reiter-ated his sincere desire that the government abolish the institution of the state rabbinate, which he considered "degrading for the spiritual rabbis" and harmful for the Jewish community.[77]

Another critical issue at the conference was the procedure used to elect the state rabbi, which many regarded as unduly cumbersome and expen-sive. There was a unanimous consensus at the congress that rabbis should be elected for a much longer term: instead of the current triennial term, they proposed to choose such rabbis, if not for life, then at least for fif-teen years. The assembly proposed that, at a minimum, rabbis with an ir-reproachable record for one to three years be permitted to remain in their post without a new election. As to the organization and supervision of the elections, one group proposed to establish a "general Jewish colle-gium" to assume the responsibilities now held by the provincial governor. That collegium could not only lighten the burden on state administration but ensure that Jews would be able to elect the rabbi of their choice with-out any external pressure from secular authorities.[78]

As to financial support for the state rabbinate, the conference saw lit-tle chance of major change. Hence most representatives concurred, if re-luctantly, that the Jewish communities would have to continue support-ing their rabbis from the kosher meat tax, although some participants voiced strong exception. The state rabbi of Ekaterinoslav, a strong opponent of the kosher meat tax, complained that the burden fell primarily on impoverished Jews, while those who held diplomas from institutions of higher education (i.e., the Jewish intelligentsia) were exempt from the tax under state law.[79] The Ekaterinoslav rabbi insisted on radical reforms before one decided how to spend the revenues.

The assembly also considered how to make the state rabbinate more attractive, to recruit more respectable, qualified candidates. Drawing on the political culture of the tsarist state, some participants proposed a special uniform for the state rabbi or awarding a symbolic medal of honor. Others proposed bestowing special prerogatives and increasing the awards for impeccable service record, as was done, for example, in the case of civil servants, military officers, and Russian Orthodox clergy. A few members suggested more practical ideas, such as providing the state rabbi with a service horse so that he could more conveniently travel long distances to perform Jewish ceremonies.[80]

After four acrimonious sessions, the congress adopted its final resolution on 22 March 1910: It proposed that all members of the Jewish prayer houses who had lived in the town for at least two years had the right to participate in the election of the state rabbi. It further recommended that a rabbi be elected to serve a term of no less than five years.[81] Spiritual rabbis were to be allowed to perform marriages and divorces and to decide religious questions in the capacity of a *moreh horaah* (*dayyan*, or rabbi). In effect, they were to gain official recognition to perform the tasks that hitherto had been the exclusive domain of the state rabbi. The congress also wanted to pay the salaries of both the state and spiritual rabbis and their assistants from the kosher meat tax and other communal levies, such as the candle tax.[82] Significantly, the congress was silent about the qualifications for the post of state rabbi: it had voted down the two proposals pertaining to secular education and the Russian language. It had also rejected the state law requiring a formal diploma from a secular educational institution by a vote of 28 to 8. Similarly, it rejected the requirement to speak the official language (Russian) by a vote of 25 to 12.[83]

While the rabbinic congress stopped short of demanding that the dual rabbinate be abolished, it did seek to improve the status of state rabbis and, most notably, to accord full legal recognition to the spiritual rabbinate.

The Family Question: Marriage and Divorce

A commentator once observed that "the ceremonial laws of Judaism embrace the entire life of a Jew, regulating his diet and intimate family life . . . much more than it does among other confessions."[84] Little wonder that the Orthodox rabbis fought so tenaciously to regain control from the state rabbis. Perhaps more important, the ubiquitous "family crisis," so critical to public discourse in the early twentieth century, reinforced concern by religious authorities, who associated traditional religiosity with the traditional family.

The problem of "secret marriages,"[85] which could be directly blamed on the failings of the dual rabbinate, epitomized the growing contradiction between Jewish and secular law. In the case of secret marriages, the state deemed the marriage null and void, whereas Jewish law did not. Similar discrepancies applied to other rites, such as circumcision, divorce, and burial. The problem was that the spiritual and state rabbis were bound to follow different rules. Hence, state rabbis, fearful of violating state laws, often refused to recognize "unofficial" marriages, circumcisions, divorces, or burials; according to secular law, they were to act as though the rites had never been performed. The spiritual rabbis took precisely the contrary view. From their perspective what mattered was the ritual, not its recognition or conformity with secular law.

As we have seen, this "dualism" led to enormous confusion and rank injustice, especially in the case of unions pronounced to be secret and therefore void. Thus, when a Jewish husband from such a union desired to marry another woman, he simply turned to the state rabbi (who had no record of the first marriage) and requested permission to marry for the first time. In most cases, the first wife not only lacked the legal means to reclaim her dowry and *ketubah* but had no right under Jewish law to remarry, since the rabbi had no way to compel her first husband to divorce her and at most could resort to "persuasion and exhortation."[86] The men had little incentive to comply, however, because the whole purpose of their deceptive actions was to avoid the financial consequences of divorce. In other cases, widows who sought to claim their inheritance were barred from their rightful possessions because their marriage to the deceased was not recorded in the metrical book, leaving them defenseless in a court of law.[87]

The growing number of *agunot* and "illegitimate" children and the moral implications of such actions put the issue of secret marriages high on the agenda at the rabbinic congress at a session devoted specifically to "marital matters." One group argued that secret marriages must be recognized as legally contracted unions if they had been performed according to Jewish customs—even if they had violated state laws. It also recommended that couples should be able to register their marriages in metrical books *ex post facto* (presumably without incurring a penalty) so as to prevent complications in the future. Some participants proposed that unrecorded marriages first be registered in the metrical books before any pending divorces could become legal. But others opposed this idea, declaring that it was sufficient to compel the Jews to register the divorce, given their strong proclivities against registration. Some delegates proposed that illegal marriages be submitted for review by a rabbinic court, which would confirm their validity and then have them registered by the state rabbi. One participant rejected all these reforms. In his view, the present system, which allowed only the state rabbi or his assistant to per- form ceremonies, was the only way to establish order; it was essential that authority be concentrated in a single institution.

The congress also addressed the question of "coerced" divorces, that is, cases where women accused their husbands of divorcing them against their will. The issue had repeatedly come before the Rabbinic Commis- sion. Most suits were directed against the state rabbi, a sober reminder of how ignorance or lack of moral scruples could lead to disastrous family predicaments. The congress took a firm, unequivocal position: "A unilat- eral divorce, without the agreement of the wife, will be considered as one of the most serious crimes; deceptions and bribery for this destructive form of divorce should be completely abolished in order to guard the interests of the weaker members of the Jewish family."[88] This resolution was clearly a direct response to the plight of Jewish divorcées and the flood of petitions to the Rabbinic Commission and to local rabbis. The congress did not specify the punishment but left no doubt that perpetrators of such "criminal" activity should be subjected to serious civil punishment.

The congress also addressed the problem of illegitimate children, an issue of general concern and one widely discussed in the non-Jewish press. As the delegates pointed out, the Jewish organizations had thus far failed to consider the issue (save for one rabbinic conference in Poltava province). This reticence was perhaps partly due to the relatively small number of illegitimate children, partly to the almost insurmountable legal obstacles to adoption (at least before 1906).[89] A new law of 1906 significantly moderated the harsh treatment of the unfortunate and guilt- less offspring of unwed parents but did contain a special qualification for Jews: "Adoption is permissible to individuals of any social status, without distinction of sex, except for those who by their own dignity are doomed to celibacy. . . . Jews are permitted to adopt children in the Pale of Settle- ment according to the laws of the empire, but only [children] of their own confession."[90] In light of these new legal developments, the congress pro- posed several measures to improve the position of illegitimate Jewish chil- dren. First, if the father reported the birth of an infant outside of wedlock, the child would be considered legitimate and could be registered under the name of the father and mother, as long as neither of them were tied to another marriage. Although that rule obviously disadvantaged children from an illicit, adulterous affair, the congress did seek to facilitate legiti- mation of those from a premarital sexual relationship. To record an ille- gitimate child in the family register, the father would have to file an adop- tion suit in court but only after he married the mother. The goal was to

FIG. 21. Family crisis: homeless children play cards on the street, Crimea, World War I. *Courtesy of the YIVO Institute for Jewish Research.*

encourage unwed parents to legalize their union for the sake of their children. In the event that the father denied paternity, the child would be registered under the mother's name. The Orthodox rabbis in the congress expressed deep concern about the future possibility of incest because of the child's unknown paternity; they therefore recommended that rabbis use all their influence to discover the identity of the father. If the father eventually married the child's mother, the couple would have the right to adopt their illegitimate child. Again, the congress stressed the "reward"—removing the stigma of illegitimacy—for legalizing the union.[91]

The congress also considered the problem of conversion and its impact on marriage. The delegation from Warsaw informed the congress of a recent meeting at which they had petitioned the Orthodox Church not to permit a baptism until the convert had first divorced a spouse. As in the case of secret marriages, the man who remarried according to the Christian rite often did not bother to divorce his Jewish wife, dooming her to spend her entire life as an *agunah*. Representatives from Poltava also noted that at an earlier conference of rabbis in their province, they had read an alarming article in the St. Petersburg Church periodical, *Tserkovnyi vestnik*, regarding Jewish converts whose marriages had been dissolved by the Church and who were permitted to remarry without a formal Jewish divorce.[92] The rabbis from Poltava reported that their appeals to the local governor had failed to elicit a response and that much money had been squandered in pursuing this strategy. In addition, they found that many Christian clergy found it difficult to permit a convert to perform a Jewish divorce, since they were already baptized and enjoined to have no further ties to their former coreligionists. The only recourse was to appeal to the state to show pity for the plight of Jewish women who had been condemned to eternal solitude.

The congress discussed a host of other family-related questions, but the archival record contains little concrete information. The members addressed such issues as marriages between Jews and Karaites,[93] how a *get* should be sent from an immigrant husband to his wife in Russia, and the problem of *halitsah* and the property rights of the widow. The assembly also discussed the question of bigamy, the procedure of divorcing an insane wife via a courier, abuses that could ensue from having to secure the signatures of one hundred rabbis for a divorce, and the guidelines on regulating spousal quarrels.[94]

Redefining the Rabbinic Commission

Proposals to reform the rabbinate and the Jewish family also led to an inevitable discussion about broadening the mission of the Rabbinic

Commission. Some delegates envisioned a permanent institution that would function year-round in order to examine "religious and domestic questions." Others doubted that there were enough cases to justify anything more than an annual meeting. But the congress unanimously agreed that the commission must play a more active role in Jewish life. In the words of one representative: "The Rabbinic Commission should be to the Jews what a religious consistory and higher spiritual board is for the non-Orthodox confessions." Its jurisdiction should be extended from mere "spiritual-ethical" issues (such as marriage and divorce, reforming the rabbinate, resolving disputes among rabbinic authorities) to serving as the *central* institution of Jewish religious and family affairs. It should also become the headquarters for the regulation of Jewish metrical books and records; each year, the commission was to process reports from Jewish communities throughout the empire on the total number of births, deaths, marriages, and divorces, in essence performing the tasks of a central statistical bureau. It is not entirely clear why the congress wished to assume this burden; perhaps they believed it would enhance the role of the commission, making it comparable to the consistory of Christian churches, or perhaps they hoped that the information would help the commission regulate the family more efficiently.

A more contentious issue was the membership of the future commissions. When the Orthodox delegates naturally advocated a body composed exclusively of spiritual rabbis, their proposal predictably elicited strong protests from their opponents. There also were dissenting opinions about the number of members who would convene in St. Petersburg. Some wanted twenty-three members (but did not explain why they chose this specific number); others believed that seven—one from each province in the Pale of Settlement—would suffice.[95]

It is impossible to know what might have resulted from these discussions had World War I not broken out four years later. Significantly, the Orthodox faction and intelligentsia alike wanted to establish a more hierarchical and centralized system of Jewish self-governance—from the communal organization at the grass roots to the Rabbinic Commission as a central religious-administrative body at the top. Although this aspiration emulated the efforts of many other groups in Imperial Russia, they probably stemmed also from the psychological need to unite a highly fragmented society. As G. B. Sliozberg pointed out at the 1909 rabbinic conference in Kovno, "I believe that the traditional unity of the Jews has been in the realm of myth for a long time, [and] the history of the disintegration of this unity is very lamentable. . . . Unfortunately, we have neither a community nor an organization." Turning to his fellow enlightened activists and to the Orthodox rabbis, he implored both groups to reconsider their definition of Jewish identity at a time when Russian Jewry sought to achieve a sense of communal solidarity. "We are all

Jews," he asserted, "regardless of the [degree] of religious rituals we observe; we are all [a part of Russian] Jewry, part of a community as long as we do not convert to another faith."[96] Although the press was actively debating the nature of the Jewish community, and whether it should be defined in "national" or "religious" terms, the higher ideal of the *obshchina* (literally, "commune" but used here in the larger sense of "community")[97] began to gain widespread support.[98]

Another motive was a desire for order and control, or what one headline aptly called "Community and Order."[99] After the destruction of the *kahal* in 1844, the Jews had no institutional authority to regulate their internal affairs other than the much maligned state rabbi. Although the *kahal* informally continued to function, Jews had no legally recognized entity.[100] Visions of local government reform stood high on the agenda of Russian government and society; it was hardly surprising that Jews also should seek to rebuild and revitalize self-governance, especially at the community level.[101] To fill the administrative vacuum left by the *kahal,* the rabbinic congress in St. Petersburg proposed to establish a permanent "communal administration," which would consist of elected officials, including the spiritual rabbi of the town, who would be responsible for resolving all questions pertaining to the Jewish faith.[102] Any internal conflicts in the communities would be sent to the Rabbinic Commission for review and final disposition. Intracommunal meetings also were to take place on a regular basis in order to establish a consensus and coordination. In effect, the congress sought to transform existing institutions like the communal spiritual boards *(dukhovnoe upravlenie)* and the Rabbinic Commission into permanent administrative bodies and to bestow on them greater power to ensure better organization and uniformity in Jewish internal life.

Thus, the Rabbinic Congress, despite the heterogeneity of its membership and the rancor in some debates, did reach a consensus or at least majority resolution on many important issues. Significantly, it focused primarily on three main issues: the rabbinate, marriage, and community organization. That agenda addressed the issues that were of greatest importance in the everyday lives of Jews, redefining their identity and role in imperial society. Perhaps the most striking development was the resurgence of the Orthodox rabbinate, not only in the Rabbinic Commission but also in the congress and its resolutions. In large measure, both the Orthodox and intelligentsia sought to restrict the growing intrusion of the secular state in Jewish religious life and, especially, marital life.

Russian State, Jewish Family

The state reaffirmed and sharply expanded its role in the last quarter of the nineteenth century. This reassertion of etatism and secular state interest applied to the religious sphere as well. As in the case of other confessions, state intrusion into Jewish affairs steadily broadened as the government sought to tighten its control over the volatile western borderlands. But the family issue was hardly unique to Jews; most questions—liberalization of divorce, terms of separation, status of illegitimate children, defense of women—were highly politicized and widely discussed with respect to the non-Jewish population, especially the Russian Orthodox. But state intervention did not mean tutelage. As in the case of the Christians and Muslims, the government increasingly served its own needs and interests; its primary concern was *raison d'état,* not Talmud or tradition.

Jurisdiction over Jewish Metrical Books

Following the rabbinic congress of 1910, one reporter asked Rabbi L. M. Tsirel'son of Kishinev if it would not be in the interests of the Jewish communities to hand over the registration of Jewish births, deaths, marriages, and divorces to the state bureaucrats. The rabbi disagreed. In his opinion, "taking away the right of the Jewish rabbinate to have authority over the metrical books would mean the degradation of the Jewish nation to another act of distrust." In other words, he would view such a step as a humiliating admission that the Jews (in particular, the rabbis) were unreliable and untrustworthy. In fact, Rabbi Tsirel'son pointed out that, in the Privislinskii region,[103] state officials so distrusted the rabbis, that they created a special *metricheskii chinovnik* (metrical bureaucrat) to oversee all registration. Another reason to oppose the transfer of metrical books to state control, he argued, was the inconvenience that it would cause for Jews whenever they needed copies of a birth, marriage, or death certificate. That just invited abuse and denigration: "You know perfectly well what a Jew has to endure when he turns to a government institution or to some bureaucrat." A rabbi, in Tsirel'son's view, would be more obliging about fulfilling the request of a coreligionist and would be more familiar with the individual entries, since these pertained directly to members in his community.[104]

The issue of who should manage the metrical books was hardly new. The government had first raised the issue of changing the jurisdiction over the metrical books in the early 1880s. In a questionnaire to the provincial governors, a commission to reexamine laws pertaining to the Jews inquired whether the state rabbis should be retained for the registration of metrical books.

The responses from provincial governors was almost unanimous: abolish the state rabbinate and transfer the duty to the *volost,* or city administration, or to the district police office. The governor of Minsk explained that this solution could help overcome the "uselessness of . . . the state rabbinate," particularly in light of his "distrust" of the Jews' capacity to keep the metrical books. The governor in Odessa concurred with the admonition that Jews not be permitted to adopt Christian names. In general, the provincial authorities hoped that state control of metrical records would free them from the odious task of dealing with the plethora of confusing Jewish religious practices and groups. "Free the religious lives of the Jews from the guardianship of the government," wrote the governor of Volhynia. On the basis of his familiarity with the Hasidic population in his province, the governor added that "it is necessary to abolish any interference of the administration and courts into the religious beliefs of the Jews." The governor of Podolia province, which also had a sizable number of Hasidic Jews, deemed it "useless for the government to interfere in the spiritual [lives] of the Jews" and recommended that the civil authorities take responsibility for the metrical books. The governor of Kiev offered a similar proposal for state control over Jewish registration but urged that the Jews "be left alone to pray."[105]

In the event, however, St. Petersburg did not act to assume control of Jewish metrical books. In part, it simply lacked the resources, human and financial, to assume the burden: the state administration was already overworked and awash with paperwork and did not need the additional responsibility. Nor was the registration of Jewish life events an easy task; the bureaucracy itself was plainly unprepared to ensure the proper transliteration of Hebrew and Yiddish names or to keep track of the "bewildering" Hebrew calender. State officials would also face significant communication barriers, since a substantial number of Jews in the Pale of Settlement spoke only Yiddish. Whereas a state ruling a relatively homogeneous ethnic community could secularize and establish state control over vital statistics (as Germany did under Bismark in the early 1870s), it was a task for which the undergoverned, multiconfessional Russian Empire was totally ill prepared. Finally, any such change would first require the approval and financial authorization of the bicameral State Duma and State Council. By 1910–1911, as these proposals were being advanced, that parliamentary order was no longer capable of effectively handling such a task.[106]

The Questionnaire

While the government recognized the problems inherent in assuming control over metrical books, it was hardly disposed to leave the Jewish family unregulated. But that intercession required reliable information on a subject about which most officials, especially those educated and raised outside the Pale, had only the dimmest understanding. To resolve various problematic issues, in 1893 the government sent a questionnaire to the Rabbinic Commission with the request that it clarify questions that had left ranking bureaucrats "baffled." But the questionnaire was hardly neutral; by including the phrase, "would it not be desirable," it plainly hinted at the need for change. Hence, it was as much a program of reform as an instrument for gathering information.

Moreover, the tone and substance of questions implicitly echoed familiar criticisms about the Jewish family that had circulated in government circles since the early nineteenth century. The first set of inquiries pertained to the conception of Jewish marriages. It asked, for example: "Do Jews consider marriage a religious union or simply a civil act?" This query reflected the awareness that the Jews had an unusually high divorce rate in comparison with the other religious confessions; state officials, apart from implying a "moral deficiency" in Jewish law, were seeking to ascertain whether Jews shared any kind of sacramentalist ideas that had made divorce so difficult for the Orthodox and Catholic believers. The commission confirmed that "Jewish marriages do not constitute a sacrament, as in the Christian [doctrines]" but emphasized that Jews nonetheless considered the marital union as "holy." Anxious to avert any misconceptions and to defend the sanctity of Judaism, the commission added that strict laws regulated marital life for Jews and that any violation of the basic responsibilities or trust was treated severely.[107]

The second question addressed the degrees of prohibition in marriages between relatives connected by blood or marriage. It resulted partly from the outcry in the science and medical community against the high number of consanguineous marriages among the Jews, and the discussion spilled over into the Jewish press as well.[108] As discussed earlier, the Jewish periodical *Evreiskoe obozrenie* had published an article on the hereditary diseases (i.e. glaucoma, blindness, mental illness) that resulted from such marriages.[109] Influenced by teachings of the Russian Orthodox church on consanguineous marriages[110] as well as the eugenicists' arguments, the state began to gather basic information about Jewish laws and practices, perhaps as a first step toward establishing legal impediments to such "harmful unions." Indeed, as we have seen, marriage of cousins was not uncommon among the Jews.[111] In fact, Judaism permits a range of marriages that would have been considered abominable by the Russian Orthodox or Catholic churches—for example, the union between a man and his niece or a widow and her brother-in-law.[112] Faced with the threat of state intervention, the commission left its answer on this question deliberately vague, confining its reply to a laconic remark that "marriages between the first and second degrees are prohibited by Talmudic law."[113]

Another marital "abuse" among Jews that alarmed the government was a purportedly widespread bigamy. Dr. Neumann of the Rabbinic Commission had already submitted a long report on the subject in 1879, in which he wrote that bigamy was not the accepted norm among Eastern European Jews. Nevertheless, the reformers raised the question once again: "Would it not be desirable to prohibit bigamy by the Jews"—specifically, that the perpetrators "be subjected to the same level of punishment as Christians?"[114] This "question" obviously presupposed that Jews still allowed or, at least, tolerated bigamy and that the problem was of significant proportions. In any case, the questionnaire was clearly less of an inquiry than a proposal to intercede and enforce a standard secular norm, regardless of whatever teaching might be found in the Talmud.

The state also showed a keen interest in Jewish divorce practice. The desperate and sensational petitions from Jews about unjust divorces had probably helped to stimulate bureaucratic interest and belief in the need for a fundamental reform. The concern, significantly, was long-standing. In 1854 the Jewish Committee had already raised concerns about the high rate of marital dissolution among the Jews and warned that "divorces among the Jews occur without proper grounds," thereby leading to instability in the Jewish family.[115] While the Rabbinic Commission at first found it unusual to receive a request about the specific grounds for divorce under Jewish law, the authors of the questionnaire obviously had their own agenda. Indeed, they even suggested that the government directly assume all responsibility for divorce: "Would it not be desirable to transfer Jewish divorce suits to the state courts?" To allay fears that the state wished to assume total authority over the Jewish divorce process, the reformers added that after the courts approved a divorce, the case would be returned to the local rabbi for the final formalities.[116] They noted that this procedure had already been established in tsarist Poland.[117]

Like the Russian Orthodox Church, the Rabbinic Commission sharply opposed such proposals, fully realizing that it was tantamount to abolishing Jewish autonomy in marital life and transforming Jewish divorces into a purely civil act. No doubt foreseeing that this provocative idea would elicit a negative response, state bureaucrats inquired "[then] what measures may be taken to limit the different interpretations of the rabbis regarding a divorce?"[118] In other words, how would the Jews suggest bringing uniformity in the application of Jewish laws on divorce if not through the state courts? Unveiled threats like these, reinforced by Russian public opinion strongly in favor of secularizing and liberalizing divorce, undoubtedly encouraged both Jewish rabbinic leaders and the intelligentsia, by the turn of the century, to consider the most effective means to bring more order to the Jewish family.

Although the questionnaire recycled old stereotypes about "harmful" Jewish practices, it also reflected the influence of contemporary intellectual trends that were contesting the unequal status of women in Russian society. That sentiment applied, first and foremost, to the unenviable plight of the *agunah*. This issue received considerable attention not only because liberal society *(obshchestvennost')* found the status of Jewish women particularly anomalous (at least compared with the Christian confessions) but because it was especially concerned about the ambiguous legal status and economic plight of the *agunah*. Hence, again, the government offered a reform in the guise of a question: "Does it not seem desirable to extend the rule in Article 54 to the Jews, thereby allowing the deserted spouse to file for a divorce after five years of [her husband's] absence?" The purpose of the "question" was transparent; it caused the Rabbinic Commission to formulate an evasive reply that neither challenged nor endorsed state's recommendation. "The position of the Jewish *agunah* is extremely difficult," the commission acknowledged, "[because] *halakhah* only permits such a wife to remarry after eighty years from the birth date of the missing husband or after his death has been confirmed." Her fate would depend completely on the personal discretion of the presiding rabbi. In light of all this, it conceded that "one should think that the extension of [civil law] will not meet with any general difficulty." In other words, Jewish women would utilize this law if the rabbis accepted it on the principle that "the law of the state is the law."[119]

Reflecting their familiarity with cases in which Jewish women had been divorced against their will, the state reformers proposed to invalidate unilateral divorces—that is, those that were initiated solely by the husband without the consent of the wife. In this case the Rabbinic Commission did support the idea of reform. Aware that such divorces still took place among the Jews of Russia, it could endorse reform because it involved not doctrine (such divorce had been banned by a rabbinic conference in Worms) but violation of Jewish law.[120]

On the basis of the information collected from this inquiry and other reports on Jewish family life, a group of progressive Russian jurists set out to draft one of the most radical proposals for a fundamental transformation of Jewish marital laws.

Progressive Jurists and Jewish Traditions

REFORM: MOTIVES AND GOALS

As the questionnaire clearly implied, Russian jurists were increasingly disposed to intervene in what had once been the autonomous sphere of Jewish marital law. It reflected, however, a much broader shift in the conception of the state and its role in society, especially at the lower level. Ever since the 1880s, when tsarist political culture rejected its self-abnegation of the 1860s and reaffirmed the transcendent role of the state, the government had increasingly reaffirmed its obligation to play a dynamic role, not only in industrialization and economic development but also in cultural, social, and religious affairs.

Moreover, state jurists desired to consolidate the "hodgepodge of laws" that governed the multinational and multiconfessional state through the creation of a single uniform law code. As one jurist pointed out, "The only escape from this labyrinth of contradictions, can be for the law to take upon itself the normative definition of the juridical nature of marriage and to liberate it from those external political, estate and religious restrictions that are foreign to its nature."[121] Since the codification of the *Digest of Laws* was first published in 1832, significant changes had taken place in relation to the national and religious minorities in the empire. Although separate ecclesiastical courts and authorities retained control over the family and religious law, the state had made headway in the cultural and legal integration of numerous minority groups.[122] So complex and confused was the original codex of laws, with its countless exceptions for various minorities, that even the most experienced jurist found it difficult to know which laws applied to what group. Hence, in the view of most reformers, a complete overhaul of the law code was long overdue.

Another impulse to the reform of family law was the emergence of new attitudes about marriage and especially the status and role of women. Even in the pre-reform era, elites had gradually embraced the new ethos of romanticism and sentimentalism that challenged conventional ideas about the meaning of marriage and the family.[123] This ethos of moral and sexual freedom was influential in paving the path for the "woman's question" that emerged in the late 1850s and 1860s. Especially among the radical "nihilist" generation, criticism of the patriarchal family and the subservient role of women was intense, but even state officials were dissatisfied with the problems of marriage and divorce among the Orthodox Christian population. Over the next few decades, the press and belles-lettres, as well as ethnographers and theologians, made the family and marriage into a central subject of concern. Much of the focus was on the fact that, under imperial law, a woman had no right to separate residence; indeed, a peasant whose wife had been abused and fled had the right to demand that authorities forcibly return her. And powerful novels like Leo Tolstoi's *Anna Karenina* drew attention to the problems of marriage and divorce.

And these new attitudes plainly informed the values and expectations of the "progressive jurists." However conservative the tsarist elites might be, the jurists themselves carried the secular, liberal attitudes from their legal training into state service. Sensitive to the prolific public debate about marriage and divorce and especially about the injustices to women and illegitimate children, they were determined to dismantle religious control and transfer these institutions to the more enlightened control of civil authorities.[124] One prominent Jewish lawyer, I. G. Orshanskii, for example, stressed that it was the duty of the law to safeguard the equal rights of the wife as was the practice in much of the Western world: "[The laws of European countries] represent the consistent development of the single idea of protecting the weaker member of the family from the arbitrary will of the stronger [member] through the courts, which is the sole motive that not only justifies but insistently demands government intervention in the family life of its citizens."[125]

Another jurist insisted that the law and society must assume responsibility to "defend the weak."[126] In other words, the legal code must contain special clauses to ensure equality among the respective members of the family and counteract the tendency for the strong to oppress the weak. Moreover, secular jurists increasingly came to emphasize the individuality of men and women—that is, as autonomous subjects separate from the family, endowed with their own rights and interests. That principle found unequivocal expression in the wish of the jurist A. F. Kazimir in 1884: "Each spouse is above all a person with his or her individual characteristics, temperament, and inclinations, and only then a component part of that collective entity called the family."[127] Hence, when the government established the Editing Commission to revise the Civil Code, it directed the new body to replace the "unlimited obedience to superior authority within the patrilineal kin-group" with the "the rights of individuals and the mutual obligations created by the natural and affective ties presumed to exist within the conjugal family."[128]

Although the legalists aimed their reform program primarily at the Russian Orthodox Church, it also came to encompass other religious groups, including Jews. The proposed changes to Jewish family laws bore a striking resemblance to the questionnaire sent to the Rabbinic Commission in 1893. They reflected the committee's preoccupation with the transformation of Jewish marital practices that it deemed incompatible with the new spirit of the times or with the practices of other religious confessions. As Wagner has noted, the civil code commission boldly aimed to change the basic regulations of individual religions "according to its own sense of justice, morality and progress."[129]

DRAFT PROPOSALS

The draft proposals of the Editing Commission, which were published at different points between 1896 and 1914, shocked the Jewish community. The dismay of rabbinical authorities was particularly intense. "Until now, our legislation almost never touched the marital laws of the Jews, leaving it to the domain of the rabbi," remarked one Jewish journalist, who reprinted the sections that pertained to the Jews. "This has [all] changed now," he continued, "for every condition (with the exception of a few items) pertinent to the dissolution of marriage is stipulated in the law, leaving a very limited area of jurisdiction for the rabbi."[130]

As foreseen by the draft text of these new laws, Jewish marriages would be more strictly regulated and based on free will. One priority was to prevent clandestine marriages, which often involved some illegality. Like the Russian Orthodox population, Jews would be required to announce their wedding at the groom and bride's place of residence and also in the synagogue or wherever the service was to be held. If one party had resided in the town for less than three months, the banns must also be proclaimed in the former place of residence. To ensure that there were no impediments to the marriage, the couple must present written proof that they were not bound to another marriage; if written proof was unavailable, the rabbi was to require testimonies from two trustworthy people on their behalf. Any marriage contracted through coercion (i.e., against the will of a spouse) was void; in particular, if a woman was forced into marriage while under the "power of a kidnapper," the marriage would be considered invalid. The draft code also annulled any marriage in which one of the parties had misrepresented or falsified his or her status and identity. Although such cases were rare (even for the large Russian Orthodox Church), the government, in the spirit of standardization, proposed to extend the rule to Jews as well. The reformers also proposed to deny legal force to contracts for matchmaking, perhaps to combat the problem of coercive marriages arranged by parents. Although Jewish law was still to define the permissible degrees of consanguinity, the Editing Committee warned that the final law would nevertheless demonstrate "a clear striving to expand the circle of relatives with whom marriage is forbidden." This was a transparent warning that cousin marriages and other unions between close relatives, which so upset the scientific community and the secular jurists, would not be tolerated. The government planned to retain the ban on underage marriages; however, it proposed to make an exception in the case of premarital pregnancy and to recognize an illegal marriage in such instances.[131]

The proposals on Jewish divorces were even more alarming to rabbinic authorities. Although the Editing Committee agreed to retain all the grounds for divorce that were stipulated in Jewish law, it recommended the establishment of a radical new procedure. Divorces based on mutual agreement were to be handled by a religious authority, who would register the deed in the metrical book. In such cases the couple had the right to determine custody of the child, the division of property, and other outstanding issues. In the event of contested cases, where only one of the spouses filed for a divorce, however, a secular court was to decide whether to grant the divorce. Significantly, the new code totally omitted the traditional requirement that the husband comply with the Jewish formality of delivering the *get* to his wife. If this draft proposal ever became law, the rabbis would lose all power to apply Jewish law and to contest divorce suits, whether consensual or contested. In a word, the new procedure amounted to the abolition of autonomy in Jewish marital laws.

The chief beneficiary of the reform was, without question, intended to be Jewish women, and the reform plainly reflected the severe criticism directed at their traditional status and treatment under Jewish law. Most striking of all, the draft proposed to prohibit Jewish and Muslim husbands from divorcing their wives unilaterally because "[this right] corresponds neither to the contemporary position of women nor to the equality of the rights of both spouses with respect to divorce which is recognized by all jurisdictions." The government also sought to ease the plight of the *agunah* by giving her the option to "request a divorce based on the regulations . . . of the civil court" but did not specify the number of years required since the husband's disappearance. Only if the missing spouse returned before the court had decided to permit the divorce would the marriage be considered intact. The Editing Committee also proposed to abolish the ceremony of *halitsah*. In its view, "the general civil court, which henceforth will be in charge of Jewish divorce cases, will not have any legal grounds to recognize the necessity of dissolving a marriage that does not really exist between the brother of the deceased husband and the widow." It warned any rabbi who refused to permit a *yevamah* to remarry would be held in contempt of the law. Under the mantra of moral progressivism and rationalism, the reformist jurists proposed to usurp power from rabbinic authorities in one broad stroke.

Like so much draft legislation in the final two decades of the Russian autocracy, very little won formal approval, let alone implementation. The opposition of vested interests, compounded by the structural problems of tsarist politics, especially during the Duma Monarchy, made it extremely difficult for virtually any piece of draft legislation to obtain approval and inclusion in the law books.[132] In the case of marital reform, where the inundation of petitions to the Imperial Chancellery made bureaucratic elites painfully aware of the magnitude of the problem, state officials labored for nearly two decades in a vain attempt to secularize, liberalize, and standardize the institutions of marriage and divorce. Although a few, very rare reforms were achieved—most notably, the law of March 1914, effectively legalizing separation through the issue of individual residence permits for women—the overwhelming bulk of the reform proposals remained a dead letter. Not until the Bolshevik Revolution, when the new regime hastily adopted revolutionary decrees on marriage and divorce, did the state finally assume total monopoly over the institution of marriage.[133]

Conclusion

By the early twentieth century, perceptive observers could not fail to discern three critical lines of development. First, the Orthodox camp had regained formal power—most dramatically through a takeover of the Rabbinic Commission but also through the influence that they increasingly came to exercise over the Russian state. As the Rabbinic Congress of 1910 dramatically demonstrated, even the intelligentsia recognized the importance and influence of "spiritual rabbis"; although still seeking to temper their rabbinical training with a good dose of secular education, few could deny the failings of the state rabbinate and the need to recognize the religious role of the spiritual rabbis.

Second, like Russian society, the Jews perceived a full-scale crisis on their hands. To be sure, it was markedly different from that plaguing their fellow Christian subjects; it was not hidebound ecclesiastical rules against divorce but a host of other, uniquely Jewish issues—from secret marriages to the plight of the *agunah*—that filled the agenda of Jewish meetings, congresses, and the Rabbinic Commission. Throughout these discussions ran a clear tension between traditional law and enlightened values, especially with respect to the rights and status of women. Although Jewish religious authorities and enlightened Jews endeavored to protect women when this was feasible (e.g., in the question of secret marriages), few besides ultraliberal or uninformed state rabbis directly challenged the validity of halakhah or proposed that it summarily be modified to fit modern expectations and needs.

Third, as in the case of the Russian Orthodox Church, the Jewish religious leaders thus found themselves clearly at odds with the liberal jurists seeking to restructure and "Europeanize" the family system. The tension between the jurists and Jews was transparent in the first great encounter—the questionnaire of 1893 and the response of the Rabbinic Commission. Significantly, neither vision of reform—that of the jurists nor that of the rabbis—could find realization in the latter years of the ancien régime. Each, ironically, had the power to block, divert, and veto; neither had the power to impose its own solution to the snowballing problems seen to plague the family. It was thus not only a profound crisis in the family but an utter inability of state *or* society to address and resolve those problems that characterized the final years of the Russian Empire.

Conclusion

In 1901, when Minna Rozenzon left her husband and demanded a separate passport, she declared that she could no longer live with him. She castigated the hatred he exhibited toward her son from a previous marriage, his extreme parsimony, and his "excessive demand for sexual relations, which she could not tolerate."[1] Her husband, a thirty-seven-year-old draftsman, responded by holding her solely responsible for the breakdown of their marriage. Hoping to undermine her credibility, he informed the Imperial Chancellery that his wife was a divorced woman, whereas she was his first and only wife. "That my wife Minna Viktorovna Rozenzon (Lunts by her divorced name) is really a silly wench [*vzdornaia baba*]," he declared, "can be confirmed by her first husband, Dr. Beniamin Lunts.[2]" He also criticized her role as a mother by stressing that she had abandoned her infant "to the mercy of fate" when she deserted him. "As for myself," he added, "I am not a drunk; I neither smoke nor play cards, but am a honest toiler." If his wife did not want to live with him, he defied her to initiate a divorce and declared that he was not going to grant a voluntary separate passport.

Despite that bombastic challenge, the husband evaded his wife's request for a formal divorce. Mark Rozenzon's sudden change of heart was no doubt due to the ruling of the St. Petersburg rabbi that he would have to return his wife's dowry of five thousand rubles in cash as well as the *ketubah* payment in order to finalize the divorce. To evade his responsibilities, the husband ordered the family notary in Riga to destroy the *ketubah,* which was deposited in a safe with the family's real estate deeds. As Minna's brother-in-law informed her, the notary had rejected the demand and insisted on the consent of both parties. When that ruse failed, Rozenzon offered to grant his wife a divorce under three conditions: that she promise not to file any suits against him in court; that she grant him sole custody of their son; and that she renounce any visitation rights. The

Chancellery investigator concluded that the husband was simply procras-
tinating to avoid his financial obligations and child custody battle in the
event of a divorce. Three years later, when the husband decide to end
their marriage (by offering his wife custody of their son and lump sum of
600 rubles), she rejected his offer. She needed a separate residence permit,
not a divorce, which could deprive her of her husband's right to reside in
St. Petersburg.

The Rozenzon case in late Imperial Russia was emblematic of countless Jewish marriages that had broken down irretrievably but did not
come to a formal, legal dissolution. As this study has suggested, there was
a growing discrepancy, not congruency, between marital breakdown and
the Jewish divorce rate. Indeed, modernization of the Jewish family followed a strikingly distinct pattern. Contrary to the ubiquitous tendency
in modern Europe for divorce rates to skyrocket, Jews experienced a decline from extraordinary high rates in the first half of the nineteenth century to a much lower frequency later in the second half. To be sure, the
reconfiguration of the Jewish family in Imperial Russia reflected larger
problems and processes; nevertheless, in so many fundamental ways the
"question of the Jewish family" differed radically from that of the dominant Orthodox majority.

The Unique Pattern of Marital Dissolution

Three major factors contributed to a decline in the Jewish divorce rate in
late Imperial Russia. One was the sharp rise in age at the time of the first
marriage. Whereas Jews had previously married at a young age (early
teens), by the early twentieth century this average had risen sharply.
Thus, by 1902 over 50 percent of Jewish brides entering marriage for the
first time were aged twenty-one to twenty-five; the grooms, twenty-six to
thirty. The rise was due in part to family economics, as increasing numbers of impoverished Jews had to postpone marriage until they established an independent livelihood (in contrast to the traditional system of
kest). Growing acceptance of scientific findings about the harmful influence of early marriage on health and fertility was also influential, especially among the scholarly elites, who had once tended to marry off children at unusually young ages. For example, the head of the Volozhin
yeshiva, Rabbi Naphtali Zvi Berlin, now warned that early marriages
were "medically unsound."[3]

The shift in marital age was fraught with enormous consequences for
the traditional marriage market and family relations. By the late nineteenth century, prospective spouses were more economically independent, psychologically mature, and often better educated. Matchmakers

did not melt in the lines of the unemployed, but their role had significantly contracted. Thus, in lieu of the traditional system of arranged marriages, which served family interests and strategies, self-made matches
became more common. The old power and interest of the parental family,
based on the marriage of economically dependent children, waned. Although parents still played a major role, they could no longer dictate
matches. It may well be that delayed marriages (involving more mature
and independent individuals) reduced the likelihood of a divorce, particularly since divorces were common among the "youthful." Some Jewish
women, like Dora Faivilevich, for example, specifically blamed their
young age and naïveté for accepting their parents' choices without knowing the character of their grooms.

Second, a variety of economic, legal, and social impediments deterred
couples from seeking a formal Jewish divorce. As the Rozenzon reveals,
economic considerations were particularly important for males; unless
the husband desired to remarry, separation of bed and board was a less
expensive option than returning the wife's dowry and *ketubah* payment—assets that were often invested in a family business or real estate.
As Jewish women learned to use the newly reformed court system to
press their financial claims, fear of litigation constituted a further disincentive for husbands to agree to a divorce. The legalistic language of divorce agreements in Moscow clearly reflected this apprehension: "We
have no present or future claims against each other."[4]

But wives too had reasons to prefer separation. In particular, as the Rozenzon case suggests, divorce automatically raised questions about their
legal status and, most important, their rights of residence in restricted
areas—that is, outside the Pale of Settlement. Although Minna Rozenzon
had pressed for a divorce earlier, she categorically declined her husband's
offer when she learned about the legal nightmares confronted by other
Jewish divorcées in St. Petersburg. It was no accident that the legal section
(iuridicheskii otdel) of Jewish newspapers such as *Rassvet* (Dawn) featured numerous queries from divorcées seeking to protect themselves from
expulsion or denial of their right to work outside the Pale of Settlement.

Third, a decline in rabbinical authority also undermined traditional
procedures of family dissolution. Due to legal restrictions on the use of
"coercion" (e.g., flogging, excommunication, and fines), it became increasingly difficult for rabbis to enforce female-initiated divorces (especially for
wife beating, poverty, incompatibility, and other conflicts). Armed solely
with the power of "persuasion and exhortation," rabbis found it difficult
to control recalcitrant husbands who blatantly ignored their admonitions
and even demanded exorbitant sums of money from their wives for a divorce. The inability of rabbinic authorities to impose their will prompted
some women to turn to the state for justice—actions fraught with deep

ramifications for the family and community. It represented a radical break with the past, a shocking violation of traditional norms of separateness and inclusiveness within the Jewish community. As the archival files show, female litigants learned how to utilize and manipulate the Russian administrative and legal system that, ironically, had long been viewed as a merciless oppressor of the Jewish people. Interference of the state in private marital disputes not only violated the prerogatives of Jewish religious authorities but abetted state intrusion into the domain of the Jewish family. Indeed, state involvement posed a growing threat to the final bastion of Jewish autonomy.

The problem of "authority" was further exacerbated by the creation of the "dual rabbinate" in Russia. The state rabbis were to be the state's liaison with the Jewish community, transmitting state policy and enforcing Jewish and secular law. For a host of reasons, explored at length in this study, that rabbinate proved extraordinarily ineffective and indeed counterproductive. Few had even a modicum of professional religious training; after 1873, when the only two state rabbinical schools closed their doors, even this modicum of specialized education vanished. As a result, the overwhelming majority of state rabbis were more state than rabbi; they were primarily a notary public for registering civil acts (birth, marriage, death, and divorce), with neither the time nor training nor, in most cases, the inclination to be spiritual leaders of their community. Although both liberal reformers and the *maskilim* had great hopes that the state rabbis would transform the Jewish world, they caused much confusion, turmoil, and disenchantment, even among their erstwhile supporters in the bureaucracy and Jewish intellectual circles.

Indeed, because the state empowered the untrained (the state rabbis), because it created a contradictory "dual rabbinate," it actually *increased* tension and disorder in the Russian family. The ill-advised, whimsical, and contradictory decisions of state rabbis left some Jews without a legal system, secular or Talmudic; in some cases neither the *Digest of Laws* nor halakhah regulated the Jewish family. Instead, the decisions of state rabbis were subject to bias and bribes; they spawned complex problems and acute pain for many victims. And most telling of all, the system of a dual rabbinate produced "dual law," with competing and contradictory rules and verdicts applying to such vital matters as marriage and divorce. If anything, the dual rabbinate was not dual power but systematic powerlessness and confusion. Within this legal vacuum, where authority was so confused, the Jewish family was left to its own devices. In that sense, the Jewish family, ironically, was "beyond the Pale," virtually outside either the traditional or secular system. Many social ills, such as secret marriage, were directly due to the dual rabbinate, which not only failed to solve old problems but created new ones.

New "Modern" Facets of Marital Conflict and Divorce

A declining divorce rate, however, does not automatically mean increased stability in the family. Thus, belles-lettres and memoir literature strongly suggest that family cohesion was rapidly dissolving, that marital breakdown, even if not formal divorce, was still at a very high level.[5] This growing disparity between the incidence of marital breakdown and divorce was due to gaps in the official records. They were far from complete, not so much because of deception by the record keepers as because of the sharp increase of mobility inside Russia and the emigration abroad. Those who divorced in America generally did not register their divorces in Russia, although there were a few exceptions. Moreover, the records did not include the many categories of unresolved cases—the countless *agunot,* separated couples, and annulment of illegal marriages.

But marital breakdown, if not official divorce, remained high. Some causes were traditional, such as in-law feuding, financial stress, and childlessness. But the files also show some new dynamics. Perhaps the most interesting new development was the pronounced transformation in gender relations and its impact on family stability. The new *mentalité* of more educated and economically independent women generated a lower degree of tolerance for their husbands' infidelity or abuse. In Leia (Sonya) Broun's own words: "My husband began to behave in an intolerable manner . . . [and] living with him became impossible." She succeeded in convincing the court investigator that her new acquaintance with educated circles made it increasingly repulsive to live with an "unintelligent and uncultivated" spouse. Such women, though aware that their husbands could accuse them of being "rebellious" and could dissolve the marriage at a whim, took their future into their own hands. For instance, Rivka Grinshtein and Khaia Zak deliberately enrolled in higher education courses to become economically self-reliant in the event of a divorce. Their husbands naturally expressed confusion at their wives' assertiveness and the reversal of roles, where the women initiated the separation either to retaliate against marital infidelity or to pursue educational aspirations.

Religious conversion was another significant and new factor in family conflict. Because the Russian Orthodox Church had neither interest nor sympathy for the spouse who remained faithful to Judaism and because it did not accord legal recognition to a non-Christian rite of marriage, it permitted the convert to remarry a Christian without bothering to obtain a formal Jewish divorce. This policy was extraordinarily disastrous for Jewish women, who found themselves anchored to a spouse who rejected his obligation to release her from their former marital bond. Given the disincentive of compliance (costs—above all, the return of the dowry and *ketubah*), converts simply disappeared into the Russian interior with new identities, new names, and new rights. More ambiguous was the position of "mixed" couples—converts who chose not to divorce their Jewish spouses. Until 1904 such couples had to decide whether their marriage was worth saving when threatened with loss of residence rights outside the Pale of Settlement, even if they had possessed those privileges prior to the conversion. For the Niurenbergs, the Senate resolution of 1904, which permitted them to remain in Moscow, came one minute too late. They had already dissolved their marriage in order to retain their residence rights and could no longer remarry each other because now they were from two separate faiths.

For those who did undergo formal divorce, the consequences were enormous—financial, legal, and emotional. It is little wonder then that a growing number of Jews resorted to extralegal forms such as desertion or bigamy. Our case studies indicate that Jewish law, both in theory and in practice, provided distinct avenues and methods by which a deserted husband could remarry without a formal divorce, but there were no parallel provisions for women, condemning many of them to the fate of *agunot*. That problem was neither new to the period of mass emigration, as some historians have suggested, nor was it the result of desertion alone, as we have illustrated. The crisis of the *agunah* was the many ways in which women could be put in an anchored position. They were vulnerable to husbands who refused to grant them a divorce even when they were living separately, stubborn brothers-in-law who refused to perform the ceremony of *halitsah,* and circumstances beyond their control, such as the disappearance and unconfirmed death of their husbands. Special Russian sources of the problem involved the conversion of a husband to Russian Orthodoxy and the exile of a *levir* to Siberia. In such desperate circumstances, some women rejected their fate and turned to the Russian state to seek some alternative method to overcome the strict religious prohibitions against their remarriage. Such efforts clearly alarmed rabbinic authorities, who were embroiled in their own battle with the government to retain autonomy in family law and practice.

New Alliances: The State and Orthodox Jews

In large measure because the state rabbis failed so miserably, a new form of conservative Orthodox politics steadily gained momentum in the last quarter of the nineteenth century. In part, it owed its vibrancy to popular revulsion against the state rabbinate; the campaigns for influence, most visibly in the elections to the Rabbinic Commission, offered incontrovertible evidence to the dominance of "spiritual" rabbis among the Jews. While the Russified youth may have turned to socialism and Zionism, the faithful turned wholeheartedly to the mainstays of traditional Judaism. Ironically, that resurgence gradually came to enjoy the blessing of the secular state. Whereas it had once ridiculed the very same currents for "fanaticism," a regime desperate for popular support turned increasingly to piety in a desperate, if abortive, attempt to find new pillars of support for the ancient regime. That new influence reached its acme in the critical interrevolutionary years, when the Orthodox rabbis not only won massive support in the electorate but even persuaded the state to recognize their authority and potential role in taming the "liberation movement" among Jews. They promised to instill traditional family values in the new generation, thereby weaning the youth from subversive revolutionary activities. Significantly, by 1910 the Jews still did not have a national religious organization; at most, they had the irregular Rabbinic Commission, which the Orthodox viewed as an institution for potential influence and change.

Also ironically, power and politics militated against the kinds of reforms that Jewish petitioners (especially women) sought from the Rabbinic Commission or the Russian state. The shift in political influence from the enlightened camp to the Orthodox brought a reassertion of "traditional" values, including a staunch refusal to modify the basic principles of halakhah to suit modern expectations and needs (i.e., its refusal to allow women to remarry without a *get*). To be sure, wherever possible, Jewish religious leaders endeavored to show latitude and flexibility; however, their resolutions remained within the framework of Jewish law, much to the dismay of many *agunot*. Nor could reform as envisioned by liberal jurists come from without: in contrast to its European peers, the Russian Empire proved unable to wrest control of marriage and divorce from the traditional religious authorities. The reason lay partly in the fact that the ancient regime simply lost its capacity to function, either to repress or reform. But the failure of reform, despite the ambitious efforts of its own jurists, derived from the fact that the state increasingly staked its survival on the very forces most inimical to change in basic values and institutions. In this case, that meant the Russian Orthodox Church and the Orthodox rabbinate, both of which fought reform tooth and nail.

As the regime headed toward the abyss, the people, whether Christian or Jewish, experienced profound problems in the existing family order. The problems and the underlying dynamics were radically different. But they shared a common fate: neither the regime nor the religious authorities were able or willing to address the enormous social problems undermining the very foundations of the old order.

Appendix

TABLE A.1
Seasonality of Jewish Marriages in Kiev, 1866–1870

Month	Total	Percent	Month	Total	Percent
January	22	5.6	July	23	5.9
February	28	7.0	August	70	17.8
March	35	8.8	September	17	4.3
April	20	5.1	October	29	7.3
May	45	11.5	November	32	8.4
June	42	10.5	December	27	7.1

Source: I. Pantiukhov, *Opyt sanitarnoi topografii statistiki iz Kieva* (Kiev: Izdanie Kievskogo gubernago statisticheskago komiteta, 1877), 228.

TABLE A.2
Seasonality of Jewish Marriages in Kiev, 1866–1870

Season	Total	Percent*
Winter	77	19.7
Spring	100	25.4
Summer	133	34.2
Fall	78	20.0

Source: I. Pantiukhov, *Opyt sanitarnoi topografii statistiki iz Kieva*, 228.

*Because of rounding, the percentages do not add up to 100.0.

TABLE A.3

Mortality Rate of the General and Jewish Population in 1897

Age	General Population		Jews	
	Male	Female	Male	Female
Up to 1	42.00	39.00	26.90	22.10
1–5	20.28	20.78	21.30	17.80
6–10	4.08	4.27	4.95	4.25
11–15	1.55	1.74	2.60	2.00
16–20	1.69	2.14	3.31	2.97
21–25	1.79	2.19	2.56	3.02
26–30	1.73	2.18	2.07	3.09
31–35	1.56	1.90	2.13	2.96
36–40	1.80	2.02	2.41	2.97
41–45	1.98	1.92	2.45	3.12
46–50	2.19	1.97	2.45	3.13
51–55	2.29	2.18	3.01	3.72
56–60	2.54	2.65	3.61	3.95
61–65	2.83	3.14	4.00	4.95
66–70	2.93	3.27	4.14	5.15
71–75	2.78	3.22	4.22	5.27
76–80	2.26	2.53	3.43	4.16
81–above	2.72	2.90	4.46	5.29

Source: "Naselenie," *Evreiskaia entsiklopediia*, 11:546.

TABLE A.4

Married Couples According to Age Group in the 1897 Census

Religious confession	< Age 21		Age 21–50		> Age 50	
	Male	Female	Male	Female	Male	Female
Total	34.1	57.4	64.0	42.0	1.9	0.6
Russian Orthodox	38.8	60.8	59.7	38.8	1.5	0.4
Old Believers	43.1	64.8	56.3	35.0	0.6	0.2
Roman Catholic	4.6	36.7	91.7	62.5	3.7	0.8
Protestants	11.4	31.1	84.8	67.7	3.5	1.2
Armenians	3.6	64.2	94.3	35.2	2.1	0.6
Jews	5.9	25.2	90.4	73.6	3.7	1.2
Muslims	9.9	53.3	85.0	45.1	5.1	1.6
Pagans	24.3	34.8	74.5	65.0	1.2	0.2

Source: "Naselenie," *Evreiskaia entsiklopediia,* 11:543.

TABLE A.5

Marital Status of Korostyshev Jews at Marriage (1854 and 1861)

Marital status at marriage	1854	1861
Single man with single woman	17	12
Single man with widow	1	2
Widower with single woman	1	2
Widower with widow	4	7
Marital status unknown	—	1
Total	23	24

Source: TsGIA-U, f. 663, op. 1, dd. 63 and 69.

TABLE A.6

Marital Status of Jews and Russian Orthodox in Kiev (1866–1869)

Marital status at marriage	Russian Orthodox	Percent	Jews	Percent
Single man with single woman	2196	74.1	227	58.2
Single man with widow	329	11.3	21	5.4
Widower with single woman	305	10.5	54	13.8
Widower with widow	135	4.2	88	22.5
Marital status unknown	—	—	—	—

Source: Pantiukhov, *Opyt sanitarnoi topografii statistiki iz Kieva,* 224 and 228 (see Bibliography).

TABLE A.7

Age Differences between Newly Married Couples in Korostyshev (1854 and 1861)

Age difference	1854	1861
0–5 years	18	18
6–10 years	5	1
11–15 years	—	—
16–20 years	—	4
21–25 years	—	—
Over 25 years	—	1
Total	23	24

Source: TsGIA-Kiev, f. 663, op. 1, d. 63, ll. 1–16 (Jewish metrical book of births of Korostyshev, 1854); f. 663, op. 1, d. 69, ll. 1–19 (for 1861).

TABLE A.8

Age of Marriage among Jews in Tsarist Russia

Year	Under age 21		Age 21–25		Age 26–30	
	Bride	Groom	Bride	Groom	Bride	Groom
1867	60.8	43.0	21.2	26.3	8.1	11.4
1875	55.3	26.6	27.2	36.1	7.5	15.9
1877	54.7	25.4	n.g.*	n.g.	n.g.	n.g.
1885	47.0	15.2	37.1	49.6	18.1	8.0
1887	42.2	10.9	n.g.	n.g.	n.g.	n.g.
1895	28.7	6.3	50.2	45.8	26.3	52.5
1897	25.0	5.8	n.g.	n.g.	n.g.	n.g.
1902	23.9	4.8	52.5	41.1	26.3	52.5

Source: Sara Rabinovich, "K voprosu o nachal'nom remeslennom obrazovanii evreiskikh zhenshchin," *Novyi voskhod* 5 (4 Feb.1910): 9–10; Shaul Stampfer, "Hamashmaut ha-hevratit shel nisui boser bemizrah eiropah," 77 (see Bibliography).

*n.g. = not given

TABLE A.9

Jewish Marriages and Divorces in Sixteen Russian Provinces (1857)

Province	Marriages	Divorces	Divorces per 1000 marriages	Total Jewish population
Arkhangel	5	0	0	229
Astrakhan	11	0	0	587
Bessarabia	739	172	232.7	78,772
Enisei	3	1	333.3	1124
Iakutsk	0	0	0	35
Kiev	2276	478	210.0	211,504
Kurland	271	22	81.2	25,560
Minsk	1024	134	130.9	94,664
Mogilev	771	78	101.2	107,206
Podolia	2491	288	115.6	196,174
Shemakhin	8	1	125.0	2137
Taganrog	13	1	76.9	893
Tavrida	168	25	148.8	8487
Vil'na	1058	106	100.2	69,182
Vitebsk	859	98	114.1	64,524
Volhynia	2076	330	159.0	185,058
Total	11,773	1734	147.3	1,046,136

Source: RGIA, f. 821, op. 8, d. 479, ll. 1–35 ob. Data were not available for the provinces of Kovno, Grodno, Chernigov, Ekaterinoslav, and Kherson, which were located in the Pale of Settlement.

TABLE A.10

Jewish Marriages and Divorces in Nineteen Provinces (1858)

Province	Marriages	Divorces	Divorces per 1000 marriages	Total Jewish population
Astrakhan	5	0	0	419
Bessarabia	1008	113	112.1	78,947
Chernigov	319	33	103.4	31,631
Enisei	8	1	125	1761
Iakutsk	0	0	0	40
Kazan	0	0	0	183
Kiev	2227	439	197.1	222,074
Kurland	262	19	72.5	25,641
Lifland	5	1	200	1052
Minsk	1076	143	132.9	85,122
Mogilev	780	59	75.6	108,537
Podolia	1917	271	141.4	191,847
Poltava	376	58	154.3	26511
Taganrog	18	2	111.1	711
Tavrida	92	18	195.7	7616
Viatka	1	0	0	298
Vil'na	1392	79	56.8	76802
Vitebsk	691	71	102.7	63833
Volhynia	1911	288	150.7	178,291
Total	12088	1595	131.9	1,101,316

Source: RGIA, f. 821, op. 8, d. 480, ll. 1–39.

TABLE A.11

Jewish Marriages and Divorces in Twenty Russian Provinces (1860)

Province	Marriages	Divorces	Divorces per 1000 marriages	Total Jewish population
Astrakhan	2	0	0	273
Baku	22	2	90.9	6685
Bessarabia	700	156	222.9	81,272
Chernigov	320	35	109.4	33,214
Enisei	11	3	272.7	1567
Grodno	724	85	117.4	95,437
Kazan	2	0	0	198
Kiev	1879	416	221.4	n.g.*
Kurland	289	14	48.4	26,823
Lifland	0	1	—	598
Minsk	985	126	127.9	84,834
Mogilev	708	97	137.0	112,270
Podolia	1751	217	123.9	196,980
Poltava	417	72	172.7	29,756
Taganrog	19	0	0	531
Tavrida	117	24	205.1	9702
Viatka	1	0	0	216
Vil'na	1126	76	67.5	80,125
Vitebsk	693	64	92.4	66,711
Volhynia	1996	320	160.3	187,562
Total	11,762	1708	145.2	1,014,754**

Source: RGIA, f. 821, op.8, d. 482, ll. 97 ob.; GAKO, f.804, op.1, d.55, ll. 2–64. Data were not available for Kovno, Ekaterinoslav, and Kherson.

*n.g. = not given, ** excluding Kiev Province

TABLE A.12

Jewish Marriages and Divorces in Fifteen Russian Provinces (1861)

Province	Marriages	Divorces	Divorces per 1000 marriages	Total Jewish population
Astrakhan	0	0	0	311
Baku	51	13	254.9	6671
Bessarabia	918	150	163.4	90,089
Chernigov	394	50	126.9	33,788
Enisei	23	6	260.9	1569
Grodno	826	134	162.2	93,695
Kazan	5	0	0	208
Kurland	255	13	51.0	29,627
Lifland	10	0	0	1196
Minsk	807	143	177.2	92,587
Mogilev	681	92	135.1	119,763
Poltava	449	51	113.6	31,890
Viatka	2	0	0	251
Vil'na	1182	77	65.1	81,147
Vitebsk	567	70	123.5	68,201
Total	6170	799	129.5	650,993

Source: RGIA, f. 821, op. 8, d. 483, ll. 1–29. Data were not available for Ekaterinoslav, Kiev, Kherson, Kovno, Podolia, Taganrog, Tavrida, Volhynia.

TABLE A.13

Jewish Marriages and Divorces in Eighteen Russian Provinces (1862)

Province	Marriages	Divorces	Divorces per 1000 marriages	Total Jewish population
Astrakhan	0	0	0	340
Baku	49	1	20.4	7024
Bessarabia	969	188	194.0	89,572
Chernigov	302	42	139.1	34,260
Enisei	26	2	76.9	1514
Grodno	893	113	126.5	101,612
Iakutsk	0	0	0	78
Kazan	0	0	0	169
Kiev	2364	466	197.1	297,842
Kurland	224	5	22.3	28,778
Lifland	5	2	400.0	1311
Minsk	829	107	129.1	93,383
Mogilev	802	128	159.6	127,604
Podolia	1989	203	102.1	202,882
Poltava	454	64	141.0	32,737
Viatka	5	0	0	285
Vil'na	1124	29	25.8	81,832
Vitebsk	582	48	82.5	63,168
Total	10,617	1398	131.7	1,164,391

Source: RGIA, f. 821, op. 8, d. 484, ll. 1–38 ob. Data were not available for the provinces of Kovno, Kherson, Ekaterinoslav, and Volhynia.

TABLE A.14

Jewish Marriages and Divorces in Fourteen Russian Provinces (1863)

Province	Marriages	Divorces	Divorces per 1000 marriages	Total Jewish population
Astrakhan	0	1	0	309
Baku	59	4	67.8	7422
Bessarabia	982	205	208.8	94,333
Chernigov	298	50	167.8	34,819
Enisei	22	1	45.5	1463
Kiev	2237	375	167.6	250,804
Kurland	263	14	53.2	33,598
Lifland	10	0	0	1219
Minsk	988	143	144.7	94,071
Podolia	2034	175	86.0	205,165
Poltava	432	76	175.9	34,540
Viatka	4	0	0	299
Vil'na	566	28	49.5	103,645
Vitebsk	628	12	19.1	69,034
Total	8523	1084	127.2	930,821

Source: RGIA, f. 821, op. 8, d. 485, ll. 1–28 ob.

TABLE A.15

Jewish Marriages and Divorces in Nineteen Russian Provinces (1864)

Province	Marriages	Divorces	Divorces per 1000 marriages	Total Jewish population
Astrakhan	1	1	1000	342
Baku	55	3	54.5	7097
Bessarabia	1305	151	115.7	97,700
Chernigov	317	35	110.4	35,557
Enisei	16	0	0	840
Grodno	987	109	110.4	50,938
Iakutsk	0	0	0	74
Kazan	4	0	0	87
Kiev	2499	423	169.3	253,447
Kurland	253	11	43.5	34,825
Lifland	33	11	333.3	2155
Minsk	1127	148	230.5	103,049
Mogilev	777	108	139.0	120,798
Podolia	2298	98	42.6	208,759
Poltava	295	68	137.4	29,418
Tavrida	81	0	0	10,090
Viatka	3	1	333.3	262
Vil'na	651	29	44.5	102,525
Vitebsk	588	52	88.4	68,554
Total	11,290	1248	110.5	2,005,815

Source: RGIA, f. 821, op. 8, d. 486, ll. 1–46 ob. Divorce statistics were not available for the provinces of Kovno, Volhynia, and Ekaterinoslav.

TABLE A.16

Jewish Marriages and Divorces in Sixteen Russian Provinces (1865)

Province	Marriages	Divorces	Divorces per 1000 marriages	Total Jewish population
Astrakhan	2	0	0	365
Baku	46	2	43.5	7170
Bessarabia	969	129	133.1	91,980
Chernigov	302	26	86.1	36,855
Enisei	15	4	266.7	1715
Iakutsk	1	0	0	108
Kazan	0	0	0	296
Kiev	2576	548	212.7	258,525
Kurland	266	17	63.9	35,670
Lifland	28	7	250	7317
Podolia	2181	94	43.1	211,115
Poltava	488	68	139.3	36,252
Tavrida	131	8	61.1	10,910
Viatka	5	0	0	285
Vil'na	610	51	83.6	103,958
Vitebsk	550	47	85.5	75,322
Total	8170	1001	122.5	877,843

Source: RGIA, f. 821, op. 8, d. 487, ll. 1–29.

TABLE A.17

Jewish Marriages and Divorces in Thirteen Russian Provinces (1866)

Province	Marriages	Divorces	Divorces per 1000 marriages	Total Jewish population
Astrakhan	8	4	500	425
Bessarabia	1162	125	107.6	93,412
Chernigov	357	37	103.6	37,758
Grodno	901	132	146.5	96,208
Iakutsk	0	0	0	62
Kazan	10	3	300.0	296
Kiev	2511	730	290.7	255,342
Kurland	312	24	76.9	34,116
Lifland	3	0	0	305
Podolia	2121	109	51.3	209,137
Poltava	514	78	151.8	38,862
Vil'na	572	93	162.6	107,531
Vitebsk	589	63	107.0	81,087
Total	9060	1398	154.3	954,541

Source: RGIA, f. 821, op. 8, d. 488, l. 26. The data do not include the provinces of Kovno, Ekaterinoslav, Minsk, Mogilev, Kherson, and Volhynia.

TABLE A.18

Jewish Marriages and Divorces in Eleven Russian Provinces (1867)

Province	Marriages	Divorces	Divorces per 1000 marriages	Total Jewish population
Astrakhan	3	0	0	503
Bessarabia	876	206	235.2	91,646
Chernigov	373	40	107.2	35,743
Enisei	11	1	90.9	1643
Grodno	1060	180	169.8	112,217
Iakutsk	0	0	0	39
Kurland	312	23	73.7	34,117
Poltava	477	69	144.7	49,328
Viatka	1	0	0	320
Vil'na	605	24	139.6	107,802
Vitebsk	766	100	130.5	80,419
Total	4484	643	143.4	513,777

Source. RGIA, f. 821, op. 8, d. 489, ll. 1–22.

TABLE A.19

Jewish Marriages and Divorces in Thirteen Russian Provinces (1869)

Province	Marriages	Divorces	Divorces per 1000 marriages	Total Jewish population
Astrakhan	33	0	0	439
Bessarabia	1094	156	142.6	91,246
Chernigov	373	44	118.0	31,147
Enisei	13	2	153.8	1703
Grodno	989	139	140.5	112,837
Iakutsk	0	0	0	46
Kazan	5	0	0	382
Kiev	2513	461	183.4	267,867
Kurland	268	20	74.6	35,417
Minsk	926	83	89.6	133,768
Poltava	471	74	157.1	49,869
Vil'na	647	48	74.2	107,633
Vitebsk	676	32	47.3	87,704
Total	8008	1059	132.2	921,058

Source: RGIA, f. 821, op. 8, d. 490, ll. 1–28.

TABLE A.20

Jewish Marriages and Divorces in Korostyshev (1854–1910)

Year	Marriages	Divorces	Year	Marriages	Divorces
1854	23	6	1889	28	n.g.*
1855	27	13	1890	42	10
1857	21	3	1892	32	8
1860	33	8	1895	40	16
1865	27	8	1900	48	1
1872	29	12	1905	28	1
1876	11	n.g.*	1910	15	2
1881	22	5			

Source: TsGIA-Kiev, f. 663, op. 1, dd. 63, 64, 73, 77, 81, 83, 86, 87, 89, 92, 97, 102, 107, 112, 113, 114, 118, 124, 126, 137, 145, 147, 154, 158, 162.

* n.g. = not given

TABLE A.21
Jewish Marriages and Divorces in Khar'kov (1870–1910)

Year	Marriages	Divorces	Year	Marriages	Divorces
1870	35	15	1882	50	13
1871	35	9	1883	55	12
1872	53	16	1884	59	13
1873	37	16	1885	67	12
1874	31	12	1886	52	11
1875	36	13	1887	85	14
1876	38	14	1888	49	6
1877	38	13	1889	75	11
1878	43	23	1890	61	n.g.*
1879	57	13	1901	108	12
1880	54	13	1910	182	24
1881	54	9			

Source: GAKhO, f. 958, op. 1, dd. 4–113.

* n.g. = not given

TABLE A.22
Marital Status of Jews According to the 1897 Census

Marital status	Absolute numbers		Percentage of total	
	Males	Females	Males	Females
Single	1,512,549	1,486,380	61.20	57.35
Married	908,433	934,919	35.76	36.07
Widowed	44,969	155,729	1.82	6.01
Divorced	3975	12,589	0.16	0.49
Not given	1469	2148	0.06	0.08
Total	2,471,395	2,591,761	100	100

Source: B. D. Brutskus. *Statistika evreiskogo naseleniia.* 3 vols. (St. Petersburg, 1909), 3:24.

TABLE A.23

Marital Status (in Percentage) of Different National Groups in the Russian Empire (1897)

Marital Status	Jews		Russians		Poles		Lithuanian-Latvian		German		All	
	M	F	M	F	M	F	M	F	M	F	M	F
Single	30.3	23.4	24.3	18.3	32.6	24.7	38.3	31.5	32.0	25.7	26.9	18.1
Married	66.0	64.8	69.3	67.3	63.4	62.0	57.0	54.0	64.3	62.4	67.3	67.6
Widowed	3.3	10.8	6.2	14.2	3.8	13.1	4.5	14.3	3.5	11.6	5.6	14.1
Divorced	0.3	0.9	0.1	0.1	0.1	0.1	0.1	0.1	0.1	0.2	0.1	0.1
Not given	0.1	0.1	0.1	0.1	0.1	0.1	0.1	0.1	0.1	0.1	0.1	0.1
Total	100	100	100	100	100	100	100	100	100	100	100	100

Source: B. D. Brutskus. *Statistika evreiskogo naseleniia* (St. Petersburg, 1909), 3:25.

The figures include only those of marriageable age (or 15 and above).

M, male; F, female.

TABLE A.24
**Ages of Jews Who Divorced in Khar'kov (1870–1915)
and Korostyshev (1854–1912)**

	Khar'kov		Korostyshev	
Ages	Males	Females	Males	Females
Unknown	10	10	0	0
15–20	4	34	10	28
21–25	50	101	45	45
26–30	97	91	29	32
31–35	67	72	10	11
36–40	53	40	15	13
41–45	44	17	7	4
46–50	21	6	11	5
51–55	25	2	4	1
56–60	7	0	4	2
61–65	6	0	2	1
66-above	5	0	5	0
Total	390	390	142	142

Source: The data on Jewish divorces in Khar'kov cover the years 1870–1889, 1901, 1903, 1906, 1909–1910, 1914–1915. GAKhO, f. 958, op. 1, dd. 5, 11, 16, 23, 30, 37, 44, 48, 52, 56, 60, 64, 68, 72, 76, 80, 84, 87, 91, 95, 108, 109–111, 113, 116b, 117; The data for Jewish divorces in Korostyshev include the years 1854, 1855, 1857, 1860, 1865, 1867, 1880, 1881, 1885, 1890, 1892, 1895, 1900, 1905, 1910–1912. TsGIA, f. 663, op. 1, dd. 112, 113, 114, 118, 124, 126, 128, 132, 136, 137, 140, 145, 147, 149, 158, 162–164.

TABLE A.25

Ages of Jews Who Divorced in Vil'na (1837–1864)

Year	13–25		26–30		31–50		51–older		Male and female missing
	Female	Male	Female	Male	Female	Male	Female	Male	
1837–1838	87	60	17	22	23	42	5	8	2
1845	50	30	29	37	24	29	4	11	0
1851	18	4	9	16	18	9	0	2	2
1853	25	10	9	13	13	18	3	9	0
1860	28	15	17	8	11	31	1	3	4
1864	17	8	5	9	7	10	0	2	2

Source: LVIA, f. 728, op. 2, dd. 6, 28, 273; op. 3, dd. 8, 15.

Glossary of Transliterated and Translated Terms

agunah—an "anchored woman,"—one who cannot remarry because her first marriage was not legally terminated either through divorce or the death of her husband

Ashkenaz—Hebrew name for the Germanic lands

av beit-din—head of the rabbinical court

beit-din (pl., *batei-din)*—rabbinical court of law

bet-midrash—house of study

dayyan—rabbi-judge

dukhovnyi ravvin—spiritual rabbi

erev Shabbat—Sabbath eve

Even haezer—"Rock of Help," the section of the *Shulhan Arukh* that deals with laws of marriage and divorce

forshpil—"merry entertainment" (pre-wedding celebration)

gaon—rabbinic scholar

gerushin—divorce

get—bill of divorcement

Gittin—Talmudic tractate on divorce

gubernator—provincial governor

guberniia—province

gubernskoe pravlenie—chief administrative council in a province

haggadah (pl., *haggadot)*—prayers, songs and historical passages read during the Passover meal

hakhnasat kallah (Hebrew), *hakhnoses kalleh* (Yiddish)—communal organization to assist poor brides

halakhah—Jewish law

halitsah—levirate divorce

haskalah—Jewish enlightenment

herem—excommunication

hevrah (pl., *hevrot)*—association(s)

huppah—the wedding canopy

kahal (pl., *kehalim)*—congregation, community, Jewish communal institution *kashrut*—religious dietary laws

kazennyi ravvin—state rabbi

kehilla—community, congregation

kest—free room and board provided by bride's family to the new couple

ketubah—the Jewish marriage contract

kiddushin—betrothal (sanctification)

korobochnyi sbor—kosher meat tax

lamdan—religious scholar

levir—brother-in-law

maggid—preacher

maskil (pl., *maskilim*)—enlightened Jew

melamed—teacher

metricheskie knigi—metrical books

mezonot—Hebrew word for *kest*

mikveh—ritual bath

minyan—quorum of ten individuals (composed of men in tsarist Russia)

mishpahah—family

mitnagdim—opponents of Hasidism

mitzvah (pl., *mitzvot*)—commandment, pious deed

mukat ets—accidental loss of virginity

nedunyah—dowry

neemanim—"reliable people"

ober-prokuror—chief procurator

perutah—a small copper coin

pinkasim—Jewish communal records

rabanut mitaam—crown rabbinate

ravvinskii uchastok—rabbinical district of a state rabbi

rebbe—title of a Hasidic leader

Rema—acrostic of Rabbi Moshe Isserles, author of the "glosses" to the *Shulhan Arukh*

responsa—questions and answers, rabbinic

shadkhan—male matchmaker

shadkhanit—female marriage broker

shadkhanut—marriage brokerage

shiddukh tov—good match

shochet—ritual slaughterer

shtetl—small Jewish town

Shulhan Arukh—codex of Jewish law compiled by Rabbi Joseph Caro

sivlonot—engagement gifts

takunah—ordinance

tenaim—contractual terms of betrothal

trefot—contrary to the dietary laws

treteiskii sud—arbitration court

tsaddik—a Hasidic leader

uezd—district

vaad arba aratsot—Council of the Four Land

vaadei haglilot—regional councils

yeshiva (pl., *yeshivot*)—rabbinical seminary

yevamah—a childless widow

yikhus—lineage

Notes

Introduction

1. The Rabbinic Commission was a consultative body under the Ministry of Internal Affairs (MVD), based on the model of the religious consistories in France. See below (chap. 2) for details.

2. Rossiisskii Gosudarstvennyi Istoricheskii Arkhiv (hereafter RGIA), fond 821, opis' 9, delo 62, listy 1–10b. (petition of Ita Radin to the Rabbinic Commission, 26 July 1907). The standard Russian archival notation will be used hereafter: f. (fond), op. (opis'), d., dd. (delo, dela), l., ll. (list, listy), ob. (oborot), g. (god).

3. RGIA, f. 821, op. 9, d. 62, l. 31 (petition of Isaak Radin to Rabbi Lev Kagan, 27 June 1907).

4. They cited Yebamoth 64a as the grounds for rejecting his petition.

5. Tsentral'nyi Derzhavnyi Istorychnyi Arkhiv Ukraïny, Kyïv (hereafter TsDIAK-Ukraïny), f. 335, op. 1, d. 120, l. 75.

6. Ibid.

7. The Rabbinic Comission noted that Rabbi Kagan cited the phrase "neither in the husband's nor wife's place of residency" directly from the *Shulhan Arukh, Even Haezer, 75,* commentary *Pithei-teshuvah* but took the words completely out of context. The original text addresses the problem of residency when spouses are from two different countries, towns, or villages. For more on the *Shulhan Arukh* (lit. "Prepared Table"), a codex of Jewish law compiled by Joseph Caro in 1565–66, see Louis Ginzberg, "The Codification of Jewish Law," in *On Jewish Law and Lore* (Cleveland, 1962); Isadore Twersky, "The Shulhan Aruk[h]: Enduring Code of Jewish Law," in *The Jewish Expression,* ed. Judah Goldin (New Haven, Conn., 1976), 322–43.

8. RGIA, f. 821, op. 9, d. 62, ll. 46–49, 51–52. These letters were written both in Hebrew and in Russian translation.

9. For state laws on the jurisdiction of state rabbis, see *Svod Zakonov* (1896), vol. 9, pt. 1 *(Inostrannye ispovedeniia),* arts. 1325, 1327, points 2 and 3; arts. 1328 and 1336.

10. Pauline Wengeroff (1833–1916) was born in Bobruisk, Russia. Her description of Jewish family life in Russia reveals deep social and religious divisions in society as well as the impact of modernization on traditional values and practice. See Lucy S. Dawidowicz, ed., *The Golden Tradition* (New York, 1967), 163–65.

11. B. Bagrov, "Nashi braki i razvody," *Nedel'naia khronika Voskhoda* 27 (1893): 725–28.

12. "Unzer tsol," *Der shadkhon* 1 (1905): 1.

13. Draft of an open letter from Rabbi Moshe Nahum ben Binyamin Yerusalimsky to the rabbis in the West (n.d.), as translated in Eli Lederhendler, *Jewish Responses to Modernity: New Voices in America and Eastern Europe* (New York, 1994), 96.

14. "Evreiskaia zhizn', sudebnaia khronika," *Rassvet* 12 (1910): 30–31.

15. *Polnoe sobranie zakonov Rossiiskoi imperii,* 1st series (hereafter *PSZ(1)*), 45 vols. (St. Petersburg, 1830), 10:90. See also RGIA, f. 821, op. 9, d. 17.

16. *PSZ* (1830), 10:90. See also M. Sh., "K voprosu o razvode mezhdu suprugami-evreiami pri perekhode odnogo iz nikh v pravoslavie," *Voskhoda* 1 (1892): 1–11.

17. J. Katz; *Tradition and Crisis: Jewish Society at the End of the Middle Ages* (New York, 1971). See also J. Katz, "Marriage and Marital Relations at the End of the Middle Ages," *Zion* 10 (1945–1946): 47–49 (Hebrew); "Family, Kinship and Marriage among Ashkenazim in the Sixteenth to Eighteenth Century," *Jewish Journal of Sociology* 1 (1959): xx.

18. Mark Zborowski and Elizabeth Herzog, *Life Is with People: The Culture of the Shtetl* (New York: Schocken Books, 1974 [reprint]), 288–89.

19. Sydney Stahl Weinberg, *The World of Our Mothers: The Lives of Jewish Immigrant Women* (New York, 1988); Susan Glenn, *Daughters of the Shtetl: Life and Labor in the Immigrant Generation* (Ithaca, N.Y., 1990); Ruth Gay, *Unfinished People: Eastern European Jews Encounter America* (New York, 1996).

20. Immanuel Etkes, "Marriage and Torah Study Among the Lomdim in Lithuania in the Nineteenth Century," in *The Jewish Family: Metaphor and Memory,* ed. David Kramer (Oxford, 1989), 153–78.

21. Katz, *Tradition and Crisis,* 243.

22. For a discussion of the illusive concepts of traditional versus modern families, see Jack Goody, *The Development of the Family and Marriage in Europe,* 2–3. For a juxtaposition of the "modern family" to the "traditional family," see the early work by Edward Shorter, *The Making of the Modern Family;* Peter Laslett and Richard Wall, eds. *Household and Family in Past Time.* Much of these initial findings, however, have since come under critical scrutiny and revision. Thus, family historians have rejected Shorter's assumption of "loveless unions" before the eighteenth century and suggested the possibilities of affective relations well before the "modern marriage" gained ascendancy. On the modern value of love in traditional Jewish marriages, see David Biale, "Love, Marriage and the Modernization of the Jews," in *Approaches in Modern Judaism,* ed. Marc Lee Raphael (Chico, Calif., 1983), 1–17.

23. David Biale, *Eros and the Jews: From Biblical Israel to Contemporary America* (Berkeley, Calif., 1997), x.

24. David Biale, "Eros and Enlightenment: Love against Marriage in the East European Jewish Enlightenment," *Polin* 1(1986):59–67; Alan Mintz, *Banished from Their Father's Table: Loss of Faith and Hebrew Autobiography* (Bloomington, Ind., 1989).

25. Paula Hyman, *Gender and Assimilation in Modern Jewish History: The Roles and Representation of Women* (Seattle, 1995); and "Gender and Jewish History," *Tikkun* (January–February 1988): 35–38.

26. Joan Wallach Scott, "Gender: A Useful Category of Historical Analysis," in *Feminism and History* (Oxford, 1996), 152–80; see also Mary Poovey, *Uneven Developments: The Ideological Work of Gender in Mid-Victorian England* (Chicago, 1988).

27. Hyman, *Gender and Assimilation,* 50–92; Shmuel Feiner, "Haishah hayehudiyah hamodernit: Mikre-mivhan beyahasei hahaskalah vehamodernah," *Zion* 58 (1993):453–99; Shaul Stampfer "Gender Differentiation and Education of the Jewish Woman in Nineteenth-century Eastern Europe," *Polin* 7(1992); Iris Parush, "Readers in Cameo: Women Readers in Jewish Society," *Prooftexts* 14

(1994): 2–16; Naomi Seidman, *A Marriage Made in Heaven: The Sexual Politics of Hebrew and Yiddish* (Berkeley, Calif., 1997); Israel Bartal, "'Onut' ve'ain onut'—bein masoret lehaskalah," in *Eros erusin veirusim* (Jerusalem, 1998), 225–33.

28. Anna Clark, "Comment," *Journal of Women's History* 5 (1993):115–20. For more on the debate over agency, see Elena Varikas, "Gender, Experience, and Subjectivity: The Tilly-Scott Disagreement," *New Left Review* 13 (1995): 89–101.

29. See Iulii Gessen, "Ravvinat v Tsarstve Pol'skom," *Evreiskaia entsiklopediia* (hereafter *EE*); reprint, St. Petersburg, 1991), 230–31.

30. Natalie Zemon Davis, *Fiction in the Archives: Pardon Tales and Their Tellers in Sixteenth-Century France* (Stanford, Calif., 1987), 2–3.

1. Marriage: Creating the Jewish Family

1. Devorah Baron, "Mishpahah" in *Parashiyot: sipurim mekubatsim* (Jerusalem, 1968), 11; an English translation can be found in Devorah Baron, "Family" in *The Thorny Path,* trans. and ed. Joseph Shachter (Jerusalem, 1969), 1.

2. For examples of naming children after deceased relatives, see David Assaf, "R. Israel meruzhin umekomo betoldot hahasidut bamahatsit harishonah shel hameah hatisha esreh" (Ph.D. diss., Hebrew University of Jerusalem, 1992), 250–59. Use of the patronymic, as in the deeply family-centered Slavic cultures, reinforced the consciousness of family ties, present and past. Hence, Leia Bentsionova Fuksman of Korostyshev (Kiev province) was the daughter of Rivka and Bentsion Avrumovich Fuksman, the son of Brukha and Avrum Borukhovich Fuksman, the son of. . . . (TsDIAK-Ukraïny, f. 663, op.1, d. 69, ll. 8 ob.–9; op. 1, d. 38, ll. 20 ob.–21).

3. Pauline Wengeroff, *Memoiren einer Grossmutter: Bilder aus der Kulturgeschichte der Juden Russlands im 19. Jahrhundert,* 2 vols. (Berlin, 1908–1910).

4. The biblical laws that prohibited degrees of marriage can be found in Leviticus 18:1–30. See Peter Elman, ed., *Jewish Marriage* (London, 1967), 20; Louis Epstein, *Marriage Laws in the Bible and the Talmud* (Cambridge, Mass., 1942), 220–74, 275–32. At the request of the Russian government, the Rabbinic Commission prepared a report about Jewish religious laws on prohibited degrees of marriage (RGIA, f. 821, op. 9, d. 29.).

5. *Midrash Rabbah,* Genesis 68, 4, as cited in I. Abrahams, "Marriages Are Made in Heaven," *Jewish Quarterly Review* 2 (1890): 172–73.

6. Shaul Stampfer, "Hamashmaut hahevratit shel nisuci boser bemizrah ciropah" in *Studies on Polish Jewry,* ed. Ezra Mendelsohn and Chone Shmeruk (Jerusalem, 1987), 67. The original quote can be found in *Shulhan Arukh, Even Haezer* 37, 8. See also *Kiddushin* 41a: "A man may give his daughter in betrothal when [she is] a *naarah* (a girl between the age of twelve and one day and twelve and a half years and one day). Only when [she is] a *naarah,* not when [she is] a minor. . . .One may not give his daughter in betrothal when a minor [but must wait] until she grows up and says "I want so-and-so."

7. A. Harkavy, *Responsen der Geonim* (Berlin, 1887), as cited in Israel Abrahams, *Jewish Life in the Middle Ages* (London, 1932), 182.

8. Simon Dubnow, ed., *Pinkas hamedinah o pinkas vaad hakehilot harishonot bemedinat lita* (Berlin, 1925), 8. See point 31.

9. V. O. Levanda, *Polnyi khronologicheskii sbornik zakonov i polozhenii kasaiuschchikhsia evreev* (St. Petersburg, 1874), 322.

10. Ibid. According to the *Shulhan Arukh, Yoreh Deah,* 240 (the Rema),

however, a son was not obliged to obey his father if he opposed the spouse of his choice.

11. William Wagner, *Marriage, Property and the Struggle for Legality in Late Imperial Russia* (Oxford, 1994), 61–66; Marc Raeff, "Introduction to Plans for Political Reform in Imperial Russia, 1730–1905," in his collection of essays, *Political Ideas and Institutions in Imperial Russia* (Boulder, Colo., 1994), 88–115.

12. Wengeroff, *Memoirs,* unpublished translation by Jay Harris.

13. Moshe Leib Lilienblum, *Ketavim autobiyografiyim: Hatot neurim* (Jerusalem, 1970), 88–89. Unpublished translation by Jay Harris.

14. Puah Rakowski (1865–1955) was a Zionist activist, born in Bialystok, who taught Hebrew and Russian in one of the first middle schools for Jewish girls in Warsaw in the 1890s.

15. Puah Rakowski, *Zikhroynes fun a yidisher revolutsionerin* (Buenos Aires, 1954), 22, 31–32.

16. Miriam S. Zunzer, *Yesterday: A Memoir of a Russian-Jewish Family* (New York: Harper and Row, 1978), 3.

17. The law against coerced marriages applied not only to parents but also to responsible authorities—above all, squires, who at least formally lost the right to marry off their serfs in a forcible manner.

18. V. N. Latkin, *Istoriia russkogo prava perioda imperii xviii–xix vv.* (St. Petersburg, 1909), 515–16. See also Levanda, *Polnyi khronologicheskii sbornik,* 321.

19. RGIA, f. 821, op. 8, d. 291, ll. 99–100 ob. (journal of the Rabbinic Commission, 1893).

20. Ibid., l. 100–100 ob. It cited the passage from Ketubot 46b: "A father has authority over his daughter in respect to her betrothal [whether it be concluded] by money, deed or intercourse."

21. Rakowski, *Zikhroynes,* 24–28. The young man was Puah Rakowski's uncle, who wanted to marry her instead of his cousin.

22. Chaim Tchernowitz, *Pirkei hayim: Autobiografiah* (New York: Bitzaron, 1954), 62. Rabbi Shlome Drozd was Chaim Tchernowitz's grandfather.

23. For the Lithuanian ban on clandestine marriages, see Dubnow, *Pinkas hamedinah,* 9; Shmuel A. Arthur Cygielman, *Jewish Autonomy in Poland and Lithuania until 1648* (Jerusalem, 1997), 314–15.

24. Wagner, *Marriage, Property and the Struggle for Legality,* 63.

25. LVIA, f. 447, op. 19, d. 8558, ll. 1–2 (petition of the third-guild merchant Yosel Vulfovich and Yudes Eliashberg, 28 January 1859).

26. Ibid., l. 5–6 ob. (petition of O. Fridberg and his daughter Basia, 4 February 1859).

27. The father-in-law and wife, Basia, always referred to the husband as "Markus," a more Europeanized version of his Yiddish name Mordkhelia. They also were able to sign their names in Russian, unlike the Eliashbergs, who signed in Yiddish. All these factors, in addition to their emphasis on the ideal of love, indicate that the Fridbergs may have been more acculturated than the Eliashberg family.

28. Ibid., l. 10 (Mordukh Yosel Eliashberg to the Vilna Conscience Court, 9 February 1859).

29. He was sent to a "house of corrections," which was an institution within the penal system, established in 1775 and abolished in 1884. A special section was specifically designated for children who had violated their obligations to their parents. See "Smiritel'nyi dom" in F. A. Brokgauz and I. A. Efron, *Entsiklopedicheskii slovar'* (St. Petersburg, 1900), 60:528–29. In the Eliashberg case, conflict ended in reconciliation; two years after his voluntary exile from Vil'na,

the parents informed the court that they were completely satisfied with their son's "moral reform"and requested that his good name be restored to him.

30. For examples of grooms who fled to the yeshivot to avoid a match or escape an unhappy marriage, see Nahum Meir Sheikevitsh (Shomer), *Shirei Shomer vezikhronotav* (Jerusalem, 1950); Ezekiel Kotik, *Mayne zikhroynes* (Warsaw, 1913), 11357 ff; David Biale, "Eros and Enlightenment: Love against Marriage in the East European Jewish Enlightenment," *Polin* 1 (1986): 52.

31. Barbara Alpern Engel and Clifford N. Rosenthal, eds. and trans., *Five Sisters: Women against the Tsar* (London: Routledge, 1992 [reprint]), 185.

32. Harriet Davis-Kram, "The Story of the Sisters of the Bund," *Contemporary Jewry* 5 (1980): 32.

33. Shmuel Leib Zitron, *Anashim vesofrim* (Shreberk, Vilna, n.d.), 125–26, as translated in Iris Parush, "Women as Agents of Social Change Among Eastern European Jews in the Late Nineteenth Century," *Gender and History* 9:1 (1997):72.

34. "Vnutrennaia khronika," *Russkii evrei* 2 (1879):45. Another report from Odessa related the story of a young Jewish girl from a well-to-do merchant family who ran away on Yom Kippur (taking along 600 rubles), with plans to enroll in school. See *Russkii evrei* 6 (10 October 1879):191.

35. See ChaeRan Y. Freeze, "When Chava Left Home: The Family Question and Conversion in Imperial Russia."

36. LVIA, f. 378, d. 221, g. 1862, l. 2 (report of the civil governor of Grodno to the general governor of Vil'na, 24 September 1862).

37. Hyman, *Gender and Assimilation in Modern Jewish History* (Seattle, 1995), 74–75.

38. On the pressures to reform family law, see Wagner, *Marriage, Property, and Law*, 81–137.

39. For more on the "conscience court," which was established by Catherine II, see: G. Verblovskii, "Sovestnye sudy" in *Entsiklopedicheskii slovar'*, 30:685–86.

40. The classic works on the *haskalah* movement include J. S. Raisin, *The Haskalah Movement in Russia* (Philadelphia: Jewish Publication Society of America, 1913); Raphael Mahler, *Hahasidut vehahaskalah* (Merhavya, 1961); Mordecai Levin, *Erkhei hevrah vekalkalah beideologyah shel tekufat hahaskalah* (Jerusalem, 1975). For the most recent and innovative studies, see Steven Zipperstein, "Haskalah, Cultural Change and Nineteenth-Century Russian Jewry: A Reassessment," *Journal of Jewish Studies* 25 (1983): 191–207, and *The Jews of Odessa* (Stanford, Calif., 1985); Michael Stanislawski, *For Whom Do I Toil: Judah Leib Gordon and the Crisis of Russian Jewry* (New York, 1988); Shmuel Feiner, *Haskalah vehistoriyah: Toldoteha shel hakarat-avar yehudit modernit* (Jerusalem, 1995); Immanuel Etkes, ed., *Hadat vehahaim: tenuat hahaskalah bemizrah eiropah* (Jerusalem, 1993); Mordechai Zalkin, *Baalot hashahar: Hahaskalah hayehudit baimperyah harusit bameah hatesha esreh* (Jerusalem, 2000).

41. Shmuel Feiner has convincingly argued that the *maskilim* rarely "functioned as initiators of change but rather as those who would attempt to preempt a social, historical, and cultural process that had already commenced . . . with the aim of introducing a certain order and direction to the process. "Haishah hayehudiyah hamodernit: Mikre-mivhan beyahasei hahaskalah vehamodernah," *Zion* 58 (1993):453–99.

42. Jakub Kalmanson, *Uwagi nad niniejszym stanem Żydów polskich i ich*

wydoskonaleniem (Warsaw, 1797), 51, as cited in Jacob Goldberg, "Jewish Marriage in Eighteenth-Century Poland," *Polin* 10 (1997):12.

43. Peretz Smolenskin, *Gemul yesharim*, pp. 119–20, as cited in Iris Parush, "Readers in Cameo: Women Readers in Jewish Society of Nineteenth Century Eastern Europe," *Prooftexts* 14(1994):8.

44. Judah Leib Gordon, "Kotso shel yud," in *Kol shirei Yehudah Leib Gordon*, 4 vols. (St. Petersburg, 1884), 4:6.

45. Stanislawski, *For Whom Do I Toil,* 125–28.

46. It is only fair to note that the parental role in arranged marriages did not necessarily preclude the development of "love" between couples. Indeed, some not only relied upon their parents' judgment but were pleased with the result. For instance, Wengeroff recollected the stirring of new emotions after her engagement: "My young girl's heart hardly knew the feeling of love [but] suddenly it was awakened. Scenes that I had never before been aware of came to my mind." Wengeroff, *Memoirs,* unpublished translation by Jay Harris.

47. For example, Rabbi Solomon Schwadron of Galicia permitted an engagement to be annulled without penalty because the groom found the bride "short . . . not pretty . . . and a bit repulsive." Solomon Mordecai Schawdron, *Sheelot uteshuvot marasham* (Warsaw, 1902), pt. 1, no. 195, as cited in David Biale, *Eros and the Jews: From Biblical Israel to Contemporary America* (New York, 1992), 164.

48. Immanuel Etkes, *Lita biyerushalayim* (Jerusalem: Yad Izhak Ben-Zvi, 1991), 66.

49. Rabbi Eliyahu ben Yehuda Feldman, *Der shadkhan* (Warsaw, 1913), 5. Similarly, Dora Shulner (b. 1881) recalled that the most popular matchmaker in her home town of Radomysl (Kiev province) was particularly sensitive to the romantic preferences of her clients. YIVO, RG 102, folder 7a (Dora Shulner, 1888–1921).

50. Jacob Goldberg, "Die Ehe bei den Juden Polens im 18. Jahrhundert," *Jahrbücher für Geschichte Osteuropas,* 31(1993): 483–515.

51. The professional *shadkhan* first emerged in twelfth-century Europe, concurrently with the expulsions and massacres that accompanied the Crusades. According to one seventeenth-century writer, "in earlier times, none but students of the law were *shadkhanim.*" That rabbinic scholars dominated this profession comes as no surprise, given their elite position in premodern Jewish society and the high value placed on marriage. See Abrahams, *Jewish Life in the Middle Ages,* 186.

52. Aizik Meyer Dik, *Masekhet aniyut* (Vil'na, 1878 [reprint]), 26, as cited in David Roskies, "Ayzik Meyer Dik and the Rise of Yiddish Popular Literature (Ph.D. diss., Brandeis University, 1975), 176.

53. *Shulhan Arukh, Hoshen Mishpat* 185, 10 (The Rema).

54. In the Habsburg realm the marriage broker was not paid until after the marriage, whereas in the Rhenish lands the parties paid him as soon as they concluded their negotiations. See "Shadkhan," *EJ,* 2 (1973).

55. In the Black Forest district, for example, a marriage broker received "one and a half percent on dowries of six hundred gulden" from both parties. See Abrahams, *Jewish Life in the Middle Ages,* 190. In the community of Bramberg, the marriage broker charged two thalers for the first one hundred thalers and one to one and a half percent for larger dowries. See Salo Baron, *The Jewish Community: Its History and Structure to the American Revolution* (Philadelphia, 1948), 3:208.

56. Dubnow, *Pinkas hamedinah,* 8.

57. Sholom Aleichem, "In Haste," in *The Old Country* (New York, 1946), 150.

58. Biale, "Eros and Enlightenment," 58–59.

59. Abraham Baer Gottlober, *Zikhronot u masaot* (Jerusalem, 1976), 87–88.
60. Tchernowitz, *Pirkei hayim,* 29 (a letter to his grandfather preserved in R. Chaim Tchernowitz's archive).
61. Yehuda Leib Cahan, *Yidishe folkslider mit melodyes* (New York, 1957), no. 290, as cited in Ruth Rubin, *Voices of a People. The Story of Yiddish Folksong* (New York, 1973), 110. For another song about the infamous matchmaker, see "Yidishe shidukhim" in Morderchai Shekhter's *Eliakum Zunzers verk* (New York, 1964), 65. A collection of Yiddish songs and folk sayings can also be found in I. M. Pulner's archive in Rossiiskii Etnograficheskii Muzei (henceforth REM, f. 9, op. 1, d. 17).
62. Simon Dubnow, "Vnutrenniaia zhizn' evreev v Pol'she v Litve," *Knizhki voskhoda* 4 (1900):11. Dora Shulner of Radomysl also describes a female matchmaker (Chaya Toybe) in her hometown who wore a white kerchief all week long but a golden wig on Sabbath. As noted earlier, her clients expected only the best matches from her services, especially if they had a romantic partner in mind. See YIVO, RG 102, file 7a.
63. Rose Shomer-Bachelis, *Unzer foter Shomer* (New York, 1950), 25. Puah Rakowski's grandmother, "an ardent merchant" also singlehandedly arranged the marriages of all her children. Rakowski, *Zikhroynes,* 13.
64. Chaim Aronson, *A Jewish Life under the Tsars: The Autobiography of Chaim Aronson, 1825–1888* (Towata, N.J., 1983), 109.
65. RGIA, f. 821, op. 8, d. 357, l. 10–10 ob. (Sura Litovchin Sagal vs. Abram Sagal, 18 May 1867). See also Dubnow, "Vnutrenniaia zhizn' v Pol'she i Litve," 11.
66. Nachman Mayzel, ed., *Dos Mendele buch* (New York, 1959), 49.
67. N. M. Sheikewitz, *Sheikevitshes nayer briefenshteler* (New York, 1900), i; 82–84.
68. Rakowski, *Zikhroynes,* 33.
69. Isaak Simkhovich Lur'e (b. 1875) was the administrative secretary of *ES.* TsGIA-St. Petersburg, f. 2129, op. 3, d. 101 (Autobiography of Isaak Lur'e).
70. TsGIA St. Petersburg, f. 2129, op. 3, d. 105 (correspondence between Isaak S. Lur'e and Mania (Maria) Lur'e), l. 33 (9 April 1903). The words in italics were written in large capital letters in Mania's letter.
71. Ibid., l. 21.
72. For example, see Ts. Kapelovits, *Seyfer hoyves nashim* (Vil'na, 1908), 11.
73. Tchernowitz, *Pirkei hayim,* 28.
74. For more on the Bund (established in 1897), see Ezra Mendelsohn, *Class Struggle in the Pale: The Formative Years of the Jewish Workers Movement* (Cambridge, 1970); Jonathan Frankel, *Prophecy and Politics. Socialism, Nationalism, and the Russian Jews, 1862–1917* (Cambridge, 1984), esp. pp. 171–257; Harriet Davis-Kram, "Sisters of the Bund," *Contemporary Jewry* 5:2 (1980):27–43.
75. Daniel Charney, *Vilne: Memuarn* (Buenos Aires, 1951), 67.
76. *Der shadkhon* 1 (1906):4.
77. Ibid., 3 (1906):4.
78. Ibid., 2 (1906):4.
79. Golda Meir, *My Life* (New York, 1955), 14.
80. A. Y. Bukhbinder, *A kaleh af oystsolen* (Warsaw, 1889), 5.
81. For examples, see REM, Tenishev collection, which contains routine reports about the challenges to parental authority among the peasantry. Also see published examples in *Byt velikorusskikh krest'ian-zemlepashtsev: Opisanie materialov etnograficheskogo biuro kniazia V. N. Tenisheva (na primere Vladimirskoi gubernii)*, ed. B. M. Firsov and I. G. Kiseleva (St. Petersburg, 1993), 241–50.

82. Etkes, *Lita beyerushalayim,* 65.

83. S. Gruzenburg, "O fizicheskom sostoianii evreev, chast 1," *Evreiskoe obozrenie* 2 (1884):59.

84. See David Assaf, *Derekh hamalkhut: R. Yisrael meruzin umekomo betoldot hahasidut* (Jerusalem, 1997). See also David Aron Twersky, *Sefer hayahas mitshernobil veruzhin* (Lublin, 1938).

85. Shomer-Bachelis, *Unzer foter,* 26.

86. "Es iz ambestn dos yeder mentsh zol ton nur mit zaynem glaykhn." Ayzik Meyer Dik, *Boruske der shoymer* (Vil'na, 1871) as cited in Roskies, "Ayzik Meyer Dik," 192.

87. I. J. Trunk, *Poyln,* 3 vols. (New York, 1944), 1:24.

88. Aleksander Poliakov, "Serebrianyi samovar—vospominaniia," in *Sem'ia Poliakovykh,* ed. Larisa Vasil'eva (Moscow, 1995), 34, 40–41.

89. Shomer's father-in-law sabotaged his daughter's love affair with a "fine young man," whose mother had converted, by marrying her off to a widower (Shomer-Bachelis, *Unzer foter,* 42); see also Mendell Lewittes, *Jewish Marriage. Rabbinic Law, Legend and Custom* (Northvale, N.J., 1994), 36.

90. Lucy Dawidowicz, *The Golden Tradition* (Syracuse, 1996 [reprint]), 248–56.

91. Marion Kaplan, *The Making of the Jewish Middle Class* (Oxford, 1991), 115.

92. Gruzenberg, "O fizicheskom sostoianii," 59. According to Marion Kaplan's study of Prussia, between 1872 and 1875, the rate of marriage between two relatives (per 1,000 marriages) was 10 for Catholics, 14 for Protestants, and 23 for Jews. *Making of the Jewish Middle Class,* 115.

93. "Korostyshev," *EE,* 9 (1991 [reprint]): 772–73.

94. TsDIAK-Ukraïny, f. 663, op. 1, dd. 63–111; see also YIVO, RG 102, file 7a.

95. TsDIAK-Ukraïny, f. 663, op. 1, d. 69, ll. 8 ob.–9; op. 1, d. 86, ll. 17 ob.–18; op. 1, d. 39, ll. 18 ob.–19.

96. TsDIAK-Ukraïny, f. 663, op. 1, dd. 63, 65, 73, 83, 86, 87.

97. Devorah Baron, "What Has Been," in *The Thorny Path,* 148.

98. Ia. B. Eiger, "Fizicheskoe razvitie i sanitarnoe sostoianie evreiskogo naselenie v Rossii," *Evreiskii meditsinskii golos* 3–4 (1911): 28.

99. Gruzenberg, "O fizicheskom sostoianii," 68–69.

100. Dr. Snigirev, "Materialy dlia meditsinskoi statistiki i geografii Rossii," *Voenno-meditsinskii zhurnal,* 4 (1884):34. The phrase "extreme form" was italicized in the original article.

101. George L. Mosse, *The Image of Man. The Creation of Modern Masculinity* (Oxford, 1996).

102. For a fascinating discussion of the transformation of the erotic male ideal in Jewish society, see Daniel Boyarin, *Unheroic Conduct: The Rise of Heterosexuality and the Invention of the Jewish Man* (Berkeley, 1997). According to Mosse, Otto Weiniger's *Geschlecht und Charakter* (published in 1903) did more to popularize the idea of the effeminate Jew than any other work (Mosse, 69). See also Sander Gilman, *The Jew's Body* (London, 1991).

103. Mosse, *Image of Man,* 80.

104. Ibid., 83. See also Edward Shorter, *From Paralysis to Fatigue: A History of Psychosomatic Illness in the Modern Era* (New York, 1991), 117–18.

105. Gruzenberg, "O fizicheskom sostoianii," 69–70.

106. Ibid., 73.

107. Tchernowitz, *Pirkei hayim,* 62.

108. *Obshchii svod po imperii rezul'tatov razrabotki dannykh pervoi vse-obshchei perepisi naseleniia, proizvedennoi 28 ianvaria 1897 goda* (St. Petersburg, 1905), 2:2–19, 184–205, as cited in Boris Mironov, *A Social History of Imperial Russia, 1700–1917 2 vols.* (Boulder, Colo., 2000), 1:103.

109. Hirsz Abramowicz, *Profiles of a Lost World: Memoirs of East European Jewish Life before World War II* (Detroit, 1999), 109–13. In towns like Butrimantsy (Vil'na province), Jews apparently turned to the local "Tatars" to heal mentally ill relatives with charms, herbs, and incantations.

110. Between 1900 and 1909, the medical office of the Vil'na provincial board received numerous petitions from Jews for permission to commit their family members to the Jewish hospital for mental illnesses. For sample cases, see LVIA, f. 383, op. 3, dd. 144, 159, 187, 188, and more.

111. LVIA, f. 383, op. 3, d. 3 (petition of Zusel Itskovich Mednik to the governor of Vil'na, 1900).

112. "Dowry," *EJ*, 6 (1973): 185–89.

113. Judith Hauptman, *Rereading the Rabbis: A Woman's Voice* (Boulder, Colo., 1998), 177–95; Louis M. Epstein, *The Jewish Marriage Contract. A Study in the Status of the Woman in Jewish Law* (New York 1927), 90–91.

114. Hauptman, *Rereading the Rabbis,* 181. See the Babylonian Talmud, Ketubot 68a.

115. Kotik, *Mayne zikhroynes,* 37, 47.

116. Abramowicz, *Profiles of a Lost World,* 72.

117. "If she stipulated to bring in [a dowry] of 1,000 dinarim then he [the husband] stipulates [in the *ketubah*], in corresponding fashion, that he owes her 1,500 [because he will invest these moneys and make them increase; it is the principal plus the profit that he obligates himself to return to her upon dissolution of the marriage]" (Mishnah Ketubot, 6:3).

118. For example, in 1893, Roza Moiseeva Pergamenshchik's husband invested her dowry (500 rubles) to open a new soap factory (jointly with his brother, who used his own wife's dowry for his share of the founding capital) in the town of Gadiach (Poltava province).When Pergamenshchik died childless shortly after the marriage, his brother refused to perform the rite of *halitsah* (the levirate divorce) for fear of losing the widow's dowry. As we shall see, restitution of the dowry and *ketubah* was one of most contentious issues in Jewish divorces and widowhood. RGIA, f. 821, op. 9, d. 35, ll. 9–90b (Petition of Roza Itskova Varshavsii to the governor of Poltava, 27 July 1893).

119. Moshe Leib Lilienblum, *Hatot neurim* (Jerusalem, 1970), 89, 92, 127.

120. Etkes, "Marriage and Torah Study among the *Lomdim,*" in *The Jewish Family: Metaphor and Memory* (Oxford, 1989), 161–63.

121. "If a person has been promised a large sum of money at his betrothal and has not received it, he must not abandon his bride because of it. Nor shall one quarrel too much about his wife's property, for he who does so shall not prosper, nor shall his marriage be successful, for the money that a man receives with his wife is not really his possession after all. Any man who marries for this reason is called a fortune hunter." Cited in Jacob R. Marcus, *The Jew in the Medieval World: A Source Book, 315–1791* (Cleveland, 1961), 101–2.

122. "Hakhnasat kallah," *EJ*, 7 (1973):1150.

123. The L'vov collections, although incomplete, are nonetheless diverse and rich. They include the foundations *(fondy)* of Sara Erlich, Aizik Rozenberg, the Aron family, and other societies, all of which allocated special funds to provide assistance and dowries for orphaned or impoverished girls. TsDIAL-Ukraïny, f.

701, op. 2/2, dd. 1486, 1487, 1527, 1528, 1529, 1585–96, 1725, 1736–47, 1822, 1896, 1902 (etc.).

124. TsDIAL-Ukraïny, f. 701 (Evreiskaia religioznaia obshchina, 1785–1939), op. 2/1, d. 1166, l. 88 (petitions of poor women for dowries in 1892).

125. TsDIAL-Ukraïny, f. 701, op. 2/1, d.1166, l. 25.

126. Hence, twenty-one-year-old Pauline Horn requested the *Gemeinde* of L'vov to announce her wedding in the synagogue for three consecutive Sabbaths (9, 16, and 24 August 1856) to establish that none in the community knew of any impedimenta to her marriage to Jacob Reines. TsDIAL-Ukraïny, f. 701, op. 2, d. 660.

127. In 1898, for example, the foundation of Eiseg Rosenberg had a total budget of 17,000 zlotys for an unspecified number of recipients. Individual reports show a modest level of assistance; thus, in 1908, Clara Strolr of L'vov reported receiving a small sum (1,568 kronins) from the "Philanthropic Dowry Fund." In general, Jewish law required a minimum of fifty *zuzim,* which was to be "reassessed in every generation in accordance with the economic conditions," but which could be augmented if funds were available. See *Shulhan Arukh, Yoreh Deah* 250, 2, and *Ketubot* 6,5.

128. Jacob Katz, *Tradition and Crisis: Jewish Society at the End of the Middle Ages* (New York 1993), 117. See also Jacob Goldberg, "Die Ehe bei den Juden Polens im 18. Jahrhundert," 503–7; Immanuel Etkes, *Lita beyerushalayim,* 63–84; Shaul Stampfer, "Hamashmaut ha hevratit shel nisuei boser bemizrah eiropah," 71.

129. It also may have provided a favorable environment for early childbearing, which generally took place at home into the early twentieth century. Indeed, in some households mothers and daughters gave birth simultaneously. Such was the case of Sheikewitz's wife and mother-in-law: on one occasion, the former delivered her second; the latter, her twenty-fourth. Shomer-Bachelis, *Unzer foter,* 42.

130. For the patterns of *kest* in early modern Poland, see Goldberg,"Die Ehe bei den Juden Polens," 500.

131. Among the Jewish merchant stratum *(kupechestvo)* in 1850, 79 percent of the families resided in complex households compared to 45 percent among the petty townspeple *(meshchanstvo),* reflecting the fact that support was more affordable and therefore more widespread among the wealthiest strata. See Mironov, *Social History,* 141.

132. Etkes, "Marriage and Torah Study among the *Lomdim,*" 158.

133. Two to four years was apparently the minimum for betrothal contracts in early modern Poland. A typical text read as follows: "The father of the bride . . . will provide the couple food from his table for two consecutive years after the wedding . . . and four years of free lodging in his home." Samuel ben David Moses Halevi, *Sefer nahalat shivah* (Jerusalem, 1961), 14.

134. See Biale, *Eros and the Jews,* 159. Ironically, the very same *maskilim* who castigated the institution of *kest* not only received support from their own in-laws but were critical when the latter failed to fulfill their legal obligations. Moshe Leib Lilienblum, for instance, claimed that after his years of *kest* were complete, his bankrupt father-in-law sought to sell their house in order to pay the dowry (as stipulated in the prenuptial agreement). However, his mother-in-law— demonized throughout the memoir—allegedly foiled these attempts, thereby depriving him of his rightful capital. See Lilienblum, *Hatot neurim,* 89, 92, 127.

135. Peretz Smolenskin, *Hatoeh bedarkhei hahayim* (Warsaw, 1905), 3:22 ff., as cited in Biale, *Eros and the Jews,* 159.

136. Ayzik Meyer Dik, *Seyfer hilkhoys derekh erets* (Vil'na, 1871). For a fuller discussion about this work, see David G. Roskies, "Ayzik-Meyer Dik," 135.

137. Suffice it to say, the precarious nature of Jewish occupations in the tsarist empire often jeopardized even the prenuptial agreements that were signed with the best of intentions. Events like the Polish uprising of 1863, for instance, delayed Ezekiel Kotik's marriage for a couple of years because his family temporarily lost their livelihood. See Kotik, *Mayne zikhroynes*, 1:317.

138. Shaul Stampfer, *Hayeshivah halitait behithavutah* (Jerusalem, 1995), 16, 121.

139. Rubin, *Voices of a People*, 33.

140. According to David Roskies, this tale was an Eastern European adaptation of an earlier story entitled "Ayn sheyn vunderlikh mayse fun ayner kale mit dray khosanim" (A beautiful and wonderful story of a bride and three grooms, n.p., n.d). Apparently the new, revised version appeared in thirteen editions during the nineteenth century, including one publication in Vilna in 1879, attesting to its widespread popularity. See Roskies, "Ayzik Meyer Dik," 68.

141. Stampfer, *Hayeshivah*, 51.

142. Zborowski and Herzog, *Life Is with People*, 82.

143. Gottlober, *Zikhronot umasaot*, 88.

144. Isaac Bashevis Singer, *In My Father's Court* (New York, 1966), 45.

145. Paula Hyman, *Gender and Assimilation*, 50–92; Iris Parush, "Readers in Cameo: Women Readers in Jewish Society of Nineteenth Century Eastern Europe, *Prooftexts* 14 (1994): 1–23; and "The Politics of Literacy: Women and Foreign Languages in Jewish Society of Nineteenth-Century Eastern Europe," *Modern Judaism* 15 (May 1995): 183–206.

146. Paula Hyman, "East European Jewish Women in an Age of Transition, 1880–1930)," in *Jewish Women in Historical Perspective*, ed. Judith R. Baskin, 2nd ed. (Detroit, 1998), 273–74.

147. For a history of Jewish women's education in Russia, see below, chap. 3. Daughters of elite families usually received an excellent cultural education at home; this consisted of piano lessons, calligraphy, modern languages (French, German, and Russian), and literature that included the romantic classics of Schiller, Zschokke, and Dumas.

148. Mordekhai Ben Hillel Hacohen, ed., *Kevar* (Warsaw, 1923), 207–8.

149. Parush, "The Politics of Literacy," 13. According to David Roskies, even the poorest readers could borrow these books for a minimal fee from traveling salesmen (better known as the *pakntreger*); so popular were these chapbooks that some were reportedly "read to pieces." In 1905 the Jewish section of the Russian Society for the Defense of Women in St. Petersburg reported that 212 women (mainly impoverished workers, seamstresses, and other artisans) borrowed books from its library that year, the most popular items being Tolstoy, Turgenev, Pushkin, and Dostoevsky. See RGIA, f. 1335, op. 1, d. 6, l. 10. This secular literature clearly played an important role in shaping the marital expectations of young Jewish women.

150. Parush, "Readers in Cameo," 7.

151. For more on the rabbinical establishment's response to the challenges of acculturation and transformation of traditional society, see Marc Shapiro, *Between the Yeshiva World and Modern Orthodoxy: The Life and Works of Rabbi Jehiel Jacob Weinberg, 1884–1966* (London, 1999).

152. Isaac Jacob Reines, *Kol Yaakov* (Lida, 1908), as cited in Yosef Salmon, "The Yeshivah of Lida: A Unique Institution of Higher Learning," *YIVO Annual* 15 (1974): 106.

153. Salmon, "Yeshiva," 114.

154. The program of study sought to conform to the requirements of the Russian gymnasium. Secular subjects included the Russian language (both written and spoken), history, arithmetic, geography, and the natural sciences. For more on the religious curriculum, see Salmon, "Yeshiva," 117–19.

155. Isaac Jacob Reines, *Shnei hameorot* (Piotrokow, 1913), 2(2):13.

156. For example, Marion Kaplan has shown that German Jewish women were "guardians of tradition" in the home against the inroads of acculturation and assimilation. *Making of the Jewish Middle Class,* 64–84.

157. For a comparative description of peasant marriage customs, see Christine Worobec, *Peasant Russia: Family and Community in the Post-Emancipation Period* (Princeton, 1991), 118–74; see also Barbara Alpern Engel, *Between the Fields and the City: Women, Work and Family in Russia, 1861–1914* (Cambridge, England, 1996), 13–14.

158. Gottlober, *Zikhronot,* 86.

159. For more on *Khoyves halevoves* and other conduct literature, see Roskies, "Aizik Meyer Dik," 27, 50–54.

160. Kotik, *Mayne zihkroynes,* 1:204.

161. Ibid, 2:18.

162. For the use of this term, see Dietrich Geyer, "Zwischen Bildungsbürgertum und Intelligenzija: Staatsdienst und akademische Professionalisierung im vorrevolutionäewn Russland," in Werner Conze and Jürgen Kocha, eds., *Bildungsbürgertum im 19. Jahrhundert* (Stuttgart, 1985), 207–30. I use the term to describe the small group of Jewish professionals, *zemstvo* employees, and small merchants, that emerged in the mid-nineteenth century. They experienced common, albeit fragile, ties through their elite education, high degree of russification, and new sensibilities, which emphasized individuality and self-reliance and a quest for upward socioeconomic mobility.

163. For a comparative study of "virginity and honor" in Mediterranean societies, see Jack Goody, *The Development of the Family and Marriage in Europe* (Cambridge, England, 1983), 212–21.

164. Levitats, *The Jewish Community in Russia* (New York, 1943), 132. Levitats does not cite the exact source for the quotation, but it probably came from the *beit-din* records of Williamspol, a suburb of Kovno that existed until 1884. The other *pinkasim,* which are listed in preceding paragraphs, do not fit the date of the accident.

165. Ibid., 133. Cases involving the issue of *mukat ets* also appear in the responsa literature. There are least fourteen references to the accidental loss of virginity in *Hut hameshulash,* a collection of responsa by rabbis Chaim Volozhiner, Hillel of Volozhin, and Eliezer Isaac Fried. See *Hut hameshulash,* no. 3, paragraphs 40 and 41. Another example can be found in Rabbi Elhanan Spektor's collection, *Ein Yitshak,* no. 1, paragraph 77, in which he ruled that a woman who claimed to be a *mukat ets* was forbidden to her groom if he was a Cohen (i.e., descended from the priestly class).

166. *Byt velilkorusskikh krest'ian-zemlepashtsev,* 259–60, 262–63.

167. Jewish soldiers, for instance, who were not permitted to marry until the completion of their military service, occasionally persuaded poor domestic servants to have premarital sexual relations with them after a promise of marriage. One product of such unions was Anna Pavlova, the illegitimate, half-Jewish daughter of a soldier and a laundress, who later became a famous dancer. On her background, see R. Buckle, *Nijinsky* (London, 1971), 26–27. Among the general population, illegal cohabitation had also become a major social problem by the

1890s. This topic dominated discussions in the Russian Orthodox Church, which struggled to reinforce the sacrament of marriage. See Gregory Freeze, "Church, Religion, and Society in Modern Russia."

168. For a comparative study of neighbors' responses to premarital pregnancy in England, see Mark Jackson, *Newborn Child Murder: Women, Illegitimacy and the Courts in Eighteenth-Century England* (Manchester, 1996), 60–83. See also Laura Gowing, "Secret Births and Infanticide in Seventeenth-Century England," *Past and Present* 156 (August 1997), 87–115.

169. In most cases, Jews accused their own coreligionists, although it was not unknown for Christian residents (especially servants in Jewish homes) to participate in the trial.

170. LVIA, f. 447, op. 19, d. 8827 (court report, 26 February 1863).

171. Ibid., l. 5. After the autopsy, the Vil'na district doctor also observed that the child was "full term or at least almost full term" and concluded that the cause of death was the infant's "weak development." The Vil'na medical board upheld this conclusion.

172. The woman who started the rumors, Mirli Fridmanova, testified that Gordon had been confined to her bed because she was ill for two days. For lack of proof, the court dropped the case.

173. LVIA, f. 447, op. 1, d. 28965, l. 45.

174. DAZhO, f. 24, op. 14, d. 398, l. 13 (testimony of Efrosiniia Ivanova Bondarenkova, a forty-year-old Russian Orthodox peasant).

175. Ibid., l. 20–20 ob. (protocol of Shendlia Yankeleva Iusilova, 3 March 1885).

176. For a similar case in which a premature birth led to accusations of fornication and infanticide, see LVIA, f. 447, op. 1, d. 28157 (case of Dvera Shapiro, May 1878). The Vil'na criminal court declared that Rivka Khaet (another domestic servant accused of infanticide), "under the influence of shame and fear," had deserted her infant in the outhouse where he died. LVIA, f. 448, op. 2, d. 12707, l. 4 (case of Rivka Khaet, March 1897). In the same language, the Zhitomir criminal court concluded that Leia Vaisman of Dubno gave birth to a dead baby and hid the body "out of shame and fear" (DAZhO, f. 19, op. 8, d. 144, ll. 41–42).

177. A century earlier, Jewish communal elders severely punished *both* sexes for an illicit relationship. In one instance, the courts forced a Jewish youth to sit in a cage for an entire week outside the synagogue in the town of L'vov, "not just for his own indiscretion, but also on behalf of his fiancée" whom he had since married. To be sure, such legal verdicts did not necessarily mirror social attitudes; they nonetheless reflected the moral norms that the elites sought to enforce. Z. Pazdro, *Organizacja i praktyka óydówskich sdów podwojewodzinskich w okresie 1740–1772 roku* (Lwow, 1903), 155–56 as cited in Jacob Goldberg, "Jewish Marriage in Eighteenth-Century Poland," *Polin* 10 (1997):11.

178. Tchernowitz, *Pirkei hayim*, 2.

179. Lynn Abrams and Elizabeth Harvey, "Introduction: Gender and Gender Relations in German History," in *Gender Relations in German History: Power, Agency and Experience from the Sixteenth to Twentieth Century* (Durham, 1997), 11.

180. A. P. V., "Obol'shchenia," *Entsiklopedicheskii slovar'*, 42:551. When the alleged seduction involved a minor (under 14 years old), the law treated the case as "adultery" regardless of any agreement between them; if convicted, the offender faced exile to Siberia and the deprivation of all his rights and property.

181. LVIA, f. 447, op. 1, d. 13070, l. 88 (protocol of Leia Kulkina, 1874).

182. As recent studies on seduction have shown, women sometimes sought to defend their honor by claiming that the relationship had not been consensual and that it had involved some degree of coercion. To counter any suspicions that she initiated the affair, Leah described her first sexual encounter as a violent act but did not explicitly accuse Kit of committing rape. Invoking the prevalent views of sexuality linking female physiology to female psychology, she stressed her physical helplessness to ward off Kit's initial advances (i.e., the locked door and the stifled cries) as well as her emotional "weakness," which had allowed her to succumb repeatedly to his subsequent demands for sex. Significantly, female litigants made frequent references to a "weak mind" *(neumnyi rassudok)*, a self-effacing but clever strategy that shifted the blame to their "female nature" and exploited a gender bias that judges and juries took at face value. For comparative studies, see Susanna Burgharz, "Tales of Seduction, Tales of Violence: Argumentative Strategies before the Basel Marriage Court," *German History* 17:1 (1999): 41–56; Miranda Chaytor, "Husband(ry): Narratives of Rape in the Seventeenth Century," *Gender and History* 7:3 (1995):378–407.

183. The father may well have cut Leah's hair upon learning that she was pregnant.

184. LVIA, f. 448, op. 1, d. 30612, l. 3 (protocol of Yakov Zelikovich Khaskes, 21 July 1909).

185. As lower-class women, especially the unskilled, migrated in ever larger numbers to urban areas, the state forced "women who traded in vice" *(promyshliaiut nepotrebstvom)* to register and remain under police surveillance. Barbara Engel notes that state regulation of prostitution empowered government physicians and police to draw "the boundary between casual sexuality and professional prostitution and to judge who transgressed it." On female subjectivity and the regulation of prostitution in Russia, see Laura Engelstein, *The Keys to Happiness. Sex and the Search for Modernity in Fin-de-Siècle Russia* (Ithaca, N.Y., 1992), 71–75; Sonya Bernstein, *Sonia's Daughters* (Berkeley, 1995). Social fears about the spread of prostitution among Jewish women prompted the creation of a Jewish section within the Russian Society for the Protection of Women (Rossiiskoe Obshchestvo Zashchity Zhenshchin) in 1901. See RGIA, f. 1335, op. 1, dd. 2 and 6.

186. LVIA, f. 448, op. 1, d. 30612 (letter of Berta Gutman to Yasha Khaskes, 27 May 1909).

187. LVIA, f. 445, op. 1, d. 2192, l. 10 (letter of Ita Khana Zarkh, 5 September 1897).

188. The plaintiff, who worked for an apothecary in Vil'na, accused Zarkh of a "dissolute lifestyle" and having "sexual relations with many young men who are ignorant and troublemakers before the law." Ibid., l. 2.

189. On the development of Hasidism, see Gershon D. Hundert, ed., *Essential Papers on Hasidism. Origins to Present* (New York, 1991); Ada Rapaport-Albert, ed., *Hasidism Reappraised* (London, 1996); Immanuel Etkes, *Tenuat hahasidut bereshitah* (Tel Aviv, 1998). On the mitnagdic movement, see Immanuel Etkes, *Yahid bedoro: Hagaon mivilnah, demut vedimui* (Jerusalem, 1998).

190. Louis Jacobs, "Hasidic Prayer," in *Essential Papers on Hasidism* (New York, 1991), 330–31.

191. Gershom Scholem, "*Devekut* or Communion with God," in *Essential Papers on Hasidism* (New York, 1991), 278.

192. Ada Rapoport-Albert, "God and the Zaddik as the Two Focal Points of Hasidic Worship," in *Essential Papers on Hasidism* (New York, 1991), 299–329.

193. Aaron Wertheim, "Traditions and Customs in Hasidism," in *Essential Papers on Hasidism* (New York, 1991), 363–98.

194. Tchernowitz, *Pirkei hayim,* 10.

195. Ibid., 6. Levitats provide a broader discussion of "the association" *(hevrah)* in Russian Jewish life in the early nineteenth century. *Jewish Community of Russia,* 105–22.

196. Mordechai L. Wilensky, "Hasidic-Mitnaggedic Polemics in the Jewish Communities of Eastern Europe. The Hostile Phase," in *Essential Papers on Hasidism* (New York, 1991), 263.

197. Wengeroff, *Memoirs.* Unpublished translation by Jay Harris.

198. Kotik, *Mayne zihkroynes,* 1: 204, 349, 353.

199. Lilienblum, *Ketavim autobiyografiyim,* 98.

200. Zborowski and Herzog, *Life Is with People,* 277.

201. Gottlober, *Zikhronot umasaot,* 89.

202. Kotik, *Mayne zikhroynes,* 1:38.

203. REM, f. 9, op. 1, d. 9, l. 92.

204. See Worobec, *Peasant Russia,* 151.

205. I. Pantiukhov, *Opyt sanitarnoi topografii statistiki iz Kieva* (Kiev, 1877), 228. See Appendix, tables A.1 and A.2.

206. REM, f. 9, op. 1, d. 1, l. 204.

207. Lewittes, *Jewish Marriage,* 83.

208. REM, f, 7, op 1, d. 1656, l. 4.

209. RGIA, f. 821, op. 150, d. 366, l. 45 (materials on the Jews of the southwest regions in 1871).

210. Lewittes, *Jewish Marriage,* 83.

211. Pantiukhov, *Opyt Sanitarnoi,* 399.

212. See the discussion starting in Ketubot 5b.

213. REM, f. 9, op. 2, d. 9, ll. 122, 202.

214. RGIA, f. 821, op. 150, d. 366, l. 45. See also Zborowski and Herzog, *Life Is with People,* 279.

215. REM, f. 9, op. 2, d. 9, ll. 101, 110.

216. RGIA, f. 821, op. 150, d, 366, l. 45 ob.

217. RGIA, f. 821, op. 150, d. 366, ll. 45ob-46 (ethnographic report of Jewish weddings in the Ukrainian provinces).

218. REM, f. 9, op. 2, d. 9, ll. 113, 120.

219. The "ritual bath" was also a common custom among the peasantry; see Worobec, *Peasant Russia,* 161. In Ukraine, a klezmer band and close friends often escorted the Jewish bride to the *mikveh,* where elderly women instructed her in her wifely duties (e.g., the laws of *niddah,* separating the tithes from the *challah,* and lighting the candles). In the town of Propoisk (Belorussia), the bride's mother, friends, and a midwife accompanied her to the ritual bath. REM, f. 9, op. 2, d. 9, ll. 132–33.

220. Devorah Baron, "Trifles," in *The Thorny Path,* 43.

221. REM, f. 9, op. 2, d. 9, l. 134.

222. In some regions, the hair was shaved after, not before the wedding ceremony. For the law against shaving Jewish women's hair, see M. I. Mysh, "Rukovodstvo k russkomu zakonodatel'stvu," *Voskhod* 5 (1890): 93.

223. REM, f. 9, op. 2, d. 9, ll. 155–94.

224. In tsarist Russia, as in most modern European countries, the betrothal *(kiddushin)* occured along with the marriage *(nisu'in),* not on two separate occasions. See Jacob Katz, *Tradition and Crisis,* 114, and Abraham H. Freiman, *Seder*

kiddushin venisuin aharei hatimat hatalmud (Jerusalem, 1944–45; reprint 1964), 28–30.

225. There was no fasting if the wedding took place on the new moon. *Khana veshivah baneihah* (Vil'na, 1904), 220.

226. Lewittes, *Jewish Marriage,* 86.

227. A *perutah* was a small copper coin.

228. In 1905, for example, Borukh Leshchiskii of Ekaterinoslav discovered that, because of his frivolous "mock betrothal" with the daughter of a certain Katz, he could not marry another woman until he delivered a formal bill of divorcement to his first "wife." RGIA, f. 821, op. 8, d. 296, ll. 60–62.

229. Biale, *Women and Jewish Law* (New York, 1984), 80–81.

230. RGIA, f. 821, op. 8, d. 291, ll. 92–93.

231. Freiman, *Seder kiddushin venisuin,* 207–8. For the wedding benedictions, see Lewittes, *Jewish Marriage,* 92–93.

232. Zborowski and Herzog, *Life Is with People,* 282–83.

233. Ibid., 284.

234. Rubin, *Voices of a People,* 121.

235. In the maskilic literature, this was one of the most traumatic moments in the life of a young man. For one groom, the sudden intrusion of inquisitive adults caused a premature ejaculation and trauma. See Biale, "Childhood, Marriage and the Family," in *The Jewish Family: Myth and Reality,* ed. Steven M. Cohen and Paula E. Hyman (New York, 1986), 49; and Alan Mintz, *Banished from Their Father's Table: Loss of Faith and Hebrew Autobiography* (Bloomington, Ind., 1989), 25–28.

236. REM, f. 9, op. 2, d. 9, l. 236.

237. According to Kotik's memoir, the week-long celebrations allowed the family to have parties for different groups of the town population "according to a long-standing custom" (Kotik, *Mayne zihkroynes,* 1:346).

238. Victoria Khiterer, *Dokumenty sobrannye evreiskoi istoriko-arkheograficheskoi komissiei, vseukrainskoi akademii nauk* (Kiev and Jerusalem, 1999), 39 (secret memorandum of the Kiev governor, 12 November 1865).

239. The pud was equivalent to 16.38 kg or approximately 36 lb.

240. Khiterer, *Dokumenty,* 40.

241. Exceptions included agricultural colonists and soldiers who needed permission from secular authorities to marry.

242. The transition was even more traumatic in the child marriages, practiced mainly by the Jewish scholarly elite, who married off children in their early teens. These weddings signified an ambiguous "intermediary" stage between childhood and adulthood, not a transition from adolescence to maturity. Some maskilic writers questioned whether the boys even experienced childhood before becoming grooms. For an analysis of concept of childhood in Eastern Europe, see Anne Lapidus Lerner, "Lost Childhood in East European Hebrew Literature," in *The Jewish Family: Metaphor and Memory* (Oxford, 1989), 95–112. See also David Biale, "Childhood, Marriage, and the Family," 49.

243. For an introduction to Russian census materials, see Ralph S. Clem, ed., *Research Guide to the Russian and Soviet Censuses* (Ithaca, N.Y., 1986); Goldberg, "Die Ehe," 498–99.

244. Goldberg, "Die Ehe," 498.

245. For the statute of the Lithuanian Council, see Dubnow, *Pinkas hamedinah,* no. 968, 266. The 1830 law setting the minimum age of marriage is in *Polnoe sobranie zakonov Rossiiskoi imperii, vtoraia seriia* (hereafter, PSZ[2]), 5: no.

3807, p. 740. To avoid confusion, the state explicitly applied the minimum age of marriage to Jews in the Statute of 1835. P. Levanda, *Polnyi khronologicheskii sbornik,* 360–63. My sample drew upon metrical books of Korostyshev and Vil'na for every fifth year; whenever records for the pertinent year were unavailable, because they were either missing or temporarily inaccessible, the materials from the nearest available years were used instead.

246. Biale, "Childhood, Marriage and the Family," 45–61

247. Gottloher, *Zikhronot,* 80.

248. Simon Dubnow, *History of the Jews in Russia and Poland* (Hoboken, N.J., 1925), 1:380.

249. For recent studies that question traditional assumptions about early marriages among Jews, see Stampfer, *Hayeshivah halitait,* 220–30. He argues that these arrangements were not made out of economic or sexual necessity but because it was an honor for the bride's parents to support the young groom in his Torah studies; Stampfer, "Hamashmaut hahevratit shel nisuei boser," 76; Andrejs Plakans and Joel M. Halpern, "An Historical Perspective on Eighteenth Century Jewish Family Household in Eastern Europe," in *Modern Jewish Fertility,* ed. Paul Ritterband (Leiden, 1981), 16–32; Goldberg, "Die Ehe," 483–515. The classic work on Jewish marriages in Eastern Europe is Jacob Katz, "Family, Kinship and Marriage among Ashkenazim in the Sixteenth to Eighteenth Century," *Jewish Journal of Sociology* 1 (1959):3–22; see also the sections on marriage and family (chaps. 14 and 15) in Katz, *Tradition and Crisis.*

250. See Goldberg, "Die Ehe," 510.

251. LVIA, f. 728, op. 2, d.2 (1837–38). The ages were missing for three single brides for these year, and one exceptional bride was registered as thirteen years old. This file was the earliest preserved metrical book of marriage in Vil'na.

252. Simon Dubnow contended that "in spite of law, embodied in the Statute of 1835, which fixed the minimum age of the bridegroom at eighteen (and that of the bride at sixteen), the practice of early marriages continued as before. Parents arranged marriages between children of thirteen and fifteen." *History of the Jews in Russia and Poland,* 1:112.

253. LVIA, f. 728, op. 3, d. 6 (1851). Of the 93 grooms marrying for the first time, 32 (34.4 percent) were between the ages of 18 and 20; 32 (34.4 percent) between 21 and 24; 19 (20.4 percent) between 25 and 29; and 10 (10.8 percent) over 30 years old. The age was missing for one entry, which would bring the exact number of single grooms to 94.

254. TsDIAK-Ukraïny, f. 663, op. 1, d. 63 (1854).

255. Mironov, *Social History,* 1: 68.

256. For a discussion of early marriage among Jews in the early modern period, see Jacob Katz's classic essay, "Nisuim vehayei ishut bemotsaei yamei habeinayim," *Zion* 10 (1944–45):22–24. See also Israel Halperin, "Nisuei behalah bemizrah eiropah," *Zion* 27 (1962): 55.

257. Babylonian Talmud, Yevamot 62b; Biale, *Women and Jewish Law,* 66.

258. Katz, *Tradition and Crisis,* 120; Mitterauer and Kagan, *The European Family: Patriarchy to Partnership 1400 to Present* (Chicago, 1982), 119.

259. Goldberg, "Die Ehe," 499–500.

260. See Appendix, table A.3.

261. In his demographic study of Kiev, I. Pantiukhov was responding to a report by G. Smolenskii, who claimed that greater concern for child rearing among Jews and parental sacrifice led to a lower rate of mortality among Jewish children.

262. I. Pantiukhov also argued that data compiled by two ethnographers,

Bobrovskii (who studied demographic patterns in Grodno province) and Zelenskii (who focused on the province of Minsk), showed a similar pattern of higher Jewish child mortality than the surrounding Christian population.

263. On the poor urban conditions (e.g., impure drinking water and poor hygiene) that helped to spread the cholera epidemic, see Michael Hamm, "Continuity and Change in Late Imperial Kiev," in *The City in Late Imperial Russia*, ed. Michael Hamm (Bloomington, Ind., 1986), 88–91.

264. M. Ptukha, *Smertnost' 11 narodnostei evropeiskoi Rossii v kontse XIX veka* (Kiev, 1928), 23–24, 27. See also Mironov, *Social History*, 1:101.

265. During the eighteenth century there were at least three such instances—in 1754, 1764, and 1793—when Jews hastily married off children even as young as eight years. The responsa literature indicates that after the rumors subsided, rabbinical authorities received numerous inquiries about dissolving these unions, many of which had never been consummated because of the couple's young age. See Halperin, "Nisuei behalah bemizrah eiropah," 38–52.

266. The edict obliged Jews to serve a twenty-five year military service like other subjects in the empire. The original statute is in V. Levanda, *Polnyi khronologicheskii sbornik zakonov*, 193–200. By the following year, Nikolai Novosil'tsev, the chief administrator of Poland, reported that the Jews of Grodno and Vil'na province had begun to marry off their small children (even ten-year-olds) in response to rumors that the state also planned to ban the marriages of minors. Iulii Gessen, *Istoriia evreiskogo naroda v Rossii* (Moscow and Jerusalem, 1993 [reprint]), 2:26. For more on Jews and military conscription, see Stanislawski, *Nicholas I and the Jews: The Transformation of Jewish Society* (Philadelphia, 1983), 13–34.

267. M. Veiner, ed., *Yisroel Aksenfelds verk* (Kharkov-Kiev, 1931), 1:143–96.

268. Halperin, "Nisuei behalah bemizrah eiropah," 36.

269. Simon Dubnow, "Evrei v Rossii v epokhu evropeiskoi reaktsii (1815–1848)," in *Evrei v Rossiiskoi Imperii XVIII–XIX vekov*. (Moscow, 1995), 355.

270. The Yiddish title was *Di shtot Heres* (Vil'na 1868). I thank Samuel Goldin for sharing the *yizkor-bukh* of his hometown, Niesvisz, with me.

271. Ibid., 8.

272. Mitterauer and Kagan, *European Family*, 118–19. For the classic essay on Western European marriage patterns, see John Hajnal, "European Marriage Patterns in Perspective," in *Population in History*, 101–43. For recent research on Western European marriage patterns, see George Alter, "New Perspectives on European Marriage in the Nineteenth Century," *Journal of Modern History* 16 (1991): 1–5.

273. Sara Rabinovich [Rabinowitsch], "K voprosu o nachal'nom remeslennom obrazovanii evreiskikh zhenshchin" *Novyi voskhod* 5 (4 February 1910): 9–10; and [Sara Rabinowitsch], "Heiraten der Juden im Europäischen Russland vom Jahr 1857 bis 1902," *Zeitschrift für Demographie und Statistik der Juden* 5(1909): fasc. 9–12. See Appendix, table A.8.

274. LVIA, f. 728, op. 3, d. 1474 (1895).

275. TsDIAK-Ukraïny, f. 663, op. 1, d. 92.

276. Sara Rabinovich [Rabinowitsch], "K voprosu o nachal'nom remeslennom," 9.

277. See Appendix, table A.8.

278. Mordechai Aaron Guenzburg, *Aviezer* (Vil'na, 1863), 75.

279. Mintz, *Banished from Their Father's Table*, 28. According to Num. 5:11–31, the *sotah* (wayward wife) must undergo the ordeal of bitter waters to prove her innocence or guilt.

280. Guenzburg, "O fizicheskom sostianii evreev," 76.

281. Biale, *Eros and the Jews,* 163–64.

282. Naphtali Zvi Berlin, *Heamek davar* (Vil'na, 1879–80), commentary on Exod. 1:7 as translated in Biale, "Eros and Enlightenment," 164. The biblical passage dealt with the high fertility rates among the Israelites in Eygpt, increasing the population several-fold: "The children of Israel were fruitful and swarmed and increased and became very very strong, and the land became filled with them."

283. Biale, "Eros and Enlightenment," 164.

284. Stampfer, *Hayeshivah halitait behithavutah,* 46, 322.

285. For examples, see TsIAM, f. 2372, op. 1, d. 28, ll. 82, 155, 155 ob, 167, 184, 185, 194, 220 ob., 296 ob., 300. To be sure, some medical students married *before* they completed their degree; for instance, see l. 64 (the groom was a 24-year-old student) and 1. ob.

286. For the 1870s, see TsIAgM, f. 2372, op. 1, d. 28, ll. 130, 134, 137 (an exceptional pharmaceutical chemist who married at the age of 22), 143, 164. For the requirements of their training, see Brokgaus-Efron, *Entsiklopedicheskii slovar',* 35:318–19.

287. TsIAM, f. 2372, op. 1, d. 28, ll. 134, 173, 198, 316. Clearly, some took longer to learn the basic skills (i.e, preparing a prescription), thus delaying their ability to marry and establish economic independence.

288. TsIAM, f. 2372, op. 1, d. 71 (the bride was 32 at the time of first marriage), 131, 207, 310, 330.

289. For example, a 25-year old female who was taking courses at the St. Petersburg Nikolaev Military Hospital married a 27-year-old student enrolled in the medical faculty in Moscow. See TsIAM, f. 2372, op. 1, d. 28, l. 330.

290. The 1804 "Statute Concerning the Jews," for instance, stipulated that the Jews must leave the countryside within three years (Levanda, *Polnyi khronologicheskii sbornik zakonov,* 54–60). The Russian government was to wage a constant battle against the Jewish liquor business, as is reflected in the countless prosecutions of Jews for illegal distillation *(vinokurenie)* in the Vil'na criminal courts. For examples, see LVIA, f. 447, op. 1, dd. 25365, 28327, 28333, 28344.

291. Arcadius Kahan, *Essays in Jewish Social and Economic History* (Chicago, 1986), 28.

292. Ezra Mendelsohn, *Class Struggle in the Pale* (Cambridge, England, 1989), 6. According to Mendelsohn, the overrepresentation of Jewish tailors could be explained partly by the religious prohibition *(shatnez)* against wearing clothing made of more than one fabric. By employing a coreligionist, Jews could ensure that this ordinance was not violated.

293. This overconcentration of Jews in consumer goods was also due to their exclusion from higher-paying mechanized factories. Mendelsohn attributes the exclusion to the problem of Sabbath rest, lack of technical skills, monopolies by non-Jewish workers, and fears of "the Jewish workers' revolutionary potential." *Class Struggle,* 20–22.

294. Ibid., 3–4.

295. G. B. Sliozberg, *Pravove i ekonomicheskoe polozhenie evreev v Rossii* (St. Petersburg, 1907), 17.

296. Mendelsohn, *Class Struggle,* 11.

297. Since the labor legislation of 1897, which limited factory labor to 11½ hours, did not apply to the private artisan shops, working hours and conditions

were not regulated. According to Jewish socialist newspapers, a journeyman in Minsk earned about three rubles a week.

298. A case study of a strike at the Gal'pern (Halpern) match factory in Pinsk shows that single female labor was often essential to the household economy, thus forcing the women to delay marriage. See LVIA, f. 446, op. 3, d. 234 (1901–1902).

299. Mendelsohn, *Class Struggle*, 13; A. Korev, ed., "Vilenskaia gubernaia," in *Materialy dlia geografii i statistiki Rossii sobrannye ofitserami general'nago shtaba* (St. Petersburg, 1863), 3:392.

300. "Iz Belostoka," *Vpered* 23 (15 December 1875):723.

301. According to the fifth revision census, which did not include women, there were 576,000 registered Jews in Poland-Lithuania. Simon Dubnow reports that there were 617,032 Jews in those regions in 1788 but agrees with the Polish historian Thaddeus Chatzki that this figure underestimates the actual number of Jews, which was approximately 900,000 (including women and those who evaded official the census). See V. M. Kabuzan, *Narody Rossii v pervoi polovine xix v.: Chislennost' i etnicheskii sostav* (Moscow, 1992), 162; Dubnow, *History of the Jews in Russia and Poland*, 263–64.

302. Mironov, *Social History*, 1:108; E. I. Kaipsha, "Dvizhenie narodonaseleniia v.Rossii s 1848 po 1852 god," in *Sbornik statisticheskikh svedenii o Rossii, izdavaemyi Russkim geograficheskim obshchestvom* (St. Petersburg, 1858), 3:429–64.

303. Rebecca Himber Berg, "Childhood in Lithuania," in *Memoirs of My People*, ed. Leo Schwarz (Philadelphia, 1943), 269.

304. Gruzenberg, "O fizicheskom sostianii evreev, chast' 2," 22.

305. Ibid.

306. V. A. Manassein, *Vrach* 41 (1882).

307. See table VI in Simon Kuznets, "Immigration of Russian Jews to the United States," *Perspectives in American History* 9 (1975), 63; Jacob Lestchinsky, "Problems der Bevölkerungs-Bewegung bei den Juden," *Metron* 6 (1 June 1927):80–164. The figures for the general Russian population can be found in B. Ts. Urlanis, *Rost naseleniia v Evrope* (Moscow, 1941), 414–15.

308. Kaplan, *Making of the Jewish Middle Class*, 42.

309. This chart appears in Mironov, *Social History*, 1:107.

310. DAZhO, f. 19, op. 8, d. 144, l. 19. (protocol of Leia Vusmanova, 15 July 1869).

311. A. O. Afinogenov, *Zhizn' zhenskogo naseleniia Riazanskogo uezda v period detorodnoi deiatel'nosti zhenshchiny* (St. Petersburg, 1903), 57; Mironov, *Social History*, 1:86–87.

312. Hauptman, *Rereading the Rabbis*.

313. Sirkes, Responsa, no. 99.

314. One priest from Novgorod complained that mothers breast-fed their children beyond the two years that he considered the legitimate limit: "Mothers continue to nurse their children up to four or five years, sometimes nursing other women's children, or toothless pups, not to mention extracting their own milk and other unnatural practices." See F. V. Giliarovskii, *Issledovanie o rozhdenii i smertnosti detei v Novgorodskoi gubernii* (St. Petersburg, 1866), 50, as cited in Mironov, *Social History*, 1:87.

315. Kaplan, *Making of the Jewish Middle Class*, 44–45.

316. Mironov, *Social History*, 1:128.

317. Abortions were not legalized until 1920 in Russia. Under certain circumstances, they were legal, but such permission was rare: during the period

1840–1890, there were only 247 legal abortions in the entire empire. Presumably, illegal abortions were more widespread, but given the legal prohibition (and stiff punishment), it is impossible to tell how often Jews or Gentiles resorted to the services of an amateur abortionist. Mironov, *Social History,* 84.

318. LVIA, f. 448, op. 1, t. 2, d. 5228, ll. 45 ob.–46.

319. According to one study, the average life expectancy at birth for Jews in European Russia was 36.6 years for men and 41.4 years for women in 1896–97. This was higher than for Russians (27.5 for men and 29.8 for women), Ukrainians (36.3 for men and 39.9 for women), and Belorussians (35.5 for men and 36.8 for women) but lower than for the Baltic nationalities: Lithuanians (41.1 for men and 42.4 for women); Estonians (41.6 for men and 44.6 for women); Latvians (43.1 for men and 46.9 for women). The national average for the Russian Empire was 31.3 for men and 33.4 for women. M. Ptukha, *Smertnost' 11 narodnostei Evropeiskoi Rossii v kontse XIX veka* (Kiev, 1928), 37–38.

320. See Appendix, table A.5. These figures did not include any divorced individuals.

321. See Appendix, table A.6.

322. The new wife reassured herself that her toil would not be in vain for hers was a "holy task," like that of a ministering angel:

> This merit is much greater than that of bringing up your own children, because the attachment that you have for your own children is natural; all animals have it. The hen raises her own children but she has no instinct to care for strange chicks, so she pecks at the stranger and chases it away. . . . The stepmother is likened to the ministering angels and that is why her reward is so great. Therefore you will repay her. . . . So, kindhearted father, purify my heart from all bad traits, especially anger and hatred, and plant in me goodheartedness and nobility.

Rivka Zakutinsky, *Techinas. A Voice from the Heart as Only a Woman Can Pray* (New York, 1992), 400–5.

323. Judah Loeb Benjamin Katsenelson, *Mah sherau enai veshamu oznai* (Jerusalem, 1947), 7–9.

324. Davidowicz, *Golden Tradition,* 276.

325. TsGIA-K, f. 663, op. 1, d. 69, ll, 6 ob.–8; 17 ob.–18 (metrical book for 1861).

326. See Appendix, table A.7.

327. The original quote can be found in Mishnah Ketubot, 5:6. The frequency of sexual relations depended on a man's occupation so that "he should be able to practice his trade and also fulfill his marital obligation." Hence, a camel driver was required to perform his conjugal duties once every month, the sailor once every six months, donkey drivers once a week, workmen, twice a week, and "one who is at leisure, once a day." See Biale, *Women and Jewish Law,* 130; Shlomo Riskin, *Women and Jewish Divorce: The Rebellious Wife, the Agunah and the Right of Women to Initiate Divorce in Jewish Law—A Halakhic Solution* (New York: 1989), 6–7.

328. Riskin, 5, as found in Mishnah Ketubot 5:5.

329. Tchernowitz, *Pirkei hayim,* 21–22.

330. The Hasidic pilgrimages were based on the Talmudic injunction to visit the rabbi personally for the three pilgrimage festivals (Passover, Shavuot, and Sukkot), as well as the new moon and Sabbaths (Rosh hashanah 16b).

331. Hyman, *Gender and Assimilation,* 67; for more on Jewish women's work in Eastern Europe, see Charlotte Baum, "What Made Yetta Work? The Economic Role of Eastern European Jewish Women in the Family," *Response: A Contemporary Jewish Review* 18 (1973):32–38; Susan Glenn, *Daughters of the Shtetl: Life and Labor in the Immigrant Generation* (Ithaca, N.Y., 1990), 32–38.

332. For comparative studies on the gender division of labor in Europe, see Karen Hausen, "Family and Role Division: The Polarization of Sexual Stereotypes in the Nineteenth Century, an Aspect of the Dissociation of Work and Family Life," in *The German Family. Essays on the Social History of the Family in Nineteenth and Twentieth Century Germany,* ed., Richard Evans and W. R. Lee (Totowa, N.J., 1981), 51–83; Jane I. Lewis, ed., *Love and Labor: Women's Experiences of Home and Family, 1850–1940* (Oxford, 1985); Robert Gray, "Factory Legislation and the Gendering of Jobs in the North of England, 1830–1860," *Gender and History* 5 (spring 1992): 56–80; Carol E. Morgan, "Gender Constructions and Gender Relations in Cotton and Chainmaking in England: A Contested and Varied Terrain," *Women's History Review* 6 (1997): 367–81.

333. Kotik, *Mayne zikhroynes,* 1:8.

334. GAKO, f. 2, op. 210, d. 612, l. 1 (report of Kiev provincial board to the governor of Kiev, 12 December 1893).

335. LVIA, f. 448, op. 1, d. 29314 (13 November 1909). For other suits in 1910 involving false scales (the majority involved female defendants), see: f. 448, op. 1, d. 30776 (Khana A. Mintz); d. 30777 (Sora A. Zaks); d. 30781 (Mire M. Toptak), and countless others.

336. Laws regulating insults to the personal honor of government officials *(oskorblenie vlasti)* fell under Statutes 394 and 395 of the Civil Code. See "Oskorblenie vlasti," *Entsiklopedicheskii slovar'* 43:280–82.

337. See James Scott, *Domination and the Arts of Resistance: Hidden Transcripts* (New Haven, Conn., 1990).

338. LVIA, f. 448, op. 1, d. 105 (indictment act, 13 December 1885).

339. For other examples, see LVIA, f. 448, op. 1, d. 30854 (case of Sheina Katsenelson); f. 448, op. 1, d. 29966 (case of Ginda Levin, 1909); f. 448, op. 1, d. 2781 (case of Taube Zyndel, 1887); f. 448, op. 1, d. 68 (case of Khana Katz, 1884), and many more.

340. LVIA, f. 448, op. 1, d. 3055 (case of Khaia Gurvich, 1909).

341. The conflict ensued after the woman attempted to prevent the peasant from disturbing her children, who were attempting to study in the adjoining room. Interestingly, the incident transpired without any mention of her husband (away on business); he surfaced belatedly and only demanded restitution of costs (doctor's bills). DAZhO, f. 19, op. 9, d. 84, ll. 182–84 (Khaia Toby Shnaidmel' vs. the peasant Fedor Pilipchuk, 27 March 1878–14 May 1880).

342. LVIA, f. 447, op. 1, d. 4672.

343. LVIA, f. 448, op. 2, d. 8841 (petition of Rivka Osherovna Berkovna Ryndziunskaia, 1885).

344. Glenn provides a useful description of Jewish women's work in the shtetl but does not place the discussion in the broader context. *Daughters of the Shtetl,* 8–49.

345. I. Pantiukhov, *Opyt,* 306.

346. DAZhO, f. 65, op. 1, d. 178.

347. Parush, "Politics of Literacy," 189.

348. Rakowski, *Zikhroynes,* 12.

349. Tchernowitz, *Pirkei hayim,* 31. Chaim Tchernowitz himself admitted

that he was a failure in his father-in-law's business and "always spoiled everything in the store."

350. To be sure, there were numerous exceptions where Jewish women undertook the task of traveling to other towns on business trips. According to Tchernowitz, his paternal grandmother, Chaya Frieda (the daughter of R. Yohanan Deich of Polotsk), once gave birth to a son in a cart, on her way to attend a fair in a distant town. She entrusted the infant to a wet nurse and promised to pick him up on her way back from business. When she returned, however, Chaya Frieda was convinced that her child had been switched and gave him up to be raised by another family. Tchernowitz, *Pirkei hayim*, 35.

351. Isaac Meyer Dyk, *Feigele der Maggid* (Vil'na, 1860), as translated in Glenn, *Daughters of the Shtetl*, 15–16.

352. See folksong in Miriam Zunser, *Yesterday: A Memoir of a Russian Jewish Family* (New York, 1978), 153–54.

353. Khaia Shenker, a Jewish domestic servant who worked for a Jewish arrendator in Vladimir-Volynsk (Volhynia province) became pregnant with the child of a Russian peasant, Nikolai Panaev, who worked as a steward in the Berenshtein household. DAZhO f. 19 op. 9, d. 32, ll. 2–33 (case of Khaia Shinker, 12 March 1875–9 February 1878).

354. "Sasha, a Russian who [had] worked in our house for years," Chagall recalled, "was very strict about the dietary laws and watched over the Sabbath as if it were her own Sunday." Bella Chagall, "Burning Lights," in *First Encounter* (New York, 1983), 26.

355. S. Fuenn, "Deputatsiia evreiskogo naroda," *Voskhod* 3 (1905):57.

356. RGIA, f. 821, op. 9, d. 139, l. 213 (report of Mr. Kogan to the Jewish Committee in Ekaterinoslav, 1881).

357. Tchernowitz, *Pirkei hayim*, 37.

358. Lilienblum, *Hatot neurim*, 106, 108.

359. Etkes, *Lita beyerushalayim*, 67.

360. For a theoretical discussion about gender hegemonies, see Sherry Ortner, *Making Gender. The Politics and Erotics of Culture* (Boston, 1996), 139–72.

361. Daniel Boyarin, *Unheroic Conduct. The Rise of Heterosexuality and the Invention of the Jewish Man* (Berkeley, Calif., 1997); Naomi Seidman, *A Marriage Made in Heaven: The Sexual Politics of Hebrew and Yiddish* (Berkeley, Calif., 1992).

362. Boyarin, *Unheroic Conduct*, 151; Ortner, *Making Gender*, 142.

363. "Zhenskii vopros u evreev," *Vestnik russkikh evreev* 1 (2 January 1873): 1–5.

364. *Russkii evrei* 3 (1884):3.

365. For a fuller discussion of this critique, see Hyman, *Gender and Assimilation*, 69–71; Mordekhai Levin, *Erkhei hevrah vekalkalah beideologyah shel tekufat hahaskalah* (Jerusalem, 1975), 151–53; Biale, *Eros and the Jews*, 160–61.

366. S. Y. Abramovitsch, "The Brief Travels of Benjamin the Third," in *Tales of Mendele the Book Peddler*, ed., Dan Miron and Ken Friedan (New York, 1996), 321.

367. Dan Miron, Introduction to *The Tales of Mendele the Book Peddler*, iv (see n. 366).

368. For the restructuring of domestic relations (reflected in the evolving status of servants), see the discussion and reference to the general literature in Angela Rustemeyer, *Dienstboten in Petersburg und Moskau, 1861–1917* (Stuttgart, 1996), 9–24.

369. Biale, *Eros and the Jews*, 161.

370. See the discussion of the limits of maskilic visions of female emancipation in Shmuel Feiner, "Haishah hayehudit hamodernit," *Zion* 58 (1993):453–99.

371. Biale, "Eros and Enlightenment: Love Against Marriage in the East European Jewish Enlightenment," *Polin* 1 (1986):63.

2. Bringing Order to the Jewish Family

1. RGIA, f. 1269, op. 1, d. 48, l. 2–2 ob. (report of the Jewish Committee to the MVD Department of Agriculture, 15 May 1854).

2. The intrusion of the government into the most intimate family and social events—religious holidays births, marriages, divorces, deaths—signaled the emergence of the modern state and its effort to impose social discipline, limit excesses, and maximize productivity. In the German case, the government "tried to impose uniform regulations, least disruptive to the normal rhythm of life and work, on betrothals, weddings and funerals." See M. Raeff, *The Well-Ordered Police State* (New Haven, Conn., 1983), 70–92. This phenomenon, first evident in the German cameralist state in the seventeenth century, began to shape Russian policy from the early eighteenth century (under Peter the Great) and thereafter remained a powerful influence on secular absolutist rule.

3. The formal title of the Jewish Committee *(Evreiskii kommitet)* was the Main Committee for the Ordering of the Jews *(Glavnyi komitet ob ustroistve evreev)*.

4. RGIA, f. 1269, op. 1, d. 48, l. 2–2 ob.

5. H. J. Matz, *Pauperismus und Bevölkerung: Die gesetzlichen Ehebeschränkungen in den süddeutschen Staaten während des 19. Jahrhunderts* (Stuttgart, 1980).

6. It bears noting that similar concerns pervaded state anxiety about the dissenting Old Believers, who, outside the control of church *and* state, freely contracted and dissolved marriages with scant attention to church canon or state edict. See G. L. Freeze, "Bringing Order to the Russian Family: Marriage and Divorce in Imperial Russia, 1760–1860," *Journal of Modern History* 62 (1992):709–46.

7. RGIA, f. 1269, op. 1, d. 48, l. 2–2 ob. Of particular interest is the important economic role accorded to Jewish women by the Nikolaevan state.

8. On his expedition through the famine-stricken provinces of Belorussia, Senator Gavrila R. Derzhavin (1743–1816) denounced the practice of early marriages among the Jews and noted that "although they are fertile, they are weak." G. R. Derzhavin, *Sochineniia*, ed. Ia. Grot, 9 vols. (St. Petersburg, 1878), 9:281.

9. In this important respect, Russia formed a striking contrast to most other European states, which had sought to "secularize" the family and marriage by placing them under the direct control of the state.

10. W. Molinskii, *Theologie der Ehe in der Geschichte* (Aschaffenburg, 1976); E. Kühn, *Entwicklung und Diskussion des Ehescheidungsrechts in Deutschland* (Hamburg, 1974); W. Molls, *Das Institut der Eheaufhebung* (Bonn, 1972); H. G. Hesse, *Evangelisches Ehescheidungsrecht in Deutschland* (Berlin, 1960); Thomas Safley, *Let No Man Put Asunder: The Control of Marriage in the German Southwest—a Comparative Study, 1550–1600* (Kirksville, Mo., 1984); M. Erle, *Die Ehe im Naturrecht des 17. Jahrhundert* (Göttingen, 1952); S. Jensko, *Scheidung und Trennung von Tisch und Bett nach französischen Recht* (Mannheim, 1984); J. Muhlsteiger, *Der Geist des Josephinischen Eherechts* (Vienna, 1967).

11. Freeze, "Bringing Order," 709–46.

12. Roderick Phillips, *Putting Asunder: A History of Divorce in Western Society* (Cambridge, 1988), 175–85, 257, 410, 422.

13. Freeze, "Bringing Order," 722.

14. A. N. Golitsyn was first chief procurator of the Holy Synod (1803–1816), then Minister of Education and Spiritual Affairs (1817–1824); as the emperor's chief agent in the religious domain, he had a powerful role in shaping state religious policy.

15. For divorce figures on the Netherlands and Belgium, see Phillips, *Putting Asunder,* 408–9. For data regarding Europe in general, see the articles on individual countries in Robert Chester, ed., *Divorce in Europe* (Leiden, 1977).

16. For a summary of data on divorces granted by the Orthodox Church, see Wagner, *Marriage, Property and the Struggle for Legality in Late Imperial Russia* (Oxford, 1994), 70.

17. Freeze, "Bringing Order," 716–17.

18. For complaints about the common-law marriages of the Old Believers, see Freeze, "Bringing Order," 746, n. 132.

19. For the institutional development of the Orthodox Church, see G. L. Freeze, *The Russian Levites: Parish Clergy in the Eighteenth Century* (Cambridge, Mass. 1977), 46–77.

20. A three-tiered administrative system governed Polish Jewry: the local councils *(kehalim),* the regional councils *(vaadei haglilot),* and finally, the supreme Council of the Four Lands *(vaad arba aratsot).* Lithuanian Jewry had their own Council of the State of Lithuania *(vaad medinat lita).* A collection of the council's regulations can be found in Simon Dubnow, *Pinkas hamedinah* (Berlin, 1925). For more on the functions each institution, see Shmuel Ettinger, "The Council of the Four Lands," in *The Jews of Old Poland* (London, 1993), ed. C. Abramsky et al., 205–11; J. R. Marcus, "The Council of the Four Lands," in *The Jews in the Medieval World: A Source Book* (Cleveland, 1961), 205–11. For an example of communal election procedures, see Meir Bałaban, "Die Krakauer Judengemeinde-Ordnung von 1595 und ihre Nachträge," *Jahrbuch der jüdisch-literarischen Gesellschaft* 10 (1895):309, 314–17.

21. For a description of the administrative structure in Poznan before the Cossack uprisings and decline of the community, see Bernard D. Weinryb, "Studies in the Communal History of Polish Jewry II," *PAAJR* 15 (1945): 93–127; for a collection of annotated sources on Jewish communal structures, see Shmuel Arthur Cygielman, *Yehudei polin velita* (Jerusalem, 1991).

22. Bałaban, *Beit yisrael bepolin* (Jerusalem, 1948–53), 58.

23. For examples of Jewish cases that ended up in the *zamek* (castle) courts, see Rosman, *The Lord's Jews* (Cambridge, Mass., 1990), 56–61. The majority of these suits involved serious monetary matters, civil and criminal litigation between Jews and non-Jews and finally, cases against the *kahal.*

24. Rosman, *The Lord's Jews,* 198.

25. Goldberg, *Jewish Privileges in the Polish Commonwealth* (Jerusalem, 1988).

26. The 1645–46 budget in Poznan indicates that the salaries for rabbis, sextons, physicians, and others (5.8% of the total budget) came from the so-called special collections. See B. Weinryb, "Studies in Communal History," 124–25.

27. Hundert, *Jews in a Private Polish Town,* 94–95.

28. Edward Fram, *Ideals Face Reality: Jewish Law and Life in Poland 1550–1655* (Cincinnati, 1997), 43. Joel Sirkes, *Responsa,* no. 9.

29. Menachem Elon, "Power and Authority: Halachic Stance of the Traditional Community and Its Contemporary Implications," in *Kinship and Consent*, ed. Daniel J. Elazar (Washington, D.C., 1983), 191.

30. Fram, *Ideals Face Reality*, 49, citing Solomon Luria, *Yam shel Shelomoh* (Warsaw, 1850), Ketubbot 2, 42.

31. Jacob Katz, *Goy shel shabbat* (Jerusalem, 1984), 73–83; Fram, *Ideals Face Reality*, 60.

32. The most striking example was the state peasantry, the target of far-reaching reform by P. D. Kiselev—the very same Kiselev who chaired the Jewish Committee. Among his comprehensive reforms: restrict peasant infrastructure, build schools, raise productivity, and improve moral and religious life. See N. M. Druzhinin, *Gosudarstvennye krest'iane i reforma P. D. Kiseleva*. 2 vols. (Moscow, 1946–58).

33. Benzion Dinur, "The Origins of Hasidism," in *Essential Papers on Hasidism*, ed. Gershom Hundert (New York, 1991), 109–13.

34. Fram, *Ideals Face Reality*, 57, citing Luria, *Yam shel shelomoh* (Warsaw, 1850), Kiddushin 2, 19.

35. Dinur, "Origins of Hasidism,"106 (citing R. David Karo of Zborów, *Ohel rahel* [Szklow, 1790], 19b).

36. Examples of complaints about the activities of the *kahal* can be found in the Kiev oblast archive: DAKO, f. 1248. op.1, d. 758 (complaints against the recruiting method of the *kahal* of Zhornitsk, 1842–1857); d. 759 (abuse of the *kahal* in recruitment, 1842–1862); f. 2, op. 1, d. 13863 (petition of the Jews of Lipets against their *kahal* for illegal recruitment, 1840); f. 2, op. 1, d. 13676 (petition of Nukhim Kushner against the *kahal* of Uman for illegally taking his son as a recruit, 1840); f. 2, op. 1, d. 13626 (complaints of the Jews of Lipovets against the abuses of their *kahal* in recruitment).

37. The ukaz of 1786 made provisions for a *treteiskii sud* (arbitration court) or the *beit-din*, which was reconfirmed in the Statute on Jews in 1804 (article 49). For more on the rabbinical courts in Russia, see I. G. Orshanskii, *Evrei v Rossii* (St. Petersburg, 1879), 363–73.

38. "Beit-din," *EE*, 4 (1991 [reprint]):410.

39. A. A. Alekseev, *Ocherki domashnei i obshchestvennoi zhizni evreev, ikh verovanie, bogosluzhenie, prazdniki, obriady, Talmud i kagal* (St. Petersburg, 1896), 214.

40. Ibid.

41. "Beit-din," *EE*, 4:412.

42. For more on the rise of Hasidism, see P. S. Marek, "Krizis evreiskogo samoupravleniia i Hasidizm," *ES* 12 (1928), 45–101; Simon Dubnow, *Toldot hahasidut* (Tel Aviv, 1931); I. Orshanskii, "Mysli o khasidizme," *Evrei v Rossii* (St. Petersburg, 1977), 311–45; Benzion Dinur, *Bemifneh hadorot* (Jerusalem, 1955), 83–227; Gershon Hundert, ed., *Essential Papers on Hasidism*. The Hasidic-mitnagdic conflict is examined closely in Mordecai L. Wilensky, *Hasidim umitnagdim* (Jerusalem, 1970); see also W. Z. Rabinowitsch, *Lithuanian Hasidism* (London, 1970).

43. See Shmuel Ettinger, "The Hasidic Movement," in *Essential Papers on Hasidism* (New York, 1991), 236–37.

44. R. Avigdor wrote the petition seven years after his removal from office by the Hasidim of Pinsk. See Rabinowitsch, *Lithuanian Hasidism*, 43–48.

45. David Assaf, *Derekh hamalkhut*, 61. For more on the "secondary" *tsaddikim*, see Assaf, "Mivolhin litsfat: Dyokano shel R. Abraham Dov meovruch (manhig hasidi bamahatsit harishonah shel hameah ha-19)," *Shalem* 2 (1992): 223–79.

46. See Lederhendler, *Road to Modern Jewish Politics* (New York, 1989),

46–47, for the idea of the transformation of the Jewish community into several Jewish communities.

47. Orshanskii, *Evrei v Rossii,* 315.

48. TsGIA-K, f. 442, op.191, d. 7, ch. 2, l. 225–25 ob.

49. B. Weinryb, "Studies in Communal History," 113–14. See Hebrew documents nos. 45–47 on p. 17 for cases in which these petitions for marriage were rejected by the communal authorities. For similar restrictions in the city of Krakow, see M. Bałaban, "Der Krakower Judengemeinde Ordnung," 329.

50. For an example, see RGIA, f. 821, op. 8, d. 363.

51. Mendele Moykher Sforim, "The Little Man," in *The Three Great Classic Writers of Modern Yiddish Literature,* ed. Marvin Zuckerman et al. (Malibu, Calif., 1991), 147.

52. Simon Dubnow, "Istoricheskie soobshcheniia," *Voskhod* 4(1901):3.

53. RGIA, f. 1269, op. 1, d. 15, l. 30 (report of P. D. Kiselev to Personal Section of His Imperial Majesty's Chancellery regarding the reasoning behind the creation of the state rabbinate and Rabbinic Commission, 26.11.1855).

54. RGIA, f. 821, op. 8, d. 283, l. 28.

55. RGIA, f. 1269, op. 1, d. 15, l. 31 ob.

56. RGIA, f. 1269, op. 1, d. 15, l. 36; f. 821, op. 8, d. 283, l. 28 (retrospective report of the MVD on the history of the Rabbinic Commission and state rabbinate, 8 August 1861).

57. RGIA, f. 1269, op. 1, d. 15, l. 33–33 ob.

58. Dubnow, *History of the Jews in Russia and Poland* (New York, 1975), 2:56.

59. Lederhendler, *Road to Modern Jewish Politics,* 74, 151.

60. Ibid., 73.

61. RGIA, f. 1269, op. 1, d. 15 (report of Count P. D. Kiselev, "Regarding the Proposal for the Location of the Rabbinic Commission in Zhitomir," n.d.).The committee did not explain why it chose Zhitomir, but it probably took several circumstances into account. First, Zhitomir was the provincial capital of Volhynia province and the center of a large Jewish population. According to the poll tax census of 1847, that province alone had 141 Jewish communities (the majority being Hasidic) with a total population of 174,457. Moreover, Zhitomir was geographically accessible to the surrounding provinces of Kiev, Podolia, Minsk, and Grodno—all having sizable Jewish communities. In effect, by planting the new institution in the heartland of Russian Jewry, the government hoped to drive a wedge into the Jewish infrastructure and to establish an effective link between St. Petersburg and Jewish communities.

62. RGIA, f. 1269, op. 1, d. 14, l. 18–18 ob.

63. RGIA, f. 821, op. 8, d. 280, l. 10b. (decree of His Imperial Majesty on the statues of the Rabbinic Commission, 1 July 1848). See section 3, point 15, regarding the transference of cases from the MVD to the Rabbinic Commission. The committee resolved that all "private" suits were to be submitted to the local governor, who, in turn, would decide whether the case merited the attention of higher officials in St. Petersburg.

64. RGIA, f. 1269, op. 1, d. 15, ll. 19 ob. –20.

65. See A. E. Presniakov, *Apogei samoderzhaviia* (Leningrad, 1925). Although more recent scholarship has emphasized the Nikolaevan era as one of "pre-reforms," the tendencies of *étatisme* and bureaucratic centralization were still pervasive. For a summary of the revisionist literature, see W. Bruce Lincoln, *Nicholas I: Emperor and Autocrat of All the Russias* (London, 1978).

66. The status of *pochetnyi grazhdanin* was first established in 1832 as an

urban status, partly to reduce the massive ennoblement by creating an intermediate privileged category. Like the nobility, its members were exempted from the onus of the poll tax, conscription, and corporal punishment.

67. The tiny merchant strata, which were defined by their property and assets, enjoyed special privileges; divided into different categories, this small group dominated city affairs and economy. For a detailed account, see Manfred Hildermeier, *Bürgertum und Stadt in Rußland, 1760–1870* (Cologne, 1986).

68. See Phyllis Cohen Albert, *The Modernization of French Jewry: Consistory and Community in the Nineteenth Century* (Waltham, 1977), 45.

69. The Department of Spiritual Affairs of Foreign Faiths was established on 8 February 1832 from an earlier institution, the Chief Administration of Spiritual Affairs of Foreign Faiths. It consisted of three divisions: the first handled Catholic affairs; the second, all other confessions (Protestants. Muslims, Jews, Buddhists, and the like); and the third, cases brought before the Senate and other ministries. For detailed reference to the pertinent legislation, see "Departament dukhovnykh del inostrannykh ispovedanii, Ministerstvo vnutrennikh del," *Gosudarstvennost' Rossii,* 2 vols. (Moscow, 1990), 2:31.

70. *Ministerstvo vnutrennikh del: istoricheskii ocherk* (St. Petersburg, 1901), 92.

71. RGIA, f. 821, op. 8, d. 280, l. 1–1 ob.

72. M. Kreps, "Ravvinskaia Komissia" *EE,* 13 (1991 [reprint]):234.

73. RGIA, f. 821, op. 8, d. 293, l. 149 ob.

74. M. R., "Neskol'ko slov o ravvinskoi komissii," *Vestnik russkikh evreev* 12(1872):365–67.

75. RGIA, f. 821, op. 8, d. 293, l. 166.

76. Among them were a merchant, Bernshtein, from Odessa; Rabbi D. Orshanskii of Poltava; Rabbi Shimon Merkel of the village of Birzhi (Belorussia); and finally, Dr. Cherol'zon from the Baltic provinces.

77. RGIA, f. 1269, op. 1, d. 15, ll. 35–36 (petition of Dinaburgskoe Jewish society to the Ministry of Interior, undated).

78. M. Morgulis, "K istorii obrazovaniia russkikh evreev (III)," 326–27.

79. RGIA, f. 821, op. 8, d. 293, l. 166 ob.

80. Morgulis, "K istorii obrazovaniia russkikh evreev (III)," 326–27; RGIA, f. 1269, op. 8, d. 293, 166 ob.

81. V. O. Levanda, *Polnyi khronologicheskii sbornik zakonov* (St. Petersburg, 1874), 349.

82. For more on the status of Russian soldiers, see E. K. Wirtschafter, *From Serf to Russian Soldier* (Princeton, N.J., 1990).

83. RGIA, f. 1269, op. 1, d. 15, ll. 28–29 (memorandum from Sergei Lanskoi to P. D. Kiselev, 8 November 1853).

84. Ibid.

85. RGIA, f. 821, op. 8, d. 281, ll. 8–11 ob. (memorandum from P. D. Kiselev to the Ministry of Interior, "Regarding the Rabbinic Commission and Provincial Rabbinate," 26 November 1855).

86. RGIA, f. 821, op. 1, d. 281, l. 53 ob. (letter of the military governor of Kiev, Podolia, and Volhynia to the Minister of Interior, 3 July 1856).

87. RGIA, f. 821, op. 8, d. 282, l. 13 (letter of the governor of Kiev, Podolia, and Volhynia to the Minister of Interior regarding the specific qualities sought in the members of the Rabbinic Commission, 11 December 1856).

88. For more on Abraham Neumann, see A. Drabkin, "Abraam Neiman, [Neumann]" *EE,* 11 (1991 [reprint]): 656; RGIA, f. 821 op. 8, gg. 1852–1854, d. 396 (confirmation of A. Neumann as the [state] rabbi of Riga); f. 821, op. 8, gg.

1858–1864, d. 400 (promotion of A. Neumann and his family to the status of honorary citizen); f. 821, op. 8, g. 1863, d. 417 (confirmation of A. Neumann as [state] rabbi of St. Petersburg); f. 821, op. 8, gg. 1864–1866 (appointment of Rabbi Neumunn as an official in the general mission on Jewish affairs by the St. Petersburg general-governor).

89. For more on Y. Z. Rapaport, see Lederhendler, *Road to Modern Jewish Politics*, 77–79.

90. For a list of the other candidates, see RGIA, f. 821, op. 8, d. 281, ll. 60 ob.–76, 126–27.

91. RGIA, f. 821, op. 8, d. 282, l. 13–13 ob. (letter of the governor of Kiev, Podolia and Volhynia to the Minister of Interior, 11 December 1856).

92. Richard Stites, *The Women's Liberation Movement in Russia: Feminism, Nihilism and Bolshevism* (Princeton, 1968), 29–63.

93. RGIA, f. 821, op. 8, d. 282, l. 39 ob.

94. Ibid.

95. Morgulis, "K istorii obrazovaniia russkikh evreev," 330.

96. Ibid., 331.

97. Ibid.

98. The third meeting of the commission included previous members, such as Abraham Neumann (chairman), Iakov Barit, and Y. Z. Rapoport, and several new ones, including I. E. Landau (the state rabbi of Kiev), G. Barats (a graduate of the state rabbinical school in Zhitomir), and A. Maidevskii of Poltava province. I. E. Gintsburg and two "learned Jews" from the Ministry of the People's Education—I. Zeiberling (St. Petersburg) and S. J. Fuenn (Vil'na)—also participated in these proceedings.

99. RGIA, f. 821, op. 9, d. 10 (Feiga Gelefonova vs. Rabbi Shaperinskii).

100. Ibid., l. 13 ob. Since *halitsah* was required only when there was no off-spring whatsoever, her excuse had no grounds.

101. Ibid., l. 14 ob.

102. RGIA, f. 821, op. 8, d. 283, l. 35–35 ob. (decree of the Senate to the MVD regarding the transferral of the Gelefonova suit to the Rabbinic Commission, undated).

103. Ibid., l. 19. See the discussion beginning on *Shulhan Arukh, E.H.* 17, 3. That the Rabbinic Commission required a written certificate of death actually exceeded the requirement in Jewish law, which mandated only the *testimony* of two competent witnesses. It approximated, instead, the requirements of state law.

104. To alleviate the agonizing position of the *agunah*, Jewish law sometimes permitted the testimony of those who were usually ineligible to serve as witnesses. See Biale, *Women and Jewish Law*, 104–5. This was clearly not the position of the rabbis in their decision about Feiga Gelefonova's fate.

105. RGIA, 821, op. 8, d. 283, l. 20–20 ob.

106. It cited *Shulhan Arukh, E.H.* 17, 2.

107. Morgulis, "K istorii obrazovaniia russkikh evreev," 334–35.

108. For the most comprehensive study on the Jewish rabbinate in Russia, see Azriel Shochat, *Mosad 'harabanut mitaam' berusyah;* see also Shochat, "Yahas hatsibur el harabanim hanikhei batei hamidrash lerabanim," in *Hadat veha-hayim* (Jerusalem, 1993), 240–68.

109. Levanda, *Polnyi khronologicheskii sbornik*, 53–59.

110. Shochat, *Mosad 'harabanut mitaam,'* 9.

111. By contrast, divorces were *not* entered into the metrical books of Russian

Orthodox communities. The difference, no doubt, stemmed from the fact that, whereas the local rabbi was empowered to dissolve marriages, only the central church authorities could do so in the case of the Russian Orthodox.

112. Levanda, *Polyni khronologicheskii sbornik,* 303; DAmK, f. 16, op. 469, d. 9 (polozhenie o evreiakh, 15 April 1835).

113. DAmK, f. 16, op. 469, d. 9, l. 12 (article 90).

114. Ismar Schorsch, "Emancipation and the Crisis of Religious Authority: The Emergence of the Modern Rabbinate," in *From Text to Context: The Turn to History in Modern Judaism* (Hanover, N.H., 1994), 10.

115. Levanda, *Polnyi khronologicheskii sbornik,* 800.

116. DAmK, f. 16, d. 469, d. 9, l. 12 ob.

117. Ibid. Perhaps the law meant to say "the repayment of the *ketubah*" because a woman was deprived of her dowry only on rare occasions.

118. On the poll tax censuses and metrical books in Imperial Russia, see B. M. Kabuzan, *Narodonaselenie Rossii v XVIII i v pervoi polovine XIX v.* (Moscow, 1963).

119. DAmK, f. 16, d. 469, d. 9, l. 12.

120. Levanda, *Polnyi khronologicheskii sbornik,* 445. The official oath for state rabbis (published in 1838) confirmed Jewish suspicions that they were nothing more than informers: "I will direct all the Jews, using all the means that is within me, to fulfill their obligations: obedience to civil authorities and the preservation of social order and peace. . . . I will not permit or hide anything harmful or contrary to the laws of the empire, and I will observe everything that pertains to the interests and usefulness of the supreme authorities, to preserve strictly any secrets entrusted to me and, in general, to conduct myself and behave [in a manner] incumbent on a good and loyal citizen." The rabbinic oath was remarkably similar to the oath required by the Russian Orthodox clergy. See Freeze, *The Russian Levites,* 29–31.

121. Shochat, *Mosad 'harabanut mitaam,'* 10.

122. Ibid., 9, 12.

123. During the first three years, students took secular courses equivalent to the curriculum of a Russian pre-gymnasium (e.g., Russian, arithmetic, geography) and traditional Jewish subjects such as the Pentateuch with the commentaries of Rashi, the early Prophets, the book of Proverbs, and so forth. The next four years were devoted to more advanced gymnasium subjects (e.g., history, physics, foreign languages) and basic halakhic texts. At the end of these seven years, students could choose to enroll in the one-year pedagogical course for teachers or the three-year program of rabbinical training. See DAZhO, f. 396, op. 1, d. 1, l. 1 (statutes of the Zhitomir rabbinical school, 1844).

124. I. L. Levanda in *Voskhod* 4 (1881):86.

125. *Kol kitvei Mendele Mokher Seforim* (Jerusalem, 1952), 237, as cited in Shochat, *Mosad 'harabanet mitaam,* 23.

126. The list of famous *maskilim* who graduated from the schools includes such figures as N. I. Bakst, H. Barats, M. Morgulis, A. Paperna, I. Soloveichik, I. Levanda, and A. Landau. See M. Stanislawski, *Tsar Nicholas I and the Jews* (Philadelphia, 1983), 107.

127. *PSZ(2),* 32:31, 831 (23 August 1857); Levanda, *Polnyi khronologicheskii sbornik zakonov,* 880; M. I. Mysh, "Rukovodstvo k russkomu zakonodatel'stvu o evreiakh," *Voskhod* (May 1890):89.

128. To promote mobility and enable youths to pursue any career (based on their abilities, not their social origin), from the late 1850s the government gradu-

ally dismantled or lowered many of the barriers to matriculation and service. One of the first targets of reform was the army: military service and officer training were now open to non-nobles and graduates of non-elite schools.

129. RGIA, f. 821, op. 8, d. 408, l. 51–510b (undated memorandum from the general-governor of Vil'na, Grodno, and Kovno to the Ministry of Interior).

130. Ibid, l.1 (letter of general governor of Vil'na, Grodno, and Kovno provinces to the Ministry of Interior, 17 November 1859).

131. For a review of the state rabbi's function and responsibilities, see also Iulii Gessen, "Ravvinat" EE, 13: 226–27; Levanda, Polnyi khronologicheskii sbornik, 370–74; G. B. Sliozberg, Sbornik deistvuiushchikh zakonov (St. Petersburg, 1909), 121–23; M. I. Mysh, "Rukovodstvo k russkomu zakonodatel'stvu," Voskhod 5 (1890):89–96.

132. Gessen, "Ravvinat" EE, 13 (1991 [reprint]): 227. See also Azriel Shochat, "Yahas hatsibur al harabanim hanikhei batei hamidrash lerabanim," in Hadat vehahayim (Jerusalem, 1993), 240–68.

133. Shochat, Mosad 'harabanut mitaam,' 31. Letter of Isaac ben Yakov to Yitshak Baer Levinson in Fun noetn over, translated into Hebrew in Hakerem (1889):42–49; J. L. Lipschitz also discusses this letter in Zikhron Yaakov (Frankfurt, 1924), 177–79.

134. RGIA, f. 821, op. 8, d. 408, ll. 5 ob.–6, 13–130b.

135. Shochat, Mosad 'harabanut mitaam,' 30.

136. RGIA, f. 821, op. 8, d. 408, l. 8 (petition of the Vil'na Jewish Community to S. S. Lanskoi, Minister of Interior, 11 October 1859).

137. For more on Iakov (Yankel Kovenskii) Barit, see Hillel Steinscheider, Ir Vil'na (Vil'na, 1900), 62–67; Lederhendler, Road to Modern Jewish Politics, 78, 143–44.

138. RGIA, f.821, op.8, d. 405 (petition compiled by Feitel' Bliumenfel'd, to the Ministry of Interior, 1 April 1859). Other signatories to the document included "those who completed the special rabbinical course" (Isaak Sagal, Feitel Bliumenfel'd, and Lev Binshtok); rabbinic candidates (A. Brik, Kh. Pesig, and M. Sheftel'son); visiting rabbinic faculty of the first and second special rabbinic courses (Kulisher, Morgulis, and Gokhtman).

139. RGIA, f. 821, op. 8, d. 408, l. 7 (report from Nazimov to the Ministry of Interior).

140. RGIA, f. 821, op. 8, d. 407 (letter of the governor of Novorossiisskaia and Bessarabskaia provinces to the Ministry of Interior, 4 November 1859).

141. For a description of the conflict over Rabbi Schwabacher, see Zipperstein, The Jews of Odessa (Stanford, 1985), 86–95.

142. RGIA, f. 821, op. 8, d. 407.

143. See DAmK, f. 16, op. 469, d. 19, l. 13.

144. Shochat, Mosad 'harabanut mitaam,' 110; see also "Obzor evreiskoi pechati," Nedel'naia khronika Voskhoda 44 (1898): 1636.

145. DAKO, f. 1, op. 146, d. 43, ll. 10–11 (petition of pharmaceutical assistant Rudol'f V. Rakobshchik to the Kiev provincial board, received on 15 September 1906. For the Senate rulings on the Oksman and G. Largman cases (both pharmacists), see Khronika evreiskoi zhizni 16 (1905):30.

146. DAKO, f. 1, op. 146, d. 43, l. 27–270b. (decree of the state Senate to the Kiev provincial board, 20 June 1906). The Senate ruled: "(1) that in accordance with the decision of the Senate (30 May 1903–28 May 1904) in the Oksman case, a person who has completed four classes in gymnasium could occupy this post; (2) that according to the circular of the Ministry of Interior from 5 February

1876, pharmacists could only take apprentices who had finished four classes of gymnasium; and (3) that in such cases, the law is obliged to recognize the right of the pharmacist's apprentice to the post of state rabbi, all the more so to a pharmaceutical assistant."

147. See G. L. Freeze, *The Parish Clergy in Nineteenth-Century Russia: Crisis, Reform, Counter-Reform* (Princeton, 1983), 339–448; P. A. Zaionchkovskii, *Rossiiskoe samoderzhavie v kontse XIX v.* (Moscow, 1970); T. Taranovsky, "The Politics of Counter-Reform: Autocracy and Bureaucracy in the Reign of Alexander III" (Ph.D. diss., Harvard University, 1976).

148. That shift accompanied significant new strains in Russian-German relations, including the Russian equivalent of a *Kulturkampf* against the Lutheran Church in the Baltics. For a detailed account, see Michael Haltzl, *Der Abbau der deutschen ständischen Selbstverwaltung in den Osteeprovinzen Russlands: ein Beitrag zur Geschichte der russischen Unifizierungspolitik, 1855–1905* (Marburg, 1977).

149. See M. I. Mysh, "Rukovodstvo k russkomu zakonodatel'stvu o evreiakh," 89–90.

150. Shochat, *Mosad 'harabanut mitaam,'* 110.

151. *Hador* 21(1901): 35.

152. S. Levin, *Mezikhronot chai,* 99.

153. "Ravvinskii tsenz," *Budushchnost'* (1901):322.

154. *Nedel'naia khronika Voskhoda* 4(1885):13.

155. *Hamelits,* Kislev (1896):1 cited in Shochat, *Mosad 'harabanut mitaam,'* 11.

156. Eli Lederhendler, "Modernity without Emancipation or Assimilation? The Case of Russian Jewry " in *Assimilation and Community: The Jews in Nineteenth-Century Europe,* ed. Jonathan Frankel and Steven Zipperstein (New York, 1992), 324.

157. Shochat, *Mosad 'harabanut mitaam,'* 99, 111.

158. *Nedel'naia khronika Voskhoda* 2 (1883): 19

159. DAOO, f. 16 , op. 108, d. 51, l. 2–20b.

160. Levanda, *Polnyi khronologicheskii sbornik zakonov,* 800.

161. A careful search through state archive records (including all the collections listed in the bibliography) in Lithuania produced only a few files on conflicts between the state and spiritual rabbinate; by contrast, Ukrainian archives contain a plethora of such cases.

162. DAZhO, f. 19, op. 6, d. 372, l. 18 (testimony of Ovruch state rabbi, I. L. Tveifel, 11 June 1873); ll.13–14 (testimony of I. Shneierson's neighbor, forty-four-year-old Mordukh Shmiolovich Bronshtein, Ovruch second-guild merchant, n.d.).

163. TsGIA-K, f. 442, op. 191, d. 7, ch. 2, l. 219 (journal of the Kiev provincial board, 13 September 1877); l. 222 ob.

164. He pointed out that according to Jewish law, the marriage of widowers, widows, and divorcées did not take place in a synagogue but in the home. Ibid., l. 223.

165. TsGIA-K, f. 442, op. 191, d. 7, ch. 2, l. 225–25 ob.

166. DAZhO, f. 19, op. 9, d. 718 (trial of Rabbi Berlo Khamer in the Rovno district court, Volynskaia province, 22 August 1876–6 June 1877).

167. Ibid., l. 5 (testimony of Rabbi Berlo L. Khamer, resident of village Stepan, 17 April 1877); l. 13 and 19 (stenogram of the trial, 20 May 1877).

168. *PSZ(2),* 28: 27, 172. The harshness of the punishment varied according to the frequency of the crime. Thus, spiritual rabbis or others who violated a state rabbi's jurisdiction for the first time received a prison sentence of two to six

months; for the second infringement, they could be taken as a military recruit without the regular physical exam or test, or if they were not suited for military service, the state could sentence them to ten to twenty years in "civilian penal brigades."

169. Levanda, *Polnyi khronologicheskii sbornik zakonov*, 800. See also Rabbi N. Gershengorn, "K voprosu o evreiskikh metricheskikh knigakh," *Nedel'naia khhronika Voskhod* 1–2 (1899):7–8.

170. DAZhO, f. 67 (Volhynia Provincial Board), op. 1, d. 686, l. 1 (15 May 1905–10 December 1905).

171. TsGIA-K, f. 442, op. 191, d. 7, ch. 2, l. 3–30b. (petition of first-guild merchant's grandson, Lipa Isserlis, and Mariam Tsetlin to the general governor of Kiev, Podolia, and Volhynia provinces, 8 April 1892).

172. "Marriages of Jewish newcomers to a town are not permitted unless they have written permission from the rabbi of their town or village, with whom the jurisdiction lies." Levanda, *Polnyi khronologicheskii sbornik*.

173. TsGIA-K, f. 442, op. 191, d. 7, ch. 2, l. 5 (note in Hebrew from Rabbi Dobrov to the cantor, 30 December 1891).

174. DAKO, f. 158, op. 150, d. 536 l. 1–1 ob. (petition of Lipa Froima Gol'dberg to the Kiev provincial board, 12 December 1916).

175. For a sample inquiry, see *Evreiskii mir* 21 (1910): 35.

176. "Otvety podpishchikam," *Novyi Put'* 30 (1916): 19.

177. For the political and intellectual context, see the discussion in Wagner, *Marriage, Property, and Law*, 101ff.

178. *Svod Zakonov Rossiiskoi Imperii*, 9 ("Zakon o sostoianii"): 770 and 915. See also L. M. Aizenberg, "Ob ispravlenii dopushchennykh v evreiskikh metricheskikh knigakh oshibok," *Evreiskii mir* 14–15 (1911): 42–43.

179. For examples of these petitions, see DAKO, f. 1, op. 139, d. 146, ll. 1–2 (petition of Man Lisianskii to the city board of Vasil'kov for the correction of his name, registered as Menashe in the metrical book of marriage [16 February 1901]); f. 1, op. 140, d. 1233, ll. 36ff. (on the correction of names in the metrical books of the Berdichev state rabbi), and more.

180. *Hapisgah* 10 (1904): 143, cited in Shochat, *Mosad 'harabanut mitaam,'* 111.

181. The provincial board subsequently filed an appeal against the state prosecutor's decision. See M. M. "Senatskaia praktika: po voprosam ob otvetstvennosti ravvinov, chlenov evreiskikh dukhovnykh pravlenii i bozhnichikh dozorov za prestupleniia dolzhnosti," *Voskhod* 2 (1897):1–7.

182. *Nedel'naia khronika Voskhoda* 4 (1885):32.

183. Ibid.

184. Mysh, "Rukovodstvo k russkomu zakonodatel'stvu," 93.

185. TsGIA-K, f. 442, op. 1, d. 354, l. 14 (case of Rabbi Manus Shur vs. the Kolkov Jewish community, 1890). He was referring specifically to *Svod zakonov* (1857 edition), vol. 11, articles 1086–87.

186. Vl. Temkin. "O ravvinskoi komissii (chast 2)," *Rassvet* 7 (1910): 5–8.

187. Levanda, *Polnyi khronologicheskii sbornik zakonov*, 800.

188. See *Svod zakonov*, 9: articles 851–53; reprinted in Levanda, *Polnyi khronologicheskii sbornik*, 372.

189. RGIA, f. 821, op. 9, d. 18, l. 20; *Svod zakonov*, vol. 11, article 1086.

190. RGIA, f. 821, op. 9, d. 18, l. 16 ob.

191. See Arcadius Kahan, *Essays in Jewish Social and Economic History* (Chicago, 1986).

192. RGIA, f. 821, op. 8, d. 357.

193. RGIA, f. 821, op. 9, d. 41 (case of Rivka Adzhiashvili vs. Rabbi Shalash-vili. 1895–1909).

194. According to *Shulhan Arukh, E.H.*, 75, the commentary of Rav Isaac ben Sheshet, 81, read as follows: "If he [the husband] cannot live and support himself, his wife is forced to go to the place where he desires."

195. Although the archival file uses the Russian phrase "that the wife is *un-faithful* to the husband," the original text in *Shulhan Arukh E.H.*, 77, refers to the *moredet*, or "a wife who *rebels* against her husband."

196. See the discussion beginning in *Shulhan Arukh, E.H.*, 75.

197. See *Shulhan Arukh, E.H.*, 77.

198. See *Shulhan Arukh, E.H.*, 141.

199. RGIA, f. 821 op. 9 d. 41 (letter from the provincial state rabbi of Kutaisi province to the military governor, 21 June 1895).

200. RGIA, f. 821, op. 8, d. 296, ll. 11–12 (journal of the Rabbinic Commission, 1910, on the B. Pekker vs. Rabbi Perel'man case). See also Genesis 1:28 and *Shulhan Arukh, E.H.*, 1,1 (section on procreation). Note that several citations to E.H. are incorrect in the archival document and do not pertain to the topic under discussion (e.g. *E.H.* 109, 8).

201. Unfortunately, the rabbi provided a cryptic citation to *Sedei hemed*, pp. 527 and 11 (published in Warsaw in 1891).

202. RGIA, f. 821, op. 8, d. 296, ll. 13–14; see also *Shulhan Arukh, EH*, 152, 10.

203. Shochat, *Mosad 'harabanut mitaam,'* 110.

204. *Hador* (1 Elul 1911): 4.

205. See the case of Ita Radin vs. Rabbi Lev Kagan in the introduction.

206. "Delo ravvina L. A. Kagana," *Budushchnost'* 40 (1902): 794.

207. TsGIA-K, f.335, op.1, d. 120, l. 256 (14 July 1907).

208. RGIA, f. 821, op. 9, d. 13, ll. 21–22 (Malka Malamud vs. Rabbi Lev Kagan).

209. RGIA, f. 821, op. 9, d. 62 (summarized above). For another case involving Rabbi Kagan, see the Pechenik and Sverdlova case in "Delo ravvina L. A. Kagana," *Budushchnost'* 40 (1902): 794.

210. RGIA, f. 821, op. 9, d. 13, l. 21 ob. For a similar case in which a state rabbi concluded a divorce without the consent of the wife, see Revka Bagrova vs. Rabbi Deichman, RGIA, f. 821, op. 8, d. 289, ll. 55–88 ob. (journal of the Rabbinic Commission for 1879).

211. RGIA, f. 821, op. 8, d. 291, l. 53 ob.; f. 821, op. 9, d. 22. Mandating cooperation by litigants in divorce cases was a problem for all confessions. Given the limited secular authority of religious bodies, litigants, especially those inclined to resist divorce, found that the most efficacious defense was simply not to cooperate with the proceedings. For a typical case involving the Orthodox Church, which presumably had far more worldly influence in coercing compliance, see G. L. Freeze, "*Kyrlov vs. Krylova:* 'Sexual Incapacity' and Divorce in Tsarist Russia," in *The Human Tradition in Modern Russia,* ed. William B. Husband (Wilmington, Del., 2000), 5–17.

212. RGIA, f. 821, op. 9, d. 13, l. 21 ob.

213. TsGIA-K, f. 442, op. 590, d. 2 (complaint of Duvid Fridman, Nakhman Glozman, and others from the village of Lugin, Volhynia province, to the governor, 5 Januaury 1879).

214. In one complaint, Rabbi Shur demanded fourteen rubles for a copy of

the death certificate (TsGIA-K, f. 442, op. 1, d. 354, l. 4). Apart from the legal defense (there was no contract to violate), Shur slyly invoked an ideological trope, portraying himself as someone locked in "a struggle against Jewish exclusivism and harmful tendencies of the Kolkov Jewish community" (ibid., l. 14). For obvious reasons, Shur feared that the community would not reelect him as state rabbi; he evidently hoped to persuade the government to leave him in his post without another election.

215. DAKO, f. 2, op. 145, d. 526 (case of Rabbi Fridman).

216. DAKO, f. 2, op. 176, d. 16 (denunciation of Rabbi Yankel Tverskii by M. Makurov).

217. TsDIAK-Ukraïny, f. 442, op. 141, d. 189, ll. 3–3 ob. (27 February 1842).

218. For another example of corruption in the state rabbinate, see the case of Rabbi Manus Shur, who issued false metrical certificates and conducted illegal marriages, TsGIA-K, f. 442, op. 543. d. 354, l. 1–14 (20 December 1890).

219. TsGIA-K, f. 442, op. 138, d. 53 (petition of Tsipi Satanovskaia, 2 March 1833); RGIA, f. 821, op. 9, d. 16 (petition of Sara Shternfeld, 9 November 1887). Although there were official models stipulating "how to write a petition," most archival files were highly individualistic, personal, and unique. See also Sarah Hanley, "Engendering the State," *French Historical Studies* 16 (1989): 4–27.

220. All this was a direct result of the judicial reform of 1864; by the late nineteenth century, many authorities bewailed a rampant "litigiousness," whereby ordinary subjects routinely and frequently resorted to the courts to press their demands, even for minor matters and often at the expense of community solidarity.

221. See G. L. Freeze, *From Supplication to Revolution: A Documentary Social History of Imperial Russia* (Oxford, 1988), pt. 3.

222. "Evreiskaia zhizn," *Rassvet* 40 (1909):24. For the Talmudic quotation, see *Kiddushin* 13, and also *Shulkhan Arukh, E.H.* 0,3.

223. "Evreiskaia zhizn," *Rassvet* 40 (1909):24.

224. RGIA, f. 821, op. 8, d. 357, l. 10–11 (report of the governor of Poltava to the Ministry of Interior regarding Abram Sagal vs. Sura Litovchin, 18 May 1867).

225. RGIA, f. 821, op. 8, d. 357 l. 5 (decision of the *beit-din,* 5 August 1866).

226. RGIA, f. 821, op. 8, d. 357, l.14 (copy of a statement signed in Russian by Abram Meerov Sagal in the presence of the *beit-din,* 7 August 1866).

227. RGIA, f. 821, op. 8, d. 357, l. 14 (statement by Avram Sagal signed in Hebrew and Russian, 25 September 1866).

228. The Poltava governor wrote to the Kremenchug police: "I instruct you to enforce the following: oblige Sagal to return to his wife and live with her or to pay her alimony of 10 rubles in addition to monthly child support that he owes her until the son is 14 years old. . . . Based on this instruction, arrest him immediately and demand money from him." RGIA, f. 821, op. 8, d.357, l. 8 (undated document).

229. RGIA, f. 821, op. 8, d. 357, ll. 1–2 ob. (petition from Kremenchug second-guild merchant Meer Sagal [the father of Abram Sagal] to the Ministry of Interior, undated).

230. RGIA, f. 821, op. 8, d. 357, l. 11 (reply from the governor of Poltava to the Ministry of Interior, 18 May 1867).

231. RGIA, f. 821, op. 8, d. 357, l. 18 (decree of the Senate, 17 February 1868).

232. B. Bogrov, "Nashi braki i razvody," *Nedel'naia khronika Voskhoda* 27 (1893): 725–28.

233. Ibid.

234. RGIA, f. 821, op. 9, d. 17, l. 62 (journal of the Rabbinic Commission, 1884 session). The commitee members included G. I. Rabinovich (chairman), Mogilever, Barats, Tottesman, Katelovker, Simkhovich, and Mileikovskii.

235. *Nedel'naia khronika Voskhoda* 46 (14 November 1893): 1218–20.

236. *Kitvei Yehuda Leib Gordon: Shirah* (Tel Aviv, 1956). The original poem was written in 1879, after the disillusionment with the Russian government and state rabbinate set in among the Jewish intelligentsia.

237. Y. L. Gordon, "Kotso shel yud," *Kitvei Yehuda Leib Gordon: Shirah* (Tel Aviv, 1956), 129–40. In this poem, the husband sends his wife a *get* before his tragic death on his sea voyage to America. But when the *get* finally arrives in Russia, the rabbi (who was trained in the finest yeshiva in Volozhin) discovers a missing letter in the husband's name and invalidates the divorce, whereby the wife becomes an *agunah* and can never remarry.

3. Marital Breakdown and Divorce

1. Devorah Baron, "Mishpahah," *Parashiyot*, 32.

2. Ibid., "Ktanot," 43; "Kritut," 182–85. For the Russian-Hebrew journals that published her works, see G. G. Branover, ed., *Rossiiskaia evreiskaia entsiklopediia*, 2 vols. (Moscow: EPOS, 1994), 1:87.

3. For the classic romantic depiction of the Jewish family in Eastern Europe, see Mark Zborowski and Elizabeth Herzog, *Life Is with People: The Culture of the Shtetl* (New York, 1962). Perhaps the most influential work to shape contemporary American perceptions of the family in the shtetl has been the musical, *Fiddler on the Roof*. For a discussion about the impact of this Broadway musical and film on Jewish memory, see Steven Zipperstein, *Imagining Russian Jewry. Memory, History, Identity* (Seattle, 1999), 16–39.

4. Abraham Mapu, *Mikhtavim* (26 October 1862), 133, as cited in Biale, "Eros and Enlightenment: Love Against Marriage in the East European Jewish Enlightenment," *Polin* 1 (1986):62.

5. Mordechai Aaron Guenzburg, *Aviezer* (Vil'na, 1863), 104.

6. Roderick Phillips, *Putting Asunder: A History of Divorce in Western Society* (Cambridge, England, 1988), 317.

7. For the impact of this process in other historical contexts, see Lynn Abrams, "Companionship and Conflict: The Negotiation of Marriage Relations in the Nineteenth Century," in *Gender Relations in German History: Power, Agency, and Experience from the Sixteenth to the Twentieth Century* (Durham: Duke University Press, 1997); David Sabean, *Property, Production and Family in Neckarhausen, 1700–1870* (Cambridge, 1990); R. Griswold, *Family and Divorce in California, 1850–1900: Victorian Illusions and Everyday Realities* (Albany, 1982); James Hammerton, *Cruelty and Companionship: Conflict in Nineteenth Century Married Life* (London, 1992).

8. V. Maksimov, *Zakony o razvode pravoslavnogo i nepravoslavnogo i razdel'nom zhitel'stve suprugov s raz"iasneniiami Pravitel'stvuiushchego Senata i tsirkuliarnymi i separatnymi ukazami Sviateishego Sinoda* (Moscow, 1909), 281.

9. Phillips, *Family Breakdown in Late Eighteenth-Century France: Divorces in Rouen, 1702–1803* (Oxford, 1980), 44–104; Nancy Cott, "Divorce and the Changing Status of Women in Eighteenth-Century Massachussetts," *William and Mary Quarterly*, 33 (1976):586–614; Sheldon S. Cohen, "To Parts of the World

Unknown: The Circumstances of Divorce in Connecticut, 1750–1797," *Canadian Review of American Studies* 11 (1980):275–93.

10. Phillips, *Putting Asunder,* 28–29.

11. In the Jewish case, a divorce was only recognized following the proper delivery of the *get* (bill of divorcement) to the wife (or her agent) by the husband (or his agent) in the presence of two witnesses.

12. Phillips, *Putting Asunder,* 4–6.

13. Ibid., 14.

14. For general works on the development and position of the Catholic Church on marriage and divorce, see G. H. Joyce, *Christian Marriage: An Historical and Doctrinal Study* (London, 1948); Charles E. Smith, *Papal Enforcement of Some Medieval Marriage Laws* (Baton Rouge, La., 1940).

15. The Gospel of Matthew had raised the possibility of divorce "for the cause of fornication" (Matthew 5:32; 19:9), a qualifying clause that cast some ambiguity on the absolute indissolubility of marriage.

16. J. Waterworth, trans., *Canons and Decrees of the Council of Trent* (London, 1948), 195.

17. Maksimov, *Zakony o razvode* (Moscow, 1909), 139, 258–59.

18. G. L. Freeze, "Bringing Order to the Russian Family. Marriage and Divorce in Imperial Russia," *Journal of Modern History* 62 (1990), 713, 719.

19. Maksimov, *Zakony o razvode,* 8.

20. Freeze, "Bringing Order," 719.

21. William Wagner, *Marriage, Property and the Struggle for Equality in Late Imperial Russia* (Oxford, 1994), 68, 70.

22. Freeze, "Bringing Order," 724, 745.

23. See Steven Ozment, *When Father Ruled: Family Life in Reformation Europe* (Cambridge, Mass., 1983).

24. Phillips, *Putting Asunder,* 44, 90. A collection of case studies on divorces during the time of John Calvin can be found in Robert M. Kingdon, *Adultery and Divorce in Calvin's Geneva* (Cambridge, Mass., 1995).

25. Maksimov, *Zakony o razvode,* 153.

26. Ibid., 278 (Karaite laws on divorce), 190 and 314 (Muslim laws on divorce). For the Jewish law on divorces by mutual consent, see *Shulhan Arukh, Even Haezer* hereafter *Shulhan Arukh, E.H. (Pithei teshuvah),* 134, 9; David Werner Amram, *The Jewish Law of Divorce According to Bible and Talmud* (Philadelphia, 1896), 39–40; "Divorce," *EJ,* 6:126.

27. Maksimov, *Zakony o razvode,* 278.

28. Salo Baron, *A Social and Religious History of the Jew,* 18 vols. (New York, 1952), 2:218; RGIA, f. 821, op. 821, d. 289, l. 109 ob. ("explanation" of the Rabbinic Commission regarding Jewish marriage and divorce, 13 March 1979).

29. Isaiah M. Gafni, "The Institution of Marriage in Rabbinic Times," in *The Jewish Family, Metaphor and Memory* (Oxford, 1989), 15.

30. Gittin 90b; Malachi 2:13–14.

31. Ibid., 119,3.

32. Judith Hauptman, *Rereading the Rabbis: A Woman's Voice* (Boulder, Colo., 1998), 103. See Gittin 90a–b.

33. Ze'ev Falk, *Jewish Matrimonial Law in the Middle Ages* (Oxford, 1966), 115, 116.

34. RGIA, f. 821, op. 8, d. 293, l. 198 (report of the St. Petersburg rabbinic congress in 1910).

35. See chap. 4 for details.

36. RGIA, f. 821, op. 9, d. 29, l. 6 ob. The discussion about the virginity of the bride begins in *Shulḥan Arukh, E.H.* (hilkhot ketubot), 68.

37. *Shulḥan Arukh, E.H.,* 68, 7.

38. The reference cited in the report of the Rabbinic Commission is incorrect; the correct citation is unclear from the context.

39. The requirement for eyewitnesses commenced in 1805; it was intended to be a public humiliation, which in turn would discourage casual divorce and deter fallacious confessions of adultery (done solely to secure dissolution of the marriage).

40. Num. 5:12.

41. Biale, *Women and Jewish Law* (New York, 1984), 189. See Sotah 27b.

42. For a comprehensive treatment of the "moredet" question, see Shlomo Riskin, *Women and Jewish Divorce: The Rebellious Wife, the Agunah and the Right to Initiate Divorce in Jewish Law, A Halakhic Solution* (Hoboken, N.J., 1989), 3–4. The quote is from Mishnah Ketuboth, 1:2.

43. Ibid., 5.

44. Ibid., 131; *Shulḥan Arukh, E.H.,* 77, 2.

45. Riskin, *Women and Jewish Divorce,* 131.

46. Rabbis were to warn the woman and give her a chance to return to her husband, but some state rabbis who were ignorant of Jewish law permitted divorces without waiting for the wife to respond. For examples, see chap. 2.

47. RGIA, f. 821, op. 9, d. 29, l. 6 ob.; *Shulḥan Arukh, E.H.,* 154, 12.

48. Yebamoth, 64a.

49. Yebamoth, 65b.

50. Ibid. For a full discussion of these grounds for divorce, see the discussion in the *Shulḥan Arukh, E.H.* 154.

51. Amram, *Jewish Law of Divorce,* 45.

52. Ibid., 46. For Maimonides' views, see his treatise *Gerushin,* 10, 23.

53. For example, see RGIA, f. 821, op. 8, d. 296, ll. 81–86. A metrical book for divorce in the city of Khar'kov registered a single divorce based on the "insanity of the wife" (see DAKhO, f. 958, op. 1, g. 1885, d. 80, ll. 2 ob.–3).

54. RGIA, f. 281, op. 8, d. 296, ll. 81–86.

55. Biale, *Women and Jewish Law,* 84–85. For the laws, see *Shulḥan Arukh, E.H..,* 154, 1 and also Ketuboth, 77a.

56. Amram, *Jewish Law of Divorce,* 68. See the opinion of Rabbi Solomon ben Adereth in *Shulḥan Arukh, E.H.,* 20, 3 (The Rema or Rabbi Moses Isserles).

57. DAKhO, f. 958, op. 1, g. 1901, d. 108, ll. 6 ob.–7; LVIA, f. 728, op. 2, d. 6, g. 1837–38.

58. DAKhO, f. 958, op. 1, g. 1901, d. 108, ll. 6 ob.–7. It is unclear from the file whether the husband was unable or simply unwilling to support his estranged wife any longer.

59. Amram, *Jewish Law of Divorce,* 69.

60. *Shulḥan Arukh, E.H.,* 76, 11.

61. Biale, *Women and Jewish Law,* 122.

62. For more on the tension between Torah study and marital obligations in the Talmud, see Daniel Boyarin, *Carnal Israel: Reading Sex in Talmudic Culture* (Berkeley, Calif., 1993), 134–66.

63. Amram, *Jewish Law of Divorce,* 71 as cited from Moses Isserles, *Darkhei Moshe, Tur, E.H.* starting on 154, 3.

64. Biale, *Women and Jewish Law,* 95.

65. Amram, *Jewish Law of Divorce*, 65.

66. RGIA, f. 821, op. 8, d. 289, l. 129 ob.–130.

67. For more on Jewish women who turned to the state for redress of marital grievances, see ChaeRan Y. Freeze, "The Litigious *Gerusha*: Jewish Women and Divorce in Imperial Russia," *Nationalities Papers* 25:1 (1997): 89–101.

68. A. A. Alekseev, *Ocherki domashnei i obshchestvennoi zhizni evreev*, 218; "Beit-din," *EE*, 4 (1991 [reprint]): 106–13.

69. *Shulhan Arukh, E.H.*, in Seder haget following section 154.

70. RGIA, f. 821, op. 8, d. 369, ll. 1–14 (divorce suit of Getsel and Gita Borshch).

71. *Shulhan Arukh, E.H.*, Seder haget, 2, notation 7.

72. Ibid., Seder haget, 9.

73. Ibid., Seder haget, 10 and 12.

74. The discussion about the delivery of the *get* begins in *Shulhan Arukh, E.H.*, 132.

75. The following section comes from *Shulhan Arukh, E.H.*, Seder haget, 2 (notation 7), 9–15, 39–96.

76. The numerical value of the Hebrew word *get* was 12—hence, the twelve lines of the text.

77. This entire section comes from RGIA, f. 821, op. 9, d. 289, ll. 37, 39, 41–43, 46 ob.–47, 52, 54, *Sara Shnaper vs. Yankel Shnaper*.

78. *Shulhan Arukh, E.H.*, Seder haget, 101.

79. Amram, *Jewish Law of Divorce*, 142.

80. Phillips, *Putting Asunder*, 315.

81. Throughout, divorce rate means divorces per 1,000 marriages; although imprecise, it is the index most often used in the literature and provides a useful correlation between the absolute numbers of divorce and the demography of a given group.

82. LVIA, f. 728, op. 2, d. 6, l. 15 (data for 19 October 1837–1838).

83. LVIA, f. 728, op. 2, d. 28 (data for 1845).

84. *Izvlecheniia iz otcheta po vedomstvu dukhovnykh del pravoslavnogo ispovedaniia* (St. Petersburg, 1837–63).

85. Mordechai Aaron Guenzburg, *Aviezer* (Vil'na, 1863), 104.

86. Yehudah Shereshevskii, *Kur lezahav* (Vil'na 1858), 214.

87. Israel Yuval, "Takanot neged ribui gerushin begermanyah bemeah ha-15" *Zion*, 48:2 (1983): 177–215.

88. Jacob Goldberg, "Jewish Marriage in Eighteenth-Century Poland," *Polin* 10 (1997): 9.

89. S. Staszic, *Ród ludzki*, ed. Z. Daszkowski and B. Suchodolski, iii (Warsaw, 1959), 288–89 as cited in Jacob Goldberg, "Jewish Marriage," *Polin* 10 (1997): 9.

90. Ibid., 9–10.

91. Goldberg, "Jewish Marriage," 11–12. For example, the author described a case in which a Jewish resident of Tarnów complained that he suspected a local Jewish delegate to the regional council of having a sexual affair with his wife ("he was seen to leave her at midnight dressed only in a shirt and a Polish nobleman's robe"). He also cited records of *mukat ets* (the accidental loss of virginity), couples who engaged in premarital sex, sexual liaisons between Jewish men and Polish women or Jewish wives and Polish townsmen.

92. Thus, the conscience court handled such matters as infanticide (e.g., the case of Tsipe Beniaminovna, accused of killing her newborn infant in 1845, in LVIA, f. 456, op. 2, d. 219), sexual licentiousness (e.g., the 1850 file on Sora Katsevna, accused of fornication and living "a depraved life" [ibid., d. 107]),

rape (e.g., the 1845 case of Noselia Gordon, based on the accusation of Rivka Gol'dinova [ibid., d. 894]), and even bestiality (the 1842 case of Leib Movshovich Anellevich, seen "on a cow in an improper position" [ibid., d. 175]).

93. LVIA, f. 456, op. 2, d. 1124, ll. 18–19 (counterpetition of Pesia Bershtelova, 1851).

94. Although Moses Isserles' glosses to the *Shulhan Aruch* did not compel a man to divorce his wife after ten years of childlessness (so that he could fulfill the commandment of procreation), it was not uncommon in Vil'na for men to dissolve their marriages on these grounds until the mid-nineteenth century. See *Shulhan Aruch, E.H.,* 1,3.

95. The Statutes of 1804 prohibited Jews from leasing taverns, pubs, or inns, part of a broader policy of forced expulsions from the rural areas. Although the law was observed largely in the breach, it began to have a detrimental impact on the economy of the western provinces. In 1845, the government introduced a new "compromise," which permitted only Jewish guild merchants to engage in the vodka trade. As a result, Stanislawski observes that although common townspeople *(meshchane)* sold vodka illegally, they were gradually driven out of the market. The Jewish economy was exacerbated by the decline of seasonal fairs and the distribution of factory products directly to customers, making the role of peddlers and traveling traders obsolete. Michael Stanislawski, *Tsar Nicholas I and the Jews* (Philadelphia, 1983), 170–82.

96. As the metrical books reveal, some men were forced to divorce their spouses for wife beating, violating Jewish laws, cursing their in-laws, and behaving indecently. In all these cases, the Vil'na *beit-din* authorized the marital dissolution.

97. Grodno, Kovno, Ekaterinoslav, Tavrida, Poltava, Kherson, and Chernigov.

98. RGIA, f. 821, op. 8, d. 482, ll. 1–17 ob. See table 3.3.

99. Kovno, Kherson, and Ekaterinoslav were not included.

100. Wagner, *Marriage, Property and Law,* 70.

101. See Figure 11.1 in Roderick Phillips, *Putting Asunder,* cited in Paul H. Jacobson and Pauline F. Jacobson, *American Marriage and Divorce* (New York, 1959), 90; *Historical Statistics of the United States, 1789–1945,* 49.

102. RGIA, f. 821, op. 9, d. 479. ll. 15–16 (Kishinev), l. 19 (Vil'na).

103. For the exact rates, see Appendix, tables A.9–A.17.

104. Immanuel Etkes, "Marriage and Torah Study among the *Lomdim,*" in *The Jewish Family, Metaphor and Meaning,* 154.

105. RGIA, f. 821, op. 8, d. 291, l. 92.

106. For these figures, see Simon Kuznets, "Immigration of Russian Jews to the United States: Background and Structure," *Perspectives in American History* 9(1975): 35–124, esp. pp. 116–17.

107. The regional difference is probably exaggerated because Jews in Vil'na were less meticulous about recording divorce, perhaps because local officials there were less frenetic about enforcing registration (above all, to control urban migration) than in the southwest. There is even some confirmation in modern practices; according to Aryeh Edrei, similar patterns of noncompliance with registration laws persist among the *mitnagdim* in present-day Israel.

108. DAKO, f. 1, op. 142, d. 926. ll. 1–148.

109. TsGIA, f. 633, op. 1, dd. 63–204. See Appendix, table A.21.

110. DAKhO, f. 958, op. 1, dd. 3–117. See Appendix, table A.21.

111. See Appendix, tables A.20, A.21.

112. LVIA, f. 728, op. 3, dd. 82, 89 (there were corrections added on the last page

of the metrical book that are not included in the calculations). Similarly, in 1871, there were 39 divorces to 269 marriages, a rate of 145.0 (dd. 89, 90, 91, 1176).

113. LVIA, f. 728, op. 3. dd. 1090, 1091, 1410.

114. *Nedel'naia khronika Voskhoda* 20 (15 May 1882), 534–55; translated in Mendes-Flohr and Reinharz, *The Jew in the Modern World* (Oxford, 1980), 309.

115. LVIA, f. 728, op. 4, d. 376; RGIA, f. 821, pp. 8, d. 49, ll. 19–21.

116. See Appendix, tables A.22 and A.23.

117. Wagner, *Marriage, Property, and Law,* 70.

118. Letters between Isaac Lur'e, the administrative secretary for *Evreiskaia starina,* and his teenage nephew, Arush Khavkin of Moscow, reflect a growing ethnic consciousness among some acculturated youth. In a letter dated 18 December 1916, Khavkin admitted: "No, I am not acquainted with our language, national literature, or the history of the Jews. . . . In childhood, I studied Hebrew and spoke it fairly fluently but I only studied it because my father insisted on it. . . . A national consciousness was completely absent in me . . . [in fact] I was ashamed that I was a Jew." Lur'e sent him a copy of Simon Dubnow's book, which the young man had requested. TsGIA-St. Petersburg, f. 2129, op. 3, d. 106.

119. See Appendix, table A.24.

120. See Appendix, table A.21.

121. TsDIAK-Ukraïny, f. 663, op. 1, d. 132, ll. 4 ob.–5.

122. See table 1.1.

123. Shaul Stampfer, "Remarriage among Jews and Christians in Nineteenth-Century Eastern Europe," *Jewish History* 3 (1988): 86.

124. D. Brutskus, *Statistika evreiskogo naseleniia* (St. Petersburg, 1909): 24.

125. Phillips, *Putting Asunder,* 318.

126. There have been exceptions (as in Stalinist Russia) whereby the state, for its own reasons, artificially imposed barriers in an attempt to stem the divorce revolution. Still, the dominant pattern, since the early nineteenth century, has been for the divorce rate to grow, sometimes at a spectacular pace.

127. ChaeRan Y. Freeze, "The Litigious Gerusha: Jewish Women and Divorce in Imperial Russia," *Nationalities Papers* 25:1 (1997):89–101.

128. Kantseliariia ego Imperatorskogo Velichestva po prinatiiu proshenii (1884–1917).

129. For more on this body, see S. N. Pisarev, *Uchrezhdenie po priniatiiu i napravleniiu proshenii i zhalob, prinosimykh na Vysochaishee imia, 1810–1910* (St. Petersburg, 1911).

130. Russian law defined a woman's status on the basis of her father's (prior to marriage) or her husband's; hence, separation, entailing no dissolution of the marital nexus, served to protect any privileges while insulating the woman from the obligatory cohabitation.

131. LVIA, f. 728, op. 2, d. 6, g. 1837–8.

132. RGIA, f. 821, op. 9, d. 16, l. 16. Letter from Sara Shternfel'd to the Rabbi of Kovno, translated from Hebrew into Russian (30 June 1881).

133. M. G. Gershfel'd, "K voprosuo zhenskom obrazovanii u evreev," *Russkii evrei,* 6(1880):205.

134. RGIA, f. 821, op. 8, d. 289, l. 66 (testimony of Grigorii Bagrov).

135. Wengeroff, *Memoirs,* unpublished translation of *Memoiren einer Grossmutter* by Jay Harris.

136. RGIA, f. 1412, op. 228, d. 23, l. 56.

137. Abraham Simchah Sachs, *Horeve veltn* (New York, 1917), 12–13.

138. RGIA, f. 1412 (His Imperial Majesty's Chancellery for the Receipt of Petitions), op. 223, d. 49, ll. 1–4.

139. LVIA, f. 728, op. 2, d. 6.

140. RGIA, f. 1412, op. 213, d. 1, l. 1.

141. Chaim Tchernowitz, *Pirkei hayim* (New York, 1954), 27.

142. RGIA, f. 1412, op. 213, d. 36, ll. 1–7.

143. Lilienblum, *Ketavim autobiyografiyim: Hatot neurim* (Jerusalem, Bialik Institute, 1970), 124.

144. RGIA, f. 821, op. 8, d. 289, l. 66.

145. For the law regarding the obligation to support needy parents, see *Svod zakonov* (1857), x, pt. 1, art. 194.

146. RGIA, f. 1412, op. 223, d. 49, l. 4 ob. Letter of response from Solomon Meerson to charges brought against him by his wife.

147. As in the case of pre-reform state courts (and the Orthodox Church), judges relied on the formal written evidence and were strictly forbidden to exercise personal discretion, even when common sense told them that the evidence was patently false, manufactured, and illogical.

148. RGIA, f. 821, op. 8, d. 349, ll. 1–22 ob. Yankel M. Maizil'son vs. Meer Aizinshtat (2 November 1857–25 July 1858).

149. Gottlober, *Zikhronot umasaot* (Jerusalem, 1976), 243, 245.

150. Ben Zion Dinur, introduction to *Mikhtavei Avraham Mapu* (Jerusalem, 1970), 21, 29. There are more than forty letters from Avraham Mapu to his brother concerning his first marriage and divorce.

151. RGIA, f. 1412, op. 223, d. 49, l. 4.

152. LVIA, f. 456, op. 2, d. 1075, ll. 88, 104.

153. LVIA, f. 728, op. 2, d. 77 (1845).

154. Zborowski and Herzog, *Life Is with People,* 300.

155. See chap. 4 about the growing legal consciousness among Jewish women in Russia.

156. Wagner, *Marriage, Property and Law,* 95. Not until 1914 did the state finally modify its passport laws to permit, on a routine basis, separate residence and hence *de facto* marital separation for women of all faiths.

157. Although a few sensational cases made headlines, these seem to be the exception; provincial files, at least, do not indicate substantial attempt to recover fugitive wives. What women needed was less protection against forcible return than a passport to reside separately in the cities.

158. RGIA, f. 1412, op. 231, d. 1, ll. 1–22 (case of Dora Faivilevich, 1912). As David Sabean's study of property and family in Neckarhausen has shown, the transformation of marriage from a patriarchal, economy-based union to a companionate partnership led some husbands to use physical violence to reassert their diminishing control over their *Herrschaft.* Sabean, *Property, Production, and Family in Neckarhausen, 1700–1870* (Cambridge, 1990), 133–38.

159. For another example, see RGIA, f. 821, op. 9, d. 16, l. 16.

160. RGIA, f. 821, op. 9, d. 16, ll. 16–17.

161. RGIA, f. 821, op. 8, d. 291, ll. 17–18.

162. RGIA, f. 821, op. 9. d. 54, l. 69.

163. The problem of wife-beating figured far more prominently among the general Russian population in the official records, especially from the lowest social strata. For example, out of 1899 total petitions filed to the Imperial Chancellery for the Receipt of Petitions, 1523 or 80 percent of the suits were from

wives of peasants (including factory workers) and members of unprivileged urban estates. Petitions from wives of the nobility, civil officials, and officers only constituted twelve percent of those who applied for a separate passport. Wagner, *Marriage, Property and Law,* 97.

164. RGIA, f. 1412, op. 223, d. 49, l. 1.

165. The ages of husbands, who were forced to divorce their wives, ranged from 20 to 50.

166. Levitats, *The Jewish Community in Russia, 1772–1844,* 209.

167. Nancy Tomes, "'A Torrent of Abuse:' Crimes of Violence Between Working-Class Men and Women in London," *Journal of Social History* 11:3 (1978):328–49.

168. James Hammerton, *Cruelty and Companionship: Conflict in Nineteenth-Century Married Life* (New York, 1992).

169. For more on public responses to alcoholism, see Patricia Herlihy, *The Alcoholic Empire: Vodka and Politics in Late Imperial Russia* (Oxford, 2001).

170. RGIA, f. 1412, op. 1, d. 734, ll. 1–9 (Petition of Dveira Aizikovich to the Imperial Chancellery for the Receipt of Petitions (3 June 1882–1884).

171. RGIA, f. 821, op. 9, d. 18, ll. 16–17. Poliakov versus Poliakov; f. 821, op. 8, d. 291, l. 9 ob.–10 ob. (Journal of the Rabbinic Commission in 1893).

172. Phillips, *Putting Asunder,* 344.

173. See Keith Thomas, "The Double Standard," *Journal of the History of Ideas* 20 (1959):210 ff; G. R. Quaife, *Wanton Wenches and Wayward Wives* (London, 1979).

174. TsDIAK-Ukraïny, f. 442, op. 160, d. 42, ch. 1, l. 482

175. RGIA, f. 1412, op. 219, d. 15, l. 2 (petition of Khaia Sima Zak, 8 February 1889).

176. In the end, the wife punished her husband by withholding their child from him even though their separation agreement permitted the father to see his daughter for two weeks every year. See ibid., l. 70 (signed affidavit of Khaia Zak permitting her husband to see his daughter), l. 90. (complaint of Girsh Zak against his wife for withholding their daughter from him, 31 August 1900).

177. TsDIAK-Ukraïny, f. 442, op. 160, d. 42, ch. 1, l. 482.

178. In response, the Rabbinic Commission outlined the following process of "Jewish penance": "for greater transgressions [e.g. adultery resulting in the birth of an illegitimate child], the guilty individual was to be subjected "to forty days of fasting, in addition to begging for alms, . . . spread out over a period of three to six months or more, depending on the [individual's] health." The adulterer was required "to abstain for one to two years from social entertainment, feasts and hot beverages and to read the book of Psalms once every month." A minor form of penance involved "twenty days of fasting, together with begging for alms over a period of six to twelve months or more, depending on the individual's health"; the rest of the penance was similar to one described above. For the penance *(epitimiia)* of Russian Orthodox, see Gregory L. Freeze, "Public Penance in Imperial Russia: A Prosopography of Sinners," in *Seeking God: The Recovery of Religious Identity in Orthodox Russia, Ukraine, and Georgia,* ed. Stephen K. Batalden (DeKalb, 1993), 53–82.

179. RGIA, f. 821, op. 8, d. 496.

180. Significantly, the authorities virtually ceased to prosecute those who cohabited; such prosecutions gradually disappear in 1880s and 1890s, with a formal abrogation of punishment finally being issued in 1902.

181. RGIA, f. 1412, op. 213, d. 101, ll. 1–236 ob. (case of Leia Broun,

1900–1901). The Imperial Chancellery abrogated its former decision and gave the father custody of the two children when it found out the wife was having an affair with a revolutionary.

182. RGIA, f. 1412, op. 221, d. 2, l. 29.

183. RGIA, f. 1412, op. 228, d. 23, l. 56. (petition of Ester Saet to the Imperial Chancellery)

184. Lynn Abrams, "Companionship and Conflict," *Gender Relations in German History*, 115.

185. For a rereading of rabbinic texts about procreation from a woman's perspective, see Judith Hauptmann, *Rereading the Rabbis*, 130–46.

186. LVIA, f. 1240, op. 1, d. 36, l. 2 ob.

187. Anne L. Lapidus, "Lost Childhood in East European Hebrew Literature," in *The Jewish Family: Metaphor and Memory*, 99.

188. Debate over adoption became an important public issue in the late Imperial period. Essentially, the strict prohibition derived from state *soslovie* (estate) law, which ascribed status to a child on the basis of the father's juridical status at the moment of birth; a socially conservative state was highly reluctant to allow large-scale changes in status (as adoption inevitably entailed). For more on adoption in Imperial Russia, see Wagner, *Marriage, Property and Law*, 72–73.

189. RGIA, f. 1412, op. 8, d. 312, l. 1 (13 October 1909). Unfortunately, the file contained no resolution to their case—in all likelihood, an indication that the petition was rejected.

190. The Chancellery received numerous petitions from Jews seeking to adopt various family members who became orphaned through the tragic deaths of their parents. For examples, see RGIA, f. 1412, op. 8, d. 299 (petition of Dvoira Zelikman to adopt her orphaned grandson); f. 1412, op. 9, d. 319 (petition of Hillel Iozifovich to adopt his orphaned grandson); f. 1412, op. 2, d. 499 (petition of Siman Belin to adopt a daughter).

191. Devorah Baron, "Family," *The Thorny Path* (Jerusalem, 1969), 31.

192. RGIA, f. 821, op. 8, d. 289, ll. 90–92 ob.(Grinshtein vs. Grinshtein, December 1875).

193. Judith R. Baskin, "Rabbinic Reflections on the Barren Wife," *Harvard Theological Review* 82:1 (1989):112.

194. Unfortunately, the reference in the file to *Sedei hemed* was incorrect and I have been unable to locate the correct passage.

195. For example, see entry no. 8 in the 1860 metrical book of divorce. LVIA, f. 728, op. 2, d. 273.

196. Rose Shomer-Bachelis, *Unzer foter Shomer*, 14–15.

197. The Russian Orthodox Church allowed annulment (if the mental illness was premarital, hence precluding a valid marital sacrament) but not divorce for postmarital insanity. By the late nineteenth century calls to liberalize steadily gained in popularity, but did not elicit a change until the Church Council of 1917–1918. See Gregory Freeze, "L'Ortodossa russa e la crisi della famiglia," in *L'autunno della Santa Russia*, ed. Adalberto Mainardi (Magnano, 1999), 79–118.

198. RGIA, f. 821, op. 8, d. 296, l. 85 ob.

199. Dr. Nikolai Pirogov (1810–1881) was a prominent surgeon who became deeply involved in the debate on women's education, starting in the mid-nineteenth century. His works can be found in N. I. Pirogov, *Sevastopol'skie pis'ma i vospominaniia* (Moscow, 1950); *Sobranie sochinenii*, 8 vols. (Moscow, 1957–1960); and *Sochineniia*, 2 vols. (St. Petersburg, 1900). For the Pirogov society, see Nancy M. Frieden, *Russian Physicians in an Era of Reform and Revolution, 1856–1905*

(Princeton, N.J., 1981), and John F. Hutchinson, *The Cleansing Hurricane: Politics and Public Health in Revolutionary Russia, 1890–1918* (Baltimore, 1990).

200. RGIA, f. 821, op. 8, d. 296, l. 81–86.

201. Both factors—premarital insanity and fraudulent representation—*were* valid grounds for divorce for the Russian Orthodox Church; that may have served as the model for the suit here.

202. RGIA, f. 821, op. 8, d. 366, ll. 1–28 (Kissin vs. Mysh divorce suit). In the end, Kissin moved to Lodz, where he persuaded another rabbi to grant the divorce. Later, in response to an inquiry from the Rabbinic Commission, he claimed to have secured the signatures of 100 rabbis from Austria-Hungary and Poland and that his local rabbi in Kovno had recognized the signatures as valid.

203. Phillips, *Putting Asunder,* 511.

204. After Anton Alekseev Davidov (formerly David Gofberg) converted to Orthodoxy in 1851, he immediately abandoned the Pale and his Jewish wife, moving to Khar'kov (to which Jewish merchants were admitted only during the great commercial fairs). RGIA, f. 821, op. 8, d. 348, l. 1.

205. RGIA, f. 797 (Chancellery of the Chief Procurator *[ober-prokuror]* of the Holy Synod), op. 92, d. 120, l. 7 (statute of 9 April 1851, citing a law first enacted by the state in 1835).

206. Ibid., ll. 8 ob.–9 (decision of the Senate on the Rubenshtern and Brozgal case, 27 August 1852).

207. Ibid., l. 4 (report of the governor of Moscow, 31 August 1899).

208. Ibid., ll. 10–11 (case of Isaak Gurkov; his first petition was filed on 18 March 1892).

209. Ibid., ll. 5 ob.–6 ob. (proposal of the chief procurator and Senate, 2 January 1901).

210. Ibid., ll. 21–22 ob.

211. Ibid.

212. Ibid., ll. 22 ob.–23, 33–36 ob. By the time the Senate had resolved to permit the Niurenbergs to reside in Moscow in 1904, the couple had already divorced, apparently in order to retain their residence permits. Upon the dissolution of their marriage, they could not marry each other again unless the wife converted to Christianity.

213. "Post-reform" *(poreformennyi)* is the shorthand term for describing Russian state and society after the Great Reforms of the 1860s.

214. Wagner, *Marriage, Property, and Law,* 85.

215. For the women's movement in the empire, see the survey account in Richard Stites, *The Women's Liberation Movement* (Princeton, 1968), 64–232.

216. Michael Stanislawski, *For Whom Do I Toil? Judah Leib Gordon and the Crisis of Russian Jewry* (Oxford, 1988), 125.

217. David Biale, "The Jewish Family in the East European Jewish Enlightenment," 55; see also "Zhenskii vopros u evreev," *Vestnik russkikh evreev* 1(1873):1–5.

218. A. Zeidder, "O zhenskom obrazovanii," *Rassvet* 40 (1861):638–39; I. Likub, "Chastnoe evreiskoe devich'e uchilishche," *Rassvet* 4 (1860):54; *Russkii evrei* 3 (1884):3–5; E. Iampol'skaia, "Nechto o zhenskom obrazovanii u evreev," *Russkii evrei* 20 (1880):780–81.

219. *Russkii evrei* 7 (17 October 1879):218–19; see also A. Zeidder,"O zhenskom obrazovanii," 638–39.

220. RGIA, f. 821, op. 9, d. 2, l. 6 (Report of the Rabbinic Commission, composed of Zagel Rappoport, Yankel Barit, Solomon Gurovich, and Abram Chlenov).

221. Ibid., l. 8. The commission defined the ideal wife as the "woman of valor" described by King Solomon in Proverbs.

222. Christine Johanson, *Women's Struggle for Higher Education in Russia, 1855–1900* (Kingston, 1987), 29. For general studies on the development of women's education in Russia, see E. Likhacheva, ed., *Materialy dlia istorii zhenshogo obrazovaniia v Rossii, 1856–1880* (St. Petersburg, 1901); Ruth Dudgeon, "Women and Higher Education in Russia, 1855–1905" (Ph.D. diss., George Washington University, Washington, D.C., 1975).

223. Johanson, *Women's Struggle*, 29–30.

224. A list of some of these private Jewish women's schools can be found in V. E. Kel'ner and D. A. El'iashevich, eds. *Literatura o evreiakh na russkom iazyke, 1890–1947* (St. Petersburg, 1995), 346–58.

225. DAOO, f. 42, op. 1, dd. 6–32.

226. "Iuridicheskii otdel," *Evreiskii mir* 4 (1910): 3.

227. "Vnutrenniaia khronika," *Russkii evrei* 6 (10 October 1879):191.

228. Sara Rabinovich, "K zhenskomu voprosu u evreev," *Evreiskii mir* 1 (1909):26.

229. The school had far lower proportions of Roman Catholics (3.2 percent), Lutherans (3.0 percent), and miscellaneous other groups (1.6 percent).

230. These figures are confirmed by the Russian-Jewish press: see "Evreiki-studentki," *Rassvet* 37 (1880):1465–66. For a brief biography of one of the first Jewish women (Anna Gertsenshtein) to complete her education in the medical-surgical hospital in Nikolaev, see "Pervaia evreika-studentka v Rossii," *Russkii evrei* 27 (188):1071–72.

231. Johanson, *Women's Struggle*, 45, 69, 82–83. For examples of Jewish women who successfully completed their medical courses and began their careers in Zhitomir, see DAZhO, f. 67, op. 4, d. 93 (Polina Kulisher); f. 67, op. 4, d. 74 (Gilda Rukhel Kaminer). There are over twenty-five files of Jewish women doctors and nurses in this collection.

232. "Vnutrenniaia khronika," *Russkii evrei* 2 (1879):45.

233. Johanson, *Women's Struggle*, 25. For her autobiography, see Toby W. Clyman and Judith Vowles, eds., *Russia Through Women's Eyes. Autobiographies from Tsarist Russia* (New Haven, Conn., 1996), 158–85.

234. RGIA, f. 1412, op. 215, op. 104, ll. 1–5 ob. (petitions of Chaim Grinshtein, 1 December 1899 and Revka Grinshtein, 17 November 1901).

235. Yeshaya Heshl Perelstein, *Zikhronot shel naar toeh* (*Memoirs of an Errant Man*), as translated by Eli Lederhendler, in *Jewish Responses to Modernity* (New York, 1994), 64.

236. Pauline Wengeroff, *Memoirs,* unpublished translation by Jay Harris.

237. Marion Kaplan, *The Making of the Jewish Middle Class* (Oxford, 1991), 64–84.

238. Isaac Bashevis Singer, *In My Father's Court* (New York, 1966), 51.

239. Wengeroff, *Memoirs,* unpublished translation by Jay Hams.

240. Singer, *In My Father's Court,* 288.

241. RGIA, f. 1412, op. 213, d. 101, l. 133.

242. See Barbara Engel, *Between the Fields and the City* (Cambridge, England, 1996).

243. For example, while 43 percent of Jewish grooms were under the age of twenty years in 1867, by 1895 over 50 percent of men were over twenty-five years of age at first marriage. Later marriage was also true of Jewish brides: by 1902, more than three-fourths of Jewish women were over twenty years old at

their first marriage, and of this group almost one-third were over twenty-five. See Appendix, table A.8.

244. According to one study by the Jewish Colonization Association in 1898, there were 76,548 registered Jewish women artisans or 15.3 percent of the total number Jewish artisans in Russia. Of these, 53,964 (approximately 70 percent) of the female artisans worked in the garment industry as milliners, modistes, tailors, seamstresses, and stocking makers. See Sara Rabinovich, "K vo prosu o nachal'nom remeslennom obrazovanii evreiskikh zhenshchin," 9–10. The original data can be found in Jewish Colonization Association, *Recueil de matériaux sur la situation éonomique des Israelites de Russie,* 2 vols. (Paris, 1906–1908), 1:251, 255, 285.

245. Arcadius Kahan, "Impact of Industrialization in Tsarist Russia," in *Essays in Jewish Social and Economic History,* ed. Roger Weiss (Chicago, 1986), 65, n. 14.

246. The official report of the Imperial Chancellery showed that the husband's actual age according to the metrical books was eighty-six and the wife's age was thirty-three—a fifty-three-year age gap. According to the government's investigation, the husband received a pension of six rubles a month.

247. RGIA, f. 1412, op. 219, d. 11, l. 1–22 (case of Dveira Gita Zaets, 22 August 1905).

248. Sara Rabinovich, "K voprosu o nachal'nom remeslennom obrazovanii evreiskikh zhenshchin, 9–19; and "K zhenskomu voprosy u evreev (po povodu zhenskogo s"czda)," *Evreiskii mir* 1 (1909):27–28.

249. Biale, "The Jewish Family in the Eastern European Jewish Enlightenment," 57, citing Abraham Mapu, *Mikhtavim* (26 October 1862), p. 133.

250. David Biale, "The Jewish Family in the East European Jewish Enlightenment," 57.

4. Kritut: Negotiating the Divorce Agreement and Unresolved Issues

1. RGIA, f. 821, op. 8, d. 289, ll. 55–88 ob.

2. RGIA, f. 1412, op. 1, d. 734.

3. M. G. Gershfel'd, "K voprosu o zhenskom obrazovanii u evreev," *Russkii evrei,* 6 (1880):205.

4. "Dowry," *EJ,* 6 (1973):186.

5. RGIA, f. 821, op. 8, d. 291, ll. 92–93 (journal entry of the Rabbinic Commission regarding the proper form and meaning of the Jewish marriage contract, 21 December 1893). According to Jewish law, the proportion of the increment was subject to local customs; normally, it varied from one-third to one-half of the total amount of the dowry.

6. Amram, *The Jewish Law of Divorce* (Philadelphia, 1896), 122.

7. Epstein, *The Jewish Marriage Contract* (New York, 1927), 210–12.

8. Ibid., 213; Ketuboth 72 a–b, Gittin 90b, Sotah 25b, Ketuboth 7, 6–7.

9. Ibid., 213; Ketuboth 71a, 72a.

10. Lilienblum, *Hatot neurim* (Jerusalem, 1970).

11. RGIA, f. 821, op. 9, d. 289, ll. 29 ob.–35 ob. (journal of the Rabbinic Commission,1879). Gitlia Kramer filed a suit against her husband in a Volyhnia state court for divorcing her against her will based on his accusation that she did not observe Jewish laws of *niddah.*

12. Riskin, *Women and Jewish Divorce* (Hoboken, N.J., 1989), 131. For the original quote, see *Shulhan Arukh, E.H. 77, 2.*

13. In this case, the wife is entitled to the entire *nikhsei tson barzel,* which is the "capital value of the property at the time of [the husband's] receipt thereof, even if it should suffer loss or depreciation." Even if this property had been stolen or lost, the husband was responsible for paying its entire value. She also had the right to retrieve her *nikhsei melog* ("plucked property"), which was "property of which the principal remained in the wife's ownership but the fruits thereof were taken by the husband so that he had no responsibility or rights in respect of the principal, both its loss and gain being only hers." See: Riskin, *Women and Jewish Divorce,* 132–33; "Dowry," *EJ* 6 (1973):186–87.

14. Riskin, *Women and Jewish Divorce,* 133.

15. Epstein, *Jewish Marriage Contract,* 214. For a more detailed description of these defects (such as the definition of a mole that is regarded as a bodily defect), see Ketuboth 75a,

16. It is not clear how strictly or frequently such rules were invoked; the archives, at any rate, hold few references to them.

17. RGIA, f. 821, op. 8, d. 291, ll. 87–88. In 1872, the *Vilenskii vestnik* also observed that the accessibility of the new courts prompted many Jews in Vil'na to abandon the traditional *beit-din* in favor of the secular courts. "Ob otnoshenii vilenskikh evreev k sudu," *Vilenskii vestnik* 241 (1872).

18. Ibid., l. 89 ob.

19. See ChaeRan Y. Freeze, "The Litigious *Gerusha:* Jewish Women and Divorce in Imperial Russia," *Nationalities Papers* 25:1 (1997):89–401.

20. For example, see Beatrice Farnsworth, "The Litigious Daughter-in-Law: Family Relations in Rural Russia in the Second Half of the Nineteenth Century," in Beatrice Farnsworth and Lynn Viola, eds., *Russian Peasant Women* (Oxford: Oxford University Press, 1992), 89–106. In the biannual reports filed by low-ranking "deans" of the Church, there were numerous complaints about the "profusion of frivolous litigation," which allegedly exacerbated social tensions and led to corruption in the courts. See Gregory Freeze, "Russian Orthodoxy on the Periphery: Decoding the Raporty Blagochinnykh in Lithuania Diocese," in B. Anan'ich et al., eds., *Problemy vsemirnoi istorii* (St. Petersburg, 2000), 127.

21. For examples of suits filed in the Zhitomir civil courts, see DAZhO, f. 24, op. 3, g. 1888, d. 1134 (suit of T. E. Fogelia and her daughter to receive the inheritance left by the late husband); f. 24, op. 7, d. 153 (suit of a widow, E. I. Gershberg, to receive her rightful property and money out of her husband's estate); f. 24, op. 3, g. 1888, d. 764 (suit of the widow of B. A. Gokhfel'd). For a complete list of civil suits regarding property and monetary disputes over wills and last testaments, see f. 24, opisi 2–10, where virtually every third item involved a Jewish case.

22. For examples, see DAZhO, f. 170, op. 1, d. 265 (Leia Keizerman vs. Itsak Leib and Ester Rozenbaum for unpaid services valued at 10 rubles) and f. 170, op. 1, d. 322 (Rukhli Vakser vs. Leib and Khana Unikel for 10 rubles).

23. Examples of suits brought by relatives against each other can be found in DAZhO, f. 24, op. 7, d. 117 (confirmation of the decision of the arbitration court in the altercation between A. Zil'bershvein and B. Zil'bershvein in 1900); f. 24, op. 7, d. 1453 (confirmation of the decision of the arbitration court in the altercation between Ia. Fel'dman and I. Fel'dman).

24. DAZhO, f. 62 (Zhitomir City Board), op. 1, d. 989, ll. 1–60 (Rozentsvaig vs. Rabinovich, 1877–1885).

25. For a good example, see DAZhO, f. 24, op.2, d. 145 (suit of Rozalii D. Eske against her husband, L. Yakovlev Eske, for 1,570 rubles in 1880).

26. By the late nineteenth century there was a significant contingent of Jewish attorneys, especially in the two capitals. In St. Petersburg, 22 percent of all sworn lawyers and 42.5 percent of attorneys-in-training were Jewish in 1889. *Vysochaishe uchrezhdennaia pri Ministerstve Iustitsii Kommisiia* (St. Petersburg, 1897), 113–14. See also William Pomeranz, "'Profession or Estate'? The Case of the Russian Pre-Revolutionary *Advokatura*," *Slavic and East European Review* 77:2 (April 1999): 251–53; Benjamin Nathans, "Beyond the Pale: The Jewish Encounter with Russia" (Ph.D. diss., University of California, Berkeley, 1995), 248–340.

27. TsIAM, f. 1457, op. 1, d. 40, l. 9. This was the standard language used in most of the divorce petitions.

28. RGIA, f. 821, op. 9, d. 137, l. 50 (report of the Jewish Committee in Volhynia province, 1881). The main complaint was about the exploitation of Christian peasants by the so-called Jewish lawyers, who were allegedly well versed in neither the Russian language nor the law.

29. RGIA, f. 821, op. 8, d. 356, ll. 1–2 ob.

30. Lewittes, *Jewish Marriage* (Northvale, N.J., 1994), 264.

31. For example, see TsIAM, f. 1457, op. 1, d. 20, l. 5.

32. The vast statistical reports from 1864, filed from parishes across the realm, show that most priests had an income of 200 to 300 rubles per annum, supplemented by a small plot of land. See RGIA, f. 804, op. 1, razdel 3, dd. 1–420. Even the "ideal" income—calculated by a dissident priest, I. S. Belliustin—brought only a per capita income of 80.88 rubles. See I. S. Belliustin, *Description of the Clergy in Rural Russia. The Memoir of a Nineteenth-Century Parish Priest* (Ithaca, N.Y.: Cornell University Press, 1985), 201.

33. RGIA, f. 821, op. 8, d. 356, l. 4.

34. Ibid., l. 5. The Senate requested the Ministry of Interior to make the appropriate inquiries about the nature of the rabbinic courts.

35. A. Granat, *Nastol'nyi entsiklopedicheskii slovar'*, 8 vols. (Moscow: A. A. Levenson, 1897), 8:4805.

36. For example, the Commission sent Grigorii and Revka Bagrov back to an arbitration court to resolve the issue of the wife's maintenance and child support. RGIA, f. 821, op. 8, d. 289, l. 88 ob.

37. RGIA, f. 821, op. 9, d. 33, l. 5 ob.

38. Ruth Rubin, *Voice of a People: The Story of Yiddish Folksong* (New York, 1973), 112–13.

39. B. Brutskus, *Statistika evreiskago naselentia* (St. Petersburg, 1909), 3:26. Specifically, the proportion of divorced women residing in cities (approximately 1.1 percent of the total Jewish population of marriageable age, or over sixteen) was far greater than the same category living in rural areas (0.3 percent). By contrast, there was no such difference in the empire at large, where the proportion of all divorced women in the Russian empire was 0.3 percent of the entire population of marriageable age in the cities and 0.3 percent in the rural areas. It is also plausible that divorced women migrated to the cities in search of new husbands or anonymity.

40. RGIA, f. 821, op. 9, d. 18, ll. 1–47; f. 821, op. 8, d. 291. By the time that Ester Poliakov's petition regarding the divorce had reached the Rabbinic Commission in 1893, her husband had already remarried.

41. RGIA, f. 1412, op. 231, d. 1, ll. 5–6. (report of the governor of Odessa to the Imperial Chancellery, 31 March 1912).

42. RGIA, f. 821, op. 8, d. 291, ll. 30–34. The law that the rabbi quoted was from the "Ustav grazhanskogo sudoproizvodstva," vol.10, p. 2, article 130. ob.–34.

43. The standard phrase used for most divorce settlements in Moscow in the late nineteenth century was as follows: "We do not have any present or future claims (*pretenzii*) against one another." See TsGIA, f. 1457, op. 1, d. 20 for examples.

44. Ibid., l. 1 ob.

45. The case had already been examined by a rabbinic court of Grodno, the provincial governor's office, the police administration, and the civil court, all of which rejected her claims that the divorced had been coerced.

46. RGIA, f. 821, op. 8, d. 360, l. 1 (petition of townswoman from Grodno, Meita Z. Liubich, 1 May 1870). The fifty-two-year-old husband, Zel'man Liubich, remarried almost a year after their divorce.

47. TsIAM, f. 1457, op. 1, d. 20, l. 4.

48. Unfortunately, the file does not include the conclusion of the case, so it is unclear whether the wife accepted his terms or elected to undergo a formal divorce hearing.

49. At bottom, this anarchy derived from the absence of detailed, systematic state laws; that lacuna in turn resulted from the confessional (not state) control over divorce and, no doubt, the fact that the dominant state church, Russian Orthodoxy, allowed few divorces and no separation. Hence, partners were left to negotiate and, if that failed, to appeal to state courts, local officials, or the government—or even the emperor.

50. RGIA, f. 821, op. 8, d. 291, ll. 84 ob.–89. A complete discussion of the Jewish laws on child custody and support can be found in Ketuboth 65b and *Shulhan Arukh, E.H.,* 82. In Russia a daughter "came of age" when she married, a son when he turned sixteen.

51. See Ketubot 101b–103a.

52. Roderick Phillips, *Putting Asunder: A History of Divorce in Western Society* (Cambridge, 1988), 273.

53. The petitions sent to the Moscow state rabbi, Jacob Maze, show that husbands rarely assumed sole custody of their children. See TsIAM, f. 1457, op. 1, dd. 11, 16, 20, 26, 34, 40, 44, 50, 57, 64,65, 34.

54. TsIAM, f. 1457, op. 1, d. 16, l. 40. The Rozens were married on 1 May 1903 and divorced in December 1908.

55. In 1911 (the year that the couple signed their agreement), the Moscow consistory reported 83 conversions from Judaism to Russian Orthodoxy in Moscow (of a total of 1,651 for the entire empire). The next year, that figure increased to 120. See *Vsepoddaneishii otchet ober-prokuror po vedomstvu dukhovnykh del pravoslavnogo ispovedanie za 1911* (St. Petersburg, 1912), 60–63; *Vse. otchet . . . za 1912* (St. Petersburg, 1913), 64–66.

56. TsIAM, f. 1457, op. 1, d. 64, l. 17–17 ob.

57. *Svod zakonov,* 9:1385.

58. LVIA, f. 605, op. 2, d. 1919.

59. TsIAM, f. 1457, op. 1, d. 20, l. 34–34 ob. They were married on 13 June 1903 and divorced in January 1911.

60.TsIAM, f. 1457, op. 1, d. 64, l. 17–17 ob.

61. As early as 1834, women like Sora Shmukler asked the governor-general of Vil'na to enforce the decision of the *beit-din,* which had awarded her 24 rubles for child support. The ex-husband claimed that he could not pay the required sum and had allegedly given her his personal property with an equivalent value

After a brief investigation by the police, the state returned the case to the *kahal*. The file does not indicate the final disposition of the case. LVIA, f. 378, d. 1330, g. 1837 (no opis number for 1837).

62. For example, see RGIA, f. 821, op. 8, d. 289, l. 88 ob.

63. RGIA, f. 821, op. 8, g. 1870, d. 361, ll. 1–9.

64. RGIA, f. 821, op. 8, d. 296, l. 110 ob.

65. For example, the police arrested the father, Avram Moorovich Sagal, for failing to pay the 144 rubles he owed to his wife and child. RGIA, f. 821, op. 8, d. 357, ll. 1–2 ob.

66. TsGIA-St. Petersburg, f. 2129, op. 3, d. 149 (agreement between the Kopel'mans drafted by the lawyer Sliozberg, 1897).

67. RGIA, f. 1412, op. 227, d. 40, l. 32–32 ob.

68. RGIA, f. 821, op. 8, d. 355, l. 1. The law was taken from the 1859 edition of the Digest of Military Orders *(Svod voennykh postanovlenii)*, article 2340, appendix 129, p. 11, bk. 1.

69. DAZhO, f. 160 (Volynskii prikaz obshchestvennogo prizreniia), op. 1, d. 441 (20 June 1891–27 July 1891, petition of Iudes Golodoi); f. 160, op. 1, d. 332 (7 June 1880–15 July 1880, petition of Basia Feldman); f. 160, op. 1, d. 421 (26 March 1891–24 April 1892, petition of Sura Rivka Kavruka).

70. DAZhO, f. 160, op. 1, d. 421, l. 1.

71. Ibid., l. 1–1 ob. (petition to the Starokonstantin district court from Leia Nezdatna, 28 January 1880).

72. DAZhO, f. 24 (Zhitomir district court) op. 14, d. 32, ll. 1–161 (8 October 1880–11 February 1881).

73. Since the system of hereditary social status *(soslovie)* in Imperial Russia required strict observance of the father's status, the regime sought to avoid the proliferation of elite status and confusion among the disprivileged poll tax population. This system was so rigid that, if the father was ennobled (e.g., through bureaucratic service), only children born *after* that point held the rank of noble; all those born earlier retained the father's earlier station. For more on the *soslovie* system, see Gregory Freeze, "The *Soslovie* (Estate) Paradigm and Russian Social History, *American Historical Review* 91:1 (1986):11–36.

74. RGIA, f. 1412, op. 3, d. 325, l.5. (petition of legal lawyer Rafael L'vov Veisman, resident of Tomsk, 2 September 1902). Veisman apparently did not marry his lover because he did not want to convert to the Russian Orthodox faith.

75. RGIA, f. 1412, op. 3, d. 931, l. 2–2 ob.

76. The laws on adoption can be found in Sloizberg, *Sbornik deistvuiushchikh zakonov o evreiakh* (St. Petersburg, 1909), 107.

77. TsIAM, f. 1457, op. 1, d. 64, l. 17.

78. RGIA, f. 1412, op. 219, d. 15, ll. 77–101 ob. In this case, the wife had married her husband for love and against her parent's wishes, only to discover that he was having an affair with another woman. For more details of the case, see chap. 3.

79. RGIA, f. 821, op. 223, d. 49, l. 2 (petition of Anna Meerson to the Imperial Chancellery, 28 June 1903).

80. RGIA, f. 1412, op. 213, d. 101, l. 133 (letter of Iosif Moiseevich Broin to his son, Viktor Broin, undated). Broin's second child was a four-year-old daughter.

81. RGIA, f. 1412, op. 3, d. 933, l. 1 (petition of David Moiseevich Vurgraft and Dyshel Khaimova Vurgraft, 27 September 1907).

82. In general, the state was exceedingly reluctant to permit any change of status or even name—a clear reflection of its desperate attempt to gain some

control over the mass of population. For the problem of changing names (primarily to avoid embarrassing and shameful family names), see Andrew Verner, "What's in a Name: Of Dog-killers, Jews and Rasputin," *Slavic Review,* 53 (1994): 1046–70.

83. Wagner, *Marriage, Property and Law,* 47–63.

84. Ibid., 63.

85. "Peterburgskaia letopis'," *Khronika voskhoda* 41(1899):1271–72. When the Department of Police raised the question of a divorced Jewish woman's rights and status in 1872, the Ministry of the Interior recommended the principle that a wife retain her husband's status be applied to Jewish divorcées. See RGIA, f. 821, op. 8, d. 365, ll. 1–9.

86. Although located in the Pale of Settlement, the city of Kiev was formally closed to ordinary Jews; only special privileged categories could obtain residency rights in the city.

87. RGIA, f. 821, op. 8, d. 365, l. 9. The decision of the Senate was based on article 100 of the civil law, vol. 10, p. 1 (published in 1887).

88. *Budushchnost'* 41 (1902): 813.

89. RGIA, f. 1405, op. 103, d. 9373 (complaint of Sora Fridman, 1902).

90. See st. 5, t. 9, Zak. Sost. (1876).

91. This position had several precedents, including the case of Sore Khana Peznik, who married a townsman from Lida. Her numerous attempts to register in Krondstadt, where her father (a retired soldier) resided, were to no avail; she was expelled and sent back to the Pale of Settlement. RGIA, f. 1405, op. 103, d. 9373, l. 11 ob.

92. Women living under extremely difficult conditions could appeal to the emperor for renewed residence rights, although the Senate did not define what those conditions entailed.

93. Another article reported: "We would like to clarify the point that women, who have independent rights of residence outside the Pale of Settlement can keep their children with them—sons until they come of age, and daughters until they marry." *Khronika voskhoda* 38 (1899):1203.

94. RGIA, f. 1405, op. 103, d. 9373, l. 11 ob.

95. DAKO, f. 1, op. 148, d. 83, ll. 1–7 (petition of Iankel Srul Gofman to the governor of Kiev, 30 April 1914). For Gofman's army record, see l. 2–2 ob.

96. DAKO, f. 1, op. 147, d. 268, ll. 1–6.

97. RGIA, f. 1405, op. 103, d. 9373, ll. 7–8.

98. RGIA, f. 1312, op. 240, d. 96, ll. 1–22.

99. RGIA, f. 1405, op. 103, d. 9373, l. 10.

100. LVIA, f. 447, op. 1, d. 6021.

101. LVIA, f. 448, op. 1, d. 7571.

102. The metrical books of Odessa reveal that a significant proportion of Jewish men and women married Moldavian and Turkish subjects (almost every other entry in the metrical book of marriages for 1875). Examples can be found in DAOO, f. 39, op. 2, g, 1875, d. 3, ll. 2–4 ob., 6 ob.–7 ob., 9–16 ob.

103. RGIA, f. 1269, op. 1, d. 56, l. 2.

104. Ibid., l. 4. Apparently, Jewish women did not need permission from the state to marry foreigners but had to inform local officials in order to change their status and paperwork.

105. *Svod zakonov,* 9:1408.

106. Ibid.

107. RGIA, f. 1269, op. 1, d. 56, l. 4–8 ob.

108. "Senatskaia praktika" *Budushchnost'* 29 (1901): 569.

109. The Senate sent its final resolution to the Bessarabian provincial board on 22 January 1901.

110. There are numerous cases of Jewish soldiers who were forcibly baptized. After the state passed the "Law of Tolerance" in 1905, the synod and local consistories received petitions from converts who desired to return to Judaism. For example, see RGIA, f. 797, op. 76, d. 401.

111. TsDIAK-Ukraïny, f. 442, op. 157, d. 994, 1. 12 (petition of Rukhli S. Shor to the gubernator of Kiev, 21 December 1846). It is interesting that Rukhli Shor pointed to her gender as the source of her gullibility, perhaps to gain sympathy from the state.

112. "Sudebnaia khronika, delo o podloge v metricheskoi knige," *Kievlianin*, 245 (1890): 9.

113. See also *Shulhan Arukh, E.H.*, 6,1.

114. Biale, *Women and Jewish Law*, 71.

115. RGIA, f. 821, op. 8, d. 296, ll. 52–52 ob.

116. See chap. 2 for the dubious character of state rabbis in the "new areas of settlement," such as Simferopol and Kherson.

117. RGIA, f. 821, op. 8, d. 296, ll. 52 ob.–53 ob.

118. The decision not to prosecute stemmed from the fact that Perel'man had not violated state law. It also noted that he had correctly rejected Iudelia Katz's demand for a divorce, since only the local rabbi in the permanent place of residence could dissolve a marriage.

119. See the discussion beginning in *Shulhan Arukh, E.H.*, 6,1.

120. RGIA, f. 821, op. 8, d. 296, l. 54.

121. Other examples of couples who confronted this dilemma can be found in Isaac Metzker, *A Bintel Brief* (New York, 1971).

122. Phillips, *Putting Asunder*, 296. Significantly, however, it was very uncommon for a Russian Orthodox marriage to be annulled on grounds of bigamy; in 1913, for example, only two annulments each year were based on bigamy. See *Vsepoddanneishii otchet za 1913 god*, appendix 14.

123. The only, partial exception is a study of unregistered marriages (bigamies and otherwise); see chap. 2.

124. "Dopuskaet-li iudaizm i zhelaiut-li evrei mnogozhenstva?" *Vestnik russkikh evreev* 23 (1871): 775–76.

125. *Russkii evrei*, 10 (5 March 1880): 362–69.

126. Significantly, the principal problem was male, not female, bigamy; although Russia distinguished between male and female (*dvoezhenstvo* and *dvoemuzhie, mnogozhenstvo* and *mnogomuzhie*), it is the set of male categories that predominate, of course.

127. RGIA, f. 821, op. 8, d. 289, l. 3 ob.

128. Ibid., l. 3.

129. Ibid., l. 9.

130. Ibid., l. 10 ob. The report did not provide citation for this principle, but it corresponds to the ruling of Raba in Yevamoth 65a.

131. Rabbi Neumann made a vague reference to a certain Rabbi Kogan, but the quote appears to be from Yevamoth 65a.

132. RGIA, f. 821, op. 8, d. 289, l. 11 ob.

133. Rabbi Neumann cited the *Shulhan Arukh, E.H.*, 1,9.

134. The Ministry of the Interior occasionally sent circulars to the various provincial governors to remind them of this new regulation. See *Novyi voskhod* 14 (2 March 1910): 11.

135. RGIA, f. 821, op. 9, d. 13, l. 2.

136. "O mnogozhenstve," *Rassvet* 35 (1909): 27–28.

137. D. Margolis, "Evrei Kavkaza," *Evreiskaia mysl'* 35 (23 August 1918):5–7.

138. The state made another exception for Jews in the Caucasus, most notably in its decision to waive the minimum age requirement.

139. RGIA, f. 821, op. 8, d. 291, l. 4–88 ob.

140. The bigamist was, however, liable to secular punishment; should the *beit-din* find him guilty, government prosecutors could indict him and, if successful, insist upon the standard state punishment.

141. Biale, *Women and Jewish Law*, 104.

142. Unfortunately, Hertzberg does not indicate the source for the 100,000 figure. See his *The Jews in America* (New York, 1989).

143. "Draft of an Open Letter (Kol-koyre) to the Rabbis in the West" (undated) from Rabbi Moshe Nahum ben Binyamin Yerusalimsky of Tomashpol', Podolia, translated in Eli Lederhendler, *Responses to Modernity: New Voices in America and Eastern Europe* (New York, 1994), 96.

144. Based on a search of *agunah*, without any suffixes, on the Bar-Ilan responsa database. For example, see Yitshak Elhanan Spektor, *Sefer Beer Yitshak, Even Haezer*, no. 5. Some samples of responsa from the Polish lands before 1648 can be found in Shmuel A. Cygielman. *Yehudei polin velita ad shenat 1648* (Jerusalem, 1991), 618, 628, 621, 625; see also D. B. Ashkenazi, *Noda beshearim* 1 (1859), no. 13.

145. See Arodys Robles and Susan Cotts Watkins, "Immigration and Family Separation in the U.S. at the Turn of the Twentieth Century," *Journal of Family History*, 13:3 (1993):191–211.

146. See the case of Leia Broun in the preceding chapter.

147. DAKO, f. 2, op. 240, d. 597, l. 3 (petition of Vera Portugalov to the governor of Kiev, 30 November 1894).

148. *Hamelits* 166 (25 July 1893):4.

149. RGIA, f. 821, op. 9, d. 59, l. 2–64 ob.

150. Divorce on grounds of malicious desertion jumped from 24 cases in 1860 to 633 in 1866; the numbers later declined but were still substantial by the end of the century (380 in 1900). They subsequently dropped sharply, amounting to just 2 *(sic!)* in 1913. See *Izvlecheniia is vsepoddanneishego otcheta ober-prokurora po vedomstvu pravoslavnogo ispovedaniia za 1860 god* (St. Petersburg: Sinodal'naia tipografiia, 1862); *Izvlecheniia iz vsepoddanneishego otcheta ober-prokurora po vedomstvu pravoslavnogo ispovedaniia za 1866 god* (St. Petersburg: Sinodal'naia tipografiia, 1868); *Vsepodanneishii otchet ober-prokurora po vedomstvu pravoslavnogo ispovedaniia za 1913 god, prilozhenie*, no. 14).

151. See Shaul Stampfer, "Patterns of Internal Jewish Migration in the Russian Empire," in *Jews and Jewish Life in Russia and the Soviet Union*, ed., Yaacov R'oi (Portland, Ore., 1995), 15–27.

152. "Letter of M. N. Yerusalimsky to the Rabbis in the West" (undated), as translated in Lederhendler, *Jewish Responses to Modernity*, 96.

153. See R. S. Friedman, "Send Me My Husband Who Is in New York City: Husband Desertion in the American Jewish Immigrant Community, 1990–1926," *Jewish Social Studies* 44:1 (winter 1982): 1–18.

154. Paula Hyman, "Gender and the Immigrant Jewish Experience," in *Jewish Women in Historical Perspective*, ed. Judith Baskin (Detroit, 1981).

155. RGIA, f. 821, op. 9, d. 12, ll. 2–3 ob. (petition of Bassia Semenova Freizarov to the Rabbinic Commission, 22 December 1883).

156. "Kol Agunah," *Hamelits* 5 (3 February 1881):107–8.

157. "Agunah," *Hamelits* 21 (26 May 1870):154.

158. For example, see *Hamelits* 4 (1870):4. Statistics on crime involving Jews can be found in Ivan Stanislavich Bloikh, *Sravnenie material'nogo byta nravstvennogo sostoianiia naseleniia v cherte osedlosti evreev* (St. Petersburg, 1891), vols. 1–5. See also LVIA, f. 447, op. 19, d. 3197 (the discovery of a murdered Jewish man in the forest in 1852).

159. DAKhO, f. 958, op. 1, g. 1872, d. 15, ll. 6 ob.–7; op. 1, g. 1871, d. 10, ll. 3 ob.–4, 4 ob.–5; op. 1, g. 1870, d. 4, ll. 13 ob.–14; op. 1, g. 1874, d. 29, ll. 2 ob.–3; op. 1, g. 1880, d. 59, ll. 9 ob.–10.

160. In one case, a man granted his wife a conditional divorce with the stipulation that if he sent a letter with sixty zlotys within three years, she remained his wife. Much to the wife's dismay, however, he sent her twenty zlotys and disappeared; the decision now rested on the local rabbinical court to decide whether the woman was a divorcée or an *agunah*. See Levitats, *Jewish Community*, 133.

161. It bears noting that some Eastern European rabbis, out of sympathy for the plight of widows, accepted the testimony of a single witness. Individuals who were normally ineligible to serve as witnesses according to Jewish law included slaves; women (although their testimonies could be accepted in some cases involving *agunot*); underage children; the deaf, dumb, mute, blind and insane; transgressors of the law; relatives and close family members; and Gentiles (although their depositions were admitted in specified cases).

162. Levitats, *Jewish Community*, 134. The original responsum can be found in Rabbi D. Menkis, *Anaf ets avot* (1900), nos. 1 and 8.

163. Levitats, *Jewish Community*, 134.

164. See below for an explanation about this ritual ceremony.

165. Yitshak Elhanan Spektor, *Ain Yitzhak, Even Haezer*, no. 19. Part of the text can be found in Solomon B. Freehof, *A Treasury of Responsa* (Philadelphia, 1963), 288–91.

166. As Feiga Gelefonova quickly discovered, it was a difficult task to produce solid evidence to satisfy an overly fastidious rabbi. For details, see chap. 2. RGIA, f. 821, op. 9, d. 10 (Feiga Gelefonova vs. Rabbi Shaperinskii).

167. Ilia Orshanskii, *Russkoe zakonodatel'stvo o evreiakh* (St. Petersburg, 1877), 106.

168. RGIA, f. 797, op. 90, d. 47, ll. 4–17 ob. (Department of the Imperial Chancellery for the Receipt of Petitions to the Ober-procurator of the Holy Synod, 22 August 1886).

169. See Deut. 25: 5–10.

170. RGIA, f. 821, op. 8, d. 354, ll. 3–6 (report about the ceremony of *halitsah*). In the original biblical text, the brother's widow would spit on the *levir*'s face, but in Russia this was considered too humiliating, so women resorted to spitting on the ground instead.

171. Sometimes the brother-in-law who had converted to Christianity refused to perform what he considered a primitive and degrading ritual and the childless widow (his sister-in-law) was forbidden to remarry. On 22 May 1886, the governor of Odessa received a complaint from Sara Gener against three rabbis who refused to give her permission to remarry until she received a levirate divorce from her converted *levir*. Investigation of the case revealed that the former state rabbi of Odessa, S. L. Schwabacher, who had his doctorate from Lemberg, had erroneously instructed her to remarry on the grounds that a convert was not permitted to perform the ritual of *halitsah*. Despite Gener's protests against the inequity of her circumstances, the Rabbinic Commission rejected her suit on the

grounds that a "yevamah is chained to her levir until he releases her through the rite of *halitsah*." RGIA, f. 821, op. 8, d. 291, ll. 42–45 ob. For a more detailed discussion about the rite of *halitsah* in the event that a *levir* converts to Christianity, see RGIA, f. 821, op. 9, d. 14, ll. 1–15.

172. Ibid.

173. Ibid.

174. RGIA, f. 821, op. 9, d. 21, ll. 6–36 ob. (petition of Gitla Mogilevskaia to the Rabbinic Commission, 26 June 1893).

175. RGIA, f. 821, op. 9, d. 35, ll. 1–22. In one case, the brother-in-law had transferred all of his assets to his mother-in-law's name so that the *yevamah* could not receive any support from him. RGIA, f. 821, op. 9, g. 1910, d. 72 (Faiva Chaim Lipkovich, on behalf of his daughter Leia, vs. Beniamin Poverennyi). See also "Otvety na voprosy iz oblasty T., evreiskago pravo" *Novyi voskhod* 18 (1912):41–42.

176. RGIA, f. 821, op. 9, d. 7.

177. RGIA, f. 821, op. 9, d. 56, l. 2.

178. RGIA, f. 821, op. 8, d. 296, l. 56. (journal of the Rabbinic Commission on the Osel'ka case).

179. Ibid., l. 15. (letter signed by abovementioned rabbis, Nissan, 1895).

180. Ibid. See *Shulhan Arukh, E.H.,* 77 ff. For another case in which a rabbi rejected a deserted husband's petition for remarriage, see RGIA, f. 821, op. 8, g. 1910, d. 296. (Iosel El'baum vs. Rabbi Smerkovich).

181. RGIA, f. 821, op. 9, d. 37, l. 2.

182. RGIA, f. 821, op. 8, d. 291, l. 167 ob.

183. No less striking was the commission's decision in another case: a deserted husband inquired whether the state law permitting Russian Orthodox to remarry after the absence of a spouse for five years pertained to the Jews. The commission reluctantly ruled that some clauses in the state law could apply to men but not to women, presumably on the grounds that the woman's disappearance denied him his right to serve the bill of divorcement. RGIA, f. 821, op. 8, g. 1892, d. 291 (inquiry of Khaim Leib Muller, whose wife had been missing for eight years).

184. This decision not only landed him in prison for five months (for bigamy) but gave his wife ample evidence to press for material support, which a state court mandated him to pay. RGIA, f. 821, op. 9, d. 13, g. 1884, l. 1 ob.

185. Draft of a letter to be sent to the rabbis of Brest-Litovsk and Vil'na about the upcoming Rabbinical Commission, from R. Moshe Nahum Yerusalimsky (n.d.) as cited in Lederhendler, *Jewish Responses to Modernity,* 92.

5. Quandaries of Family Reform: Old Foes, New Alliances

1. Rabbi Yaakov Halevi Lipschitz, *Zikhron Yaakov* (Frankfurt, 1924), 2:203. The original saying went: "Ten measures *(kabin)* of wisdom descended to the world, nine were taken by Palestine and one by the rest of the world. Ten *kabin* of beauty descended to the world: nine were taken by Jerusalem and one by the rest of the world. Ten *kabin* of wealth descended to the world; nine were taken by the early Romans and one by the rest of the world" (Kiddushin 49b).

2. The term *Orthodox* is used here to describe the new socioreligious system and thought that emerged in Russia during the period of Nicholas I as a response to religious and cultural heterodoxy. Michael Stanislawski put it best when he defined the "Orthodox" as "a self-conscious traditionalist society battling its enemies on their own ground, often with their own tools, organized by leaders armed

with a vigilant new strategy and militant new ideology." One important aspect of this new Orthodoxy was the cease-fire between the Hasidim and *mitnagdim* to create a united front against the *maskilim*. See Stanislawski, *Tsar Nicholas I and the Jews* (Philadelphia, 1983), 148–54.

3. See RGIA, f. 821, op. 8, d. 437, which contains several applications for the positions in state service as learned Jews and translators. For a list of Jewish personnel in the state bureaucracy, see Eli Lederhendler, *The Road to Modern Jewish Politics* (New York, 1989), 93 (a list of censors of Hebrew and Yiddish books), 94 (learned Jews), 75–76 (a list of members of the first Rabbinic Commission).

4. See Mordechai Zalkin's discussion of the term *maskilim, Baalot hashahar* (Jerusalem, 2000); see also Zipperstein, *The Jews of Odessa* (Stanford, 1985), 11–13. For more on Jewish politics in late Imperial Russia, see Christoph Gassenschmidt, *Jewish Liberal Politics in Tsarist Russia* (New York, 1995).

5. See Eli Lederhendler, *Jewish Responses to Modernity. New Voices in America and Eastern Europe* (New York, 1995), 67–76.

6. The literature on the Russian "pre-revolution" of 1905–1917 is immense. For a convenient introduction, see Manfred Hildermeier, *Die Russische Revolution, 1905–1921* (Frankfurt, 1989); Abraham Ascher, *The Revolution of 1905*, 2 vols. (Stanford, Calif.: Stanford University Press, 1988–92). For collective statements by the principal social categories, see Gregory Freeze, *From Supplication to Revolution* (Oxford, 1988), pt. 3. For a classic treatment, see the collection of Menshevik essays in *Obshchestvennye dvizheniia v nachale XX veka*, 4 vols. (St. Petersburg, 1909).

7. "Public appeal by the rabbis of this city, Vilna" (1903) as translated in Eli Lederhendler, *Jewish Responses to Modernity*, 74–76.

8. For the classic account, focusing on government response, see P. A. Zaionchkovskii, *Krizis samoderzhaviia* (Moscow, 1964).

9. Lederhendler, *Road to Modern Jewish Politics*, 50.

10. M. L. Lilienblum, "Petah tikva," *Hakol* 22 (1878), col. 157, as translated in Lederhendler, *Road to Modern Jewish Politics*, 150. It is also quoted by Rabbi Yaakov Lifschitz in *Zikhron Yaakov*, 2:204.

11. Lifschitz, *Zikhron Yaakov*, 2:203.

12. Ibid., 2:207.

13. "Ravvinskaia komissiia," *EE*, 13 (1991 [reprint]):234.

14. Lifschitz, *Zikhron Yaakov*, 2:207.

15. During the early nineteenth century, for example, prominent rabbis, such as R. Haim of Volozhin, R. Yehoshua-Heshl Ashkenazi of Lublin, R. Shnuer Zal'man of White Russia, and others, functioned as political representatives and leaders of their communities. For a discussion about their activities and attitudes toward rabbis as *shtadlanim*, see Lederhendler, *Road to Modern Jewish Politics*, 68–74.

16. See the discussion about bigamy and state courts in chap. 4.

17. The seven cases (discussed in chaps. 3 and 4) included four divorce suits—those of Sura and Yankel Shnaper; Grigorii and Rivka Bagrov, Gitlia and Lubish Kramer, and Khaia and David Grinshtein; the remaining three cases were general discussions about marriage and divorce. RGIA, f. 821, op. 8, d. 289 (journal of the Rabbinic Commission, 1879).

18. The brief summary of each case can be found in the journal of the Rabbinic Commission in RGIA, f. 821, op. 8, d. 289. See also *Hamelits*, 4 (23 January 1879): 71; 9 (27 February 1879): 182; 11 (13 March 1879):225–26, 227–28.

19. David L. Beithilel, *K predstoiashchim vyboram v ravvinskuiu kommissiiu* (St. Petersburg: Tip. A. G. S'erkina, 1893), 1, citing the *Vilenskii vestnik*.

20. Ibid., 1–9.

21. Lifschitz, *Zikhron Yaakov,* 2:208.

22. See Jonathan Frankel, *Prophecy and Politics. Socialism, Nationalism, and the Russian Jews, 1862–1917* (Cambridge, England, 1981); Yisrael Bartal, "Bein haskalah radikalit lesotsializm yehudi," in *Hadat vehahaim,* 328–35; Henry Tobias, *The Jewish Bund in Russia from Its Origins to 1905* (Stanford, Calif., 1972); Ezra Mendelsohn, *Class Struggle in the Pale: The Formative Years of the Jewish Workers Movement in Tsarist Russia* (Cambridge, England, 1970).

23. The liberation movement *(osvoboditel'noe dvizhenie)* was the all-class, multinational movement that emphasized the notion of "two Russias,"—that of the state, that of society. At least until the fall of 1905, it enabled a broad spectrum of opposites—from gentry *frondeurs* to terrorists—to unite again autocracy. See G. L. Freeze, "The Shift in Russian Liberalism, 1901–1903," *Slavic Review* 28 (1969):81–91.

24. Again, in this case, the Orthodox were referring to the broader group of Jewish intelligentsia, not simply the small subgroup of *maskilim.*

25. Lifschitz, *Zikhron Yaakov,* 2:77.

26. Rabbi Tsvi Hirsh Rabinovich (1851–1911) was the son of the illustrious Rabbi Yitshak Elhanan Spektor of Kovno.

27. Rabbi Samuil Mogilever (1824–1898) was born in Vitebsk province and was trained not only in Jewish law but in Jewish religious-philosophical and secular literature. He became the rabbi of Belostok in 1883 and remained until his death. See I. B., "Samuil Mogilever," *EE,* 11(1991 [reprint]: 147–49; *Hamelits* 27 (1898); I. Nissenbaum, *Rabbenu Shmuel Mohilever* (Berdichev, 1898).

28. "Ravvinskaia Komissiia," *EE,* 13 (1991 [reprint]):234.

29. RGIA, f. 821, op. 8, d. 293, l. 151 ob.–152.

30. For example, in their discussion of the "deserted husband" (case of Khaim Muller), the commission cited not only the *Shulhan Arukh* but the responsa of Rabbi Meir of Rothenberg and Ezekiel Landau *(Noda beyehudah),* and the commentaries of Hatam Sofer on *Even haezer.* They also routinely relied on Maimonides (e.g., *Yad hahazakah*). RGIA, f. 821, op. 8, d. 291 (journal of the Rabbinic Commission for 1893–1894).

31. RGIA, f. 821, op. 8, dd. 14, 27, 29, 32.

32. Lifschitz, *Zikhron Yaakov,* 208–9.

33. For more on the Law of Associations and the explosion of self-organization by sundry groups, see Freeze, *From Supplication to Revolution,* 197–309.

34. The twenty-five participants included numerous distinguished rabbinic leaders, such as Rabbis Hirsh Itsakovich Rabinovich (Tzvi Hirsh Rabinovich) of Kovno, Khaim E. Grodzinskii of Vilna, Leizer Gordon of Tel'shi (Kovno province), Khaim Iosif Soloveichik of Brest-Litovsk, and others.

35. This is not a description but legal status; see the description in chap. 2.

36. RGIA, f. 821, op. 8, d. 293, ll. 41–58.

37. Letter from Rabbi Moshe Yerusalimsky to Rabbi Avraham-Mordechai of Gur, spring 1909, as translated in Eli Lederhendler, *Jewish Responses to Modernity,* 89–90.

38. "S"ezde ravvinov v Vil'ne" *Rassvet* 18 (1909):19.

39. RGIA, f. 821, op. 8, d. 293, ll. 59–64.

40. "Evreiskaia zhizn'," *Rassvet* 2 (1910):32–34.

41. "Ravvinskaia kommissia," *EE,* 13 (1991 [reprint]):234.

42. Vl. Temkin, "O ravvinskoi komissii" *Rassvet* 5 (1910):3–5.

43. Ibid.
44. No citation is given for the place or date of publication.
45. A. Davidson, "Klerikal'noe dvizhenie" *Rassvet* 13 (1910):4–6.
46. The Hasidic rabbi Borukh (from one of the dynasties of the Ba'al Shem Tov) had once made a similar argument when he tried to stop Rabbi Shneur Zalman from raising funds to assist his coreligionists who had been expelled from the villages of White Russia in 1808. "God will save us," he had contended, to which his fellow rabbi replied that Israel must not rely on miracles and "seek God's favor with deeds." Lederhendler, *Road to Modern Jewish Politics,* 69.
47. Davidson, "Klerikal'noe dvizhenie," 6.
48. Copies of articles about the 1910 election in the Russian-Jewish press can be found RGIA, f. 821, op. 8, d. 293, ll. 343–48.
49. "Evreiskaia zhizn'" *Rassvet* 50 (1909):21–22.
50. Ben Chaim, "Zakonoproekt o ravvinate i evreiskikh obshchinakh," *Novyi put',* 11–12 (1916):14–16.
51. RGIA, f. 821, op. 1, d. 296 (journal of the Rabbinic Commission of 1910).
52. *Nedel'naia khronika Voskhoda,* 6 (8 February 1898), 194.
53. Ia. Katsenel'son, "K ravvinskomu voprosu," *Voskhod* 6 (1904):172.
54. See chap. 2.
55. Katenel'son, "K ravvinskomu voprosu," *Voskhod* 6 (1904):175; M. M. "Nedavniaia politika i kazennyi ravvinat," *Russkii evrei* 2 (1883) 11
56. N. N. "Eshche k ravvinskomu voprosu," *Russkii evrei* 18 (1880):691.
57. Ibid. See also D. Polonskii, "O nalichnom sostave evreiskogo dukhovenstva," *Evreiskaia khronika,* 16 (1911): 5–10.
58. Katsenel'son, "K ravvinskomu voprosu," *Voskhod* 7 (1904): 158–59.
59. G. Sliozberg used the word *dvoevlastie* (dual power) to describe the system of the dual rabbinate in his article, "Vybory v ravvinskuiu kommissiiu," *Novyi Voskhod* 3 (21 January 1910):3–5. The term, of course, acquired greater currency and fame during the 1917 revolution.
60. Lifschitz, *Zikhron Yaakov,* 3:154; Shochat, *Mosad 'harabanut mi taam berusyah'* (Haifa, 1976), 131.
61. Shochat, *Mosad,* 132; Lifschitz, *Zikhron Yaakov,* 3:156.
62. In Russian, the society was called in Obshchestvo dlia prosveshcheniia evreev. This society, established in October 1863 by an elite group of Jews in St. Petersburg, had the goal of spreading enlightenment among the Jews. For more information, see "Obrazovania," *EE* 13 (1991 [reprint]):59–60.
63. Shochat, *Mosad 'harabanut mitaam,'* 132–33.
64. Lifschitz, *Zikhron Yaakov,* 3:156.
65. For example, see RGIA, f. 821, op. 150, d. 381, l. 287 ob.
66. Lifschitz, *Zikhron Yaakov,* 3:157.
67. Shochat, *Mosad 'harabanut mitaam,'* 131–32. See chap. 2 for a more detailed discussion of these requirements.
68. The question of the dual rabbinate was raised in the Vil'na conference of 1909 and Kovno conference of November 1909. In these meetings, the main focus of the discussion was on the material support of the spiritual rabbis.
69. The list of participants can be found in RGIA, f. 821, op. 150, d. 390, ll. 4–5. See also "O ravvinskom s"ezde," *Rassvet* 50 (1909):10–11.
70. The other subjects to be discussed were the spiritual boards of the prayer houses; organization of a Jewish religious "commune"; the centralization of Jewish philanthropic societies, such as burial societies; the religious education and

upbringing of Jewish youth; and various means to strengthen observance and faith among the Jewish population. See "O ravvinskom s"ezde," *Rassvet* 50 (1909): 10–11.

71. In 1899–1902, Stolypin served as the provincial marshal of the nobility for Kovno province.

72. "Deputatsiia ravvinskago s"ezda u P. A. Stolypina," *Rassvet* 12 (1910): 28.

73. RGIA, f. 821, op. 8, d. 293, ll. 186 ob.–187 (report of the Rabbinic Congress). The reference to the capitalist Jews was an interesting remark especially in light of the growing "class" consciousness in revolutionary circles.

74. Ibid., l. 187 ob.

75. "Ravvinskii s"ezd," *Rassvet* 12 (1910):24–26.

76. The *tsaddik* noted that if the situation called for it, he had no doubt that "they [the rabbis] *will* speak Russian *(Zi velen . . . reden russish)*." In other words, he believed that most rabbis knew enough Russian to work through circumstances that required them to speak the state language. (All the words in italics were italicized in the original).

77. "Posle ravvinskago s"ezda: U Liubavichskago tsadika," *Evreiskii mir* 15–16 (1910): 21–25.

78. RGIA, f. 821, op. 1, d. 8, l. 188–88 ob.

79. "Ravvinskaia komissiia," *Evreiskii mir* 13 (1910):35.

80. RGIA, f. 821, op. 1, d. 8, l. 188 ob.

81. "Ravvinskii s"ezd," *Rassvet* 12(1910):24–26.

82. Ibid., 13(1910) 25–30.

83. Ibid., 12(1910):24–26.

84. F. Gets, "Organizatsiia evreiskoi obshchiny," *Voskhod* 4 (1905): 65.

85. A "secret marriage" was one in which the Jewish couple married without the permission of the state rabbi or failed to have the deed recorded in the metrical book. For details, see above, chap. 2.

86. N. N., "K ravvinskomu voprosu," *Russkii evrei*, 11 (1879):382–83.

87. N. N. "Eshche k ravvinskomu voprosu," *Russkii evrei* 19 (1880): 729.

88. RGIA, f. 821, op. 8, d. 293, l. 197. See also "Programma s"ezda pri ravvinskoi komissii," *Novyi Voskhod,* 9 (910):18.

89. According to one study of illegitimate births in Mogilev between 1876 and 1885, there was a considerably lower percentage of out-of-wedlock births among Jews (0.3 percent of the total number of births) than among the Christian population (9.1 percent). See "Fizicheskoe razvitie i sanitarnoe sostoianie evreiskogo naseleniia v Rossii," *Evreiskii meditsinskii golos* 3–4 (1911):19–21. Another study by I. Pantiukhov showed similar patterns among Jewish and Christian illegitimate births in Kiev province between 1866 and 1870. For this five-year period, Pantiukhov discovered 107 total out-of-wedlock births (1 illegitimate birth out of 457 legal births). Among the much larger Russian Orthodox population, the number of illegitimate births rose from 399 in 1867 to 525 in 1870. *Opyt sanitarnoi topografii i statistiki,* 217, 223.

90. Sliozberg, *Sbornik deistvuiushchikh zakonov o evreiakh,* 107.

91. RGIA, f. 821, op. 8, d. 293, l. 198

92. Ibid., l. 199 ob. For more on the church's position on Jewish converts and divorce, see: M. Sh. "K voprosu o razvode mezhdu suprugami-eveiami pri perekhode odnogo iz nikh v pravoslavie," *Voskhod* 1 (1892):1–11.

93. Rabbi Tsirel'son contended that marriages between Jews and Kararites must be viewed as invalid, although both spouses were required to obtain a divorce

to dissolve the marriage. He noted that such marriages were especially common in southern Russia, often generating confusion about the "religious" identities of the children. The members of the congress concurred that rabbis should not be permitted to perform these "interfaith" marriages. See "Ravvinskaia komissiia," *Novyi Voskhod,* 13 (1910):16.

94. RGIA, f. 821, op. 8, d. 293, ll. 198–200 ob.

95. Ibid., l. 97.

96. "Otchet o soveshchanii evreiskikh obshchestvennykh deiatelei, proiskhodivshem v Kovne 19–22-go noiabria 1909," *Evreiskii mir* 11–12 (1909):35–37.

97. The Russian word literally means commune, but it is used here in the sense of community.

98. Debates about the nature of the Jewish *obshchiny* dominated the press in 1910. For examples, see "K sporu o tipe evreiskoi obshchiny," *Evreiskii mir,* 4 (28 January 1910):1–6; "K voprosu o konfessional'nom kharakter evreiskoi obshchiny," *Evreiskii mir,* 8 (25 February 1910): 1–5; "Ob organizatsii evreiskoi obshchiny,"*Evreiskaia nedelia* 6 (1910):5–7; "Ravvinskoi vopros i reforma obshchiny," *Novyi voskhod,* 11 (1910):1–3; "Eshche ob obshchin," *Novyi voskhod,* 8 (1910):1–4.

99. G. Bogrov, "Obshchina i poriadok," *Russkii evrei* 3 (1883):84–87; 4 (1883):5–9; 5(1883):7–11; 8 (1883):5–9; 10 (1883):5–7; 13 (1883):5–8; 14 (1883):4–7; 17 (1883):4–9.

100. "Ob organizatsii evreiskoi obshchiny," *Evreiskaia nedelia* 6 (1910): 5.

101. For the salience of this issue in the Duma Monarchy, see Francis W. Wcislo, *Reforming Rural Russia: State, Local Society and National Politics, 1855–1914* (Princeton, N.J., 1990).

102. "Ravvinskii s"ezd," *Rassvet,* 12 (1910):25.

103. The ten provinces of Tsarist Poland, administratively called a *namestnichestvo* until 1875 and a *general-gubernatorstvo* thereafter.

104. "Ravvinskaia komissia. Beseda s predsedatelem ravvinskom komissii, Kishinevskim ravvinom L. M. Tsirel'sonom," *Evreiskii mir* 9 (1910): 16–17.

105. RGIA, f. 821, op. 150, d. 381, ll. 142–97.

106. Geoffrey Hosking. *The Russian Constitutional Experiment* (Cambridge, England, 1973).

107. RGIA, f. 821, op. 8, d. 290, l. 20.

108. See S. Gruzenberg, "O fizicheskom sostoianii evreev," *Evreiskoe obozrenie,* 3 (1884):63–73.

109. Ibid.

110. Although the Russian Orthodox Church formally subscribed to a ban on marriage within the "levitical degrees," in practice it formally allowed marriages within the sixth and seventh degrees and tolerated marriages in the fourth and fifth degrees. It categorically forbade any closer kinship. See Gregory Freeze, "Bringing Order to the Russian Family: Marriage and Divorce in Imperial Russia," *Journal of Modern History,* 62 (1990): 727–28.

111. See above, chap. 1.

112. Lewittes, *Jewish Marriage,* 20–21.

113. RGIA, f. 821, op. 8, d. 290, l. 20.

114. Ibid.

115. RGIA, f. 1269, op. 1, d. 48, ll. 2–2 ob. See chap. 2 for more details.

116. In an attempt to square the circle, precisely the same kind of proposal— really tantamount to establishing state control, rendering religious control purely

symbolic—informed plans with respect to the Russian Orthodox population. The device, which first appeared in an abortive reform of ecclesiastical justice in 1871, returned repeatedly in the final decades of the ancien régime. See Gregory Freeze, *Religion and Society in Modern Russia,* vol. 1 (forthcoming).

117. RGIA, f. 821, op. 8, d. 290, l. 22–22 ob.

118. Ibid., l. 23.

119. Ibid., ll. 21–23.

120. Ibid. l. 20.

121. Wagner, *Marriage, Property and Law,* 127, citing Tiutriumov in *Zamechaniia o nedostatkakh deistvuiushchikh grazhdanskikh zakonov: Izdanie redaktsionnoi kommissii po sostavleniiu grazhdanskago ulozheniia,* no. 26 (St. Petersburg, 1891), 25.

122. For example, see Robert Paul Geraci, "Window on the East: Ethnography, Orthodoxy, and Russian Nationality in Kazan," (Ph.D. diss., University of California at Berkeley, 1995) on state efforts to integrate the non-Russian peoples in the eastern parts of the empire. A study on the Karaites in Russia would provide much-needed information for a comparative analysis.

123. The writings of George Sand and other Western social theorists, for example, which became popular in Russia after the mid-1830s, inspired romantic notions about mutual love and respect in marriage, shifting the emphasis away from "economic and social considerations in marriage" to the importance of "individual emotions, feelings, and self-fulfillment." For details and references, see Wagner, *Marriage, Property and Law,* 95. More important, the "emancipation of the heart" was not only a privilege reserved for men but also a woman's right. See Richard Stites, "Women and the Russian Intelligentsia: Three Perspectives," in *Women in Russia,* ed. Dorothy Atkinson (Stanford, Calif., 1977), 40; and *Women's Liberation Movement in Russia.*

124. For a discussion of the education and background of these progressive jurists, see Wagner, *Marriage, Property, and Law.*

125. Ibid., 111, as cited in I. G. Orshanskii, "Lichnyi i imushchestvenniia otnosheniia suprugov," in *Issledovaniia po russkomu pravu semeinomu i nasledstvennomu* (St. Petersburg, 1877), 194–98.

126. Wagner, *Marriage, Property, and Law,* 112.

127. Ibid., 125.

128. William Wagner, "Family Law, the Rule of Law, and Liberation in Late Imperial Russia," *Jahrbücher für Geschichte Osteuropas* 43 (1995):525.

129. Wagner, *Marriage, Property, and Law,* 160–61.

130. "Zakonoproekt po evreiskomu semeistvennomu pravu," *Budushchnost'* 38 (1902): 748–49.

131. Ibid., 748–50.

132. See, for example, the discussion and references in the following: Gregory L. Freeze, "Subversive Piety: Religion and the Political Crisis in Late Imperial Russia," *Journal of Modern History,* 68 (1996): 309–50; L. G. Zakharova, "Krizis samoderzhaviia nakanune revoliutsii 1905 g.," *Voprosy istorii,* 1972, no. 8: 119–40; A. Ia. Avrekh, *Tsarizm nakanune sverzheniia* (Moscow, 1989); Andrew Verner, *Nicholas II and the Crisis of Russian Autocracy* (Princeton, N.J. 1990).

133. For state policy after 1917, see the discussion and literature in Wendy Z. Goldman, *Women, the State and Revolution: Soviet Family Policy and Social Life, 1917–1936* (Cambridge, England, 1993).

Conclusion

1. RGIA, f. 1412, op. 227, d. 40, l. 30 (protocol of Minna Rozenzon).
2. Ibid., l. 24.
3. Biale, "Eros and Enlightenment," *Polin*, I (1986): 58.
4. TsGIAgM, f. 1457, op. 1, d. 40, l. 9.
5. For example, images of a Jewish family in "crisis" in the late nineteenth century permeated the writings of the Hebrew author Isaac Dov Berkowitz and his contemporaries. See Avraham Holz, *Isaac Dov Berkowitz: Voices of the Uprooted* (Ithaca, N.Y., 1973), 11–12.

Bibliography

ARCHIVAL SOURCES

Derzhavnyi arkhiv Kharkivskoï oblasti (DAKhO)
f. 958   Kantseliariia Khar'kovskoi oblasti, metricheskie knigi o evreiakh

Derzhavnyi arkhiv Kyïvskoï oblasti (DAKO)
f. 1   Kievskoe gubernskoe pravlenie
f. 2   Kantseliariia Kievskogo gubernatora
f. 10   Blagotvoritel'nost'
f. 185   Vasil'kovskii gorodskoi magistrat
f. 804   Kievskii gubernskii statisticheskii komitet (1835–1916)
f. 1238   Svedeniia ob imushchestvennom polozhenii evreev
f. 1248   Tarashchanskii gorodovoi magistrat
f. 1459   Novofastovskoe evreiskoe obshchestvo (1857–1864)
f. 1788   Kollektsiia dokumental'nykh materialov evreiskikh obshchestvennykh
          organizatsii

Derzhavnyi arkhiv Odeskoï oblasti (DAOO)
f. 4   Odesskaia gorodskaia duma
f. 16   Odesskaia gorodskaia uprava
f. 36   Odesskoi gorodovoi ravvinat
f. 37   Khersonskoi dukhovnoi konsistorii
f. 42   Kantseliariia popechitelia Odesskogo uchebnogo okruga

Derzhavnyi arkhiv Zhytomyrskoï oblasti (DAZhO)
f. 1   Volynskaia dukhovnaia konsistoriia
f. 9   Mirovye sudy Zhitomirskogo sudebnomirovogo okruga
f. 17   Volynskaia palata grazhdanskogo suda
f. 18   Volynskaia palata ugolovnogo suda
f. 19   Volynskaia soedinnenaia palata ugolovnogo i grazhdanskogo suda
f. 24   Zhitomirskii okruzhnoi sud
f. 67   Volynskoe gubernskoe pravlenie
f. 70   Kantseliariia Volynskogo gubernatora
f. 118   Volynskaia kazennaia palata
f. 160   Volynskii prikaz obshchestvennogo prizreniia
f. 396   Zhitomirskoe ravvinskoe uchilishche

Derzhavnyi arkhiv mista Kyïeva (DAmK)
f. 17   Kievskaia gorodskaia duma
f. 163   Kievskaia gorodskaia uprava
f. 164   Kievskii gorodskii sirotskii sud
f. 242   Kievskoe blagotvoritel'noe obshchestvo pomoshchi bednym
          (1884–1911)

f. 253   Priiut dlia kreshchennykh v pravoslavnnuiu veru evreiskikh detei
          (1871–1884)

Tsentral'nyi istoricheskii arkhiv Moskvy (TsIAM)
f. 16   Kantseliariia Moskovskogo general-gubernatora
f. 2372   Knigi dlia zapiski brakosochetavshikhsia i razvedshikhsia evreevv Moskve

Tsentral'nyi derzhavnyi istorychnyi arkhiv Ukraïny, Kyïv (TsDIAK-Ukraïny)
f. 127   Kievskaia dukhovnaia konsistoriia
f. 325   Novo-Mirgorodskaia evreiskaia sinagoga
f. 356   Kantseliariia Nikolaevskogo voennogo gubernatora (1850–1900)
f. 403   Evreiskaia sinagoga v g. Brodintsa
f. 404   Evreiskaia sinagoga v. kolonii Izrailovka
f. 405   Evreiskaia sinagoga v. kolonii Sagaidaki
f. 442   Kantseliariia Kievskogo, Podol'skogo i Volynskogo general-
          gubernatora
f. 460   Elisavetgradskii evreiskii kagal
f. 663   Korostyshevskii ravvinat
f. 1160   Skvirskii ravvinat
f. 1162   Tarashchanskii ravvinat
f. 1164   Kievskii ravvinat
f. 1266   Ivankovskii ravvinat

Tsentral'nyi derzhavnyi istorychnyi arkhiv Ukraïny, L'viv (TsDIAL Ukraïny)
f. 701   Evreiskaia religioznaia obshchina

Tsentral'nyi gosudarstvennyi istoricheskii arkhiv, St. Petersburg (TsGIA-St.
          Petersburg)
f. 2129   Evreiskoe istoriko-etnograficheskoe obshchestvo
f. 2179   I. Roikhel

Rossiiskii gosudarstvennyi istoricheskii arkhiv, St. Petersburg (RGIA)
f. 797   Kantseliariia ober-prokurora
f. 821   Departament dukhovnykh del inostrannykh ispovedanii, MVD
f. 1269   Evreiskii komitet
f. 1286   MVD departament politsii ispol'nitel'noi
f. 1326   Kantseliariia Peterburgskogo general-gubernatora
f. 1405   Ministerstvo iustitsii
f. 1412   Kantseliariia ego Imperatorskogo Velichestva

Lietuvos Valstybes Istorijos Archyvas, Vilnius (LVIA)
f. 387   Kantseliariia Vilenskogo, Kovenskogo, i Grodnenskogo general-gubernatora
          g. Vil'na
f. 388   Vilenskii gub. statisticheskii komitet
f. 446   Prokuror Vilenskoi sudebnoi palaty g. Vil'na
f. 447   Vilenskaia soedinennaia palata grazhdanskogo i ugolovnogo suda
f. 448   Vilenskii okruzhnoi sud g. Vil'na
f. 456   Vilenskii sovestnyi sud
f. 605   Litovskaia pravoslavnaia dukhovnaia konsistoriia Vil'na
f. 620   Vilenskii evreiskii kagal g. Vil'na
f. 728   Vilenskii evreiskii ravinat

f. 1215   Pravlenie Vilenskoi evreiskoi obshchiny

Rossisskii etnograficheskii muzei (REM)
f. 9   Arkhiv I. M. Pulnera

YIVO Institute for Jewish Culture (YIVO)
RG 41   Jewish Customs (Vil'na Archives)
RG 46   Lithuanian Consistory of the Russian Orthodox Church
RG 102 Autobiographies, American-Jewish
RG 126 Genealogy and Family History

NEWSPAPERS, JOURNALS, AND PERIODICALS

Budushchnost'
Den'
Der shadkhon
Evreiskaia biblioteka
Evreiskaia nedelia
Evreiskaia semeinaia biblioteka
Evreiskaia starina
Evreiskaia zhizn'
Evreiskii golos
Evreiskii meditsinskii golos
Evreiskii mir
Evreiskoe obozrenie
Gal-ed
Hamelits
Heavar
Kievskaia mysl'
Kievskaia starina

Kievskii telegraf
Nedel'naia khronika Voskoda
Novyi put'
Novyi voskhod
Perezhitoe
Rassvet
Russkii evrei
Varskavskie gubernskie vedomosti
Varskavskii dnevnik
Varshavskoi politseiskoi gazety
Vestnik Russkii evrei
Vestnik Volyni
Volyn'
Volynskie gubernskii vedomosti
Voskhod
Yidishe folksblat
Zion

PRIMARY SOURCES

Aronson, Chaim. *A Jewish Life under the Tsars: The Autobiography of Chaim Aronson, 1825–1888.* Totowa, N.J.: Allanheld, Osmun, 1983.

Berlin, Moisei Iosifovich. *Ocherk etnografii evreiskogo narodonaseleniia v Rossii, sostavlennoi soglasno programmy, idzannoi v 1852 imperatorskim russkim geograficheskim obshchestvom.* St. Petersburg: V. Bezobrazov, 1861.

Bloikh, Ivan Stanislavich. *Sravnenie material'nogo byta i nrastvennogo sostoianiia naseleniia v cherte osedlosti evreev i vne ee: Tsifrovyne dannye i issledovaniia po otnosheniiu k evreiskomu voprosu.* 5 vols. St. Petersburg, 1891.

Bloshtein, A. *Koch-buch für Jüdische frauen.* Vil'na: L. L. Matsa, 1896.

Brafman, Iakov. *Kniga kagala.* 2nd ed. St. Petersburg, 1875.

Brutskus, B. *Statistika evreiskogo naseleniia: raspredeleniia po territorii, demografii i kul'tura: Priznaki evreiskogo naseleniia po dannym perepisi 1897 g.* St. Petersburg, 1909.

Caro, Joseph. *Shulhan Arukh, Even Haezer.* Jerusalem, 1966.

Chagall, Bella. *First Encounter.* Translated by Barbara Bray. New York: Schocken Books, 1983.

Chekhov, Mikhail Pavlovich. *Zakony o evreiakh: Spravochnaia knizhka dlia evreev i dlia uchrezhdenii, vedauishchikh del o evreiakh.* Iaroslavl', 1899.

Chernigovskaia Gubernskaia Komissiia po Evreiskomu Voprosu. *Trudy Chernigovskoi komissii po evreiskomu voprosu.* Chernigov, 1881.

Cygielman, Shmuel Arther. *Yehudei Polin veLita.* Jerusalem: Zalman Shazar Center for Jewish History, 1991.

Derzhavin, G. R. *Sochinenii.* Edited by Ia. Grot. 9 vols. St. Petersburg, 1878.

Doklad komissii izbrannoi prigovorom poverennykh odesskogo evreiskogo obshchestva ot 1 Sentabriia 1877. Odessa, 1878.

Dubnow, Simon. *Pinkas hamedinah o pinkas vaad hakehilot harishonot bemedinat lita.* Berlin: Ayanot, 1925.

Efros, I. M. *Dokladnaia zapiska Moskovskomu evreiskomu obshchestvo ot i. M. Eforsa.* Moscow, 1890.

Epstein, Barukh Halevi. *Mekor Barukh: Korot hayei avotai vehayei ani, yahad im zikhronotai mehayei hador hakodem.* New York: Hayil, 1953.

Evreiskoe statisticheskoe obshchestvo, P. M. Klipchin, ed. *Evreiskoe naselenie Rossii po dannym 1897 g. i po noveishim istochnikam.* Petrograd: Kadima, 1917.

Feldman, Eliyahu ben Yehuda Leib. *Der shadkhan.* Warsaw, 1913.

Freiman, A. H. *Seder kiddushin venisuin aharei hatimat hatalmud: Mehkar histori-dogmati bedinei Yisrael.* Jerusalem, 1964.

Fuenn, Samuel Joseph. *Kiryah neemanah, korot adat Yisrael beir vilna.* Vilna, 1915.

Gessen, Iulii, and V. Z. Fridshtein. *Sbornik zakonov o evreiakh s raz"asneniem po opredeleniiam Pravitelskago Senata.* St. Petersburg, 1904.

Gimpel'son, Iakov. *Zakony o evreiakh: Sistematicheskii obzor deistvuiushchikh zakonopolozhenii o evreiakh.* 2 pts. St. Petersburg, 1914–15.

Gottlober, Avraham Baer. *Zikhronot umasaot.* 2 vols. Jerusalem: Bialik Institute, 1976.

Guenzburg, Mordechai David. *Aviezer.* Vil'na, 1863.

Halevi, Samuel ben David Moses. *Sefer nahalat shivah.* Jerusalem, 1961.

Halpern, Israel, ed. *Pinkas vaad arba aratsot.* Jerusalem: Bialik Institute, 1945–46.

Kalisz, Ita. *Etmolai.* Ramat Gan: Kibbutz Hameuhad, 1970.

Katzenelson, Judah Loeb Benyamin. *Mah sherau enai veshamu oznai, zikaron miyemei hayai.* Jerusalem: Bialik Institute, 1947.

Komissiia po Ustroistvu Byta Evreev. *Materialy.* 2 pts. St. Petersburg, 1879.

Korngold, Sheyne. *Zikhroynes.* Tel Aviv: Farlag Idepress, 1970.

Kotik, Ezekiel. *Mayne zikhroynes.* 2 vols. Berlin: Klal Verlag, 1922.

LaZenik, Edith. *Such a Life.* New York: William Morrow and Company, 1978.

Levanda, V. O. *Polyni khronologicheskii sbornik zakonov i polozhenii kasaiushchikhsiia evreev ot ulozheniia tsaria Alekseia Mikhailovicha do nastoiashchago vremeni ot 1649–1873 g.* St. Petersburg: Tipografiia K. V. Trubnikova, 1874.

Levin, E. B. *Sbornik ogranichitel'nykh zakonov i postanovlenii o evreiakh po 1-e Iulia 1902.* St. Petersburg, 1902.

Lifschitz, Yaakov Halevi. *Zikhron Yaakov.* 3 vols. Frankfurt am Main, 1924.

Lilienblum, Moshe Leib. *Ketavim autobiyografiyim: Hatot neurim.* Jerusalem: Bialik Institute, 1970.

Lozinskii, S. G. *Opisanie del byvshago arkhiva ministerstva narodnogo prosveshcheniia. Kazennye evreiskie uchilishcha.* Petrograd, 1920.

Mahler, Raphael. *Yidn in amolikn Poyln in likht fun tsifern: Di demografishe un sotsial-ekonomishe struktur fun Yidn.* Warsaw: Yidishbukh, 1958.

Maimon, Solomon. *Solomon Maimon: An Autobiography.* Translated by J. Clark Murray. London, 1888.

Meir, Golda. *My Life.* New York: G. P. Putnam, 1955.

Ministerstvo vnutrennikh del: istoricheskii ocherk. St. Petersburg: Tipografii Ministerstva vnutrennikh del, 1901.

Pantiukhov, I. *Opyt sanitornoi topografii statistiki i Kieva.* Kiev: Izdanie Kievskogo Gubernskogo Statisticheskogo Komiteta, 1877.

Rakowski, Puah. *Zikhroynes fun a yidisher revolutsionerin.* Buenos Aires: Tsentral Farband, 1954.

Rogovin, Lev Mir. *Sistematicheskii sbornik deistvuiushchshikh zakonov o evreiakh.* St. Petersburg: V. P. Anisimov, 1913.

Sankt-Peterburgskaia Evreiskaia Obshchina, *Otchet pravleniia Sankt-Peterburgskoi evreiskoi obshchiny.* St. Petersburg, 1873–92.

Sbornik materialov ob ekonomicheskom polozhenii evreev v Rossii. 2 vols. St. Petersburg, 1904.

Sbornik reshenii ravvinskoi komissii sozyva 1910 goda. St. Petersburg, 1912.

Shekhter, Mordechai. *Elyakum Zunzers verk.* New York: YIVO, 1964.

Sliozberg, G. B. *Sbornik deistvuiushchshikh zakonov o evreiakh.* St. Petersburg: Tip. M. Ia. Minkova, 1909.

Spektor, Yitshak Elhanan. *Sefer Beer Yitshak.* Jerusalem, 1970.

Sperber, Miriam. *Miberdichev ad yerushalayim: Zikhronot levet ruzin.* Jerusalem, 1980.

Steinschneider, Noah Hillel Maggid. *Ir Vilna,* pt. 1. Vil'na, 1900.

Tchernowitz, Chaim. *Pirkei hayim: Autobiografuah.* New York: Bitzaron, 1954.

Twersky, Aron David. *Sefer hayahas mitshernobil veruzin.* Lublin, 1938.

Vasil'eva, Larisa. ed. *Sem'ia Poliakovykh.* Moscow: Atlantida, 1995.

Waldman, Bess. *The Book of Tziril: A Family Chronicle.* Marblehead, Mass.: Micah Publications, 1981.

Wengeroff, Pauline. *Memoiren einer Grossmutter.* Berlin: M. Poppelauer, 1913–19.

Zunser, Miriam S. *Yesterday. A Memoir of a Russian-Jewish Family.* New York: Harper and Row, 1978.

SELECTED SECONDARY SOURCES

Abrahams, Israel. *Jewish Life in the Middle Ages.* London: Edward Goldston, 1932.

———. "Marriages Are Made in Heaven." *Jewish Quarterly Review* 2 (1890):172–73.

Adler, Ruth P. *Women of the Shtetl: Through the Eyes of Y. L. Peretz.* Cranbury, N.J.: Associated University Press, 1980.

Alekseev, A. A. *Obshchestvennaia zhizn' evreev, ikh nravy, obychai i predrazsudki.* Novgorod, 1868.

———. *Ocherki domashnei i obshchestvennoi zhizni evreev, ikh verovanie, bogosluzhenie, prazdniki, obraidy, Talmud i kagal.* St. Petersburg, I. L. Tuzov, 1896.

Abramsky, C., M. Jachimczyk, and Antony Polonsky. *The Jews in Old Poland.* London: I. B. Tauris, 1993.

Anderson, Michael. *Family Structures in Nineteenth-Century Lancashire.* Cambridge: Cambridge University Press, 1971.

Amram, David Werner. *The Jewish Law of Divorce According to the Bible and*

Talmud with Some Reference to Its Development in Post-Talmudic Times. Philadelphia: Edward Stern and Co., 1896.

Aronson, I. M. *Troubled Waters: The Origins of the 1881 Anti-Jewish Pogroms in Russia.* Pittsburg, University of Pittsburgh Press, 1990.

Ascher, Abraham. *The Revolution of 1905.* 2 vols. Stanford, Calif.: Stanford University Press, 1988–92.

Assaf, David. *Derekh hamalkhut: R. Yisrael meruzin umekomo betoldot hahasidut.* Jerusalem: Zalman Shazar Center, 1997.

Assaf, Simha. "Lekorot harabanut beashkenaz, polin velita." *Reshumot* 2(1927):259–300.

Bałaban, Meir. *Beit Yisrael bepolin.* Edited by Israel Halpern. 2 vols. Jerusalem: Hamahlakah leinyene hanoar shel Hahistadrut Hazionit, 1948–1953.

Bartal, Israel, and Isaiah Gafni, eds. *Eros, erusin, veirusim: miniyut umishpahah bahistoryah.* Jerusalem: Zalman Shazar Center for Jewish History, 1998.

Baron, Devorah, *Parashiyot: Sipurim mekubatsim.* Jerusalem: Bialik Institute, 1968.

Baron, Salo. *The Jewish Community: Its History and Structure to the American Revolution.* 3 vols. Westport, Conn.: Greenwood Press, 1942.

———. *The Russian Jew under Tsars and Soviets.* New York: Macmillan, 1964.

Beitgilel, David L. *K predstoiashchiim vyboram v ravvinskuiu kommissii.* St. Petersburg, Tip. M. Ia. Minkova, 1909.

Beletskii, A. *Vopros ob obrazovanii evreev v tsarstvovanie Imperatora Nikolaia I.* St. Petersburg: Russkaia Shkola, 1894.

Biale, David. "Childhood Marriage and the Family in the Eastern European Jewish Enlightenment." In *The Jewish Family: Myth and Reality.* Edited by Steven M. Cohen and Paula Hyman. New York: Holmes & Meier, 1986.

———. "Eros and Enlightenment: Love against Marriage in the East European Jewish Enlightenment." *Polin* 1 (1986):59–67.

———. *Eros and the Jew: From Biblical Israel to Contemporary America.* New York: Basic Books, 1992.

———. "Love, Marriage and the Modernization of the Jews." In *Approaches to Modern Judaism.* Edited by Marc Lee Raphael. Chico, Calif.: Scholars Press, 1983.

———. "The Lust for Asceticism in the Hasidic Movement." In *Jewish Explorations of Sexuality.* Edited by Jonathan Magonet. Oxford: Berghahn Books, 1995.

Biale, Rachel. *Women and Jewish Law: The Essential Texts, Their History, and Their Relevance for Today.* New York: Schocken Books, 1984.

Breitowitz, Irving A. *Between Civil and Religious Law: The Plight of the Agunah in American Society.* Westport, Conn.: Greenwood Press, 1993.

Clements, Barbara Evans, et al. *Russia's Women: Accommodation, Resistance, Transformation.* Berkeley: University of California Press, 1991.

Daiches, Samuel. *Divorce in Jewish Law.* London, 1926.

Davidowicz, Lucy S. *The Golden Tradition: Jewish Life and Thought in Eastern Europe.* New York: Schocken Books, 1967.

Dubnow, Simon M. *History of the Jews in Russia and Poland.* 3 vols. Philadelphia, 1916–20.

———. *Toldot hahasidut.* Tel Aviv, 1943.

Eisenbach, Artur. *The Emancipation of the Jews in Poland, 1780–1870.* Oxford: Basil Blackwell, 1991.

Elon, Menachem. *Jewish Law: History, Sources, Principles. Hamishpat haivri.* 3 vols. Philadelphia: Jewish Publication Society, 1994.

Engel, Barbara Alpern. *Between the Fields and the City: Women, Work, and Family in Russia, 1861–1914.* Cambridge: Cambridge University Press, 1994.

Epstein, Louis M. *The Jewish Marriage Contract: A Study in the Status of the Woman in Jewish Law.* New York: Jewish Theological Seminary of America, 1927.

Etkes, Immanuel, ed. *Hadat vehahayim: Tenuat hahaskalah hayehudit bemizrah eiropah.* Jerusalem: Zalman Shazar Center for Jewish History, 1993.

———. *Lita biyerushalayim.* Jerusalem: Yitshak ben-Tsvi, 1991.

———. *Tenuat hahasidut bereshitah.* Tel Aviv: Misrad habitahon, 1998.

———. *Yahid bedoro: Hagaon mivilnah, demut vedimui.* Jerusalem: Zalman Shazar Center, 1998.

Ettinger, Shmuel. *Bein polin verusyah.* Jerusalem: Bialik Institute, 1994.

Falk, Ze'ev. *Jewish Matrimonial Law in the Middle Ages.* Oxford: Oxford University Press, 1966.

Farnsworth, Beatrice, and Lynne Viola. *Russian Peasant Women.* Oxford: Oxford University Press, 1992.

Feiner, Shmuel. "Haishah hayehudiyah hamodernit: Mikre-mivhan beyahasei hahaskalah vehamodernah." *Zion* 58 (1993):453–99.

Fishman, David. *Russia's First Modern Jews: The Jews of Shklov.* New York: New York University Press, 1995.

Frankel, Jonathan. *Prophecy and Politics: Socialism, Nationalism, and the Russian Jews, 1862–1917.* Cambridge: Cambridge University Press, 1981.

Freehof, Solomon B. *The Responsa Literature.* Philadelphia: Jewish Publishing Society of America, 1959.

Freeze, Gregory L. "Bringing Order to the Russian Family: Marriage and Divorce in Imperial Russia, 1760–1860." *Journal of Modern History* 62 (1990): 709–46.

———. "The Soslovie (Estate) Paradigm and Russian Social History." *American Historical Review* 91:1 (1986):11–36.

Fried, Jacob, ed. *Jews and Divorce.* New York: Ktav Publishing House, 1986.

Friedan, Nancy M. *Russian Physicians in an Era of Reform and Revolution, 1856–1905.* Princeton, N.J.: Princeton University Press, 1981.

Frierson, Cathy. "Razdel: The Peasant Family Divided." *Russian Review* 46 (January 1987):35–51.

Fuks, V. Ia. *Materialy po evreiskomu voprosu.* St. Petersburg, 1893.

Galant, I. *Cherta evreiskoi osedlosti.* Kiev, 1910.

Gessen, Iulii. *Istoriia evreiskogo naroda v Rossii.* Moscow: Moskovskaia tipografiia, 1993 [reprint].

———. *Zakony zhizn'. Kak sozidalis' ogranichitel'nye zakony o zhitel'stve evreev v Rossii.* St. Petersburg: Pravo, 1911.

Ginzberg, Louis. *On Jewish Law and Lore.* Cleveland: World Publishing Co., 1962.

Gitelman, Zvi. *Centuries of Ambivalence: The Jews of Russia and the Soviet Union, 1881 to the Present.* New York: Schocken Books, 1988.

Glenn, Susan. *Daughters of the Shtetl. Life and Labor in the Immigration Generation.* Ithaca, N.Y.: Cornell University Press, 1990.

Gol'dberg, Isidor Aleksandrovich. *K voprosu o mnogozhenstve u evreev.* St. Petersburg, n.d. (mr5).

Goldberg, Jacob. "Die Ehe bei den Juden Polens im 18. Jahrhundert." *Jahrbücher für Geschichte Osteuropas* 31 (1993):483–515.

———. *Jewish Privileges in the Polish Commonwealth: Charters of Rights Granted to Jewish Communities in Poland-Lithuania in the Sixteenth to Eighteenth Centuries.* Jerusalem: Israel Academy of Sciences and Humanities, 1985.

———. "Nisuei hayehudim bepolin hayeshanah bedaat hakahal shel tekufat hahaskalah." *Gal-ed* 4–5 (1978):25–33.

Goody, Jack. *The Development of the Family and Marriage in Europe.* Cambridge: Cambridge University Press, 1983.

Greenberg, Louis. *The Jews in Russia: The Struggle for Emancipation.* 2 vols. New Haven, Conn." Yale University Press, 1944, 1951.

Gurvich, S. B. *Moiseevo-ravvinskoe zakonodatel'stvo. K istorii razvitiia evreiskogo brakorazvodnogo prava.* St. Petersburg: Iu. B. Rozenberg, 1882.

Hajnal, J. "European Marriage Patterns in Perspective." In *Population in History: Essays in Historical Demography,* ed. D. E. C. Eversley. London: Edward Arnold, 1965.

Halpern, Israel, "Nisuei behalah bemizrah eiropah," *Zion* 27 (1962):36–58.

———. *Yehudim veyahadut bemizrah Eiropah, mehkarim betoldoteihem.* Jerusalem: Magnes Press, 1968.

Hamm, Michael. ed. *The City in Late Imperial Russia.* Bloomington: Indiana University Press, 1986.

Haut, Irwin. *Divorce in Jewish Law and Life.* New York: Sepher-Herman Press, 1983.

Herlihy, Patricia. *Odessa: A History, 1794–1914.* Cambridge, Mass.: Harvard University Press, 1986.

Heschel, A. J. *The Earth Is the Lord's: The Inner World of the Jews in Eastern Europe.* New York: H. Schuman, 1958.

Hundert, Gershon David. "Approaches to the History of the Jewish Family in Early Modern Poland." In *The Jewish Family: Myths and Reality,* edited by S. M. Cohen and P. E. Hyman, pp. 17–28. New York: Holmes & Meier, 1986.

———. ed. *Essential Papers on Hasidism.* New York: New York University Press, 1991.

———. "Jewish Children and Childhood in Early Modern East Central Europe." In *The Jewish Family: Metaphor and Memory,* edited by D. Kraemer, pp. 18–94. Oxford: Oxford University Press, 1989.

———. *The Jews in a Polish Private Town. The Case of Opatów in the Eighteenth Century.* Baltimore: John Hopkins University Press, 1992.

Hyman, Paula. *Gender and Assimilation in Modern Jewish History: The Roles and Representations of Women.* Seattle: University of Washington Press, 1995.

Johanson, Christine. *Women's Struggle for Higher Education in Russia, 1855–1900.* Kingston and Montreal: McGill-Queen's University Press, 1987.

Kabuzan, V. M. *Narodonaselenie Rossii v XVIII-pervoi polovine XIX v. (po materialam revisii).* Moscow: Karnovich, 1963.

Kahan, Arcadius. *Essays in Jewish Social and Economic History,* edited by Roger Weiss. Chicago: University of Chicago Press, 1986.

Kaplan, Marion. *The Making of the Jewish Middle Class. Women, Family and Identity in Imperial Germany.* Oxford: Oxford University Press, 1991.

Karnovich, Evgenii Petrovich. *Evreiskii vopros v Rossii.* St. Petersburg: Tip. A. A. Kraevskogo, 1864.

Katz, Jacob, "Family, Kinship and Marriage among Ashkenazim in the Sixteenth to Eighteenth Century." *Jewish Journal of Sociology* 1 (1959).

———. "Nisuim vehayei ishut bemotsaei yamei habeinayim," *Zion* 10 (1944–1945):22–54.

———. *Out of the Ghetto: The Social Background of Jewish Empancipation.* Cambridge, Mass.: Harvard University Press, 1973.

———. *Tradition and Crisis: Jewish Society at the End of the Middle Ages.* New York: New York University Press, 1993.

Klier, John D. "The Ambiguous Legal Status of Russian Jewry in the Reign of Catherine II." *Slavic Review* 35 (1976):504–17.

———. "The Concept of 'Jewish Emancipation' in a Russian Context." In *Civil Rights in Imperial Russia,* ed. Olga Crisp and Linda Edmonson. Oxford: Oxford University Press, 1989.

———. *Russia Gathers Her Jews. The Origins of the Jewish Question in Russia, 1772–1825.* DeKalb, Il.: Northern Illinois University Press, 1985.

———. *Imperial Russia's Jewish Question, 1855–1881.* Cambridge: Cambridge University Press, 1995.

Klier, John, and Shlomo Lambroza, eds. *Pogroms: Anti-Jewish Violence in Modern Russian History.* Cambridge: Cambridge University Press, 1991.

Korf, S. A. *Dvorianstvo i ego soslovnoe upravlenie za stoletie, 1762–1855 godov.* St. Petersburg, 1906.

Krutikov, M. *Evreiskie prazdniki.* Moscow: Korona, 1890.

Kuznets, Simon. "Economic Structure and Life of the Jews." In *The Jews: Their History, Culture and Religion,* edited by Louis Finkelstein. 2:1597–1666. New York: Harper and Brothers, 1960.

Latkin, V. N. *Istoriia russkogo prava perioda imperii xviii–xix vv.* St. Petersburg: Tipografiia Montvida, 1909.

Lederhendler, Eli. "Modernity without Emancipation or Assimilation? The Case of Russian Jewry." In *Assimilation and Community: The Jews in Nineteenth-Century Europe,* ed. Jonathan Frankel and Steven Zipperstein. Cambridge: Cambridge University Press, 1991.

———. *The Road to Modern Jewish Politics.* New York: Oxford University Press, 1989.

Lerner, Anne Lapidus. "Lost Childhood in East European Hebrew Literature." In *The Jewish Family. Metaphor and Memory,* edited by D. Kraemer, pp. 95–112. Oxford: Oxford University Press, 1989.

Lerner, Osip M. *Evrei v Novorossiiskom krae. Istoricheskii ocherki. Po dannym iz arkhiva byvshego novorossiiskogo general-gubernatora.* Odessa, 1901.

Leshchinskii, Iakov. *Evreiskii narod v tsifrakh.* Berlin, 1922.

Levin, Sabina. "Beit sefer lerabanim bevarshah, 1826–1863" *Gal-ed* 11(1989):35–58.

Levitats, Isaac. *The Jewish Community in Russia, 1772–1844.* New York: Columbia University Press, 1943.

———. *The Jewish Community in Russia, 1844–1917.* New York: Columbia University Press, 1943.

Lewittes, Mendell. *Jewish Marriage. Rabbinic Law, Legend, and Custom.* Northvale, N.J.: Jason Aronson, 1994.

Lincoln, Bruce. *The Great Reforms: Autocracy, Bureaucracy and the Politics of Change in Imperial Russia.* DeKalb, Ill.: Northern Illinois University Press, 1990.

———. *Nicholas I: Emperor and Autocrat of All the Russias.* Bloomington: Indiana University Press, 1978.

Lion, A. *Khronika umstvennogo i nravstvennogo razvitiia Kishinveskikh evreev 1773 g. po 1890 g. i obzor evreiskikh blagotvoritel'nykh ichrezhdenii v Bessarabskoi gubernii.* Kishinev, 1891-92.

Löwe, Heinz-Dietrich. *The Tsars and the Jews. Reform, Reaction and Antisemitism in Imperial Russia, 1772–1917.* Singapore: Harwood Academic Publishers, 1993.

Lowenstein, Steven. "Ashkenazic Jewry and the European Marriage Pattern: A Preliminary Survey of Jewish Marriage Age." *Jewish History* 8 (1994):162.

Mahler, Raphael. *Toldot hayehudim bePolin ad hame'ah ha-19*. Palestine: Hashomer Hatzair Worker's Book Guild, 1946.

Maksimov, V. *Zakony o razvode*. Moscow, 1909.

Margolis, M. G. *Organizatsiia evreiskoi obshchiny*. St. Petersburg: Tip. V. Andersona i G. Loitsianskogo, 1910.

———. *Voprosy evreiskoi zhizni. Sobranie statie*. St. Petersburg, 1889.

Markov, V. *Polozhenie evreev v Rossii*. Moscow, 1906.

Meyer, Michael. *Response to Modernity. A History of the Reform Movement in Judaism*. New York: Oxford University Press, 1988.

Mintz, Alan. *Banished from Their Father's Table: Loss of Faith and Hebrew Autobiography*. Bloomington: Indiana University Press, 1989.

Miron, Dan. *A Traveler Disguised: A Study of the Rise of Modern Yiddish Fiction in the Nineteenth Century*. New York: Shocken Books, 1973.

Mitterauer, Michael, and Alexander Kagan. "Russian and Central European Family Structure: A Comparative View." *Journal of Family History* 7 (1982):103–29.

Mysh, M. I. *Rukovodstvo k russkim zakonam o evreiakh*. 2nd ed. St. Petersburg, 1892.

Orbach, Alexander. *New Voices of Russian Jewry: A Study of the Russian-Jewish Press of Odessa in the Era of the Great Reforms, 1860–1871*. Leiden: Brill, 1980.

Orlovsky, Daniel T. *The Limits of Reform: The Ministry of Internal Affairs in Imperial Russia, 1802–1881*. Cambridge, Mass.: Harvard University Press, 1981.

Orshanskii, I. G. *Evrei v Rossii. Ocherki ekonomicheskogo i obshchestvennogo byta russkikh evreev*. St. Petersburg, 1877.

———. *Russkoe zakonodatel'stvo o evreiakh. Ocherki i issledovaniia*. St. Petersburg, 1877.

Osherovitch, Mendel. *Shtetl un shtetlekh in Ukraine*. 2 vols. New York, 1948.

Outhwaite, R. B. *Marriage and Society: Studies in the Social History of Marriage*. New York: St. Martin's Press, 1981.

Parush, Iris. "The Politics of Literacy: Women and Foreign Languages in Jewish Society of 19th-Century Eastern Europe." *Modern Judaism* 15 (1995):188–90.

———. "Readers in Cameo: Women Readers in Jewish Society." *Prooftexts* 14 (1994).

Phillips, Roderick. *Family Breakdown in Late Eighteenth-Century France: Divorces in Rouen, 1792–1803*. Oxford: Oxford University Press, 1980.

———. *Putting Asunder. A History of Divorce in Western Society*. Cambridge: Cambridge University Press, 1988.

Pintner, W. M., and D. K. Rowney. *Russian Officialdom: The Bureaucratization of Russian Society from the Seventeenth to the Twentieth Century*. Chapel Hill: University of North Carolina Press, 1980.

Pipes, Richard. "Catherine II and the Jews: The Origins of the Pale of Settlement." *Soviet Jewish Affairs* 5 (1975):3–20.

Pisarev, S. N. *Uchrezhdenie po priniatiiu i napravleniiu proshenii i zhalob, prinosimykh na Vysochaishee imia, 1810–1910*. St. Petersburg, 1911.

Plakans, Andrejs, and Joel M. Halpern, "An Historical Perspective on Eighteenth Century Jewish Family Households in Eastern Europe," In *Modern Jewish Fertility*, ed. Paul Ritterband. Leiden: E. J. Brill, 1981.

Polonskii, D. Ia. *Evreiskie prosvetitel'nye i blogotvoritel'nye uchrezhdeniia goroda Sevastopolia*. Sevatopol', 1911.

Popovich. G. *Polozhenie zhenshchin v Biblieskoi sem'e i obshchestve.* Kiev, 1915.
Pozner, S. V. *Evrei v obshchei shkole. K istorii zakonodatel'stva i pravitel'stvennoi politiki v oblasti evreiskogo voprosa.* St. Petersburg: Razum, 1914.
Rabinowitsch, W. Z. *Lithuanian Hasidism from Its Beginnings to the Present Day.* London: Vallentine, Mitchell, 1970.
Raeff, Marc. *Political Ideas and Institutions in Imperial Russia.* Boulder, Colo.: Westview Press, 1994.
———. *The Well-Ordered Police State. Social and Institutional Change through Law in the Germanies and Russia, 1600–1800.* New Haven, Conn.: Yale University Press, 1983.
Raisin, Jacob S. *The Haskalah Movement in Russia.* Philadelphia, 1913.
Ransel, David. ed. *The Family in Imperial Russia.* Urbana: University of Illinois Press, 1978.
———. *Mothers of Misery: Child Abandonment in Russia.* Princeton, N.J.: Princeton University Press, 1988.
Riasanovsky, N. V. *A History of Russia.* 3rd ed. Oxford: Oxford University Press, 1977.
———. *Nicholas I and Official Nationality in Russia, 1825–1855.* Berkeley: University of California Press, 1959.
Riskin, Shlomo. *Women and Jewish Divorce: The Rebellious Wife, the Agunah and the Right of Women to Initiate Divorce in Jewish Law, a Halakhic Solution.* Hoboken, N.J.: Ktav Publishing House, 1989.
Roggers, Hans J. "The Beilis Case: Antisemitism and Politics in the Reign of Nicholas II." *Slavic Review* 25 (1966):615–29.
———. *Jewish Policies and Right-Wing Politics in Imperial Russia.* Berkeley: University of California Press, 1986.
Rosman, M. J. *The Lord's Jews Magnate: Jewish Relations in the Polish-Lithuanian Commonwealth during the Eighteenth Century.* Cambridge, Mass.: Harvard University Press, 1990.
Rotshtein, L. O. *Po povodu vyborov obshchestvennogo ravvina v g. Odesse.* Odessa, 1903.
Rubin, Ruth. *Voices of a People: The Story of Yiddish Folksong.* New York: McGraw-Hill Book Co., 1973.
Sabean, David. *Property, Production, and Family in Neckarhausen, 1700–1870.* Cambridge: Cambridge University Press, 1990.
Schorsch, Ismar, ed. *From Text to Context: The Turn to History in Modern Judaism.* Hanover, N.H.: University Press of New England for Brandeis University, 1994.
Seidman, Naomi. *A Marriage Made in Heaven: The Sexual Politics of Hebrew and Yiddish.* Berkeley: University of California Press, 1997.
Shigarin, Nikolai Dmitrievich. *Evreiskie gazety v Rossii.* St. Petersburg, 1879.
Shochat, Arziel. "Hahanhagah bekehilot Rusyah im bitul hakahal." *Zion* (1979):143–223.
———. *Mosad 'harabanut mitaam' berusyah.* Haifa: University of Haifa, 1976.
———. *Im hilufei tekufot.* Jerusalem: Bialik Institute, 1960.
Silber, Jacques. "Some Demographic Characteristics of the Jewish Population in Russia at the End of the Nineteenth Century." *Jewish Social Studies* 42 (1980):269–80.
Skal'kovskii, A. A. *Odessa 84 god tomu nazad i teper'.* Odessa, 1878.
Slutsky, Yehudah. "Beit hamidrash lerabanim bevilna." *Heavar* 7 (1960):29–40.
———. *Tenuat hahaskalah beyahadut rusyah.* Jerusalem: Zalman Shazar Center, 1977.

Soloveitchik, Hayim. *Sheelot u teshuvot: Makor histori.* Jerusalem: Zalman Shazar Center, 1990.

Springer, A. "Gavrill Derzhavin's Jewish Reform Project of 1800." *Canadian-American Slavic Studies* 10 (1976):1–24.

Stampfer, Shaul. "Gender Differation and Education of the Jewish Woman in Nineteenth-Century Eastern Europe." *Polin* 7 (1992):63–87.

———. "Hamashma'ut hahevratit shel nisuei boser bemizrah eiropah." In *Studies on Polish Jewry,* edited by Ezra Mendelsohn and Chone Shmeruk. Jerusalem: Zalman Shazar Center, 1987.

———. "L'amour et la famille chez les Juifs d'Europe orientale à époque moderne." In *La Société Juive à travers l'histoire,* edited by Shmuel Trigano. Paris: 1992.

———. "Remarriage among Jews and Christians in Nineteenth-Century Eastern Europe." *Jewish History.* 3:2 (fall 1988): 85–114.

———. *Hayeshivah halitait behithavutah.* Jerusalem: Zalman Shazar Center, 1995.

Stanislawski, Michael. *For Whom Do I Toil? Judah Leib Gordon and the Crisis of Russian Jewry.* Oxford: Oxford University Press, 1988.

———. "Jewish Apostasy in Russia: A Tentative Typology." In *Jewish Apostasy in the the Modern World,* edited by Todd M. Endelman. New York, 1987.

———. *Tsar Nicholas I and the Jews: The Transformation of Jewish Society in Russia, 1825–1855.* Philadelphia: Jewish Publishing Society of America, 1983.

Stites, Richard. *The Women's Liberation Movement in Russia: Feminism, Nihilism, and Bolshevism, 1860–1930.* Princeton, N.J.: Princeton University Press, 1968.

Stoianov, A. N. *Semeinoe pravo i nasledovanie u evreev: Etiud po istorii zakonodatel'stva.* Kharkov, 1884.

Stone, Lawrence. *The Family, Sex and Marriage in England 1500–1800.* New York: Harper and Row, 1977.

Tarnovich, G. *Opyt sovremennoi i osmotritel'noi reformu v oblasti iudaizma v Rossii.* Odessa, 1868.

Vaisenberg, S. A. *Imena iuzhno-russkikh evreev.* Moscow, 1913.

Vol'piang-Smolenskaia, G. *Evreiskaia zhenshchina, ee rol' i polozhenie v istorii evreiskogo naroda.* Vilna, 1900.

Yaney, G. L. *The Systemization of Russian Government: Social Evolution in the Domestic Administration of Imperial Russia, 1711–1905.* Urbana: Illinois University Press, 1973.

Wagner, William B. *Marriage, Property and the Struggle for Legality in Late Imperial Russia.* Oxford: Oxford University Press, 1994.

Wall, Richard, ed. *Family Forms in Historic Europe.* Cambridge: Cambridge University Press, 1983.

Wandycz, P. S. *The Lands of Partitioned Poland, 1795–1870.* Seattle: University of Washington Press, 1974.

Weinryb, Bernard. *The Jews of Poland: A Social and Economic History of the Jewish Community in Poland from 1100–1800.* Philadelphia: Jewish Publication Society of America, 1973.

———. "Studies in the Communal History of Polish Jewry II." *Proceedings of the American Academy for Jewish Research.* 15 (1945):93–127

Wilensky, Mordecai. *Hasidim umitnagdim: Letoldot hapulmus benehem bashanim 532–575.* 2 vols. Jerusalem: Mosad Byalik, 1970.

Wirtschafter, Elise K. *From Serf to Russian Soldier.* Princeton, N.J.: Princeton University Press, 1990.

Worobec, Christine. *Peasant Russia: Family and Community in the Post-Emancipation Period.* Princeton, N.J.: Princeton University Press, 1991.

Wortman, Richard S. *The Development of a Russian Legal Consciousness.* Chicago: University of Chicago Press, 1976.

Zakutinsky, Rivka. *Techinas: A Voice from the Heart as Only a Woman Can Pray.* New York: Aura Press, 1992.

Zalkin, Mordechai, *Baalot hashahar: Hahaskalah hayehudit baimperyah harusit bameah hatesha esreh.* Jerusalem: Magnes Press, 2000.

Zborowski, Mark and Elizabeth Herzog. *Life Is with People: The Culture of the Shtetl.* New York: Shocken Books, 1962.

Zipperstein, Steven. "Haskalah, Cultural Change, and Nineteenth-Century Russian Jewry: A Reassessment." *Journal of Jewish Studies* 34:2 (1983):191–207.

———. *The Jews of Odessa: A Cultural History, 1794–1881.* Stanford, Calif.: Stanford University Press, 1985.

———. "Transforming the Heder: Maskilic Politics in Imperial Russia." In *Jewish History: Essays in Honour of Chimen Abramsky,* edited by Ada Rapoport-Albert and Steven J. Zipperstein, pp. 87–111. London: Halban, 1988.

Index